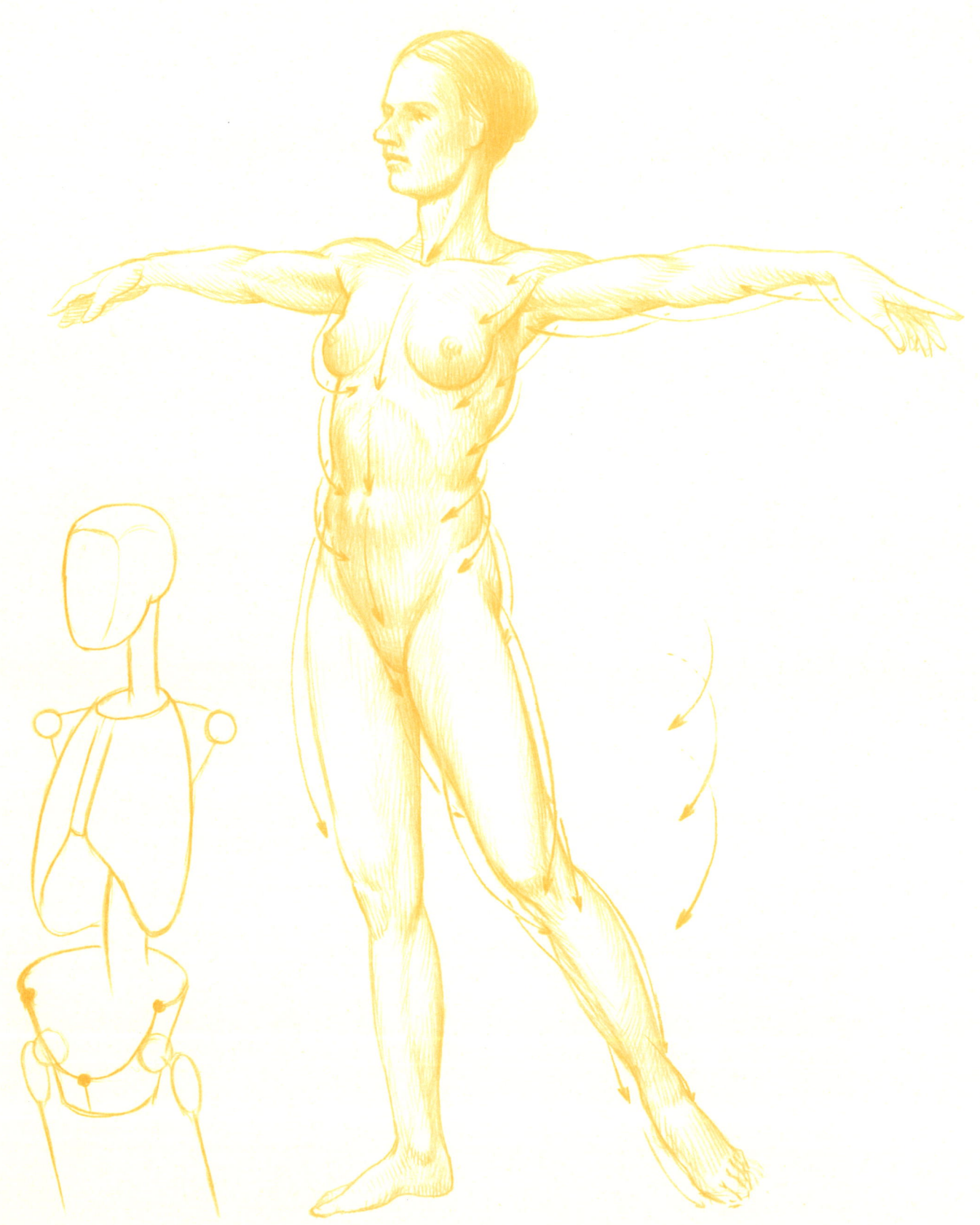

DYNAMIC HUMAN ANATOMY

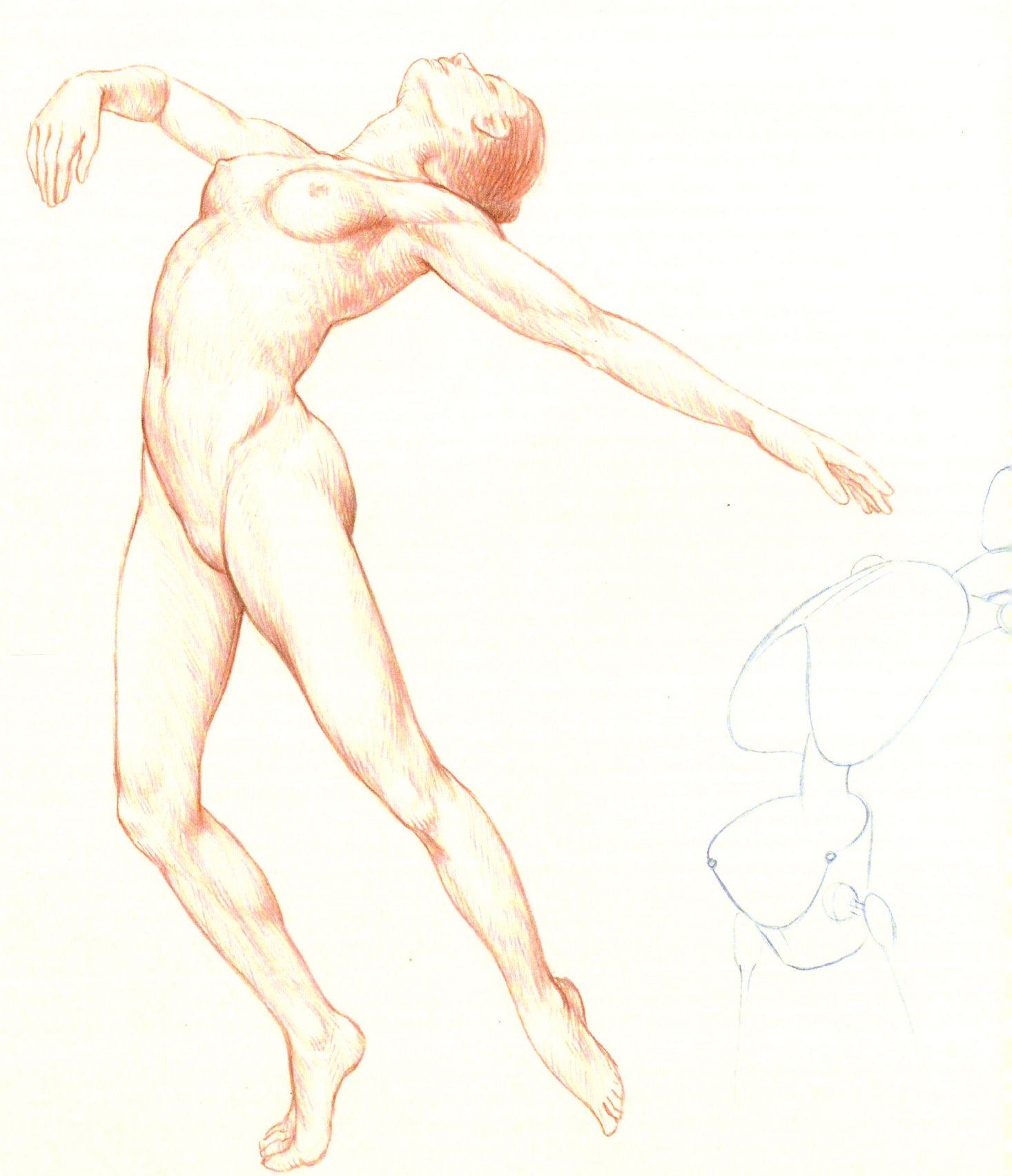

DYNAMIC HUMAN ANATOMY

AN ARTIST'S GUIDE TO STRUCTURE, GESTURE, AND THE FIGURE IN MOTION

ROBERTO OSTI

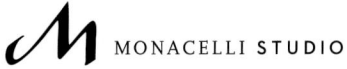

MONACELLI STUDIO

Published in the United States by Monacelli Studio,
an imprint of The Monacelli Press, a division of Phaidon

Library of Congress Cataloging-in-Publication Data

Names: Osti, Roberto, author.
Title: Dynamic human anatomy : an artist's guide to structure, gesture, and
the figure in motion / Roberto Osti.
Description: First edition. | New York : The Monacelli Press, [2021] |
Includes bibliographical references and index. | Summary: "An essential
visual guide for artists to the mastery and use of advanced human
anatomy skills in the creation of figurative art. Dynamic Human Anatomy
picks up where Basic Human Anatomy leaves off and offers artists and art
students a deeper understanding of anatomy, including anatomy in motion,
and how that essential skill is applied to the creation of fine
figurative art"-- Provided by publisher.
Identifiers: LCCN 2020029793 | ISBN 9781580935517 (hardback)
Subjects: LCSH: Anatomy, Artistic. | Human figure in art.
Classification: LCC NC760 .O884 2021 | DDC 743.4/9--dc23
LC record available at https://lccn.loc.gov/2020029793

ISBN: 978-1-58093-551-7

Printed in China

Design by Jennifer K. Beal Davis
Cover design by Jennifer K. Beal Davis
Cover illustrations by Roberto Osti

10 9 8 7 6 5 4 3

First Edition

MONACELLI STUDIO
The Monacelli Press
111 Broadway
New York, New York 10006

www.monacellipress.com

ALSO AVAILABLE

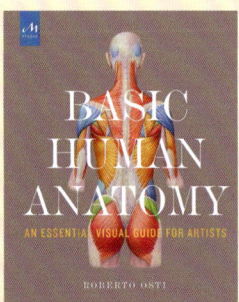

In memory of my wife, Angela Conrad, the love of my life

August 17, 1966—March 27, 2019

She was my soulmate, and she left us too soon.

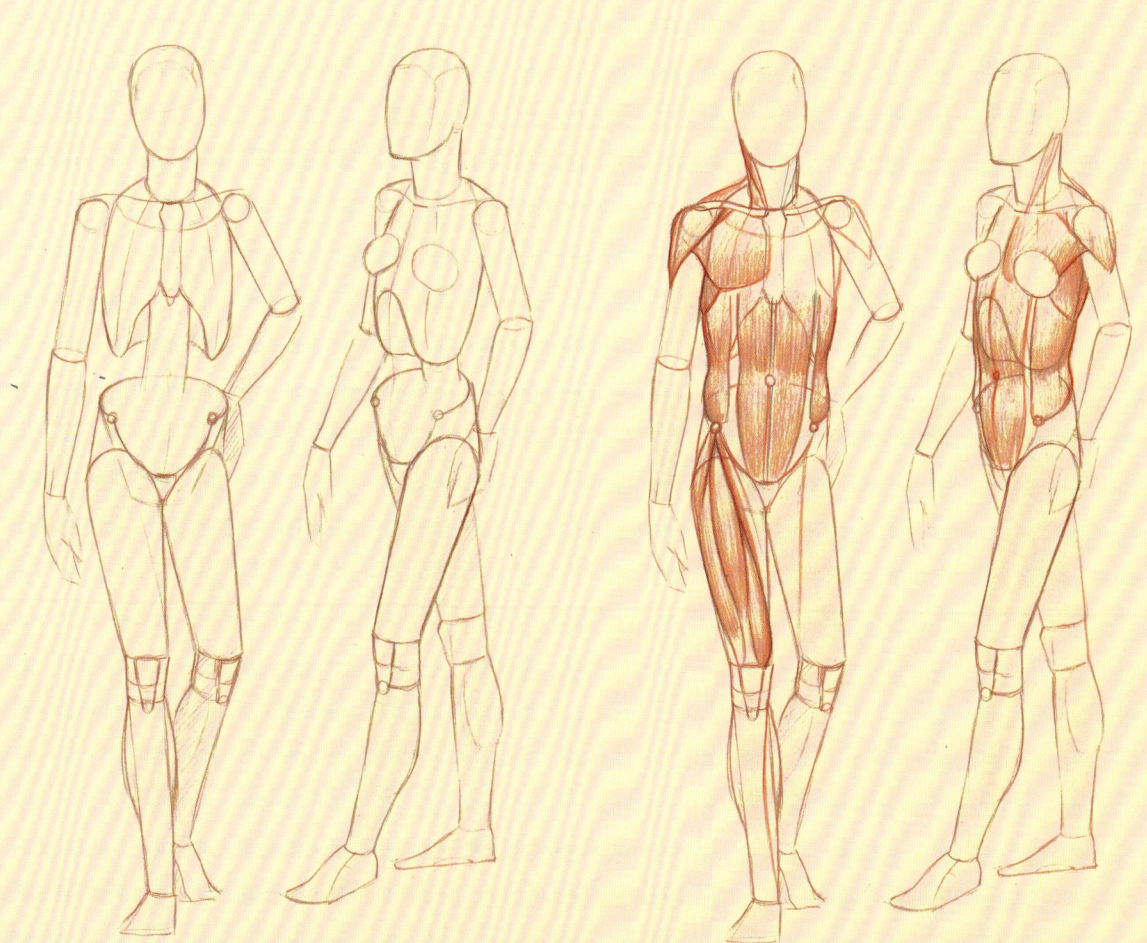

CONTENTS

FOREWORD

By Dan Thompson

In the field of anatomy, there is a nearly inexhaustible theoretical wellspring of creative agencies that play upon the sensibility and intelligence of the figurative artist. In the act of drawing, while encountering another human being in a pose, a draftsperson might perceive the figure as visually self-evident, requiring minimal examination. To others, there is an abundance of momentarily frozen evidence, comprised of some known and much unknown detail. Forms within the figure respond to other forms—as muscles react to the bony framework engaged in action. While posing, the body's physical ecosystem seems to awaken, relate, resonate, subside, and then rearrange . . . . How can the human organism be suspended in such a complex, precarious, yet breathtakingly beautiful state? How do we come to terms with the elusive phenomena that constitute the figure and tether it to itself? Why is the human body so effectively able to visually express human emotion, even while maintaining a stance that, from an engineer's perspective, might seem impossible?

Roberto Osti reveals, through a wealth of insights, how anatomy transmogrifies into force for artistic comprehension. Building upon his celebrated 2016 text *Basic Human Anatomy*, Roberto embarks on a bold journey into the more mystifying aspects of anatomical construction. By tapping into historical expositions of human form, he first articulates the manner in which mechanistic anatomy is exquisitely aligned with a natural order. He then analyzes the historic, enduring, fertile, and evolving notion of the anatomical proportional cannon. From his contemporary aesthetic experience, he promotes drawing without the use of static grids in the body. Instead, Roberto infers conclusions that facilitate the drawing of holistic form. His drawings reveal the abiding mindset of dynamic proportional relationships while recreating powerful human expression on a page.

This book reflects the uplifting state of early twenty-first century drawing education, in which many principles of are being refashioned. In lieu of gambling on an education that may involve picking up an unintentionally disharmonic form sense, students of figure drawing are immersing themselves in life rooms, devoted to the acquisition of proficiency. They know that without proving an incontrovertible aptitude for drawing, their essential artistic development is at stake. They will recognize and embrace the abundance of practical knowledge that Roberto has presented here.

Roberto's book will resonate as a touchstone for the belief that aesthetics and anatomy exist in an emerging as well as a converging realm. As this trajectory evolves, his book will serve as a vehicle for decoding the body. It will inspire other efforts to describe that which connects traditional anatomy and physiology with art-making. That artists have habitually found promise on the frontiers, between presumed fields, leads me to trust in the profound implications of this form of imaginative and intelligent seeing. Roberto enables this potential, even as his book testifies to the very real, lyrical beauty of the human being, appreciated most movingly through drawing.

Dan Thompson is Dean of Fine Arts, Studio Incamminati, Philadelphia.

INTRODUCTION

For a figurative artist, a sure sign of accomplishment is the ability to achieve a *transcendent* artwork—a work of art that conveys a sense of life or expresses psychological character. Such expertise is cultivated not only by mastering drawing techniques and practicing drawing the human form from life, but also by learning to read the many languages and intentions the human body speaks: movement, power, tension or relaxation, friendliness or aggression, and all the rest.

In my teaching, I aim to give students knowledge of the body's anatomy and mechanics in as accurate and neutral a way as possible, without influencing their artwork stylistically or aesthetically. Developing style and aesthetics is each artist's own personal artistic quest. In my figure anatomy and figure drawing classes, students learn to draw with "informed" lines that result from an analysis of the subject as opposed to a passive, imitative approach.

With this book, I set out to explore, decode, interpret, and describe the infinite dynamic, expressive, and aesthetic combinations the human form can manifest. Explaining depictions of the human figure also means defining what the human figure has represented during various historical periods. Art featuring the human figure created over millenniums tells us about the values of past cultures—just as contemporary values must always be considered when drawing, painting, or sculpting the human figure now, to make our art relevant to the times we live in.

The first two chapters of the book are dedicated to a discussion of human proportions, anatomical knowledge, cultural values, and aesthetic development in Archaic, Classical, and Hellenistic Greek art, as well as in art of the Renaissance. Chapters 3 and 4 study anatomy and the structure of the body using an approach specifically directed toward movement, dynamism, and proportional harmonies. At the core of my method, which follows the Renaissance tradition, is the study of the body's landmarks and the origin and insertion of muscles. Understanding these muscular-skeletal connections is essential to appreciating the human form's structure holistically and is indispensable for accessing the body's dynamic and aesthetic connections, concepts treated in chapters 5 and 6. Chapters 7 and 8 are devoted, respectively, to the hands and head, exploring both their structural and their expressive qualities.

Each chapter investigates a specific method of thinking and looking at the human form, giving the reader a multifaceted understanding of this infinite subject while promoting creativity and personal style. This approach is continued in chapter 9, where various drawing techniques are connected to different conceptual analyses of the human form. Armed with this knowledge, you will be able to "read" the human form in depth, appreciate its fascinating complexity, avoid a tedious and passive imitative approach, and create accurate, expressive, and aesthetically unique works of art.

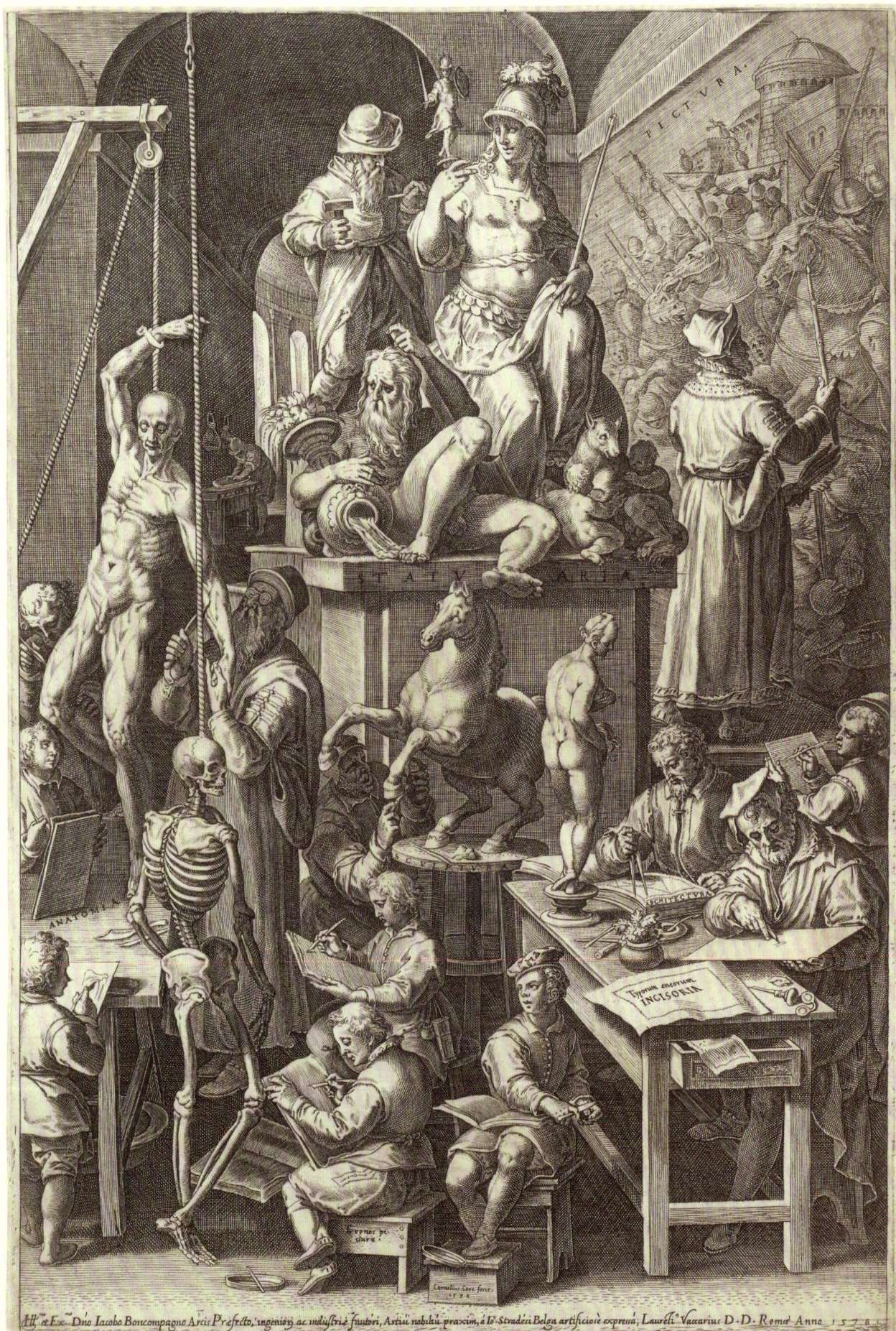

PICTVRA.

STATVARIA

ANATOMIA

ARCHITECTVRA

Typorum imprimum
INCISORIA

Ill.mo et Ex.mo D.no Iacobo Boncompagno Arcis Præfecto, ingeniorü ac industriæ fautori, Artiü nobiliü praxim, á Io. Stradensi Belga artificiose expressa, Laurent.º Vaccarius D. D. Romæ Anno 1 5 7 8 .

CHAPTER 1

AESTHETIC ANATOMY— HISTORICAL OBSERVATIONS

When the engraving opposite was created, the study of human anatomy was one of the cardinal points in the academic training of an artist. The human figure still played a dominant role in painting and would continue to do so for a few more centuries after this image was produced. The figure was charged with aesthetic and political content and was at the center of historical and religious narrative, so it was very important for the artist to have a deep understanding of the human form. The students in the engraving seem to be following the progressive method for drawing the human figure that Leon Battista Alberti had outlined more than a

OPPOSITE: Cornelis Cort (after Stradanus), *Allegory of the Arts*, 1578, engraving, 17 × 11⅜ inches (43.2 × 29.5 cm). Rijksmuseum, Amsterdam.

This engraving summarizes the artist's training in a sixteenth-century Florentine or Roman academy. Sculpture, painting, architecture, and engraving all appear, as does anatomy. Judging from the very young age of the students who are busy drawing the standing skeleton, anatomy seems to be the foundation of drawing—and probably of all the other arts, as well. Note that the anatomist (center left) is intently preparing a cadaver for the next step in his students' study of the human figure.

century earlier: start drawing the bones first, then the muscles, fat, and skin, and finally the clothing.

This chapter investigates the fundamental role played by anatomical knowledge in the creation of artworks that convincingly describe a narrative, evoke emotions, and convey cultural concepts. I emphasize how the correct depiction of the human form and its artistic interpretation based on a sound knowledge of anatomy imbues the artwork with aesthetic qualities.

THE MANY LIVES OF A TORSO

A timeless source of inspiration

Possible aesthetic interpretations of the human figure are infinite, each resulting from the cultural values of specific historical and artistic periods. Nevertheless, some artworks provide a timeless source of inspiration. Examples include the Belvedere Torso and the sculptural group called Laocoön and His Sons, both shown opposite. These two iconic masterpieces have been reinterpreted by many artists over the course of centuries. Their common denominator lies not just in their highly dramatic and expressive poses but also in the deep knowledge of human anatomy displayed by the artists who created them. In these works, aesthetic content is expressed through anatomical form.

The Belvedere Torso and the Laocoön group, rediscovered during the Renaissance, became sources of inspiration for many later artworks—for example, figures of Christ and the Virgin Mary in Michelangelo's *Last Judgment* in the Sistine Chapel. The torso of Christ, including the position of the legs, is very similar to that of the Belvedere, and Mary's pose clearly recalls that of one of Laocoön's sons being killed by snakes, although the Virgin, like Christ, is looking down in judgment on humanity whereas both Laocoön and his son, facing imminent death, look up in agony at the gods who condemned them.

Michelangelo also witnessed the rediscovery of the Domus Aurea, the long-buried "Golden House" that the emperor Nero had built as an entertainment palace for himself in Rome. Michelangelo had himself lowered on ropes into its now-underground chambers, where he saw frescos like the one of Apollo opposite, which clearly inspired him, as well.

OPPOSITE TOP LEFT: Belvedere Torso, 1st century CE copy of earlier original, marble, height 63 inches (160 cm). Vatican Museums.

OPPOSITE TOP RIGHT: Laocoön and His Sons, possible copy after a Hellenistic original from c. 200 BCE, 82 × 64 × 44 inches (208 × 163 × 112 cm). Vatican Museums.

OPPOSITE BOTTOM LEFT: Fresco, Domus Aurea, Rome.

OPPOSITE BOTTOM RIGHT: Michelangelo Buonarroti, *The Last Judgment* (detail), 1536-41, fresco. Sistine Chapel, Vatican.

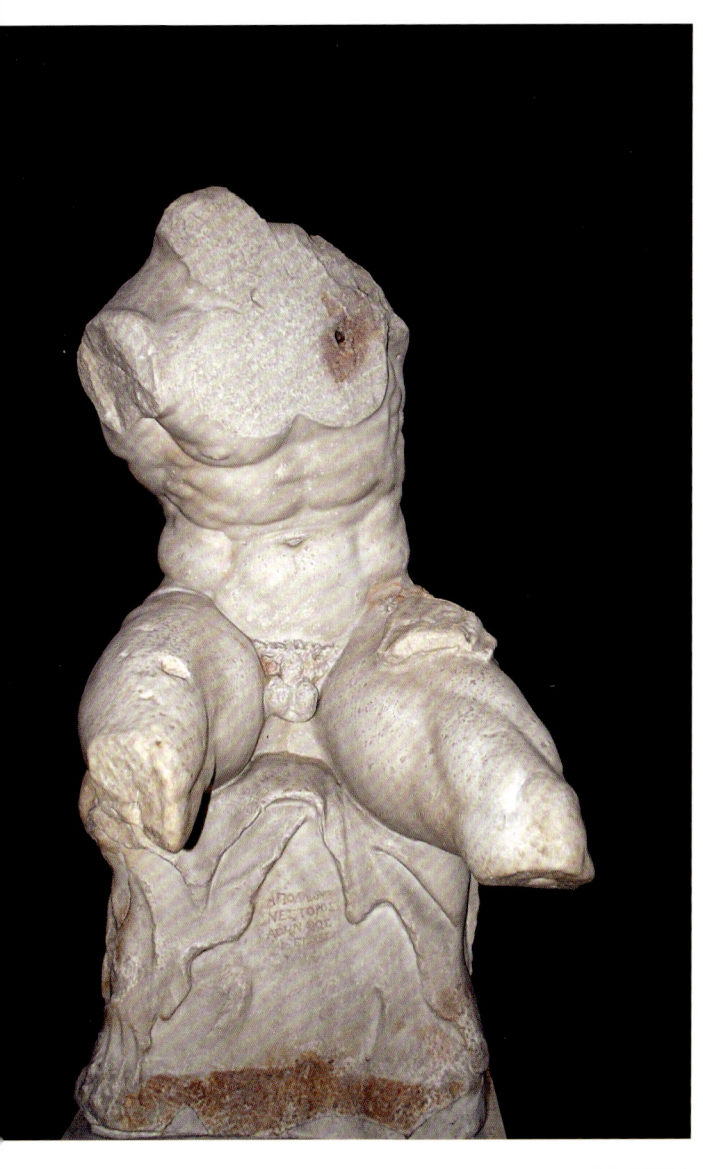

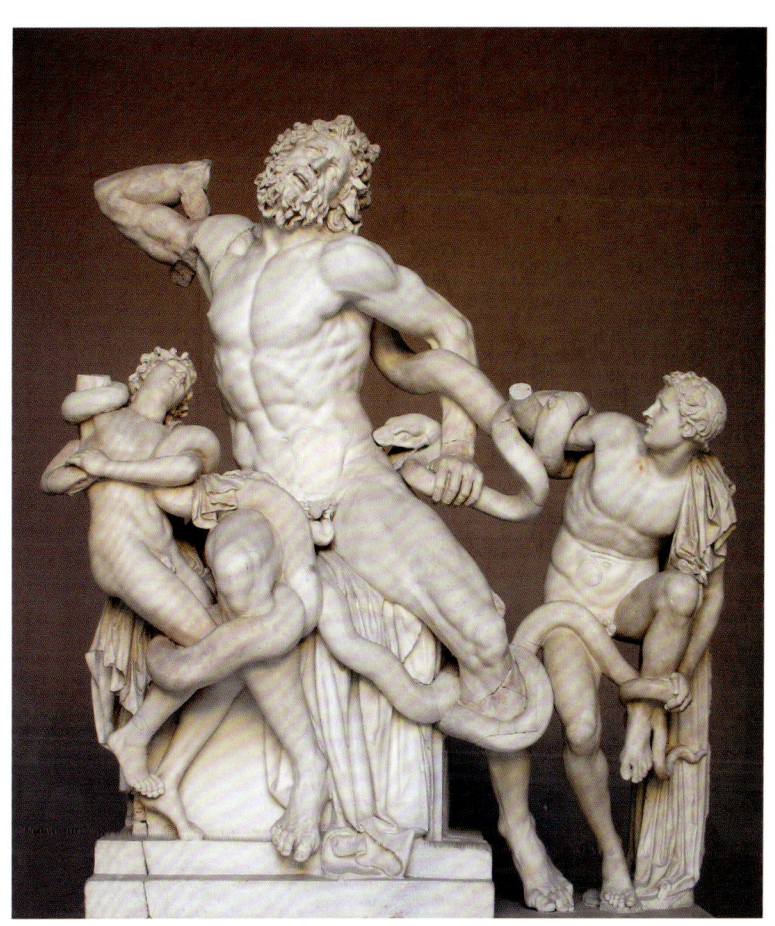

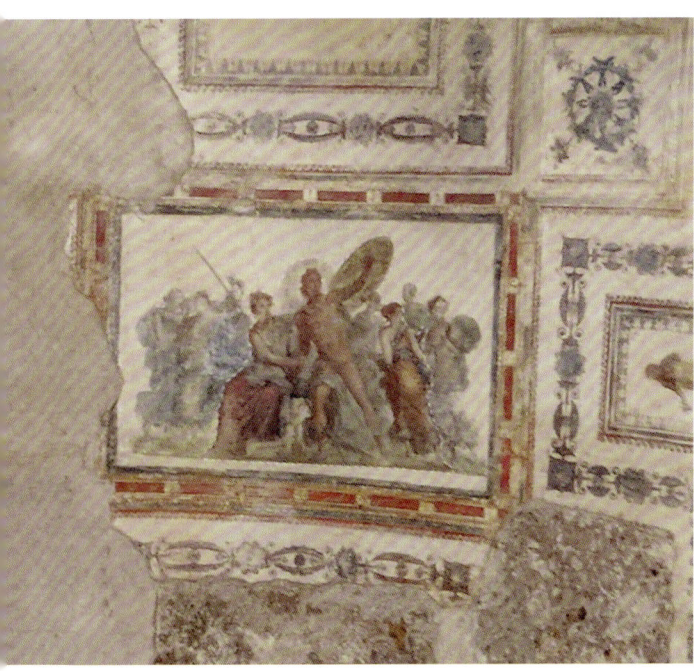

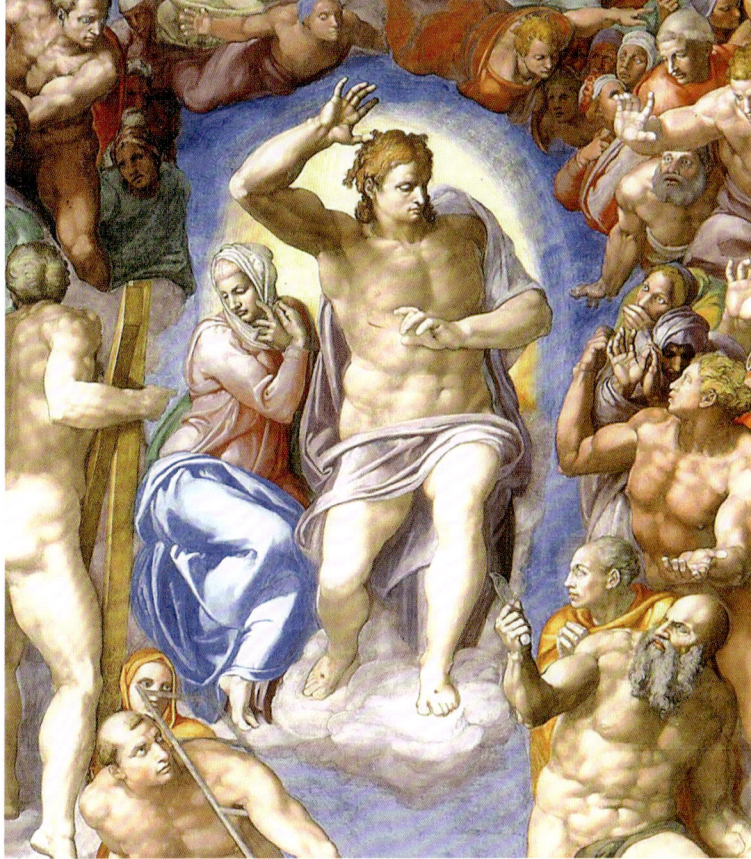

LEONARDO'S AESTHETIC ANATOMY

Leonardo da Vinci thoroughly considered anatomical detail when depicting the human figure. He studied anatomy both as a scientist and as an artist. As a scientist, Leonardo was moved by pure thirst for knowledge—he wanted to unlock the mysteries of human life. But beyond being anatomically correct, the depictions of human forms in Leonardo's artworks are beautiful. As an artist he studied anatomy with aesthetic intent. The many dissections he performed were followed by virtual reconstructions of the body through drawings charged with life, expression, and movement.

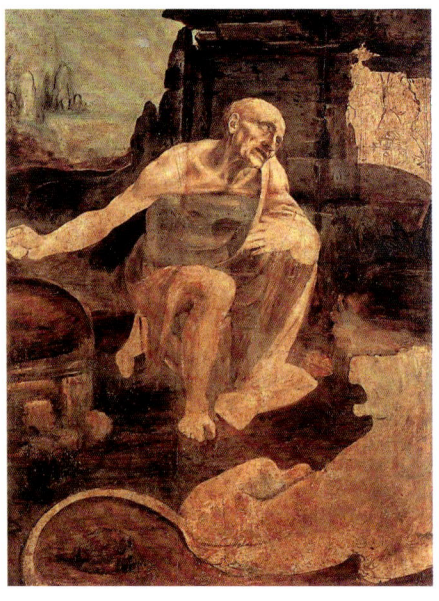
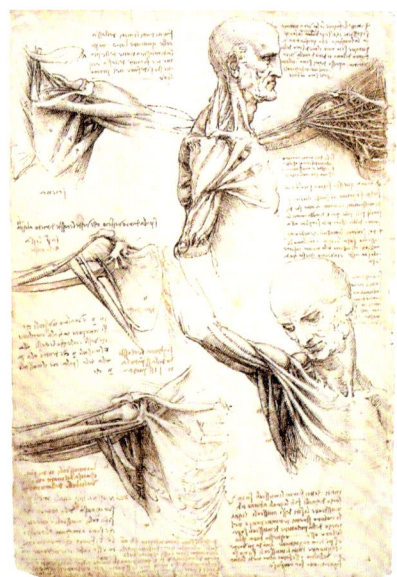
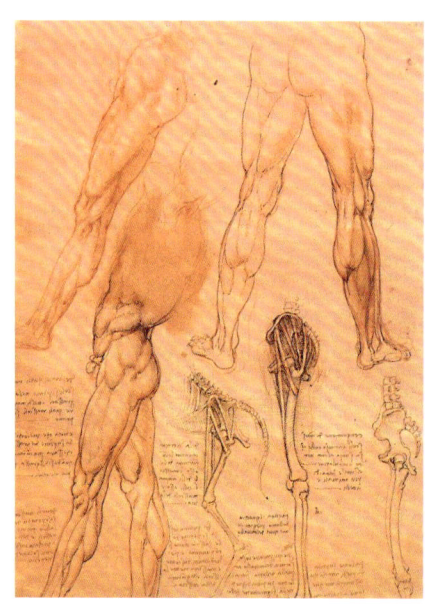
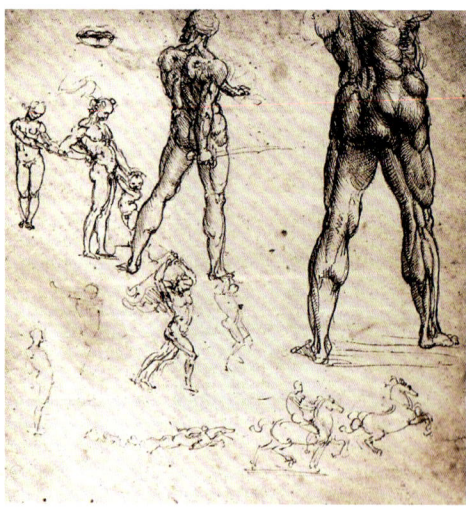

ABOVE LEFT: Leonardo da Vinci, *Saint Jerome in the Wilderness,* c. 1480, tempera and oil on walnut panel, 41 × 30 inches (103 × 75 cm). Vatican Museums.

Leonardo never finished this underpainting of Saint Jerome.

ABOVE CENTER: Leonardo da Vinci, anatomical studies of the shoulder, 1510–11, black chalk and ink on paper, 11⅜ × 7¹³⁄₁₆ inches (28.9 × 19.9 cm). Royal Library, Windsor, United Kingdom.

This page from Leonardo's Codex Atlanticus shows the incredibly modern method he used to dissect and study the human body. Because the muscles are reduced to ropelike structures, it is easier to understand their actions, origins, and insertions.

ABOVE RIGHT: Leonardo da Vinci, studies of legs of man and the leg of a horse, 1506-7, ink and red chalk on red prepared paper, 11¼ × 8¹⁄₁₆ inches (28.5 × 20.5 cm). Royal Librarian (United Kingdom).

RIGHT: Leonardo da Vinci, figure studies, c. 1505. Royal Library of Turin.

ANATOMICAL NAMES AND ACRONYMS

For beginners, the number and difficulty of anatomical names can seem overwhelming. Here are some tips on remembering muscles' names, as well as a list of common acronyms used in this book for some especially long and/or daunting names of muscles and skeletal structures.

REMEMBERING MUSCLE NAMES

Their Latin appellations are probably the biggest obstacle to learning the names of the muscles. I encourage my terrified students to use the "gym" names for muscles that have them: "lats" instead of latissimus dorsii, "quads" instead of quadriceps, "gluts" instead of glutei, "pecs" instead of pectoralis, and so on.

Understanding the meaning of the muscles' names can also help you to memorize them. Once you understand them, you can see that the names are very practical: they indicate the muscles' origin and insertion (where they begin and end), or their action, or their morphology (shape). For example, the name *sternocleidomastoid* indicates that muscle's origin at the sternum and collar bone (*cleido*) and its insertion on the mastoid process behind the ear. *Latissimus dorsii*, or "lats," means "the big one" (*latissimus*) of the back (*dorsii*). *Tensor fasciae latae* means "the muscle that tenses the side band" (i.e., the iliotibial band).

Even some very complicated muscle names become easier to remember when you understand the meanings of the Latin words. For instance, the long name *extensor carpi radialis longus* means "the muscle that extends the wrist (*carpus*) from the side of the radius," and the incredibly long name *levator alequae nasi labii superioris*

means "the muscle that lifts the wing of the nose and the upper lip."

The English word *muscle* has an interesting and somewhat comical origin. It apparently comes from the Latin word *mus,* meaning "mouse," probably because the movements of the muscles under the skin recall the movements of a mouse under a blanket.

SOME COMMON ANATOMICAL ACRONYMS

Throughout this book, and especially in labels on images, I use some common acronyms for skeletal structures and muscles that have long, complex names. Here's the list:

AIIS	anterior inferior iliac spine
ASIS	anterior superior iliac spine
ECRB	extensor carpi radialis brevis
ECRL	extensor carpi radialis longus
ECU	extensor carpi ulnaris
EPB	extensor pollicis brevis
EPL	extensor pollicis longus
FCR	flexor carpi radialis
FCU	flexor carpi ulnaris
PIIS	posterior inferior iliac spine
PSIS	posterior superior iliac spine
TFL	tensor fasciae latae

ANATOMY, AESTHETICS, AND REALISM—SCULPTURE "DISSECTED"

In the 1940s, the art historian Gisela Richter published the book *Kouroi: A Study of the Development of the Greek Kouros from the Late Seventh to the Early Fifth Century B.C.* In it, she discusses how *kouroi*—freestanding sculptures of nude young men—can be dated based on the level of realism they display. Elaborating on Richter's idea, I try in what follows to draw connections between anatomical accuracy and

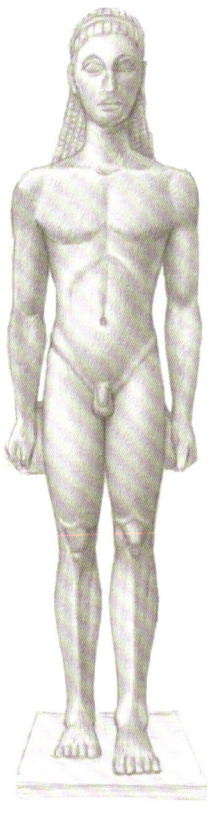

MET KOUROS
ARCHAIC (590 BCE)

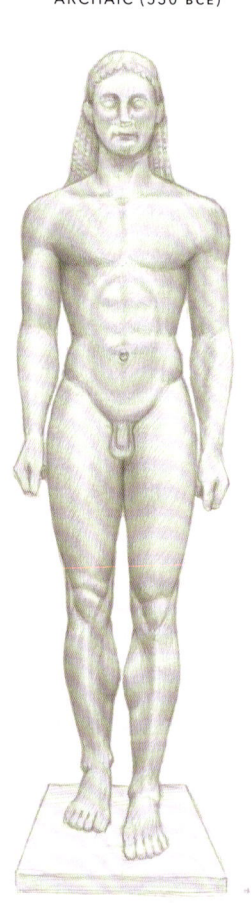

KROISOS KOUROS
ARCHAIC (530 BCE)

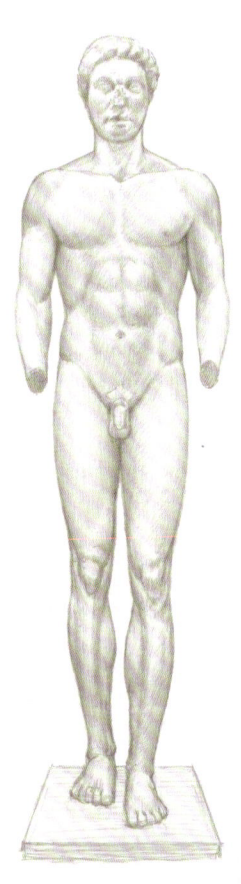

KOUROS OF ARISTODIKOS
ARCHAIC (500 BCE)

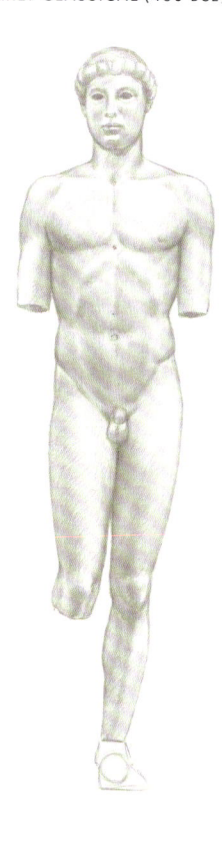

KRITIOS BOY
EARLY CLASSICAL (480 BCE)

realistic, lifelike effects and in a number of artworks from the Greek Classical period (fifth century BCE) up to the European Baroque (seventeenth century).

To do so, I have analyzed eight works from successive artistic periods with the intent of showing that increasing knowledge and accurate depiction of anatomy corresponds to an increase in an artwork's sense of life and movement and the development of a specific aesthetic. The works I've chosen are iconic and represent the highest level of technical, conceptual, and aesthetic expression of their periods.

INCREASING REALISM IN ANCIENT GREEK SCULPTURE

In ancient Greece, the sculptural depiction of the human figure changed dramatically over a the span of about five hundred years. As the level of anatomical precision increased, so did the depictions' realism, dynamism, and sense of emotional and physical life.

DORYPHOROS
CLASSICAL (440 BCE)

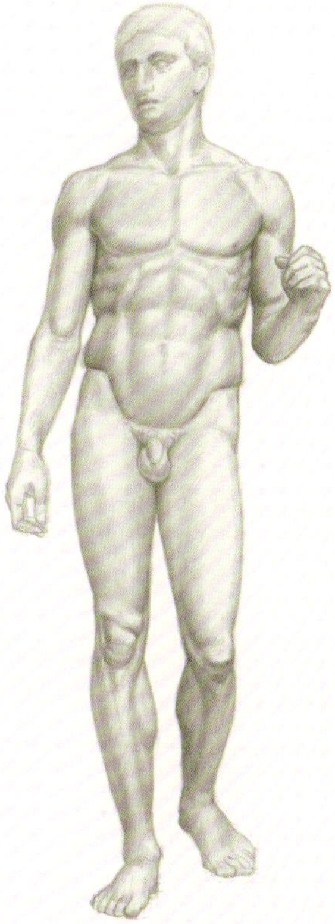

HAGIAS
LATE CLASSICAL (337 BCE)

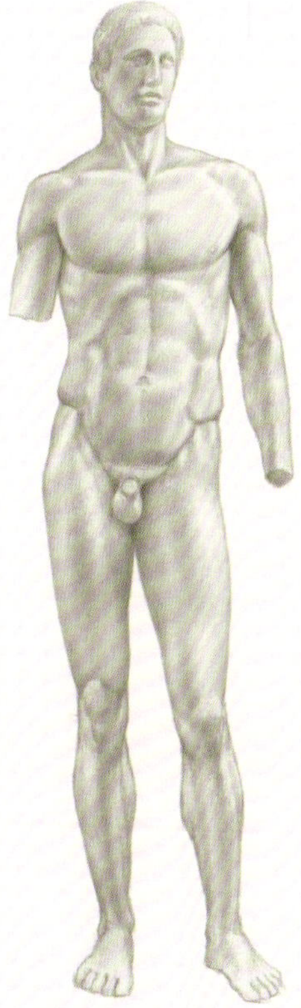

LAOCOÖN
HELLENISTIC (C. 100 BCE)

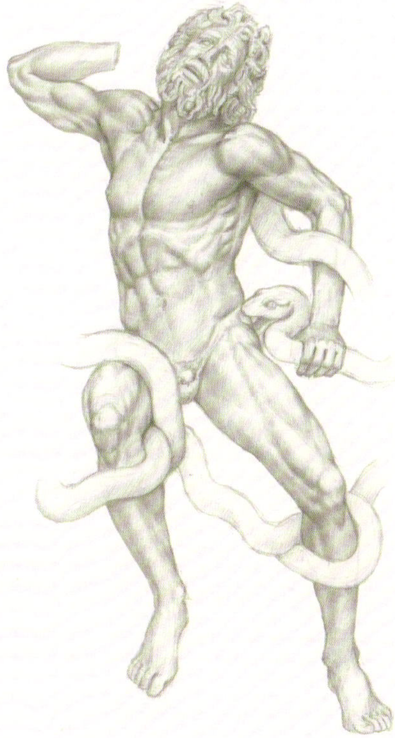

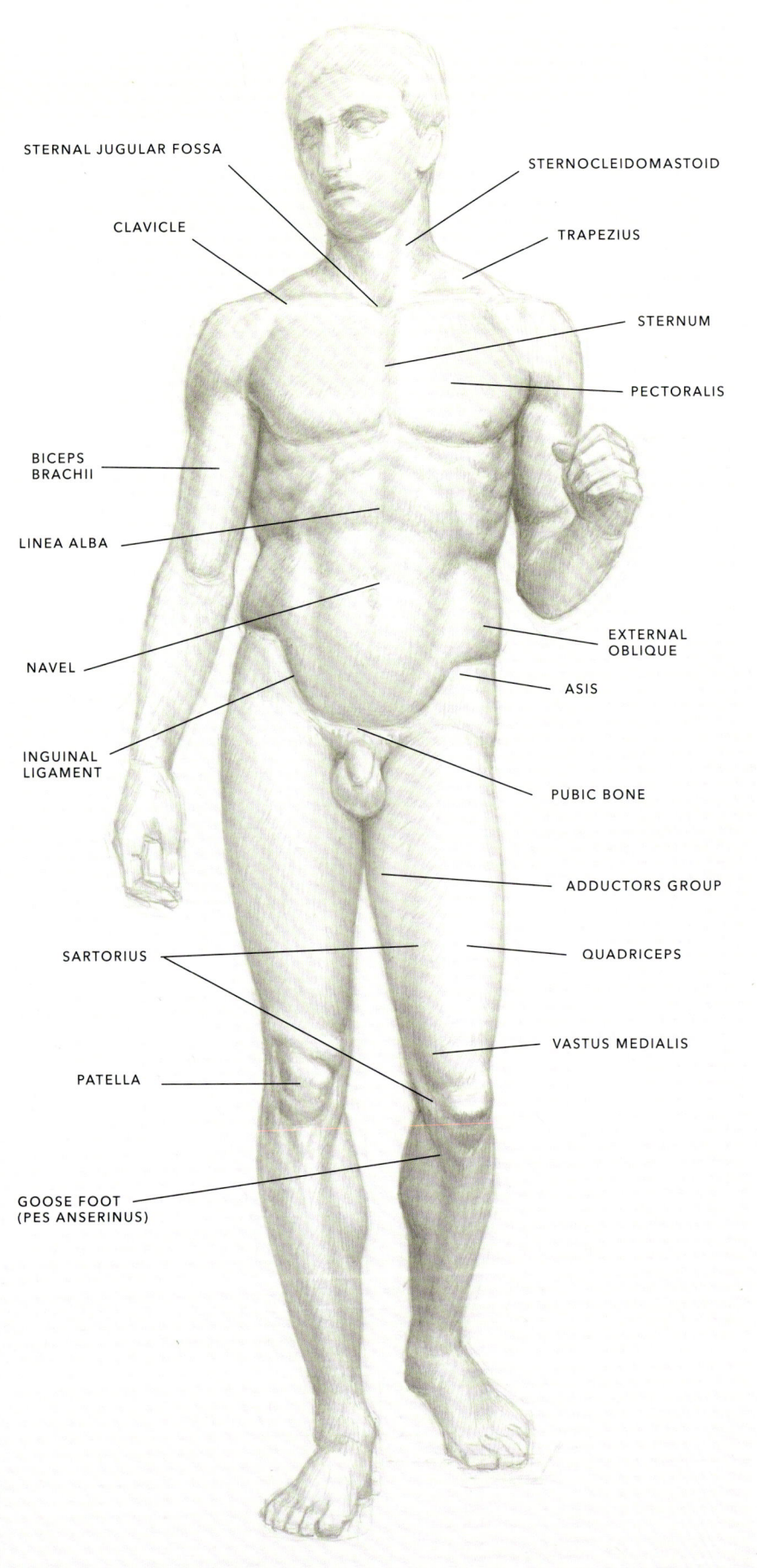

STERNAL JUGULAR FOSSA

CLAVICLE

STERNOCLEIDOMASTOID

TRAPEZIUS

STERNUM

PECTORALIS

BICEPS
BRACHII

LINEA ALBA

NAVEL

EXTERNAL
OBLIQUE

ASIS

INGUINAL
LIGAMENT

PUBIC BONE

ADDUCTORS GROUP

SARTORIUS

QUADRICEPS

VASTUS MEDIALIS

PATELLA

GOOSE FOOT
(PES ANSERINUS)

DORYPHOROS

The Doryphoros, or Spear Bearer, exhibits the proportional canons established by the Classical Greek sculptor Polykleitos in the fifth century BCE. (For more on these canons, see chapter 2.) The bronze original, dating to 440 BCE, is lost, but several Roman copies, sculpted in marble, survive. The Doryphoros's contrapposto pose and accurate (if idealized) anatomy convey a sense of impending movement and realism, and therefore of life.

All the essential skeletal and soft landmarks are properly positioned on the Doryphoros, revealing the artist's solid understanding of skeletal structure and muscular-skeletal connections. Following these landmarks, it is possible to reconstruct the skeleton of the spear bearer, as shown opposite. Although idealized in a "type" and somewhat purged of their organic aspects, the figure's muscular forms are correctly synthesized and properly positioned on the skeleton. One can speculate that the standardization of proportions and anatomical forms helped maintain certain aesthetic canons and a high level of quality in the production of this and other Classical artworks. (The identification of skeletal landmarks and muscular volumes is discussed in depth in chapters 3 and 4.)

LEFT: Rendering of Polykleitos's Doryphoros (Spear Bearer; original c. 440 BCE)

The labels on this and other drawings of sculptures that follow show that skeletal landmarks and muscular volumes are properly positioned, proving that the artists who created these works understood these anatomical connections. In my opinion, this also proves that the sculptures' forms were not obtained through mere imitation but by thorough synthesis and idealization of real anatomical structures.

OPPOSITE: Reconstructed skeleton of Doryphoros, showing skeletal landmarks

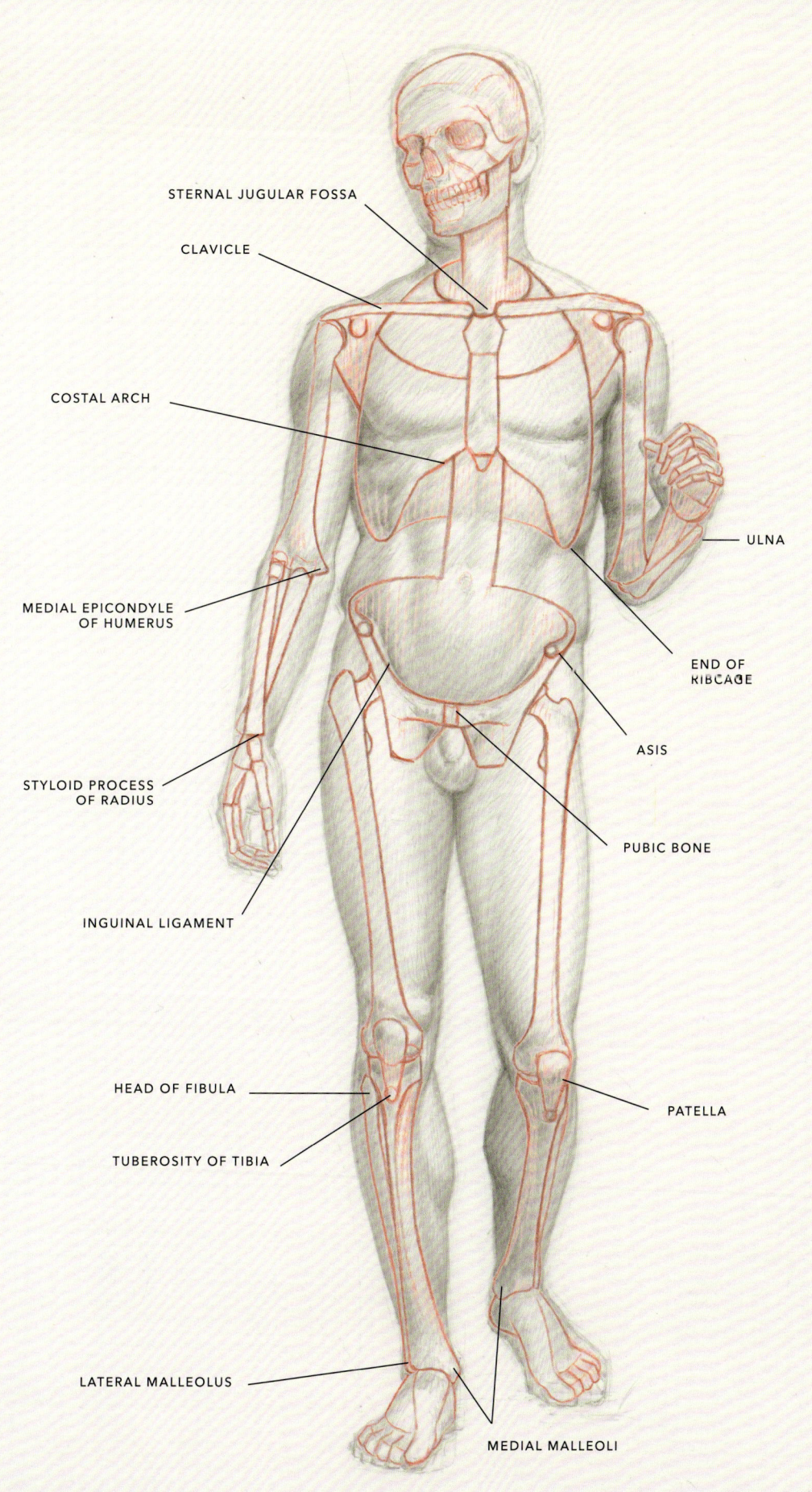

STERNAL JUGULAR FOSSA

CLAVICLE

COSTAL ARCH

MEDIAL EPICONDYLE
OF HUMERUS

STYLOID PROCESS
OF RADIUS

INGUINAL LIGAMENT

HEAD OF FIBULA

TUBEROSITY OF TIBIA

LATERAL MALLEOLUS

MEDIAL MALLEOLI

ULNA

END OF
RIBCAGE

ASIS

PUBIC BONE

PATELLA

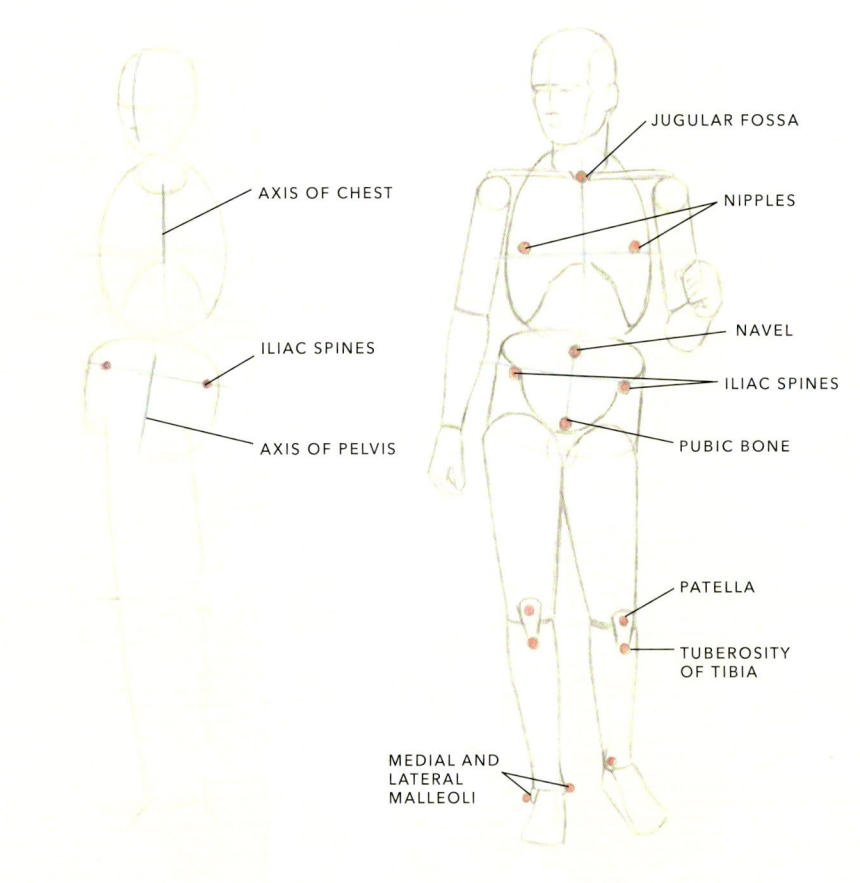

AXIS OF CHEST

ILIAC SPINES

AXIS OF PELVIS

JUGULAR FOSSA

NIPPLES

NAVEL

ILIAC SPINES

PUBIC BONE

PATELLA

TUBEROSITY
OF TIBIA

MEDIAL AND
LATERAL
MALLEOLI

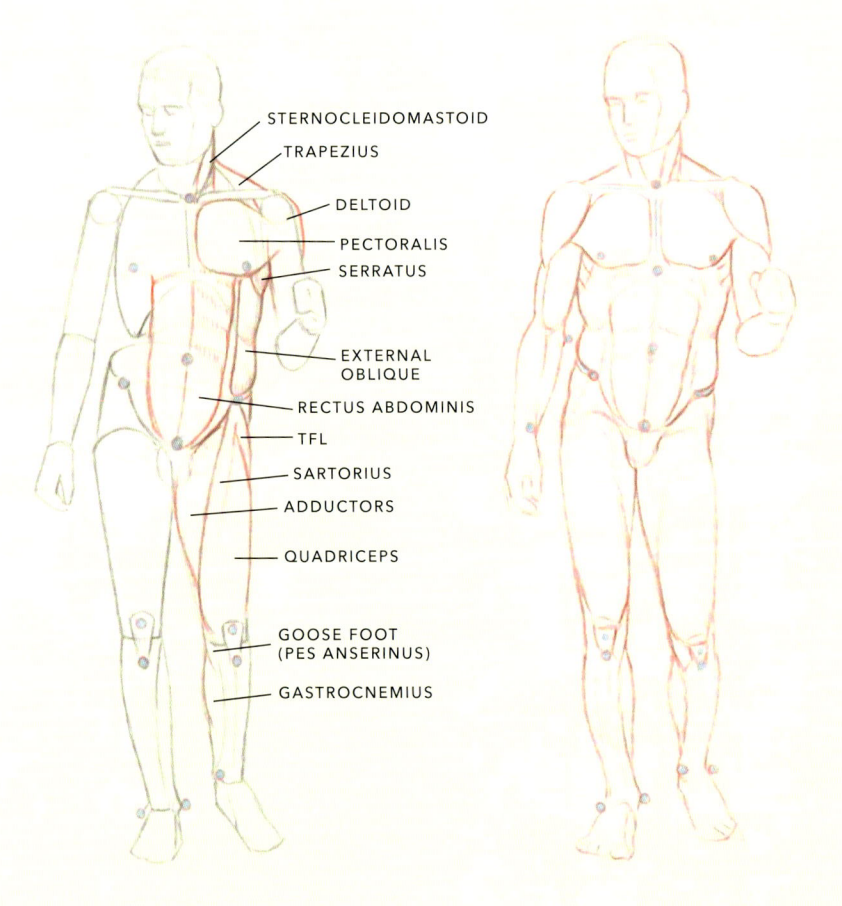

STERNOCLEIDOMASTOID

TRAPEZIUS

DELTOID

PECTORALIS

SERRATUS

EXTERNAL
OBLIQUE

RECTUS ABDOMINIS

TFL

SARTORIUS

ADDUCTORS

QUADRICEPS

GOOSE FOOT
(PES ANSERINUS)

GASTROCNEMIUS

LEFT: Sequence of Doryphoros from landmarks to external forms

With this "reverse dissection," I wanted to establish whether there is a correspondence between the skeletal and muscular structures in the Doryphoros. As you can see, it is indeed possible to reconstruct a structurally and proportionally sound skeleton using the landmarks. The muscular volumes can then be added to obtain a complete rendering of the external forms. In my opinion, this proves that the artist who created this work had a complex understanding of muscular and skeletal structures.

OPPOSITE: Rendering of Agias, by Lyssipos (c. 340 BCE)

AGIAS

The late Classical-era sculptor Lysippos created several masterpieces, one of which is this stunning statue portraying Agias, a celebrated and invincible pankration athlete. (The pankration, an event in the ancient Olympic games, was a free-form fighting sport much like today's mixed martial arts.) The original bronze, which no longer exists, dated to about 340 BCE. The figure of the Agias is more elongated overall than that of the Doryphoros, and its anatomy is slightly more detailed than that of earlier works, but the forms of the muscles still generally correspond to the type characteristic of older Classical sculptures. The modification of the proportional relationships of this new canon in relation to the previous one is also evidence of some form of systematized sculptural method and anatomical knowledge. It also creates a new aesthetic.

A celebrated, invincible athlete

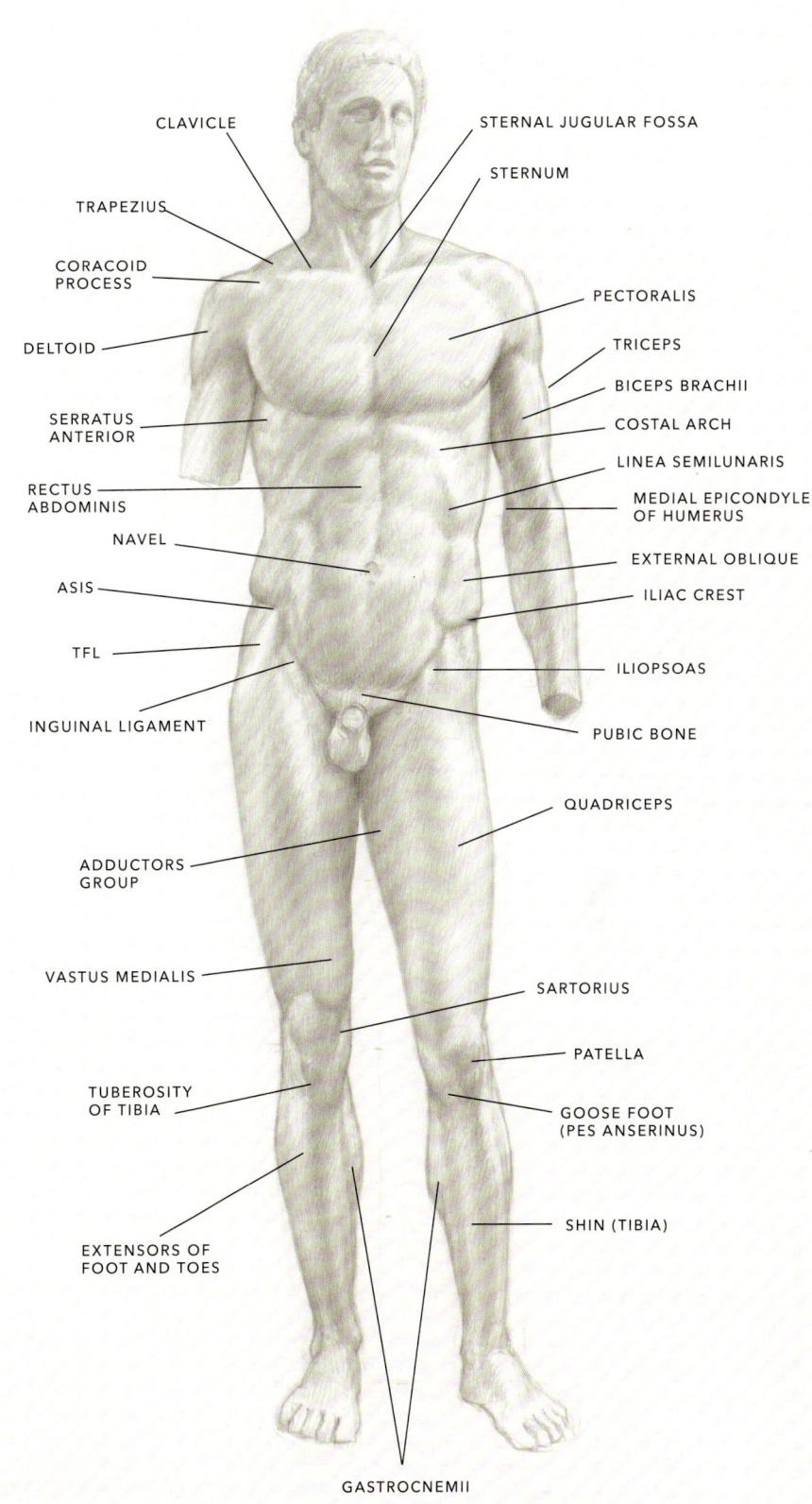

CLAVICLE
STERNAL JUGULAR FOSSA
STERNUM
TRAPEZIUS
CORACOID PROCESS
PECTORALIS
TRICEPS
DELTOID
BICEPS BRACHII
COSTAL ARCH
SERRATUS ANTERIOR
LINEA SEMILUNARIS
RECTUS ABDOMINIS
MEDIAL EPICONDYLE OF HUMERUS
NAVEL
EXTERNAL OBLIQUE
ASIS
ILIAC CREST
TFL
ILIOPSOAS
INGUINAL LIGAMENT
PUBIC BONE
QUADRICEPS
ADDUCTORS GROUP
VASTUS MEDIALIS
SARTORIUS
PATELLA
TUBEROSITY OF TIBIA
GOOSE FOOT (PES ANSERINUS)
SHIN (TIBIA)
EXTENSORS OF FOOT AND TOES
GASTROCNEMII

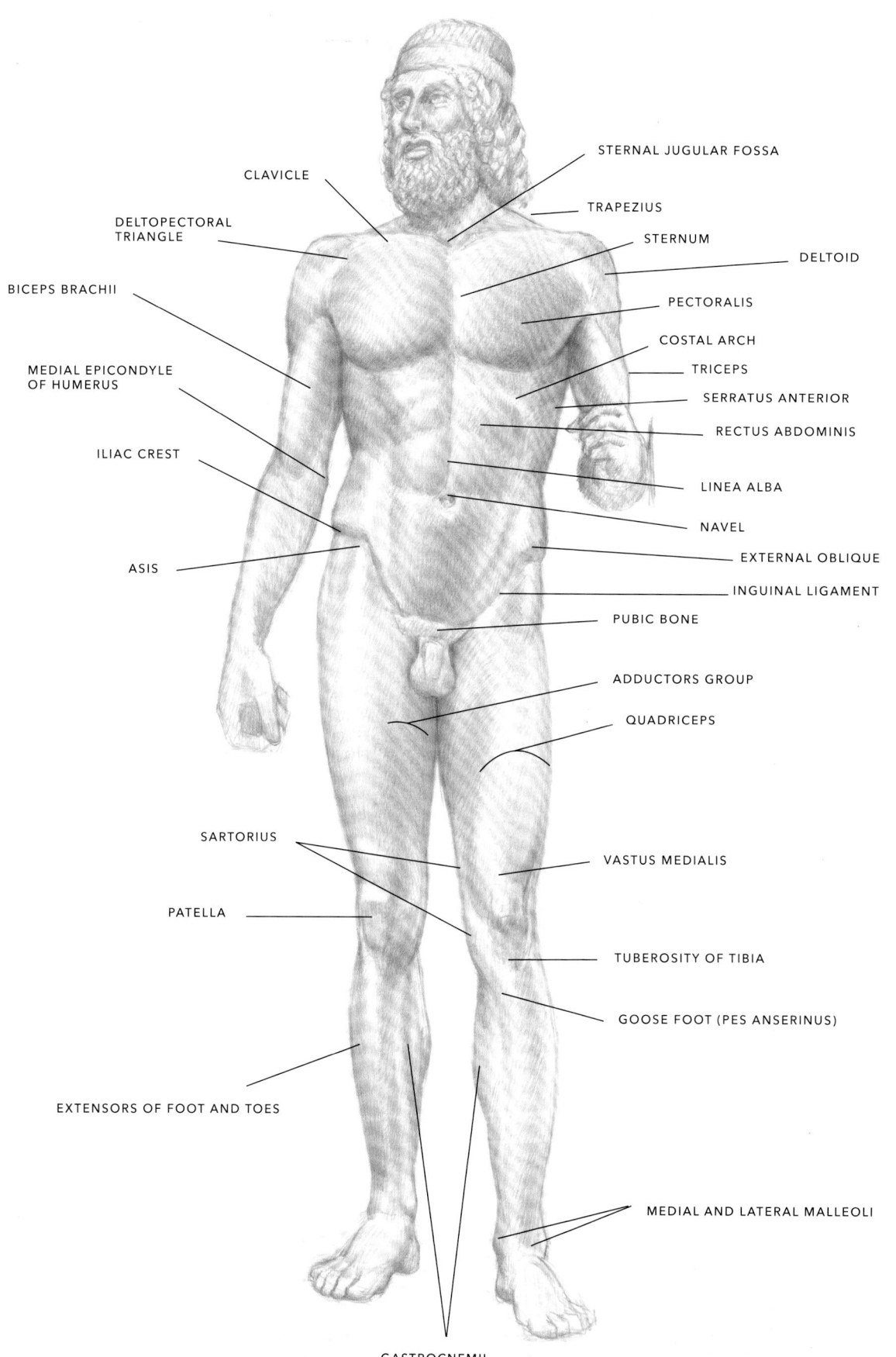

CLAVICLE

DELTOPECTORAL
TRIANGLE

BICEPS BRACHII

MEDIAL EPICONDYLE
OF HUMERUS

ILIAC CREST

ASIS

SARTORIUS

PATELLA

EXTENSORS OF FOOT AND TOES

STERNAL JUGULAR FOSSA

TRAPEZIUS

STERNUM

DELTOID

PECTORALIS

COSTAL ARCH

TRICEPS

SERRATUS ANTERIOR

RECTUS ABDOMINIS

LINEA ALBA

NAVEL

EXTERNAL OBLIQUE

INGUINAL LIGAMENT

PUBIC BONE

ADDUCTORS GROUP

QUADRICEPS

VASTUS MEDIALIS

TUBEROSITY OF TIBIA

GOOSE FOOT (PES ANSERINUS)

MEDIAL AND LATERAL MALLEOLI

GASTROCNEMII

RIACE WARRIOR

In 1972, two rare, well-preserved examples of Greek bronze sculpture were found in the Adriatic Sea off the coast of Riace, Italy. Both of these statues of warriors, dubbed *I Bronzi di Riace* (The Riace Bronzes), stand in a contrapposto pose and exhibit anatomical patterns similar to those of the Doryphoros. The forms of their pectorals, deltoids, abs, costal arches, external obliques, and inguinal ligaments correspond to the idealized types common to so many sculptures of the Classical period. Because these are original Greek works, we can deduce that the standardization of poses and of the organic forms of the body to a type is not a limitation of Roman copyists but a stylistic choice to idealize the human form.

It is difficult to ascertain with certainty what level of anatomical knowledge the sculptors of Classical Greece had—and whether they obtained their knowledge directly, by practicing dissection, or through observation of dissections, or if they relied instead on established types, perhaps supplemented by posing a real model. The Classical-era works are beautiful and powerful, but they don't display the same level of anatomical detail of later Hellenistic works like the Laocoön group or of Renaissance works whose creators acquired their knowledge through "direct experience."

Those later artists—including Pollaiuolo, Leonardo, Michelangelo, Titian, and others—attended dissections or even performed them themselves to obtain more realistic results. The Greek artists of the Classical period were not as interested in achieving such a high level of anatomical detail, probably because their works were intended to express ideal forms and models of perfection.

> A stylistic choice to idealize the human form

OPPOSITE: Rendering of one of the Riace warriors (c. 460-450 BCE)

THE VENUS PUDICA

For the Greeks, the ideal female figure (unlike the ideal male) includes forms created by fat. In the Aphrodite of Menophantos, right, the fat layers are correctly represented and positioned coherently on the muscular volumes. The bony landmarks are less visible than on male figures, but there are hints of them in all the correct places.

The term *Venus Pudica* is used to describe a pose in which the nude goddess is represented hiding her breasts and genitals. Sometimes she is exiting the water where she has been bathing; in other versions she is reaching for a towel, either to dry or to cover herself. In yet another version—called the "Crouching Venus,"—the goddess is even more embarrassed by her nudity and is portrayed in self-protective crouching pose. These poses are in strident contrast to the confident, almost exhibitionist poses of the male subjects. In a 1996 essay "The Venus Pudica: Uncovering Art History's 'Hidden Agendas' and Pernicious Pedigrees," art historian Nanette Salomon discusses how Venus, even though she is a powerful goddess, is portrayed as vulnerable and reduced to her own sexuality when shown hiding and protecting her private parts. Some other scholars, however, have characterized this pose as seductive—Venus being the goddess of love—rather than ashamed. Other female deities such as Athena (the Roman Minerva) and Hera (Juno) were not portrayed in vulnerable or seductive poses.

RIGHT: Rendering of the Aphrodite of Menophantos (1st century BCE)

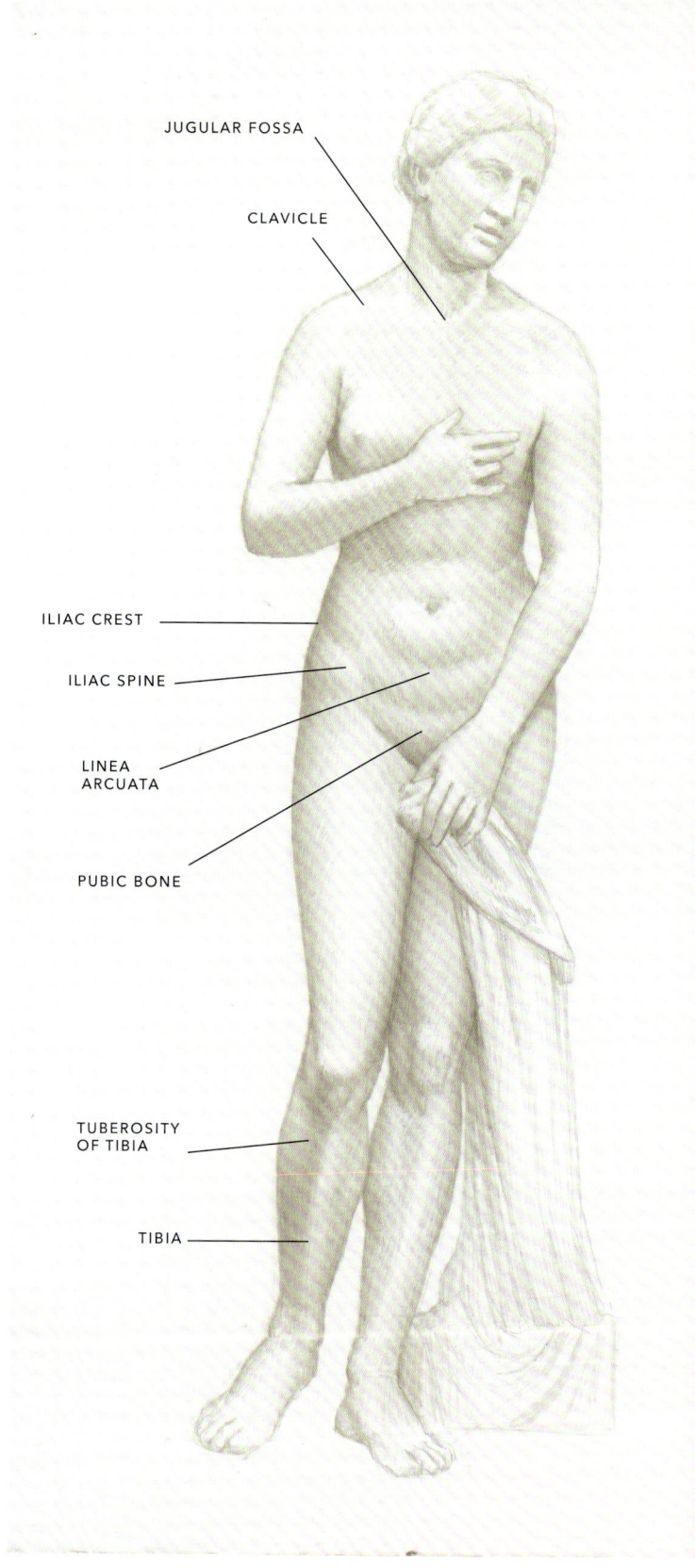

JUGULAR FOSSA

CLAVICLE

ILIAC CREST

ILIAC SPINE

LINEA ARCUATA

PUBIC BONE

TUBEROSITY OF TIBIA

TIBIA

BARBERINI FAUN

The Barberini Faun (actually a satyr) has led a very complicated life for an inanimate object: Created in Greece around 220 BCE, it was later stolen and taken to Rome. During the sixth century CE, the Roman defenders of Hadrian's Mausoleum (later known as Castel Sant'Angelo) hurled it down at the invading barbarian hordes during one of the periodic sackings of Rome. It was rediscovered in 1620 in the moat of the castle, where it had been buried beneath centuries of detritus, and it eventually entered the collection of Cardinal Maffeo Barberini. At the end of the eighteenth century it was sold to the sculptor Vincenzo Pacetti and then, after complex negotiations, was acquired by Ludwig I of Bavaria, who installed it at the Glyptothek museum in Munich, where it can be found today. Apparently, the Faun keeps sending postcards from all the places he visits to all his previous owners!

Because the head, legs, and arm of the Faun were heavily restored, I will not discuss this work too much in detail, but do note that the pose of this Hellenistic work has clear affinities with the figure of Laocoön. The Faun's head, ribcage, and pelvis are aligned along a curved axis, and his arms and legs create a vortex that hints at disquieting dreams or nightmares. Even if its muscular forms are not as exceptionally rendered as those of the Laocoön, this work displays a very good knowledge of anatomy, and its anatomical accuracy is clearly visible in the complex armpit area and the portion of the ribcage below.

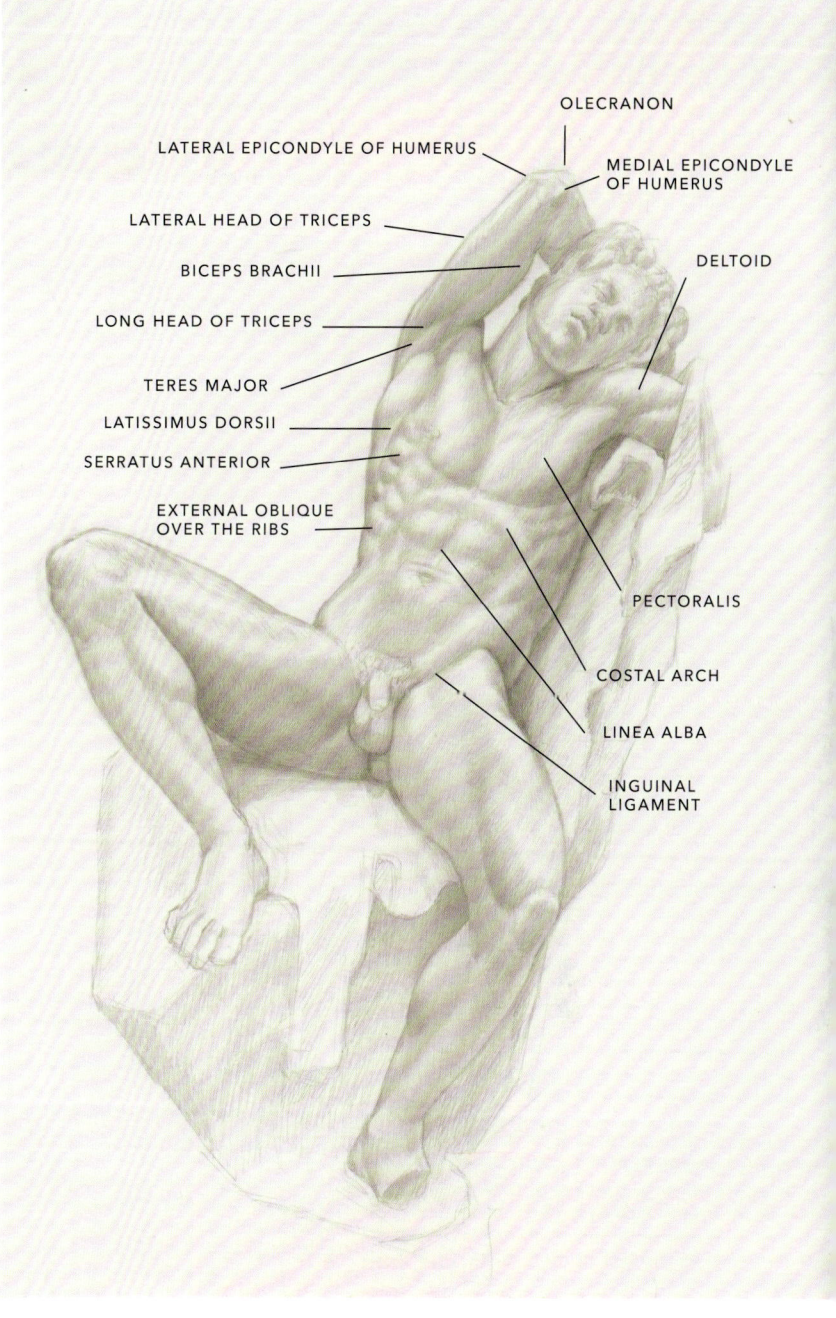

ABOVE: Rendering of Barberini Faun, c. 220 BCE

In the Barberini Faun, pose and anatomy are a vehicle to express the mysterious and powerful motions of the soul.

An inanimate
object's complicated
life

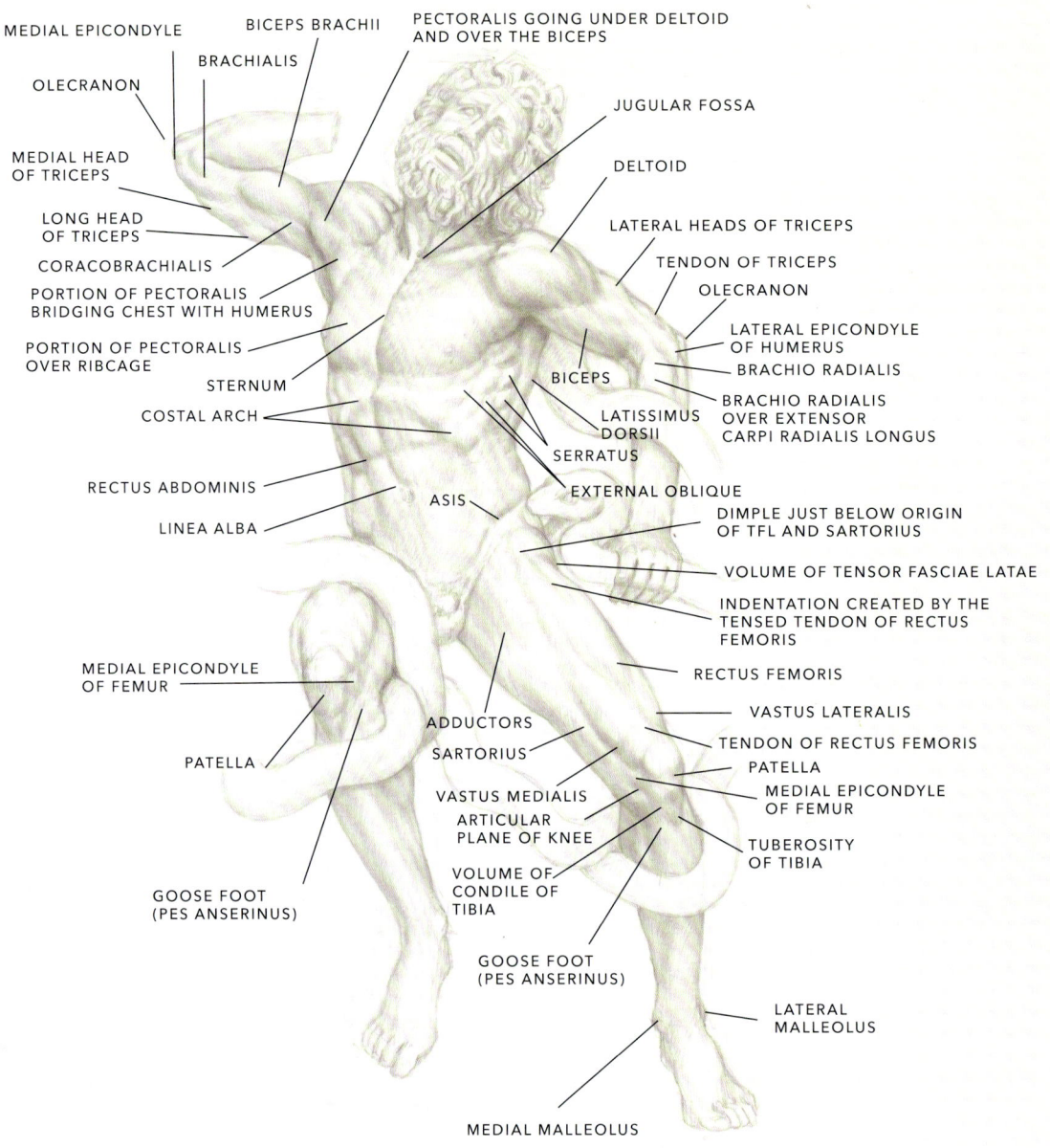

MEDIAL EPICONDYLE

BICEPS BRACHII

BRACHIALIS

PECTORALIS GOING UNDER DELTOID AND OVER THE BICEPS

OLECRANON

JUGULAR FOSSA

MEDIAL HEAD OF TRICEPS

DELTOID

LONG HEAD OF TRICEPS

LATERAL HEADS OF TRICEPS

CORACOBRACHIALIS

TENDON OF TRICEPS

PORTION OF PECTORALIS BRIDGING CHEST WITH HUMERUS

OLECRANON

LATERAL EPICONDYLE OF HUMERUS

PORTION OF PECTORALIS OVER RIBCAGE

BRACHIO RADIALIS

BICEPS

STERNUM

BRACHIO RADIALIS OVER EXTENSOR CARPI RADIALIS LONGUS

COSTAL ARCH

LATISSIMUS DORSII

SERRATUS

RECTUS ABDOMINIS

EXTERNAL OBLIQUE

ASIS

LINEA ALBA

DIMPLE JUST BELOW ORIGIN OF TFL AND SARTORIUS

VOLUME OF TENSOR FASCIAE LATAE

INDENTATION CREATED BY THE TENSED TENDON OF RECTUS FEMORIS

MEDIAL EPICONDYLE OF FEMUR

RECTUS FEMORIS

VASTUS LATERALIS

ADDUCTORS

TENDON OF RECTUS FEMORIS

PATELLA

SARTORIUS

PATELLA

VASTUS MEDIALIS

MEDIAL EPICONDYLE OF FEMUR

ARTICULAR PLANE OF KNEE

TUBEROSITY OF TIBIA

GOOSE FOOT (PES ANSERINUS)

VOLUME OF CONDILE OF TIBIA

GOOSE FOOT (PES ANSERINUS)

LATERAL MALLEOLUS

MEDIAL MALLEOLUS

ABOVE: Rendering of the Laocoön figure from the Laocoön Group, c. 2nd century BCE–1st century CE

LAOCOÖN

The Hellenistic masterpiece known as Laocoön and His Sons, or the Laocoön Group, dates from sometime between the second century BCE and the first century CE. The Roman writer Pliny the Elder attributed it to three Greek sculptors from the island of Rhodes (Agesander, Polidoros, and Athenodoros), but its creators are not known for certain. Rediscovered in 1506 during excavations in a vineyard on Rome's Esquiline Hill, it had a great impact on Michelangelo, who was one of the first Renaissance artists to see it. Soon after being dug up, it was acquired by Pope Julius II, and it remains in the Vatican Museums today.

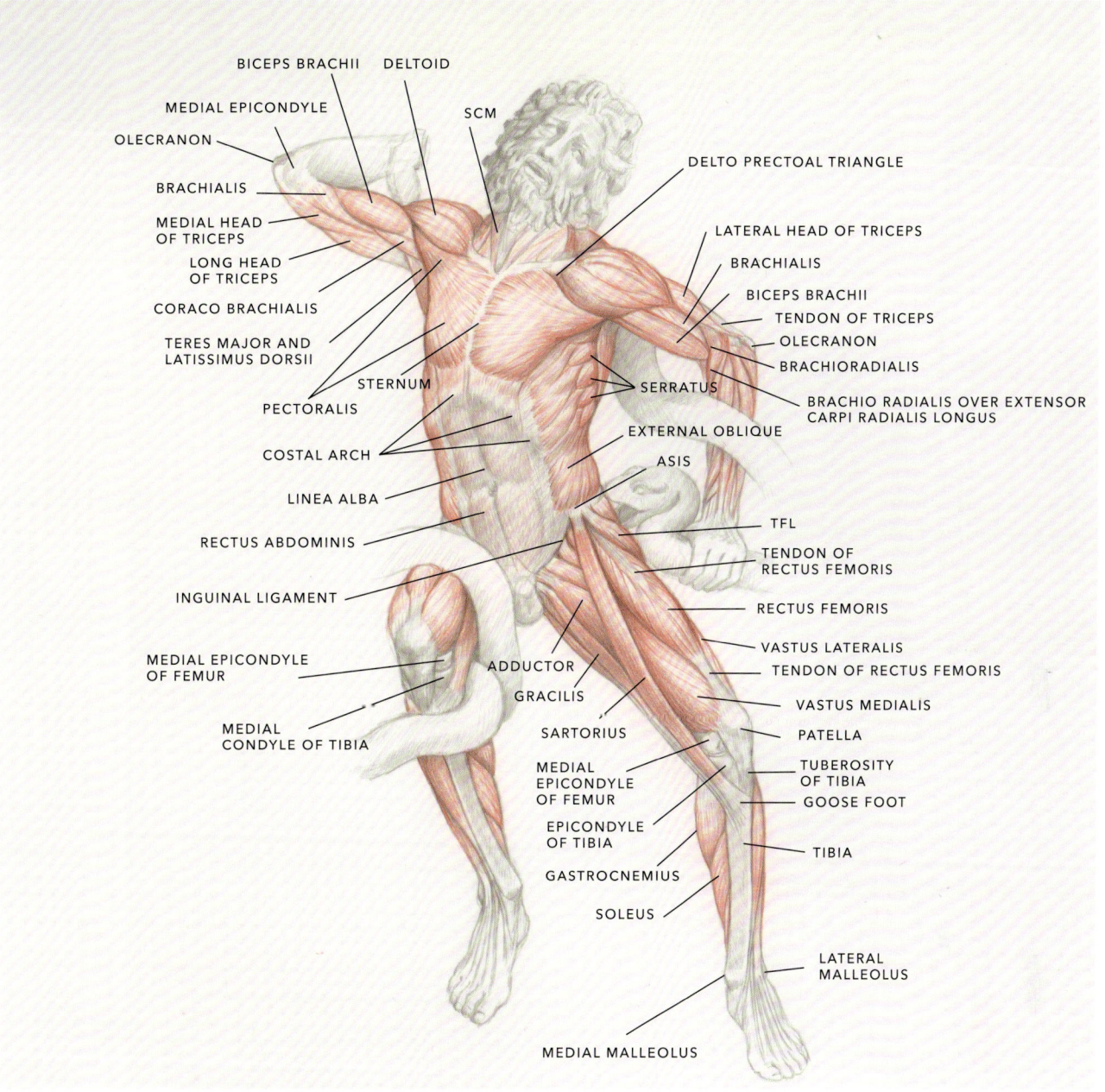

BICEPS BRACHII   DELTOID

MEDIAL EPICONDYLE

SCM

OLECRANON

DELTO PRECTOAL TRIANGLE

BRACHIALIS

LATERAL HEAD OF TRICEPS

MEDIAL HEAD
OF TRICEPS

BRACHIALIS

LONG HEAD
OF TRICEPS

BICEPS BRACHII

CORACO BRACHIALIS

TENDON OF TRICEPS

OLECRANON

TERES MAJOR AND
LATISSIMUS DORSII

BRACHIORADIALIS

STERNUM

SERRATUS

BRACHIO RADIALIS OVER EXTENSOR
CARPI RADIALIS LONGUS

PECTORALIS

EXTERNAL OBLIQUE

COSTAL ARCH

ASIS

LINEA ALBA

TFL

RECTUS ABDOMINIS

TENDON OF
RECTUS FEMORIS

INGUINAL LIGAMENT

RECTUS FEMORIS

VASTUS LATERALIS

MEDIAL EPICONDYLE
OF FEMUR

ADDUCTOR

TENDON OF RECTUS FEMORIS

GRACILIS

VASTUS MEDIALIS

MEDIAL
CONDYLE OF TIBIA

SARTORIUS

PATELLA

MEDIAL
EPICONDYLE
OF FEMUR

TUBEROSITY
OF TIBIA

GOOSE FOOT

EPICONDYLE
OF TIBIA

TIBIA

GASTROCNEMIUS

SOLEUS

LATERAL
MALLEOLUS

MEDIAL MALLEOLUS

Even though it is probably a marble copy of a bronze original, the Laocoön Group exhibits a high level of anatomical knowledge. The realism, sense of movement, and physical and psychological tension that animate the figure of Laocoön are powerfully conveyed by the bending and twisting of the body; the contraction, compression, and distension of the muscles; and the accurate depiction of the anatomy.

Examining the raised and flexed right arm, we can see the balled-up biceps brachii as it flexes. The figure's inflated deltoid shows the intramuscular lines that separate the muscle into smaller groups of fascicles as Laocoön strains to lift his arm as he fights the snakes wrapping themselves around him and his sons. Just below the

ABOVE: Laocoön écorché

As I worked on this flayed version of Laocoön, it became even more evident to me that a superficial knowledge of human anatomy would not have been sufficient to create this masterpiece. The artists clearly knew the body from the skeleton out, and a merely imitative approach would not have permitted them to reproduce the anatomy so correctly in all its forms and details.

deltoid, we see that the portion of the pectoralis bridging the chest and humerus is beautifully rendered, contributing to the action of the deltoid lifting the arm. And we can also see how the pectoralis goes under the deltoid and over the biceps as it finds its way to its insertion on the humerus. Below the biceps, the coracobrachialis, the long and medial heads of the triceps, the brachialis, the medial epicondyle of the humerus, and, finally, the olecranon are all visible.

In my opinion, this level of anatomical detail could only come from a deep knowledge of anatomy derived from anatomical dissection. Did the Greek artists practice human dissections as their Renaissance counterparts would do 1,500 years later? I don't think this can be proven. Greek physicians and anatomists such as Erasistratus and Herophilus were performing dissections in Alexandria during the fourth century BCE, but it is not clear that the anatomical knowledge they acquired was passed on to the artists. One obstacle to such a hypothetical exchange might be that artists were not considered intellectuals and had a lower social status than physicians, making a connection between them unlikely. Nonetheless, it is self-evident that sculptures of the Hellenistic period show a high level of anatomical detail usually not found in Classical works. The enhanced anatomical realism of Hellenistic artworks is indispensable to conveying the works' psychological narrative effectively and convincingly.

The Laocoön figure shows incredible anatomical precision—for example, in the raised arm and in the slightly bent left leg, from the indentation created on the rectus femoris by its tendon at the origin to the volumes of the medial epicondyle of the femur and of the medial condyle of the tibia. We can also identify the goose foot (pes anserinus) at the distal end of the sartorius, as well as the nearby tuberosity of the tibia. What makes this sculpture even more amazing is that all this anatomical correctness is coherent with the extreme straining movements of the figure.

Did the Greeks practice dissection?

THE ANATOMICAL WAXES OF LA SPECOLA

The anatomical waxes of Florence's La Specola Museum, the oldest scientific museum in the world, are some of the greatest examples of collaboration between art and science. These life-size, highly realistic waxes permitted the study of anatomy year-round to students of both medicine and art in a period when human dissections were performed only during the coldest months of the year to slow the decay of the dissected cadavers. The waxes are not just accurate in all details but also display an aesthetic aspect in their poses and facial expressions. Moreover, they show a high degree of technical execution that is not really necessary for a merely scientific tool. Anatomy and aesthetics are masterfully blended in these works.

BELOW: Anatomical models, 18th century, wax. La Specola Museum, Florence.

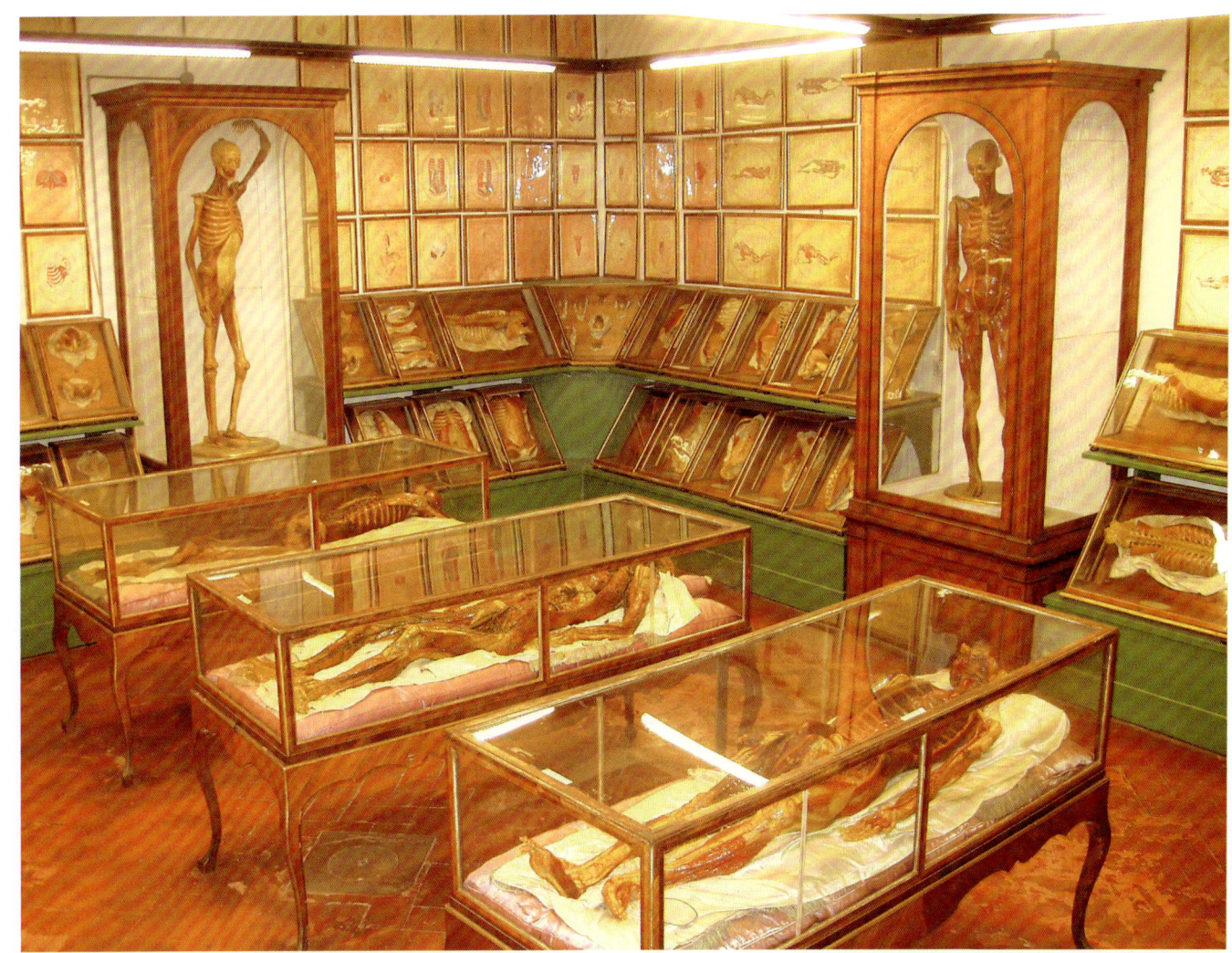

Anathomia offium corpozis humani

Os laude.i.
Os parietale.i.
Os petrofum.i.
Os parillare.i.
Os furcule.i.

Os parietale.f.
Os cozonale.f.
Os petrofum.i.
Offa paris.4.
Offa nafi.z.

Os fpatule.i.
Os adiutozij.i.

Spondiles.zot
Os furcule.i.
Os fpatule.i.
Os adlutorij.t

Cofte.rrliii.
Focile maioz.f.
Os banche.i.
Focile mioz.f.

Offa thozaci.7
os epiglotale.i
Os cozdis.i.

Os rafcete.8.
Os pectinis.4
offa digitoz.iy.

Os focile.f.:
Offa rafceti.8.
Offa pectinis.4.
offa digitozum.ty

Os fcie.i.
Os coze.i.
fpatula gëu.i.

Os pectinis des
bein des fturmbu
bels das bein der lê
dê barabifch genâ
Dalbatafar

drü fint ö bein des
arfchbübels zvelch
fin in der zal d.rrr.
£spondolen.

Os coze.i:
Rotula genu.i.
Minoz canna.i.

Minoz canna:i
Os cabab.i.

Os nauiculare.i.
Offa rafcete 4
Offa digitoz.i4.

Os cabab.i.
Os nauiculare i
Offa rafcete.4.
Offa digitorü.i.4

Maioz cãna
Minoz canna.i.
Os calcane.i.
Os calcanei.i.
Offa pectini.y.
Offa pectinis.y.

Redemption of the mortal body through art

RIGHT: "Black abdomen" figure, from *Das Buch der Chirurgia des Hieronymus Brunschwig*, Strassburg, 1497. Wellcome Historical Medical Museum, London.

This woodcut from a surgical textbook of the late fifteenth century is still deeply connected to the medieval "dance of death"—a reminder of the fragility of life. In contrast, the humanistic revolution that propelled the Italian Renaissance led to the creation of human figures that transcended death, as in Leonardo's anatomical drawings or Mantegna's *Lamentation over the Dead Christ* (opposite page).

THE REDISCOVERY OF THE HUMAN BODY IN THE RENAISSANCE

During the late Middle Ages, the practice of human dissection was revived. Dissections began at the University of Bologna around 1370, and by about fifty years later the study of human anatomy had spread to the fine arts. Many artists were now attending dissections or performing them themselves with the aim of creating

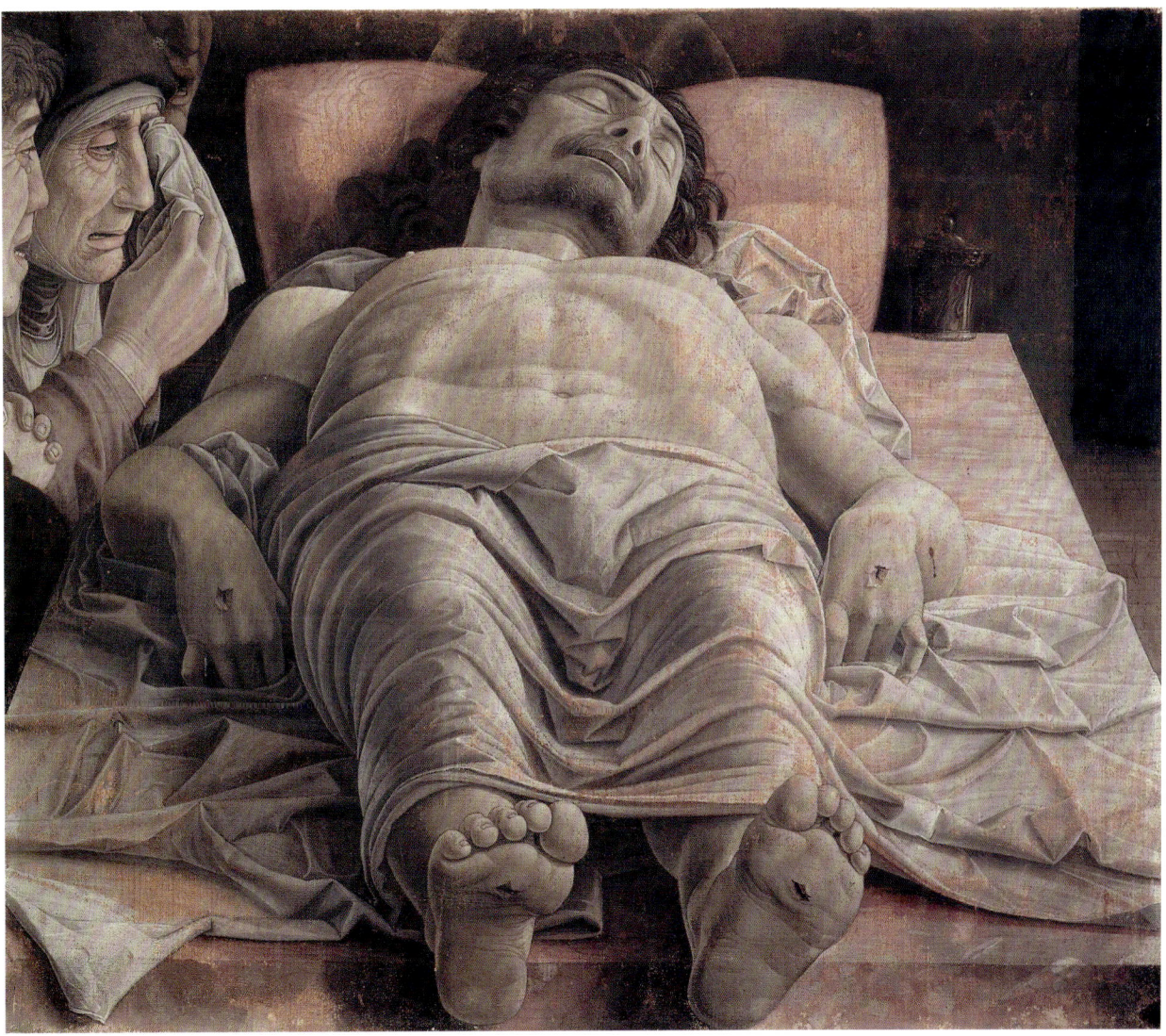

more realistic depictions of the human figure. Antonio del Pollaiuolo and Andrea Mantegna are early examples of such artists. The cadaver depicted in Pollaiuolo's *Lamentation over a Dead Hero* quite precisely recalls a body on a dissection table, as does the body of Christ in Mantegna's *Lamentation over the Dead Christ*, above.

Artists took a humanistic approach to dissection: the cadaver on the dissection table or hanging from a rope might be gruesome, but the body would be given a heroic, religious, or aesthetic meaning through art. In Jan van Calcar's woodcuts for Vesalius's *De humani corporis fabrica* (see page 40), the bodies in various stages of dissection populate an idyllic landscape; they are no longer the frightening "black abdomen" corpses of the Middle Ages, reminders of the horrors of the black death (see opposite), but instead are animated by a humanistic afflatus and represent a redemption of the mortal body, which is now glorified as an expression of the divine.

ABOVE: Andrea Mantegna, *Lamentation over the Dead Christ,* c. 1490, tempera on canvas, 26¾ × 31⅞ inches (68 × 81 cm). Pinacoteca di Brera, Brera, Italy.

MICHELANGELO'S ANATOMICAL STUDIES

Michelangelo investigated anatomy through dissections and prepared many sketches, like this one of legs, both for studying human anatomy and in preparation for specific artworks. Some of his sculptural studies of arms and the body can be seen today at Michelangelo's house in Florence, where they are preserved.

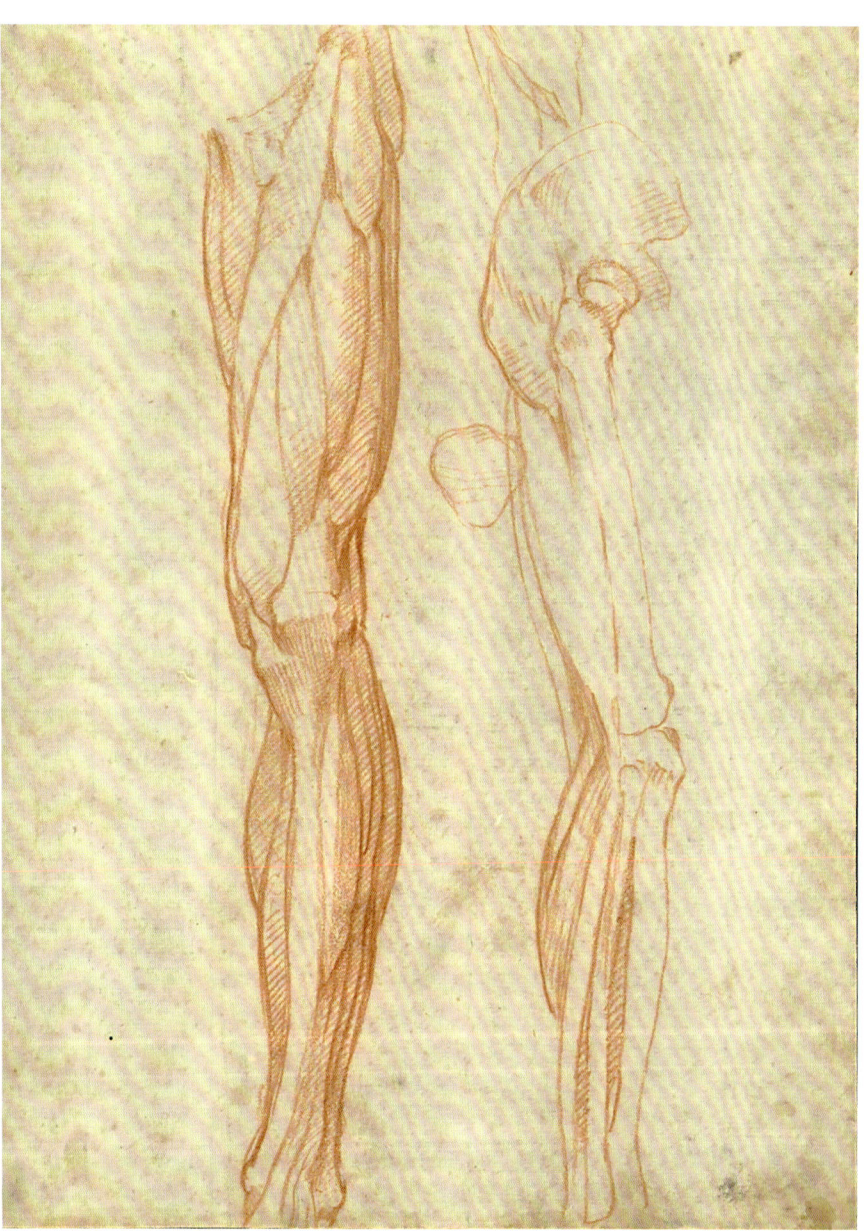

RIGHT: Michelangelo Buonarroti, study of the muscles of the left leg, seen from the front, and the bones and muscles of the right leg seen in right profile, and between them, a patella, c. 1515–20, red chalk, 10¾ × 8 inches (27.3 × 20.2 cm). Wellcome Library, London.

MICHELANGELO'S *DAVID*

During the Italian Renaissance artists applied a revolutionary method to the visual arts: direct approach, direct experience. The artists started looking at nature with a newly inquisitive eye, discarding the dogmatic or speculative methodology that characterized the approach to knowledge for most of the Middle Ages.

Mathematics, anatomy, philosophy, and direct experience were the principles that guided them. Just as artists used mathematics and perspective to create visually correct ideal landscapes, they started dissecting the human body to create more realistic depictions of the human figure. Michelangelo acquired a great deal of anatomical knowledge directly from the numerous dissections he performed, as documented by some of his anatomical drawings and beautifully expressed in works like his *David,* which displays a rare balance between ideal and organic form.

Michelangelo was impassioned about the inherent beauty of the human body, and his work shows it. Unlike the Classical sculptors of Greece and Rome, he was not interested in creating an ideal type. The anatomy of his *David,* which now stands in the Galleria dell'Accademia in Florence, is more specific, accurate, and detailed. This is visible, for example, in the ribcage and abdomen, where the ribs, costal arch, serratus anterior, and rectus abdominis are rendered with a realism that the Classical Greek and Roman sculptures do not have. Michelangelo understood and replicated with great accuracy the effect that the deep skeletal and muscular structures have on the more superficial muscular layers.

The deltoid is also more organic than in Classical figures, showing the underlying subtle volume of the coracoid process and the depression of the deltopectoral triangle. The intramuscular lines are visible in the pectoralis at the level of the sternum, and the external oblique is not so rigid and regular as those of the Doryphoros or the Riace Warriors.

A rare balance between ideal and organic form

OVERLEAF, LEFT: Rendering of Michelangelo's *David* (1501-4)

OVERLEAF, RIGHT: *David* écorché

As I did for the Laocoön, I created this écorché to demonstrate that it is possible to imaginatively flay this sculpture to reveal Michelangelo's thorough knowledge of human anatomy.

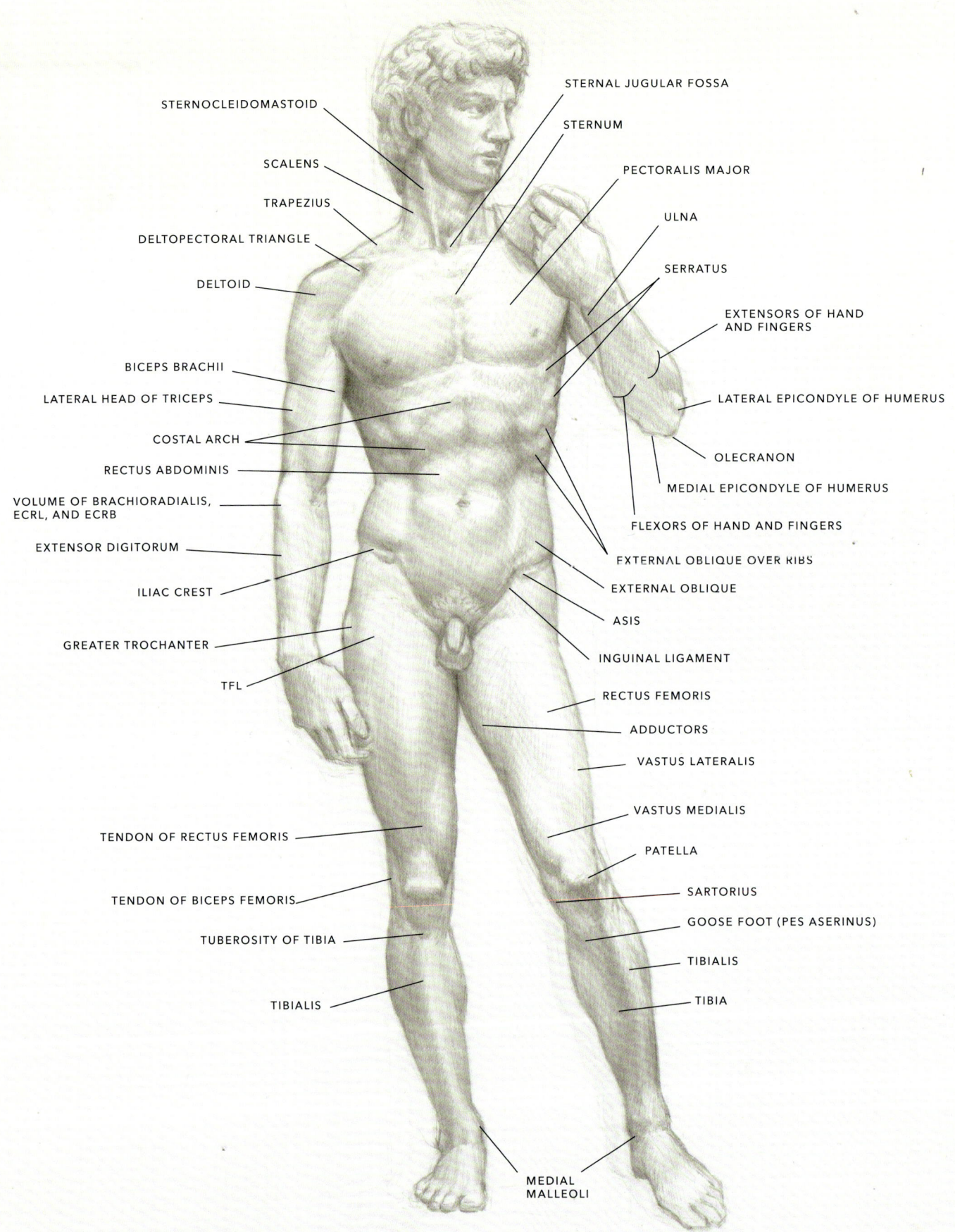

STERNOCLEIDOMASTOID

SCALENS

TRAPEZIUS

DELTOPECTORAL TRIANGLE

DELTOID

BICEPS BRACHII

LATERAL HEAD OF TRICEPS

COSTAL ARCH

RECTUS ABDOMINIS

VOLUME OF BRACHIORADIALIS,
ECRL, AND ECRB

EXTENSOR DIGITORUM

ILIAC CREST

GREATER TROCHANTER

TFL

TENDON OF RECTUS FEMORIS

TENDON OF BICEPS FEMORIS

TUBEROSITY OF TIBIA

TIBIALIS

STERNAL JUGULAR FOSSA

STERNUM

PECTORALIS MAJOR

ULNA

SERRATUS

EXTENSORS OF HAND
AND FINGERS

LATERAL EPICONDYLE OF HUMERUS

OLECRANON

MEDIAL EPICONDYLE OF HUMERUS

FLEXORS OF HAND AND FINGERS

EXTERNAL OBLIQUE OVER RIBS

EXTERNAL OBLIQUE

ASIS

INGUINAL LIGAMENT

RECTUS FEMORIS

ADDUCTORS

VASTUS LATERALIS

VASTUS MEDIALIS

PATELLA

SARTORIUS

GOOSE FOOT (PES ASERINUS)

TIBIALIS

TIBIA

MEDIAL
MALLEOLI

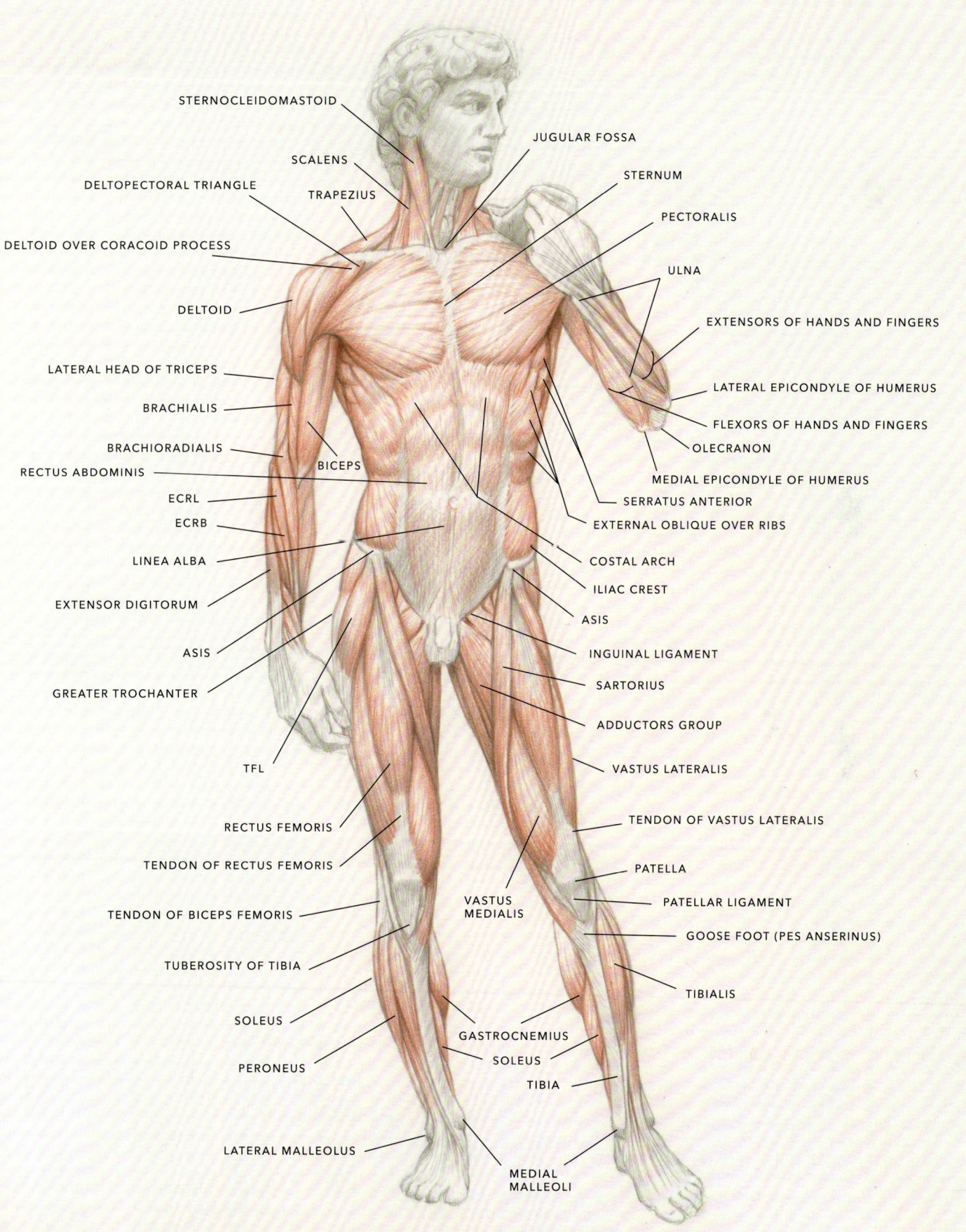

STERNOCLEIDOMASTOID

JUGULAR FOSSA

SCALENS

STERNUM

DELTOPECTORAL TRIANGLE

TRAPEZIUS

PECTORALIS

DELTOID OVER CORACOID PROCESS

ULNA

DELTOID

EXTENSORS OF HANDS AND FINGERS

LATERAL HEAD OF TRICEPS

LATERAL EPICONDYLE OF HUMERUS

BRACHIALIS

FLEXORS OF HANDS AND FINGERS

BRACHIORADIALIS

OLECRANON

RECTUS ABDOMINIS

BICEPS

MEDIAL EPICONDYLE OF HUMERUS

ECRL

SERRATUS ANTERIOR

ECRB

EXTERNAL OBLIQUE OVER RIBS

LINEA ALBA

COSTAL ARCH

EXTENSOR DIGITORUM

ILIAC CREST

ASIS

ASIS

GREATER TROCHANTER

INGUINAL LIGAMENT

SARTORIUS

ADDUCTORS GROUP

VASTUS LATERALIS

TFL

RECTUS FEMORIS

TENDON OF VASTUS LATERALIS

TENDON OF RECTUS FEMORIS

PATELLA

TENDON OF BICEPS FEMORIS

PATELLAR LIGAMENT

VASTUS MEDIALIS

GOOSE FOOT (PES ANSERINUS)

TUBEROSITY OF TIBIA

TIBIALIS

SOLEUS

PERONEUS

GASTROCNEMIUS

SOLEUS

TIBIA

LATERAL MALLEOLUS

MEDIAL MALLEOLI

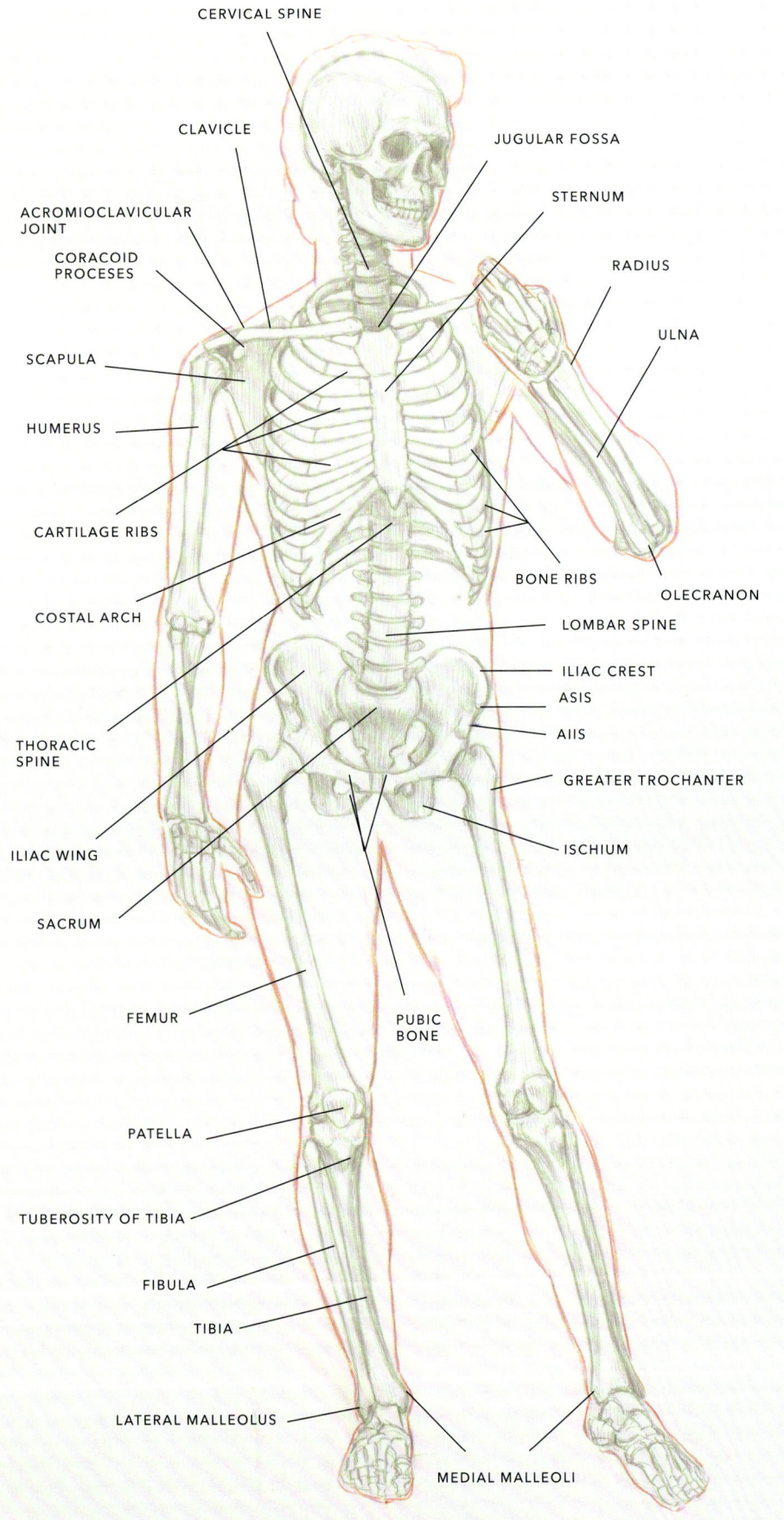

CERVICAL SPINE

CLAVICLE

JUGULAR FOSSA

STERNUM

ACROMIOCLAVICULAR JOINT

CORACOID PROCESES

RADIUS

ULNA

SCAPULA

HUMERUS

CARTILAGE RIBS

BONE RIBS

OLECRANON

COSTAL ARCH

LOMBAR SPINE

ILIAC CREST

ASIS

AIIS

THORACIC SPINE

GREATER TROCHANTER

ISCHIUM

ILIAC WING

SACRUM

FEMUR

PUBIC BONE

PATELLA

TUBEROSITY OF TIBIA

FIBULA

TIBIA

LATERAL MALLEOLUS

MEDIAL MALLEOLI

Using the same method I employed for the Doryphoros (see page 18), I reconstructed the skeleton of Michelangelo's *David* by following the bony and soft landmarks that are easily identifiable on the outside of the sculpture. The coherence between the skeletal, muscular, and external forms is evident; the muscles are also perfectly positioned over the skeleton, proving that Michelangelo had a thorough, direct understanding of structural and anatomical characteristics of the human body.

LEFT: *David* skeleton

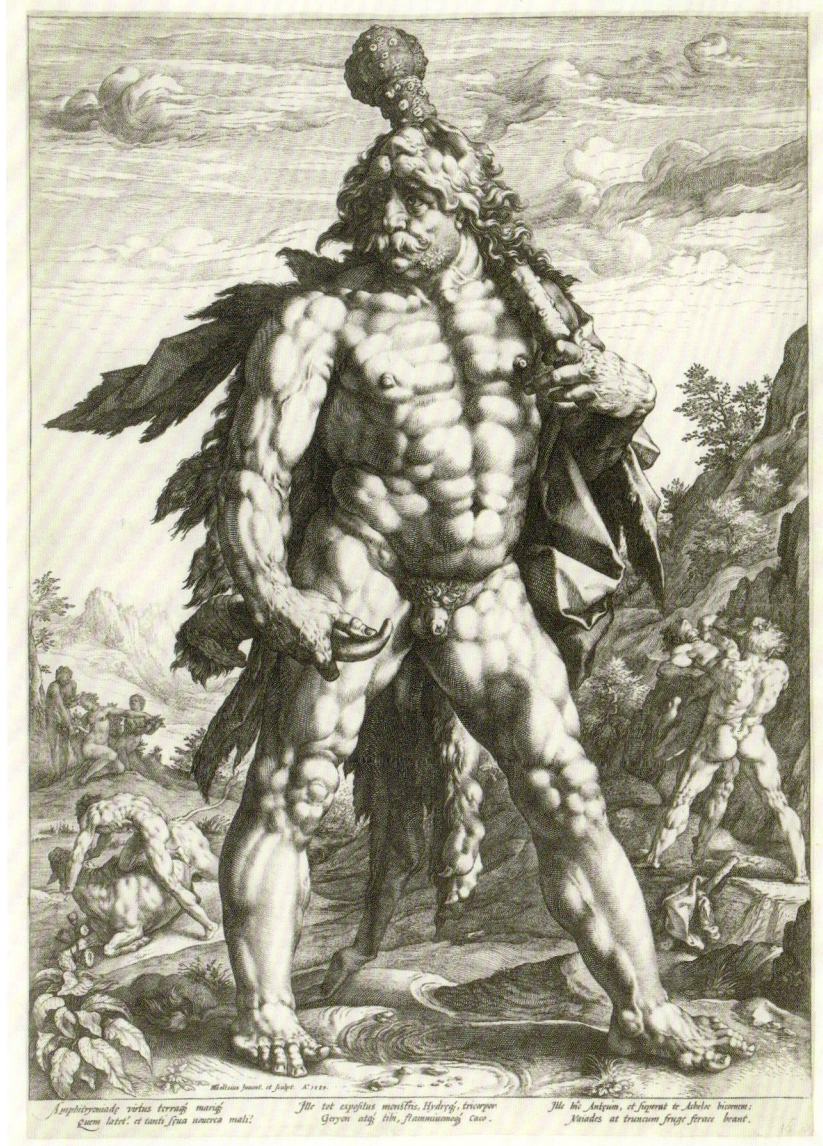

A MASTERPIECE OF *INACCURATE* ANATOMY

I am particularly fond of the work at left by the Dutch Baroque artist Hendrick Goltzius, in which the ancient mythical hero Hercules is depicted almost like a sixteenth-century German *Landsknecht* (mercenary soldier). Goltzius knew anatomy very well, as many of his works attest, but here he seems to be poking fun at the Classical tradition. Hercules's burly body resembles a sack full of sausages and eggs instead of muscles; the horn—probably ripped from the head of the Cretan Bull—mocks the tiny size of Hercules's penis. It would be interesting to create a flayed version of this work to see what new muscles would appear! It's also interesting to compare the fictitious bumps of Goltzius's Hercules to the real bumps Michelangelo depicted on the figure in his drawing of a male nude, below left.

ABOVE LEFT: Hendrick Goltzius, *The Great Hercules,* 1589, engraving, 21⅞ × 15⅞ inches (55.5 × 40.4 cm). Metropolitan Museum of Art, New York. Harris Brisbane Dick Fund, 1946.

LEFT: Michelangelo Buonarroti, *Male Nude Seen from the Back with a Flag Staff,* c. 1504, black chalk heightened with white, 10⅝ × 7¾ inches (27 × 19.6 cm). The Albertina Museum, Vienna.

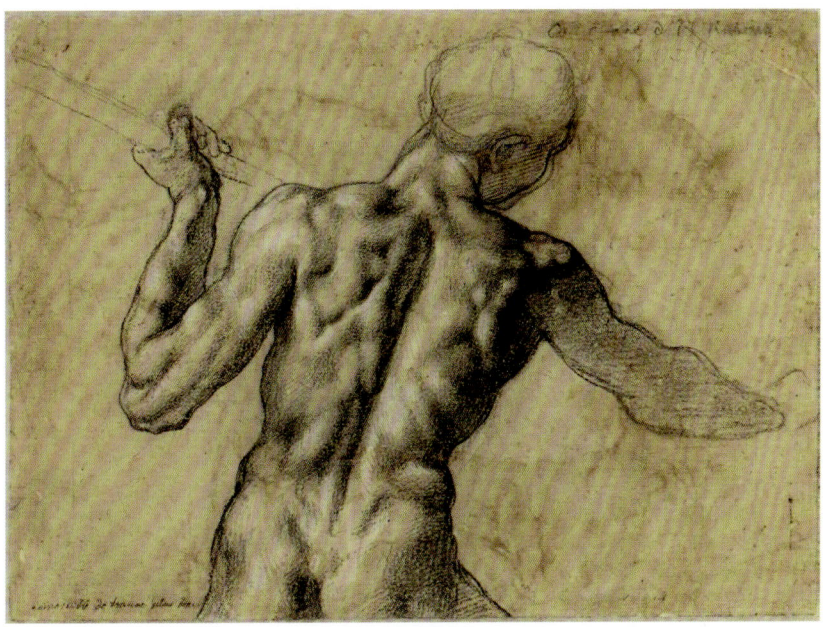

MICHELANGELO'S REBEL SLAVE

As I've mentioned, Michelangelo was one of the first to see the Laocoön Group when it was rediscovered in Rome in 1506. The contorted forms and anguished expression of the Trojan priest fighting for his life, his sons, and the safety of Troy deeply impressed and inspired him to create his own series of powerful, struggling figures. The *Rebel Slave* is one of them. The figure's physical strain is intended to visualize deep psychological tensions: the inflated muscles, which seem about to burst, are animated by passions of the soul, by erotic tension, by the struggle of the body with the soul, and by matter clashing with spirit.

Michelangelo started studying anatomy at age seventeen and practiced dissections to improve his knowledge. It is exactly because he knew anatomy so well that he could manipulate the forms of the body so masterfully. His figures, even if bulging, twisting, or stretched, are always anatomically accurate—not like the distorted figures of El Greco or the Mannerists or the powerful (and maybe sarcastic) Hercules by Goltzius (previous page), with his unreal muscular masses that make him look like a sack full of nuts. By contrast, the strong physicality of Michelangelo's figures is always based on sound anatomy, making them emotionally relatable.

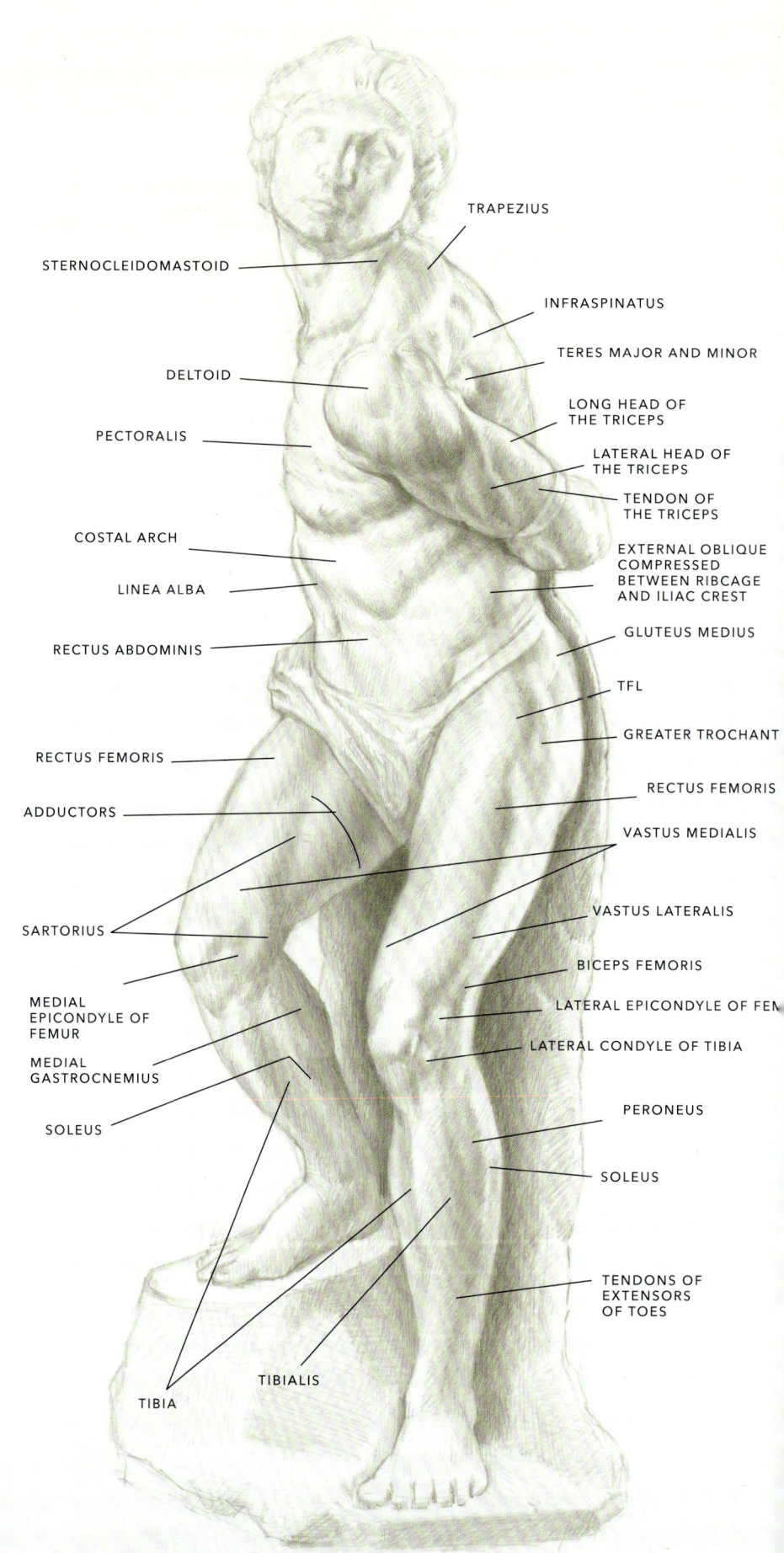

STERNOCLEIDOMASTOID

TRAPEZIUS

INFRASPINATUS

TERES MAJOR AND MINOR

DELTOID

LONG HEAD OF THE TRICEPS

PECTORALIS

LATERAL HEAD OF THE TRICEPS

TENDON OF THE TRICEPS

COSTAL ARCH

EXTERNAL OBLIQUE COMPRESSED BETWEEN RIBCAGE AND ILIAC CREST

LINEA ALBA

GLUTEUS MEDIUS

RECTUS ABDOMINIS

TFL

GREATER TROCHANT

RECTUS FEMORIS

RECTUS FEMORIS

ADDUCTORS

VASTUS MEDIALIS

VASTUS LATERALIS

SARTORIUS

BICEPS FEMORIS

MEDIAL EPICONDYLE OF FEMUR

LATERAL EPICONDYLE OF FEM

LATERAL CONDYLE OF TIBIA

MEDIAL GASTROCNEMIUS

PERONEUS

SOLEUS

SOLEUS

TENDONS OF EXTENSORS OF TOES

TIBIALIS

TIBIA

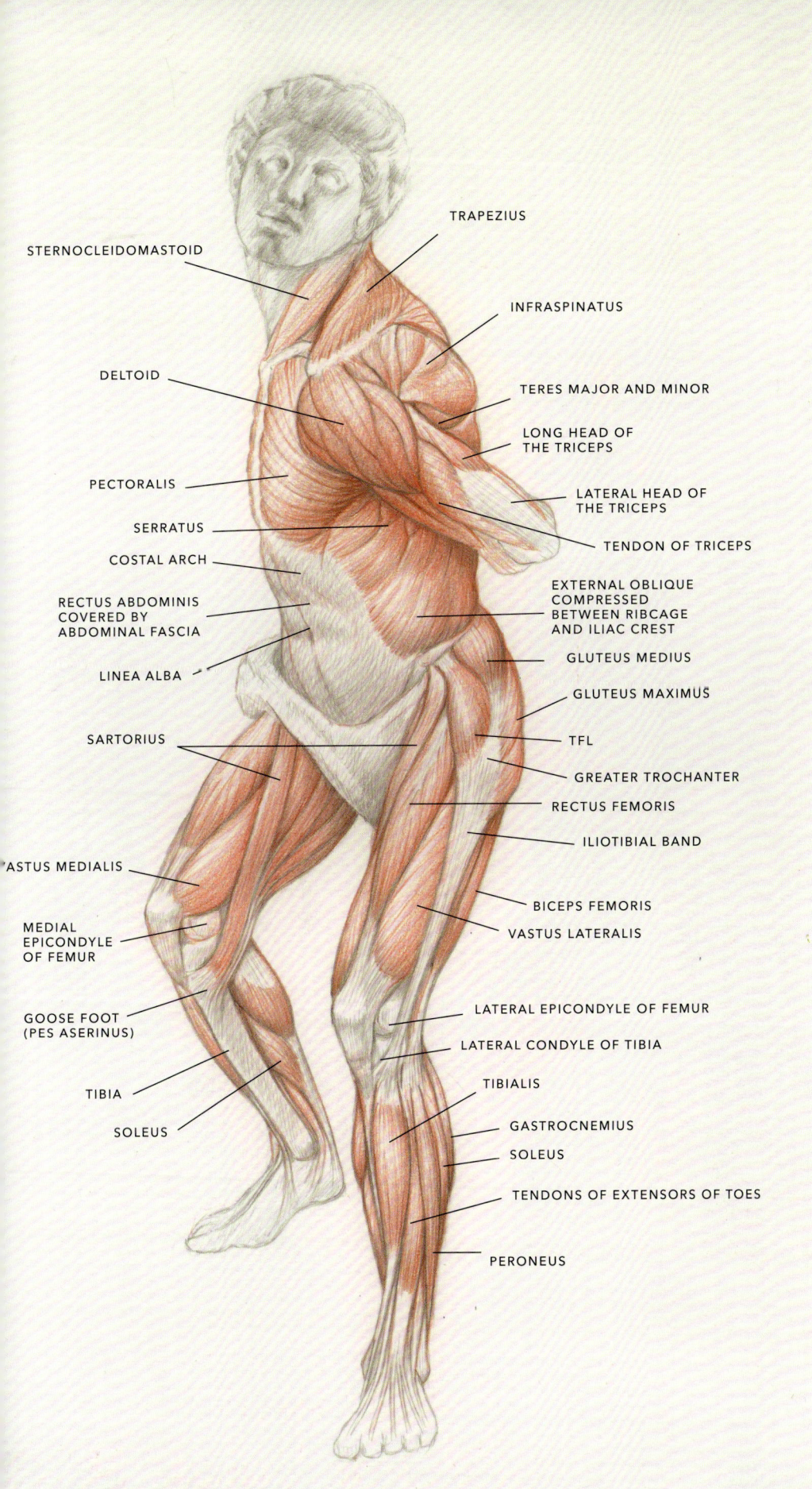

STERNOCLEIDOMASTOID

TRAPEZIUS

INFRASPINATUS

DELTOID

TERES MAJOR AND MINOR

LONG HEAD OF
THE TRICEPS

PECTORALIS

LATERAL HEAD OF
THE TRICEPS

SERRATUS

TENDON OF TRICEPS

COSTAL ARCH

RECTUS ABDOMINIS
COVERED BY
ABDOMINAL FASCIA

EXTERNAL OBLIQUE
COMPRESSED
BETWEEN RIBCAGE
AND ILIAC CREST

GLUTEUS MEDIUS

LINEA ALBA

GLUTEUS MAXIMUS

SARTORIUS

TFL

GREATER TROCHANTER

RECTUS FEMORIS

ILIOTIBIAL BAND

ASTUS MEDIALIS

BICEPS FEMORIS

MEDIAL
EPICONDYLE
OF FEMUR

VASTUS LATERALIS

LATERAL EPICONDYLE OF FEMUR

GOOSE FOOT
(PES ASERINUS)

LATERAL CONDYLE OF TIBIA

TIBIALIS

TIBIA

SOLEUS

GASTROCNEMIUS

SOLEUS

TENDONS OF EXTENSORS OF TOES

PERONEUS

Matter clashing
with spirit

OPPOSITE: Rendering of
Michelangelo's *Rebel Slave,* 1513

LEFT: *Rebel Slave* écorché

This rendering of a flayed *Rebel Slave*
shows that his inflated and twisted
forms are still based on correct human
anatomy, with each volume, form, and
bump corresponding to a specific
muscle.

ARTISTS AND ANATOMISTS

The collaboration between artists and anatomists during the sixteenth century was very fruitful. In the middle of the century, the great anatomist Andreas Vesalius authored the first complete, systematic text of human anatomy, *De humani corporis fabrica*. The work was illustrated with beautiful plates by Jan van Calcar, a Belgian artist who trained at the school of Titian in Venice.

The painting of the martyrdom of Saint Sebastian by Titian, left opposite, painted in 1570, was probably inspired both by Michelangelo's *Rebel Slave* and by images of dissections that were regularly performed in the art academies like the one at center opposite. The flayed figure from *De humani corporis fabrica*, right opposite, clearly recalls the pose of Laocoön and evokes Titian's *Saint Sebastian*, as well.

RIGHT: Plate from Andreas Vesalius's *De humani corporis fabrica* (1543)

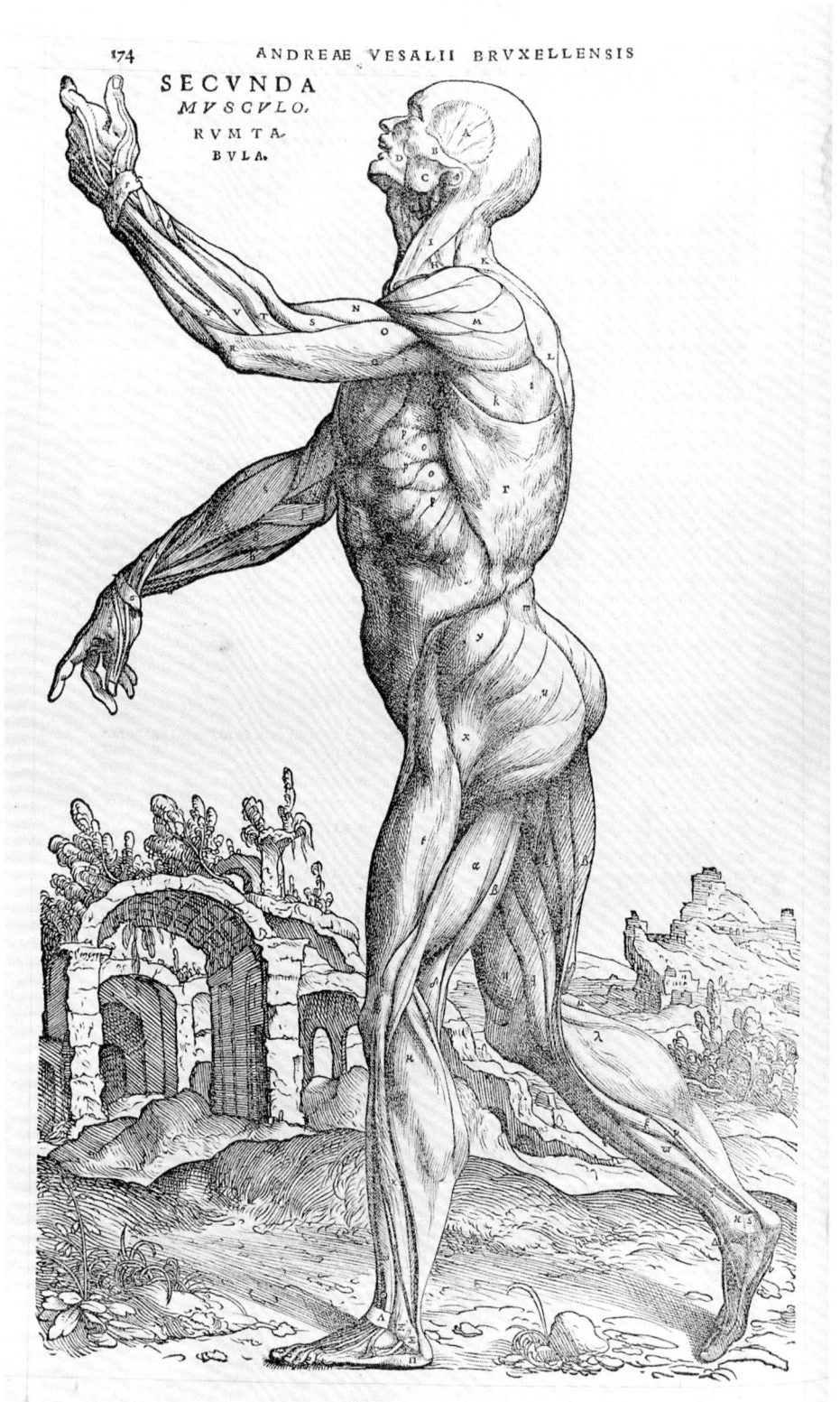

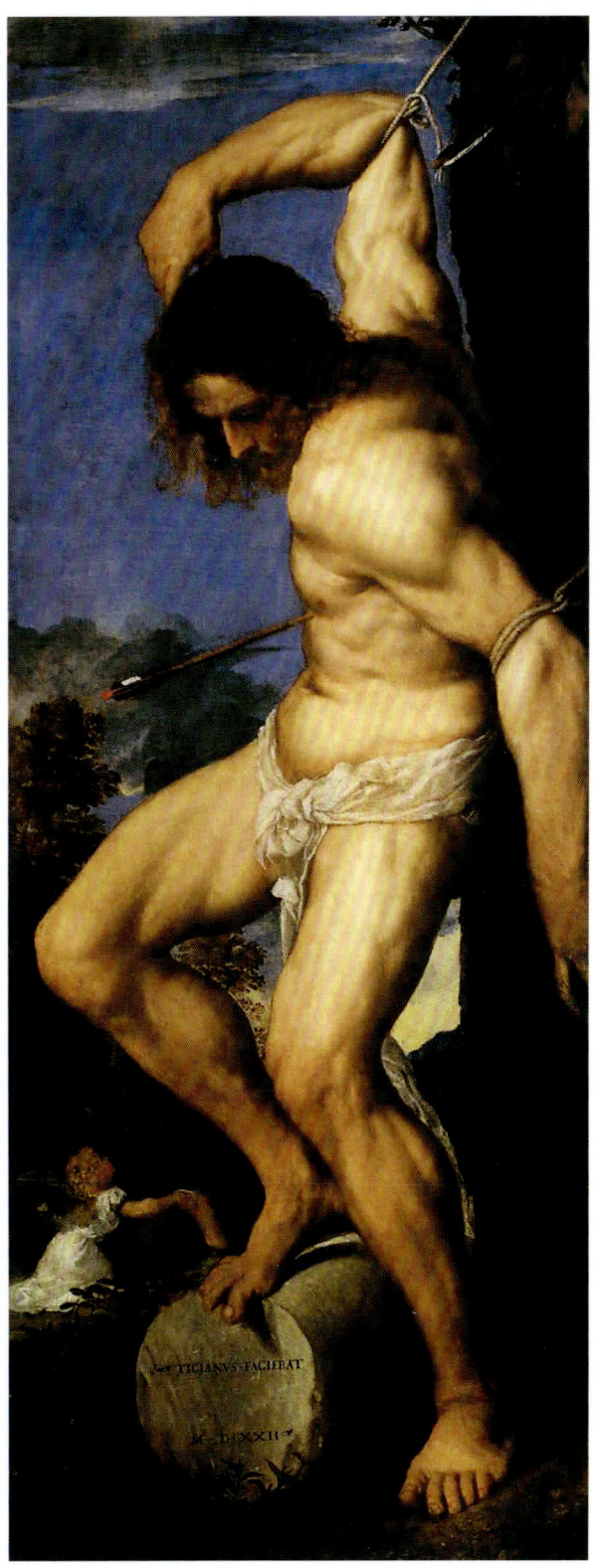

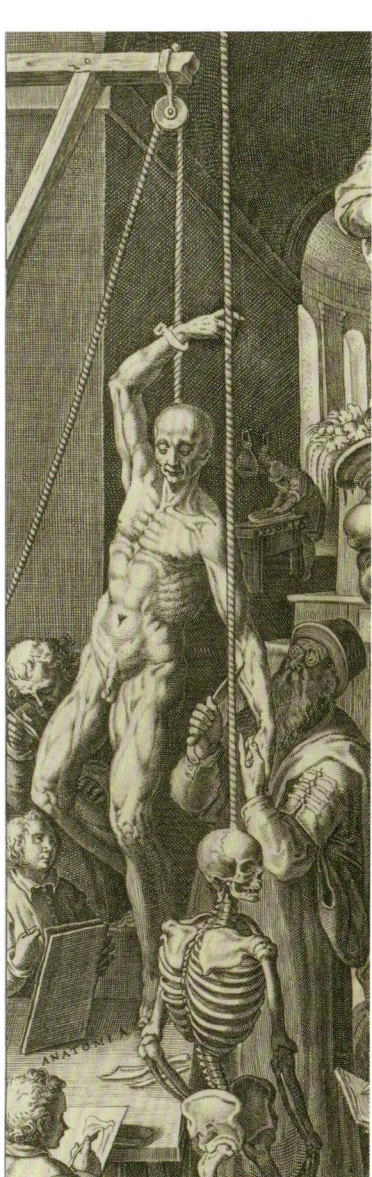

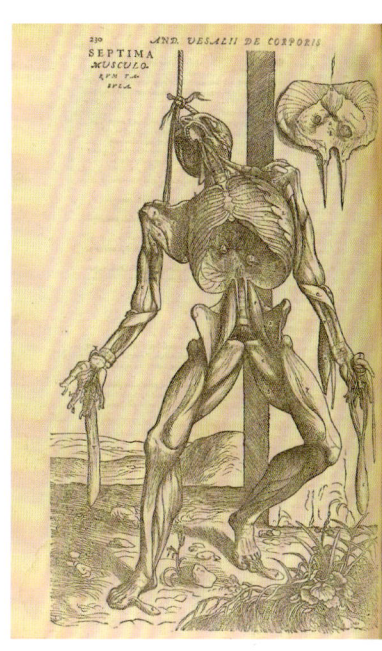

LEFT: Titian, *Saint Sebastian*, panel from the *Averoldi Polyptych (Averoldi Altarpiece)*, 1520–22, oil on canvas, 67 × 25⅝ inches (170 × 65 cm). Basilica Church of Santi Nazaro e Celso, Brescia, Italy.

ABOVE: Detail from Cornelis Cort, *Allegory of the Arts* (see page 10 for full image)

ABOVE RIGHT: Flayed figure from Vesalius's *De humani corporis fabrica*

INTER-PENETRATION IN BAROQUE ART

A term that describes the essence of Baroque art is *interpenetration*—interpenetration of light and shadow, of divine and human, of myth and reality, and of past, present, and future. For example, the Baroque painter Caravaggio challenged the physical identity of the human form with the interplay of light and shadow; he challenged time and space by projecting biblical stories and people into seventeenth-century Rome, and he challenged the insurmountable divide between human and divine by having Thomas insert his incredulous finger into Christ's chest wound in his painting *Doubting Thomas.* In Bernini's *David,* the narrative is partly expressed by the sense of movement and torsions of the body, but just as important by the intense gaze that is directed toward the implied Goliath whom David's stone is about to strike. Here, the interpenetration is between the artwork and mind of the viewer where Bernini projects the neaar-future events.

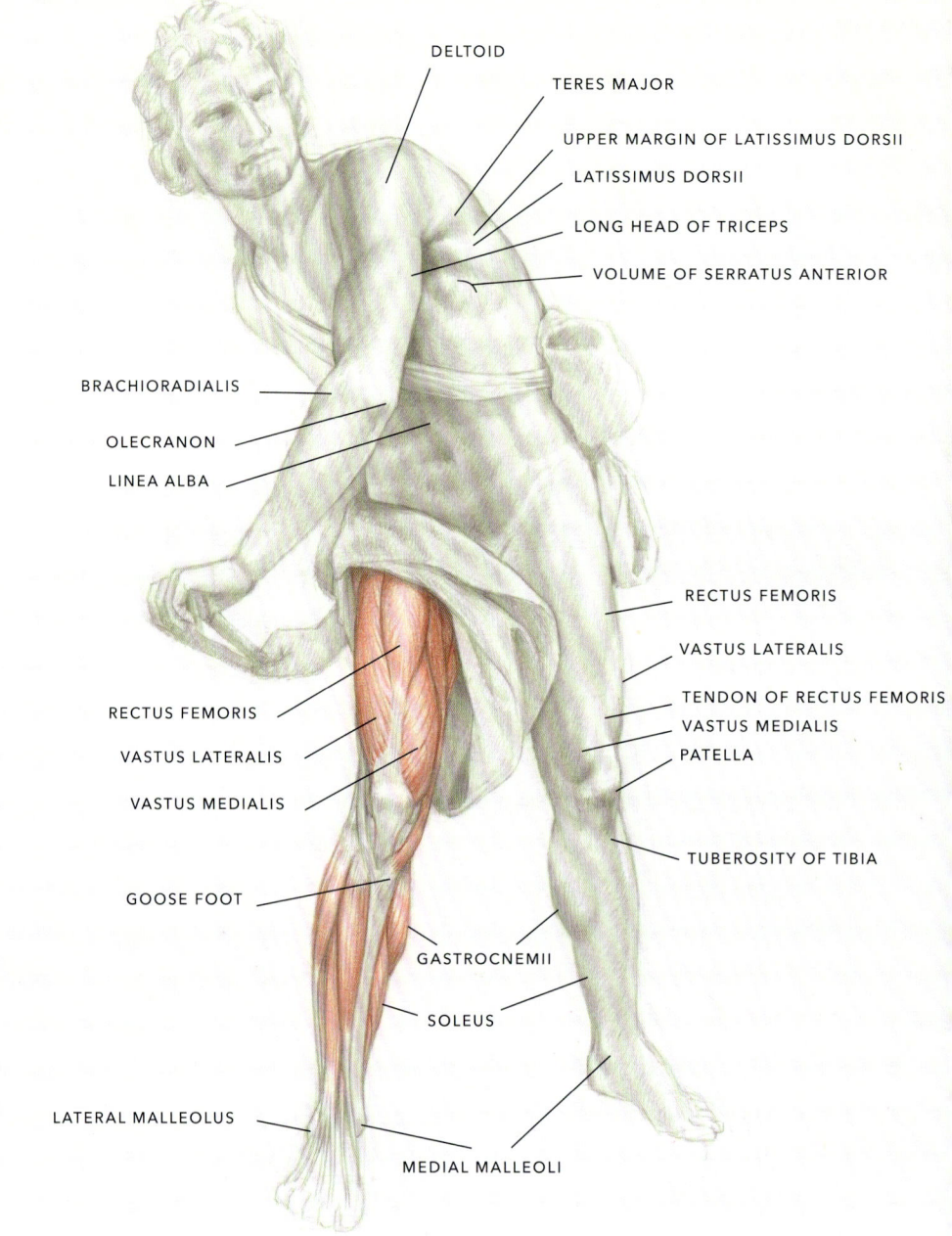

DELTOID
TERES MAJOR
UPPER MARGIN OF LATISSIMUS DORSII
LATISSIMUS DORSII
LONG HEAD OF TRICEPS
VOLUME OF SERRATUS ANTERIOR
BRACHIORADIALIS
OLECRANON
LINEA ALBA
RECTUS FEMORIS
VASTUS LATERALIS
TENDON OF RECTUS FEMORIS
VASTUS MEDIALIS
PATELLA
RECTUS FEMORIS
VASTUS LATERALIS
VASTUS MEDIALIS
TUBEROSITY OF TIBIA
GOOSE FOOT
GASTROCNEMII
SOLEUS
LATERAL MALLEOLUS
MEDIAL MALLEOLI

BERNINI'S *DAVID*

Baroque art is highly theatrical, as the sculptures of Gian Lorenzo Bernini exemplify. But Bernini's work isn't just dramatic: his *David* displays a high level of anatomical knowledge without indulging in an extremely detailed rendering. The bulging of the muscles, the twisting of the body, and even the movement of the cloth around the figure's hips convey a very convincing sense of movement. The intensity of David's gaze expresses his concentration and his intent, evoking in our mind the biblical story and its conclusion.

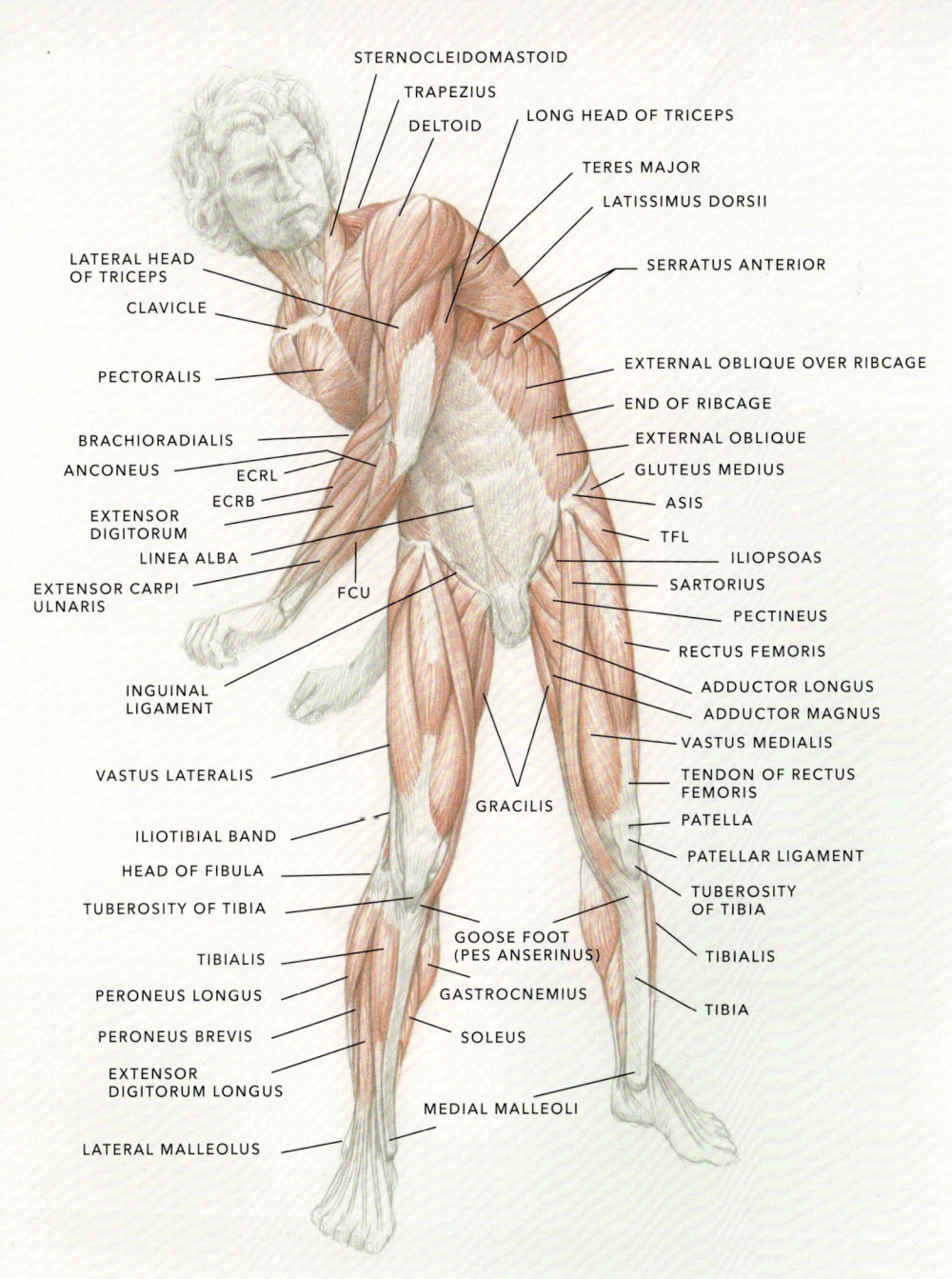

STERNOCLEIDOMASTOID
TRAPEZIUS
DELTOID
LONG HEAD OF TRICEPS
TERES MAJOR
LATISSIMUS DORSII
SERRATUS ANTERIOR
LATERAL HEAD OF TRICEPS
CLAVICLE
PECTORALIS
EXTERNAL OBLIQUE OVER RIBCAGE
END OF RIBCAGE
EXTERNAL OBLIQUE
GLUTEUS MEDIUS
BRACHIORADIALIS
ANCONEUS
ECRL
ECRB
ASIS
TFL
EXTENSOR DIGITORUM
ILIOPSOAS
LINEA ALBA
SARTORIUS
EXTENSOR CARPI ULNARIS
FCU
PECTINEUS
RECTUS FEMORIS
ADDUCTOR LONGUS
ADDUCTOR MAGNUS
INGUINAL LIGAMENT
VASTUS MEDIALIS
VASTUS LATERALIS
TENDON OF RECTUS FEMORIS
GRACILIS
PATELLA
PATELLAR LIGAMENT
ILIOTIBIAL BAND
HEAD OF FIBULA
TUBEROSITY OF TIBIA
TUBEROSITY OF TIBIA
GOOSE FOOT (PES ANSERINUS)
TIBIALIS
TIBIALIS
PERONEUS LONGUS
GASTROCNEMIUS
TIBIA
PERONEUS BREVIS
SOLEUS
EXTENSOR DIGITORUM LONGUS
MEDIAL MALLEOLI
LATERAL MALLEOLUS

A cinematic sequence of movement

The anatomical accuracy in this work is impeccable, but it is accessory to the narrative, which is always more convincing when the artwork is not hindered by technical shortcomings. Bernini does not exaggerate the physical features (as Michelangelo did in some of his works to charge them with pathos or psychological tension) but relies instead on intense facial expressions and a very realistic rendering of anatomy and movement. His *David* captures a moment in a cinematic sequence of movement, encouraging the viewer to imagine the rest of the action.

OPPOSITE: Rendering of Bernini's *David*, 1623-24, with flayed right leg

ABOVE: Écorché of Bernini's *David*

EXERCISE

One fun, engaging way to
learn the names of muscles and
their positions is to color each
muscle with a different colored
pencil and then label all the
muscles you've identified, as in
the example below, showing the
écorché of Bernini's *David*. Do
this yourself using photocopies of the three other écorchés
shown here.

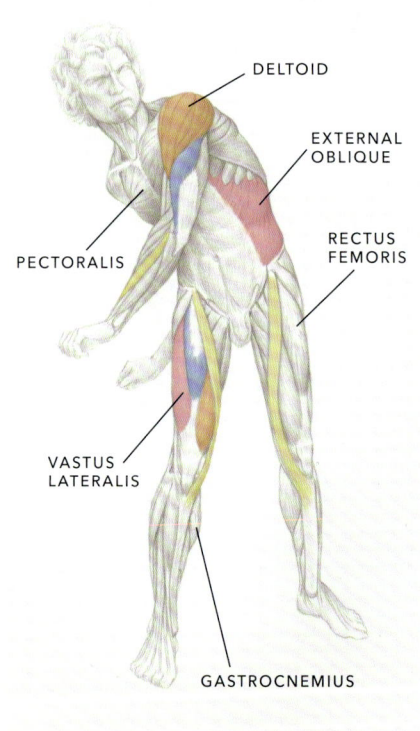

DELTOID

EXTERNAL
OBLIQUE

RECTUS
FEMORIS

PECTORALIS

VASTUS
LATERALIS

GASTROCNEMIUS

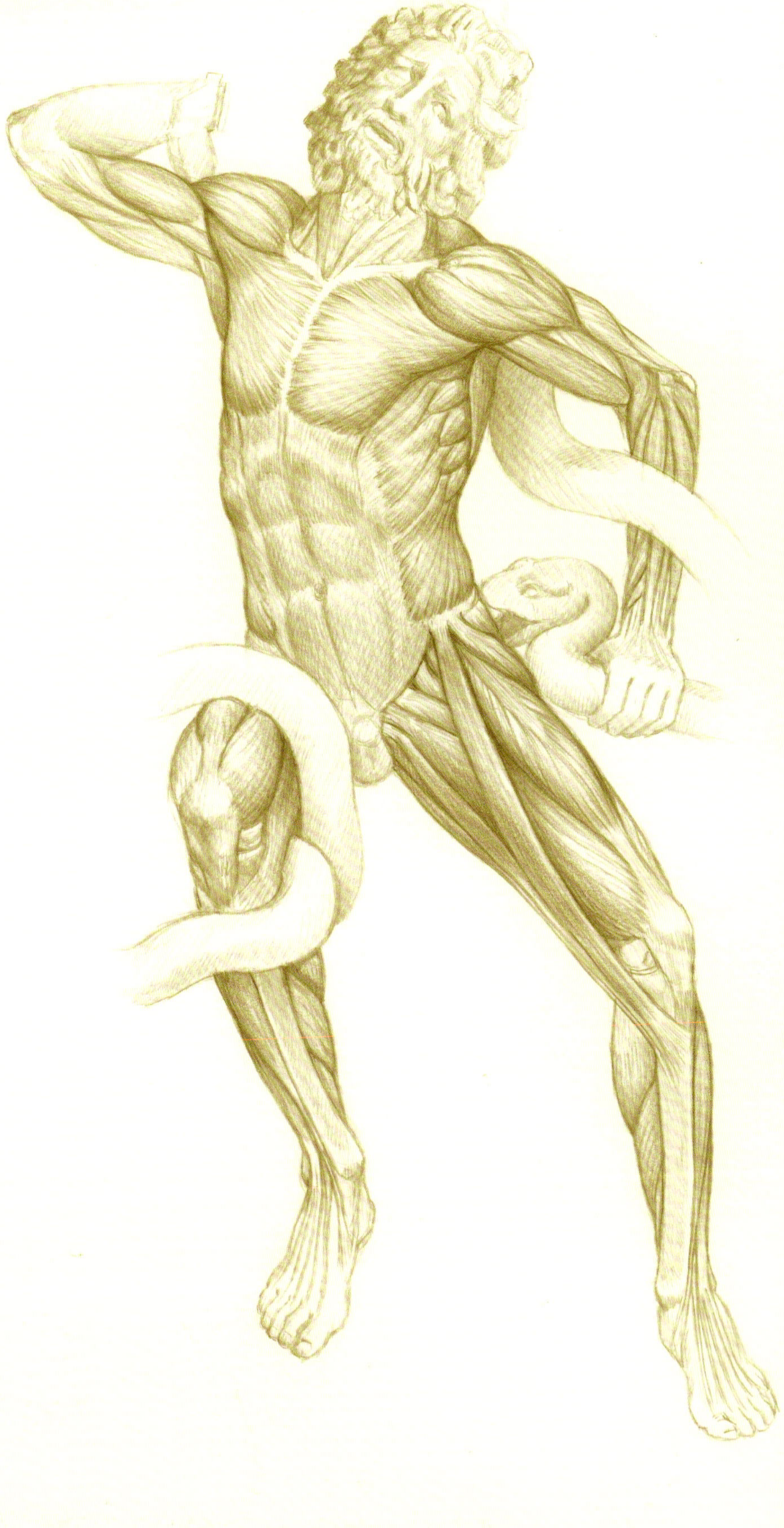

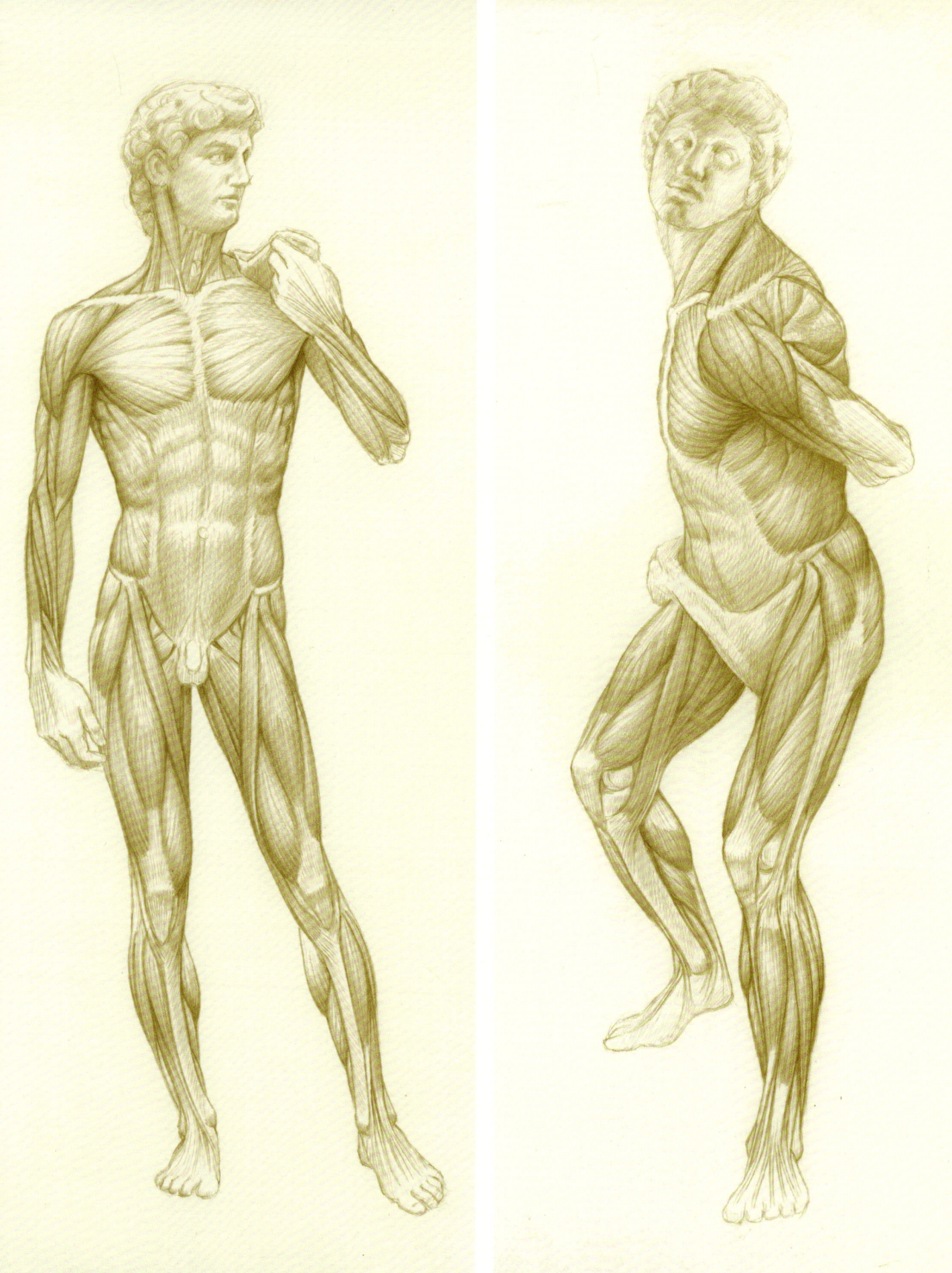

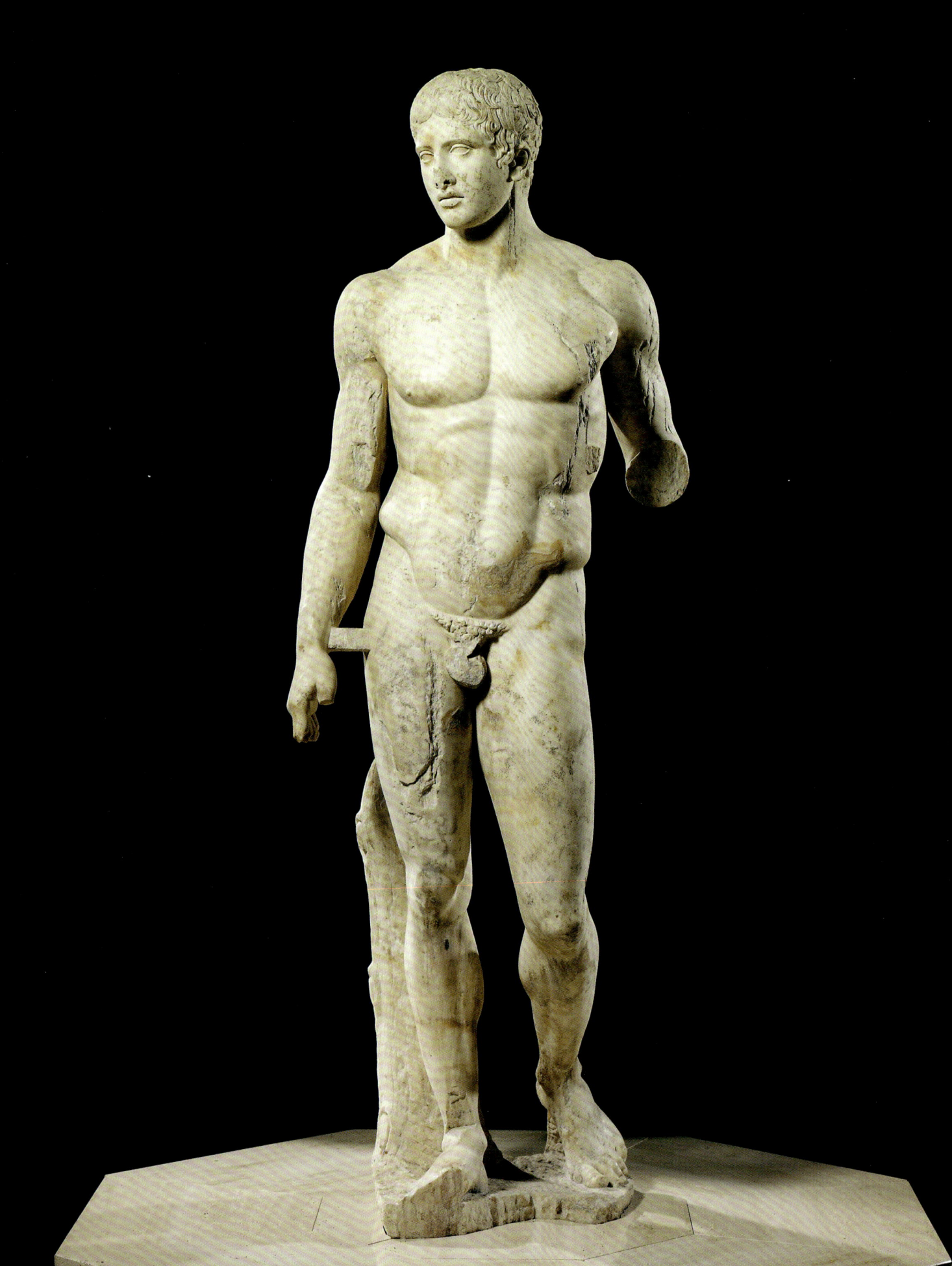

CHAPTER 2

AESTHETIC GEOMETRIES & PROPORTIONAL RELATIONSHIPS

This chapter is about applying geometry to the practice of drawing the human figure, first by using the principle of proportional relationships (meaning the typical proportions of the segments of the body in relation to each other), and then by seeing the geometric patterns and related aesthetics that can be found in the human figure. The aesthetic geometries of the human body can be inherent—meaning that they are expressed by the muscular and skeletal structures—or they can be found in a pose, a composition, or the body in movement.

OPPOSITE: Unknown Roman sculptor (after Polykleitos), Doryphoros (Spear Bearer), 50-20 BCE, marble, 78 × 19 × 19 inches (198.12 × 48.26 × 48.26 cm). Minneapolis Institute of Art, The John R. Van Derlip Fund and gift of funds from Bruce B. Dayton, an anonymous donor, Mr. and Mrs. Kenneth Dayton, Mr. and Mrs. W. John Driscoll, Mr. and Mrs. Alfred Harrison, Mr. and Mrs. John Andrus, Mr. and Mrs. Judson Dayton, Mr. and Mrs. Stephen Keating, Mr. and Mrs. Pierce McNally, Mr. and Mrs. Donald Dayton, Mr. and Mrs. Wayne MacFarlane, and many other generous friends of the Institute.

A number of Roman copies of the lost original survive today.

Proportional approaches to the human figure have been developed and used by artists since ancient times. Probably the first systematic method was developed in Classical Greece, when the human figure was idealized according to the concept of *kalokagathia,* loosely definable as the correspondence between moral rectitude and physical beauty. (The Romans would later adopt and adapt this principle as *mens sana in corpore sano,* or "a healthy mind in a healthy body.") Created by the sculptor Polykleitos in the fifth century BCE, the Doryphoros, or Spear Bearer (this chapter's opening illustration), is the epitome of this Classical ideal.

Polykleitos wrote a treatise called *The Canon,* now lost and known only indirectly through the writings of other ancient authors, that described the ideal proportional relationships of the human body. Those relationships are realized in Doryphoros, which also became known as "the Canon." This method of idealizing the human form based on sound anatomy and harmony among the various segments of the body was gradually abandoned with the advent of Christianity, when the representation of nudity—identified with paganism and sin—was suppressed.

The use of the idealized proportions and the study of anatomy for artistic purposes was not revived until the Italian Renaissance, beginning in the fifteenth century. It then became one of the core elements of art training in Western art academies for the next five hundred years. For a brief period during the twentieth century, peaking during the 1960s, this approach was purged from Western art schools, but with renewed interest in representational art, the traditional method is being recovered and is now taught in art schools and ateliers around the world.

STABILITY, UTILITY, AND BEAUTY

Renaissance artists rediscovering the Classical ideals looked back to several ancient sources. For example, Leonardo da Vinci's famous drawing known as *Vitruvian Man,* opposite, visualizes human proportions as described by the first-century BCE Roman architect and military engineer Marcus Vitruvius Pollio in his book *De Architectura*, which was widely read during the Renaissance by artists who, besides Leonardo, included the Florentine architect Filippo Brunelleschi and the German painter and printmaker Albrecht Dürer.

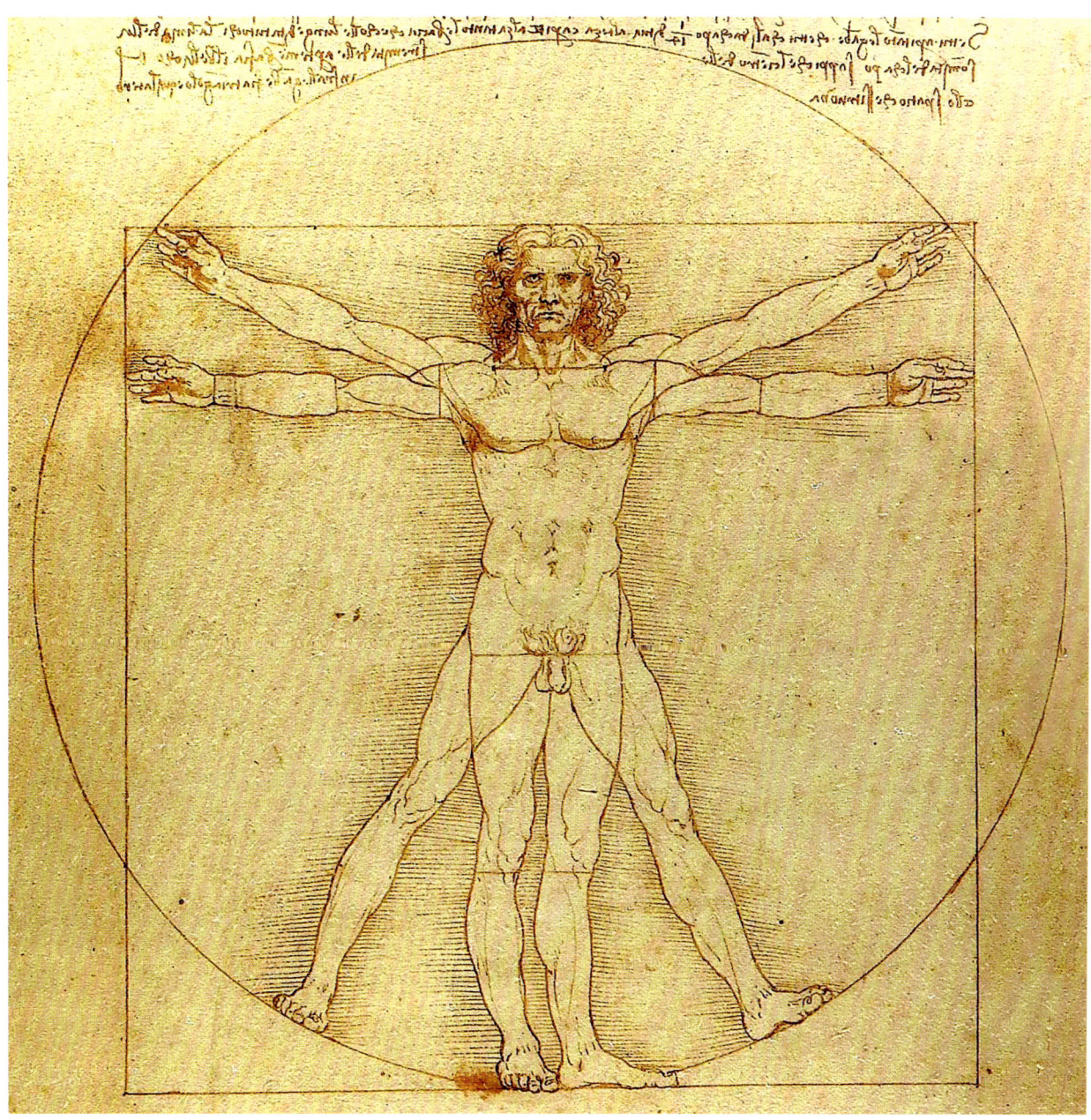

The leading principles that guided Vitruvius's architecture were stability, utility, and beauty. In his text, Vitruvius drew a correspondence between sound architecture and the structure of the human body, which is related as a whole to the space that surrounds and contains it just as the various segments of the body are related to the body that contains them. In Leonardo's *Vitruvian Man*, the section lines in the arms and legs define the proportional relationships between the various segments of the body as described by Vitruvius in his book. Vitruvius's proportions were probably the same as those established centuries earlier by Polykleitos.

ABOVE: Leonardo da Vinci, *Vitruvian Man*, c. 1490, pen and ink with wash over metalpoint on paper, 13⅗ × 10 inches (34.6 × 25.5 cm). Galleria dell'Accademia, Venice.

OTHER PROPORTIONAL SYSTEMS

Following Leonardo, other artists have systematically studied human anatomy and have developed their own proportional systems, as exemplified by the proportion studies made by Michelangelo and Dürer. And other architects besides Vitruvius have sought to harmonize the human form with the architectural space that accommodates it. In the twentieth century, the French architect Le Corbusier based his work on similar premises and created what he called the Modulor—his own version of human proportions as related to architectural space.

The method of establishing proportional relationships between parts of the body, such as the head-to-body ratio, has been used without interruption since first codified by Polykleitos. These pages show examples from the seventeenth through twentieth centuries.

RIGHT: Crisóstomo Alejandrino José Martínez y Sorli, plate for the unpublished "Atlas Anatomico," c. 1680–94, etching, sheet: 27¹⁵⁄₁₆ × 21⅛ inches (70.9 × 53.6 cm). Metropolitan Museum of Art, New York City, Mary Oenslager Fund, 2016.

Crisóstomo Alejandrino Martínez created a system for relating the parts of the body to each other. Sadly, the artist died before he could complete the work.

BELOW: Paul Marie Louis Pierre Richer, plates from *Anatomie artistique,* 1890.

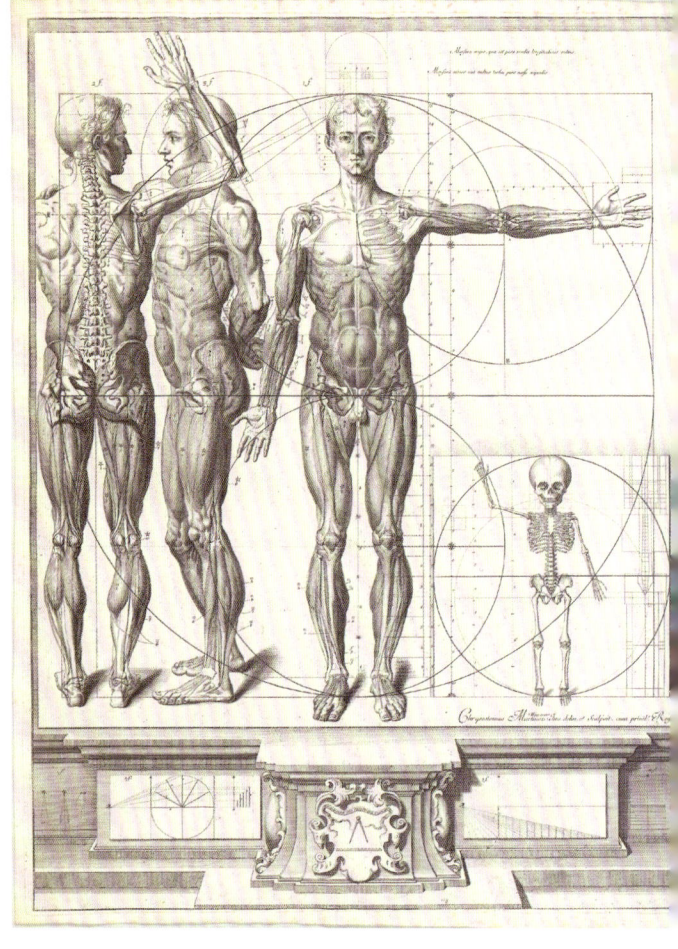

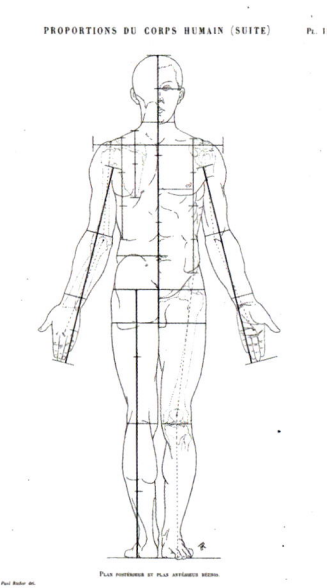

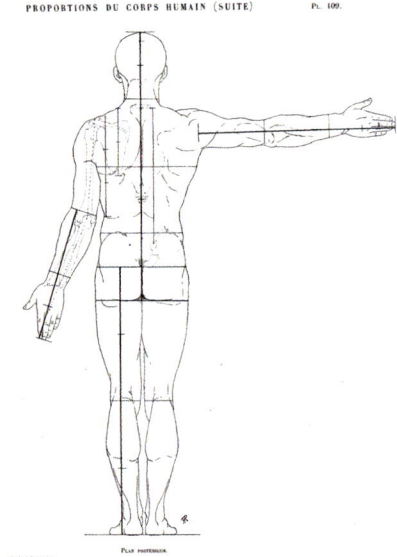

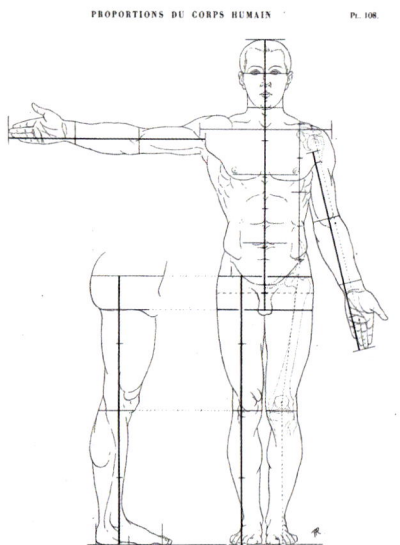

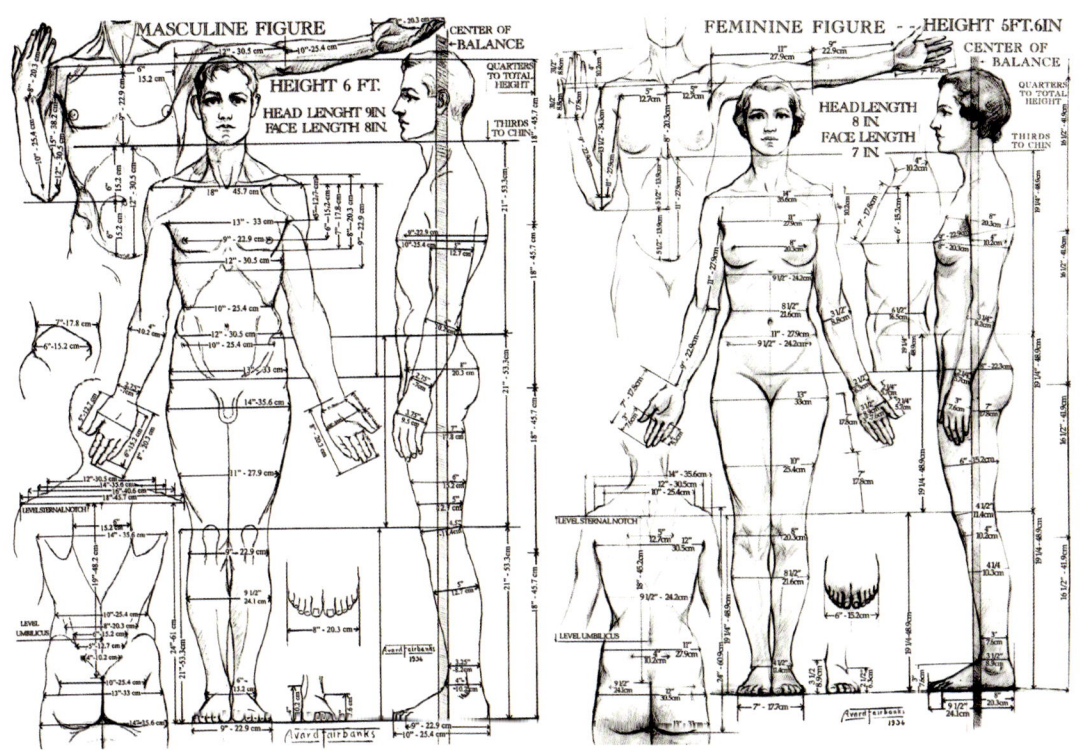

The Modulor concept of twentieth-century Swiss-French architect Le Corbusier brings us full circle, echoing Vitruvius while being informed by the Modernist revolution.

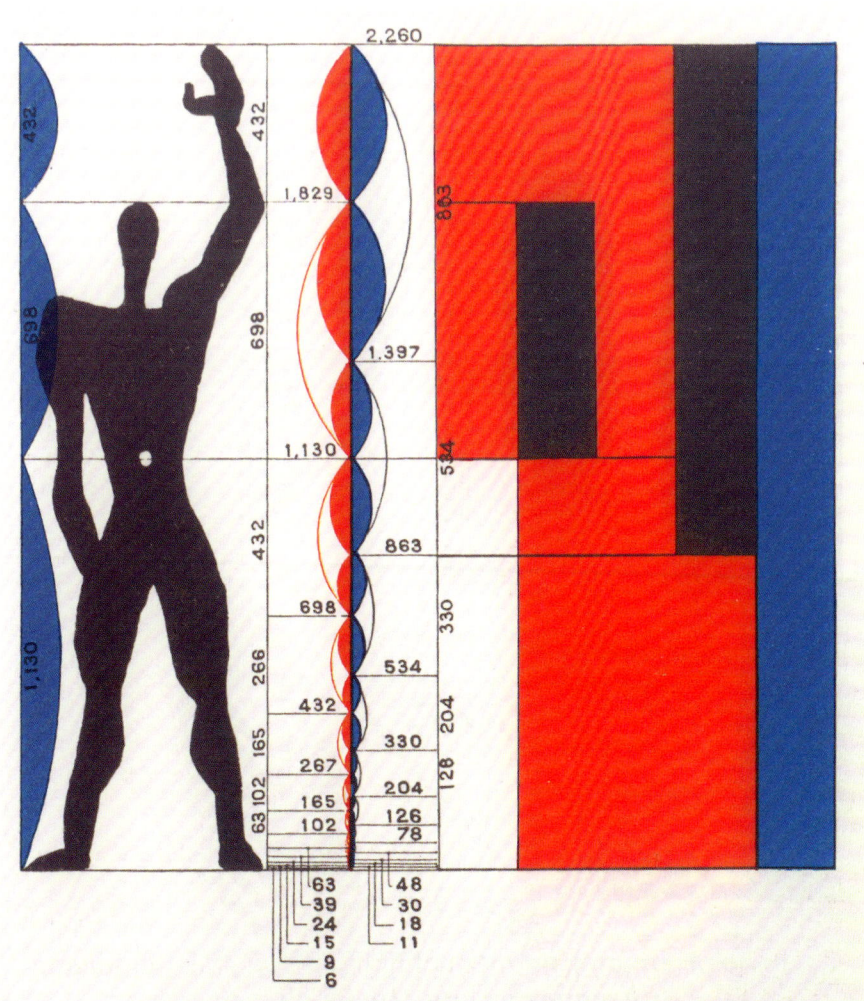

AESTHETIC GEOMETRIES

Like all organisms in nature, the human form is built according to the laws of physics and the demands of evolution. Its structure, forms, and proportions must respect specific parameters for the body to be viable. Because the laws of physics are ruled by mathematics, the structure of the human body is based on mathematics and geometry. The body's specific geometries assume an aesthetic meaning, so geometry can also be used by the artist to imbue the body with an aesthetic meaning.

Greek sculpture of the Classical era provides what is probably the first example of systematic, complex interpretation of the human form through the lenses of mathematics, geometry, and anatomy, in addition to philosophy. The artistic representation of the figure so obtained is a synthesis of organic forms and aesthetic characteristics: the body becomes a vessel carrying cultural constructs.

THE HEAD-TO-BODY RATIO

One time-honored method for establishing the proportions of the figure—a method that dates back to antiquity and is still used today—expresses the relationship of the head to the rest of the body through a ratio that measures how many times the height of the head will fit within the total height of the body. The height of the head is also used as the unit to determine the size of all the other segments of the body, expressed as multiples or fractions of the measure of the head. For example, if the measure of the head is considered to be 1, the chest will be about 1½ heads high, the hips 1 head high, the upper arm 1⅜ heads, the hand ⅞ of a head, and so on.

In the early Classical canon established by Polykleitos in the fifth century BCE, the head–to–body ratio is about 1:7½, meaning that the height of the whole body, from the top of the head to the soles of the feet, is about seven and a half heads high. In the late Classical canon associated with Lysippos in the fourth century BCE, the ratio is about 1:8. These new proportions reflect the transition from Classical to Hellenistic art. The chart opposite compares these two sets of canonical proportions.

The body imbued with aesthetic meaning

OPPOSITE: The 1:7½ ratio compared to the 1:8 ratio

The chart compares the early Classical Doryphoros (or Canon) of Polykleitos, on the left, to the late Classical Agias of Lysippos.

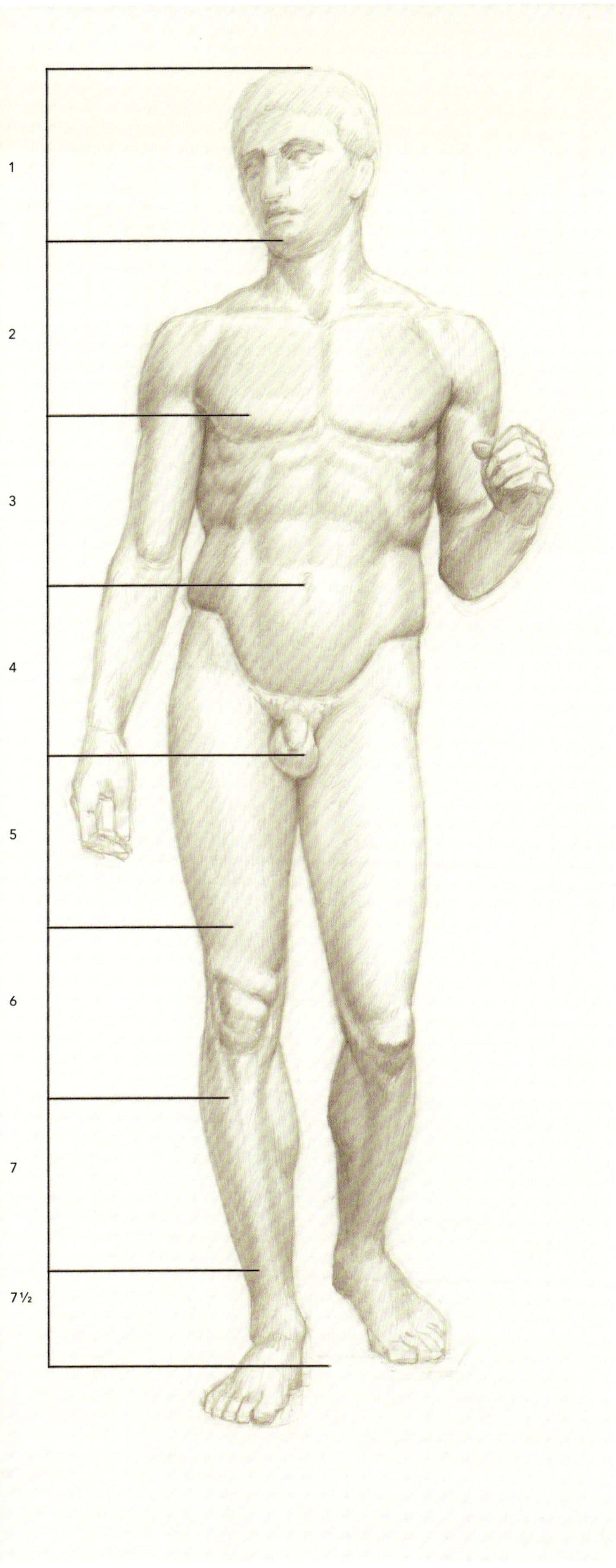

Left figure measurements:
1
2
3
4
5
6
7
7½

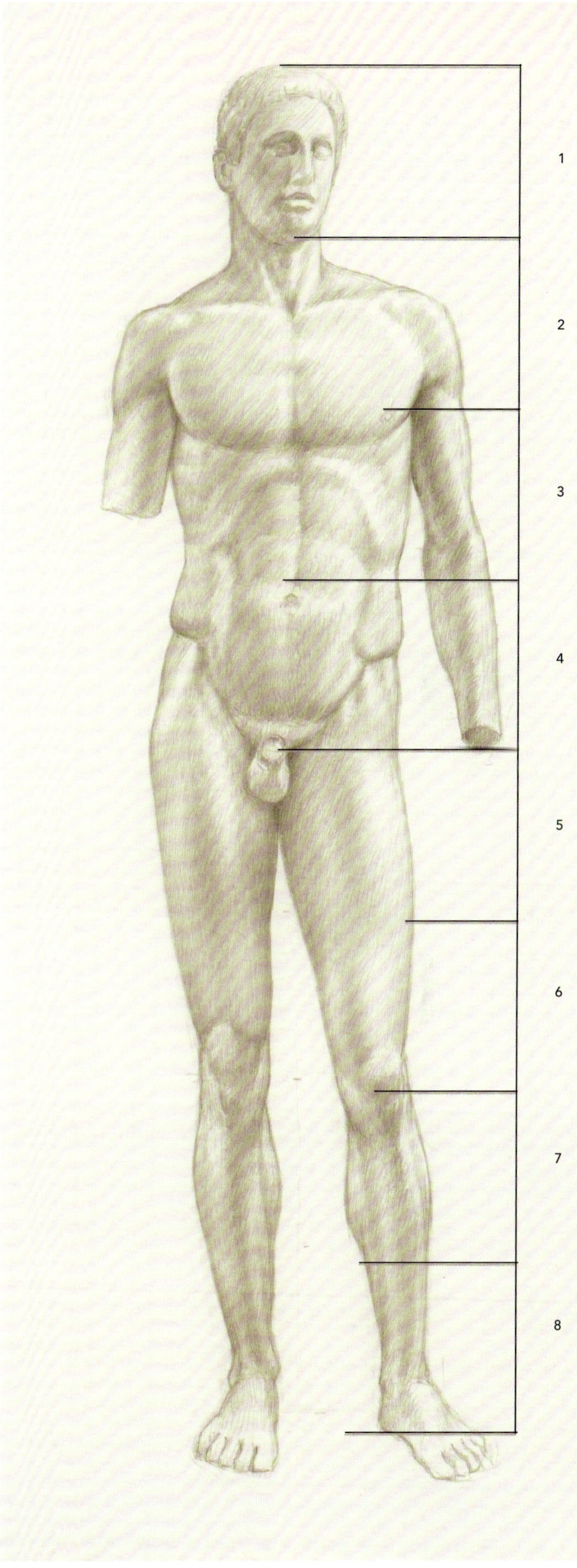

Right figure measurements:
1
2
3
4
5
6
7
8

ANOTHER POSSIBLE MODULAR SYSTEM

The fact that the sculptures of Polykleitos and Lysippos conform to these ratios does not necessarily mean, however, that the works were created using the head as the basic unit of measure. Based purely on empirical and speculative observations, I think these proportional relationships could be also obtained differently. Greek sculptors of the Archaic and Classical periods most likely used a compass and triangle to create their artworks. Using these two tools to analyze drawings and photos of a few Archaic and Classical sculptures, I identified a few geometric patterns and noticed some methodological constants that could be the basis of a different modular system for constructing the human figure.

I focused on these three sculptures: the late Archaic Kouros of Aristodikos (c. 500 BCE), the early Classical Kritios Boy (c. 480 BCE), and the work considered to be the canon of Classical proportions: the Doryphoros of Polykleitos (c. 440 BCE). Playing with a compass and a triangle over images of these works, I noticed that all three can be enclosed in five squares of the same size plus a rectangle one-half the height of one square. This could be a standardized, modular method for producing artworks that correspond to a "type" in terms of subject, pose, and anatomical form. (My intention is not to prove that the Greek artists used the method described below, but rather to show how the body can be read using a language of patterns and geometry.)

Once the five and a half squares are traced, reference landmarks for the body (see chapter 3) can be established inside each square using a compass and a triangle. Each square contains a specific segment of the body:

- The first square contains the head and neck down to the collarbone.
- The second square goes from the collarbone to the waist (end of ribcage).
- The third square goes from the waist to just below the genitals.
- The fourth square goes from just below the genitals to the knees.
- The last one and a half squares include the lower legs and feet.

OPPOSITE: Kouros of Aristodikos (Archaic period, c. 500 BCE), proposed modular construction

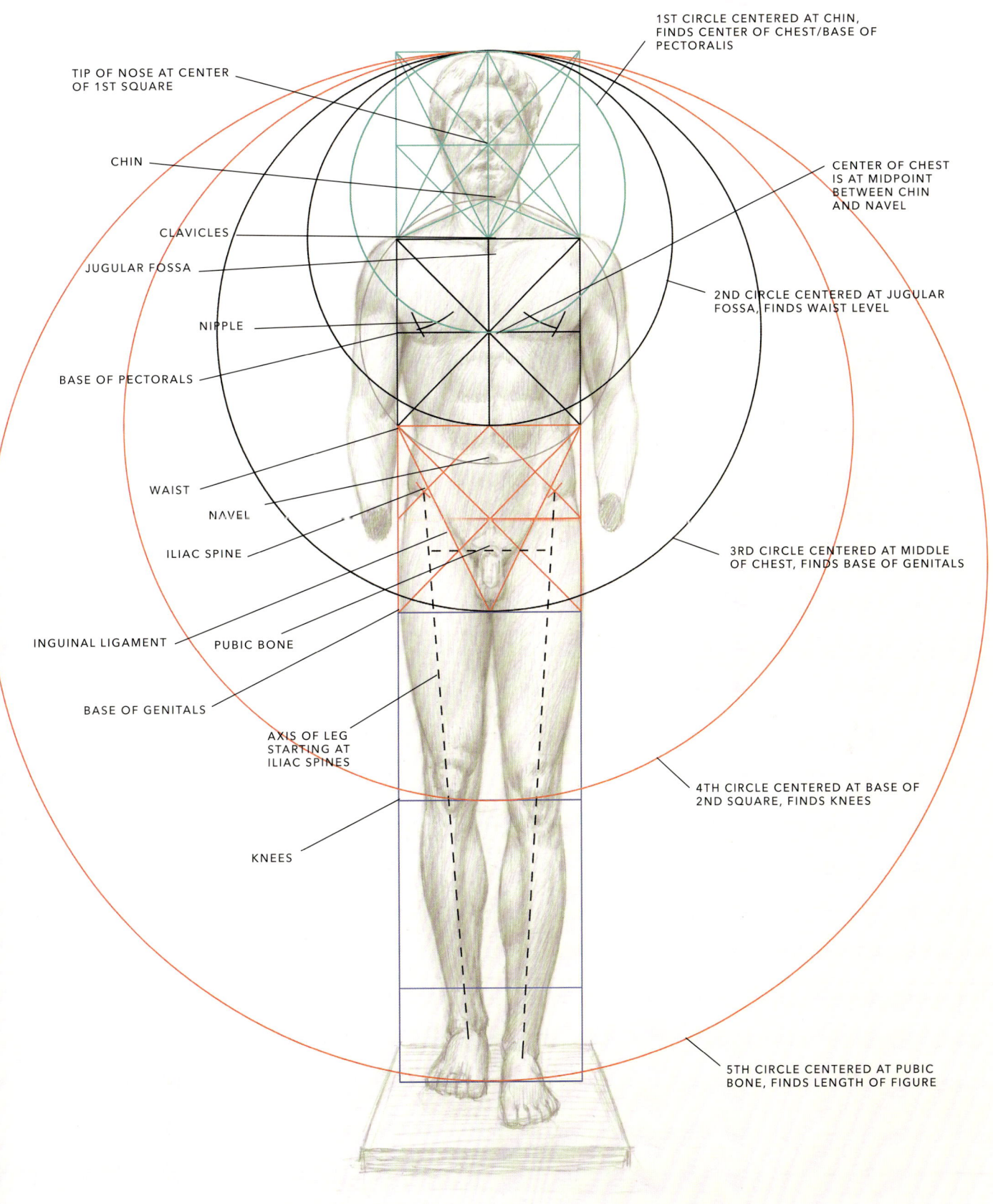

1ST CIRCLE CENTERED AT CHIN, FINDS CENTER OF CHEST/BASE OF PECTORALIS

TIP OF NOSE AT CENTER OF 1ST SQUARE

CHIN

CENTER OF CHEST IS AT MIDPOINT BETWEEN CHIN AND NAVEL

CLAVICLES

JUGULAR FOSSA

2ND CIRCLE CENTERED AT JUGULAR FOSSA, FINDS WAIST LEVEL

NIPPLE

BASE OF PECTORALS

WAIST

NAVEL

ILIAC SPINE

3RD CIRCLE CENTERED AT MIDDLE OF CHEST, FINDS BASE OF GENITALS

INGUINAL LIGAMENT

PUBIC BONE

BASE OF GENITALS

AXIS OF LEG STARTING AT ILIAC SPINES

4TH CIRCLE CENTERED AT BASE OF 2ND SQUARE, FINDS KNEES

KNEES

5TH CIRCLE CENTERED AT PUBIC BONE, FINDS LENGTH OF FIGURE

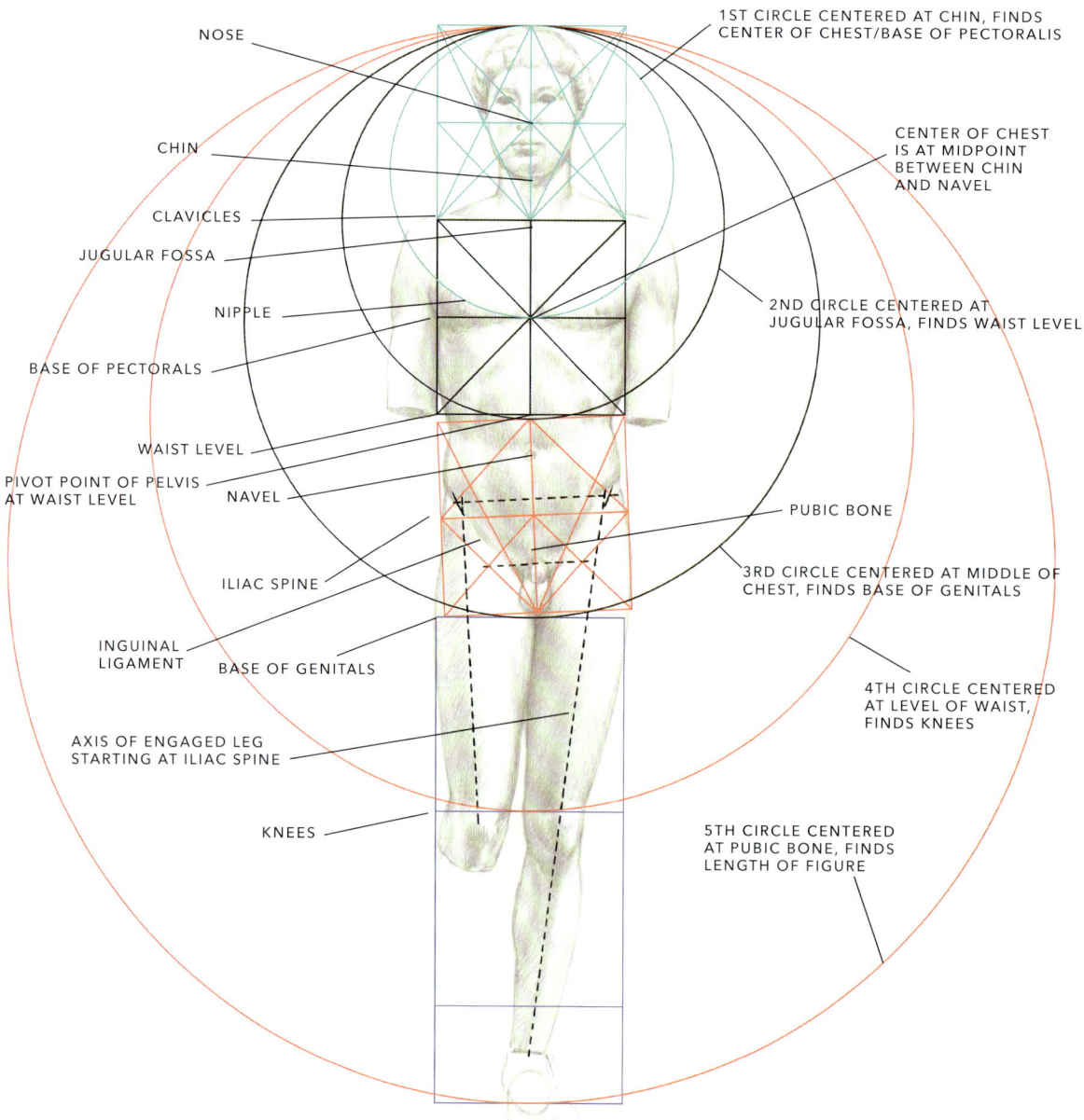

NOSE

1ST CIRCLE CENTERED AT CHIN, FINDS
CENTER OF CHEST/BASE OF PECTORALIS

CHIN

CENTER OF CHEST
IS AT MIDPOINT
BETWEEN CHIN
AND NAVEL

CLAVICLES

JUGULAR FOSSA

NIPPLE

2ND CIRCLE CENTERED AT
JUGULAR FOSSA, FINDS WAIST LEVEL

BASE OF PECTORALS

WAIST LEVEL

PIVOT POINT OF PELVIS
AT WAIST LEVEL   NAVEL

PUBIC BONE

ILIAC SPINE

3RD CIRCLE CENTERED AT MIDDLE OF
CHEST, FINDS BASE OF GENITALS

INGUINAL
LIGAMENT   BASE OF GENITALS

4TH CIRCLE CENTERED
AT LEVEL OF WAIST,
FINDS KNEES

AXIS OF ENGAGED LEG
STARTING AT ILIAC SPINE

KNEES

5TH CIRCLE CENTERED
AT PUBIC BONE, FINDS
LENGTH OF FIGURE

ABOVE: Kritios Boy, (early Classical period, c. 480 BCE), proposed modular construction

The revolutionary innovation of the contrapposto pose

The Kouros of Aristodikos, (previous page), still exhibits the typical erect, frontal Archaic pose, derived from Egyptian statuary. The squares neatly stack up along a straight central axis, but his forms are more realistic overall and the anatomy is better defined than in earlier kouroi. About twenty-five years passed between the creation of Aristodikos's kouros and that of the Kritios Boy, above. Their proportions and the method used to create them are apparently the same, but the Kritios Boy introduces the revolutionary innovation of the contrapposto pose, which seems to be obtained by pivoting the third box on a fulcrum at the base of the second box. One leg is tilted and the other is slightly flexed, but the axes of the legs still originate at the iliac spines. (For more on the contrapposto pose, see pages 182–85.)

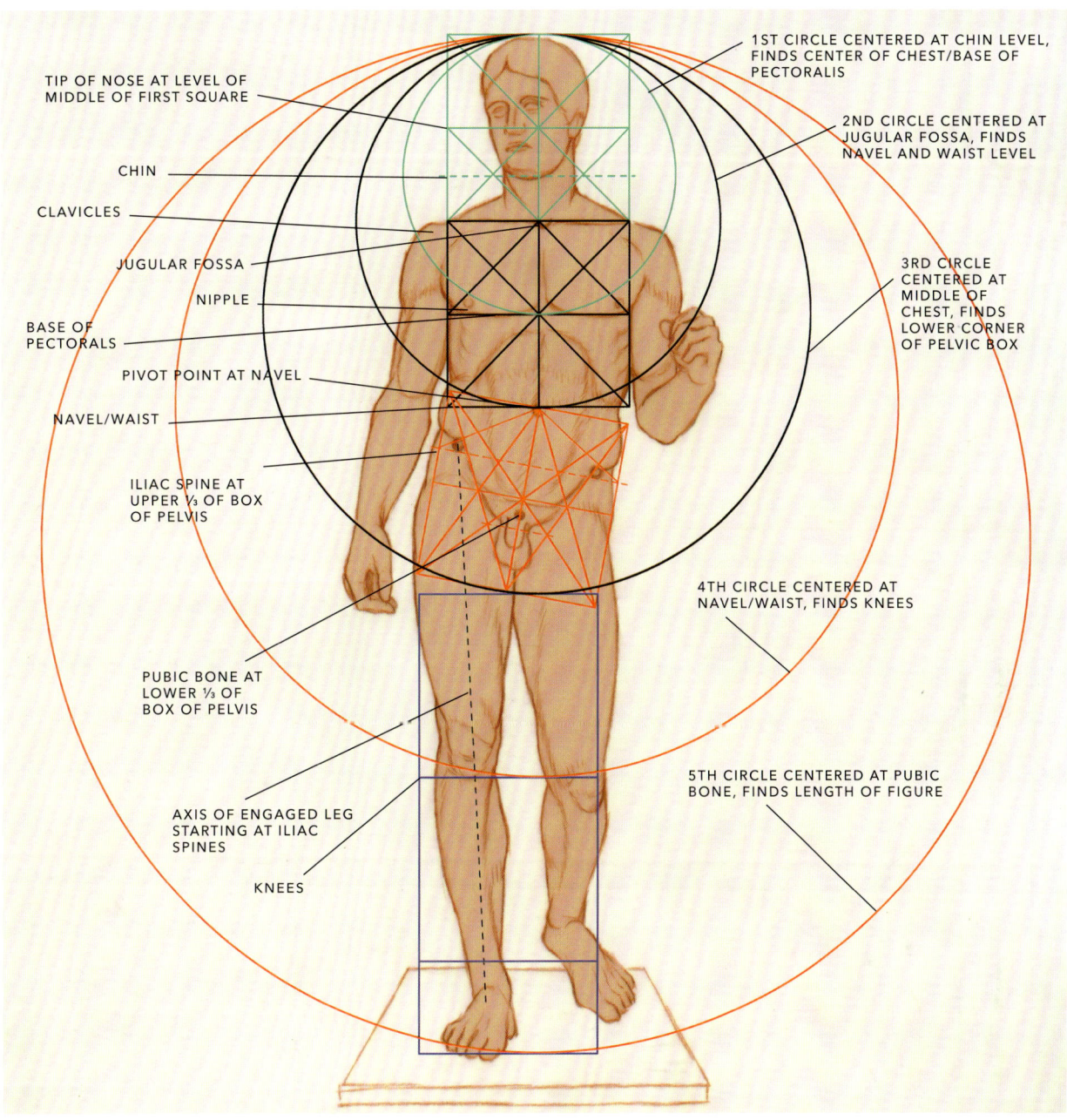

TIP OF NOSE AT LEVEL OF MIDDLE OF FIRST SQUARE

1ST CIRCLE CENTERED AT CHIN LEVEL, FINDS CENTER OF CHEST/BASE OF PECTORALIS

2ND CIRCLE CENTERED AT JUGULAR FOSSA, FINDS NAVEL AND WAIST LEVEL

CHIN

CLAVICLES

JUGULAR FOSSA

NIPPLE

BASE OF PECTORALS

3RD CIRCLE CENTERED AT MIDDLE OF CHEST, FINDS LOWER CORNER OF PELVIC BOX

PIVOT POINT AT NAVEL

NAVEL/WAIST

ILIAC SPINE AT UPPER ⅓ OF BOX OF PELVIS

4TH CIRCLE CENTERED AT NAVEL/WAIST, FINDS KNEES

PUBIC BONE AT LOWER ⅓ OF BOX OF PELVIS

5TH CIRCLE CENTERED AT PUBIC BONE, FINDS LENGTH OF FIGURE

AXIS OF ENGAGED LEG STARTING AT ILIAC SPINES

KNEES

The Doryphoros of Polykleitos still fits the five-and-a-half-squares modular construction, but a few landmarks are positioned differently from where they appear in the two previous examples: the navel is higher, now at the same level as the waist; the iliac spines are at the upper one-third of the pelvis; and the pubic bone is at the lower one-third of the pelvis. The pivot point of the pelvis is at the navel. While the Kritios Boy probably depicts an adolescent athlete, his body long and graceful, the Doryphoros is an adult and a warrior. His body is stronger, his muscles more massive, his chest wider, and the tilt of his pelvis more pronounced. The Doryphoros's contrapposto pose suggests an imminent stride more than the graceful resting pose of the Kritios Boy.

ABOVE: Doryphoros (Classical period, c. 440 BCE), proposed modular construction

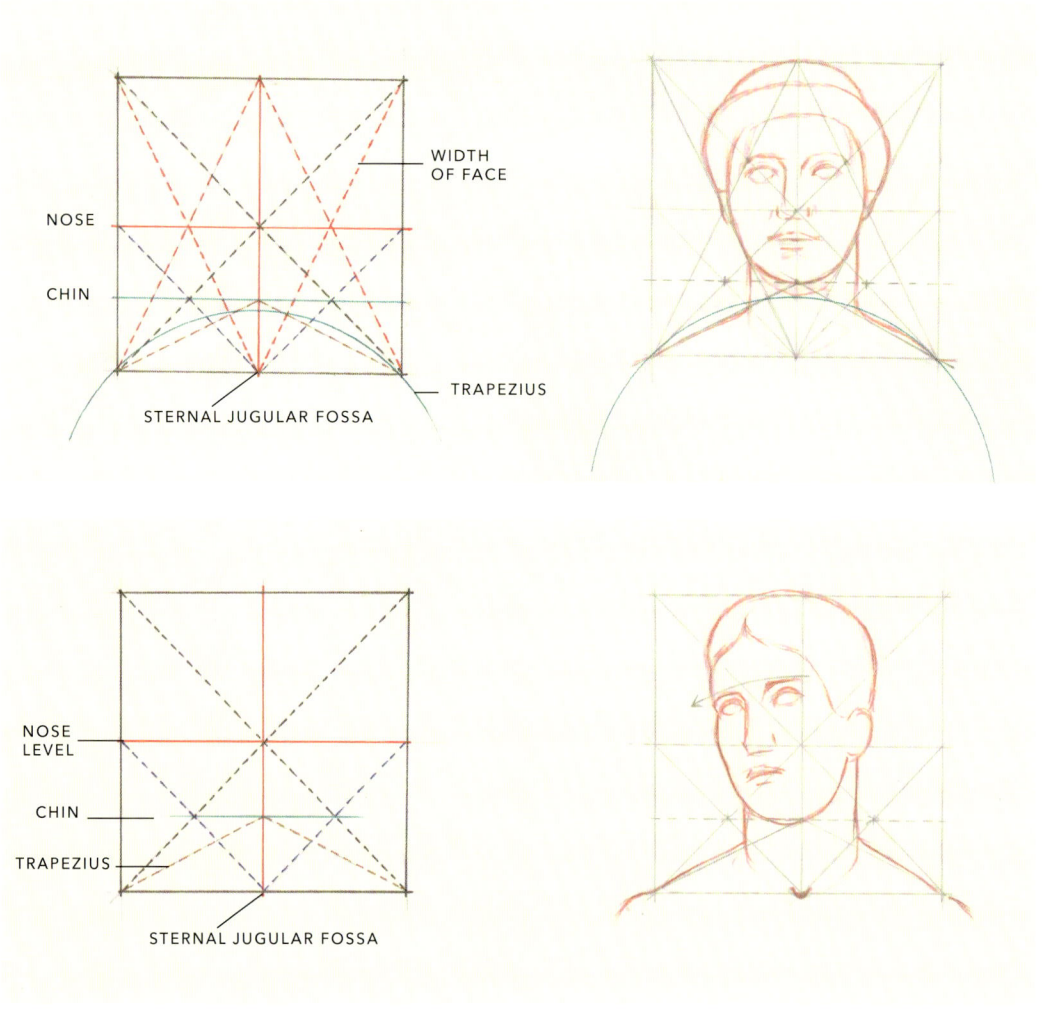

PROPORTIONS OF KRITIOS BOY AND DORYPHOROS COMPARED

In the Kritios Boy, the main landmarks are obtained in the same way and are therefore similarly positioned within the specific squares. The pelvis of the Kritios Boy is tilted, but the positions of the navel, iliac spines, inguinal ligament, pubic bone, and genitals are obtained using the same geometric coordinates.

The head of the Doryphoros has almost the same proportions as the earlier sculpture but is slightly tilted along its central axis, which starts at the base of the neck; the curvature of the brow ridge follows the arc of the tilt. The navel is positioned between the second and third boxes instead of in the third box as in the Kritios Boy. The anterior superior iliac spines and pubic bone are at the upper and lower third, respectively. These variations in the second and third boxes result in a shorter, squarer ribcage, giving the Canon a sturdier, stronger look.

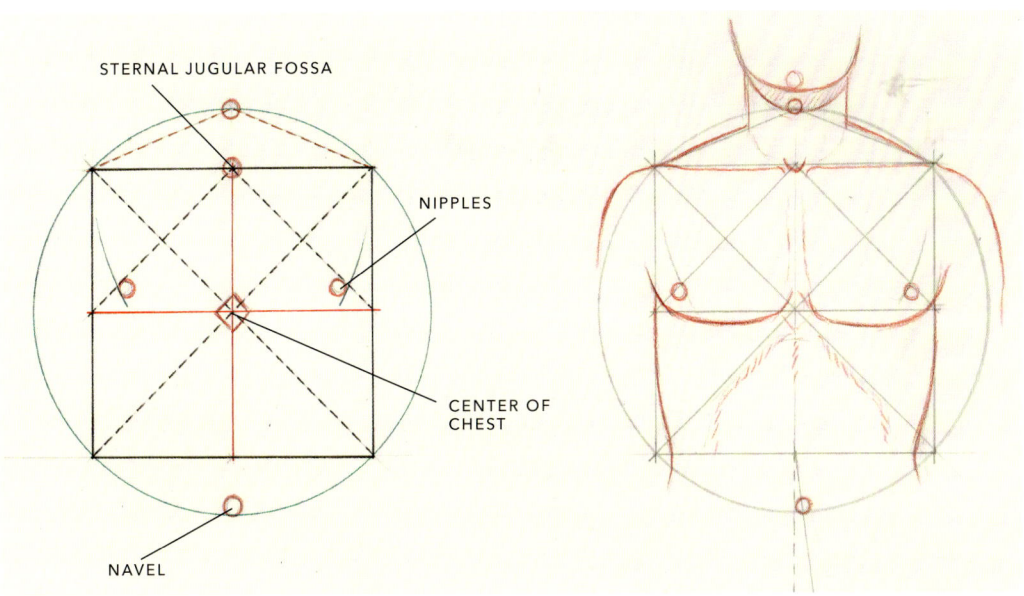

STERNAL JUGULAR FOSSA

NIPPLES

CENTER OF CHEST

NAVEL

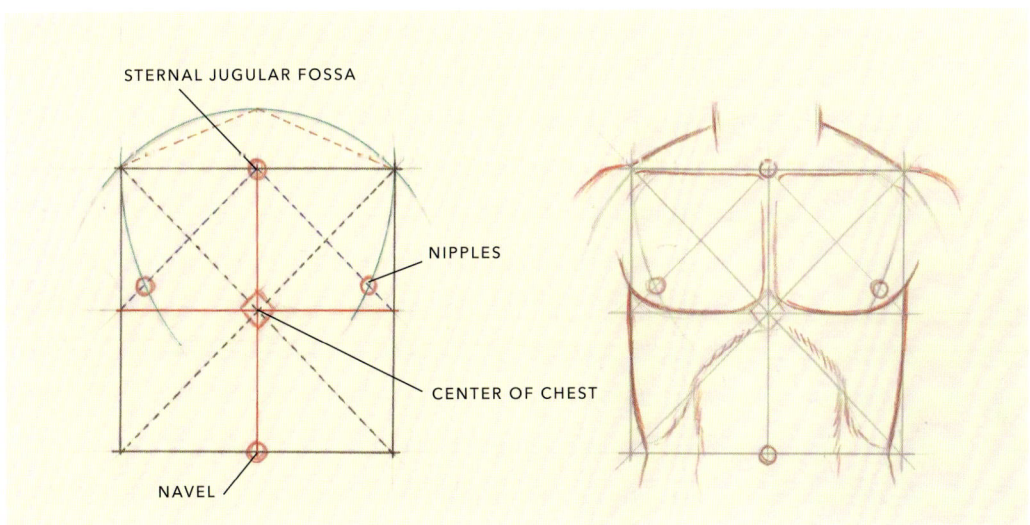

STERNAL JUGULAR FOSSA

NIPPLES

CENTER OF CHEST

NAVEL

OPPOSITE TOP: Construction of Kritios Boy head

OPPOSITE BOTTOM: Construction of Doryphoros head

The proportions of the head of the Kritios Boy and the Doryphoros seem to be obtained through variations on the same method. Starting from the center top and center bottom of the square and going to the corners of the square, diagonal lines frame the width of the face of the Kritios Boy but not of the Doryphoros because his head is slightly turned and tilted. The positions of the nose, chin, and trapezius are obtained the same way in both works.

TOP: Construction of Kritios Boy chest

ABOVE: Construction of Doryphoros chest

The nipples and sternal jugular fossa of the Kritios Boy and the Doryphoros are similarly obtained, but the Kritios Boy's navel is at the lower point of the circle while the Doryphoros's navel is at the base of the square. The smaller space between the pit of the neck and the navel gives the Doryphoros a sturdier look, with a wider chest and shoulders.

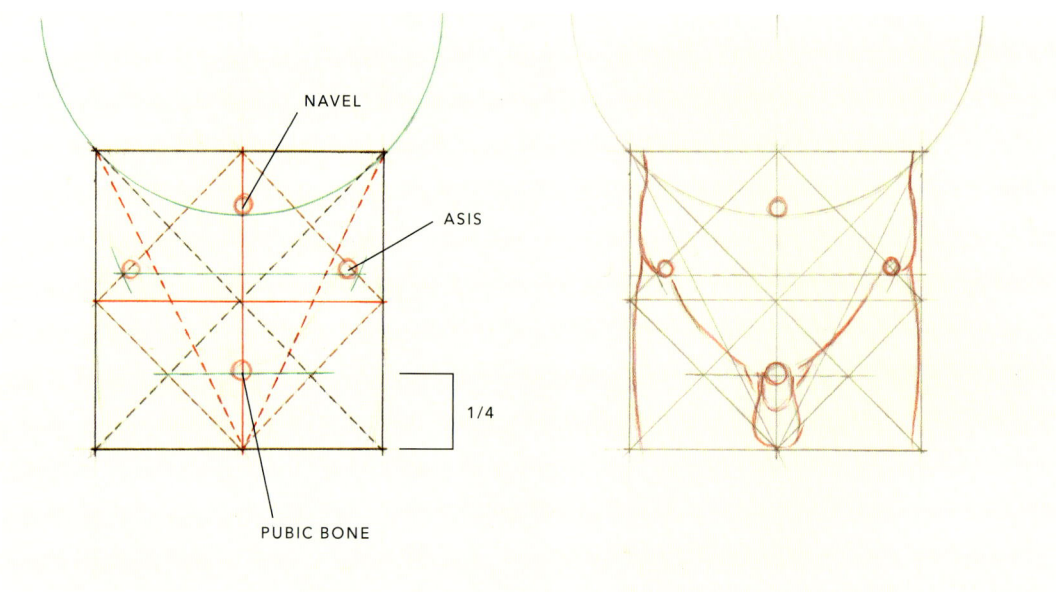

NAVEL

ASIS

PUBIC BONE

1/4

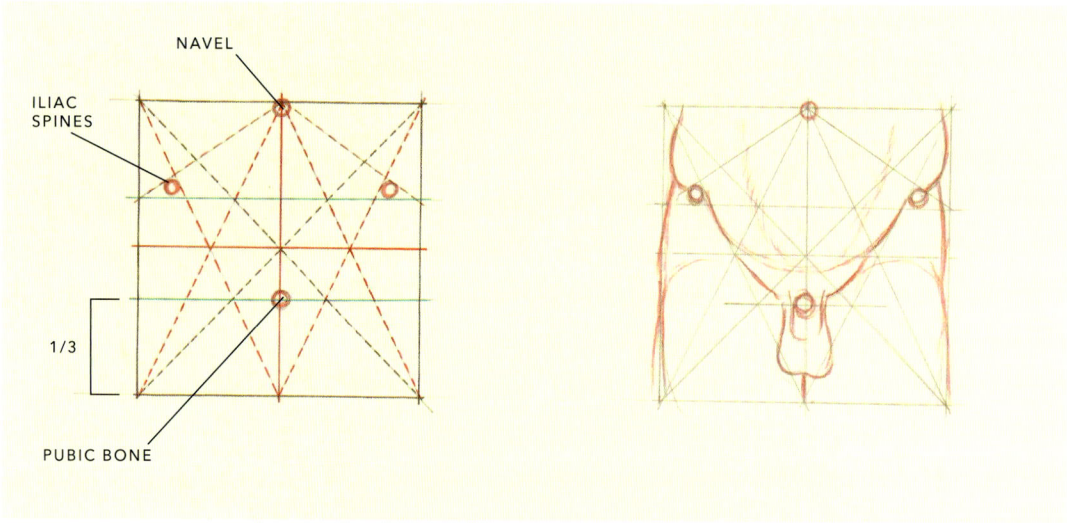

NAVEL

ILIAC
SPINES

PUBIC BONE

1/3

TOP: Construction of Kritios Boy pelvis

BOTTOM: Construction of Doryphoros pelvis

The navel, iliac spines, and pubic bone are positioned differently in the two sculptures, but they can be obtained using the same method of geometric subdivision of the square.

THE BATTLE OF THE CANONS

The two most common head-to-body ratios in humans are 1:7½ and 1:8. In the models I work with, 1:7½ is more common than 1:8, but the latter is also fairly frequent. These are not the only two possible ratios: in adults, the ratios most often vary between 1:6½ and 1:8, but yet other ratios are possible.

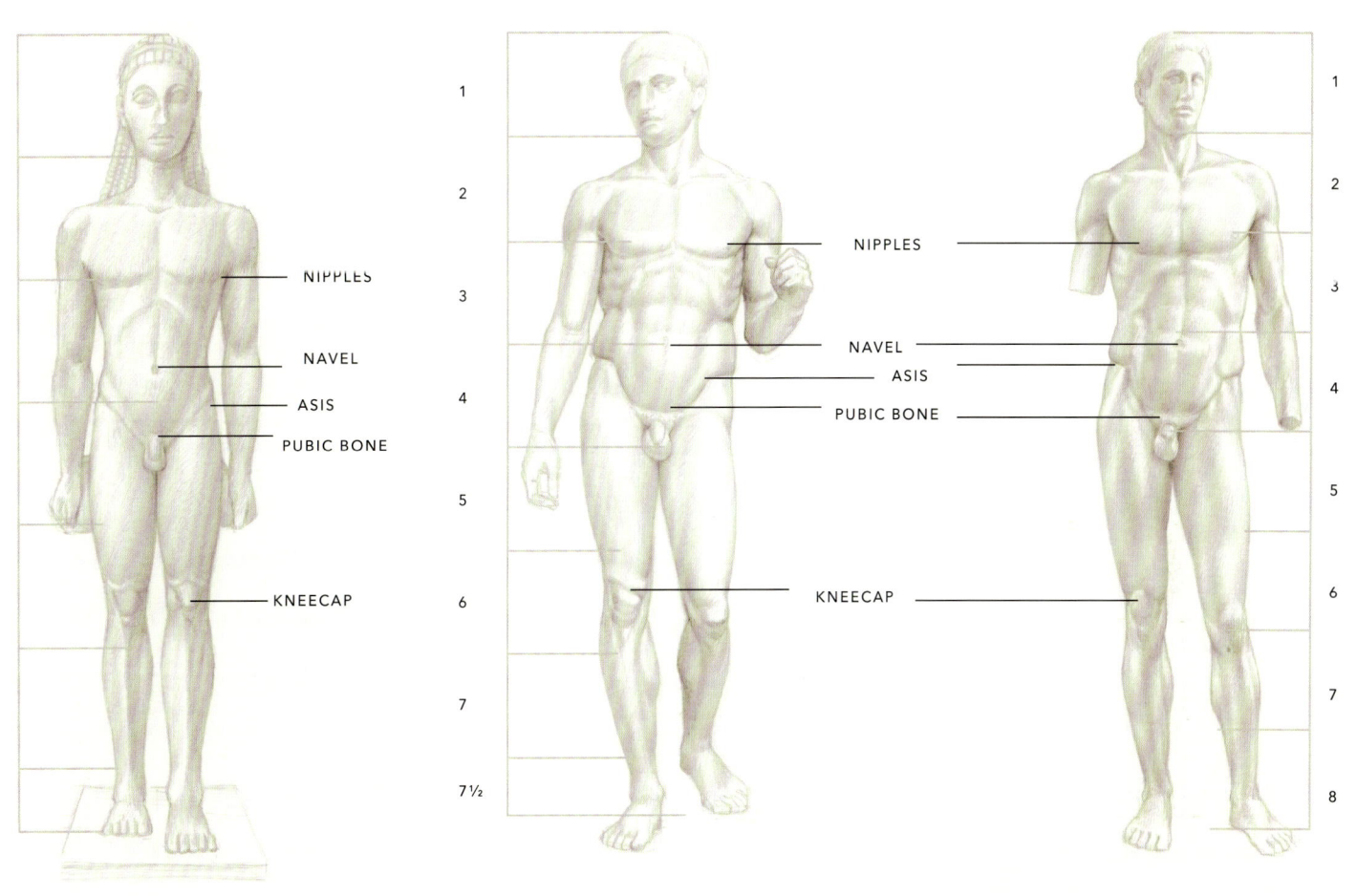

ABOVE: Comparison of head-to-body ratios

This image compares the head-to-body ratio of the Archaic Met Kouros with two Classical canons: the early Classical Doryphoros of Polykleitos and the late Classical Agias of Lysippos. For the Met Kouros the ratio is 1:6; for the Doryphoros about 1:7 or 1:7½; and for the Agias 1:8. The proportions of the kouros are those of an adolescent boy, but it is difficult to establish whether his proportions are based on a canon or the artist was following the proportions of a young model and not using a canon at all. Do notice how much Greek artists' knowledge of anatomy and technical skill evolved in the space of about one hundred years.

As we've seen, Polykleitos established the 1:7½ head-to-body ratio, the proportions visualized in his Doryphoros, which has also become known as "the Canon." These proportions give the figure a solid feel, and the Doryphoros's wide chest and muscular legs and arms convey strength and stability but not agility. As with most Classical statues of warriors, athletes, or gods, the Doryphoros's contained and balanced emotions are expressed through the correspondingly stable and self-assured pose.

The late Classical sculptor Lysippos established a new ratio of 1:8. These proportions create a more elongated figure, with a proportionally smaller head and longer legs. The Agias, Lysippos's masterpiece, memorializes a champion pankration athlete. (The pankration was a fighting sport that mixed wrestling, boxing, kicking, and choking and had practically no rules except for prohibiting biting and eye-gouging.) The body of Agias, while still conveying great physical strength, appears more agile and evokes life and movement more convincingly than the Doryphoros.

Comparing the ratios of the Doryphoros and Agias, (previous page), you can see that the first three head measures fall at about the same levels in both sculptures: the nipples are at a level one head down the from the chin, and the navel is one head lower. But then things begin to differ: in the Doryphoros, the fourth head falls below the testicles while in the Agias it reaches only to the root of the penis; the fifth head is above the box of the knees in the Doryphoros but only about halfway down the thigh in the Agias; the sixth head runs through the middle of the calf in the Doryphoros but falls at the tuberosity of the tibia in the Agias; and the seventh is at the ankles in the Doryphoros but only about halfway down the lower leg in the Agias. In the Doryphoros, the heels are seven and a half heads down, but in the Agias it takes a full eight measures of the head to reach them.

IDEAL VERSUS REAL

The head-to-body ratio can be used when drawing the figure from life, but only as an approximate guide. For example, a real model's nipples won't necessarily be located exactly at the second head mark but may be just above or below it. Similarly, the navel and the genitals may be just above or below the marks of the third and fourth heads, respectively.

When using the ratio as a guide, start the drawing by blocking in the positions of the main landmarks based on the typical proportions, first creating an approximate but structurally and anatomically sound structure that can then be refined by finding the exact positions of the landmarks on your model. In all likelihood, your model's proportions will vary, even if minimally, from those of the canon.

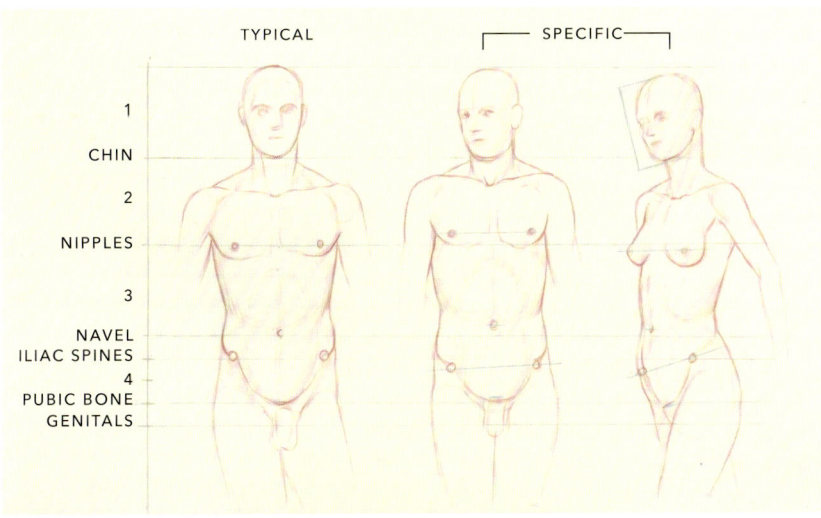

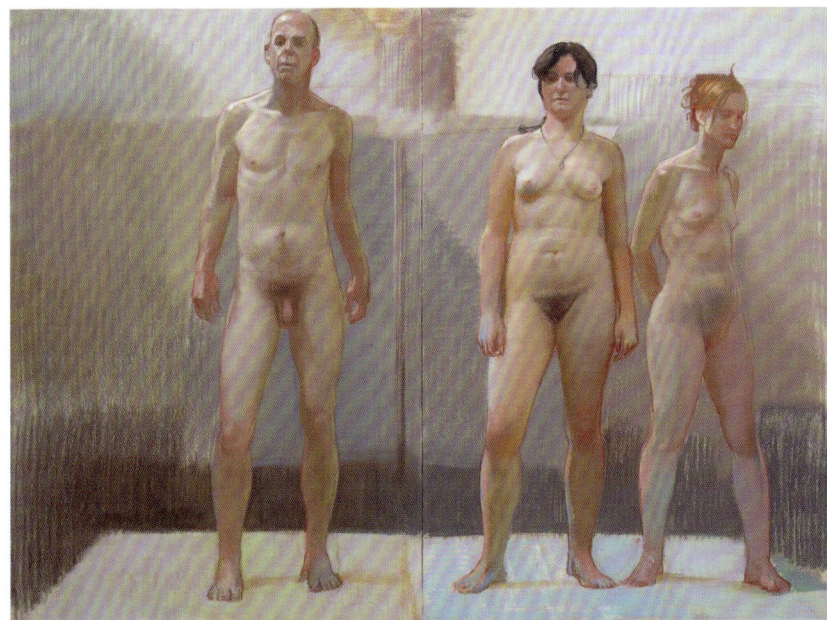

TOP LEFT: Ideal versus actual proportions

The proportional relationships of the figure on the left are those of the idealized 1:7½ canon: the nipples are one head down from the chin; the navel is two heads down from the chin; and the genitals are three heads down from the chin. The figures at center and right of the diagram represent just two possible variations encountered when drawing from life. In the figure at center, the nipples are a little above the mark of the second head, and the navel is a little higher than the level of the third head. The landmarks' position can also be affected by the pose: in the figure at right, the chin is lower because of the lowered and tilted head; the nipples are lower because breasts can vary in size and position on the chest; and the iliac spines are uneven—one higher and one lower—because of the tilt of the pelvis. When drawing the figure, the artist must adjust for these small individual and specific variations.

BOTTOM LEFT: Scott Noel, *Dave, Sue and Jessica as Adam and Eve and Lilith, Structure Evolves to Likeness*, 2010, pastel, 44 × 60 inches (111.76 × 152.40 cm). Courtesy of the artist.

This work by my friend and colleague Scott Noel effectively demonstrates the variety of body proportions that an artist can encounter. The specific proportions of these three bodies can be measured by adapting the method described in the image above.

USES OF PROPORTIONAL RELATIONSHIPS

What use are proportional relationships? Well, just knowing that the length of the hand is always slightly shorter than the height of the head, for example, or that the length of the foot is about the same or slightly longer than the height of the head promotes a more objective analysis of the forms of the figure. You move away from an imitative, passive approach when drawing toward a more informed, precise approach that captures the inherent harmonies of the human body more accurately. No more drawings with tiny feet, huge hands, or badly proportioned limbs!

I have already mentioned how the various segments of the body relate to each other proportionally. For example, the length of the segments of the limbs decreases as they move toward the extremity; in the image below, you can see that the femur (thigh bone) is longer than the tibia and fibula (bones of the lower leg), which in turn are longer than the foot. The image opposite shows the main proportional relationships of the body: the upper arm is longer than the forearm, and the forearm is longer than the hand, and so on down to the fingertips. The elbow reaches to the level of the waist, the nipples are at a measure of one head down from the chin, and the navel is two heads from the chin.

No more badly proportioned limbs!

RIGHT: Proportional relationship of bones of the leg and foot

OPPOSITE: Proportional relationships and correspondences between parts of the body

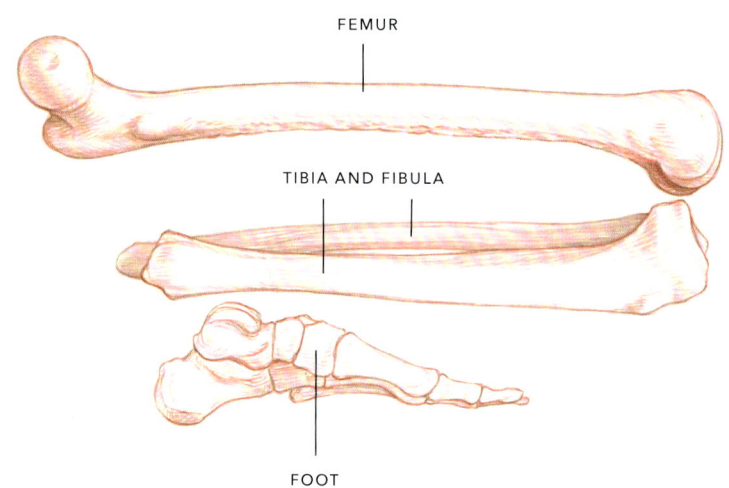

FEMUR

TIBIA AND FIBULA

FOOT

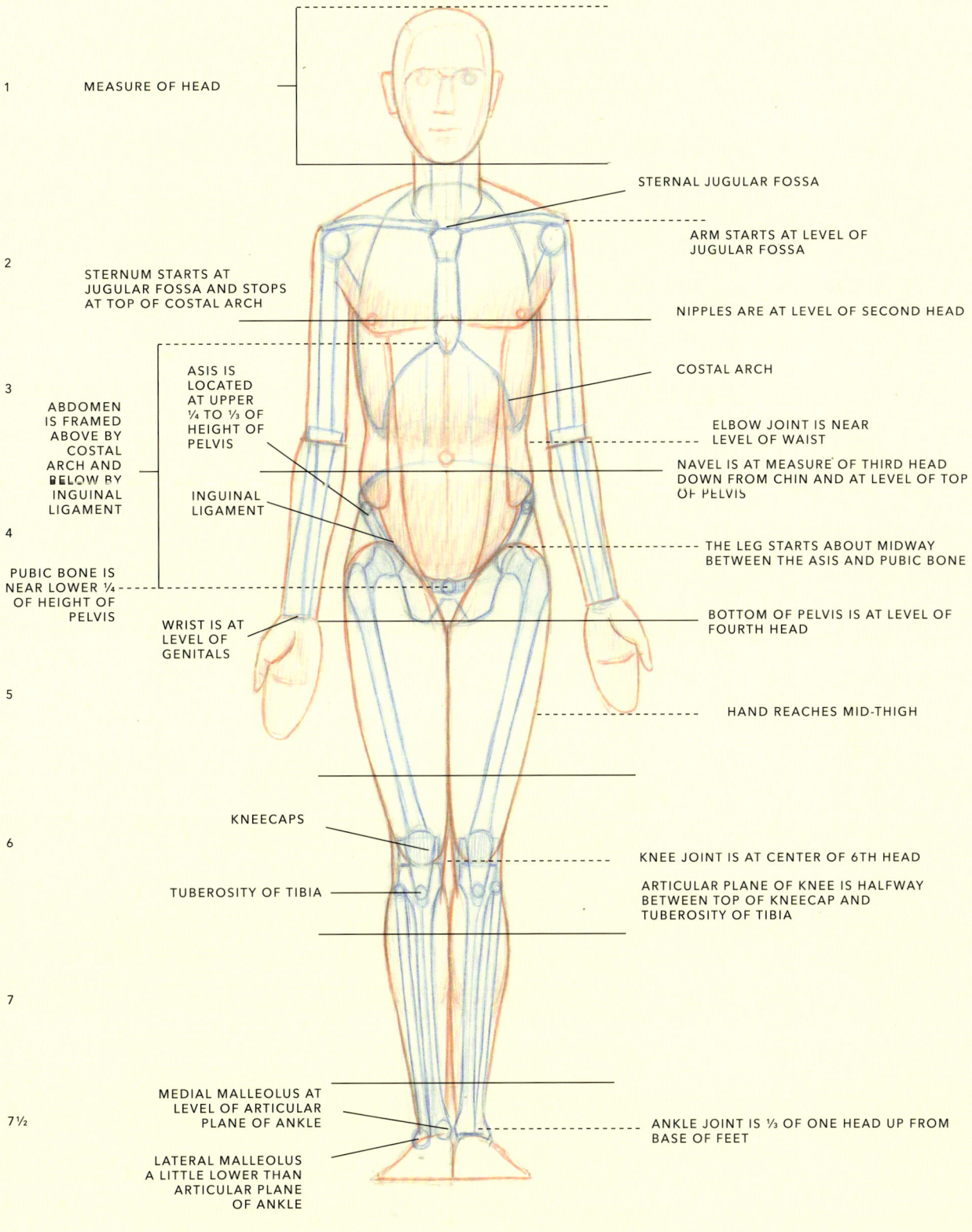

1   MEASURE OF HEAD

STERNAL JUGULAR FOSSA

ARM STARTS AT LEVEL OF
JUGULAR FOSSA

2

STERNUM STARTS AT
JUGULAR FOSSA AND STOPS
AT TOP OF COSTAL ARCH

NIPPLES ARE AT LEVEL OF SECOND HEAD

3

ASIS IS
LOCATED
AT UPPER
¼ TO ⅓ OF
HEIGHT OF
PELVIS

COSTAL ARCH

ELBOW JOINT IS NEAR
LEVEL OF WAIST

ABDOMEN
IS FRAMED
ABOVE BY
COSTAL
ARCH AND
BELOW BY
INGUINAL
LIGAMENT

NAVEL IS AT MEASURE OF THIRD HEAD
DOWN FROM CHIN AND AT LEVEL OF TOP
OF PELVIS

INGUINAL
LIGAMENT

4

THE LEG STARTS ABOUT MIDWAY
BETWEEN THE ASIS AND PUBIC BONE

PUBIC BONE IS
NEAR LOWER ¼
OF HEIGHT OF
PELVIS

BOTTOM OF PELVIS IS AT LEVEL OF
FOURTH HEAD

WRIST IS AT
LEVEL OF
GENITALS

5

HAND REACHES MID-THIGH

KNEECAPS

6

KNEE JOINT IS AT CENTER OF 6TH HEAD

TUBEROSITY OF TIBIA

ARTICULAR PLANE OF KNEE IS HALFWAY
BETWEEN TOP OF KNEECAP AND
TUBEROSITY OF TIBIA

7

MEDIAL MALLEOLUS AT
LEVEL OF ARTICULAR
PLANE OF ANKLE

7½

ANKLE JOINT IS ⅓ OF ONE HEAD UP FROM
BASE OF FEET

LATERAL MALLEOLUS
A LITTLE LOWER THAN
ARTICULAR PLANE
OF ANKLE

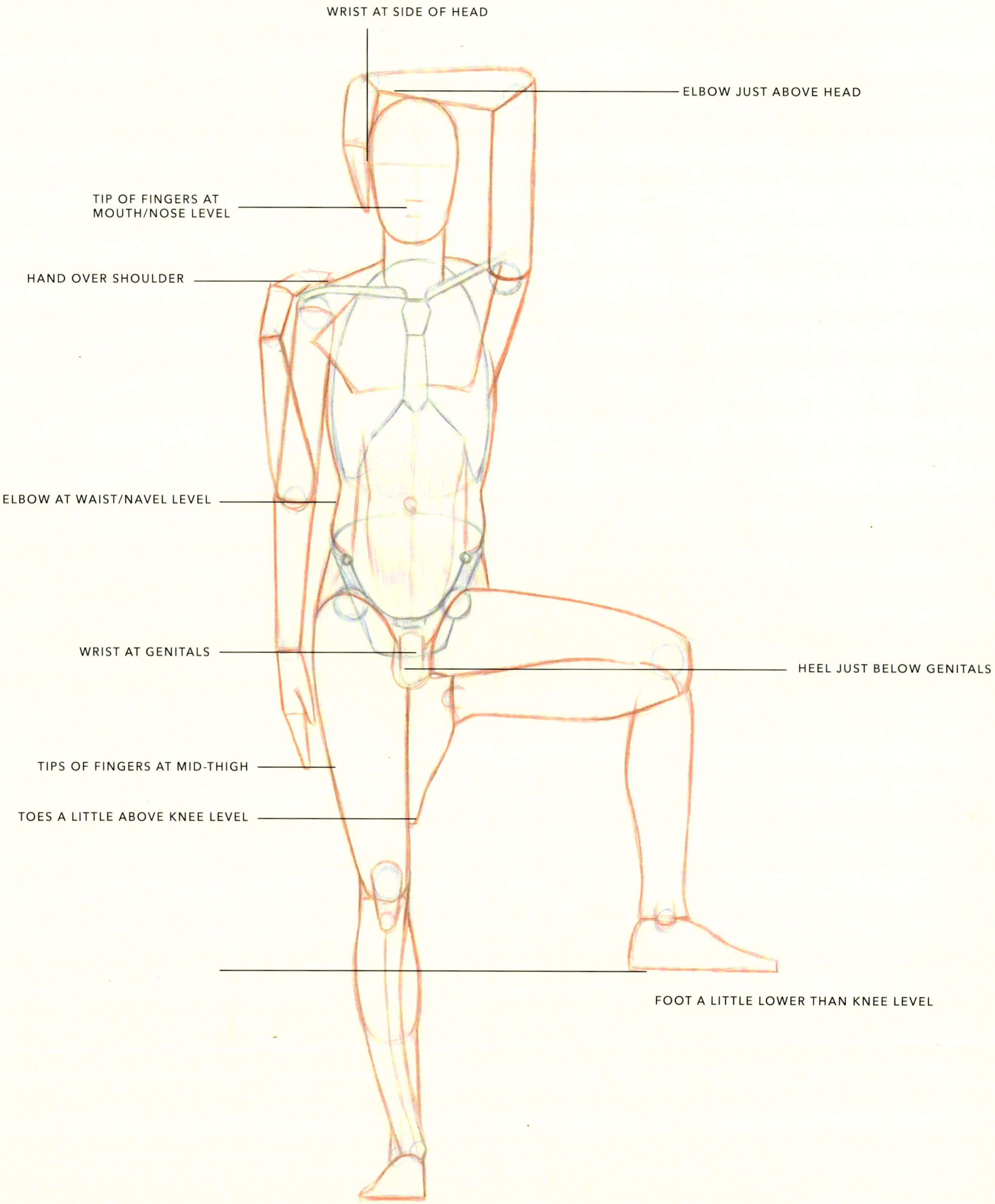

WRIST AT SIDE OF HEAD

ELBOW JUST ABOVE HEAD

TIP OF FINGERS AT
MOUTH/NOSE LEVEL

HAND OVER SHOULDER

ELBOW AT WAIST/NAVEL LEVEL

WRIST AT GENITALS

HEEL JUST BELOW GENITALS

TIPS OF FINGERS AT MID-THIGH

TOES A LITTLE ABOVE KNEE LEVEL

FOOT A LITTLE LOWER THAN KNEE LEVEL

PROPORTIONAL RELATION-SHIPS AND MOVEMENT

The proportional relationships of the figure create specific correspondences between various parts of the body when the torso, pelvis, head, or limbs are flexed, extended, or bent. The images here exemplify this concept when applied to the whole figure (idealized), the arm, and the bodies of actual models in non-foreshortened poses.

OPPOSITE: Proportional relationships with flexed limbs, front view

BELOW: Proportional relationships with flexed limbs, side view

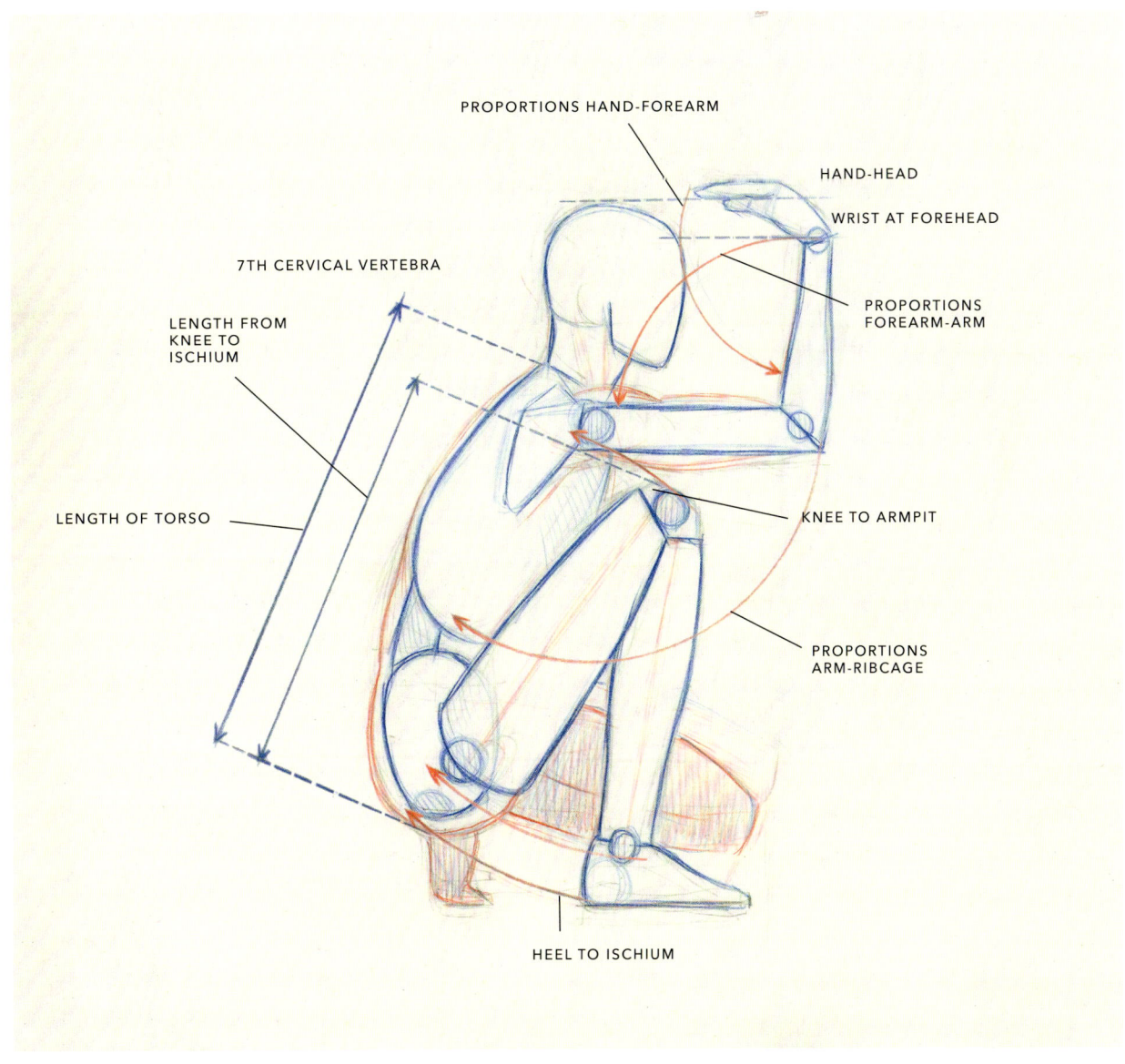

PROPORTIONS HAND-FOREARM

HAND-HEAD

WRIST AT FOREHEAD

7TH CERVICAL VERTEBRA

PROPORTIONS FOREARM-ARM

LENGTH FROM KNEE TO ISCHIUM

KNEE TO ARMPIT

LENGTH OF TORSO

PROPORTIONS ARM-RIBCAGE

HEEL TO ISCHIUM

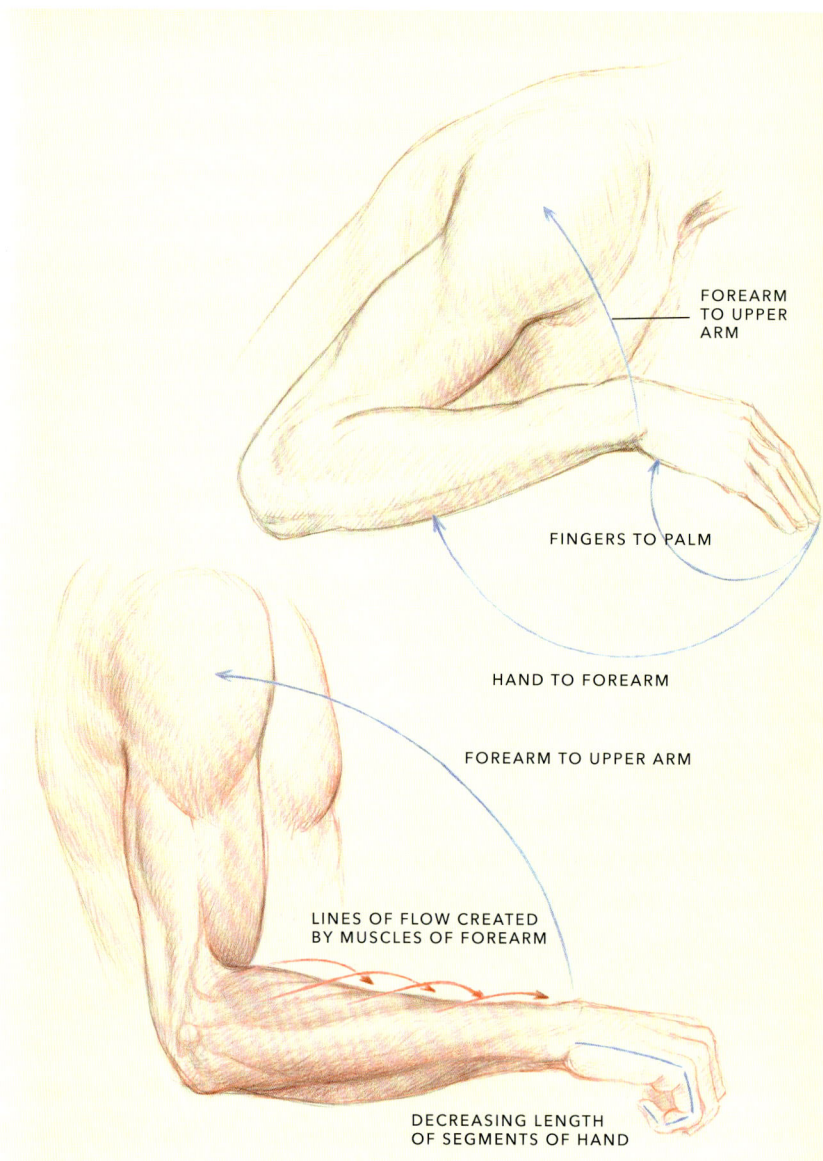

TOP: Proportional relationships of the main segments of the upper limb

When drawing the arm, all its segments must be considered in relation to each other, resulting in a harmonious whole.

RIGHT: Reading the proportional relationships in a pose

This drawing of a real model, Joseph, shows the use of proportional relationships in the whole figure when the figure is not foreshortened. Compare the height of the head with the length of the feet and hands: the hands are a little shorter than the length of the head, and the feet are a little longer than the height of the head. The heel is at the same level as the ischium, and the knees are at the armpit. The arrows indicate lines of muscular flows that can also be used to measure the various segments of the body, as, in this case, the end of the ribcage, the iliac crest, and the beginning of the thigh.

FOREARM
TO UPPER
ARM

FINGERS TO PALM

HAND TO FOREARM

FOREARM TO UPPER ARM

LINES OF FLOW CREATED
BY MUSCLES OF FOREARM

DECREASING LENGTH
OF SEGMENTS OF HAND

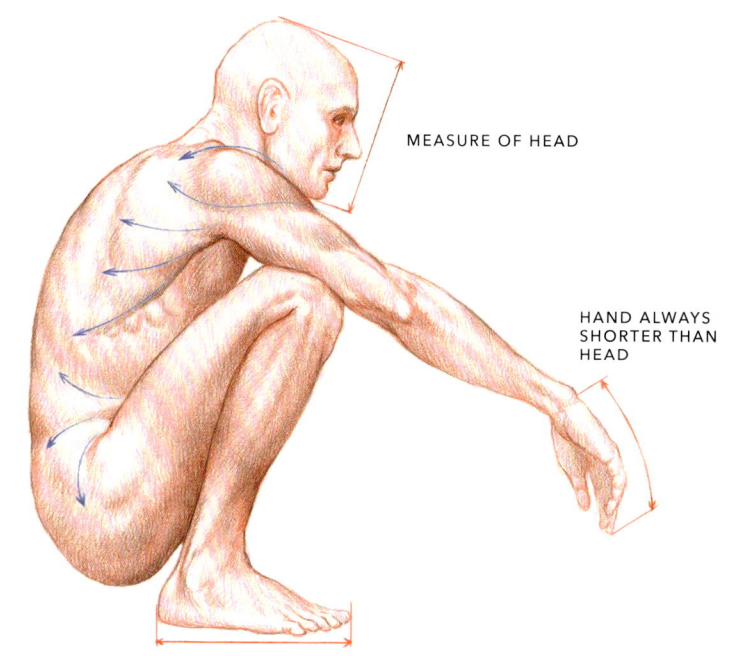

MEASURE OF HEAD

HAND ALWAYS
SHORTER THAN
HEAD

FEET ALWAYS LONGER THAN HEAD

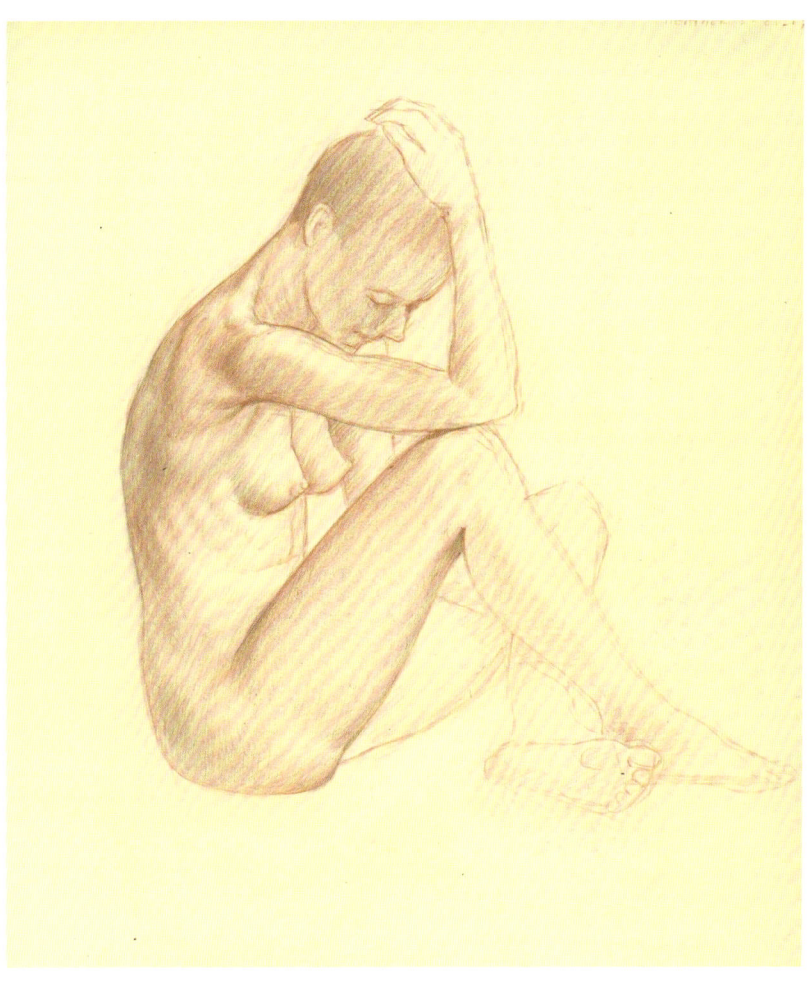

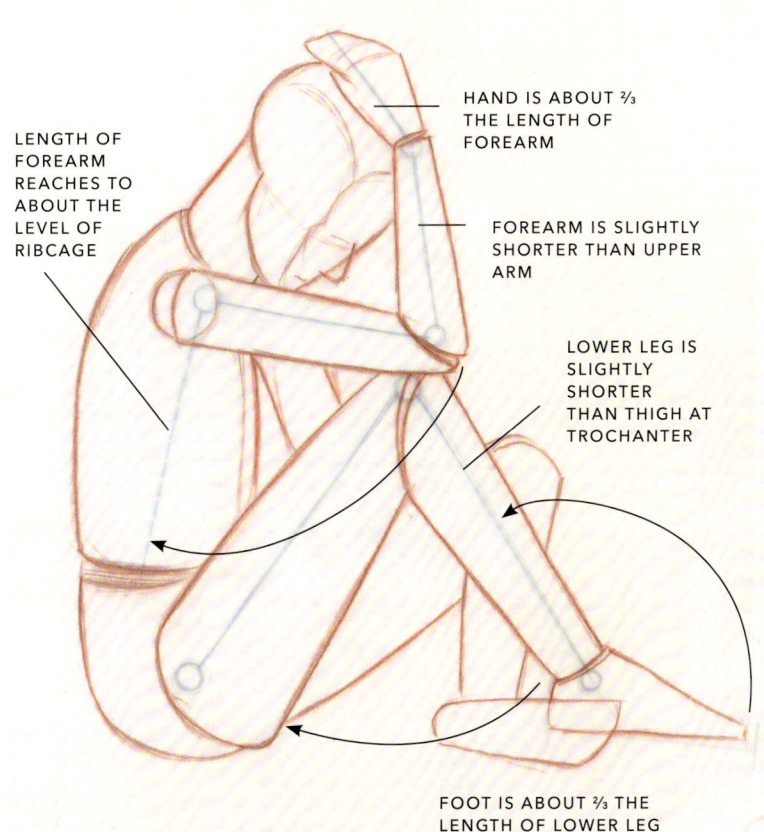

LENGTH OF
FOREARM
REACHES TO
ABOUT THE
LEVEL OF
RIBCAGE

HAND IS ABOUT ⅔
THE LENGTH OF
FOREARM

FOREARM IS SLIGHTLY
SHORTER THAN UPPER
ARM

LOWER LEG IS
SLIGHTLY
SHORTER
THAN THIGH AT
TROCHANTER

FOOT IS ABOUT ⅔ THE
LENGTH OF LOWER LEG

LEFT: Visualizing proportional relationships in a pose

These drawings of another real model, Heather, also show how to identify the correspondences between various parts of the body and how to relate them properly when drawing. The image above represents the model posing, and the image below shows how to analyze it. As you can see, this approach helps you maintain dimensional harmony between the parts of the figure.

PROPORTIONAL RELATIONSHIPS AND AESTHETIC GEOMETRIES

The geometric patterns created by the body in movement or at rest

As we have seen in the preceding drawings, when the segments of the body are reduced to simple lines, it is much easier to appreciate their actual dimensions and to see the geometric shapes, like squares or triangles, that they can create in a pose. It is much easier and more precise to evaluate the dimensions of a simple line or a geometric shape than of an organic form. Proportional relationships are the basis of the geometric patterns created by the body when in movement or in various poses at rest. The next few images demonstrate how proportional relationships can create aesthetic geometries resulting from the interaction between parts of the body or from the figure in movement, and they show how to consider them when drawing the figure.

The landmarks of the body can also be used to visualize geometric patterns for measuring the proportions of the subject, as shown in the images here. (The body's landmarks are discussed in depth in chapter 3.)

BELOW: Proportional relationships create geometric patterns

Note the spiral created by the gradually decreasing length of the segments of the arm and hand.

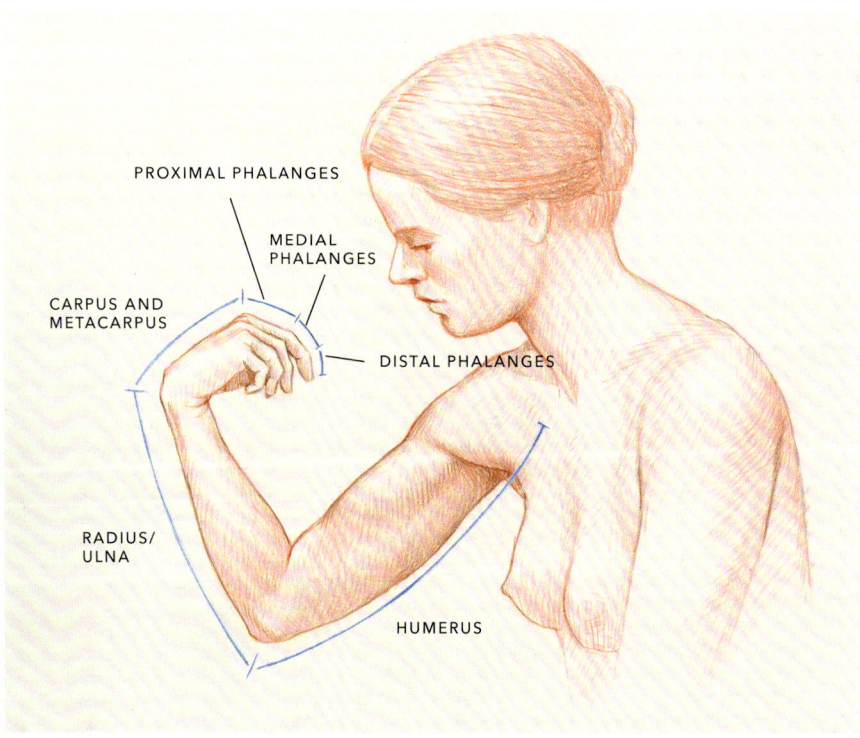

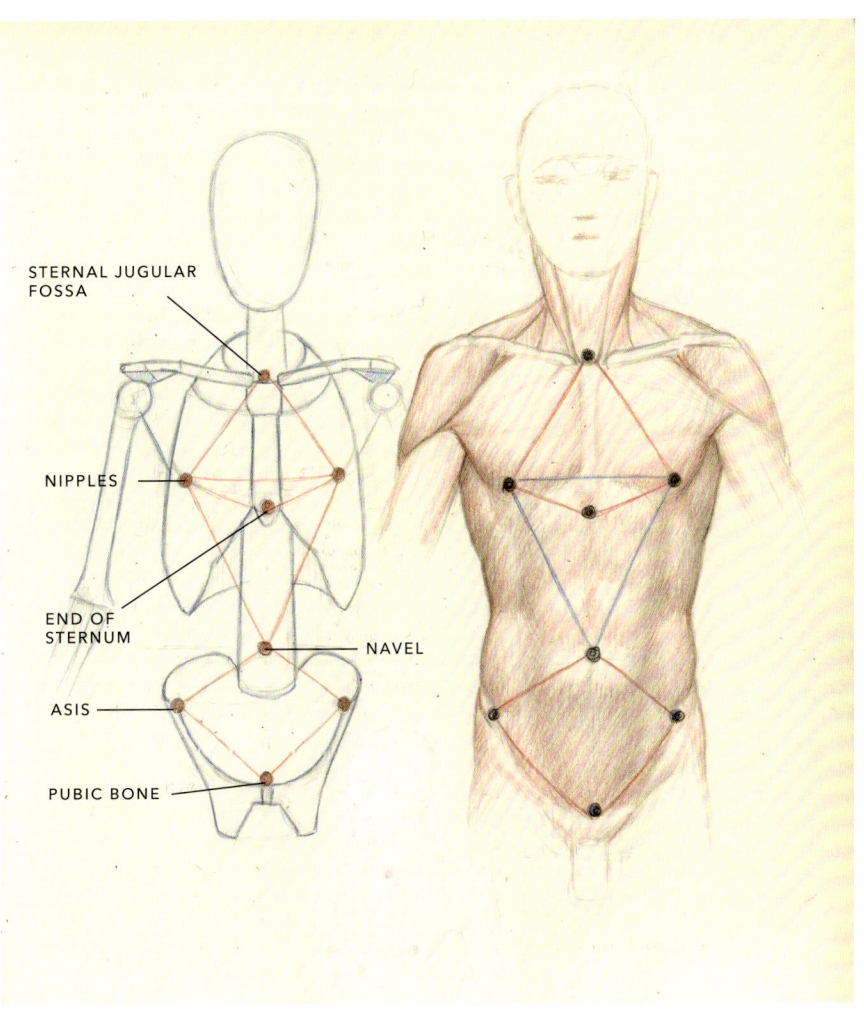

STERNAL JUGULAR
FOSSA

NIPPLES

END OF
STERNUM

NAVEL

ASIS

PUBIC BONE

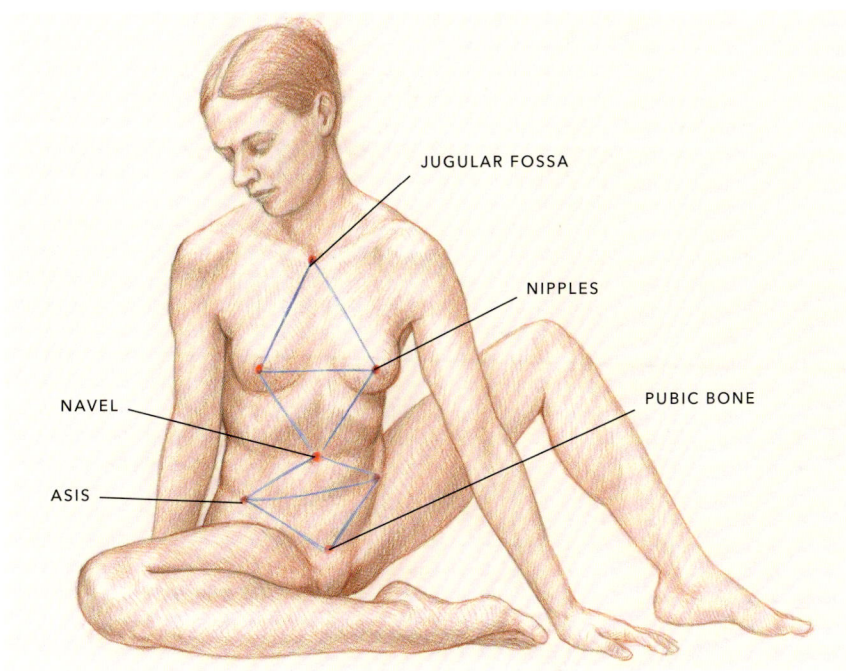

JUGULAR FOSSA

NIPPLES

NAVEL

ASIS

PUBIC BONE

TOP: Aligning landmarks creates geometric patterns

Visualizing geometric patterns in the figure using the skeletal and soft landmarks provides a more precise measure of the proportions of the figure. It is more accurate to measure and compare the length of lines or the size of geometric patterns rather than organic forms.

LEFT: Alignments of landmarks in a pose

Geometric patterns created by aligning landmarks can be used to appreciate the figure's proportions. This image shows a few examples: an equilateral triangle created by joining nipples and navel reveals that these three spots are equidistant from each other; the nipples and sternal notch produce an isosceles triangle, because the distance between the nipples is shorter than the distance between nipples and sternal notch.

Innumerable patterns can be visualized in the human figure. It's just not possible to show all of them, but the drawings here analyze the patterns that arise in a few different poses.

In the image at top right, note the gradually decreasing measures of the segments of the *P*-shaped spiral. The extended arm is the longest measure; the width of the shoulder is the second greatest; and the lengths of the upper arm, forearm, and hand grow gradually smaller.

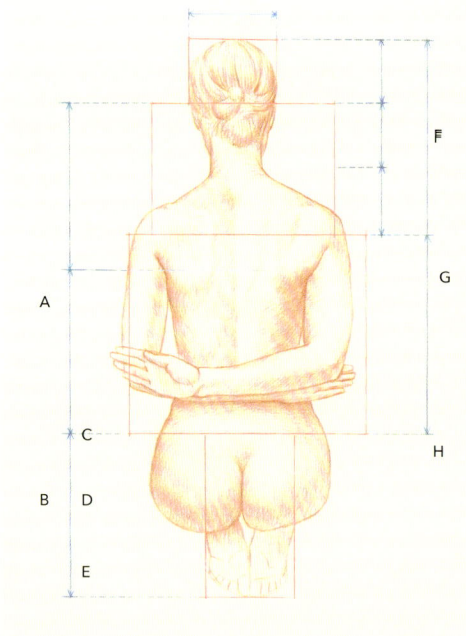

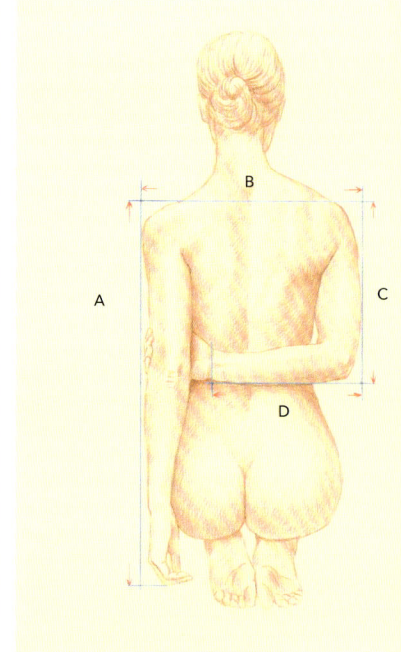

TOP LEFT: Reducing complex forms to measures

In this pose viewed from the back, the model's folded arms create a rectangular shape between the waist and shoulders; the width of this rectangle is larger than its height. The glutei and feet are contained in gradually smaller rectangular shapes, each of whose width is larger than its height. The widths of the head and feet are the same. Also note the other corresponding measures, marked with letters and that A=B, C=D=F, and F=G=H.

TOP RIGHT: Visualizing pattern in a pose

The various segments of the body can be reduced to lines to describe their length or width. These measures can then be used to find proportional relationships and geometric patterns.

RIGHT: The encasing envelope—finding the height-to-width ratio

These drawings compare the height-to-width ratios of rectangles encasing the shoulders, upper arms, and forearms of a male and a female model. In the male, the width of the rectangle is proportionally a little larger in relation to the height than in the female.

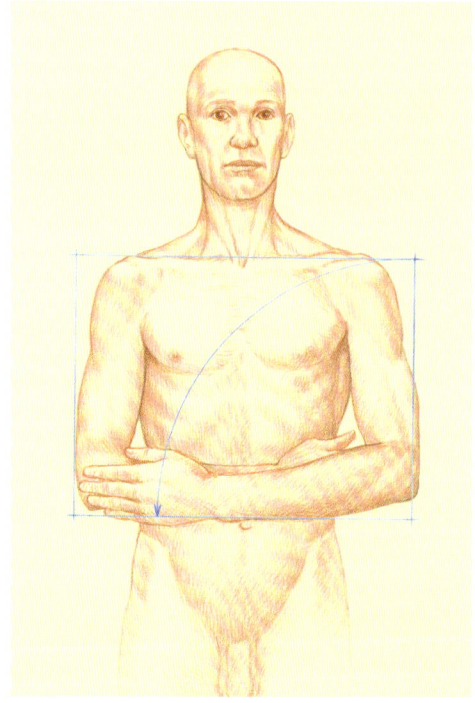

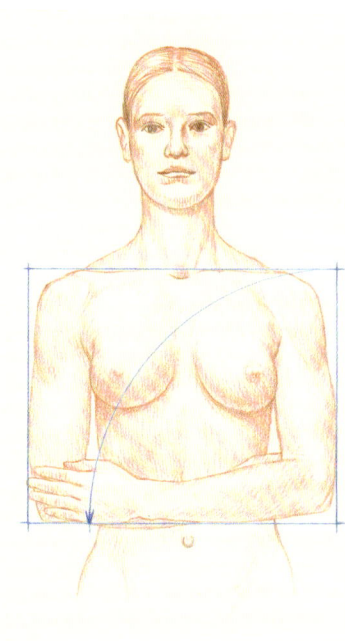

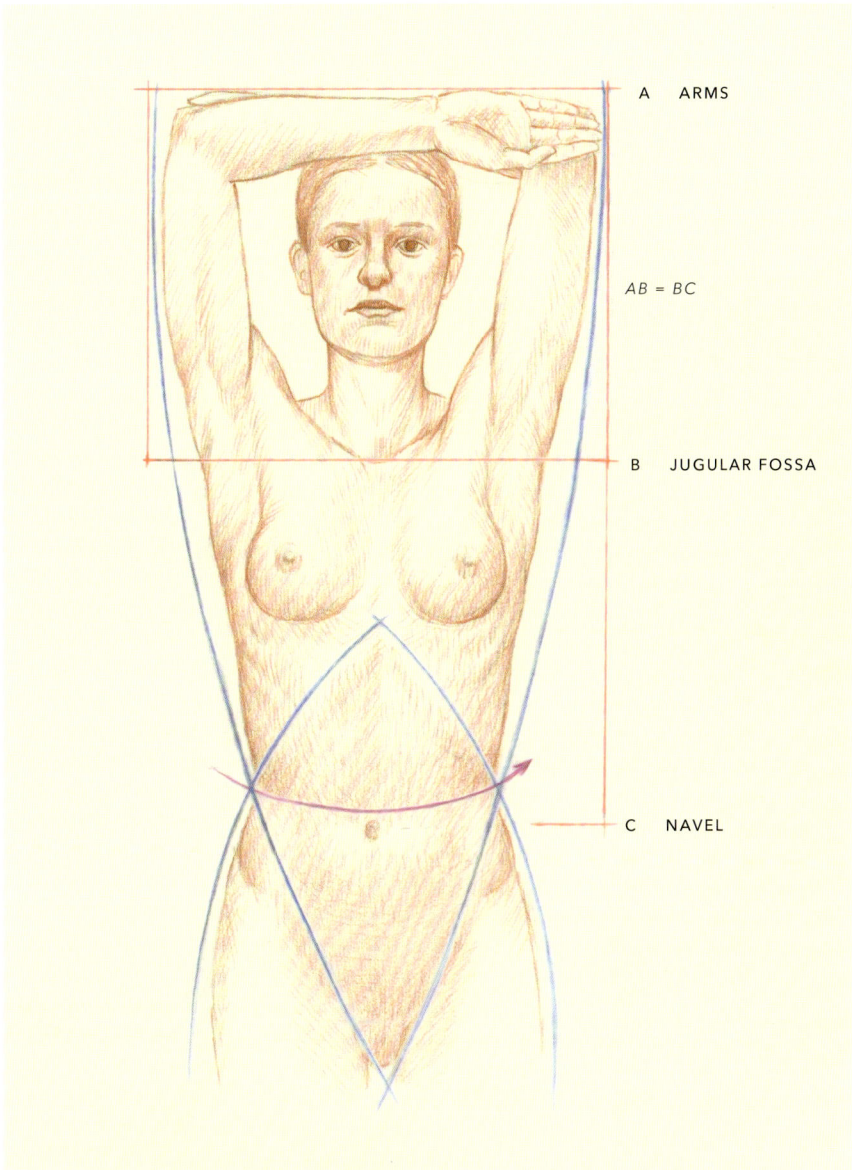

A   ARMS

AB = BC

B   JUGULAR FOSSA

C   NAVEL

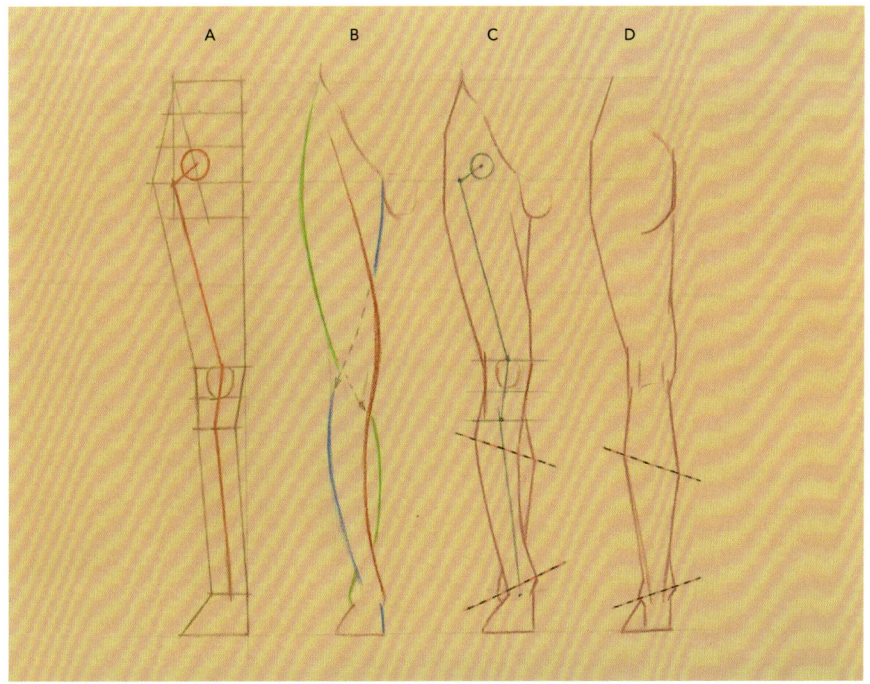

A   B   C   D

LEFT: Patterns happen!

You can find *many* patterns in a pose, but I always try to find the main ones. Note the hourglass pattern created by the two *V*-shaped patterns of the upper and lower segments of the figure.

BELOW LEFT: Different approaches to "reading" the figure

The human figure can be "read" using several different approaches. In the leg at left *(A)*, the axis of the skeleton is considered; note how the segments of the skeleton follow a zigzag line. The second leg *(B)* shows the flows created by the volumes of the main muscles of the leg. The third and fourth legs *(C and D)*, showing anterior and posterior views, focus instead on the alignments of the calves and ankles.

FINDING GEOMETRIC PATTERNS IN A POSE

Encasing or subdividing a pose with geometric shapes can be very useful in measuring the figure and establishing the compositional characteristics of the pose. In the examples here, the poses are visualized as sets of triangles. These geometric visualizations—whether of triangles, squares, rectangles, or circles—can be fairly arbitrary.

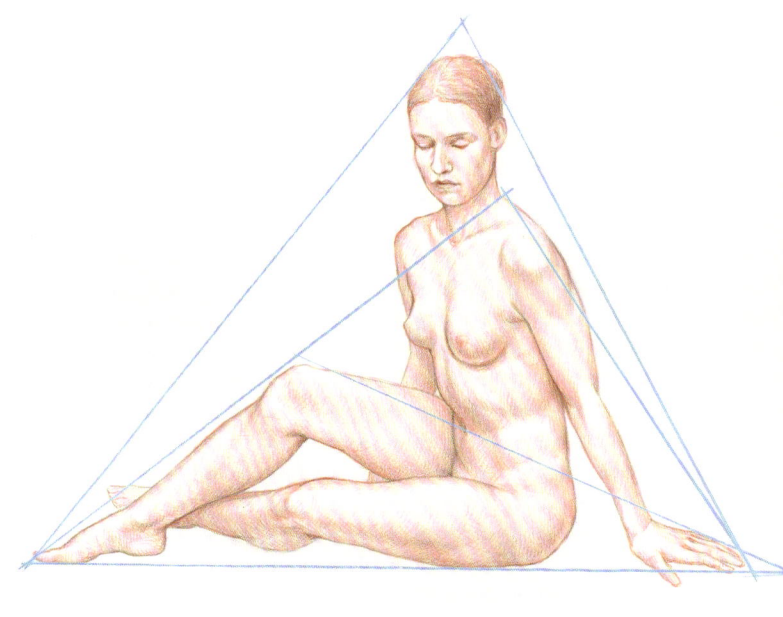

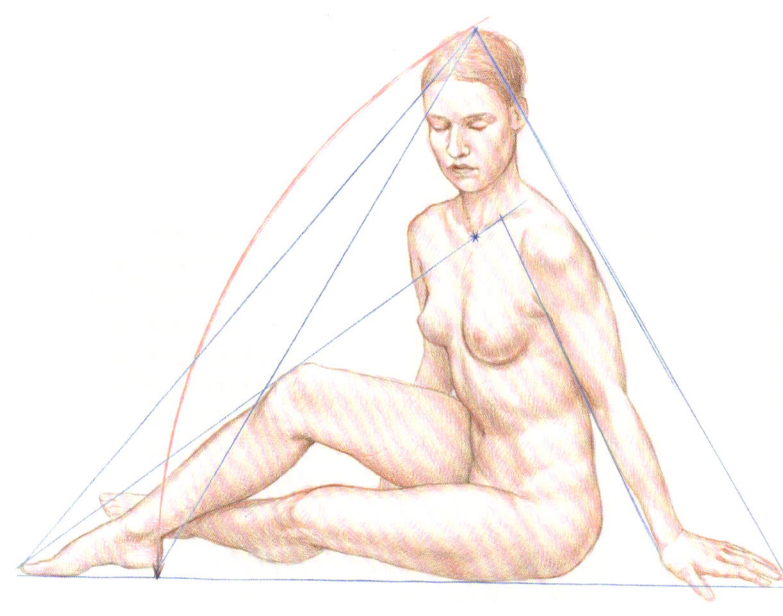

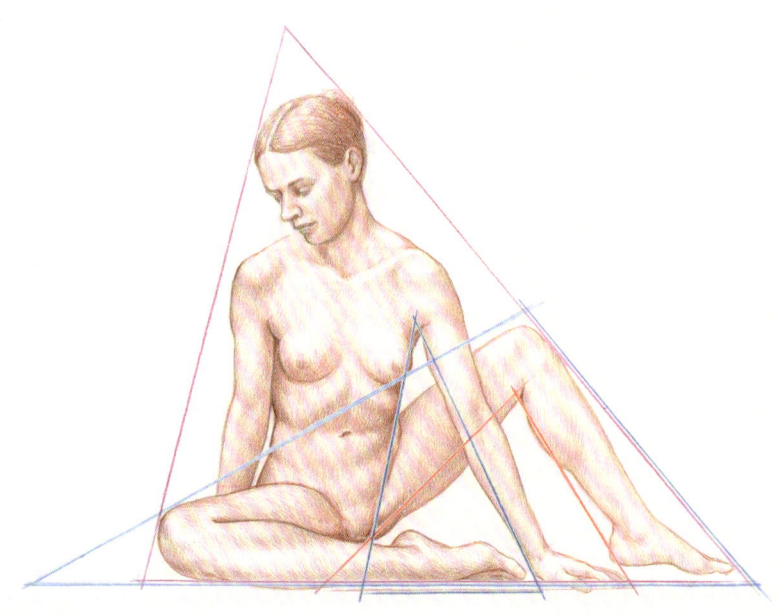

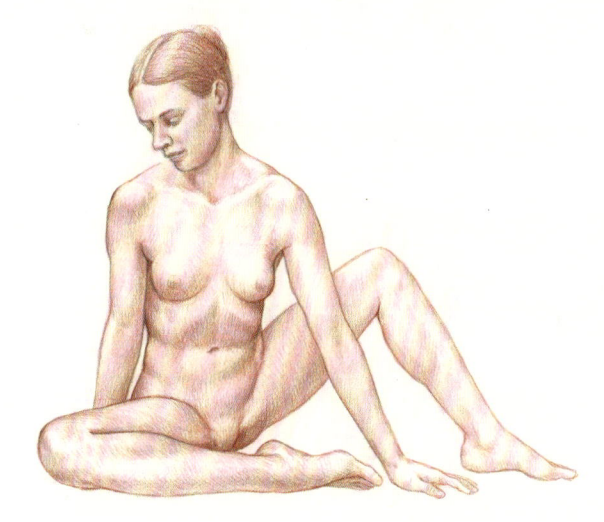

EXERCISE

Place a sheet of tracing paper over each of the images on this page and practice finding geometric patterns in each pose, as in the sidebar opposite. Don't restrict yourself to triangles. You'll be able to find patterns of circles, squares, and rectangles, as well.

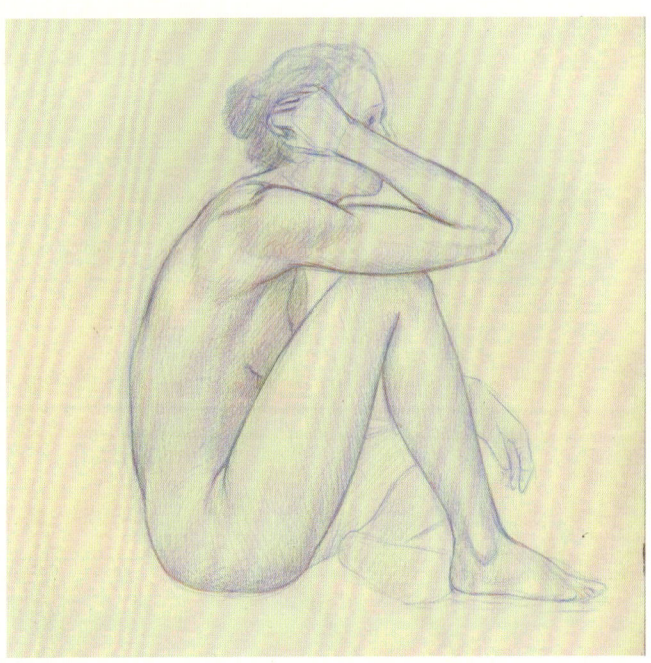

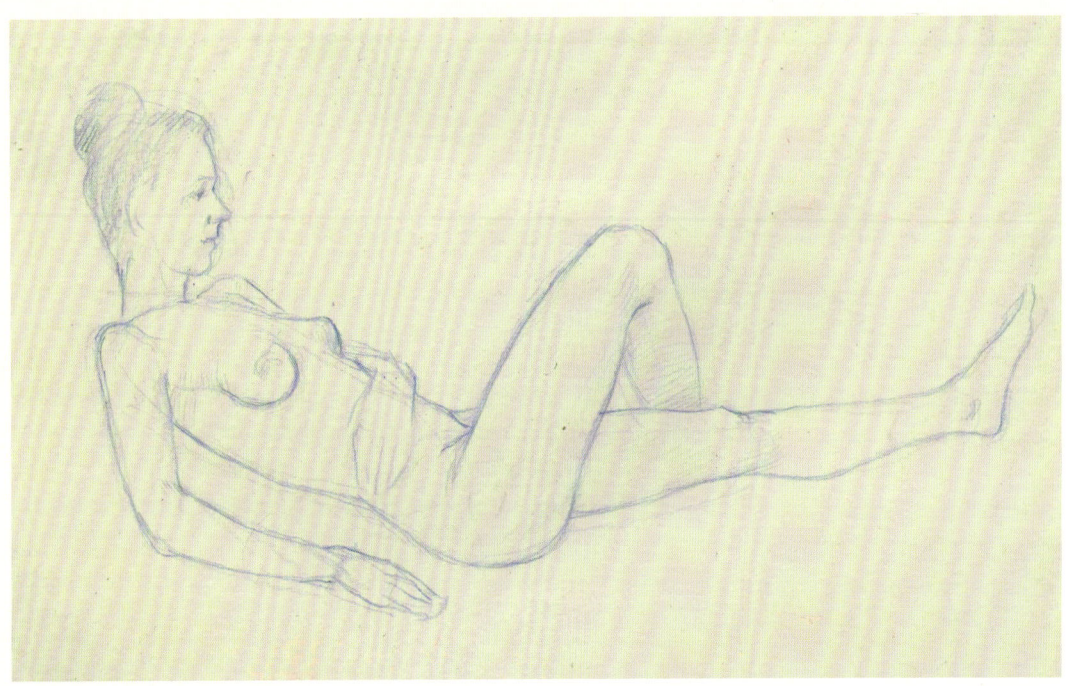

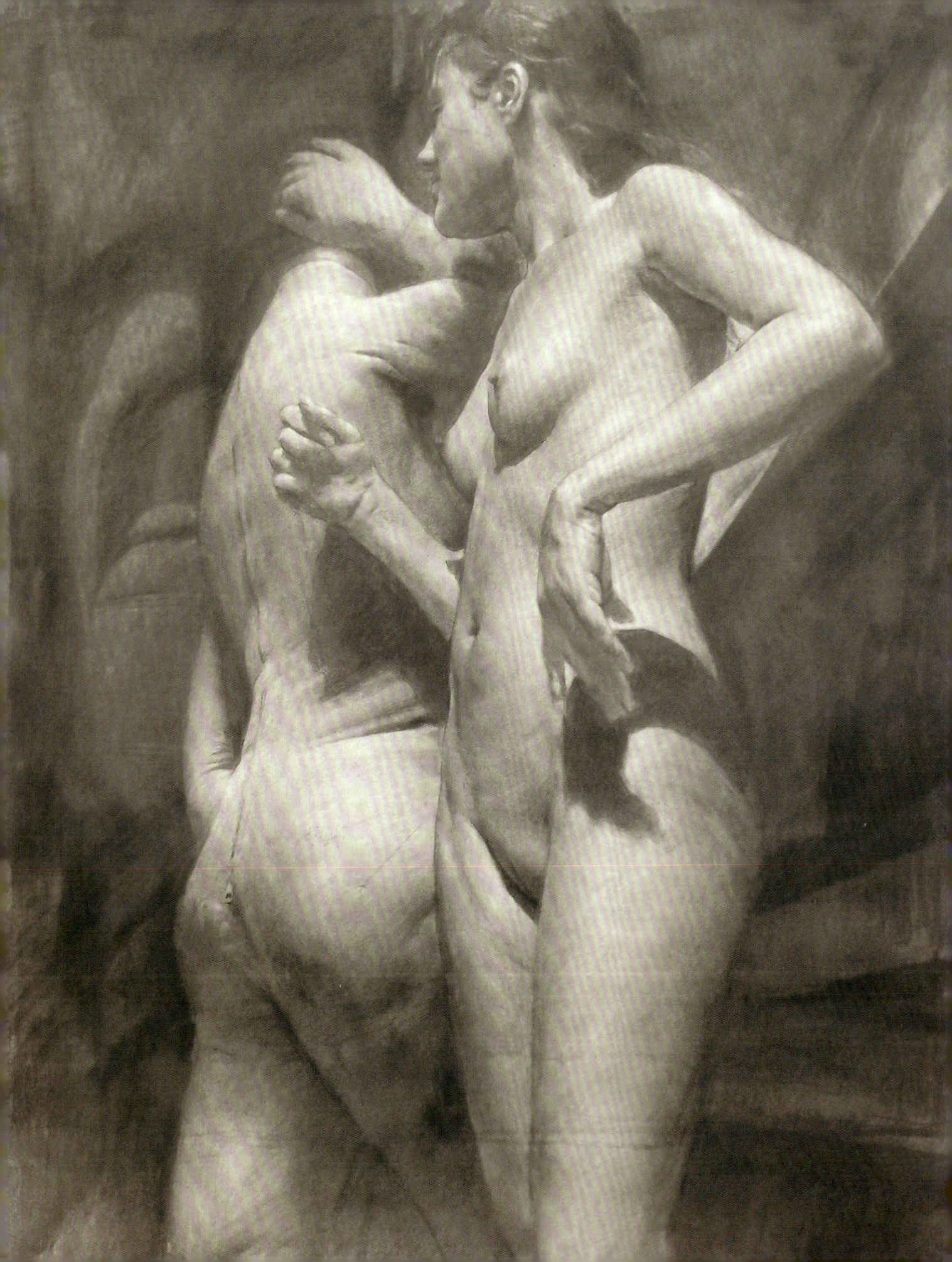

CHAPTER 3

LANDMARKS & MUSCULAR VOLUMES

Any artist who wants to master the dynamism and aesthetics of the human body needs to become acquainted with the skeletal system, its structural characteristics, and its connections with the muscular system. This chapter systematically identifies and describes the body's landmarks, muscular volumes, and muscular-skeletal connections to help you learn to use them when drawing and painting the human figure.

Why is the skeleton so important for the figurative artist? The artists of the Renaissance compared the human skeletal structure to a strong foundation that holds up a building. Without a good foundation, a building will collapse. Similarly, if the skeletal structure is not well understood and considered when drawing the figure, the artwork will also fail.

OPPOSITE: Michael Grimaldi, *Mantle,* 2019. Courtesy of the artist.

Skeletal structure—a strong foundation

BELOW: Bartolomeo Passarotti, *Self-portrait Lecturing on the Theory of Anatomical Drawing,* 1580s, ink on paper, 13⅛ x 18¼ inches (33.4 x 46.4 cm). University of Warsaw Library.

Passarotti's drawing illustrates the progressive approach I recommend.

OPPOSITE: Overview of the landmarks of the front of the torso

The blue circles mark the landmarks, both skeletal and soft, that are most easily visible on the body. The blue hatch lines mark the less visible or invisible landmarks that can be extrapolated using adjacent landmarks.

Even though the skeleton is hidden under muscular volumes and a more or less thick layer of fat, a few hints of it can be perceived just under the skin at some specific places on the body. These spots are the *skeletal landmarks,* or *bony landmarks.* Besides the skeletal landmarks, the body also displays some *soft landmarks* created by tendons or ligaments such as the linea alba and the inguinal ligament, as well as surface forms such as the navel and nipples.

By identifying the skeletal landmarks, we can reconstruct the whole skeleton and obtain a deeper understanding of the human figure, its poses, dynamism, and aesthetics. The ability to identify muscular forms on the surface of the body permits us to properly relate the muscles to the skeleton when drawing, creating more complex, expressive, and harmonious artworks.

LANDMARKS AND ANATOMY OF THE TORSO

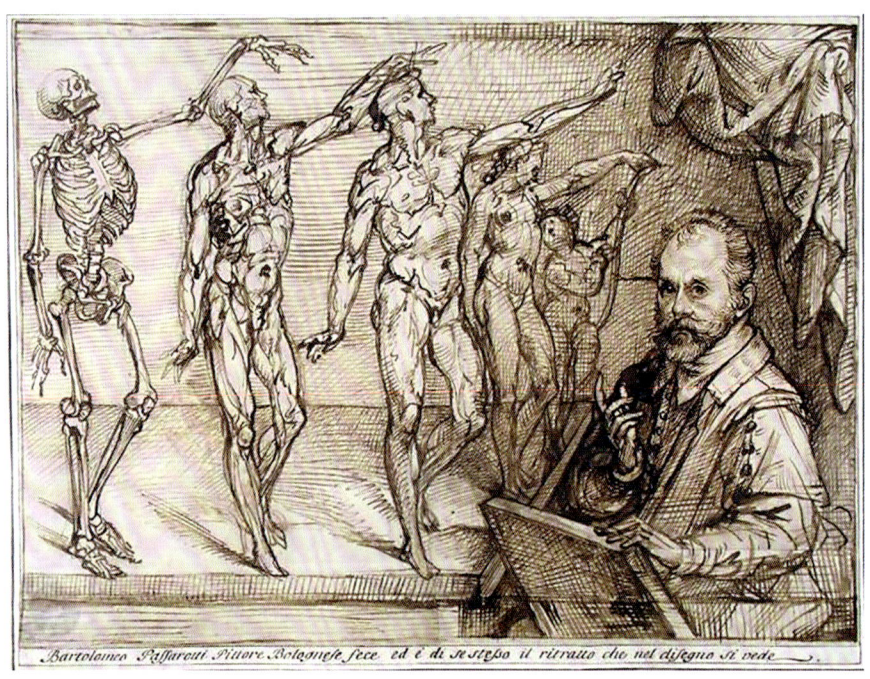

Bartolomeo Passarotti Pittore Bolognese fece ed è di se stesso il ritratto che nel disegno si vede.

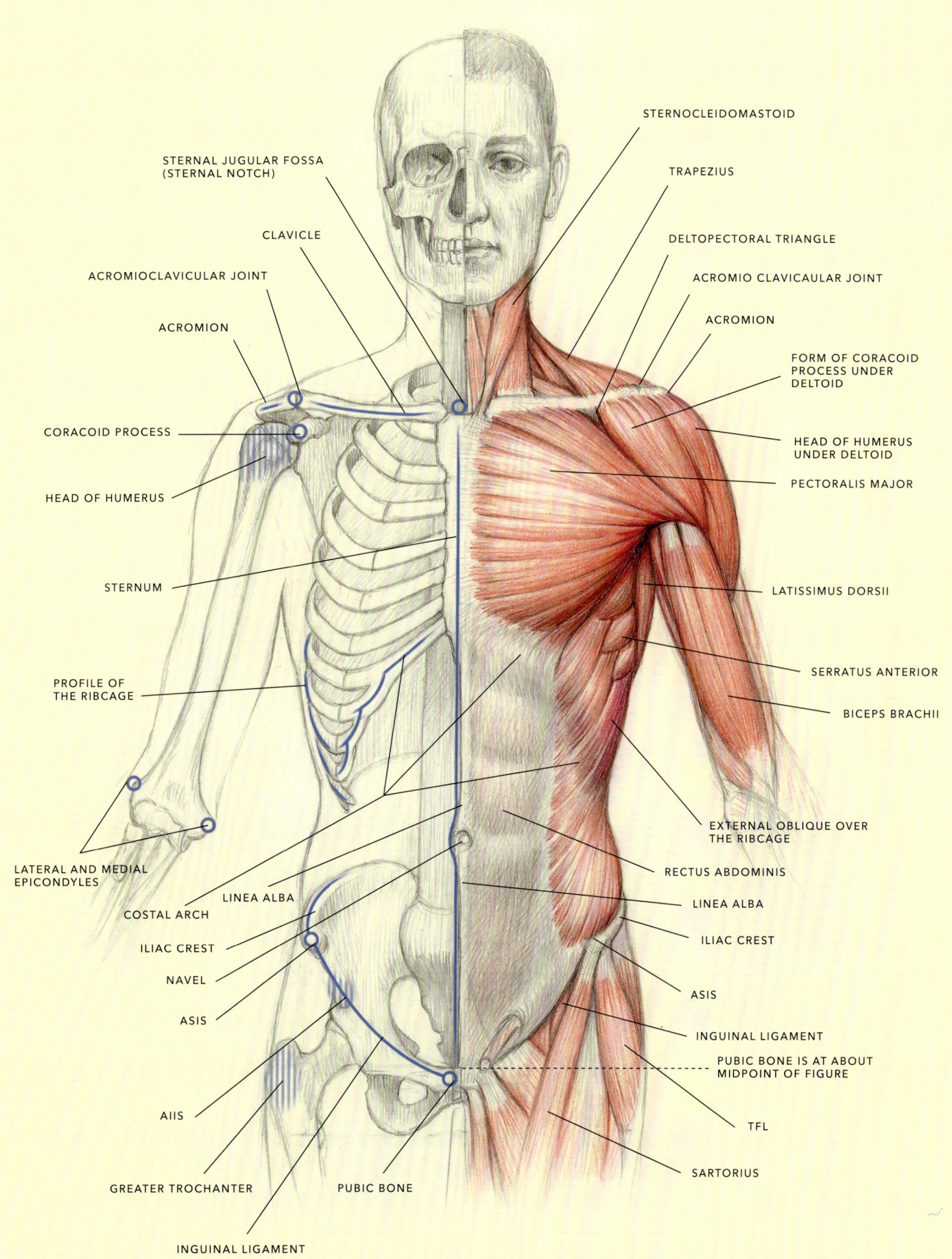

STERNOCLEIDOMASTOID

TRAPEZIUS

DELTOPECTORAL TRIANGLE

ACROMIO CLAVICAULAR JOINT

ACROMION

FORM OF CORACOID
PROCESS UNDER
DELTOID

HEAD OF HUMERUS
UNDER DELTOID

PECTORALIS MAJOR

LATISSIMUS DORSII

SERRATUS ANTERIOR

BICEPS BRACHII

EXTERNAL OBLIQUE OVER
THE RIBCAGE

RECTUS ABDOMINIS

LINEA ALBA

ILIAC CREST

ASIS

INGUINAL LIGAMENT

PUBIC BONE IS AT ABOUT
MIDPOINT OF FIGURE

TFL

SARTORIUS

STERNAL JUGULAR FOSSA
(STERNAL NOTCH)

CLAVICLE

ACROMIOCLAVICULAR JOINT

ACROMION

CORACOID PROCESS

HEAD OF HUMERUS

STERNUM

PROFILE OF
THE RIBCAGE

LATERAL AND MEDIAL
EPICONDYLES

COSTAL ARCH

LINEA ALBA

ILIAC CREST

NAVEL

ASIS

AIIS

GREATER TROCHANTER

PUBIC BONE

INGUINAL LIGAMENT

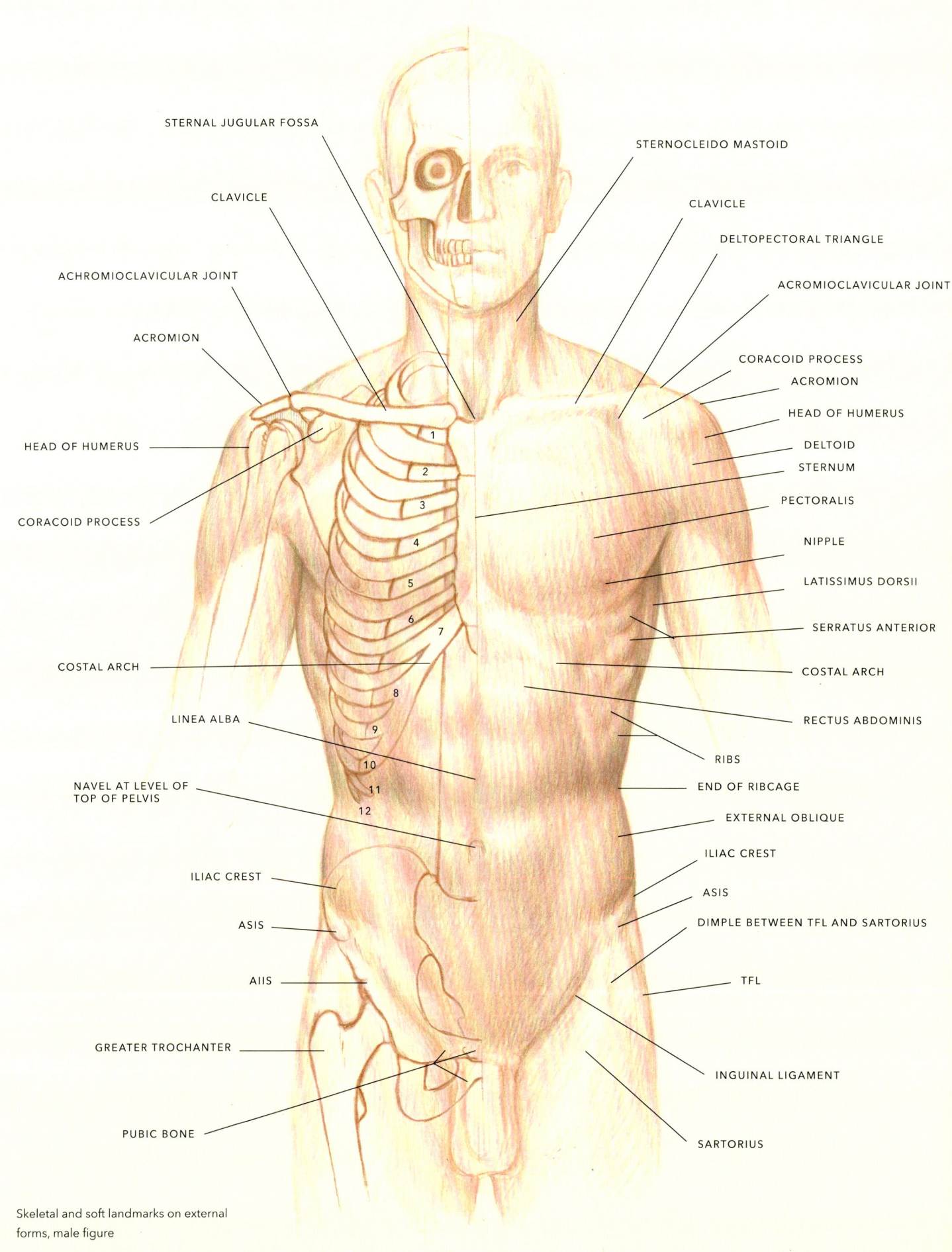

STERNAL JUGULAR FOSSA

CLAVICLE

ACHROMIOCLAVICULAR JOINT

ACROMION

HEAD OF HUMERUS

CORACOID PROCESS

COSTAL ARCH

LINEA ALBA

NAVEL AT LEVEL OF
TOP OF PELVIS

ILIAC CREST

ASIS

AIIS

GREATER TROCHANTER

PUBIC BONE

STERNOCLEIDO MASTOID

CLAVICLE

DELTOPECTORAL TRIANGLE

ACROMIOCLAVICULAR JOINT

CORACOID PROCESS

ACROMION

HEAD OF HUMERUS

DELTOID

STERNUM

PECTORALIS

NIPPLE

LATISSIMUS DORSII

SERRATUS ANTERIOR

COSTAL ARCH

RECTUS ABDOMINIS

RIBS

END OF RIBCAGE

EXTERNAL OBLIQUE

ILIAC CREST

ASIS

DIMPLE BETWEEN TFL AND SARTORIUS

TFL

INGUINAL LIGAMENT

SARTORIUS

1
2
3
4
5
6
7
8
9
10
11
12

Skeletal and soft landmarks on external
forms, male figure

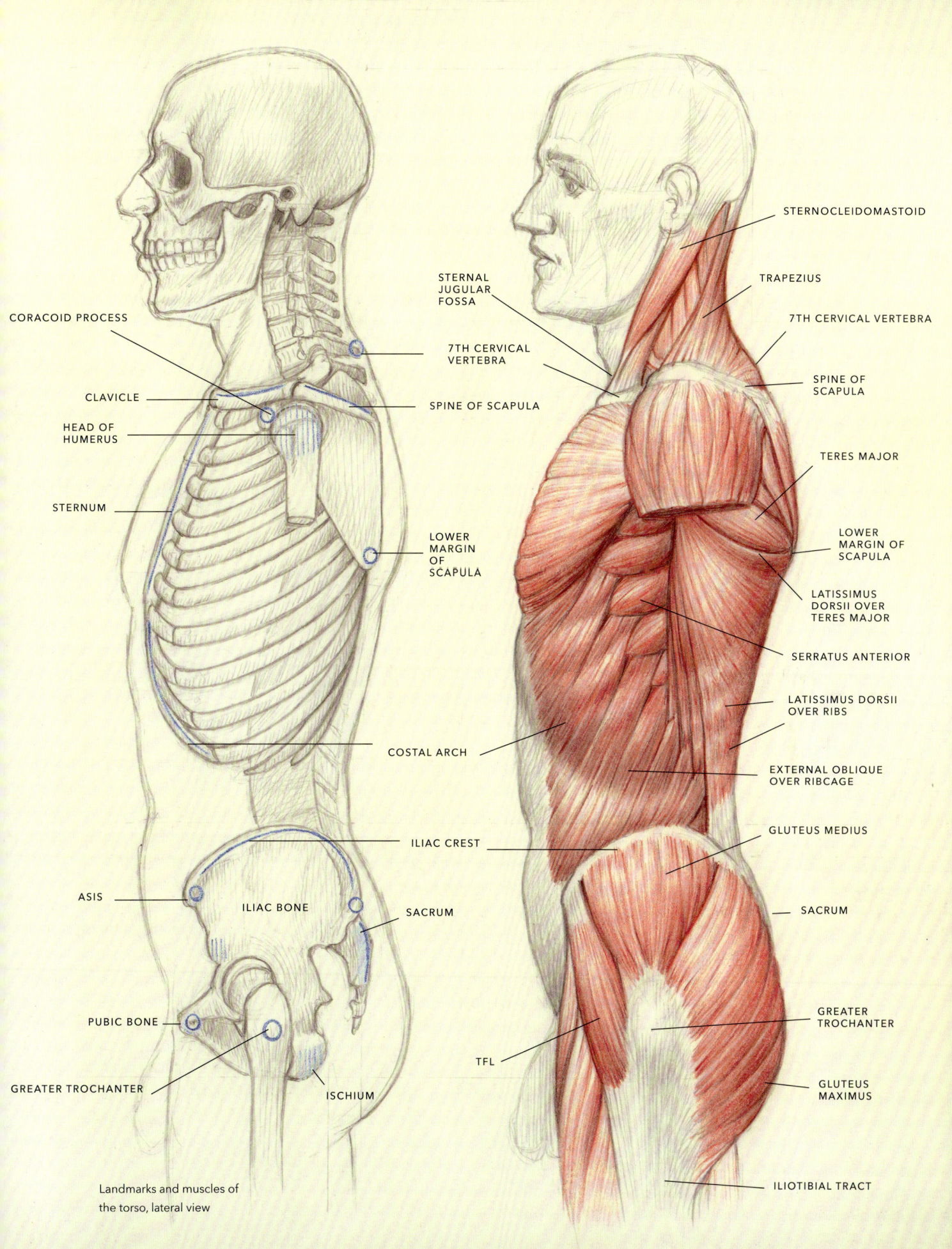

CORACOID PROCESS

CLAVICLE

HEAD OF
HUMERUS

STERNUM

STERNAL
JUGULAR
FOSSA

7TH CERVICAL
VERTEBRA

SPINE OF SCAPULA

LOWER
MARGIN
OF
SCAPULA

COSTAL ARCH

ILIAC CREST

ASIS

ILIAC BONE

SACRUM

PUBIC BONE

GREATER TROCHANTER

ISCHIUM

Landmarks and muscles of
the torso, lateral view

STERNOCLEIDOMASTOID

TRAPEZIUS

7TH CERVICAL VERTEBRA

SPINE OF
SCAPULA

TERES MAJOR

LOWER
MARGIN OF
SCAPULA

LATISSIMUS
DORSII OVER
TERES MAJOR

SERRATUS ANTERIOR

LATISSIMUS DORSII
OVER RIBS

EXTERNAL OBLIQUE
OVER RIBCAGE

GLUTEUS MEDIUS

SACRUM

GREATER
TROCHANTER

GLUTEUS
MAXIMUS

TFL

ILIOTIBIAL TRACT

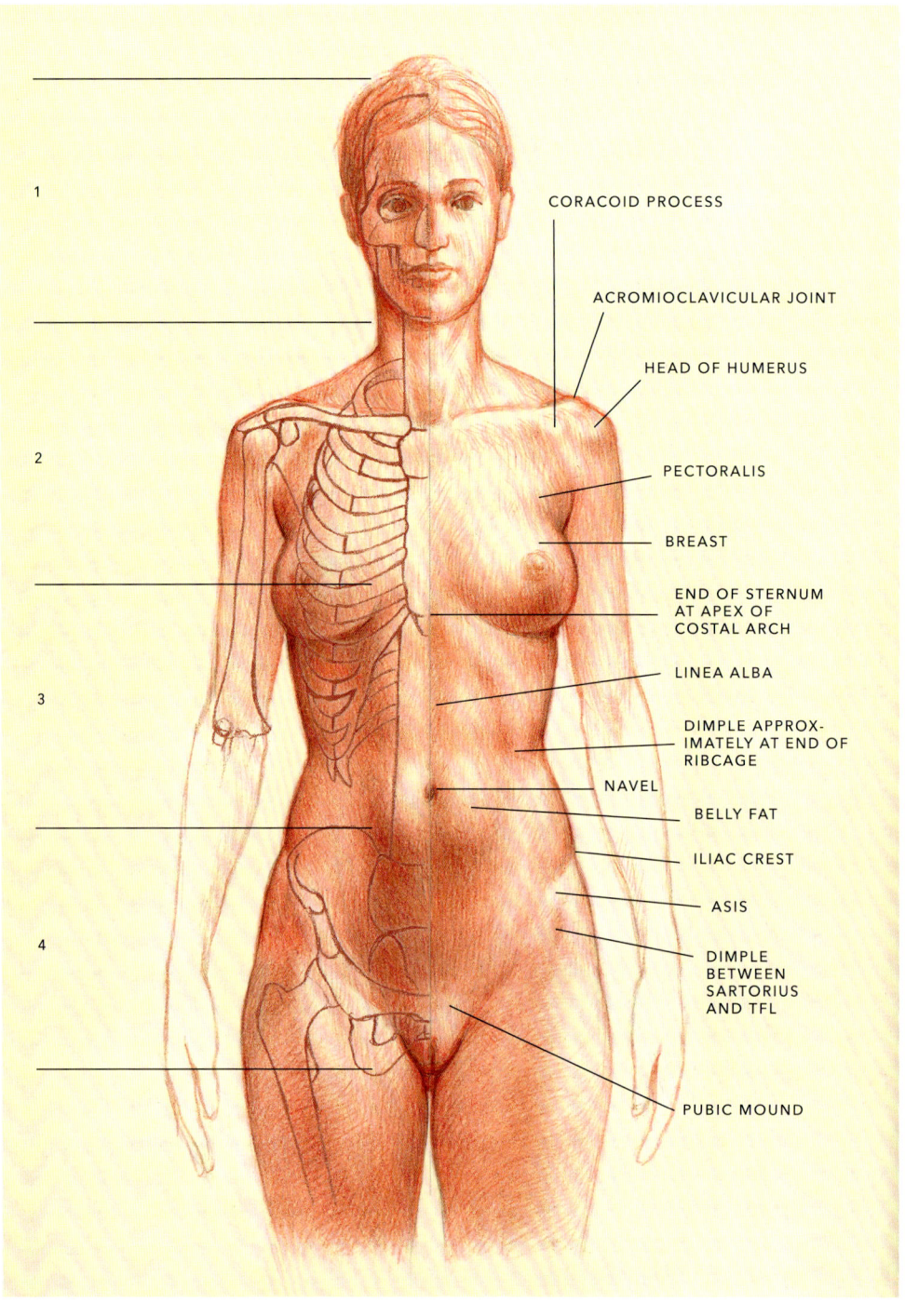

1

2

3

4

CORACOID PROCESS

ACROMIOCLAVICULAR JOINT

HEAD OF HUMERUS

PECTORALIS

BREAST

END OF STERNUM
AT APEX OF
COSTAL ARCH

LINEA ALBA

DIMPLE APPROX-
IMATELY AT END OF
RIBCAGE

NAVEL

BELLY FAT

ILIAC CREST

ASIS

DIMPLE
BETWEEN
SARTORIUS
AND TFL

PUBIC MOUND

LANDMARKS OF FEMALE FIGURE

ABOVE: Skeletal and soft landmarks on external forms, female figure

Comparing the male and female skeletons, we notice that in women the width of pelvis is usually greater than the width of the ribcage, while in men they are similar. Women's wider pelvis is also responsible for the greater inward angle of the thighs as they move toward the knees. The nipples are not necessarily at the measure of one head down from the chin because of great variation in the size of the breasts.

THE BREASTS

A single breast is not a symmetrical form. Also, various factors, such as size and age, cause the position and overall form of the breasts to vary. Because of these variables, the breasts can be positioned higher or lower on the chest; the nipple is not necessarily close to the level of the fifth rib as in men but may be higher or lower. The space between the bottom of the breasts and the top of the costal arch can help in correctly placing the breasts on a specific figure.

TOP RIGHT: Breast forms

When drawing the breast, think of a water balloon (A). The weight of the water pulls on the upper part of the balloon, stretching it, while the bottom part of the balloon widens as it is filled with water, giving it a droplike form. The nipple is usually at the peak of the form of the breast, which can be directed upward, forward, or downward (B). The side view (C) shows that the breasts lie on the inclined plane of the chest. The top view detail (D) reveals that the breasts are not usually oriented directly forward but are slightly divergent from each other because they lie on the curved form of the chest. Detail E shows that the breasts overlap the pectoralis; breast and pectoralis are two separate and distinct forms.

BOTTOM RIGHT: Size and position of breasts in relation to the measure of one head down from the chin and to the costal arch.

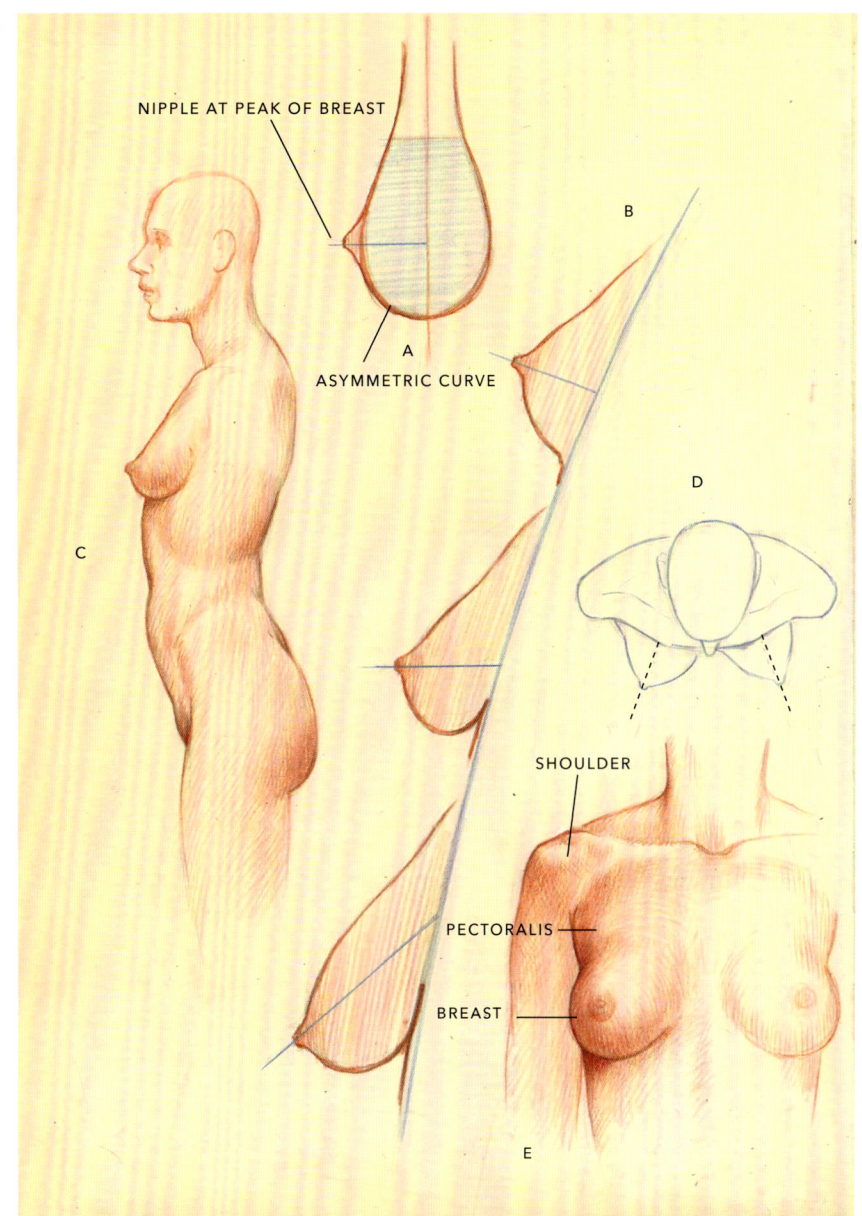

NIPPLE AT PEAK OF BREAST

ASYMMETRIC CURVE

A

B

C

D

SHOULDER

PECTORALIS

BREAST

E

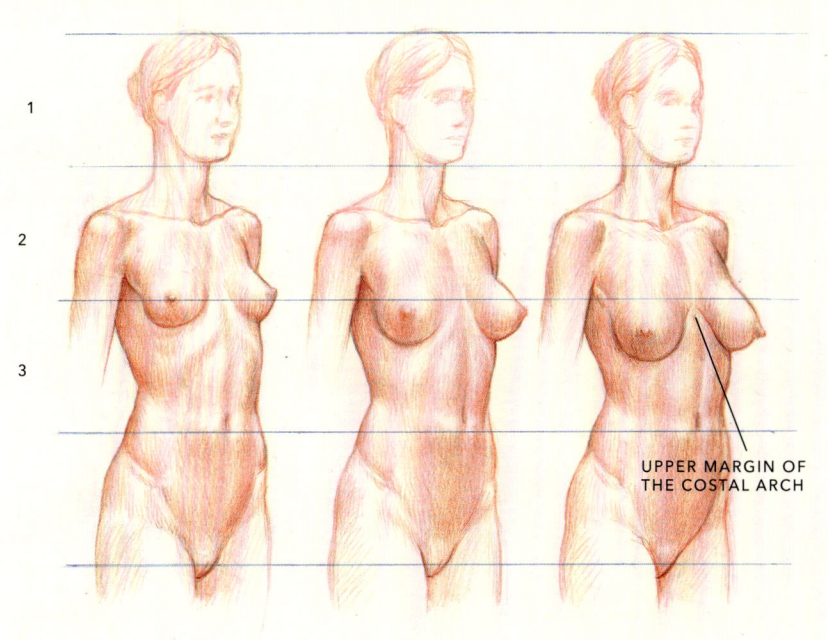

1

2

3

UPPER MARGIN OF THE COSTAL ARCH

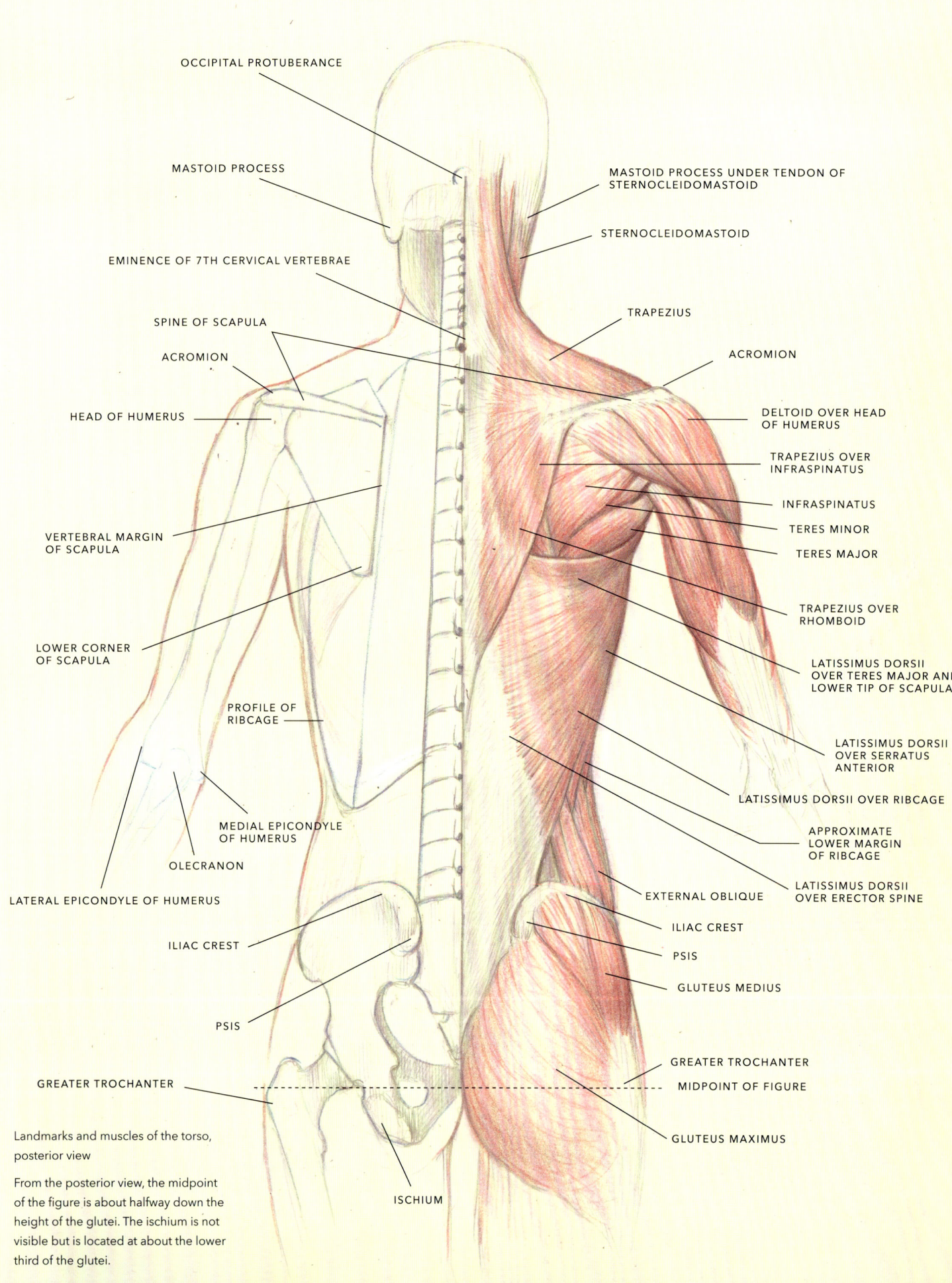

OCCIPITAL PROTUBERANCE

MASTOID PROCESS

MASTOID PROCESS UNDER TENDON OF STERNOCLEIDOMASTOID

STERNOCLEIDOMASTOID

EMINENCE OF 7TH CERVICAL VERTEBRAE

TRAPEZIUS

SPINE OF SCAPULA

ACROMION

ACROMION

HEAD OF HUMERUS

DELTOID OVER HEAD OF HUMERUS

TRAPEZIUS OVER INFRASPINATUS

INFRASPINATUS

TERES MINOR

TERES MAJOR

VERTEBRAL MARGIN OF SCAPULA

TRAPEZIUS OVER RHOMBOID

LATISSIMUS DORSII OVER TERES MAJOR AND LOWER TIP OF SCAPULA

LOWER CORNER OF SCAPULA

PROFILE OF RIBCAGE

LATISSIMUS DORSII OVER SERRATUS ANTERIOR

LATISSIMUS DORSII OVER RIBCAGE

APPROXIMATE LOWER MARGIN OF RIBCAGE

MEDIAL EPICONDYLE OF HUMERUS

LATISSIMUS DORSII OVER ERECTOR SPINE

OLECRANON

EXTERNAL OBLIQUE

LATERAL EPICONDYLE OF HUMERUS

ILIAC CREST

ILIAC CREST

PSIS

GLUTEUS MEDIUS

PSIS

GREATER TROCHANTER

GREATER TROCHANTER

MIDPOINT OF FIGURE

GLUTEUS MAXIMUS

Landmarks and muscles of the torso, posterior view

From the posterior view, the midpoint of the figure is about halfway down the height of the glutei. The ischium is not visible but is located at about the lower third of the glutei.

ISCHIUM

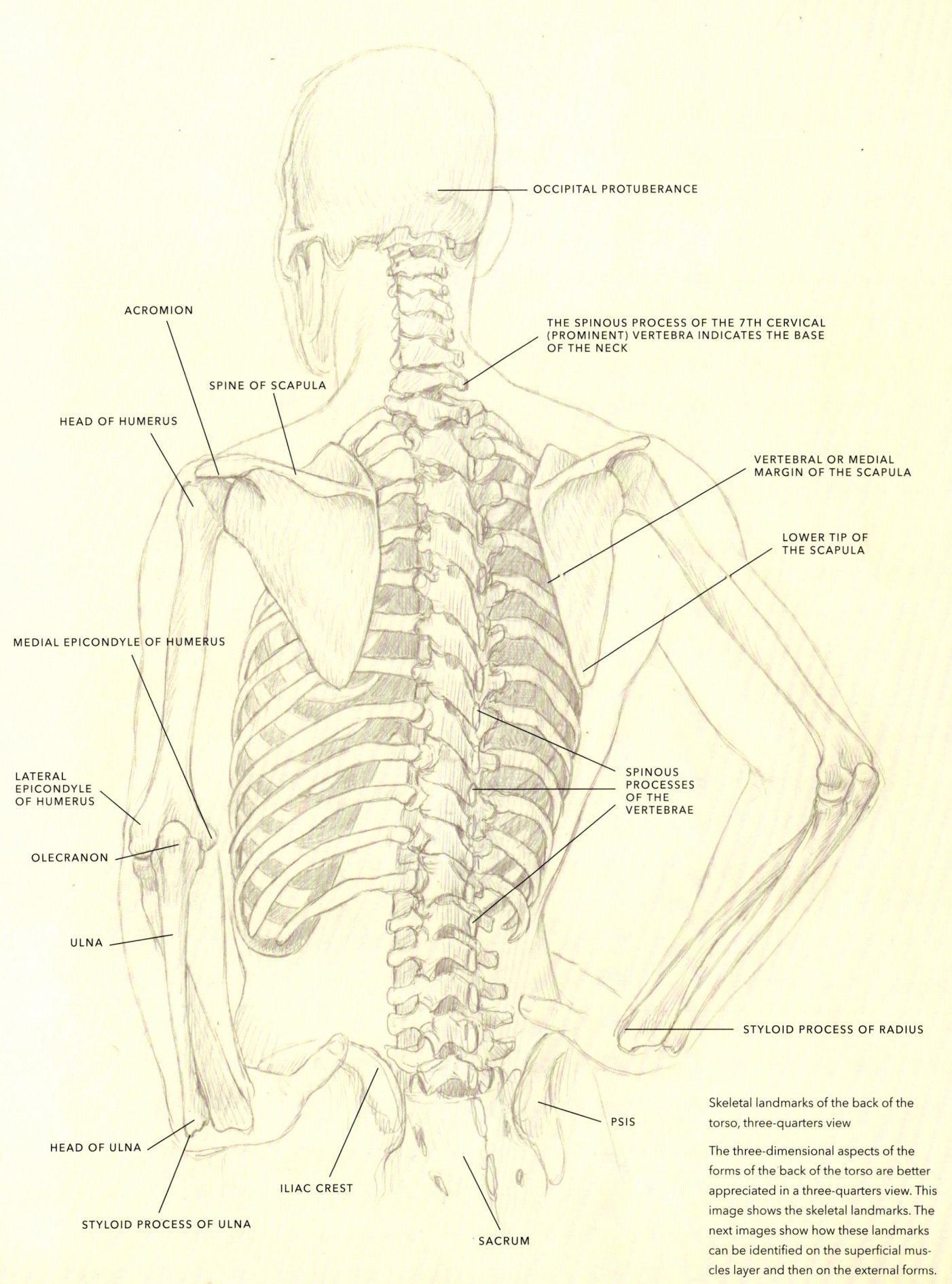

OCCIPITAL PROTUBERANCE

ACROMION

SPINE OF SCAPULA

HEAD OF HUMERUS

THE SPINOUS PROCESS OF THE 7TH CERVICAL (PROMINENT) VERTEBRA INDICATES THE BASE OF THE NECK

VERTEBRAL OR MEDIAL MARGIN OF THE SCAPULA

LOWER TIP OF THE SCAPULA

MEDIAL EPICONDYLE OF HUMERUS

LATERAL EPICONDYLE OF HUMERUS

OLECRANON

ULNA

SPINOUS PROCESSES OF THE VERTEBRAE

STYLOID PROCESS OF RADIUS

HEAD OF ULNA

STYLOID PROCESS OF ULNA

ILIAC CREST

SACRUM

PSIS

Skeletal landmarks of the back of the torso, three-quarters view

The three-dimensional aspects of the forms of the back of the torso are better appreciated in a three-quarters view. This image shows the skeletal landmarks. The next images show how these landmarks can be identified on the superficial muscles layer and then on the external forms.

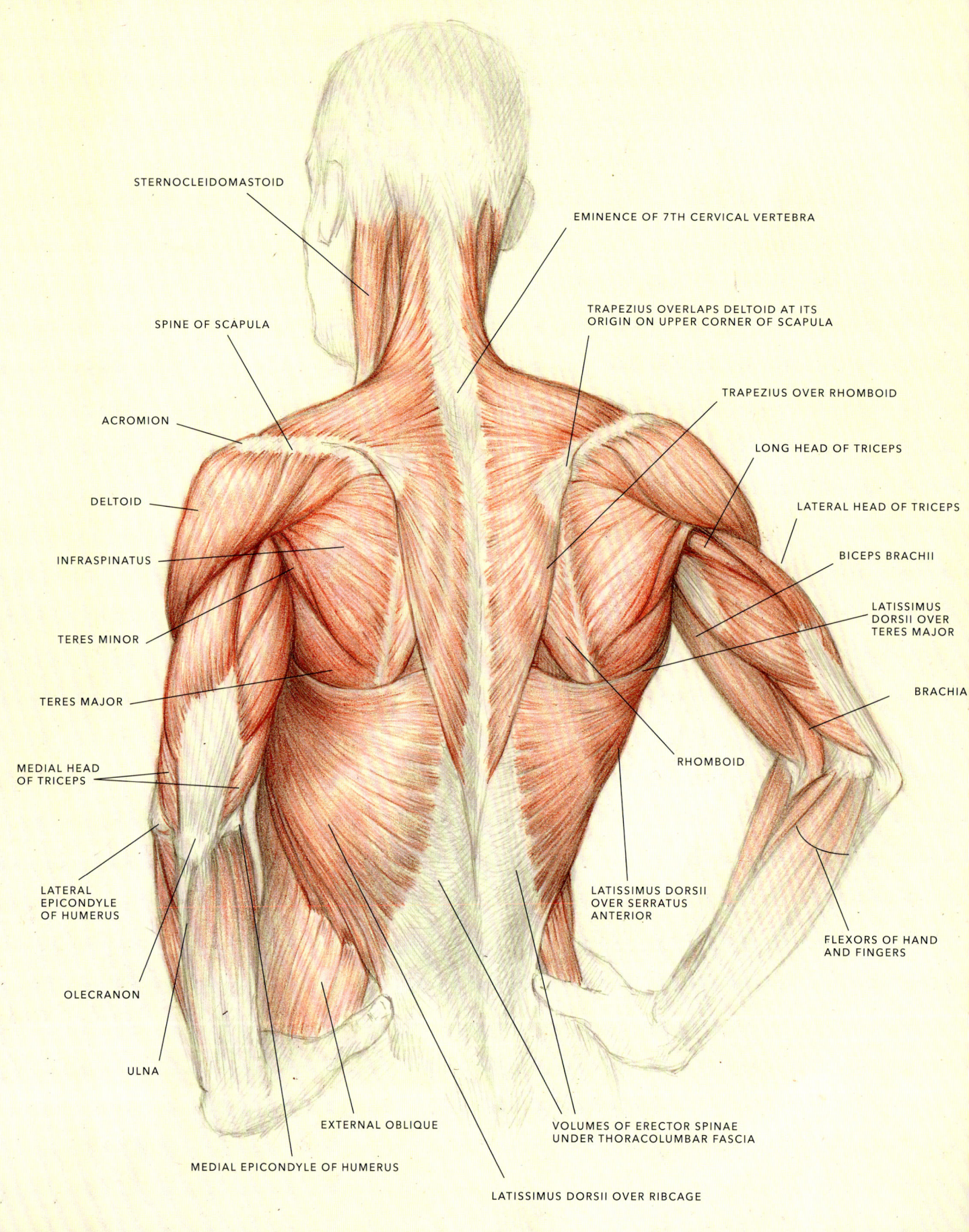

STERNOCLEIDOMASTOID

EMINENCE OF 7TH CERVICAL VERTEBRA

SPINE OF SCAPULA

TRAPEZIUS OVERLAPS DELTOID AT ITS
ORIGIN ON UPPER CORNER OF SCAPULA

ACROMION

TRAPEZIUS OVER RHOMBOID

DELTOID

LONG HEAD OF TRICEPS

INFRASPINATUS

LATERAL HEAD OF TRICEPS

BICEPS BRACHII

TERES MINOR

LATISSIMUS
DORSII OVER
TERES MAJOR

TERES MAJOR

BRACHIA

MEDIAL HEAD
OF TRICEPS

RHOMBOID

LATERAL
EPICONDYLE
OF HUMERUS

LATISSIMUS DORSII
OVER SERRATUS
ANTERIOR

FLEXORS OF HAND
AND FINGERS

OLECRANON

ULNA

EXTERNAL OBLIQUE

VOLUMES OF ERECTOR SPINAE
UNDER THORACOLUMBAR FASCIA

MEDIAL EPICONDYLE OF HUMERUS

LATISSIMUS DORSII OVER RIBCAGE

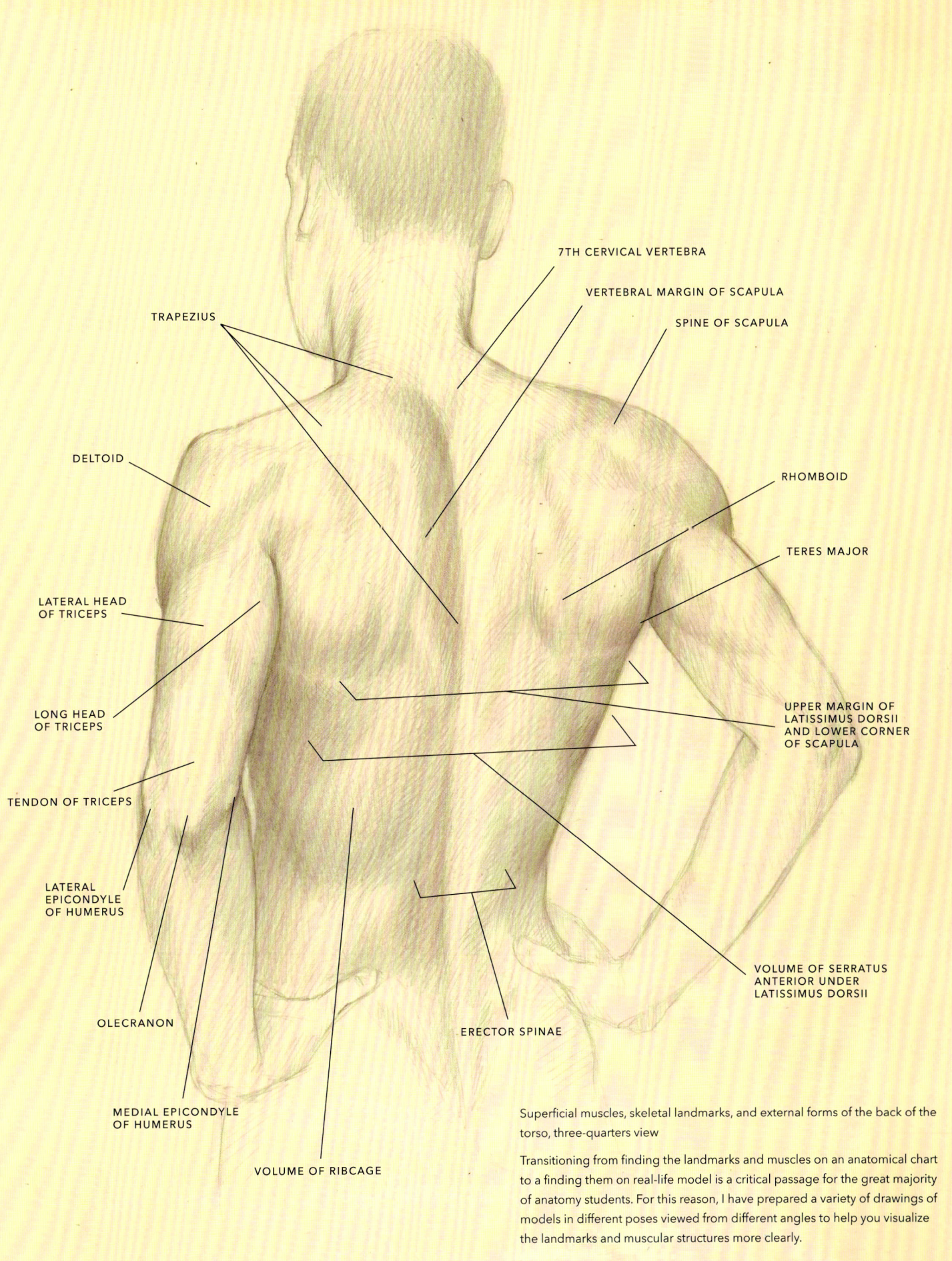

7TH CERVICAL VERTEBRA

VERTEBRAL MARGIN OF SCAPULA

SPINE OF SCAPULA

TRAPEZIUS

DELTOID

RHOMBOID

TERES MAJOR

LATERAL HEAD
OF TRICEPS

LONG HEAD
OF TRICEPS

UPPER MARGIN OF
LATISSIMUS DORSII
AND LOWER CORNER
OF SCAPULA

TENDON OF TRICEPS

LATERAL
EPICONDYLE
OF HUMERUS

VOLUME OF SERRATUS
ANTERIOR UNDER
LATISSIMUS DORSII

OLECRANON

ERECTOR SPINAE

MEDIAL EPICONDYLE
OF HUMERUS

VOLUME OF RIBCAGE

Superficial muscles, skeletal landmarks, and external forms of the back of the torso, three-quarters view

Transitioning from finding the landmarks and muscles on an anatomical chart to a finding them on real-life model is a critical passage for the great majority of anatomy students. For this reason, I have prepared a variety of drawings of models in different poses viewed from different angles to help you visualize the landmarks and muscular structures more clearly.

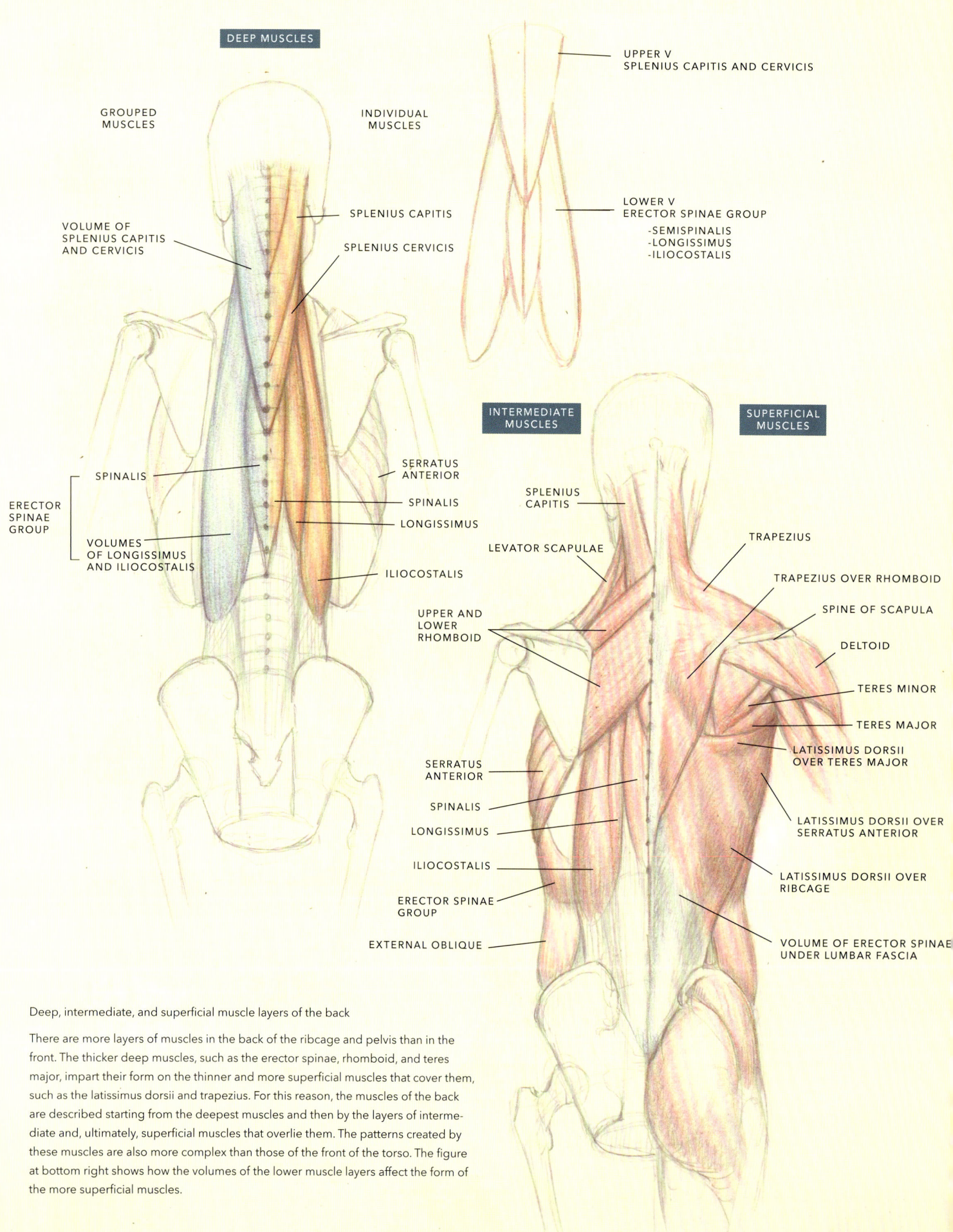

DEEP MUSCLES

GROUPED MUSCLES

INDIVIDUAL MUSCLES

VOLUME OF SPLENIUS CAPITIS AND CERVICIS

SPLENIUS CAPITIS

SPLENIUS CERVICIS

SPINALIS

ERECTOR SPINAE GROUP

VOLUMES OF LONGISSIMUS AND ILIOCOSTALIS

SERRATUS ANTERIOR

SPINALIS

LONGISSIMUS

ILIOCOSTALIS

UPPER V
SPLENIUS CAPITIS AND CERVICIS

LOWER V
ERECTOR SPINAE GROUP
-SEMISPINALIS
-LONGISSIMUS
-ILIOCOSTALIS

INTERMEDIATE MUSCLES

SUPERFICIAL MUSCLES

SPLENIUS CAPITIS

LEVATOR SCAPULAE

UPPER AND LOWER RHOMBOID

SERRATUS ANTERIOR

SPINALIS

LONGISSIMUS

ILIOCOSTALIS

ERECTOR SPINAE GROUP

EXTERNAL OBLIQUE

TRAPEZIUS

TRAPEZIUS OVER RHOMBOID

SPINE OF SCAPULA

DELTOID

TERES MINOR

TERES MAJOR

LATISSIMUS DORSII OVER TERES MAJOR

LATISSIMUS DORSII OVER SERRATUS ANTERIOR

LATISSIMUS DORSII OVER RIBCAGE

VOLUME OF ERECTOR SPINAE UNDER LUMBAR FASCIA

Deep, intermediate, and superficial muscle layers of the back

There are more layers of muscles in the back of the ribcage and pelvis than in the front. The thicker deep muscles, such as the erector spinae, rhomboid, and teres major, impart their form on the thinner and more superficial muscles that cover them, such as the latissimus dorsii and trapezius. For this reason, the muscles of the back are described starting from the deepest muscles and then by the layers of intermediate and, ultimately, superficial muscles that overlie them. The patterns created by these muscles are also more complex than those of the front of the torso. The figure at bottom right shows how the volumes of the lower muscle layers affect the form of the more superficial muscles.

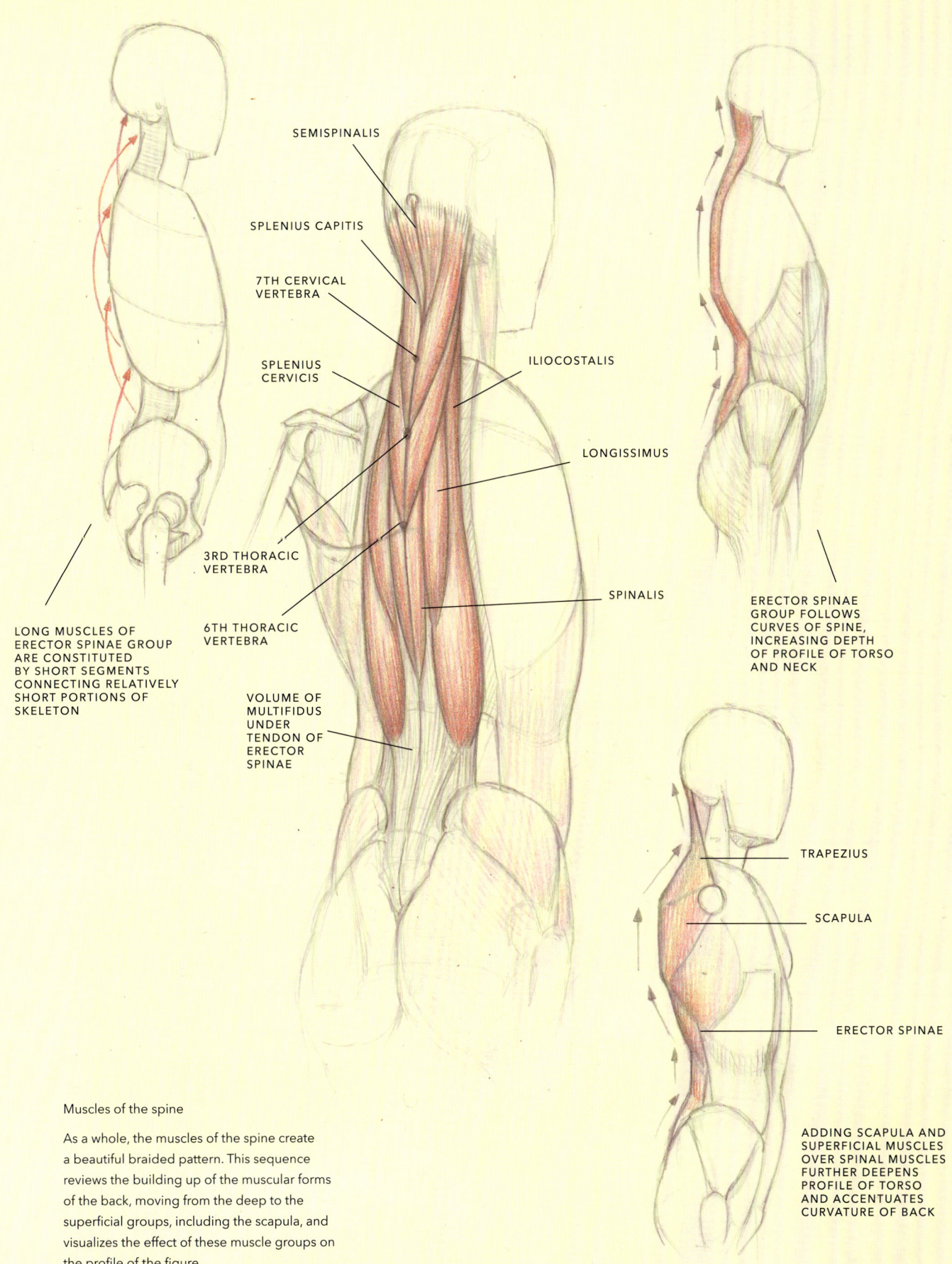

SEMISPINALIS

SPLENIUS CAPITIS

7TH CERVICAL
VERTEBRA

SPLENIUS
CERVICIS

ILIOCOSTALIS

LONGISSIMUS

3RD THORACIC
VERTEBRA

6TH THORACIC
VERTEBRA

SPINALIS

VOLUME OF
MULTIFIDUS
UNDER
TENDON OF
ERECTOR
SPINAE

LONG MUSCLES OF
ERECTOR SPINAE GROUP
ARE CONSTITUTED
BY SHORT SEGMENTS
CONNECTING RELATIVELY
SHORT PORTIONS OF
SKELETON

ERECTOR SPINAE
GROUP FOLLOWS
CURVES OF SPINE,
INCREASING DEPTH
OF PROFILE OF TORSO
AND NECK

TRAPEZIUS

SCAPULA

ERECTOR SPINAE

ADDING SCAPULA AND
SUPERFICIAL MUSCLES
OVER SPINAL MUSCLES
FURTHER DEEPENS
PROFILE OF TORSO
AND ACCENTUATES
CURVATURE OF BACK

Muscles of the spine

As a whole, the muscles of the spine create
a beautiful braided pattern. This sequence
reviews the building up of the muscular forms
of the back, moving from the deep to the
superficial groups, including the scapula, and
visualizes the effect of these muscle groups on
the profile of the figure.

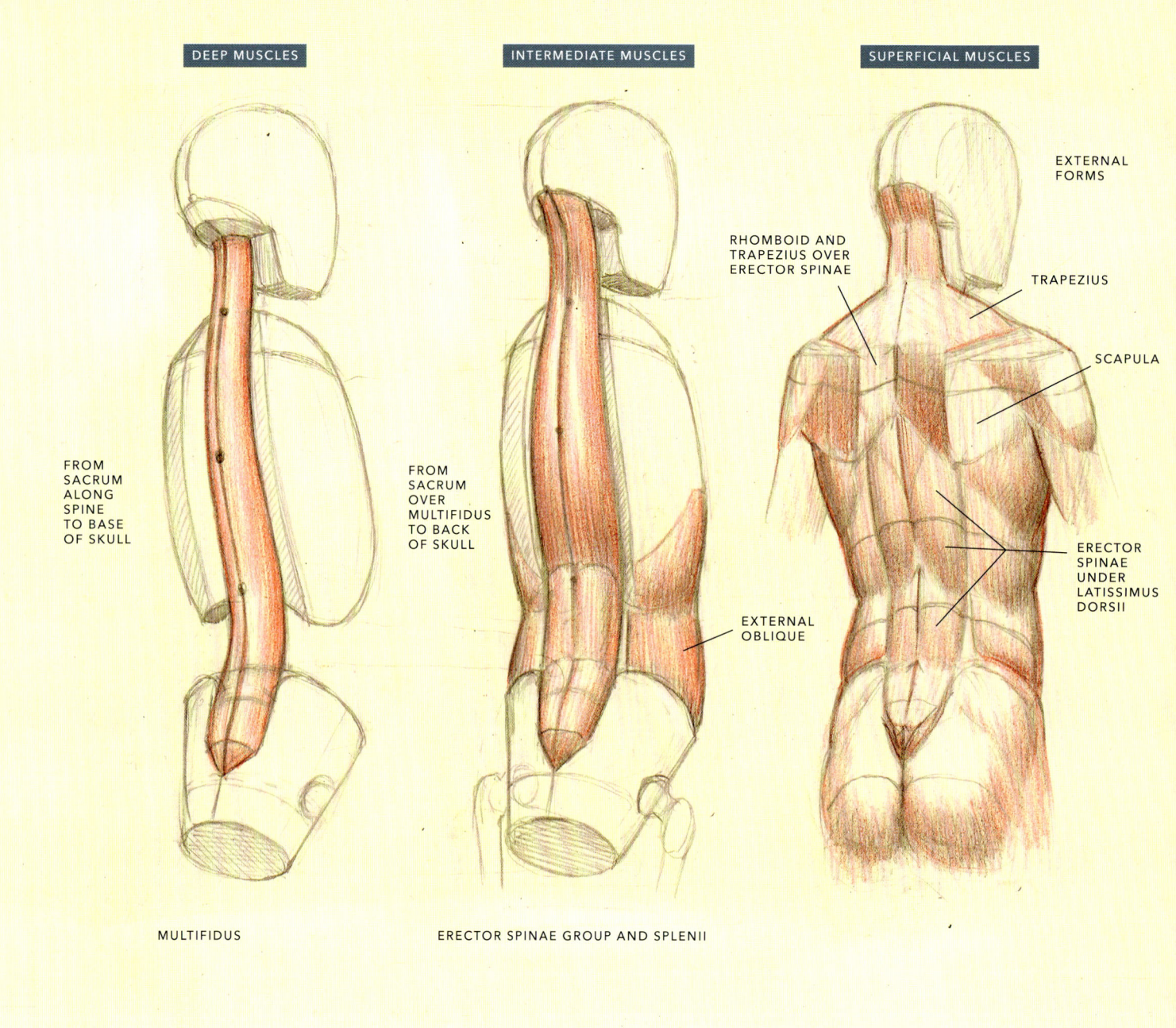

DEEP MUSCLES

INTERMEDIATE MUSCLES

SUPERFICIAL MUSCLES

EXTERNAL FORMS

RHOMBOID AND TRAPEZIUS OVER ERECTOR SPINAE

TRAPEZIUS

SCAPULA

FROM SACRUM ALONG SPINE TO BASE OF SKULL

FROM SACRUM OVER MULTIFIDUS TO BACK OF SKULL

EXTERNAL OBLIQUE

ERECTOR SPINAE UNDER LATISSIMUS DORSII

MULTIFIDUS

ERECTOR SPINAE GROUP AND SPLENII

ABOVE: Layering of the muscles of the back

The multifidus is a deep muscle that goes from the sacrum to the base of the skull, running on the side of the spine. The erector spinae group, simplified here in a single form, is positioned over the multifidus, whose volume is still visible under the tendons of the erector spinae.

LANDMARKS OF THE BACK— FEMALE-MALE COMPARISON

A woman's wider pelvis, narrower hips, and more pronounced angle between ribcage and hips create a posture different from that of the male figure, which appears straighter and has a more discernible distinction between the ribcage, waist, and pelvis.

BELOW LEFT AND CENTER: Landmarks of the back, three-quarters posterior view, female figure

BELOW RIGHT: Landmarks of the back, three-quarters posterior view, male figure

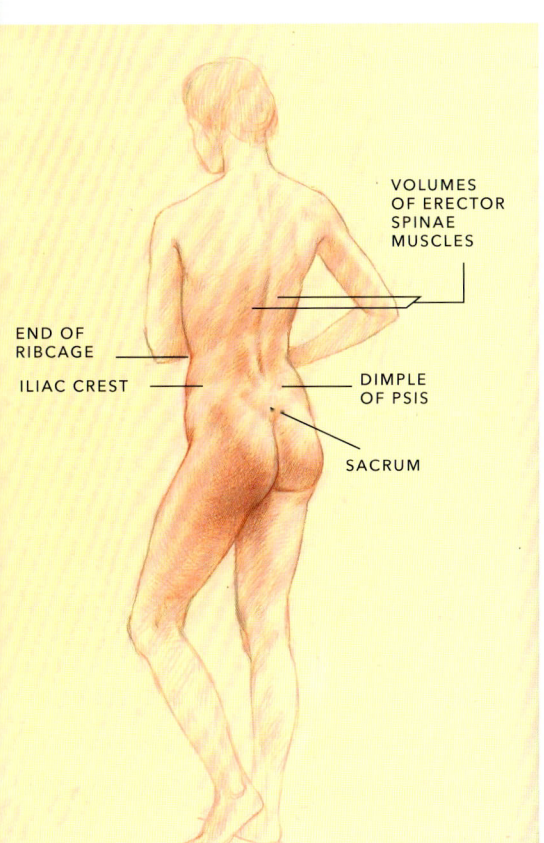

VOLUMES OF ERECTOR SPINAE MUSCLES

END OF RIBCAGE

ILIAC CREST

DIMPLE OF PSIS

SACRUM

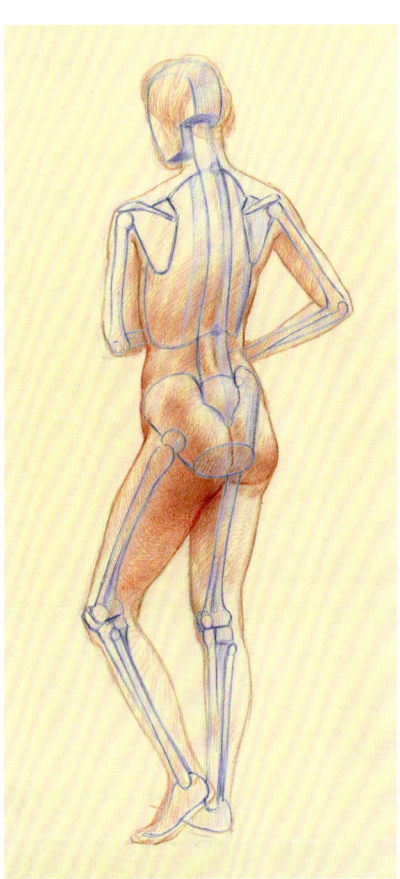

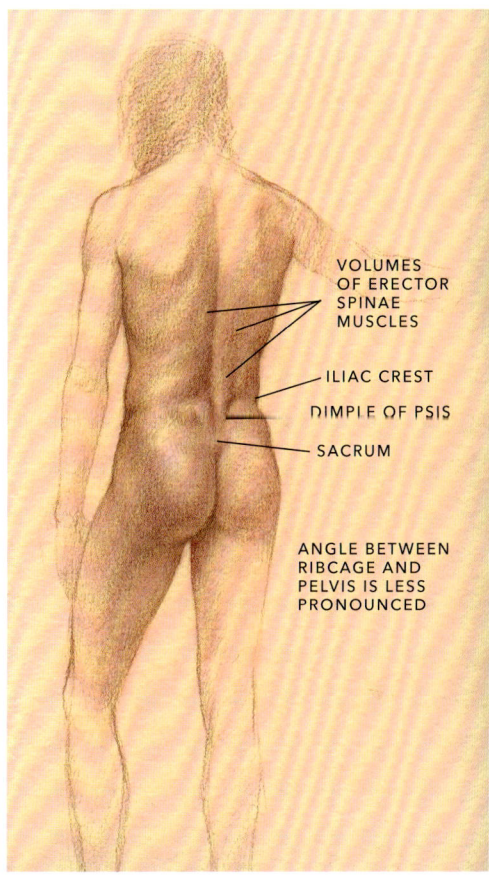

VOLUMES OF ERECTOR SPINAE MUSCLES

ILIAC CREST

DIMPLE OF PSIS

SACRUM

ANGLE BETWEEN RIBCAGE AND PELVIS IS LESS PRONOUNCED

LANDMARKS AND ANATOMY OF THE ARM

A very
challenging
subject

BELOW: Correspondence between superficial muscles and external forms, medial view of the arm with hand facing up

The great mobility of the arms makes them a very challenging subject for the artist. The images that follow analyze the arms in depth in various ways: skeleton, landmarks, muscles, stereometry, external forms, and movements.

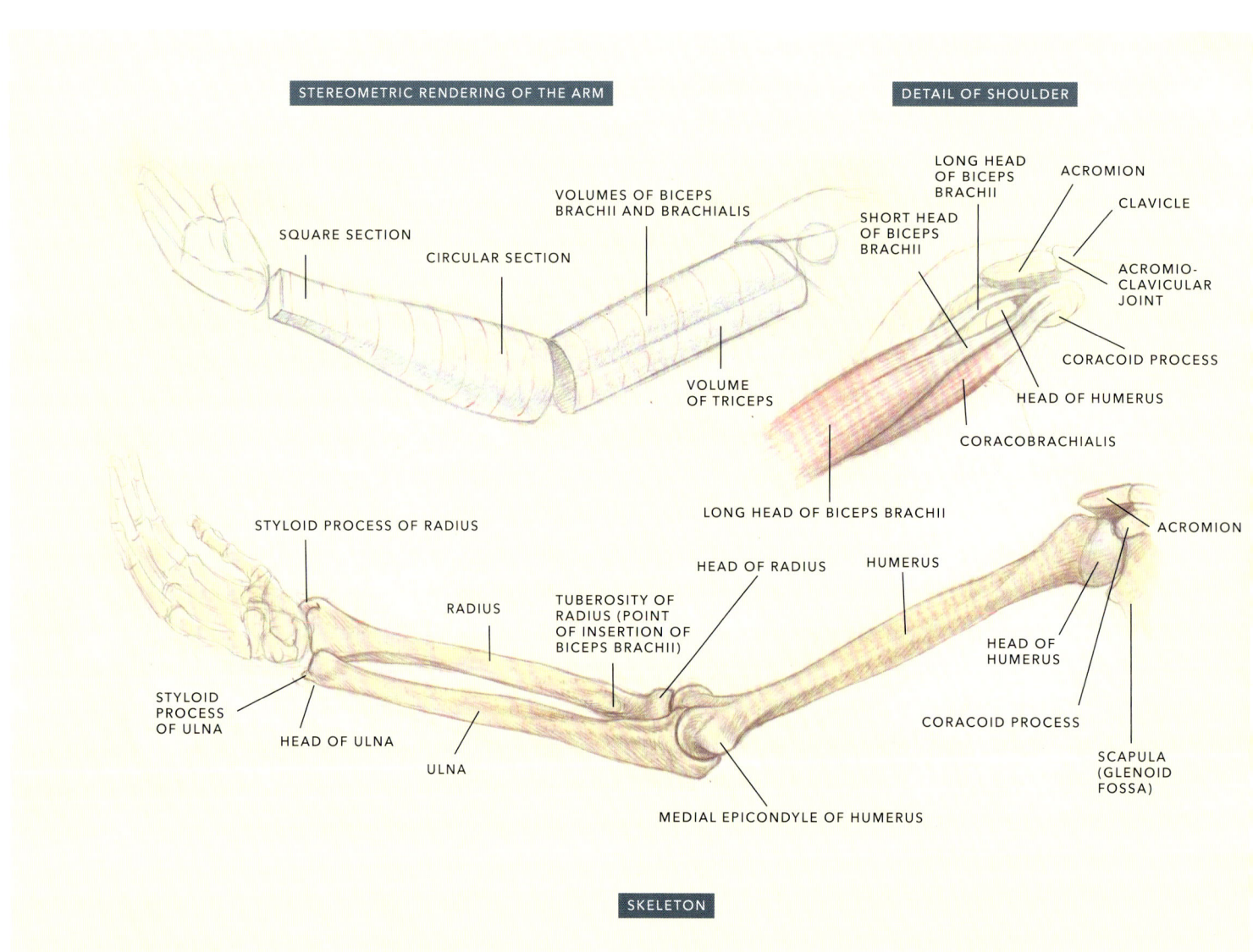

STEREOMETRIC RENDERING OF THE ARM

DETAIL OF SHOULDER

SQUARE SECTION

CIRCULAR SECTION

VOLUMES OF BICEPS BRACHII AND BRACHIALIS

VOLUME OF TRICEPS

LONG HEAD OF BICEPS BRACHII

SHORT HEAD OF BICEPS BRACHII

ACROMION

CLAVICLE

ACROMIO-CLAVICULAR JOINT

CORACOID PROCESS

HEAD OF HUMERUS

CORACOBRACHIALIS

LONG HEAD OF BICEPS BRACHII

STYLOID PROCESS OF RADIUS

RADIUS

HEAD OF RADIUS

TUBEROSITY OF RADIUS (POINT OF INSERTION OF BICEPS BRACHII)

HUMERUS

ACROMION

STYLOID PROCESS OF ULNA

HEAD OF ULNA

ULNA

HEAD OF HUMERUS

CORACOID PROCESS

SCAPULA (GLENOID FOSSA)

MEDIAL EPICONDYLE OF HUMERUS

SKELETON

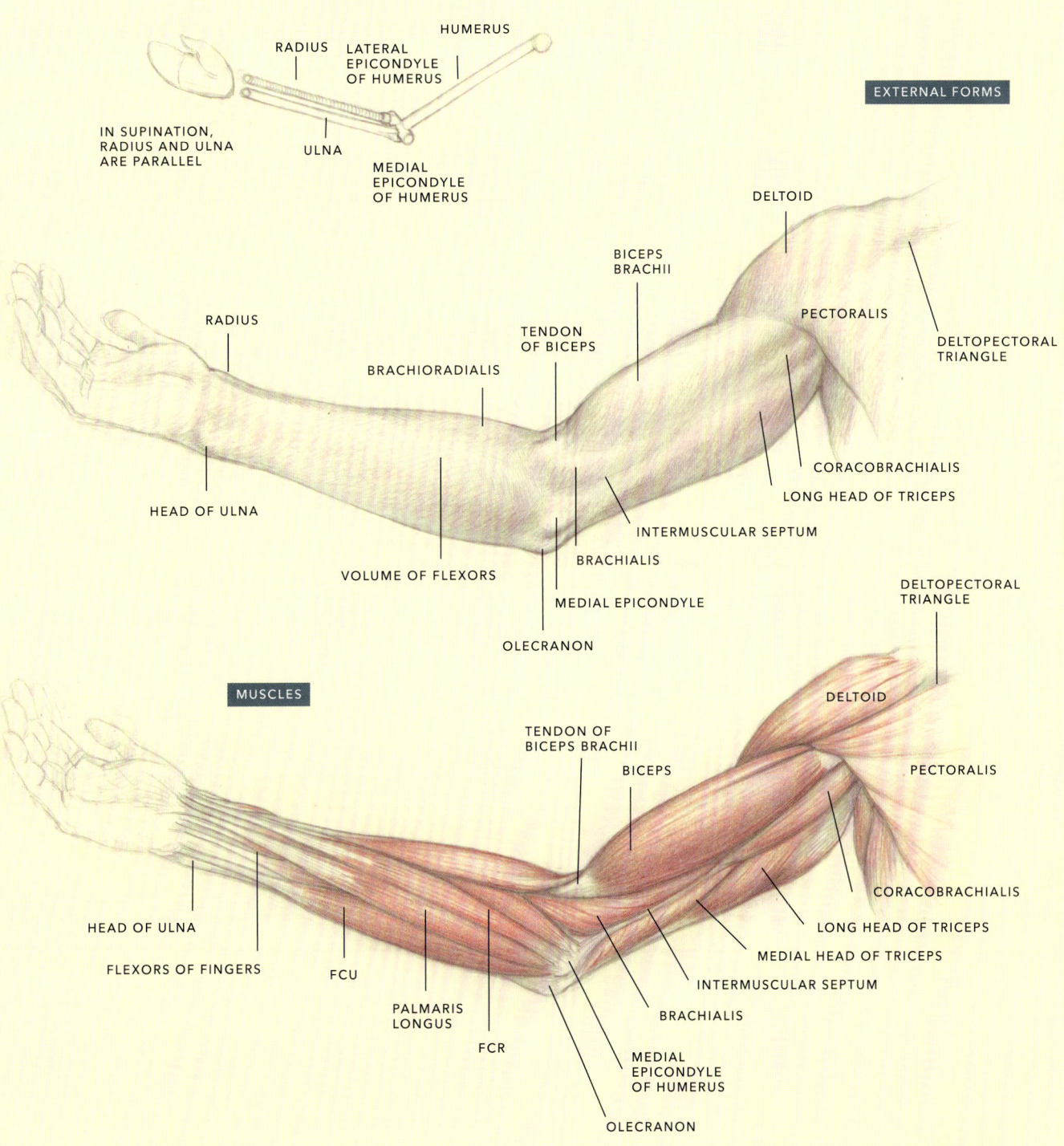

HUMERUS

RADIUS   LATERAL
EPICONDYLE
OF HUMERUS

IN SUPINATION,
RADIUS AND ULNA
ARE PARALLEL

ULNA

MEDIAL
EPICONDYLE
OF HUMERUS

DELTOID

BICEPS
BRACHII

PECTORALIS

RADIUS

BRACHIORADIALIS

TENDON
OF BICEPS

DELTOPECTORAL
TRIANGLE

HEAD OF ULNA

CORACOBRACHIALIS

LONG HEAD OF TRICEPS

INTERMUSCULAR SEPTUM

VOLUME OF FLEXORS

BRACHIALIS

MEDIAL EPICONDYLE

OLECRANON

DELTOPECTORAL
TRIANGLE

DELTOID

TENDON OF
BICEPS BRACHII

BICEPS

PECTORALIS

HEAD OF ULNA

FLEXORS OF FINGERS

FCU

PALMARIS
LONGUS

FCR

MEDIAL
EPICONDYLE
OF HUMERUS

OLECRANON

CORACOBRACHIALIS

LONG HEAD OF TRICEPS

MEDIAL HEAD OF TRICEPS

INTERMUSCULAR SEPTUM

BRACHIALIS

Correspondence between muscular and
external forms, medial view of the arm
with hand facing up

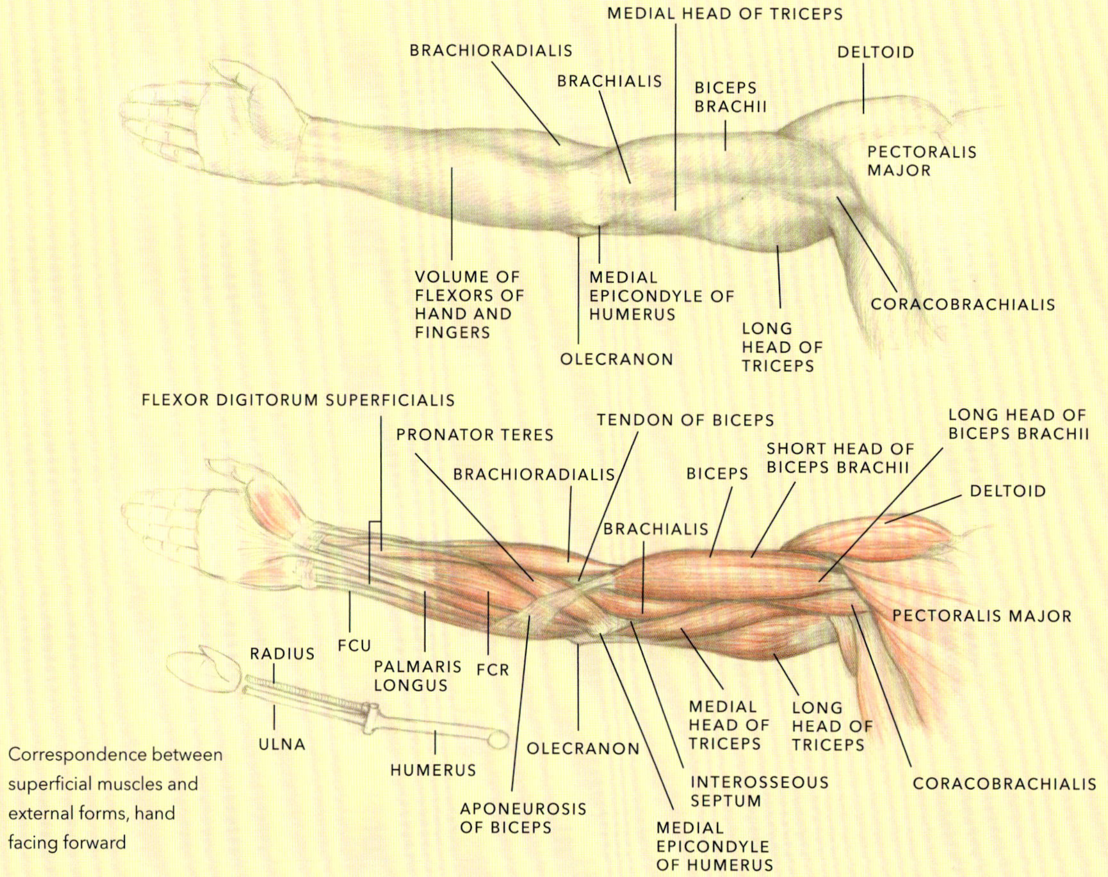

MEDIAL HEAD OF TRICEPS

BRACHIORADIALIS

BRACHIALIS

BICEPS BRACHII

DELTOID

PECTORALIS MAJOR

VOLUME OF FLEXORS OF HAND AND FINGERS

MEDIAL EPICONDYLE OF HUMERUS

OLECRANON

LONG HEAD OF TRICEPS

CORACOBRACHIALIS

FLEXOR DIGITORUM SUPERFICIALIS

PRONATOR TERES

TENDON OF BICEPS

LONG HEAD OF BICEPS BRACHII

BRACHIORADIALIS

BICEPS

SHORT HEAD OF BICEPS BRACHII

DELTOID

BRACHIALIS

RADIUS

FCU

PALMARIS LONGUS

FCR

PECTORALIS MAJOR

ULNA

HUMERUS

OLECRANON

MEDIAL HEAD OF TRICEPS

LONG HEAD OF TRICEPS

APONEUROSIS OF BICEPS

INTEROSSEOUS SEPTUM

MEDIAL EPICONDYLE OF HUMERUS

CORACOBRACHIALIS

Correspondence between superficial muscles and external forms, hand facing forward

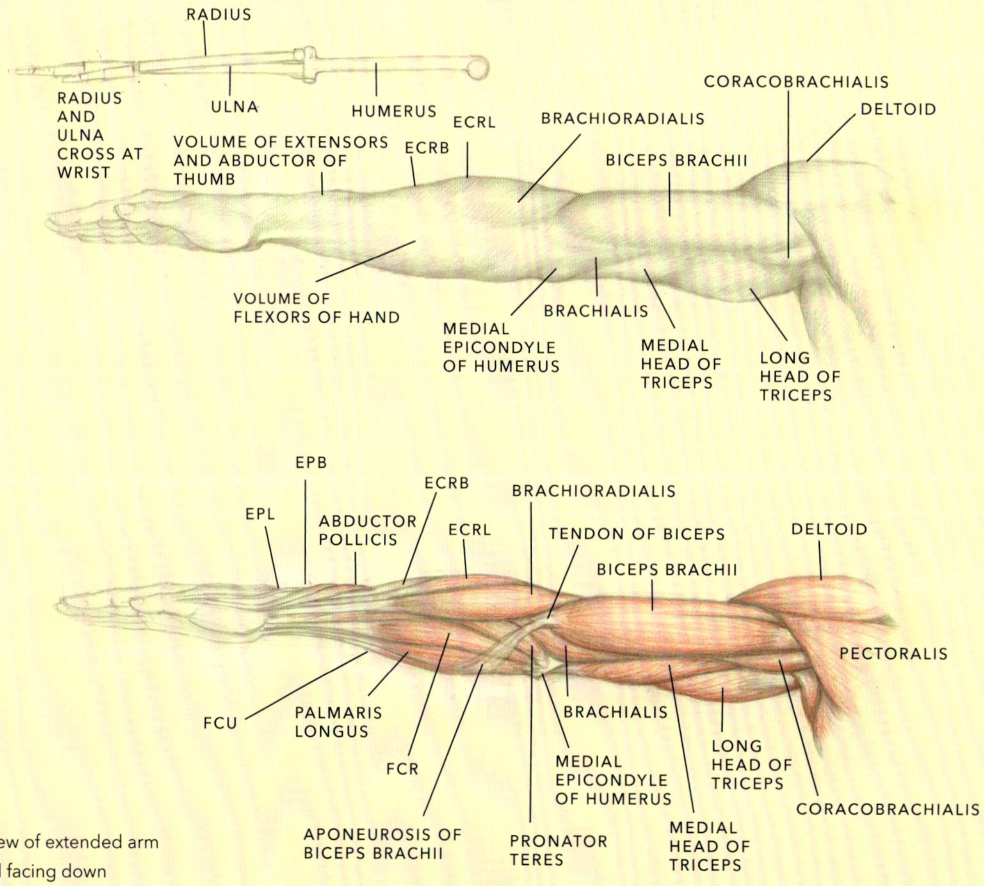

RADIUS

RADIUS AND ULNA CROSS AT WRIST

ULNA

HUMERUS

ECRL

VOLUME OF EXTENSORS AND ABDUCTOR OF THUMB

ECRB

BRACHIORADIALIS

CORACOBRACHIALIS

DELTOID

BICEPS BRACHII

VOLUME OF FLEXORS OF HAND

MEDIAL EPICONDYLE OF HUMERUS

BRACHIALIS

MEDIAL HEAD OF TRICEPS

LONG HEAD OF TRICEPS

EPB

ECRB

BRACHIORADIALIS

EPL

ABDUCTOR POLLICIS

ECRL

TENDON OF BICEPS

DELTOID

BICEPS BRACHII

FCU

PALMARIS LONGUS

FCR

BRACHIALIS

MEDIAL EPICONDYLE OF HUMERUS

LONG HEAD OF TRICEPS

PECTORALIS

CORACOBRACHIALIS

APONEUROSIS OF BICEPS BRACHII

PRONATOR TERES

MEDIAL HEAD OF TRICEPS

Medial view of extended arm with hand facing down

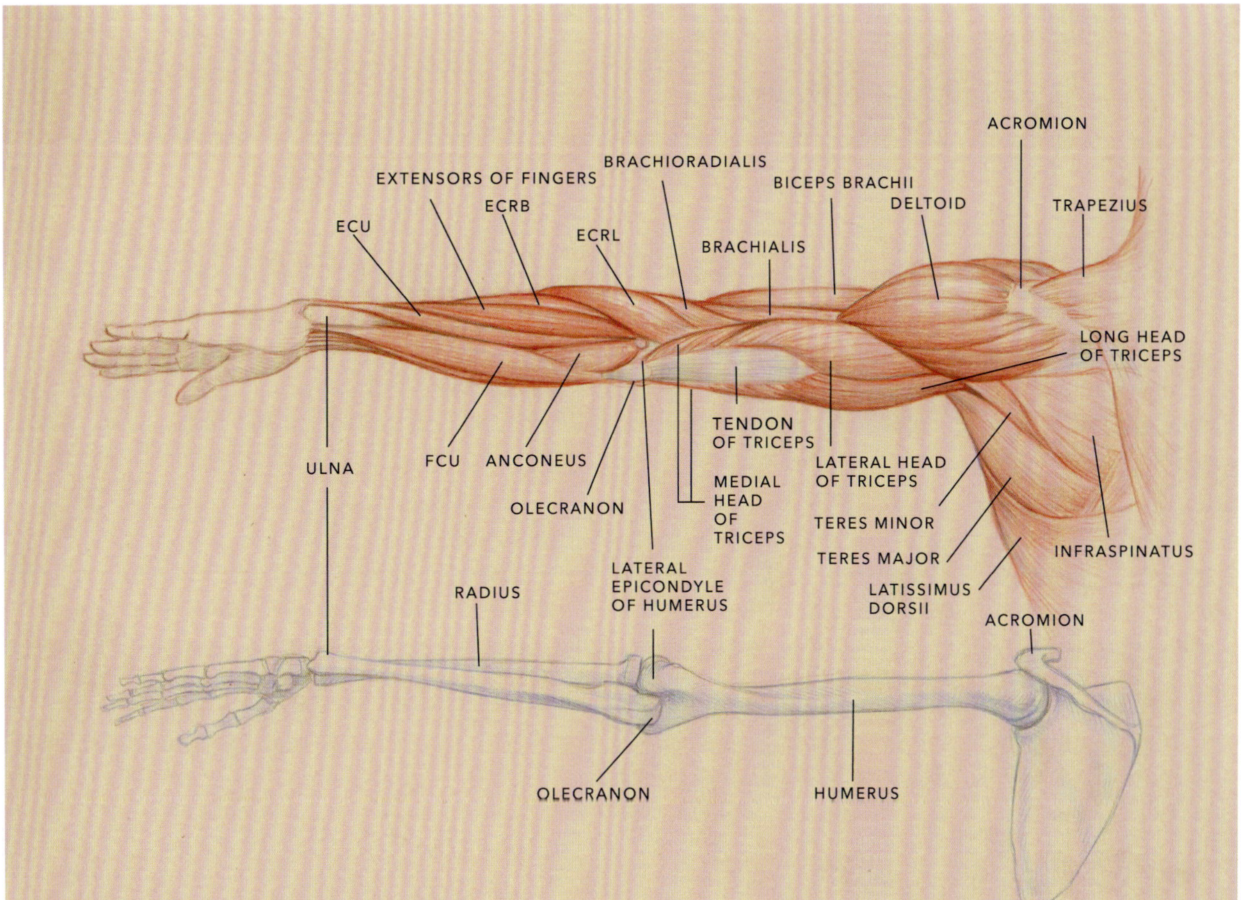

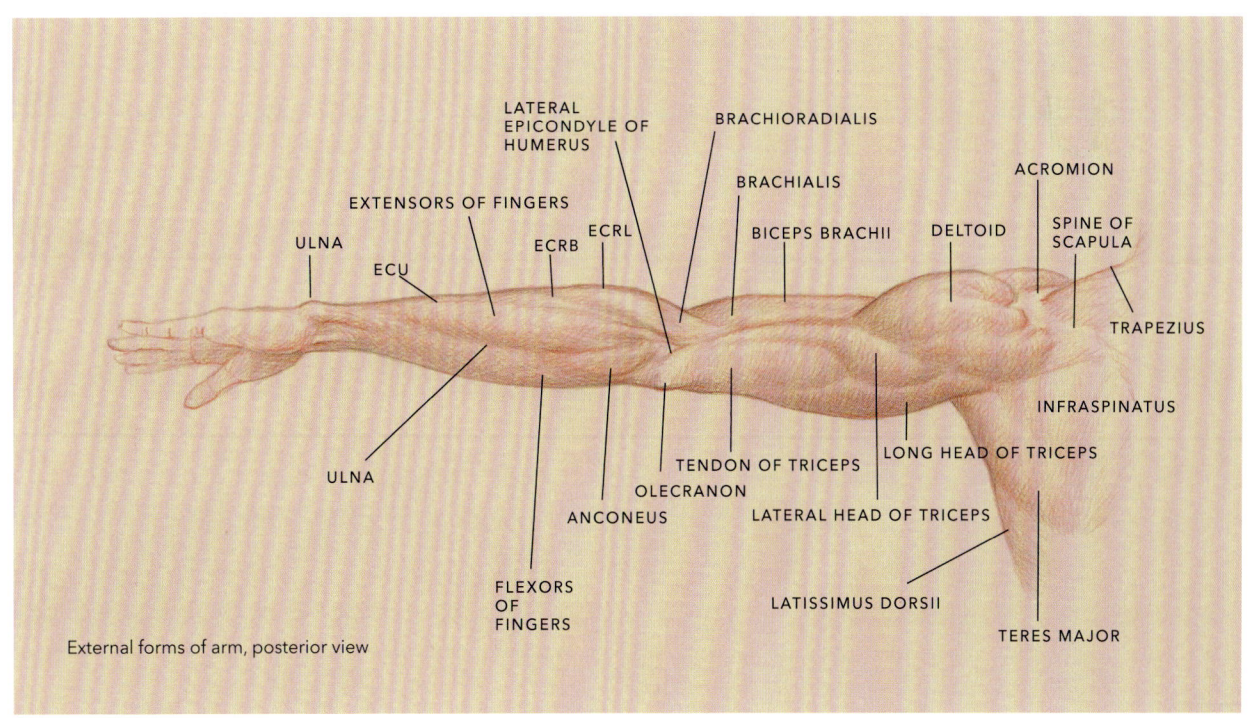

ACROMION

EXTENSORS OF FINGERS

BRACHIORADIALIS

ECRB

BICEPS BRACHII

ECU

DELTOID

TRAPEZIUS

ECRL

BRACHIALIS

LONG HEAD
OF TRICEPS

TENDON
OF TRICEPS

ULNA

LATERAL HEAD
OF TRICEPS

FCU   ANCONEUS

MEDIAL
HEAD
OF
TRICEPS

TERES MINOR

OLECRANON

TERES MAJOR

INFRASPINATUS

LATERAL
EPICONDYLE
OF HUMERUS

LATISSIMUS
DORSII

RADIUS

ACROMION

OLECRANON

HUMERUS

Skeleton and muscles of arm, posterior view

LATERAL
EPICONDYLE OF
HUMERUS

BRACHIORADIALIS

EXTENSORS OF FINGERS

BRACHIALIS

ACROMION

ECRB

ECRL

BICEPS BRACHII

DELTOID

SPINE OF
SCAPULA

ULNA

ECU

TRAPEZIUS

INFRASPINATUS

ULNA

TENDON OF TRICEPS

LONG HEAD OF TRICEPS

ANCONEUS

OLECRANON

LATERAL HEAD OF TRICEPS

FLEXORS
OF
FINGERS

LATISSIMUS DORSII

TERES MAJOR

External forms of arm, posterior view

ACROMION VISIBLE AS FLAT TOP PORTION OF SHOULDER

END OF CLAVICLE AT ACROMIOCLAVICULAR JOINT

TRAPEZIUS

CORACOID PROCESS UNDER DELTOID

CLAVICLE

HEAD OF HUMERUS UNDER DELTOID

DELTOID

RADIATING PATTERN OF PECTORALIS

CORACOBRACHIALIS

MEDIAL HEAD OF TRICEPS

LONG HEAD OF BICEPS ORIGINATES ABOVE GLENOID FOSSA OF SCAPULA

SHORT HEAD OF BICEPS

LATERAL HEAD OF TRICEPS

BICEPS BRACHII

BRACHIALIS

TENDON OF BICEPS AT INSERTION

MEDIAL EPICONDYLE OF HUMERUS

BRACHIO-RADIALIS

PRONATOR TERES

FCR

PALMARIS LONGUS

FCU

RADIUS

ULNA

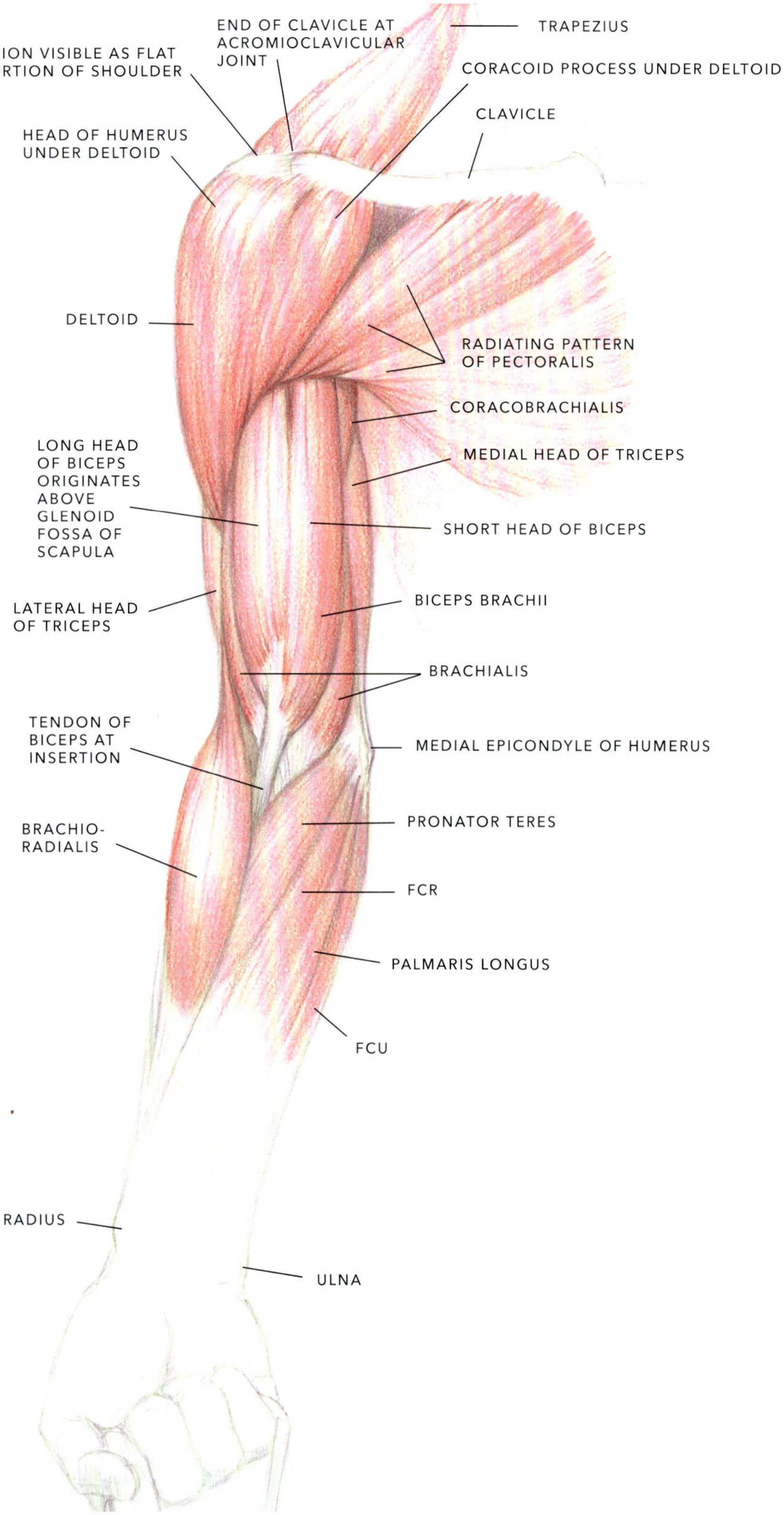

The images here and opposite show in detail the connections between the arm's skeletal structure and muscular structure, resulting in specific orientations of the external forms. Note, for example, that the extremities of the biceps are directed toward specific points: the upper extremities toward the head of the humerus and the coracoid process and the lower extremity toward the tuberosity of the radius, resulting in a slightly diagonal orientation of the axis of the biceps in relation to the axis of the humerus. As a general rule we can say that the axes of muscular volumes are *not* parallel to the axes of the bones they are connected to.

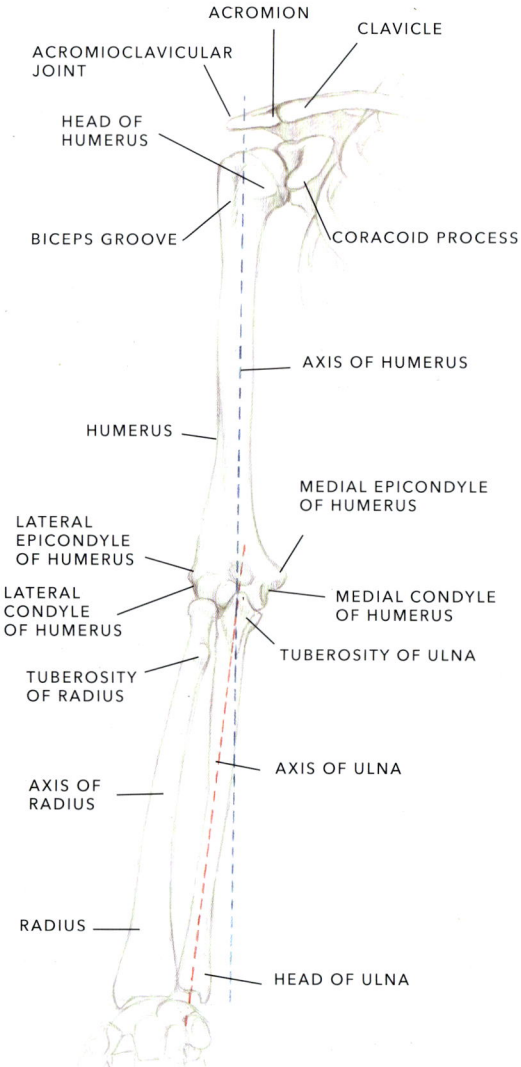

ACROMION

CLAVICLE

ACROMIOCLAVICULAR JOINT

HEAD OF HUMERUS

CORACOID PROCESS

BICEPS GROOVE

AXIS OF HUMERUS

HUMERUS

MEDIAL EPICONDYLE OF HUMERUS

LATERAL EPICONDYLE OF HUMERUS

LATERAL CONDYLE OF HUMERUS

MEDIAL CONDYLE OF HUMERUS

TUBEROSITY OF ULNA

TUBEROSITY OF RADIUS

AXIS OF RADIUS

AXIS OF ULNA

RADIUS

HEAD OF ULNA

External volumes, muscles, and landmarks of the arm, anterior view

On the larger drawing, note that the three distinctive "bumps" at the top of the deltoid are produced by the head of the humerus, the coracoid process, and the acromioclavicular joint. The smaller inset drawing shows the origin and insertion of the biceps brachii. The biceps has two origins, one at the top of the glenoid fossa and one at the coracoid process. The insertion is at the tuberosity of the radius. The main volume of the biceps brachii is oriented slightly diagonally in relation to the main axis of the radius.

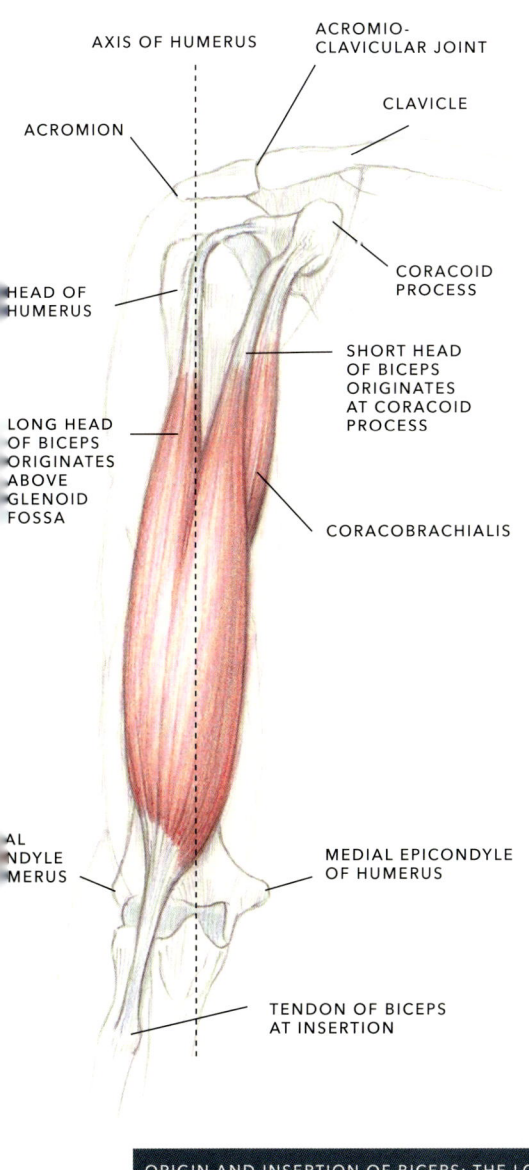

AXIS OF HUMERUS

ACROMIO-CLAVICULAR JOINT

CLAVICLE

ACROMION

HEAD OF HUMERUS

CORACOID PROCESS

SHORT HEAD OF BICEPS ORIGINATES AT CORACOID PROCESS

LONG HEAD OF BICEPS ORIGINATES ABOVE GLENOID FOSSA

CORACOBRACHIALIS

AL NDYLE MERUS

MEDIAL EPICONDYLE OF HUMERUS

TENDON OF BICEPS AT INSERTION

ORIGIN AND INSERTION OF BICEPS: THE LONG HEAD OF THE BICEPS ORIGINATES ABOVE THE GLENOID FOSSA AND THE SHORT HEAD OF THE BICEPS ORIGINATES AT THE CORACOID PROCESS. THE INSERTION IS AT THE TUBEROSITY OF THE RADIUS.

CLAVICLE

TRAPEZIUS

ACROMIOCLAVICULAR JOINT

ACROMION, VISIBLE AS FLAT TOP PORTION OF THE SHOULDER

DELTOPECTORAL TRIANGLE (SMALL DEPRESSION BELOW CLAVICLE AND BETWEEN DELTOID AND PECTORALIS)

HEAD OF HUMERUS UNDER DELTOID

CORACOID PROCESS UNDER DELTOID

DELTOID

PECTORALIS

A LINE DIVIDING TWO HEADS OF BICEPS BRACHII MIGHT APPEAR DURING FLEXION OF MUSCLE

SHORT HEAD OF BICEPS IS DIRECTED TOWARD CORACOID PROCESS

LONG HEAD OF BICEPS IS DIRECTED TOWARD HEAD OF HUMERUS

BRACHIALIS

BRACHIO-RADIALIS

MEDIAL EPICONDYLE OF HUMERUS

LATERAL EPICONDYLE OF HUMERUS NOT VISIBLE FROM FRONT BECAUSE HIDDEN BEHIND VOLUME OF BRACHIORADIALIS

TENDON OF INSERTION OF BICEPS IS DIRECTED TOWARD TUBEROSITY OF RADIUS

RADIUS (THUMB SIDE)

ULNA (PINKY SIDE)

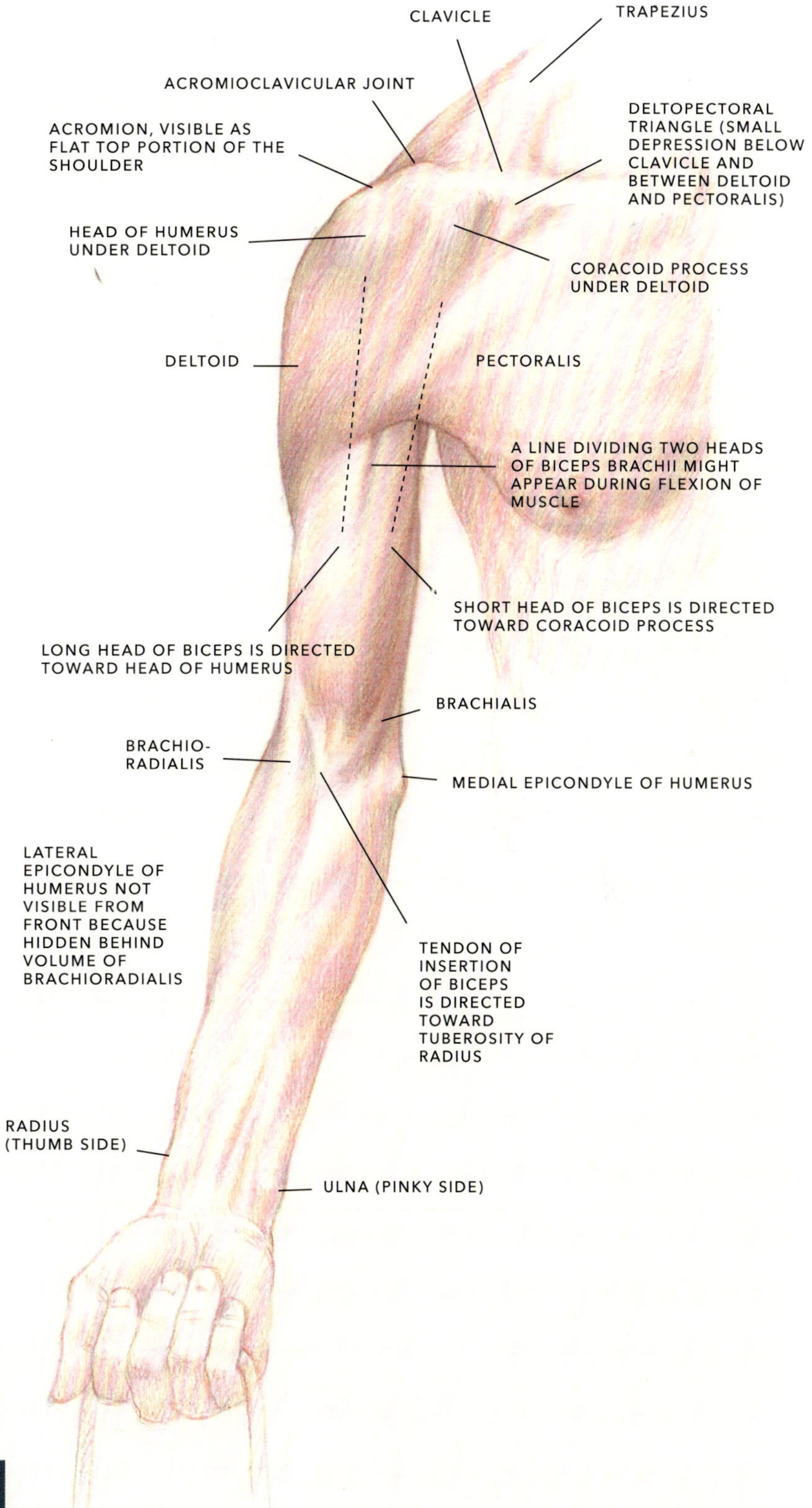

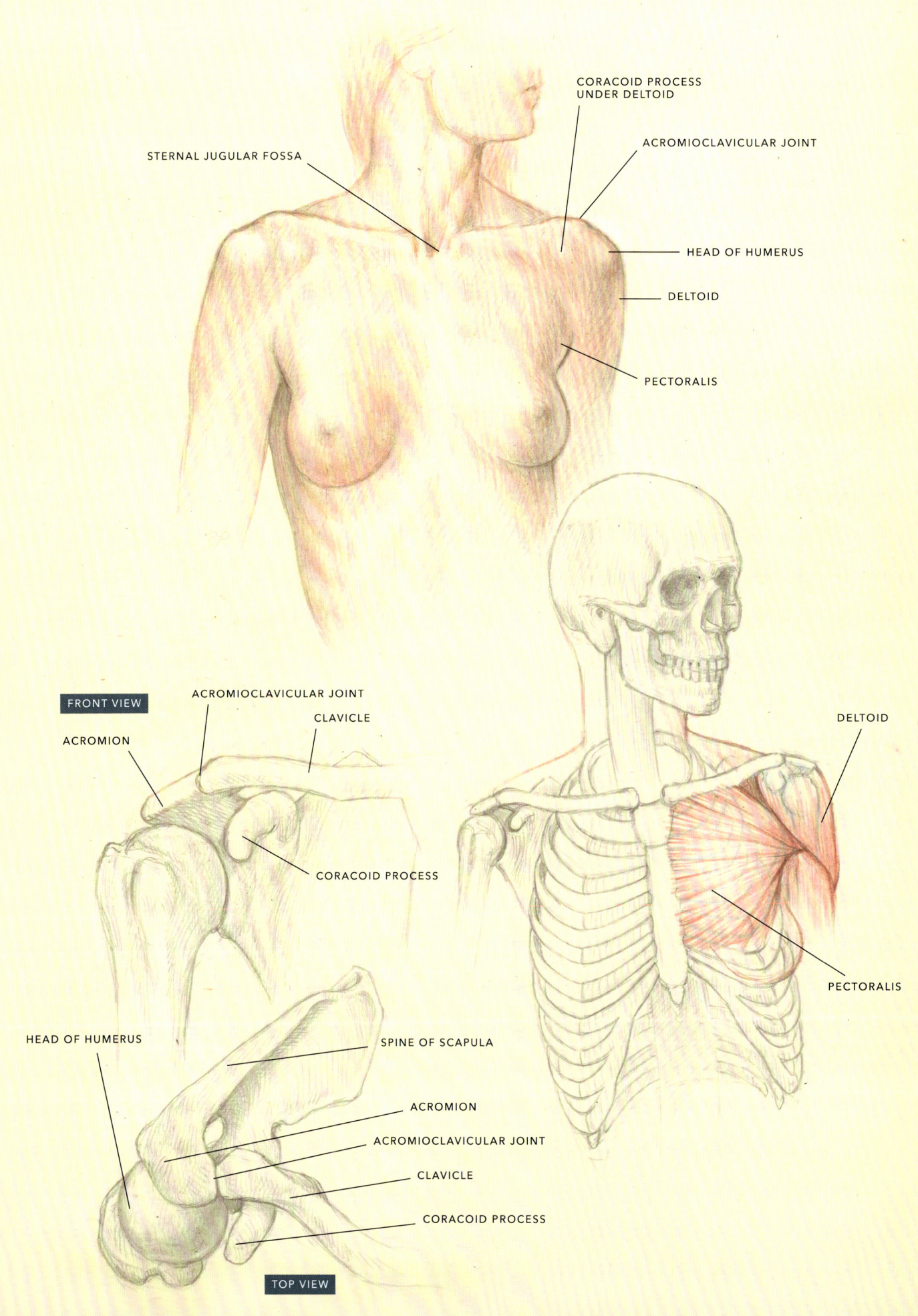

CORACOID PROCESS
UNDER DELTOID

ACROMIOCLAVICULAR JOINT

STERNAL JUGULAR FOSSA

HEAD OF HUMERUS

DELTOID

PECTORALIS

FRONT VIEW

ACROMIOCLAVICULAR JOINT

CLAVICLE

ACROMION

DELTOID

CORACOID PROCESS

PECTORALIS

HEAD OF HUMERUS

SPINE OF SCAPULA

ACROMION

ACROMIOCLAVICULAR JOINT

CLAVICLE

CORACOID PROCESS

TOP VIEW

LANDMARKS AND ANATOMY OF THE SHOULDER AND SCAPULA

The images below briefly introduce the landmarks of the shoulder and scapula. When hiring a model for figure-study practice, consider that the skeletal landmarks are more clearly visible on a lean model whose muscles are not too developed.

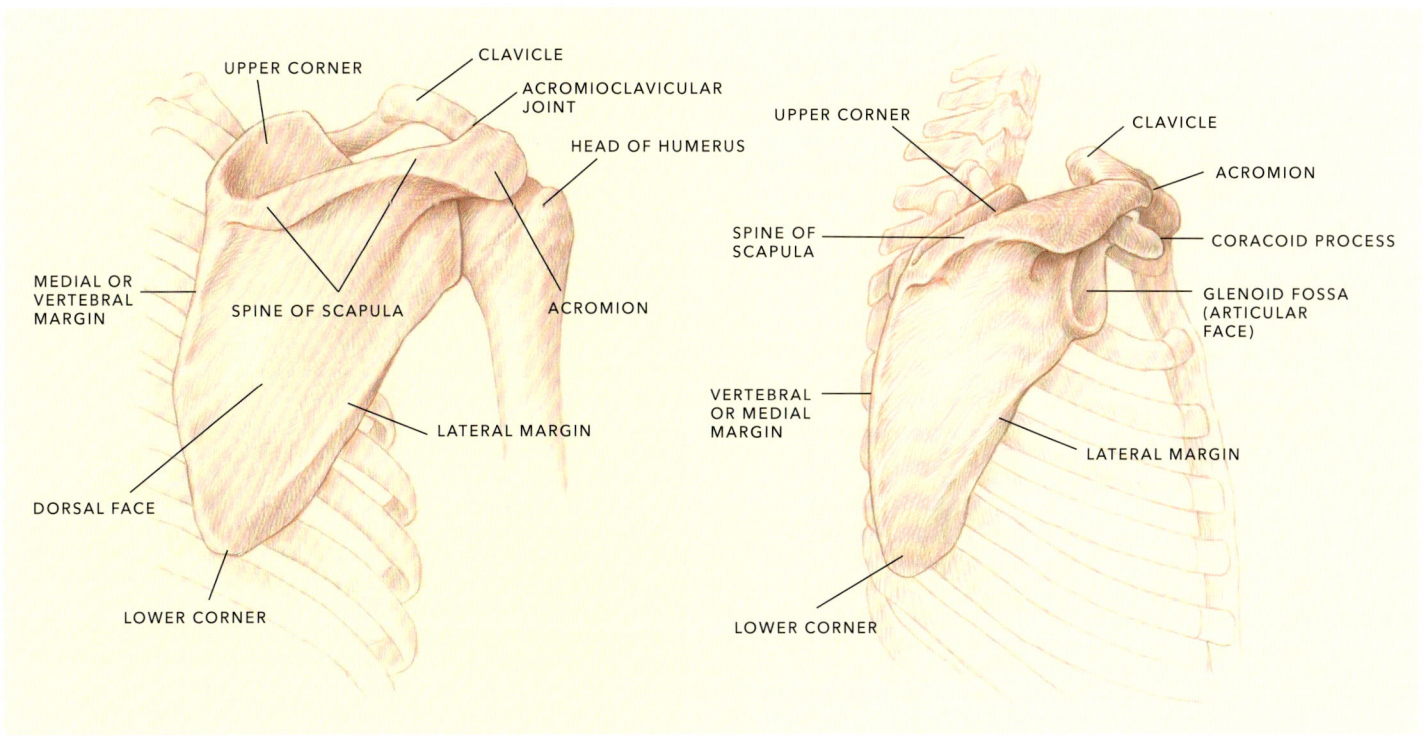

OPPOSITE: Correspondence between skeletal landmarks of the shoulder and external forms

The coracoid process and the head of the humerus create two typical rounded forms on the surface of the deltoid.

ABOVE LEFT: Scapula, posterior view

ABOVE RIGHT: Scapula, lateral view

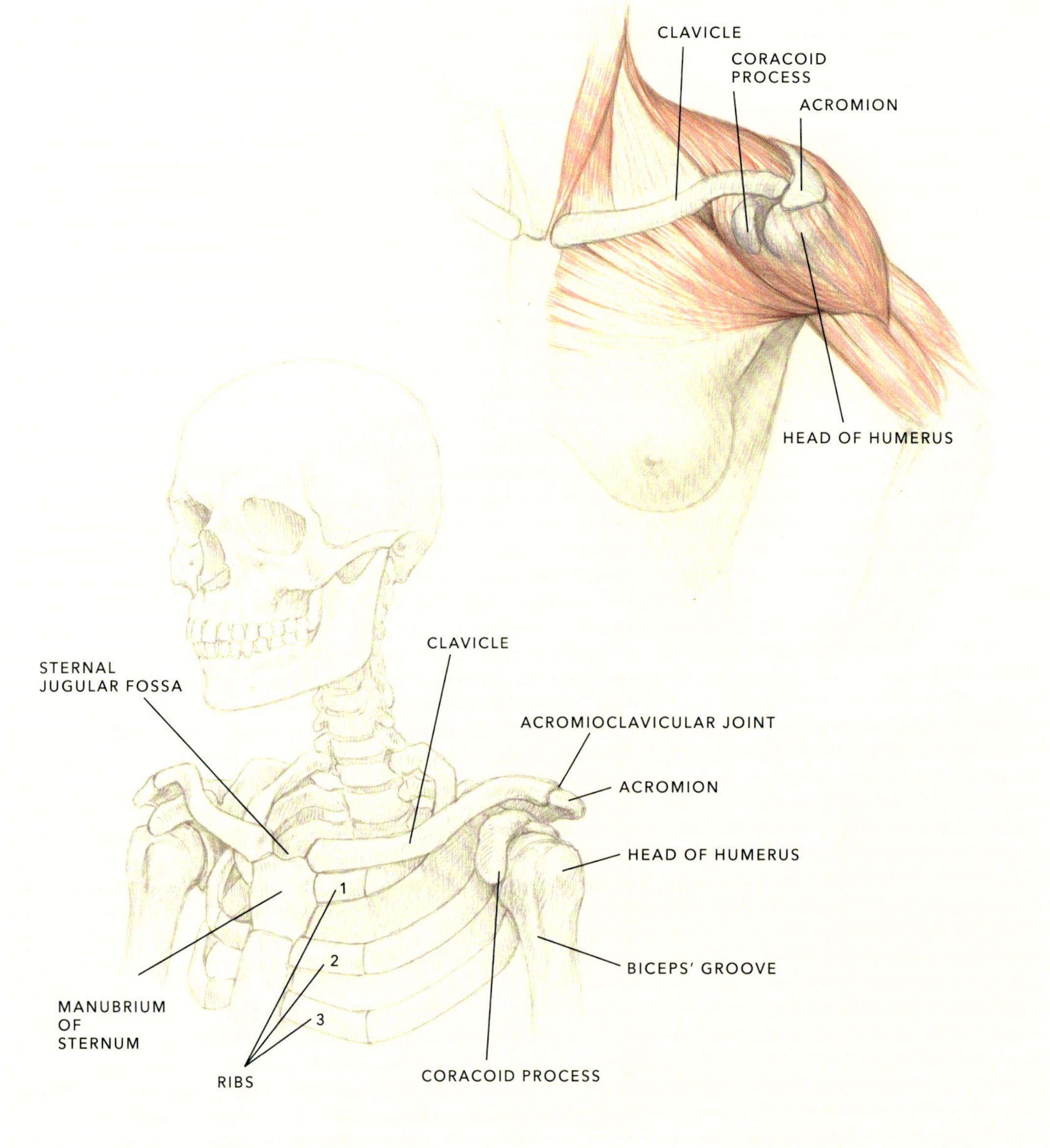

CLAVICLE

CORACOID
PROCESS

ACROMION

HEAD OF HUMERUS

STERNAL
JUGULAR FOSSA

CLAVICLE

ACROMIOCLAVICULAR JOINT

ACROMION

HEAD OF HUMERUS

BICEPS' GROOVE

MANUBRIUM
OF
STERNUM

1

2

3

RIBS

CORACOID PROCESS

ABOVE: Shoulder joint, overview, and external forms of shoulder (detail)

This top view of the shoulder shows how the underlying volumes of the head of the humerus and coracoid process affect the form of the deltoid muscle.

RIGHT: Scapula, anterior view

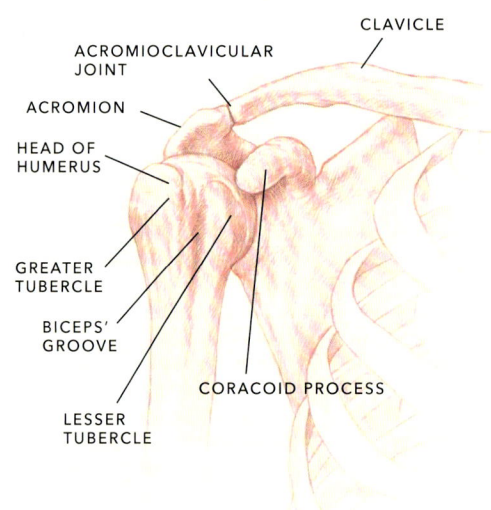

CLAVICLE

ACROMIOCLAVICULAR
JOINT

ACROMION

HEAD OF
HUMERUS

GREATER
TUBERCLE

BICEPS'
GROOVE

CORACOID PROCESS

LESSER
TUBERCLE

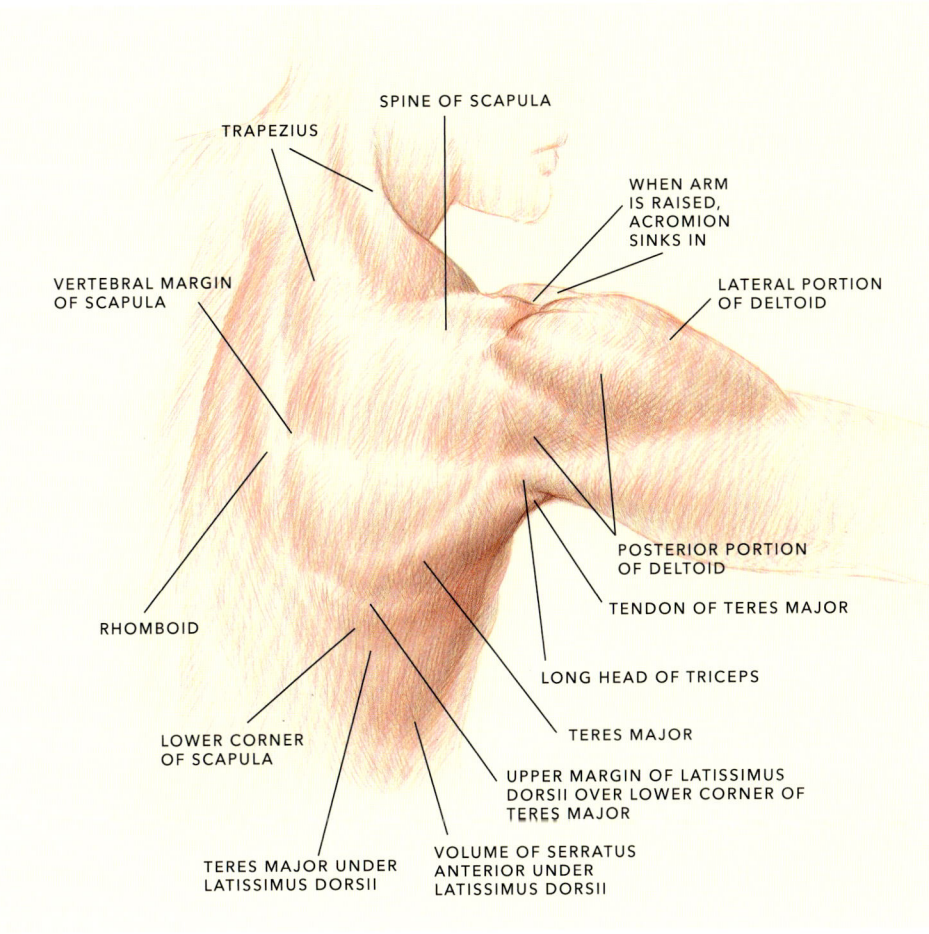

TRAPEZIUS

SPINE OF SCAPULA

WHEN ARM IS RAISED, ACROMION SINKS IN

LATERAL PORTION OF DELTOID

VERTEBRAL MARGIN OF SCAPULA

RHOMBOID

POSTERIOR PORTION OF DELTOID

TENDON OF TERES MAJOR

LONG HEAD OF TRICEPS

TERES MAJOR

LOWER CORNER OF SCAPULA

UPPER MARGIN OF LATISSIMUS DORSII OVER LOWER CORNER OF TERES MAJOR

TERES MAJOR UNDER LATISSIMUS DORSII

VOLUME OF SERRATUS ANTERIOR UNDER LATISSIMUS DORSII

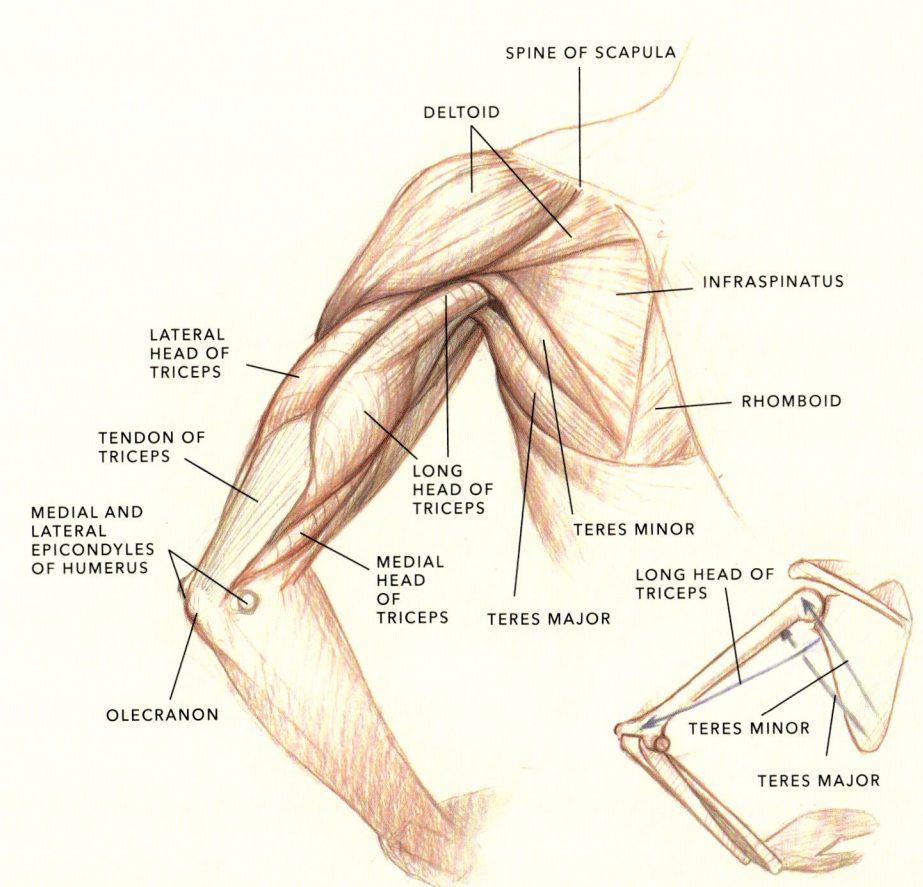

SPINE OF SCAPULA

DELTOID

INFRASPINATUS

LATERAL HEAD OF TRICEPS

RHOMBOID

TENDON OF TRICEPS

LONG HEAD OF TRICEPS

MEDIAL AND LATERAL EPICONDYLES OF HUMERUS

TERES MINOR

MEDIAL HEAD OF TRICEPS

LONG HEAD OF TRICEPS

TERES MAJOR

OLECRANON

TERES MINOR

TERES MAJOR

ABOVE: Shoulder with arm raised, posterior view

LEFT: Elbow and shoulder, posterior view

This posterior view of the shoulder shows how a pose can be studied in detail by creating a diagram of the muscles. Note how the long head of the triceps is wedged between the teres major and teres minor and how the three heads of the triceps merge on the tendon of the triceps, which then connects with the olecranon. Note also how the deltoid "wraps" over the triceps muscle.

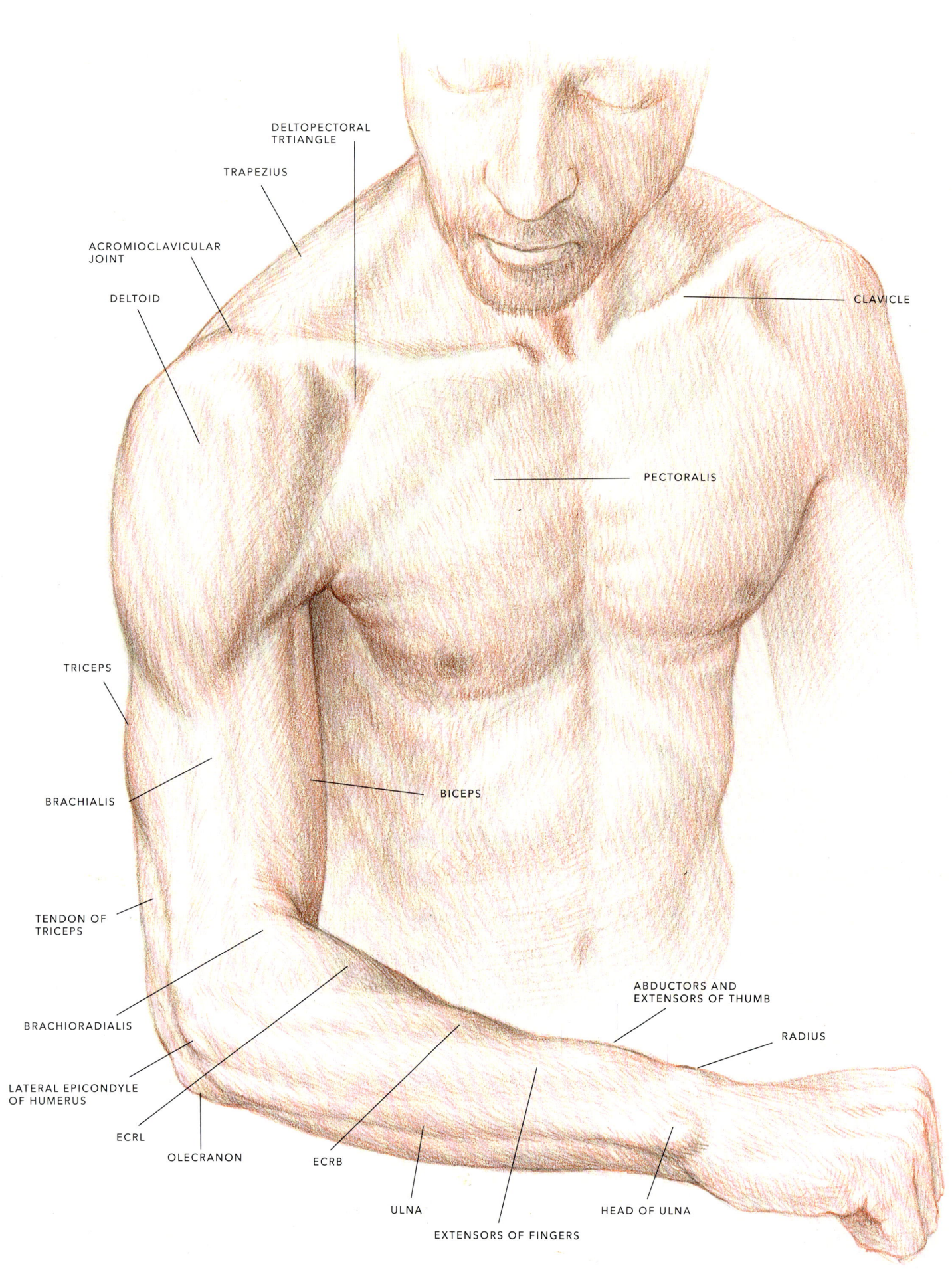

DELTOPECTORAL
TRTIANGLE

TRAPEZIUS

ACROMIOCLAVICULAR
JOINT

DELTOID

CLAVICLE

PECTORALIS

TRICEPS

BRACHIALIS

BICEPS

TENDON OF
TRICEPS

ABDUCTORS AND
EXTENSORS OF THUMB

RADIUS

BRACHIORADIALIS

LATERAL EPICONDYLE
OF HUMERUS

ECRL

OLECRANON

ECRB

ULNA

EXTENSORS OF FINGERS

HEAD OF ULNA

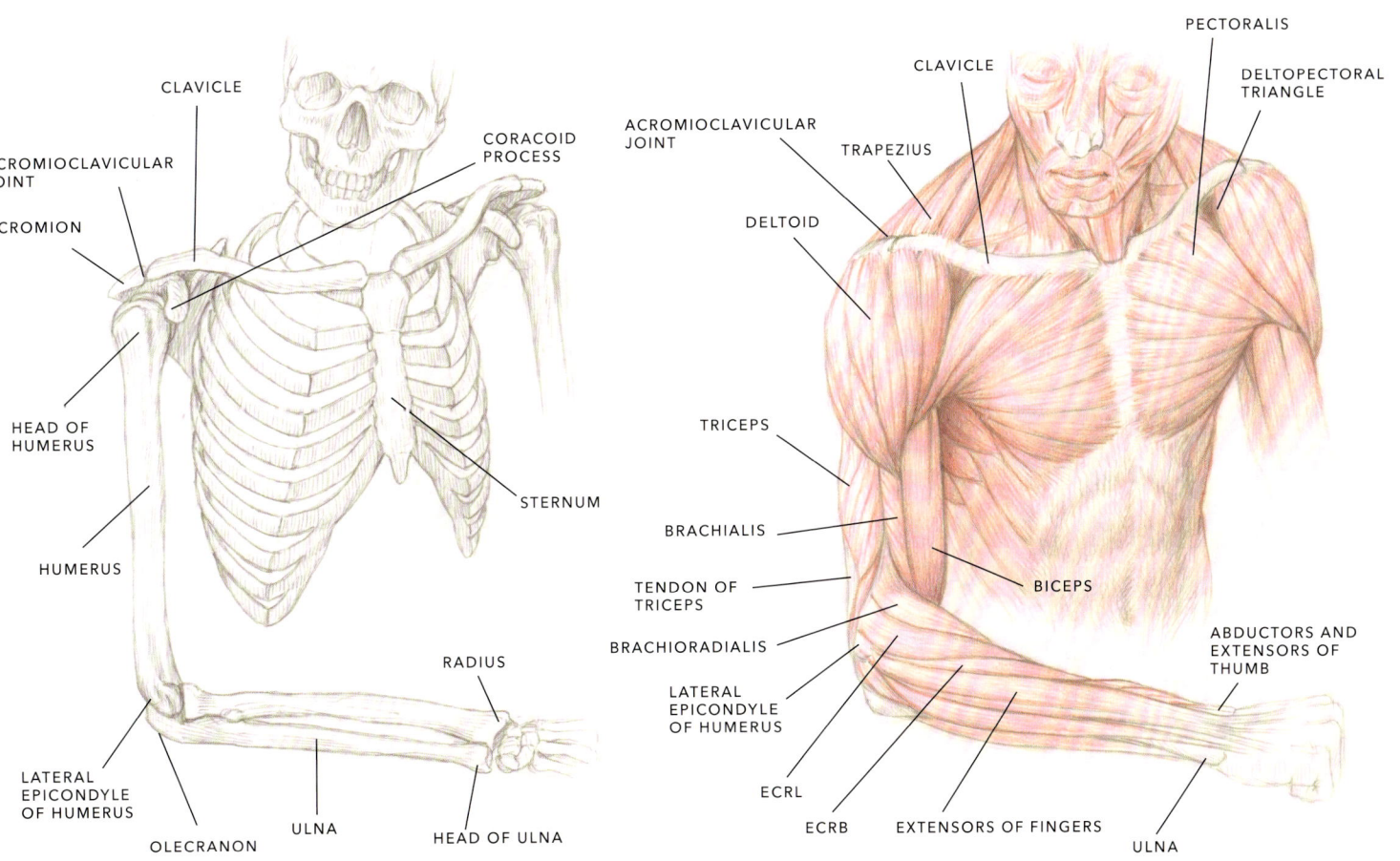

CLAVICLE

CROMIOCLAVICULAR JOINT

CROMION

HEAD OF HUMERUS

HUMERUS

LATERAL EPICONDYLE OF HUMERUS

OLECRANON

CORACOID PROCESS

STERNUM

RADIUS

ULNA

HEAD OF ULNA

ACROMIOCLAVICULAR JOINT

CLAVICLE

TRAPEZIUS

DELTOID

PECTORALIS

DELTOPECTORAL TRIANGLE

TRICEPS

BRACHIALIS

TENDON OF TRICEPS

BRACHIORADIALIS

LATERAL EPICONDYLE OF HUMERUS

ECRL

ECRB

BICEPS

ABDUCTORS AND EXTENSORS OF THUMB

EXTENSORS OF FINGERS

ULNA

OPPOSITE: Shoulder and arm, external forms

ABOVE LEFT: Skeleton and skeletal landmarks of arm and shoulder

ABOVE RIGHT: Shoulder and arm, muscle layers

The complex skeletal forms of the elbow (right) are more easily understood when reduced to essential structures; the schematic detail at left shows the various parts of the elbow joint (A) and how the humerus, radius, and ulna articulate (B).

OPPOSITE: Elbow joint and landmarks, posterior and lateral views

With the arm extended (A), the lateral and medial epicondyles of the humerus and the olecranon are aligned along a straight line. When the arm is flexed (B), the olecranon moves down; visually connecting the lateral and medial epicondyles and the olecranon produces a triangular pattern. The lateral view (C) shows the position of the joint between humerus and radius in relation to the olecranon.

THE ELBOW JOINT

There are only three landmarks in the elbow: the medial and lateral epicondyles of the humerus, which mark the end of that bone, and the olecranon, which indicates the beginning of the forearm. These landmarks give us a lot of clues about the structural and anatomical characteristics of the arm at rest and in movement. The articular plane between the upper arm and forearm is just below the level of the epicondyles; knowing this permits us to have a very good idea of where the humerus ends and its overall length.

The volume of the flexors of the hand starts on the anterior side of the medial epicondyle of the humerus, and the volume of the extensors of the hand starts on the posterior side of the lateral epicondyle of the humerus. Knowing this, we can position the main muscular groups on the forearm more correctly and can better understand the change of the forms of the forearm when transitioning, for example, from supination to pronation.

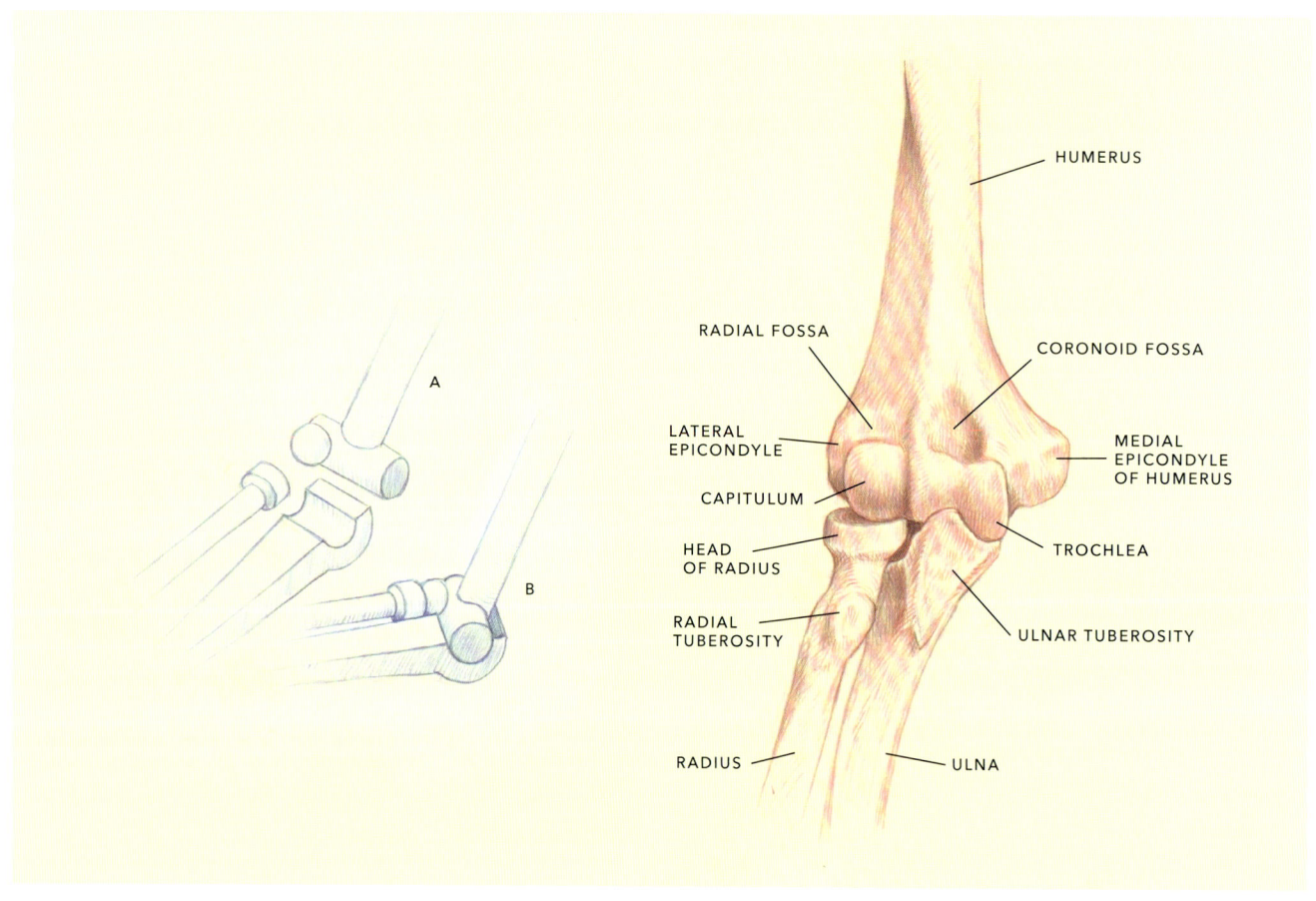

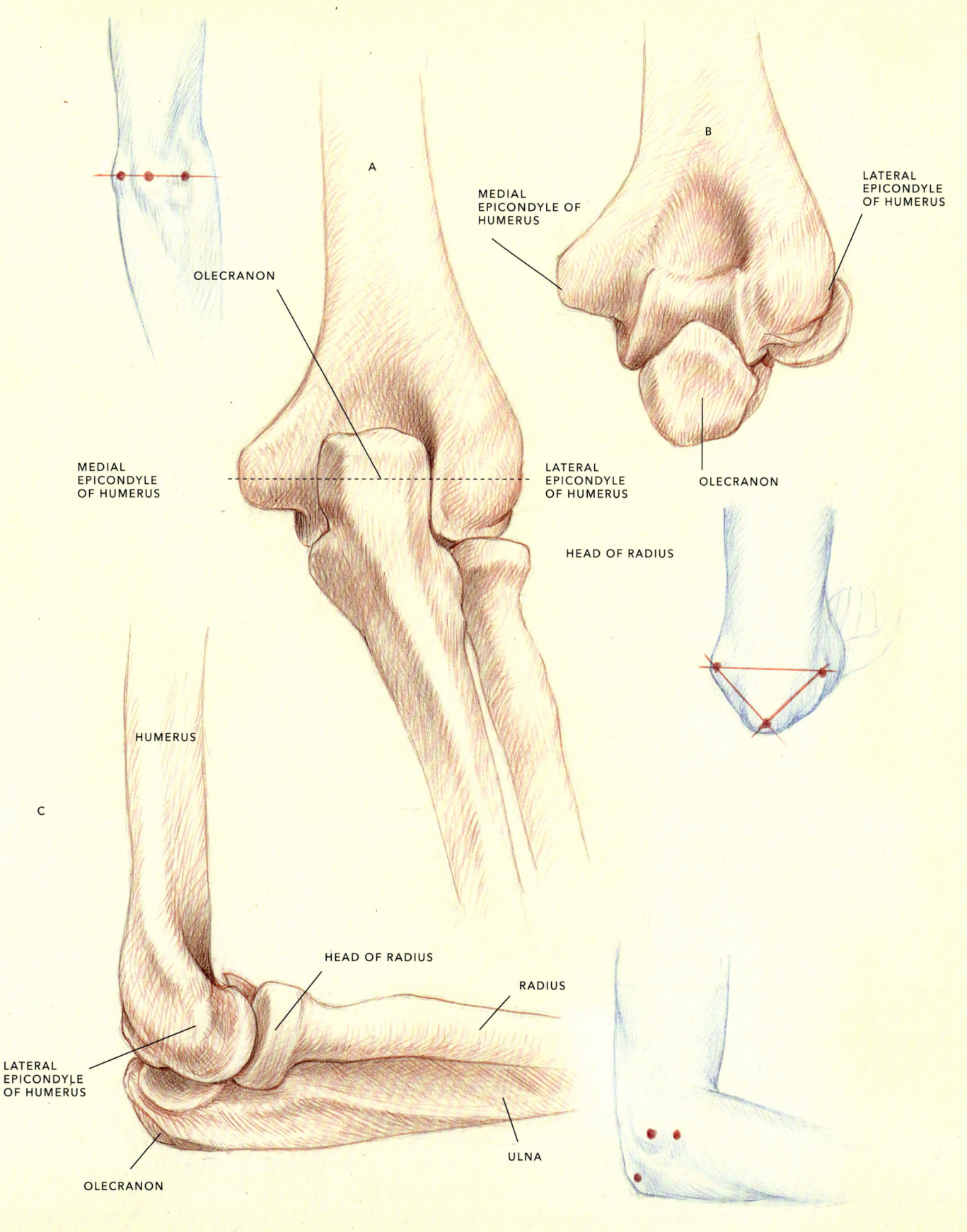

A

OLECRANON

MEDIAL
EPICONDYLE OF
HUMERUS

LATERAL
EPICONDYLE
OF HUMERUS

MEDIAL
EPICONDYLE
OF HUMERUS

LATERAL
EPICONDYLE
OF HUMERUS

HEAD OF RADIUS

B

OLECRANON

HUMERUS

C

HEAD OF RADIUS

RADIUS

LATERAL
EPICONDYLE
OF HUMERUS

ULNA

OLECRANON

LANDMARKS AND ANATOMY OF THE HIPS

The schematic renderings in this section visualize structural and anatomical aspects of the lower abdomen and hips, such as the main planes created by the muscular structures and the forms created by the interactions and overlapping of muscles and skeleton. The images show the differences between male and female figures

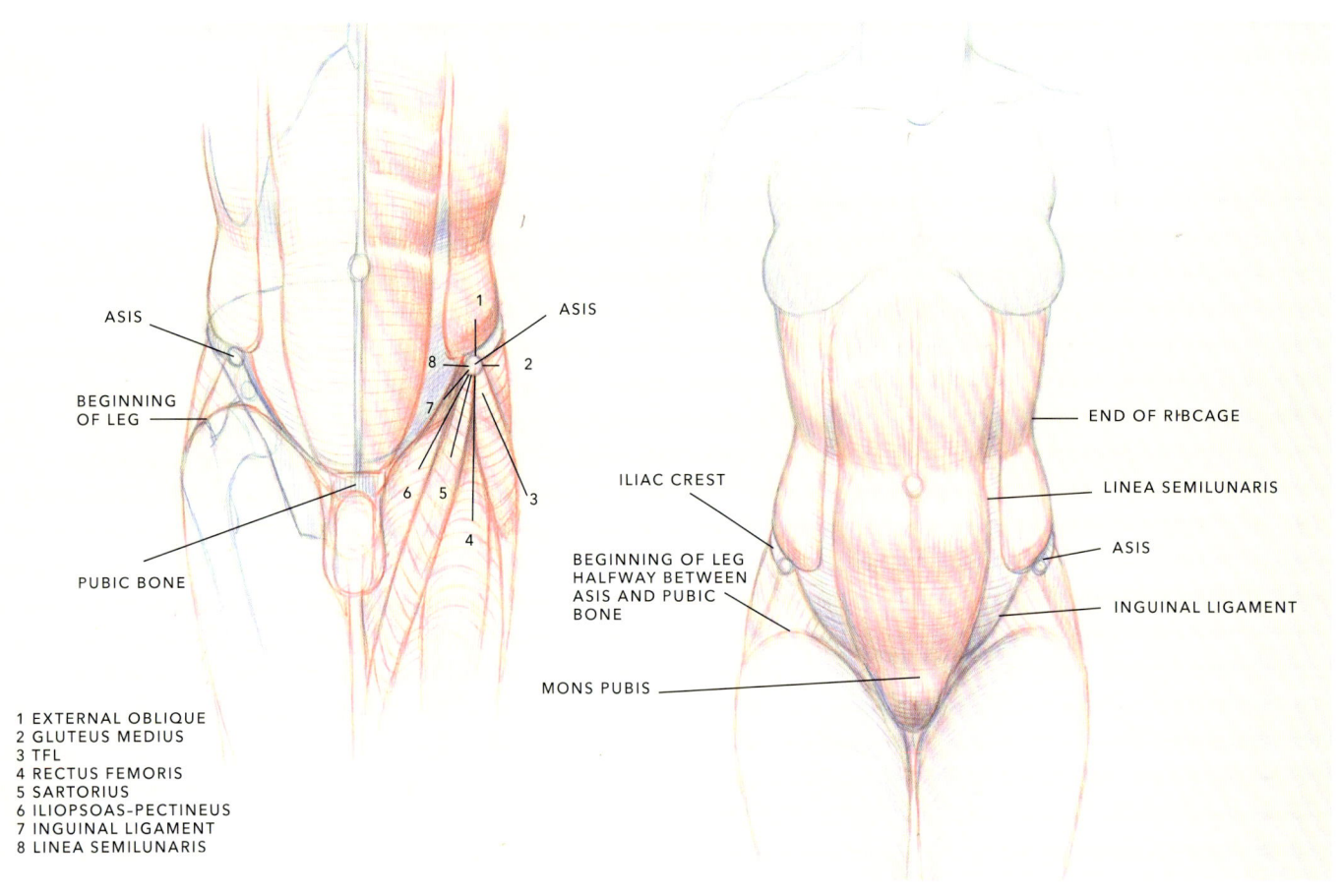

ASIS

BEGINNING OF LEG

PUBIC BONE

ASIS

1
8
7
2
6   5   3
4

1 EXTERNAL OBLIQUE
2 GLUTEUS MEDIUS
3 TFL
4 RECTUS FEMORIS
5 SARTORIUS
6 ILIOPSOAS-PECTINEUS
7 INGUINAL LIGAMENT
8 LINEA SEMILUNARIS

ILIAC CREST

BEGINNING OF LEG HALFWAY BETWEEN ASIS AND PUBIC BONE

MONS PUBIS

END OF RIBCAGE

LINEA SEMILUNARIS

ASIS

INGUINAL LIGAMENT

ABOVE: ASIS "clock"

This figure shows another advantage of knowing the landmarks: you can use the ASIS as a mnemonic device to help you remember and identify the surrounding parts. Note that in men, the inguinal ligament converges just above the base of the genitals, while in women the inguinal ligament converges at the level of the mons pubis, or pubic mound, a fatty tissue area over the pubic bone and just above the genitals.

OPPOSITE: Planes of the abdomen, pelvis, and hips

The two larger, realistic drawings visualize the planes and structures of the abdomen and hips. In the smaller, schematic drawings, note the different curves that the inguinal ligament can have in different people—a wide *U* shape, a narrower *U,* or a *V* shape. The wide *U* shape is more common in women due to their wider pelvis. Also note that the female hips, unlike the male's, are typically wider than the ribcage.

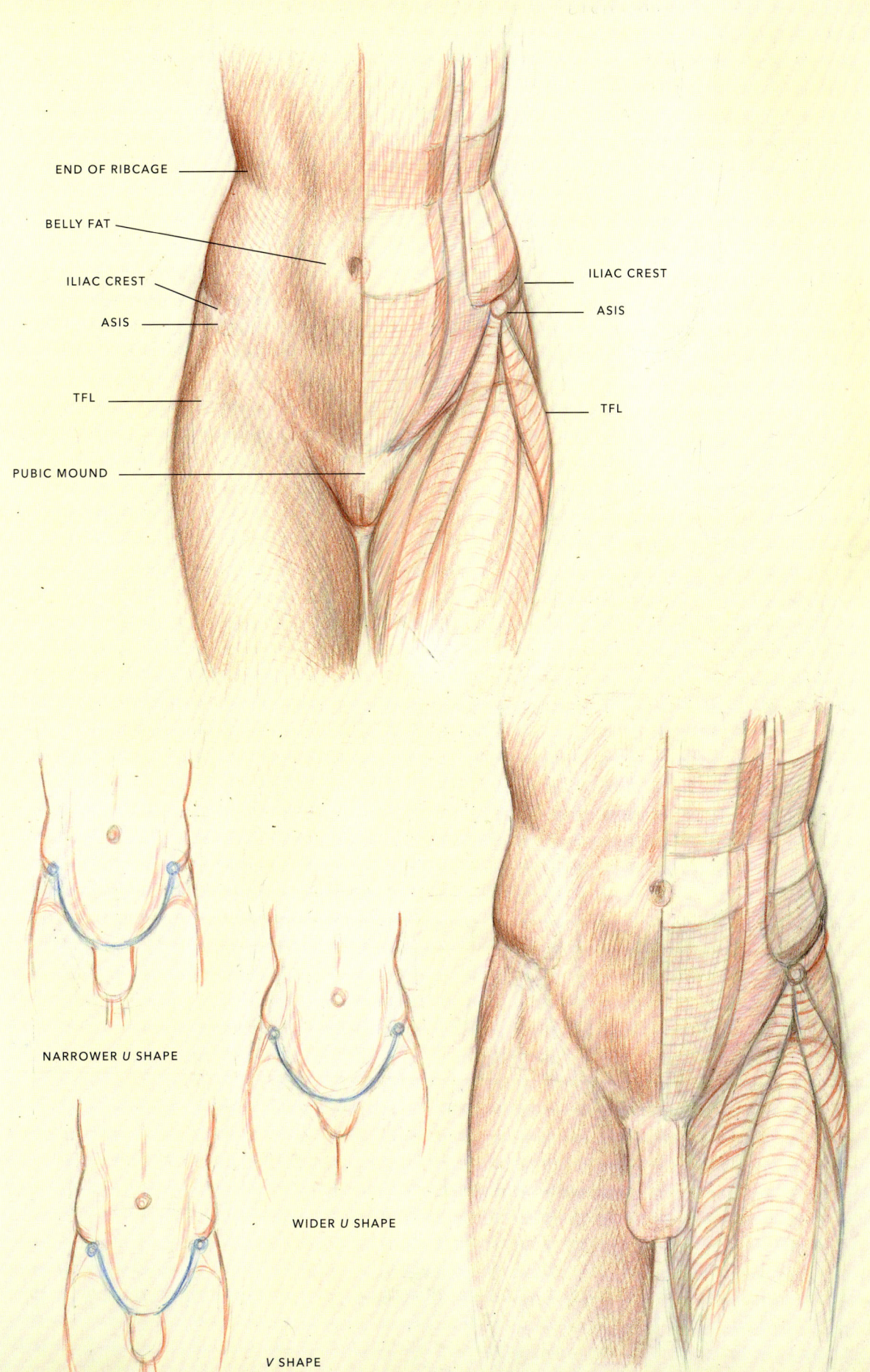

END OF RIBCAGE

BELLY FAT

ILIAC CREST

ASIS

TFL

PUBIC MOUND

ILIAC CREST

ASIS

TFL

NARROWER *U* SHAPE

WIDER *U* SHAPE

V SHAPE

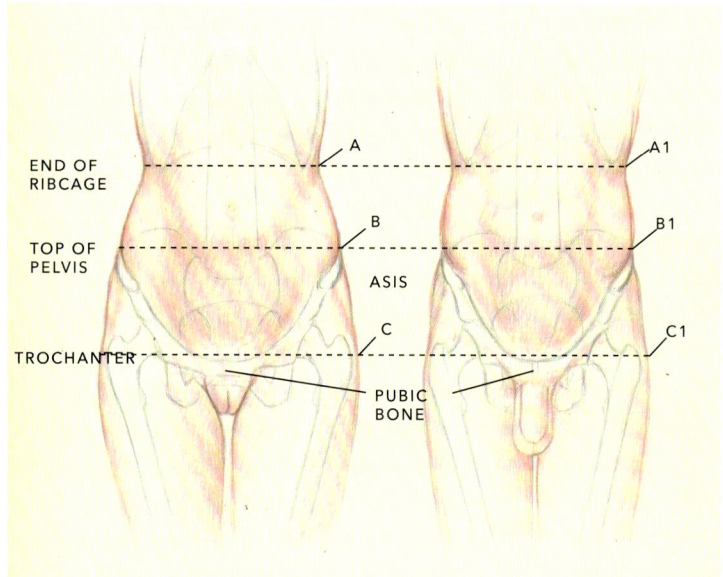

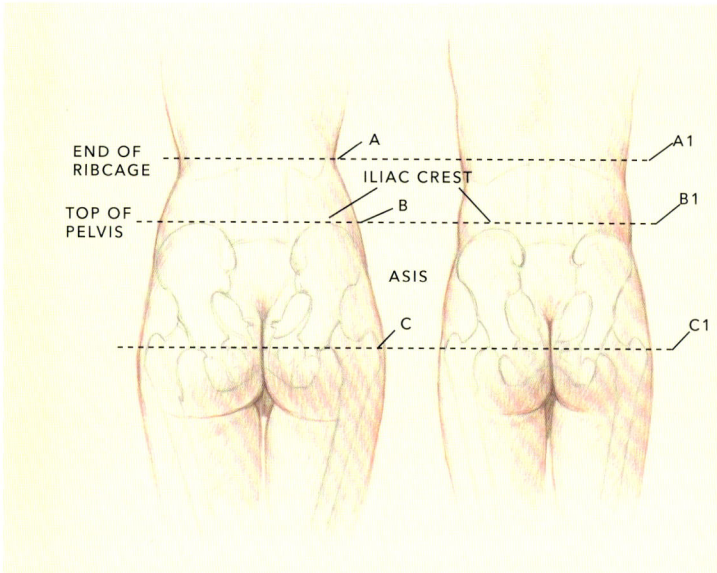

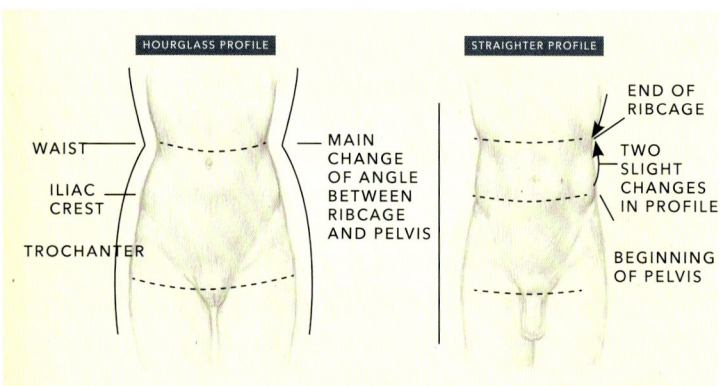

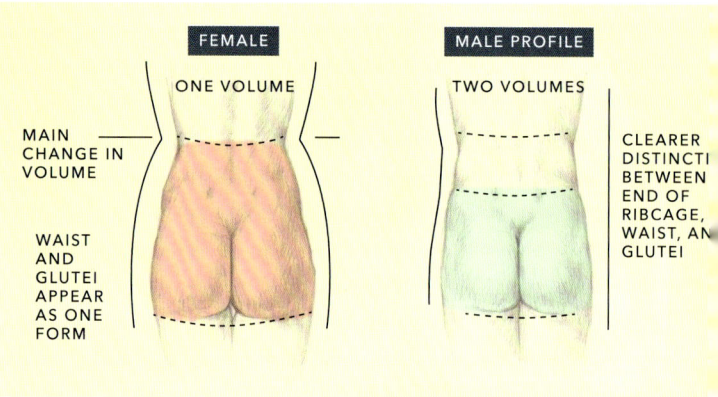

TOP LEFT: Relation between external forms and skeleton in female and male pelvis

The skeleton of the female pelvis is typically slightly wider than the male's when compared with the respective ribcages. This difference creates a typical difference in the profile of men's and women's hips, as this image shows.

ABOVE LEFT: External forms of female and male hips, anterior view

The female hips appear to be bigger than the male hips because of the different angles of the profile and the differences in size between the ribcage and pelvis.

TOP RIGHT: Relation between external forms and skeleton in female and male pelvis, posterior view

In women, the less pronounced change in angle at the waist between the ribcage and iliac crest creates the appearance of a single volume between waist and hips; in men, the passage from waist to iliac crest is more pronounced, creating three separate volumes aligned along a straighter profile.

ABOVE RIGHT: External forms of female and male hips, posterior view

LANDMARKS AND ANATOMY OF THE LEG

The images in this section show all the landmarks and the muscular–skeletal connections of the lower limbs and pelvis from the anterior, posterior, lateral, and medial views.

BELOW: Skeleton, muscles, and external forms of the female pelvis

This three-part sequence shows the deep muscles, superficial muscles, and external forms of the female pelvis, as well as the connections between the skeleton and muscles.

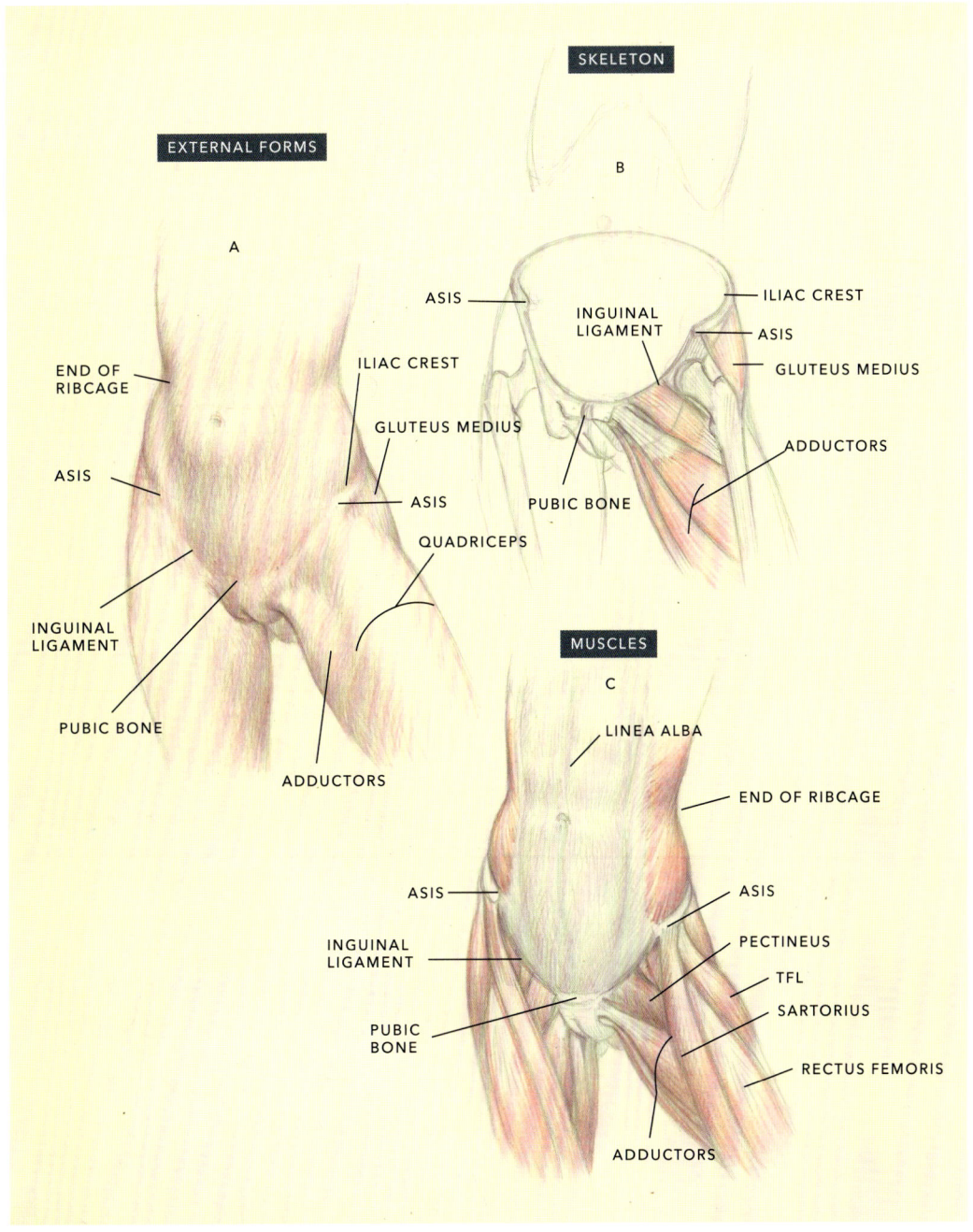

SKELETON

EXTERNAL FORMS

A

B

ASIS

INGUINAL LIGAMENT

ILIAC CREST

ASIS

GLUTEUS MEDIUS

END OF RIBCAGE

ILIAC CREST

GLUTEUS MEDIUS

ADDUCTORS

ASIS

ASIS

INGUINAL LIGAMENT

QUADRICEPS

PUBIC BONE

PUBIC BONE

ADDUCTORS

MUSCLES

C

LINEA ALBA

END OF RIBCAGE

ASIS

ASIS

INGUINAL LIGAMENT

PECTINEUS

TFL

PUBIC BONE

SARTORIUS

RECTUS FEMORIS

ADDUCTORS

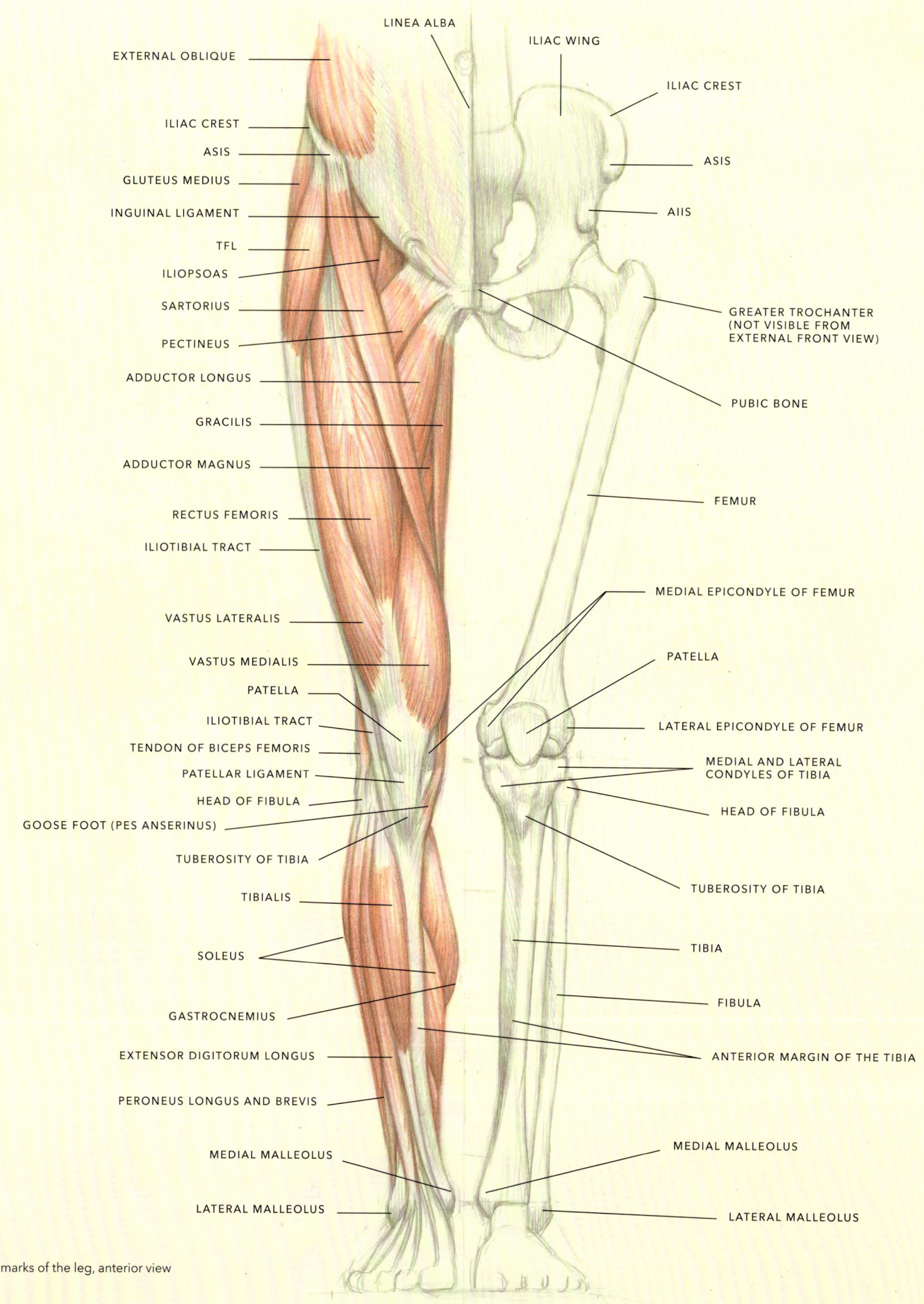

EXTERNAL OBLIQUE

LINEA ALBA

ILIAC WING

ILIAC CREST

ILIAC CREST

ASIS

ASIS

GLUTEUS MEDIUS

AIIS

INGUINAL LIGAMENT

TFL

ILIOPSOAS

SARTORIUS

PECTINEUS

GREATER TROCHANTER
(NOT VISIBLE FROM
EXTERNAL FRONT VIEW)

ADDUCTOR LONGUS

PUBIC BONE

GRACILIS

ADDUCTOR MAGNUS

RECTUS FEMORIS

FEMUR

ILIOTIBIAL TRACT

VASTUS LATERALIS

MEDIAL EPICONDYLE OF FEMUR

VASTUS MEDIALIS

PATELLA

PATELLA

ILIOTIBIAL TRACT

LATERAL EPICONDYLE OF FEMUR

TENDON OF BICEPS FEMORIS

MEDIAL AND LATERAL
CONDYLES OF TIBIA

PATELLAR LIGAMENT

HEAD OF FIBULA

HEAD OF FIBULA

GOOSE FOOT (PES ANSERINUS)

TUBEROSITY OF TIBIA

TUBEROSITY OF TIBIA

TIBIALIS

TIBIA

SOLEUS

FIBULA

GASTROCNEMIUS

EXTENSOR DIGITORUM LONGUS

ANTERIOR MARGIN OF THE TIBIA

PERONEUS LONGUS AND BREVIS

MEDIAL MALLEOLUS

MEDIAL MALLEOLUS

LATERAL MALLEOLUS

LATERAL MALLEOLUS

Landmarks of the leg, anterior view

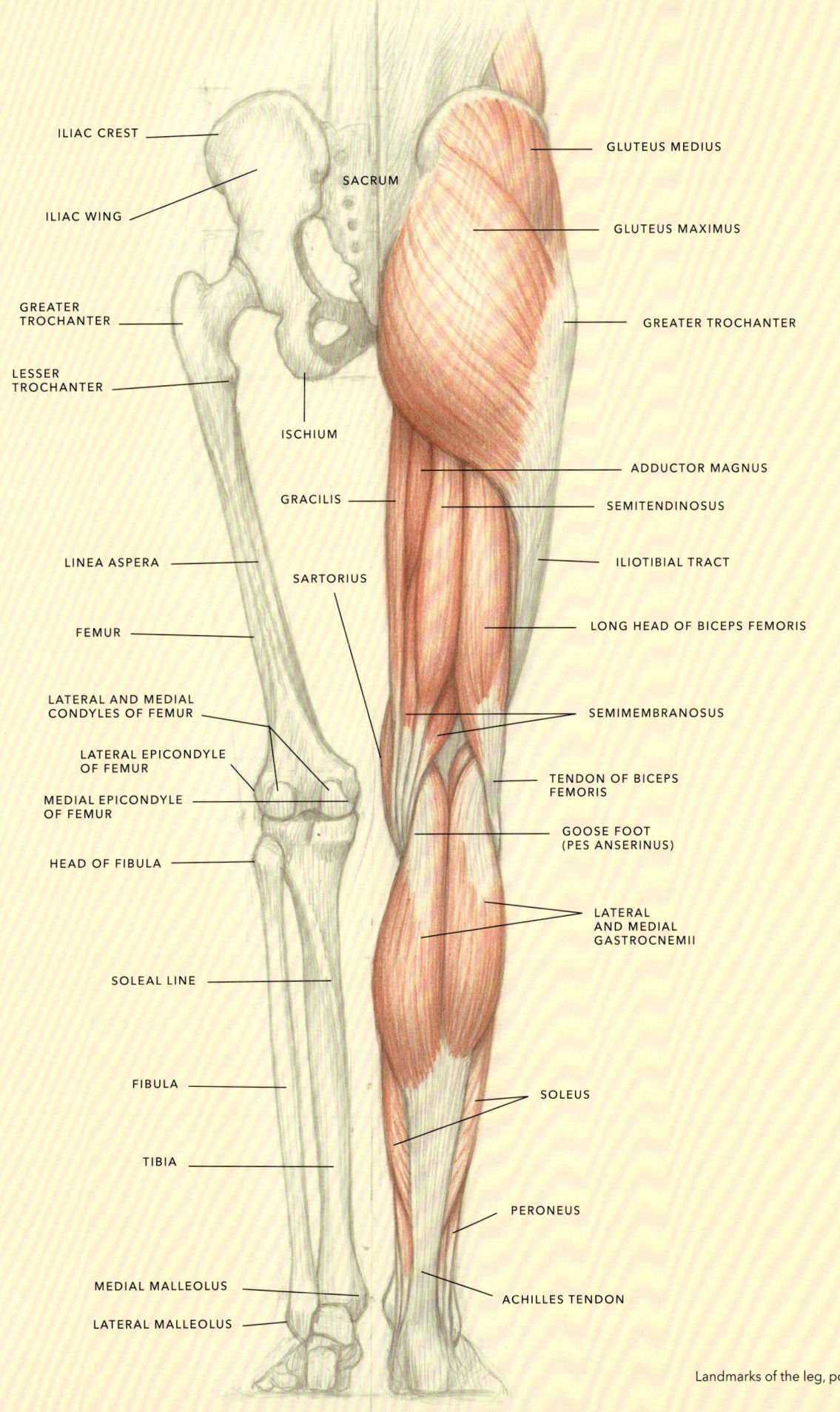

ILIAC CREST

ILIAC WING

SACRUM

GLUTEUS MEDIUS

GLUTEUS MAXIMUS

GREATER
TROCHANTER

GREATER TROCHANTER

LESSER
TROCHANTER

ISCHIUM

ADDUCTOR MAGNUS

GRACILIS

SEMITENDINOSUS

LINEA ASPERA

SARTORIUS

ILIOTIBIAL TRACT

FEMUR

LONG HEAD OF BICEPS FEMORIS

LATERAL AND MEDIAL
CONDYLES OF FEMUR

SEMIMEMBRANOSUS

LATERAL EPICONDYLE
OF FEMUR

TENDON OF BICEPS
FEMORIS

MEDIAL EPICONDYLE
OF FEMUR

GOOSE FOOT
(PES ANSERINUS)

HEAD OF FIBULA

LATERAL
AND MEDIAL
GASTROCNEMII

SOLEAL LINE

FIBULA

SOLEUS

TIBIA

PERONEUS

MEDIAL MALLEOLUS

ACHILLES TENDON

LATERAL MALLEOLUS

Landmarks of the leg, posterior view

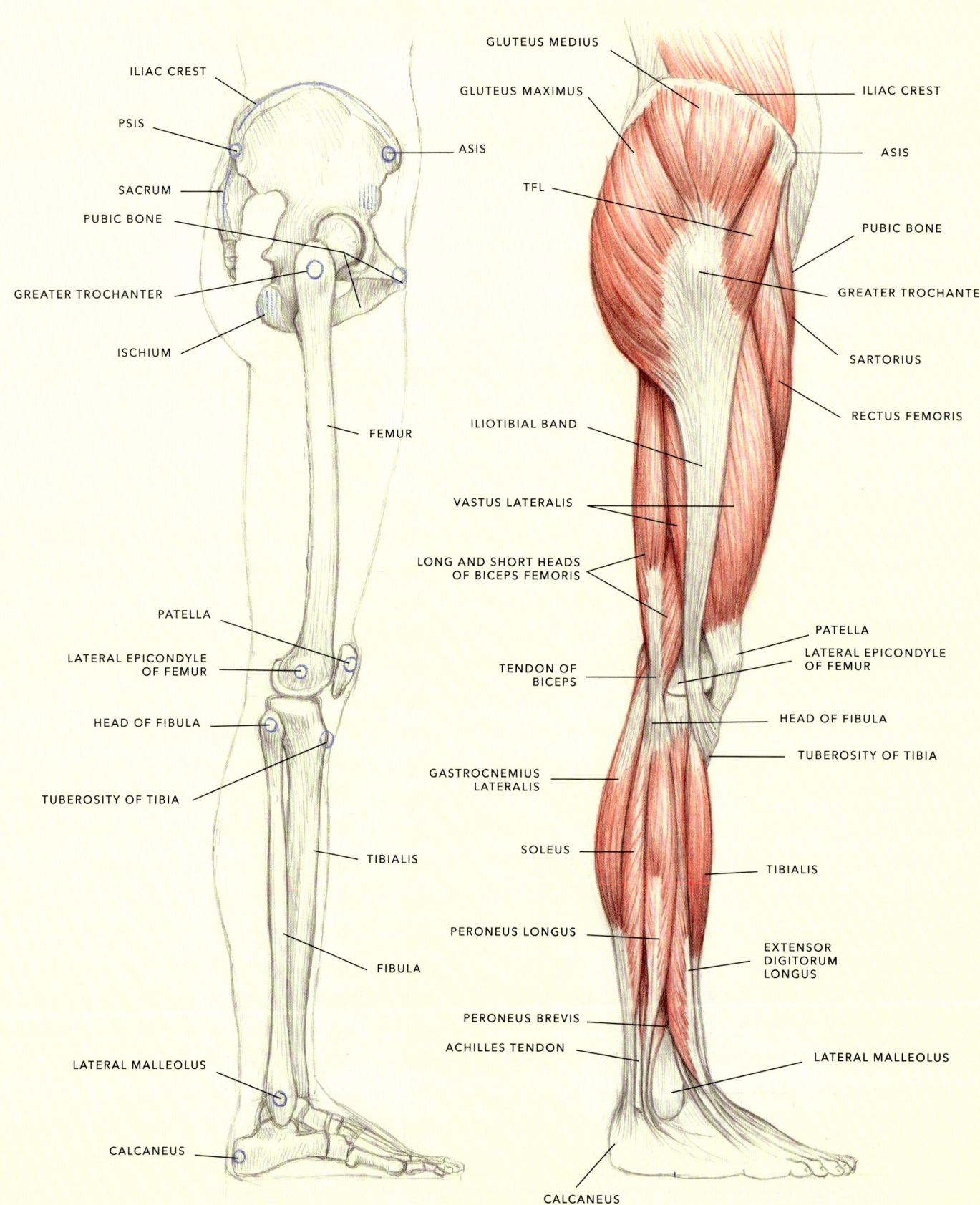

GLUTEUS MEDIUS

GLUTEUS MAXIMUS

TFL

ILIAC CREST

ASIS

PUBIC BONE

GREATER TROCHANTER

SARTORIUS

RECTUS FEMORIS

ILIAC CREST

PSIS

SACRUM

PUBIC BONE

GREATER TROCHANTER

ISCHIUM

ASIS

FEMUR

ILIOTIBIAL BAND

VASTUS LATERALIS

LONG AND SHORT HEADS
OF BICEPS FEMORIS

TENDON OF
BICEPS

PATELLA

LATERAL EPICONDYLE
OF FEMUR

HEAD OF FIBULA

TUBEROSITY OF TIBIA

PATELLA

LATERAL EPICONDYLE
OF FEMUR

HEAD OF FIBULA

TUBEROSITY OF TIBIA

GASTROCNEMIUS
LATERALIS

SOLEUS

PERONEUS LONGUS

PERONEUS BREVIS

ACHILLES TENDON

TIBIALIS

FIBULA

TIBIALIS

EXTENSOR
DIGITORUM
LONGUS

LATERAL MALLEOLUS

LATERAL MALLEOLUS

CALCANEUS

CALCANEUS

Landmarks of the leg, lateral view

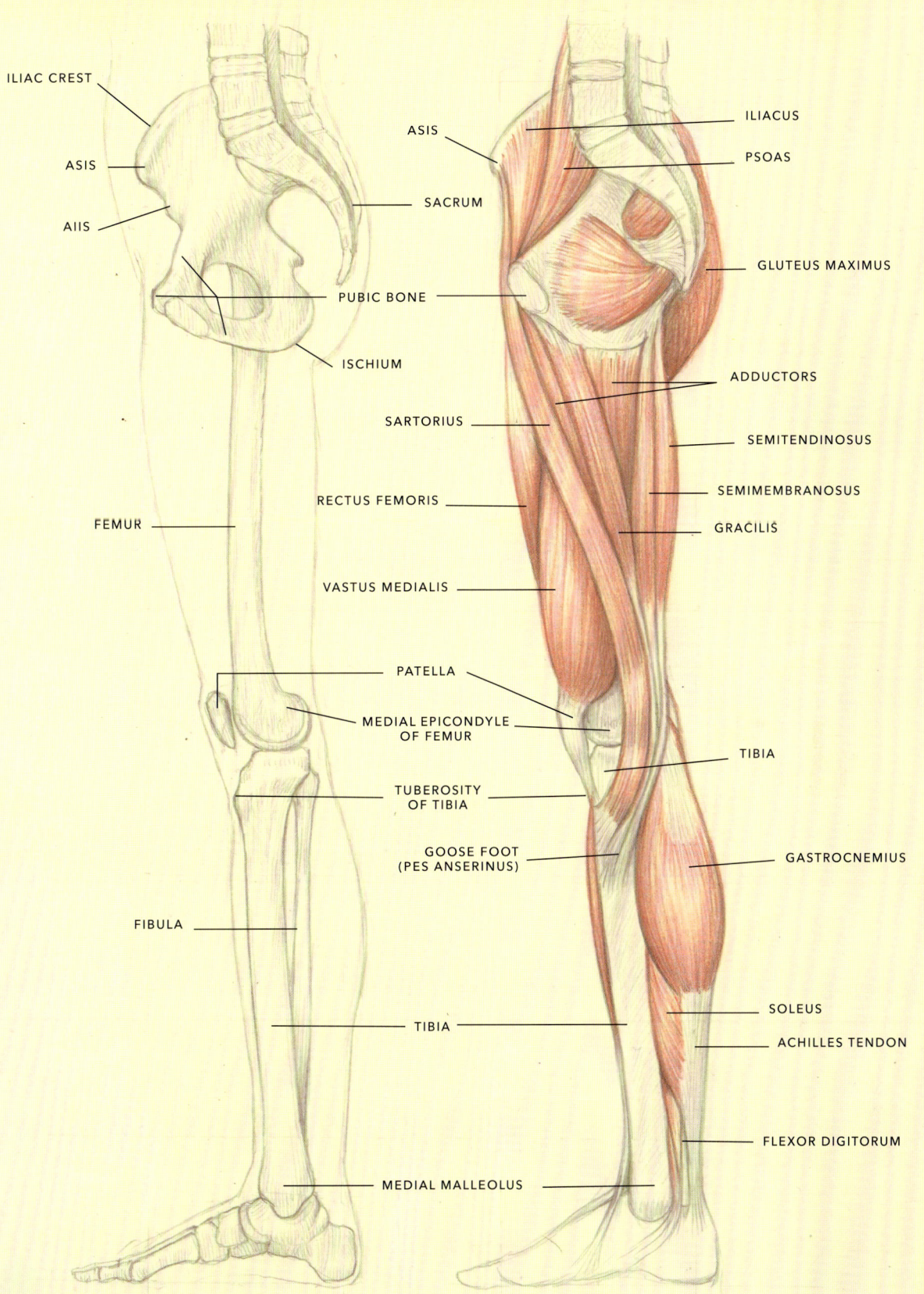

ILIAC CREST

ASIS

AIIS

ASIS

SACRUM

ILIACUS

PSOAS

GLUTEUS MAXIMUS

PUBIC BONE

ISCHIUM

ADDUCTORS

SARTORIUS

SEMITENDINOSUS

SEMIMEMBRANOSUS

RECTUS FEMORIS

GRACILIS

FEMUR

VASTUS MEDIALIS

PATELLA

MEDIAL EPICONDYLE
OF FEMUR

TIBIA

TUBEROSITY
OF TIBIA

GOOSE FOOT
(PES ANSERINUS)

GASTROCNEMIUS

FIBULA

TIBIA

SOLEUS

ACHILLES TENDON

FLEXOR DIGITORUM

MEDIAL MALLEOLUS

Landmarks of the leg, medial view

Avoid bumpy, awkward knees

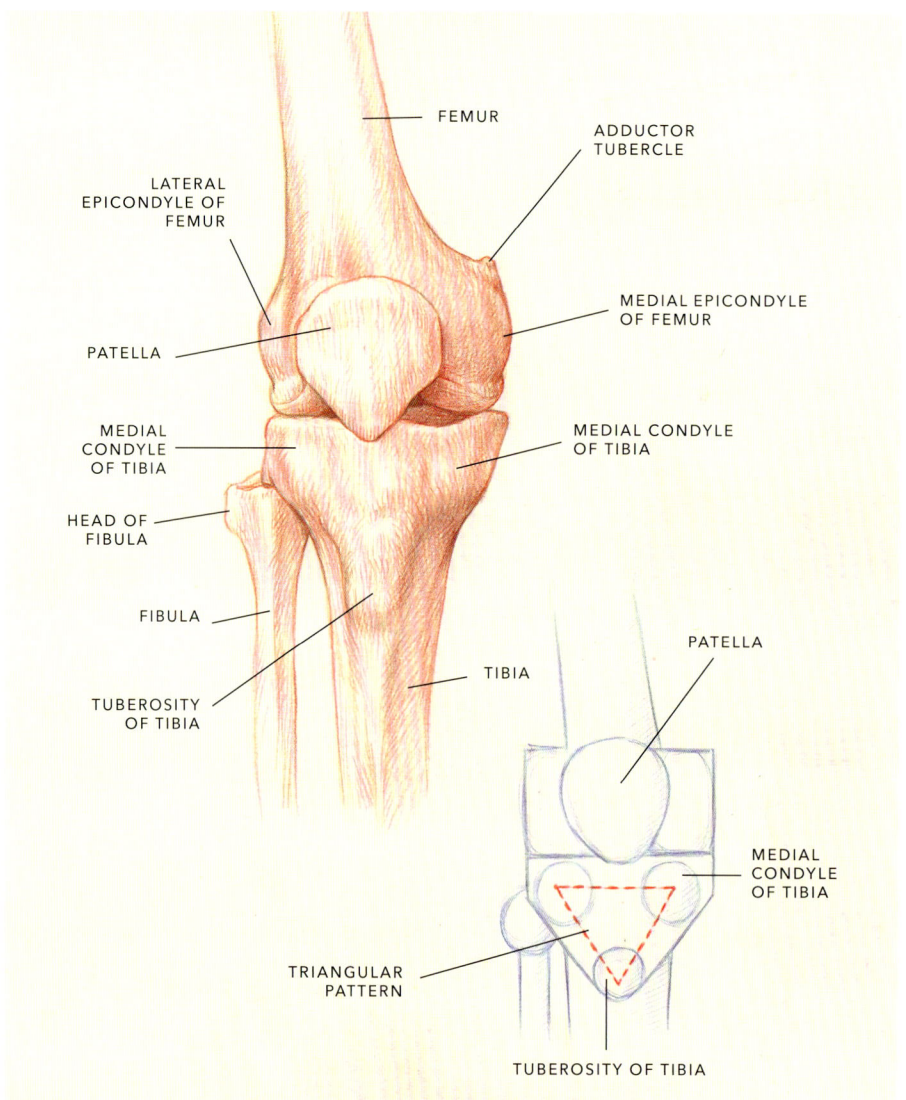

RIGHT: Skeletal landmarks of the knee, anterior view

The small inset drawing is a schematic visualization of the "bumps" of the knee.

OPPOSITE, TOP LEFT: External forms of the knee, anterior view

OPPOSITE, TOP RIGHT: External forms of the knee, posterior view

OPPOSITE CENTER: Skeletal landmarks and external forms of the knee, lateral view

OPPOSITE BOTTOM: Skeletal landmarks and external forms of the knee, medial view

LANDMARKS AND ANATOMY OF THE KNEE

The knee is amazingly complicated. Its external forms are so complex because of its many parts: tendons, muscles, bony landmarks, fatty pads, and so on. Putting any of these parts in the wrong place in a drawing will result in a bumpy, awkward knee. The images in this section show all the structures of the knee from various points of view in extended and flexed positions.

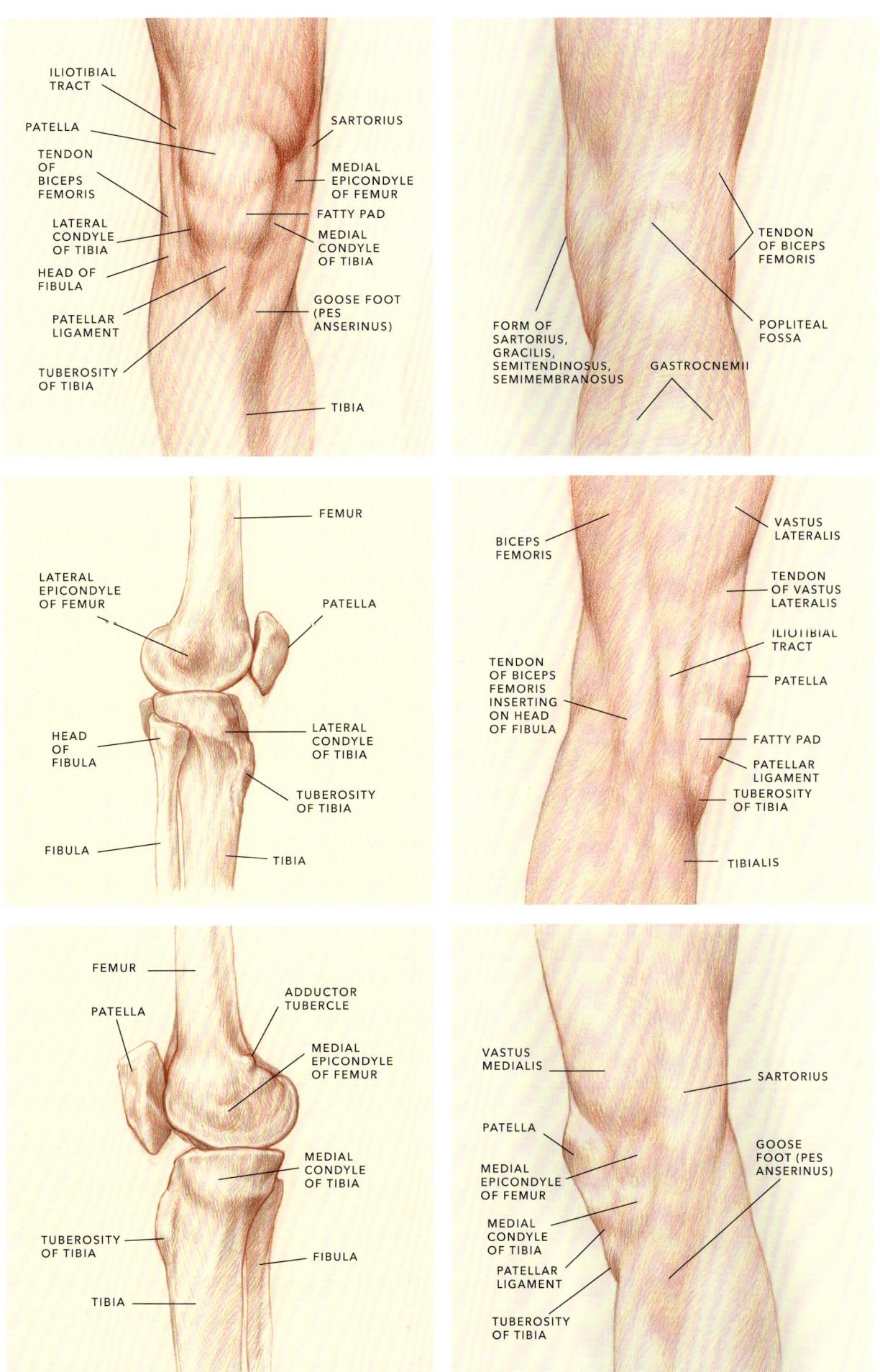

ILIOTIBIAL TRACT

PATELLA

TENDON OF BICEPS FEMORIS

LATERAL CONDYLE OF TIBIA

HEAD OF FIBULA

PATELLAR LIGAMENT

TUBEROSITY OF TIBIA

SARTORIUS

MEDIAL EPICONDYLE OF FEMUR

FATTY PAD

MEDIAL CONDYLE OF TIBIA

GOOSE FOOT (PES ANSERINUS)

TIBIA

FORM OF SARTORIUS, GRACILIS, SEMITENDINOSUS, SEMIMEMBRANOSUS

GASTROCNEMII

TENDON OF BICEPS FEMORIS

POPLITEAL FOSSA

FEMUR

LATERAL EPICONDYLE OF FEMUR

PATELLA

HEAD OF FIBULA

LATERAL CONDYLE OF TIBIA

TUBEROSITY OF TIBIA

FIBULA

TIBIA

BICEPS FEMORIS

TENDON OF BICEPS FEMORIS INSERTING ON HEAD OF FIBULA

VASTUS LATERALIS

TENDON OF VASTUS LATERALIS

ILIOTIBIAL TRACT

PATELLA

FATTY PAD

PATELLAR LIGAMENT

TUBEROSITY OF TIBIA

TIBIALIS

FEMUR

PATELLA

ADDUCTOR TUBERCLE

MEDIAL EPICONDYLE OF FEMUR

MEDIAL CONDYLE OF TIBIA

TUBEROSITY OF TIBIA

FIBULA

TIBIA

VASTUS MEDIALIS

PATELLA

MEDIAL EPICONDYLE OF FEMUR

MEDIAL CONDYLE OF TIBIA

PATELLAR LIGAMENT

TUBEROSITY OF TIBIA

SARTORIUS

GOOSE FOOT (PES ANSERINUS)

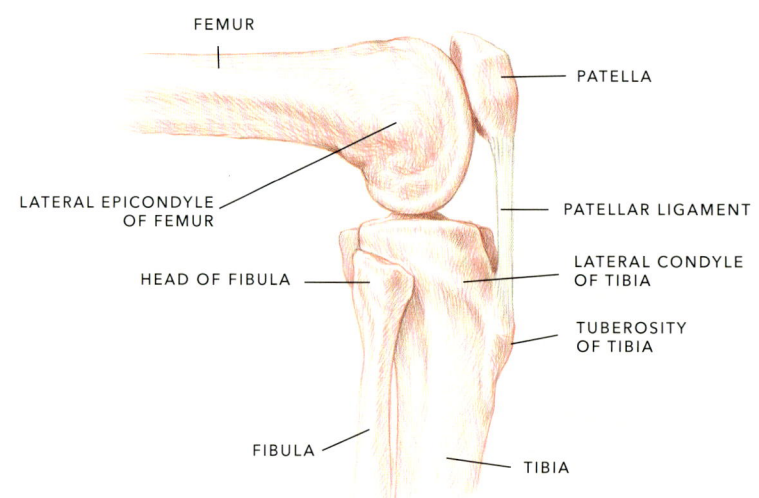

FEMUR

PATELLA

LATERAL EPICONDYLE
OF FEMUR

PATELLAR LIGAMENT

HEAD OF FIBULA

LATERAL CONDYLE
OF TIBIA

TUBEROSITY
OF TIBIA

FIBULA

TIBIA

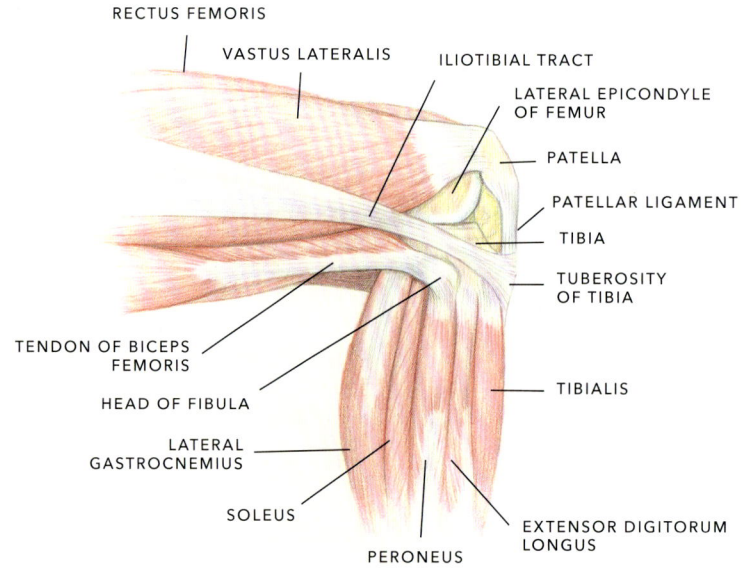

RECTUS FEMORIS

VASTUS LATERALIS

ILIOTIBIAL TRACT

LATERAL EPICONDYLE
OF FEMUR

PATELLA

PATELLAR LIGAMENT

TIBIA

TUBEROSITY
OF TIBIA

TENDON OF BICEPS
FEMORIS

HEAD OF FIBULA

TIBIALIS

LATERAL
GASTROCNEMIUS

SOLEUS

PERONEUS

EXTENSOR DIGITORUM
LONGUS

TOP: Skeletal landmarks of flexed
knee, lateral view

CENTER: Muscles of flexed knee,
lateral view

BOTTOM: External forms of flexed
knee, lateral view

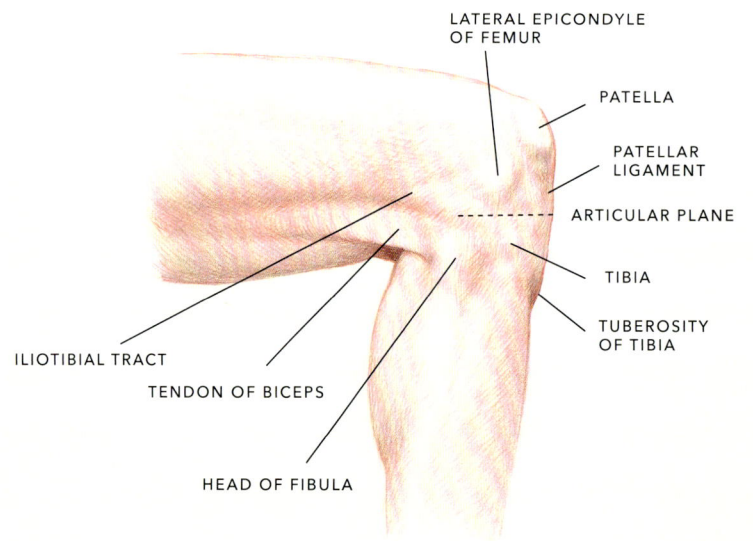

LATERAL EPICONDYLE
OF FEMUR

PATELLA

PATELLAR
LIGAMENT

ARTICULAR PLANE

TIBIA

TUBEROSITY
OF TIBIA

ILIOTIBIAL TRACT

TENDON OF BICEPS

HEAD OF FIBULA

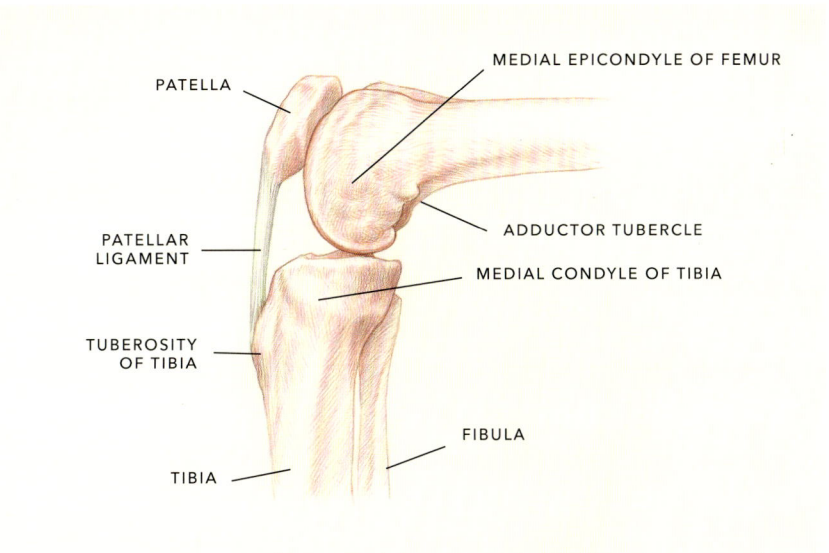

PATELLA

MEDIAL EPICONDYLE OF FEMUR

PATELLAR LIGAMENT

ADDUCTOR TUBERCLE

MEDIAL CONDYLE OF TIBIA

TUBEROSITY OF TIBIA

FIBULA

TIBIA

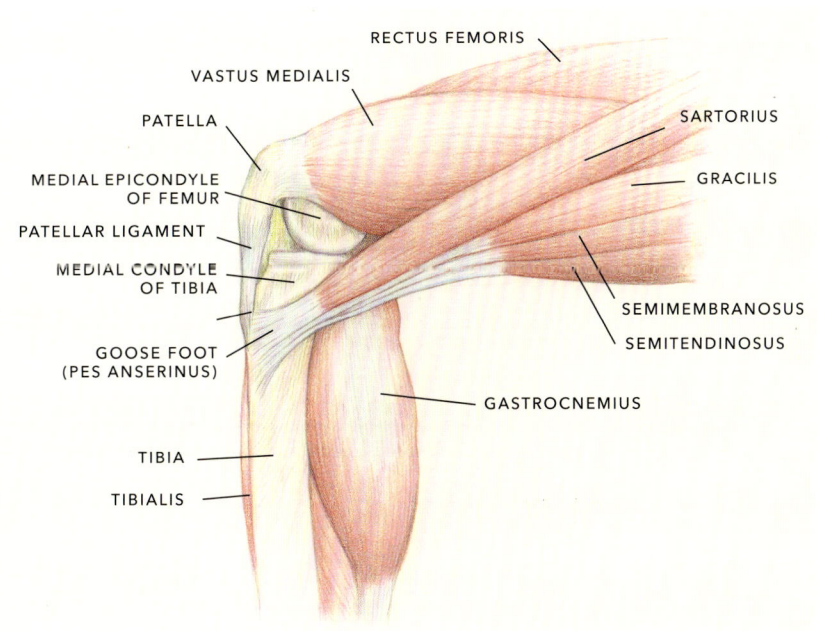

RECTUS FEMORIS

VASTUS MEDIALIS

PATELLA

SARTORIUS

MEDIAL EPICONDYLE OF FEMUR

GRACILIS

PATELLAR LIGAMENT

MEDIAL CONDYLE OF TIBIA

SEMIMEMBRANOSUS

SEMITENDINOSUS

GOOSE FOOT (PES ANSERINUS)

GASTROCNEMIUS

TIBIA

TIBIALIS

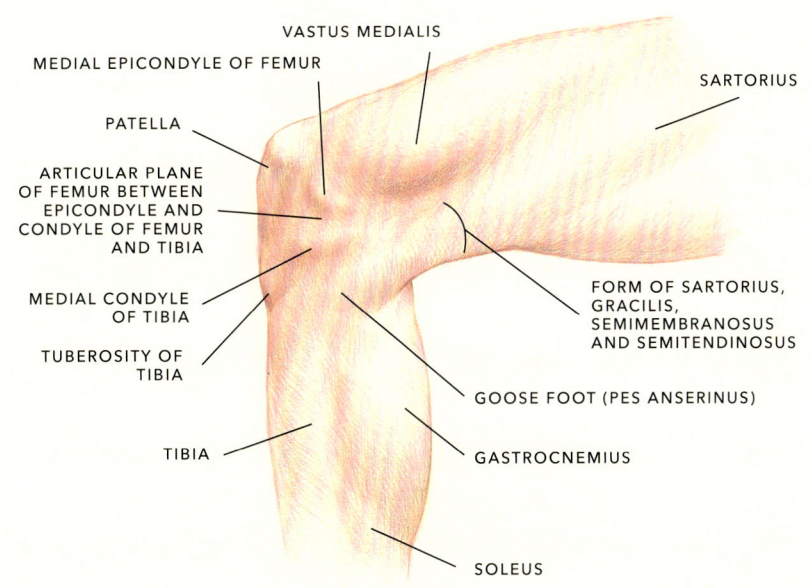

VASTUS MEDIALIS

MEDIAL EPICONDYLE OF FEMUR

SARTORIUS

PATELLA

ARTICULAR PLANE OF FEMUR BETWEEN EPICONDYLE AND CONDYLE OF FEMUR AND TIBIA

FORM OF SARTORIUS, GRACILIS, SEMIMEMBRANOSUS AND SEMITENDINOSUS

MEDIAL CONDYLE OF TIBIA

TUBEROSITY OF TIBIA

GOOSE FOOT (PES ANSERINUS)

TIBIA

GASTROCNEMIUS

SOLEUS

TOP: Skeletal landmarks of flexed knee, medial view

CENTER: Muscles of flexed knee, medial view

BOTTOM: External forms of flexed knee, medial view

117

LANDMARKS AND ANATOMY
OF THE ANKLE AND FOOT

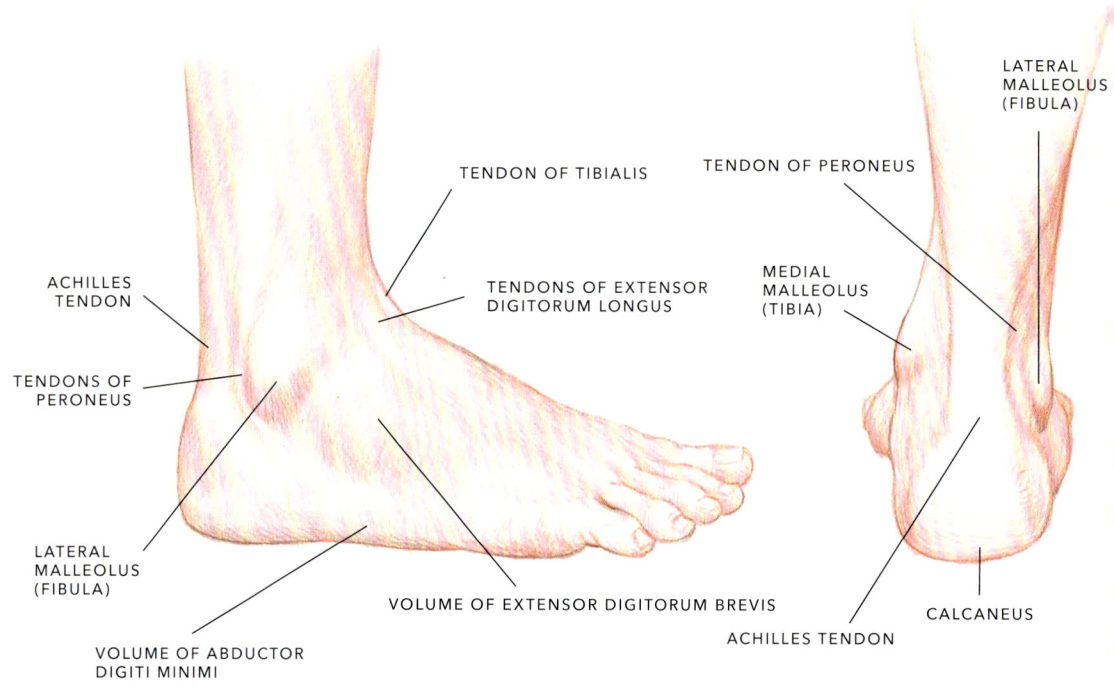

LATERAL
MALLEOLUS
(FIBULA)

TENDON OF TIBIALIS

TENDON OF PERONEUS

ACHILLES
TENDON

TENDONS OF EXTENSOR
DIGITORUM LONGUS

MEDIAL
MALLEOLUS
(TIBIA)

TENDONS OF
PERONEUS

LATERAL
MALLEOLUS
(FIBULA)

VOLUME OF EXTENSOR DIGITORUM BREVIS

ACHILLES TENDON

CALCANEUS

VOLUME OF ABDUCTOR
DIGITI MINIMI

RIGHT: External forms, skeletal
structures, and tendons of the
foot and ankle

These images allow you to compare the external forms of the
foot and ankle with the skeletal
structures and tendons as seen
from lateral, posterior, anterior,
and anterior three-quarters views.

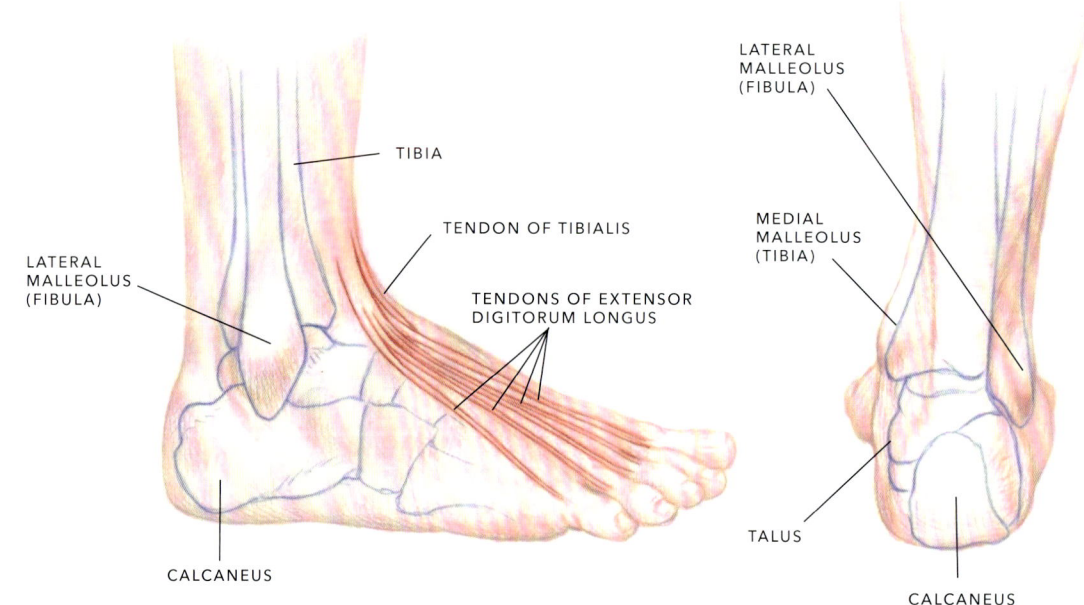

TIBIA

LATERAL
MALLEOLUS
(FIBULA)

TENDON OF TIBIALIS

TENDONS OF EXTENSOR
DIGITORUM LONGUS

LATERAL
MALLEOLUS
(FIBULA)

MEDIAL
MALLEOLUS
(TIBIA)

TALUS

CALCANEUS

CALCANEUS

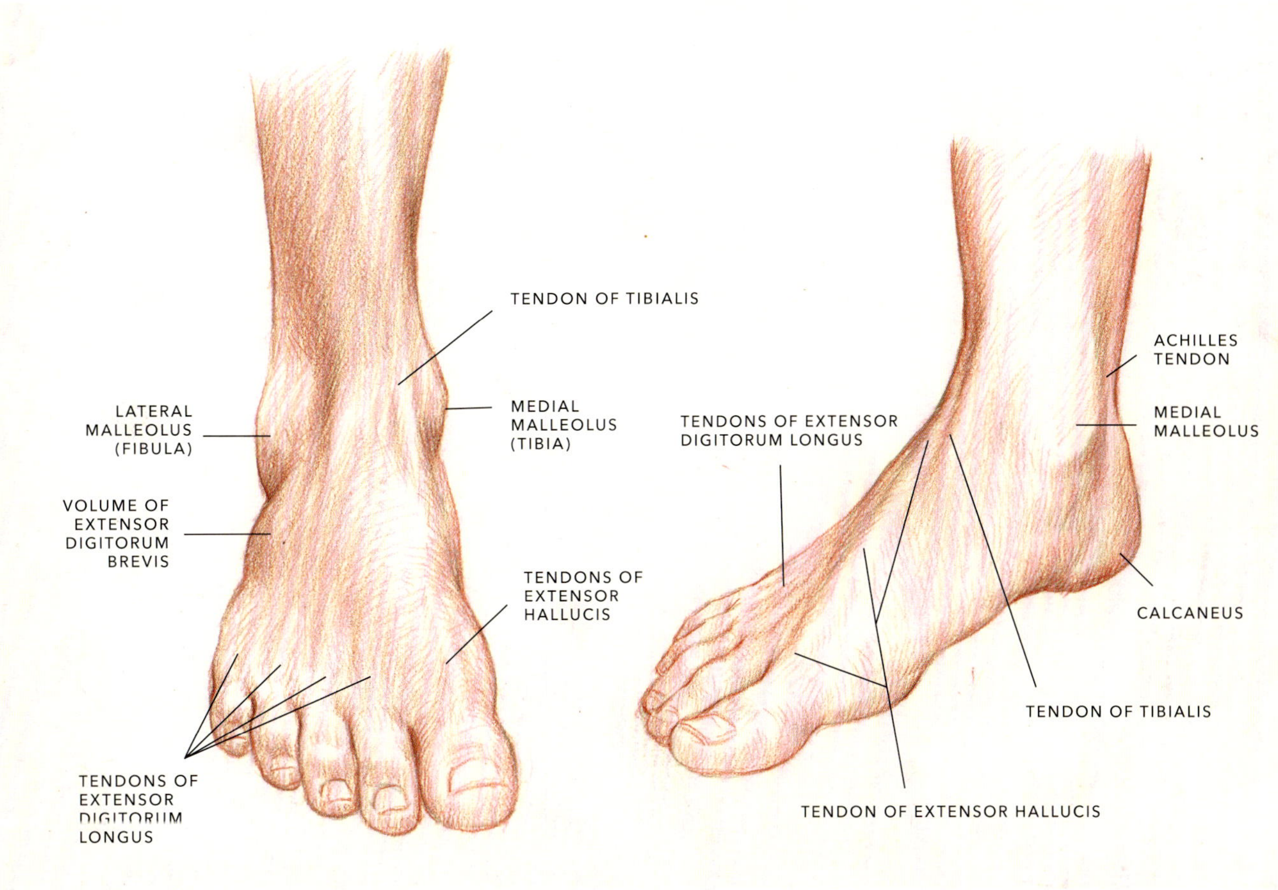

TENDON OF TIBIALIS

LATERAL
MALLEOLUS
(FIBULA)

MEDIAL
MALLEOLUS
(TIBIA)

ACHILLES
TENDON

TENDONS OF EXTENSOR
DIGITORUM LONGUS

MEDIAL
MALLEOLUS

VOLUME OF
EXTENSOR
DIGITORUM
BREVIS

TENDONS OF
EXTENSOR
HALLUCIS

CALCANEUS

TENDON OF TIBIALIS

TENDONS OF
EXTENSOR
DIGITORUM
LONGUS

TENDON OF EXTENSOR HALLUCIS

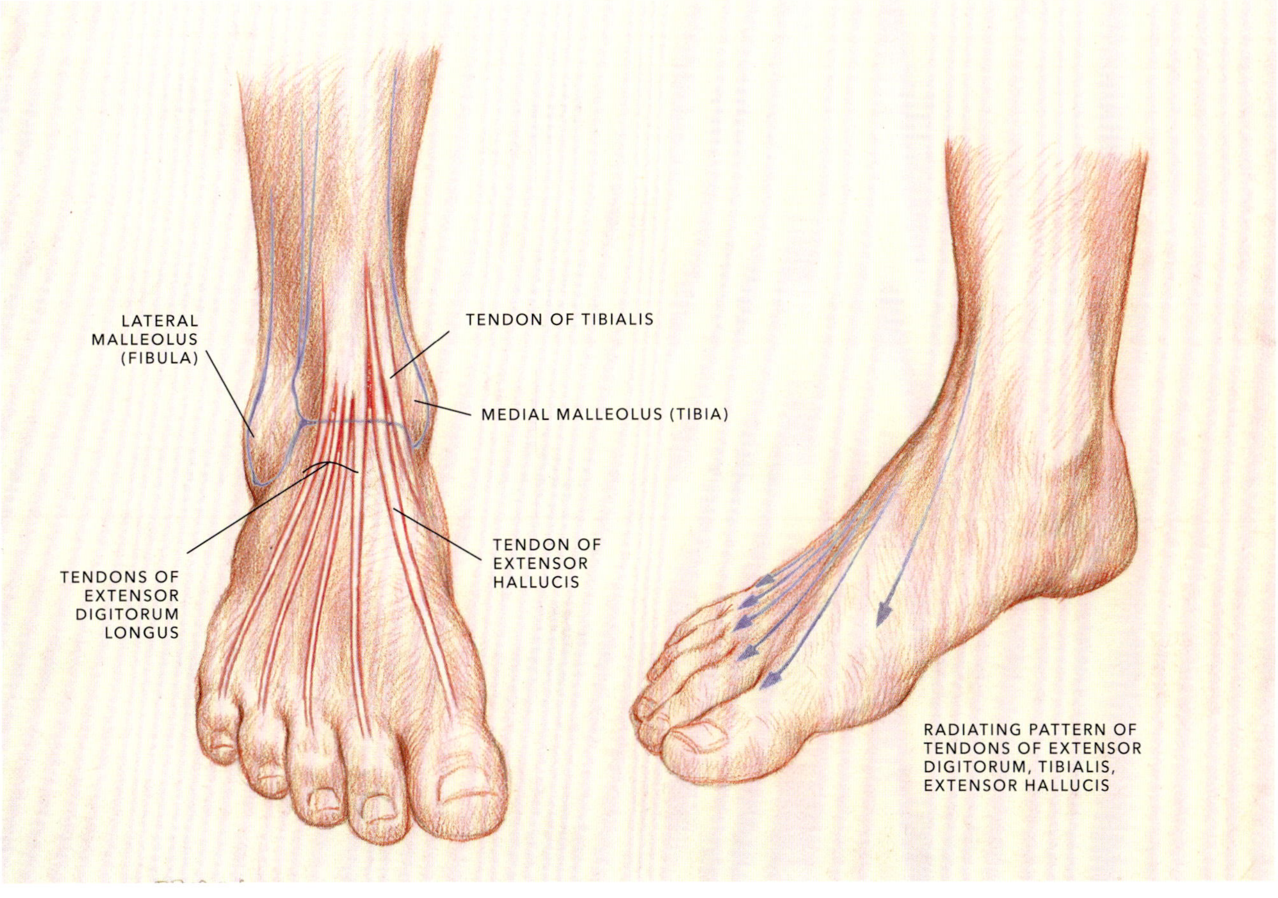

LATERAL
MALLEOLUS
(FIBULA)

TENDON OF TIBIALIS

MEDIAL MALLEOLUS (TIBIA)

TENDONS OF
EXTENSOR
DIGITORUM
LONGUS

TENDON OF
EXTENSOR
HALLUCIS

RADIATING PATTERN OF
TENDONS OF EXTENSOR
DIGITORUM, TIBIALIS,
EXTENSOR HALLUCIS

EXERCISE

Use the images on these and the following pagess to practice identifying landmarks and muscles. Make black-and-white photocopies of the blank (unlabeled) drawings and label the skeletal landmarks, soft landmarks, and muscles. To help yourself memorize them, you can also color the muscles with different colored pencils. Use the labeled images for reference.

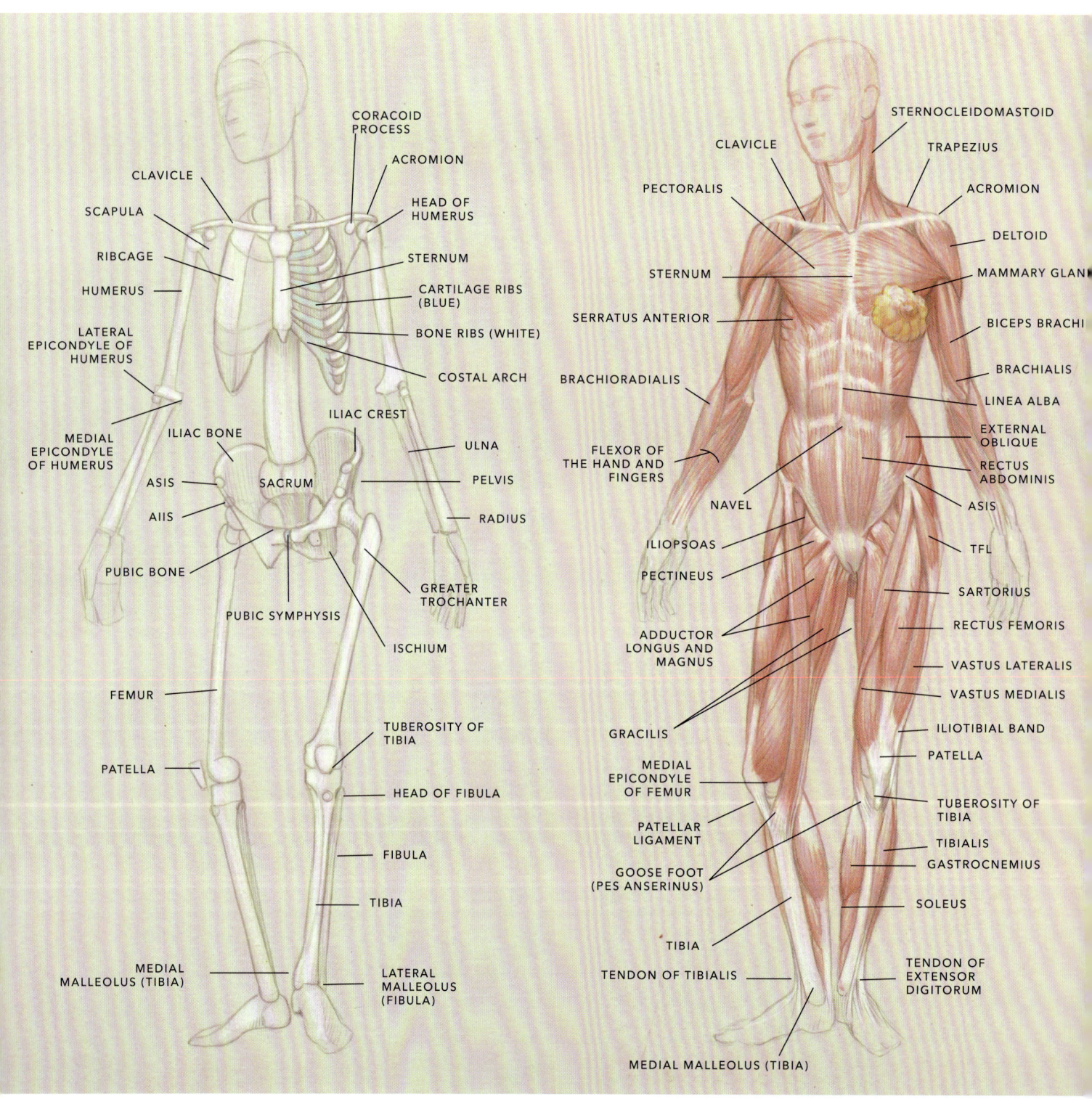

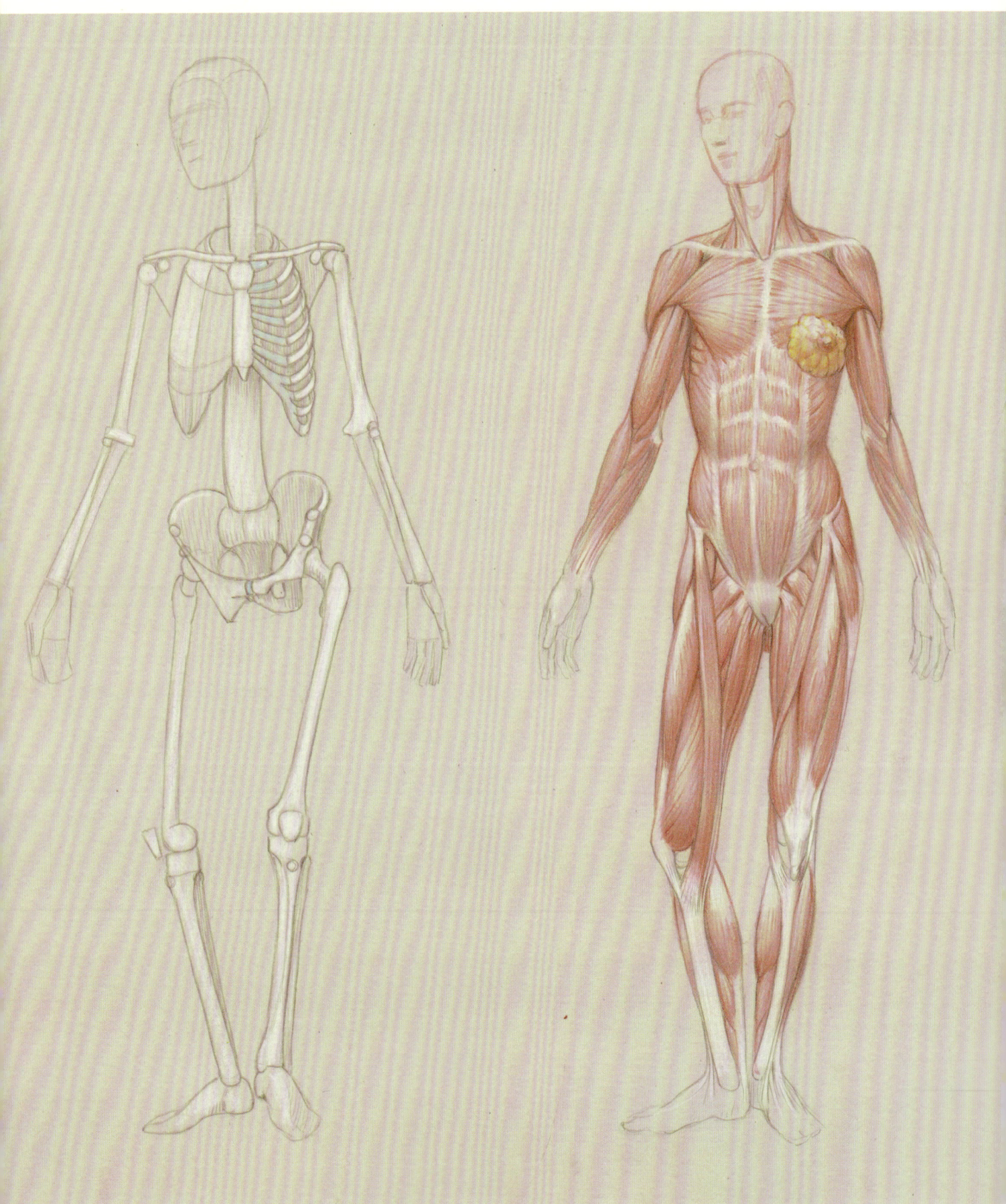

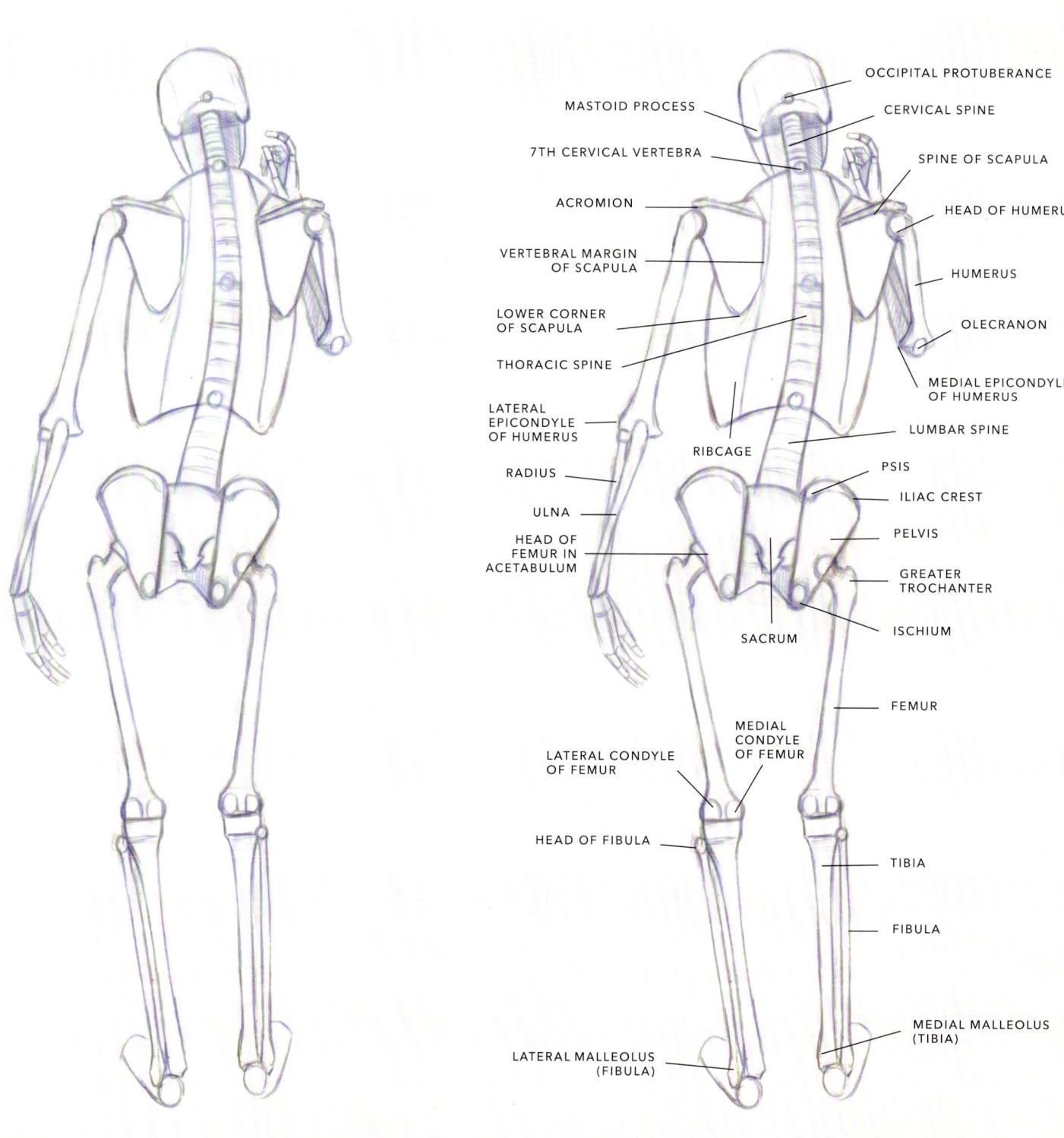

OCCIPITAL PROTUBERANCE

MASTOID PROCESS

CERVICAL SPINE

7TH CERVICAL VERTEBRA

SPINE OF SCAPULA

ACROMION

HEAD OF HUMERUS

VERTEBRAL MARGIN
OF SCAPULA

HUMERUS

LOWER CORNER
OF SCAPULA

OLECRANON

THORACIC SPINE

MEDIAL EPICONDYLE
OF HUMERUS

LATERAL
EPICONDYLE
OF HUMERUS

LUMBAR SPINE

RIBCAGE

RADIUS

PSIS

ULNA

ILIAC CREST

HEAD OF
FEMUR IN
ACETABULUM

PELVIS

GREATER
TROCHANTER

SACRUM

ISCHIUM

FEMUR

MEDIAL
CONDYLE
OF FEMUR

LATERAL CONDYLE
OF FEMUR

HEAD OF FIBULA

TIBIA

FIBULA

MEDIAL MALLEOLUS
(TIBIA)

LATERAL MALLEOLUS
(FIBULA)

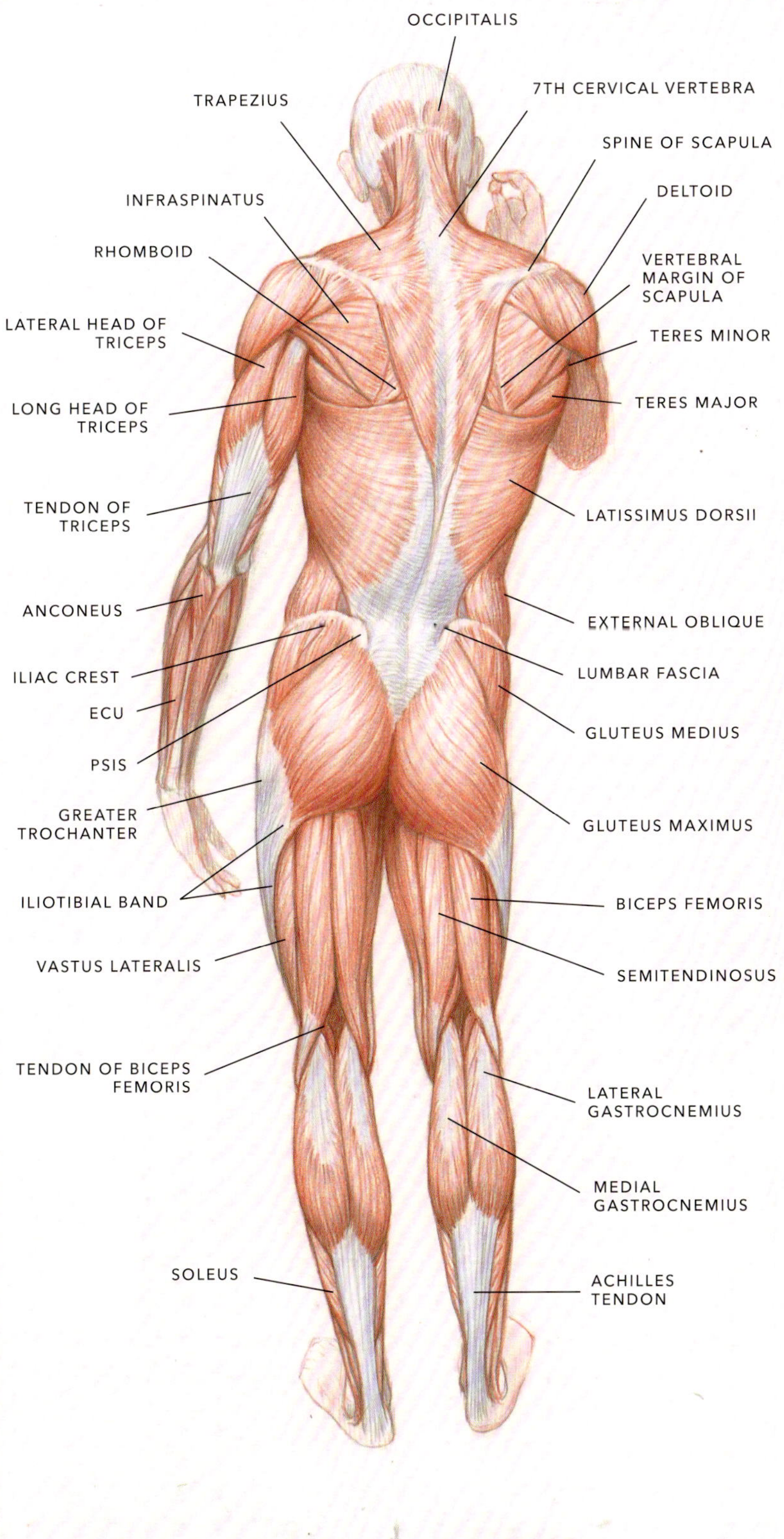

OCCIPITALIS

TRAPEZIUS

7TH CERVICAL VERTEBRA

SPINE OF SCAPULA

INFRASPINATUS

DELTOID

RHOMBOID

VERTEBRAL
MARGIN OF
SCAPULA

LATERAL HEAD OF
TRICEPS

TERES MINOR

LONG HEAD OF
TRICEPS

TERES MAJOR

TENDON OF
TRICEPS

LATISSIMUS DORSII

ANCONEUS

EXTERNAL OBLIQUE

ILIAC CREST

LUMBAR FASCIA

ECU

GLUTEUS MEDIUS

PSIS

GREATER
TROCHANTER

GLUTEUS MAXIMUS

ILIOTIBIAL BAND

BICEPS FEMORIS

VASTUS LATERALIS

SEMITENDINOSUS

TENDON OF BICEPS
FEMORIS

LATERAL
GASTROCNEMIUS

MEDIAL
GASTROCNEMIUS

SOLEUS

ACHILLES
TENDON

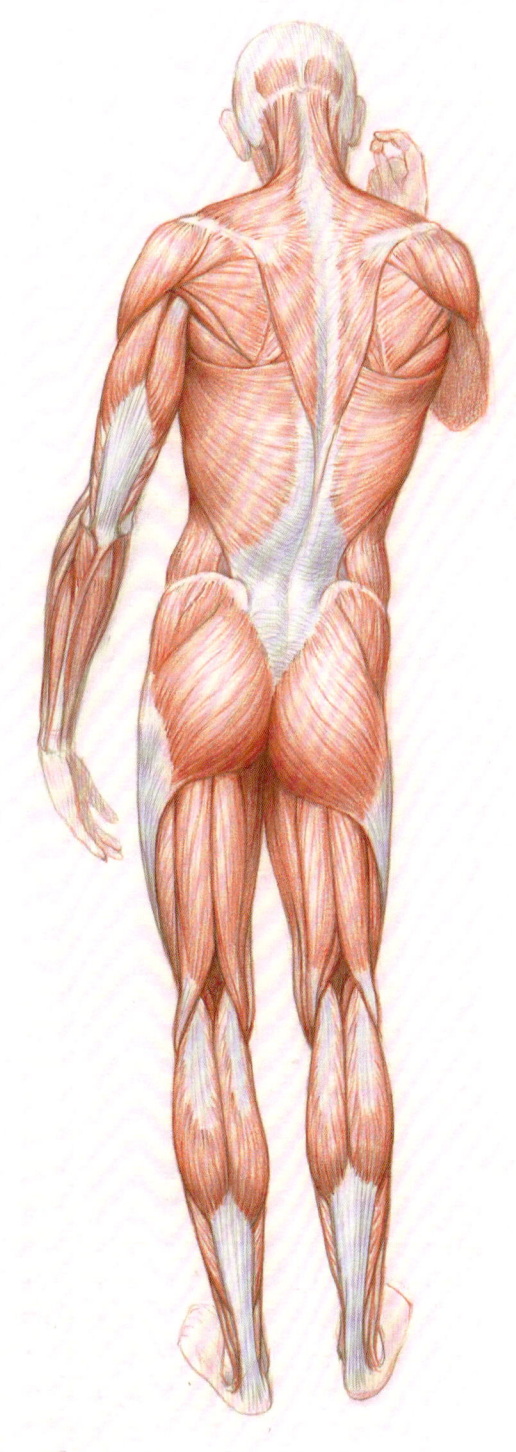

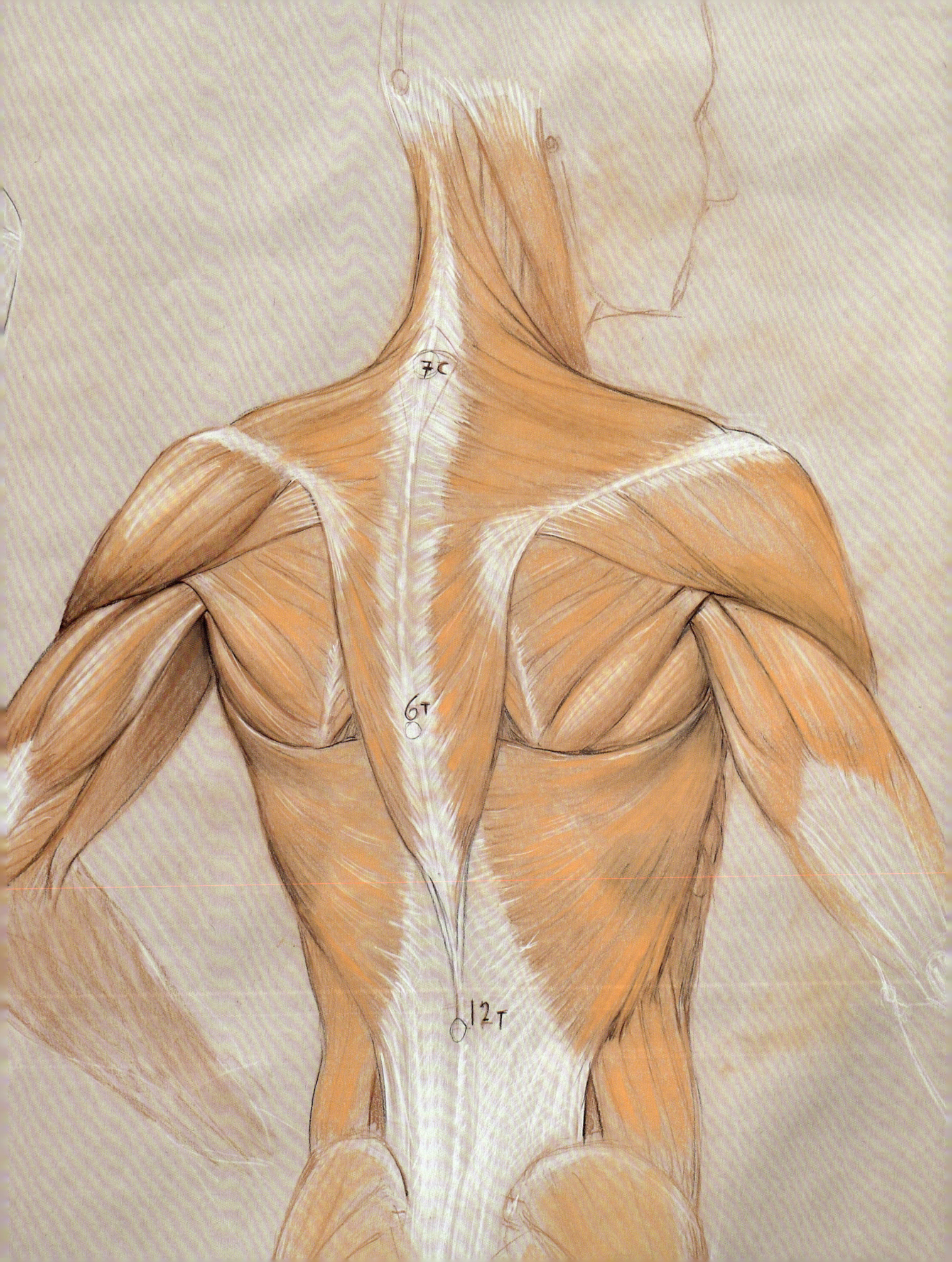

CHAPTER 4

USING LANDMARKS & PROPORTIONS IN FIGURE DRAWING

In the second chapter, you became acquainted with the structural and proportional characteristics of the body, and in chapter 3 you learned how to identify the human figure's soft and skeletal landmarks, muscles, and muscular–skeletal connections. Now we bring together these various ways of reading the figure and apply them to figure drawing.

OPPOSITE: This life-size, pastel-on-craft-paper drawing for a class demonstration shows a posterior view of the superficial muscles of the torso and arms.

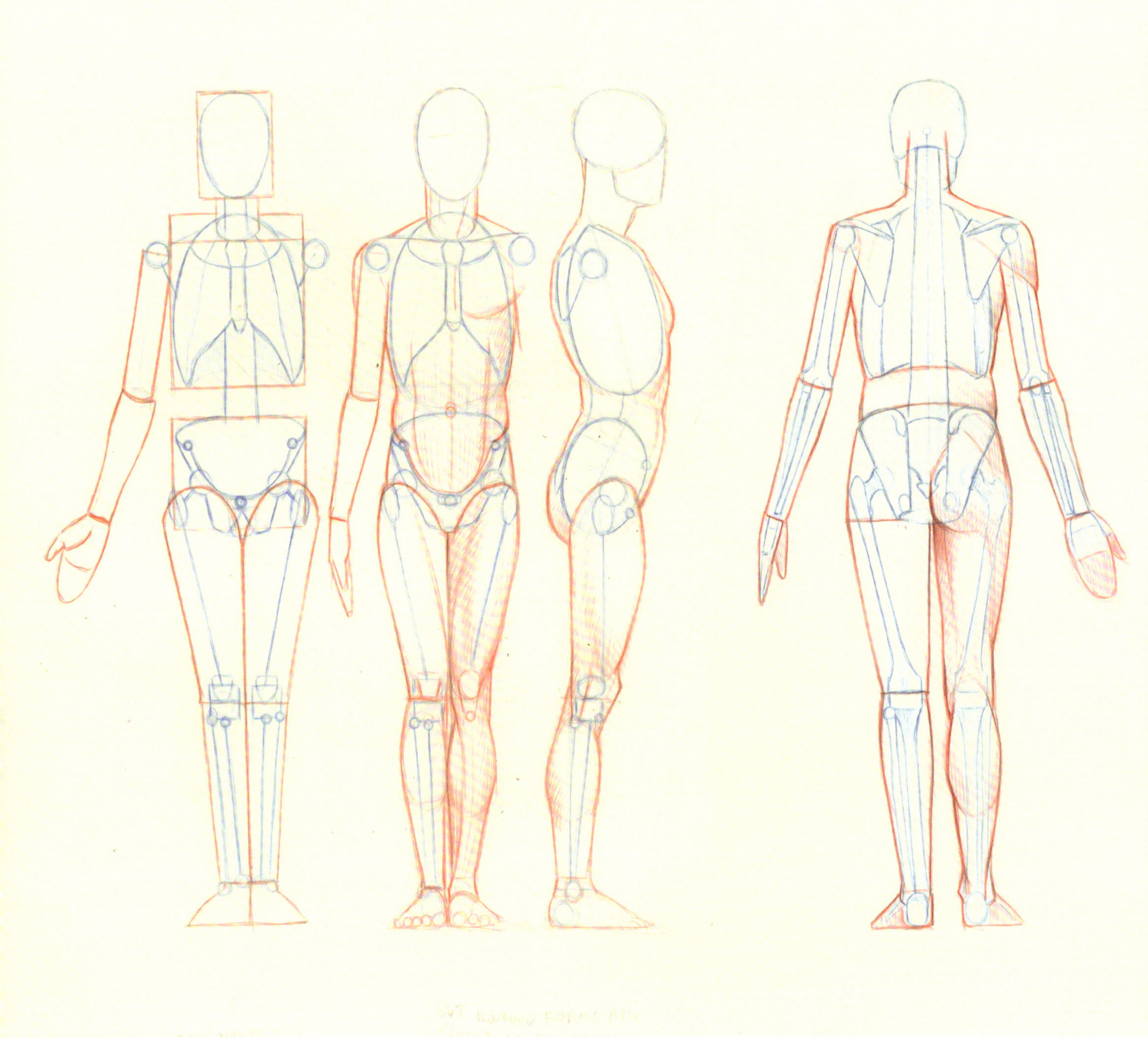

Drawing the figure more accurately

These reference charts show the stereometric volumes, proportional relationships, and landmarks of the male and female figures. Use the charts as references when creating essential renderings of the pose. The objective is to draw the figure more accurately, truly understanding it instead of just passively imitating it.

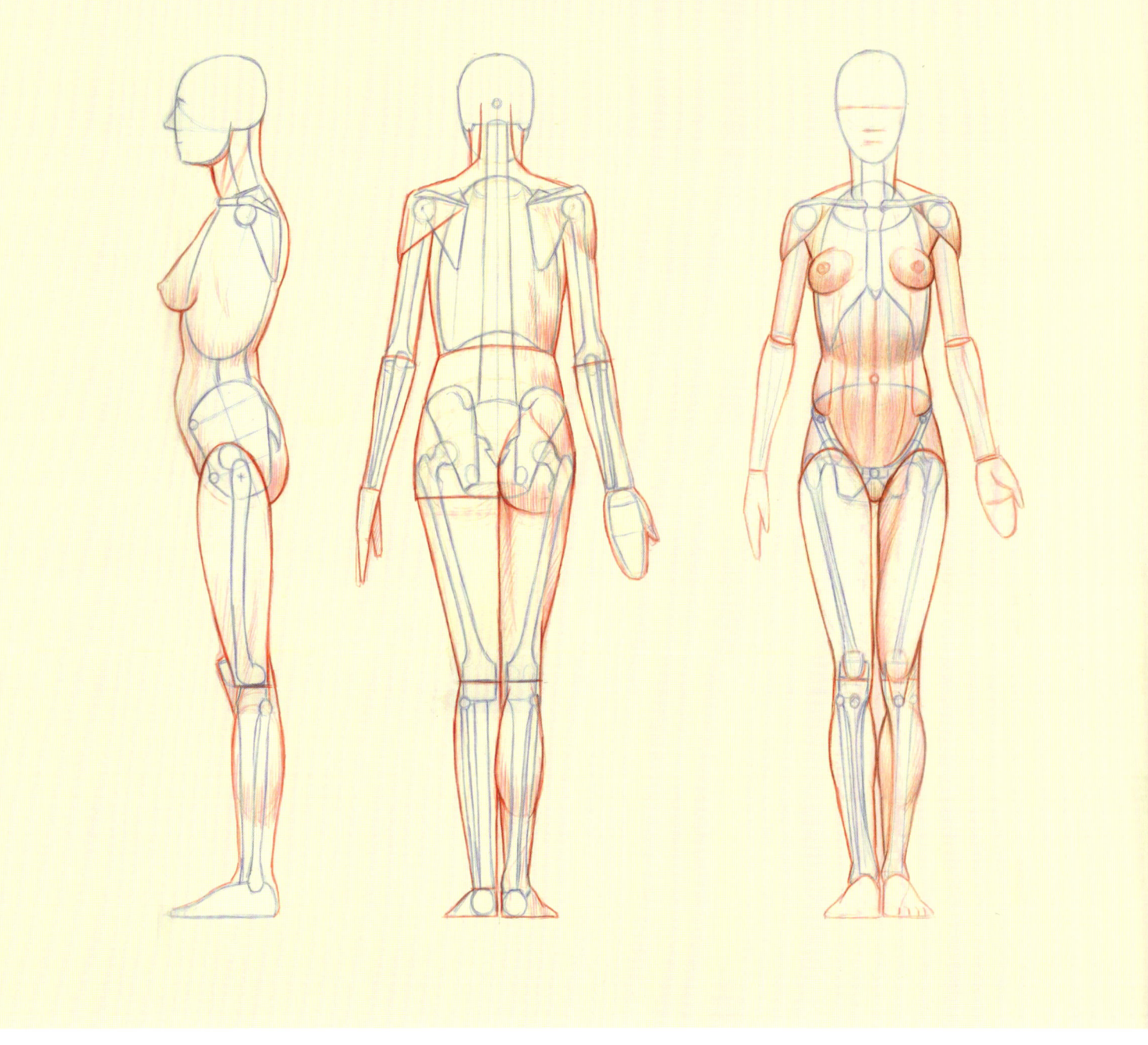

OPPOSITE: Main volumes, proportions, and landmarks of the male figure

The figure at left shows the correspondence between the stereometric rendering of the figure (in red) and the structural skeleton (in blue) that it contains. The other figures show how easy it is to quickly block in the main muscular volumes using the structural skeleton and landmarks.

ABOVE: Main volumes, proportions, and landmarks of the female figure

This chart describes the female proportions from front, side, and back views and provides an essential rendering of the muscular volumes.

USING SCHEMATIC SKELE-TONS AND STEREOMETRY

The human figure can be visualized in many ways depending on how we look at it or what aspects of the body we focus on. These three images introduce a method that focuses on the visualization of the landmarks, the proportions, and the external forms.

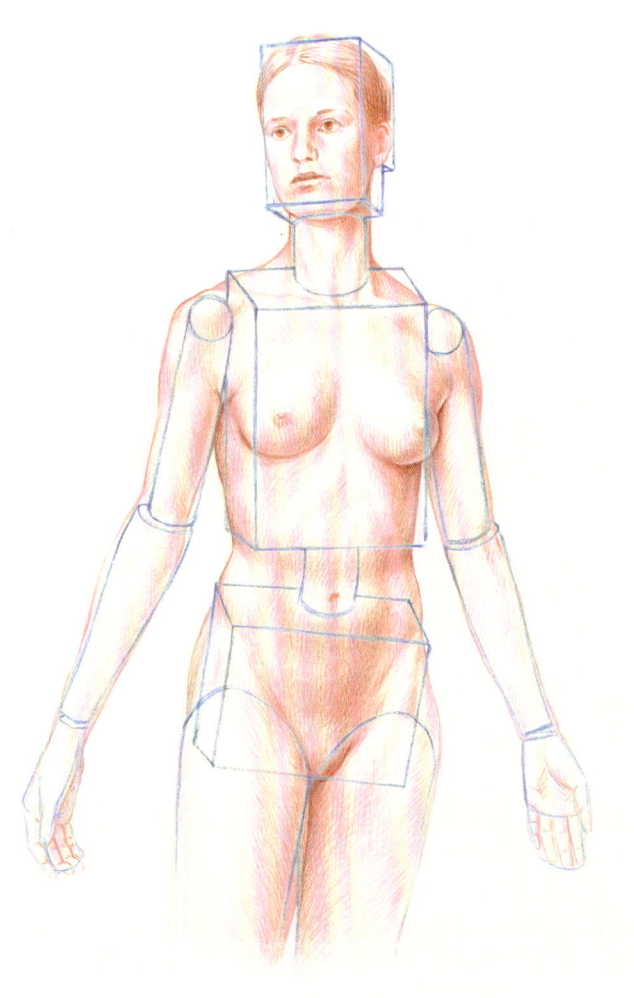

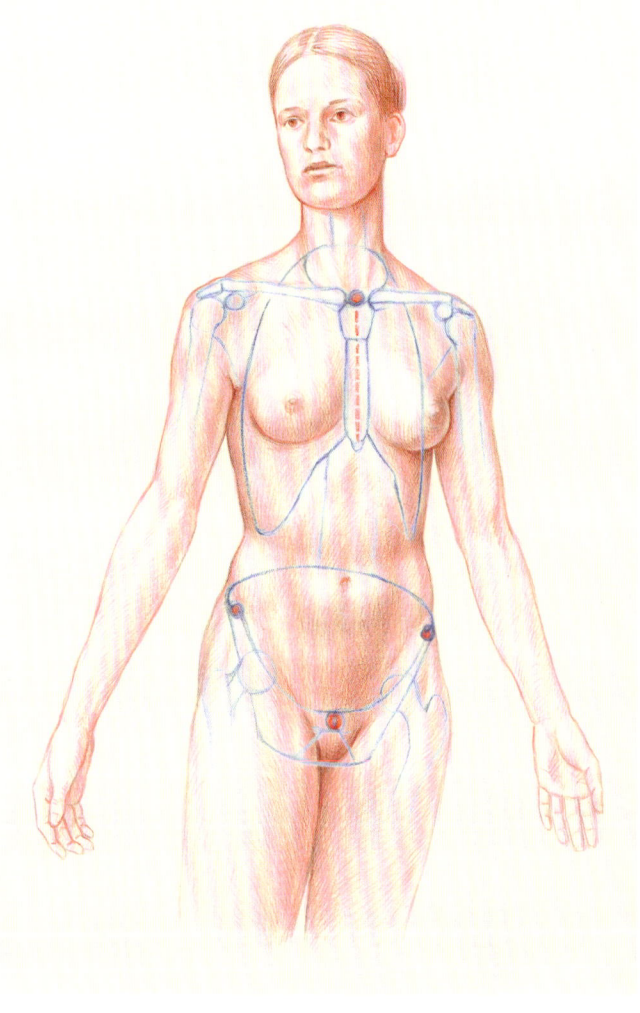

ABOVE LEFT: Stereometric volumes

Here, the stereometric volumes are sketched-in using a series of boxes.

ABOVE RIGHT: Schematic skeleton

Here, the skeleton of the torso is schematically visualized using the landmarks as anchor points.

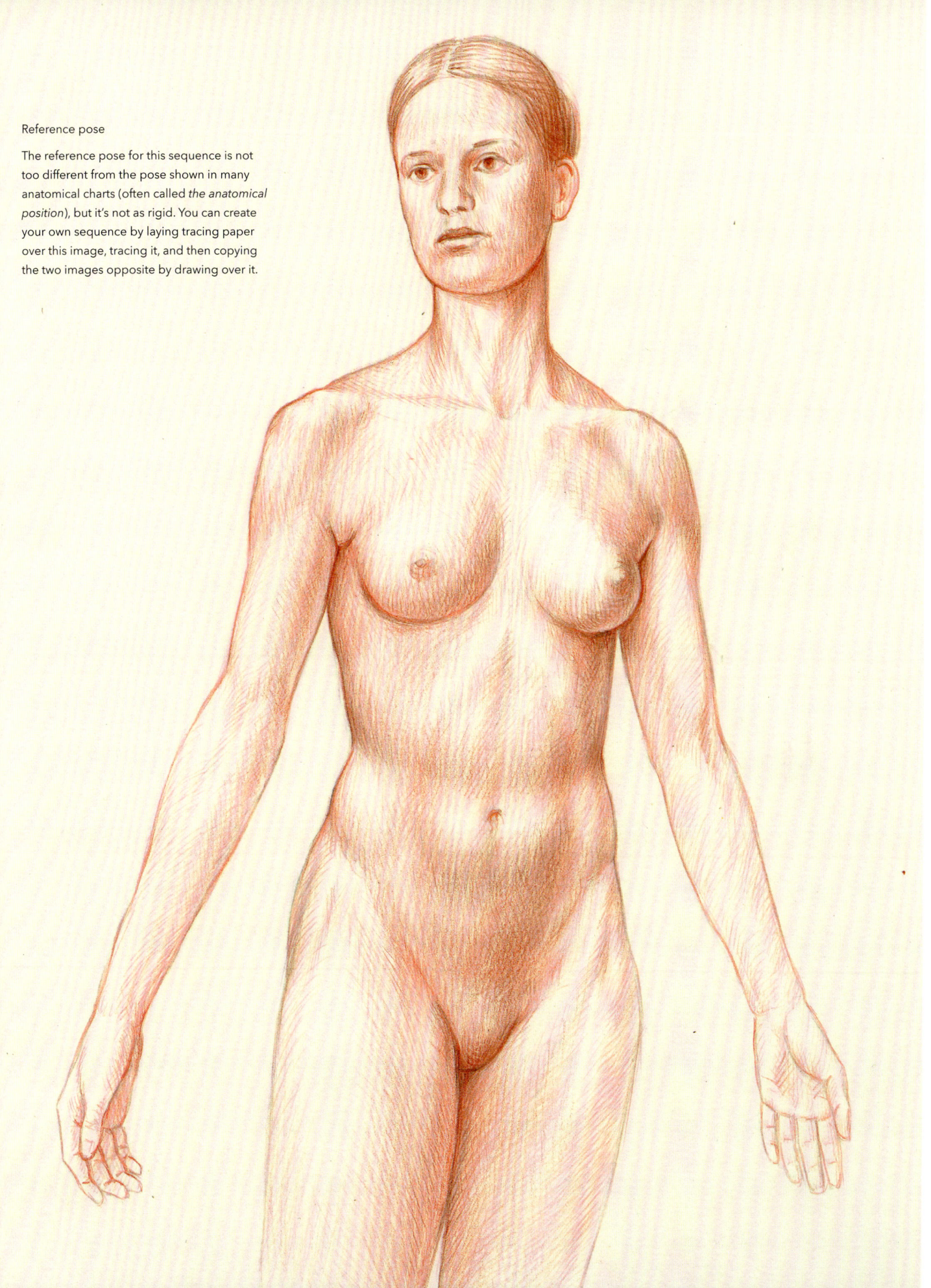

Reference pose

The reference pose for this sequence is not too different from the pose shown in many anatomical charts (often called *the anatomical position*), but it's not as rigid. You can create your own sequence by laying tracing paper over this image, tracing it, and then copying the two images opposite by drawing over it.

These images show how to employ these conceptualizations to study a pose or start a figure drawing.

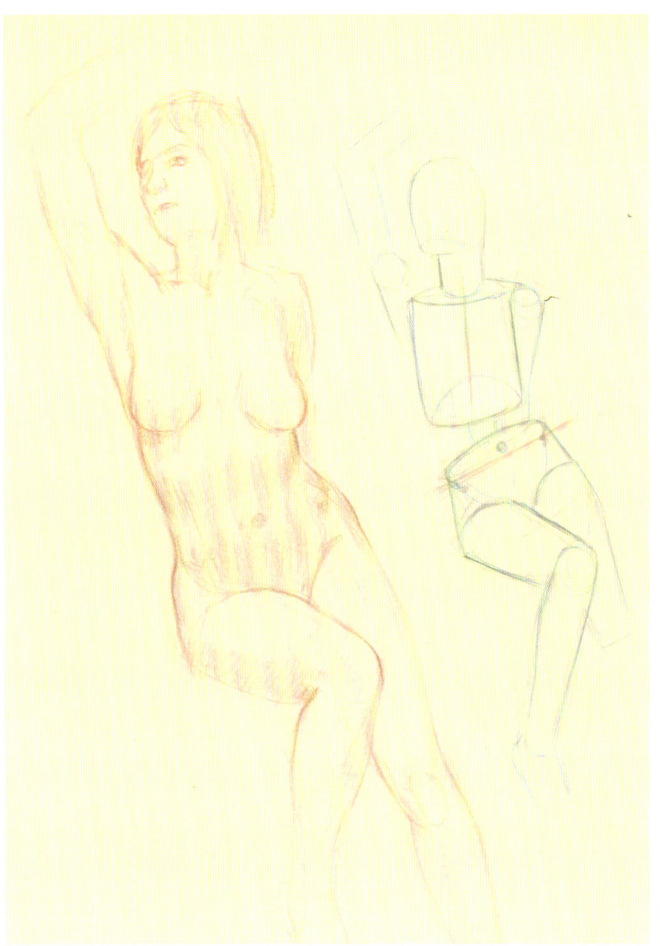

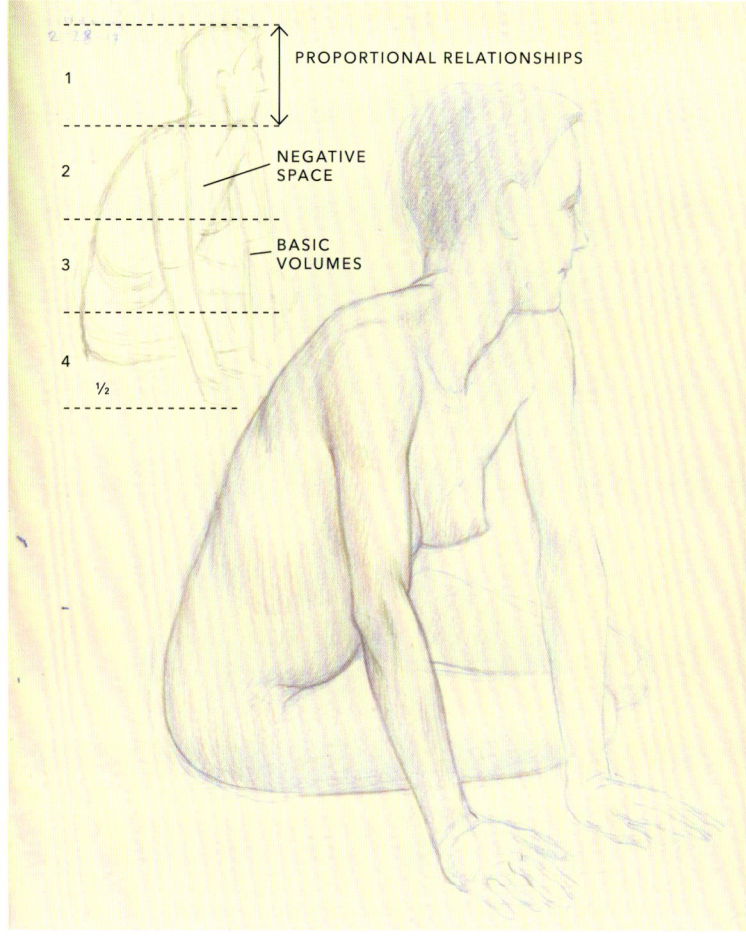

ABOVE LEFT: Using stereometry to study a pose, example 1

The pelvic tilt and the angle of the ribcage are revealed by the alignment of the iliac spines and the angle of the sternum.

ABOVE RIGHT: Using stereometry to study a pose, example 2

The visualization of the complex organic form as geometric volumes makes it much easier to appreciate the dimensions of the figure and pose.

OPPOSITE: Drawing a limb—from schematic to stereometric to organic

It is much easier to measure the length and width of a cylinder than of an actual arm. The sequence depicted in this image shows how to draw the forearm in a posterior-lateral view. Start with a quick, schematic drawing of the skeleton (A) to see where the main landmarks are and how they are oriented; then block-in the main volumes of upper arm and forearm (B); then start adding detail, subdividing the main forms in smaller muscle groups (C and D). The final image here is still semi-schematic, but it could be brought to completion by further refining the organic forms.

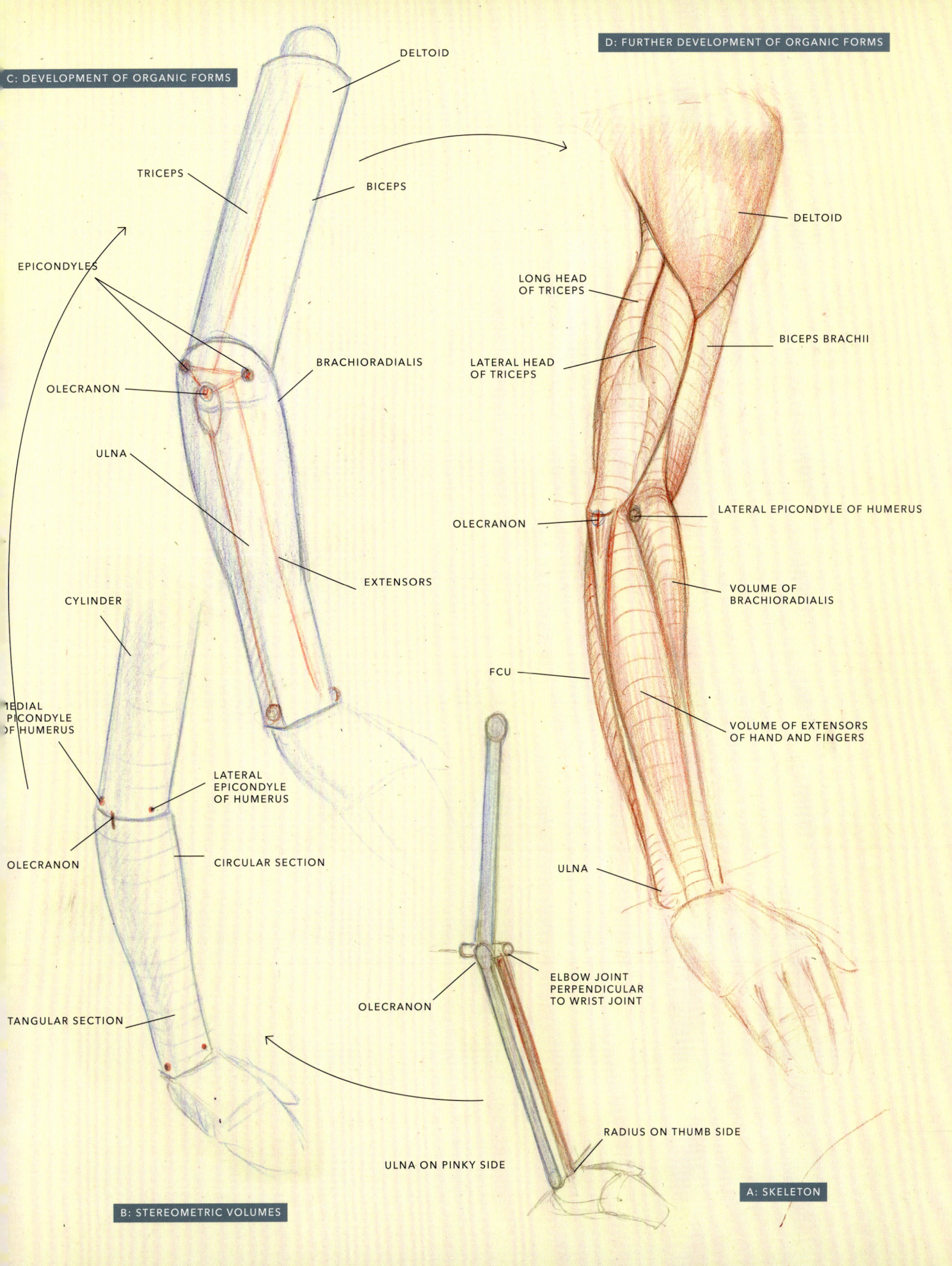

C: DEVELOPMENT OF ORGANIC FORMS

DELTOID

TRICEPS

BICEPS

EPICONDYLES

OLECRANON

BRACHIORADIALIS

ULNA

EXTENSORS

CYLINDER

MEDIAL EPICONDYLE OF HUMERUS

LATERAL EPICONDYLE OF HUMERUS

OLECRANON

CIRCULAR SECTION

TANGULAR SECTION

D: FURTHER DEVELOPMENT OF ORGANIC FORMS

DELTOID

LONG HEAD OF TRICEPS

LATERAL HEAD OF TRICEPS

BICEPS BRACHII

OLECRANON

LATERAL EPICONDYLE OF HUMERUS

VOLUME OF BRACHIORADIALIS

FCU

VOLUME OF EXTENSORS OF HAND AND FINGERS

ULNA

OLECRANON

ELBOW JOINT PERPENDICULAR TO WRIST JOINT

RADIUS ON THUMB SIDE

ULNA ON PINKY SIDE

B: STEREOMETRIC VOLUMES

A: SKELETON

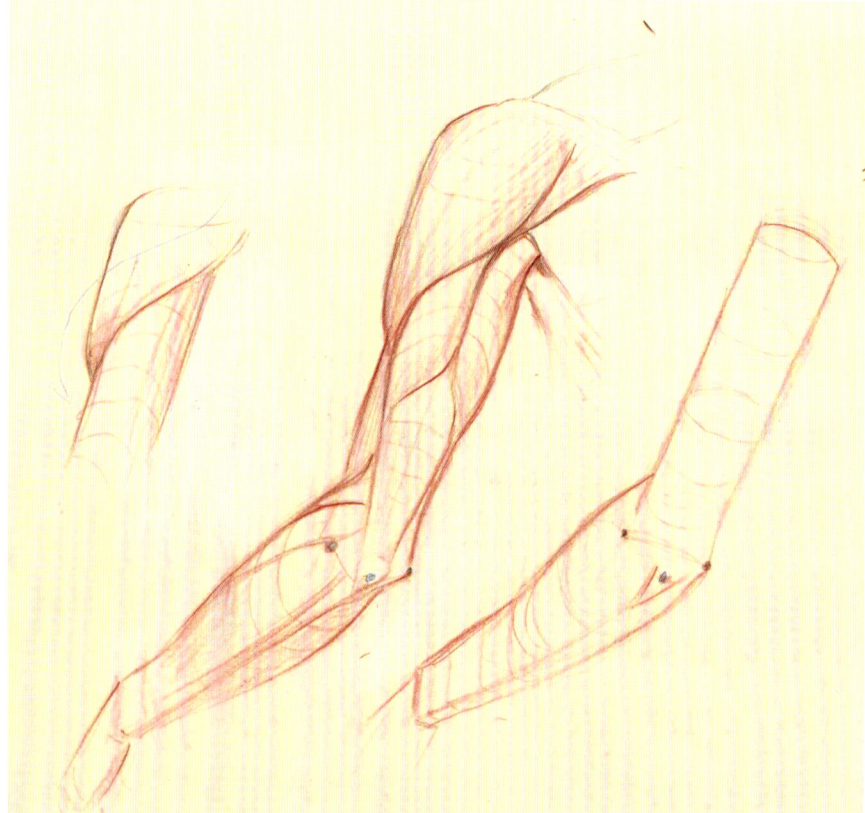

RIGHT: Considering overlapping volumes

The sequence here, which shows the arm from a different angle, emphasizes the importance of considering the three-dimensional effects of overlapping the various muscular volumes.

BELOW: Using stereometry when drawing foreshortened poses

Stereometric volumes are also very helpful when drawing a pose that is strongly foreshortened and has overlapping forms.

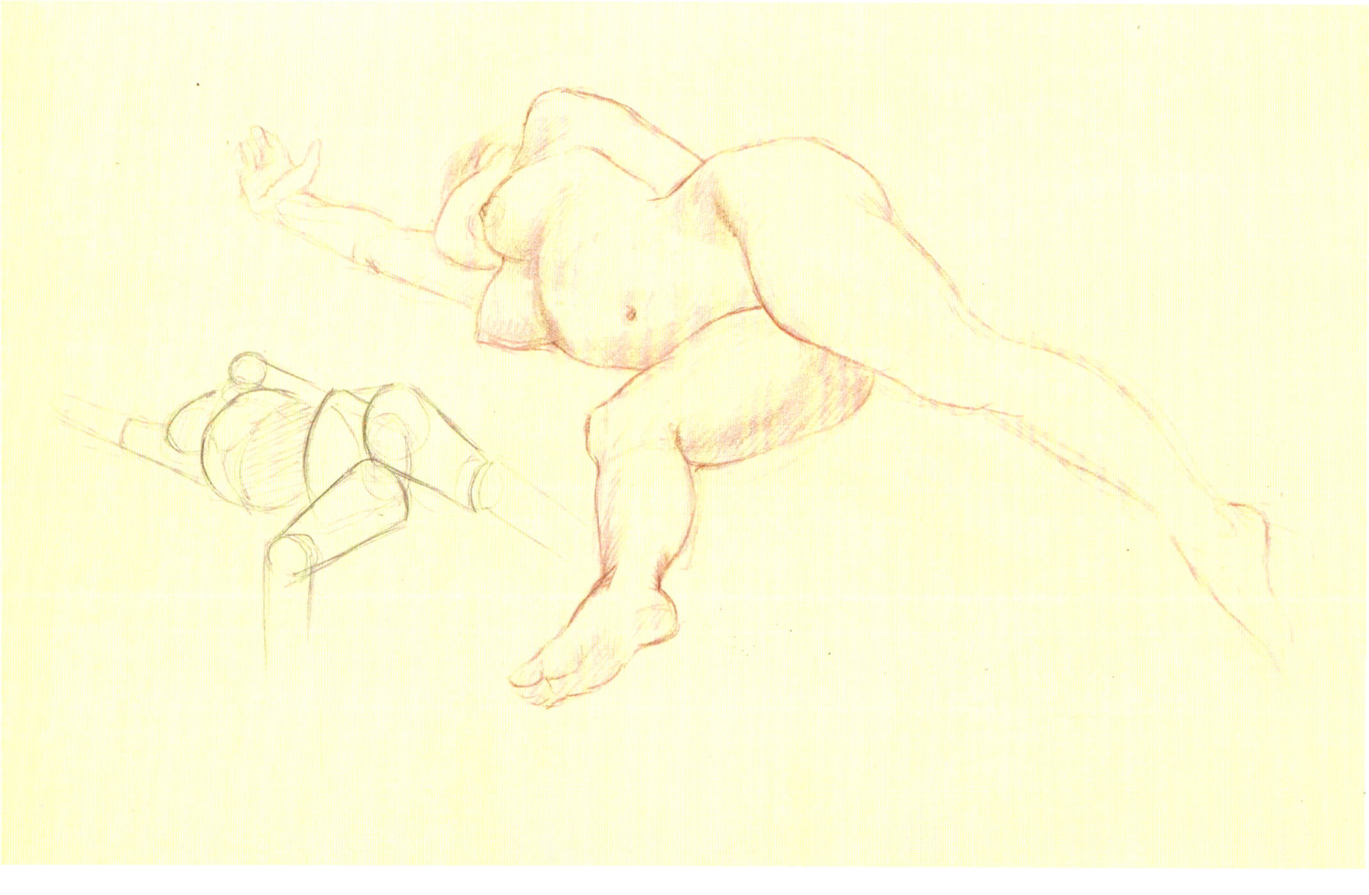

"READING" A FORESHORTENED POSE

Foreshortened poses are notoriously hard to draw. Part of the problem is that we tend not to consider the overlapping of the forms of the figure. Considering their three-dimensional characteristics when visualizing the forms of the body can help you imagine how they overlap.

This sequence visualizes the analytical process I used to "transform" an organic form into stereometric volumes. You can replicate these steps yourself.

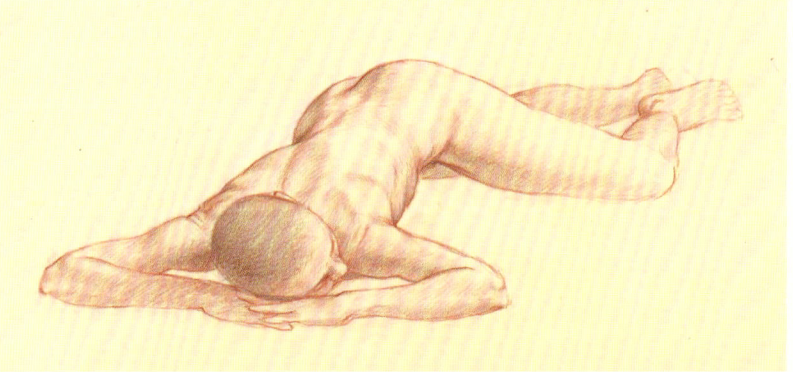

1

Pretend the drawing here is the model posing for you, and identify the positions of the joints and landmarks.

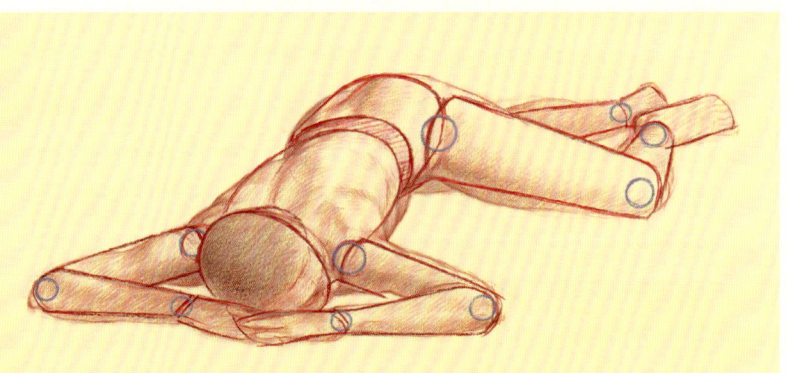

2

Once you've identified the joints, you have a better idea of the size and orientation of the various segments of the body. You can practice identifying the joints and volumes by drawing them on tracing paper layered over the image in the previous step.

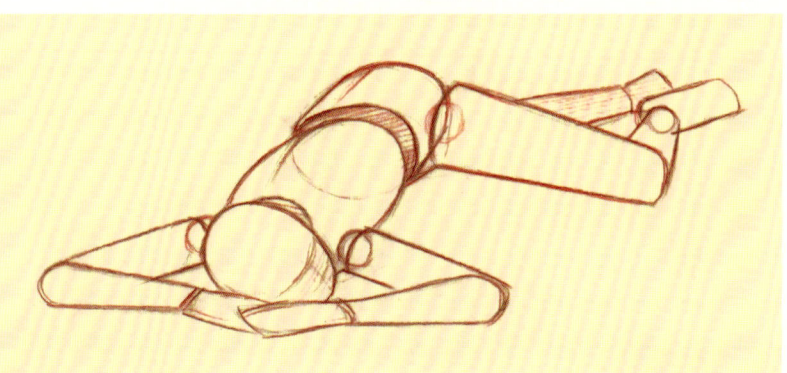

3

This image shows the result of the synthesis of the initial pose. Becase the forms of the body have been reduced to essential volumes, it is easier to appreciate how the volumes overlap in a foreshortened pose.

RECONSTRUCTING THE FIGURE FROM SKELETON TO MUSCLES

Extrapolate the skeleton from the landmarks

Now let's move toward a more organic and realistic rendering of the body, extrapolating the skeleton from the skeletal landmarks and then finding the muscular-skeletal connections. The images here are reference charts for positioning the main superficial muscular volumes over the skeleton. (You may also wish to consult the landmark and muscle charts in the previous chapter.)

RIGHT: Positioning the muscles over the skeleton, anterior view

OPPOSITE: Positioning the muscles over the skeleton, posterior view

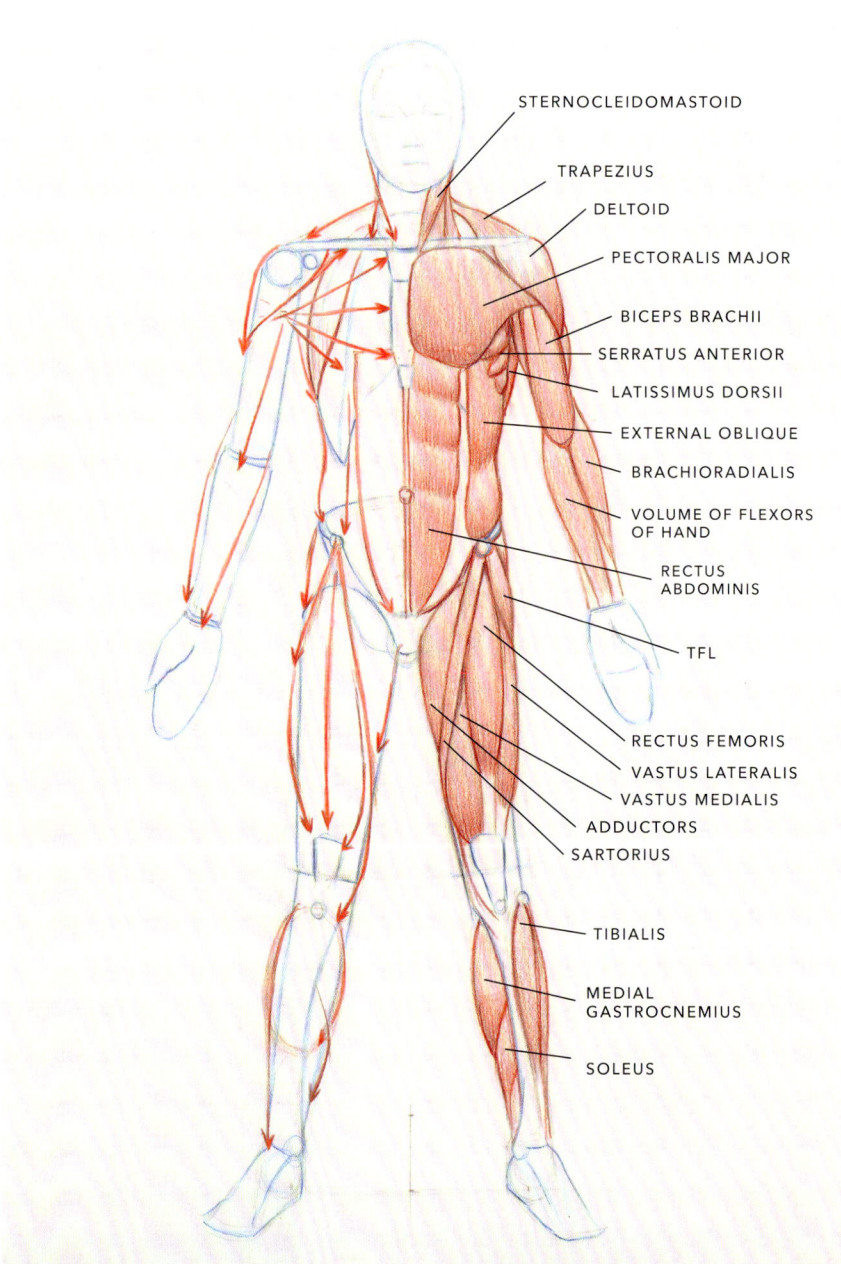

STERNOCLEIDOMASTOID

TRAPEZIUS

DELTOID

PECTORALIS MAJOR

BICEPS BRACHII

SERRATUS ANTERIOR

LATISSIMUS DORSII

EXTERNAL OBLIQUE

BRACHIORADIALIS

VOLUME OF FLEXORS OF HAND

RECTUS ABDOMINIS

TFL

RECTUS FEMORIS

VASTUS LATERALIS

VASTUS MEDIALIS

ADDUCTORS

SARTORIUS

TIBIALIS

MEDIAL GASTROCNEMIUS

SOLEUS

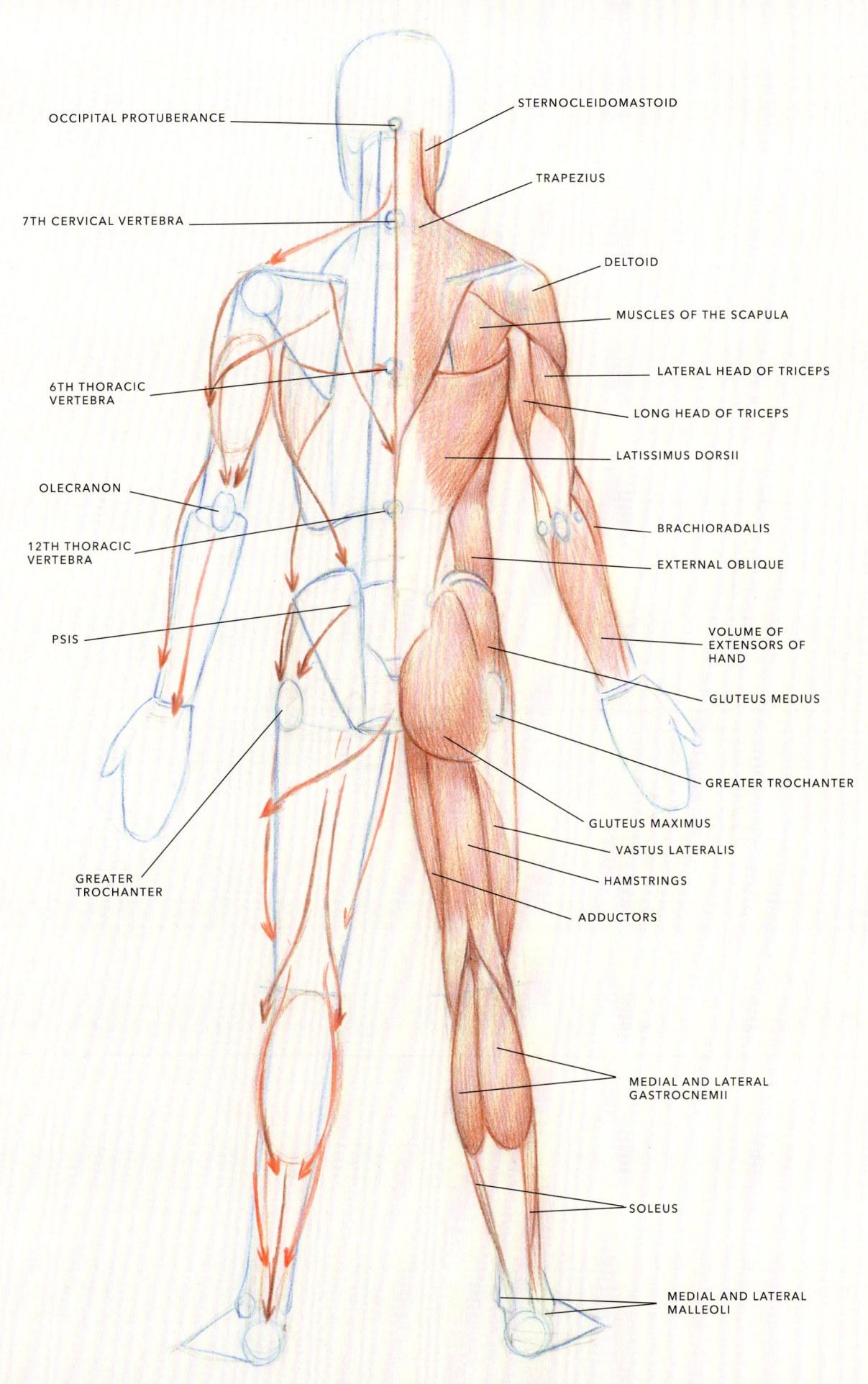

OCCIPITAL PROTUBERANCE

STERNOCLEIDOMASTOID

TRAPEZIUS

7TH CERVICAL VERTEBRA

DELTOID

MUSCLES OF THE SCAPULA

LATERAL HEAD OF TRICEPS

6TH THORACIC
VERTEBRA

LONG HEAD OF TRICEPS

LATISSIMUS DORSII

OLECRANON

BRACHIORADALIS

12TH THORACIC
VERTEBRA

EXTERNAL OBLIQUE

PSIS

VOLUME OF
EXTENSORS OF
HAND

GLUTEUS MEDIUS

GREATER TROCHANTER

GREATER
TROCHANTER

GLUTEUS MAXIMUS

VASTUS LATERALIS

HAMSTRINGS

ADDUCTORS

MEDIAL AND LATERAL
GASTROCNEMII

SOLEUS

MEDIAL AND LATERAL
MALLEOLI

Positioning the muscles over the skeleton, lateral view

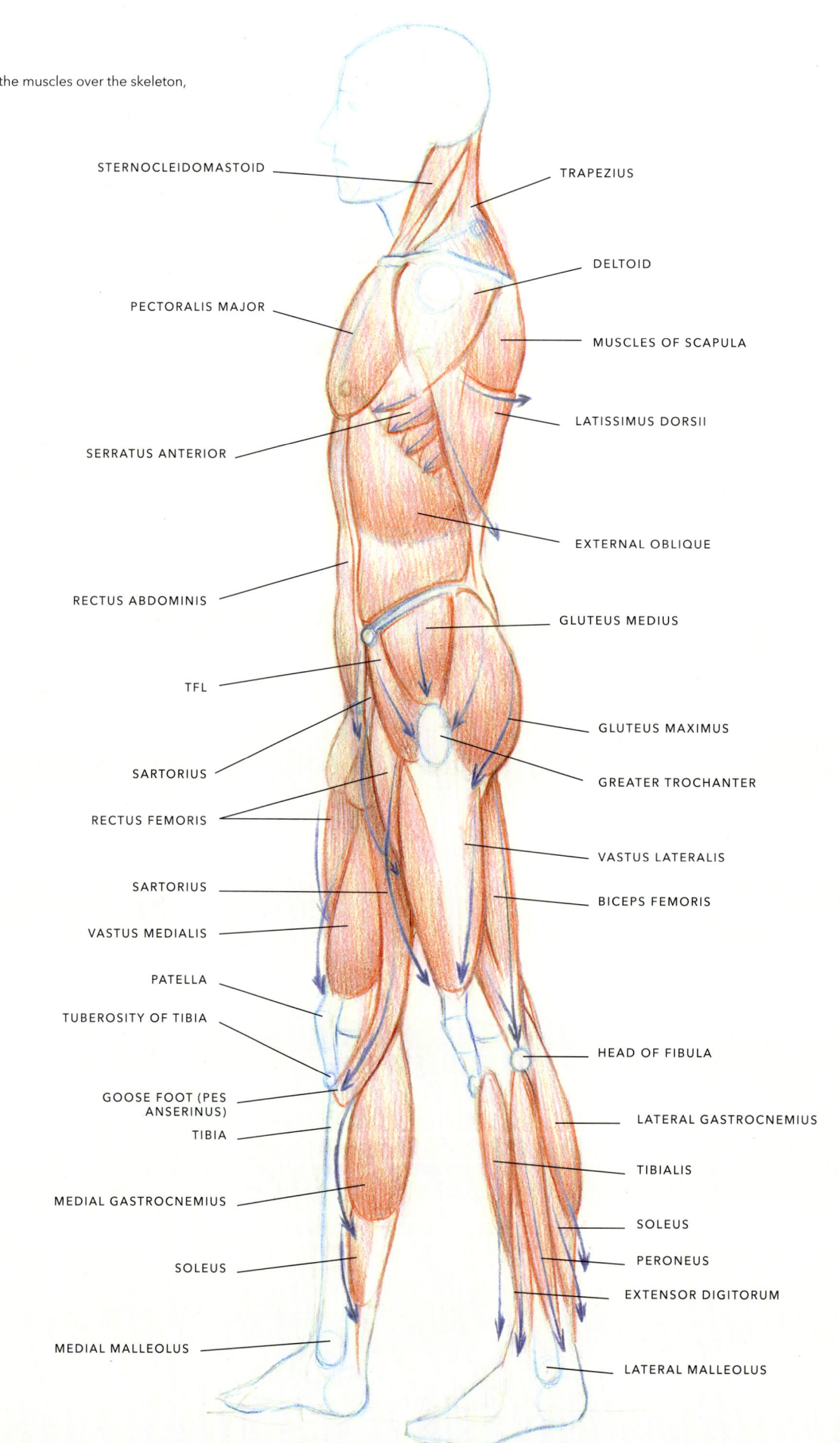

STERNOCLEIDOMASTOID

TRAPEZIUS

DELTOID

PECTORALIS MAJOR

MUSCLES OF SCAPULA

LATISSIMUS DORSII

SERRATUS ANTERIOR

EXTERNAL OBLIQUE

RECTUS ABDOMINIS

GLUTEUS MEDIUS

TFL

GLUTEUS MAXIMUS

SARTORIUS

GREATER TROCHANTER

RECTUS FEMORIS

VASTUS LATERALIS

SARTORIUS

BICEPS FEMORIS

VASTUS MEDIALIS

PATELLA

TUBEROSITY OF TIBIA

HEAD OF FIBULA

GOOSE FOOT (PES ANSERINUS)

LATERAL GASTROCNEMIUS

TIBIA

TIBIALIS

MEDIAL GASTROCNEMIUS

SOLEUS

PERONEUS

SOLEUS

EXTENSOR DIGITORUM

MEDIAL MALLEOLUS

LATERAL MALLEOLUS

The next groups of images show how to identify the skeletal landmarks in a pose and then visualize the skeleton beneath. Using an anatomically accurate figure drawing, you can locate the skeletal landmarks that appear on the surface of the figure and reconstruct the skeleton starting from those clues.

BELOW: Reconstructing the skeleton, front view

The skeletal and soft landmarks indicated in the image on the left are used to reconstruct the skeleton in the image on the right. You can practice reconstructing the skeleton by laying tracing paper over the right-hand image, tracing it, and then using the image at right as a reference. Note how the skeleton can be rendered either very structurally or more realistically.

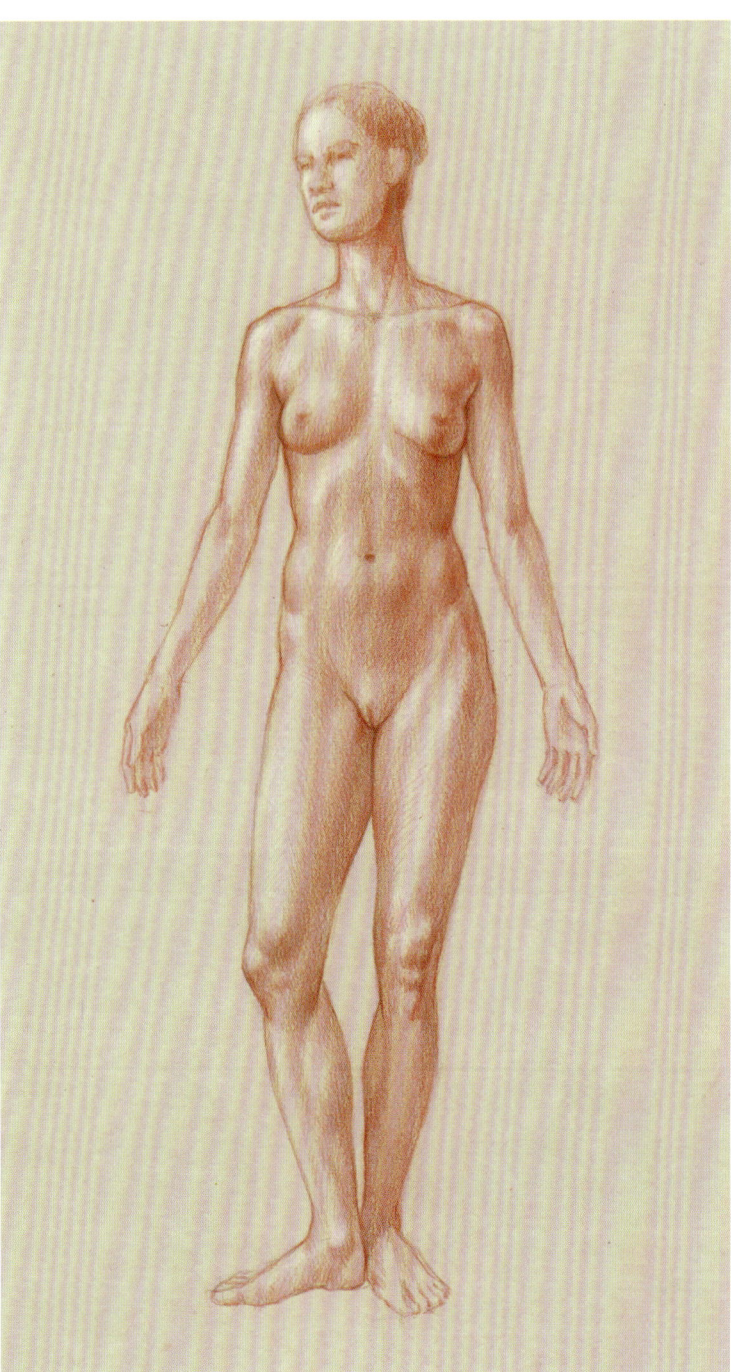

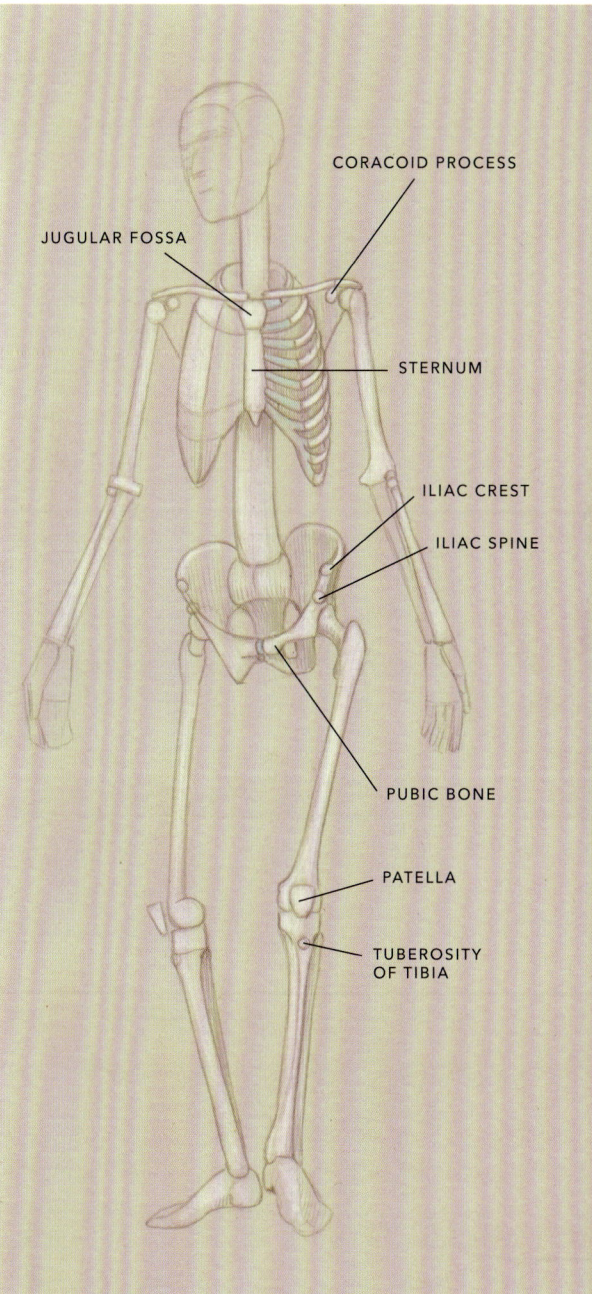

CORACOID PROCESS

JUGULAR FOSSA

STERNUM

ILIAC CREST

ILIAC SPINE

PUBIC BONE

PATELLA

TUBEROSITY OF TIBIA

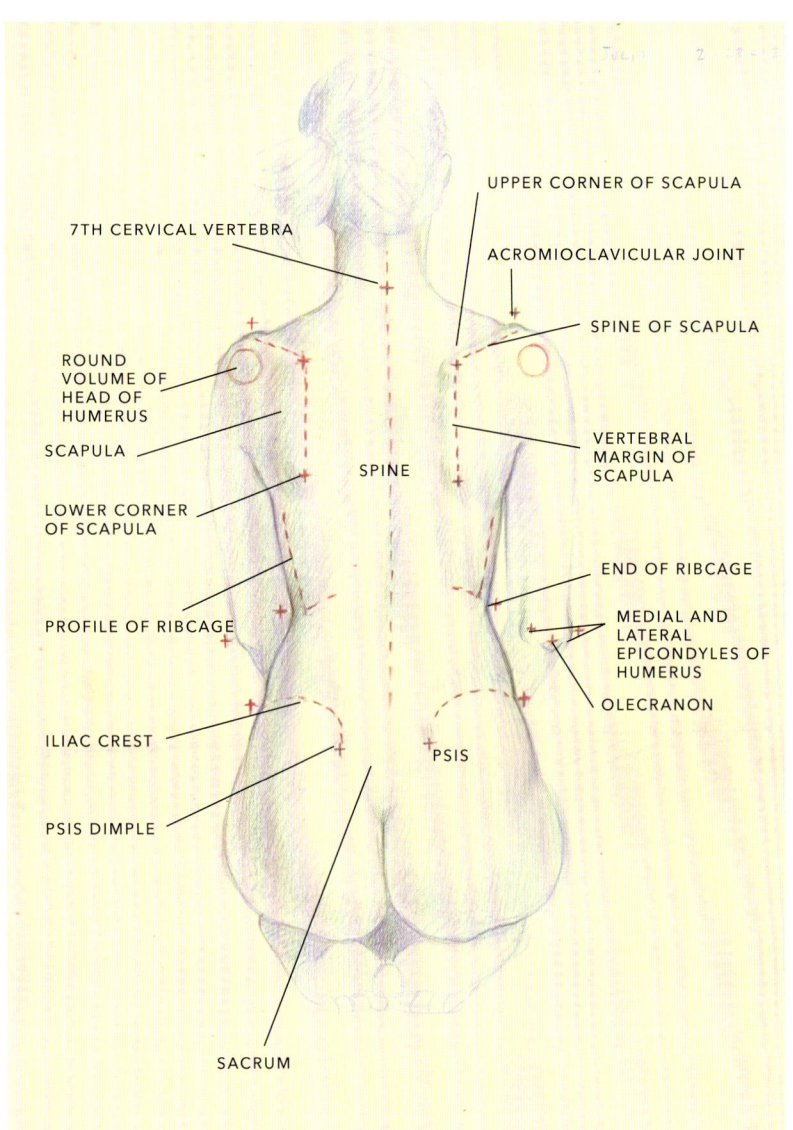

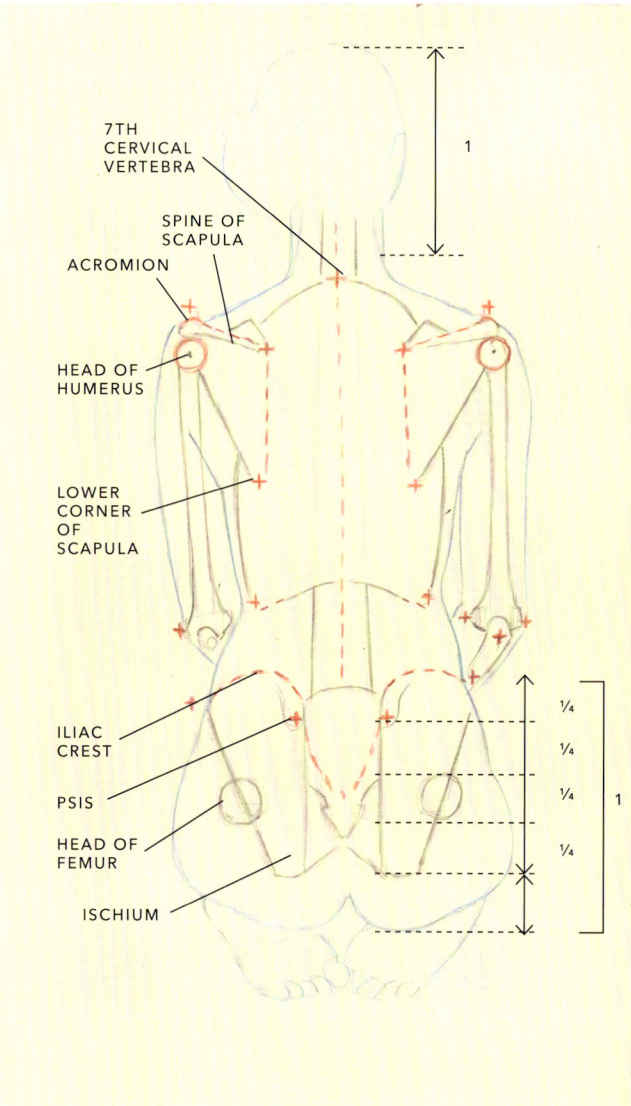

ABOVE LEFT: Reconstructing the ribcage and pelvis, back view

In the figure drawing at left, note that the 7th cervical vertebra shows like a little bump at the base of the neck, and each posterior superior iliac spine (PSIS) shows like a little dimple at the end of the curve of the iliac crest.

ABOVE RIGHT: As you can see in the drawing at right, the height of the pelvis is about the same as the height of the head. (Start measuring from the top of the iliac crest, and remember that at the bottom of the pelvis you have to allow for the volume of muscles, fat, and skin.)

A CONTEMPORARY MASTER
OF RENAISSANCE TECHNIQUE

The work of Scott Noel shows how today's figurative artists still use the Renaissance method, as described by Leon Battista Alberti, of layering muscles over the skeleton (and eventually skin and clothing over the muscles).

BELOW: Scott Noel, *Jon, Flesh over Skeleton*, 2008, pastel, 30 × 22 inches (76.20 × 55.88 cm). Courtesy of the artist.

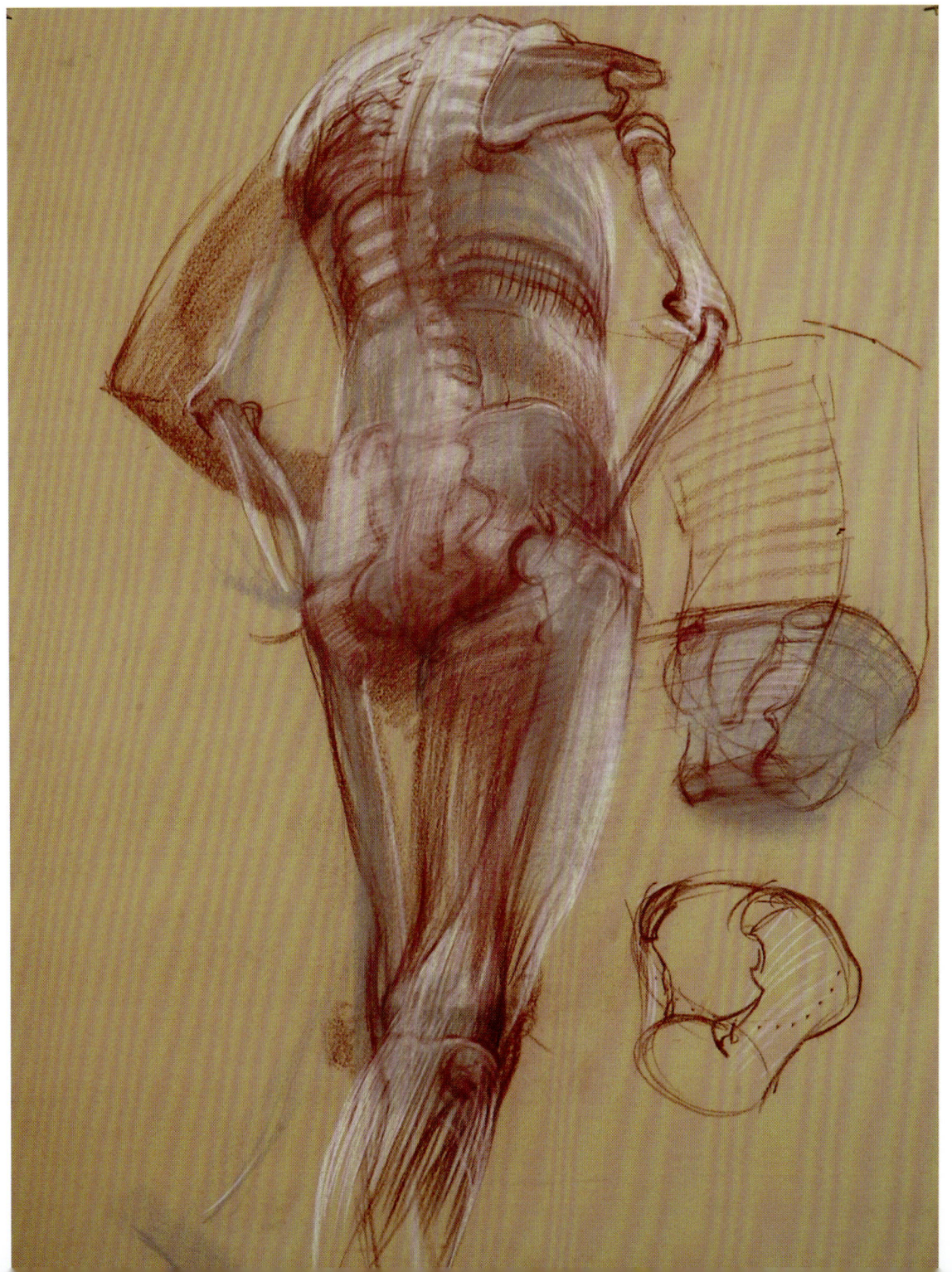

This sequence shows how to identify the skeletal landmarks visible on the figure from the lateral, or side, view and how to use them to reconstruct the skeleton and position the muscles.

OPPOSITE: Positioning the muscles of the torso, lateral view

Once the skeleton has been visualized, the muscles can be layered over it.

EXTRAPOLATING THE SKELETON AND POSITIONING THE MUSCLES

In this section, I first show how to extrapolate the skeleton from the model. Then I complete the "reverse dissection," showing how to position the muscles over the extrapolated skeleton.

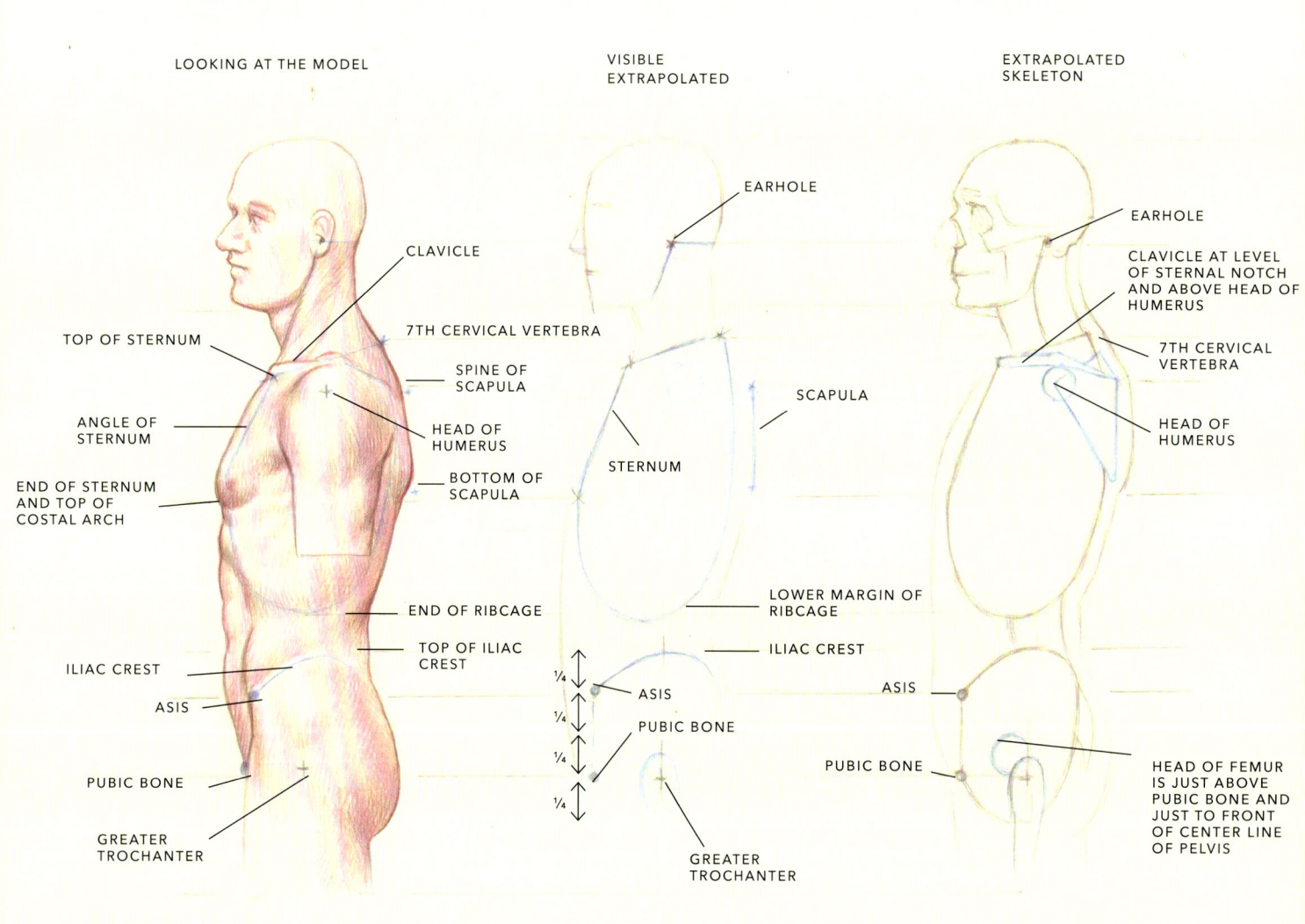

LOOKING AT THE MODEL

VISIBLE EXTRAPOLATED

EXTRAPOLATED SKELETON

CLAVICLE

TOP OF STERNUM

7TH CERVICAL VERTEBRA

SPINE OF SCAPULA

ANGLE OF STERNUM

HEAD OF HUMERUS

END OF STERNUM AND TOP OF COSTAL ARCH

BOTTOM OF SCAPULA

END OF RIBCAGE

TOP OF ILIAC CREST

ILIAC CREST

ASIS

PUBIC BONE

GREATER TROCHANTER

EARHOLE

SCAPULA

STERNUM

LOWER MARGIN OF RIBCAGE

ILIAC CREST

¼

¼

ASIS

¼

PUBIC BONE

¼

GREATER TROCHANTER

EARHOLE

CLAVICLE AT LEVEL OF STERNAL NOTCH AND ABOVE HEAD OF HUMERUS

7TH CERVICAL VERTEBRA

HEAD OF HUMERUS

ASIS

PUBIC BONE

HEAD OF FEMUR IS JUST ABOVE PUBIC BONE AND JUST TO FRONT OF CENTER LINE OF PELVIS

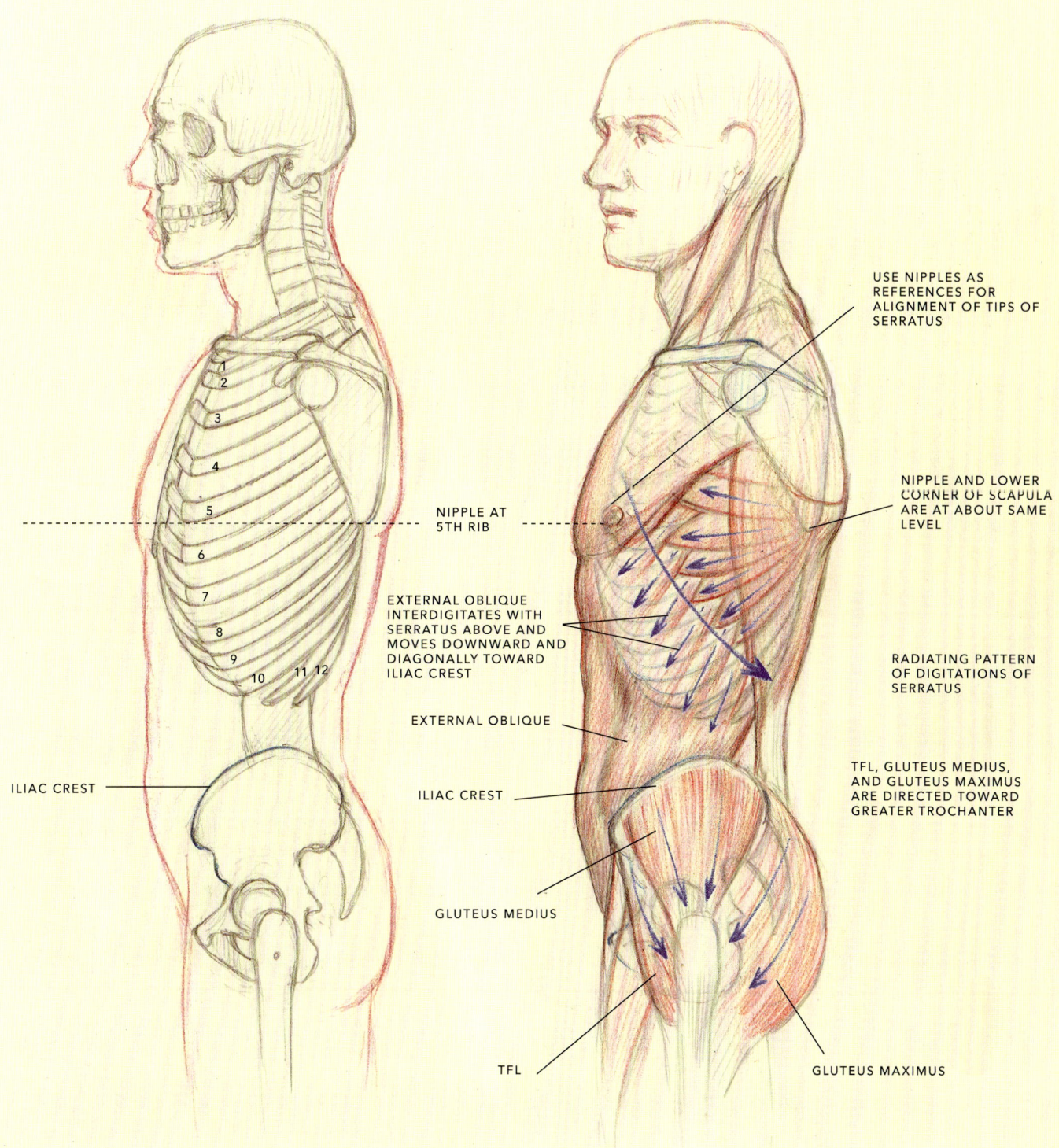

1
2
3
4
5
6
7
8
9
10   11 12

NIPPLE AT
5TH RIB

ILIAC CREST

USE NIPPLES AS
REFERENCES FOR
ALIGNMENT OF TIPS OF
SERRATUS

NIPPLE AND LOWER
CORNER OF SCAPULA
ARE AT ABOUT SAME
LEVEL

EXTERNAL OBLIQUE
INTERDIGITATES WITH
SERRATUS ABOVE AND
MOVES DOWNWARD AND
DIAGONALLY TOWARD
ILIAC CREST

RADIATING PATTERN
OF DIGITATIONS OF
SERRATUS

EXTERNAL OBLIQUE

ILIAC CREST

TFL, GLUTEUS MEDIUS,
AND GLUTEUS MAXIMUS
ARE DIRECTED TOWARD
GREATER TROCHANTER

GLUTEUS MEDIUS

TFL

GLUTEUS MAXIMUS

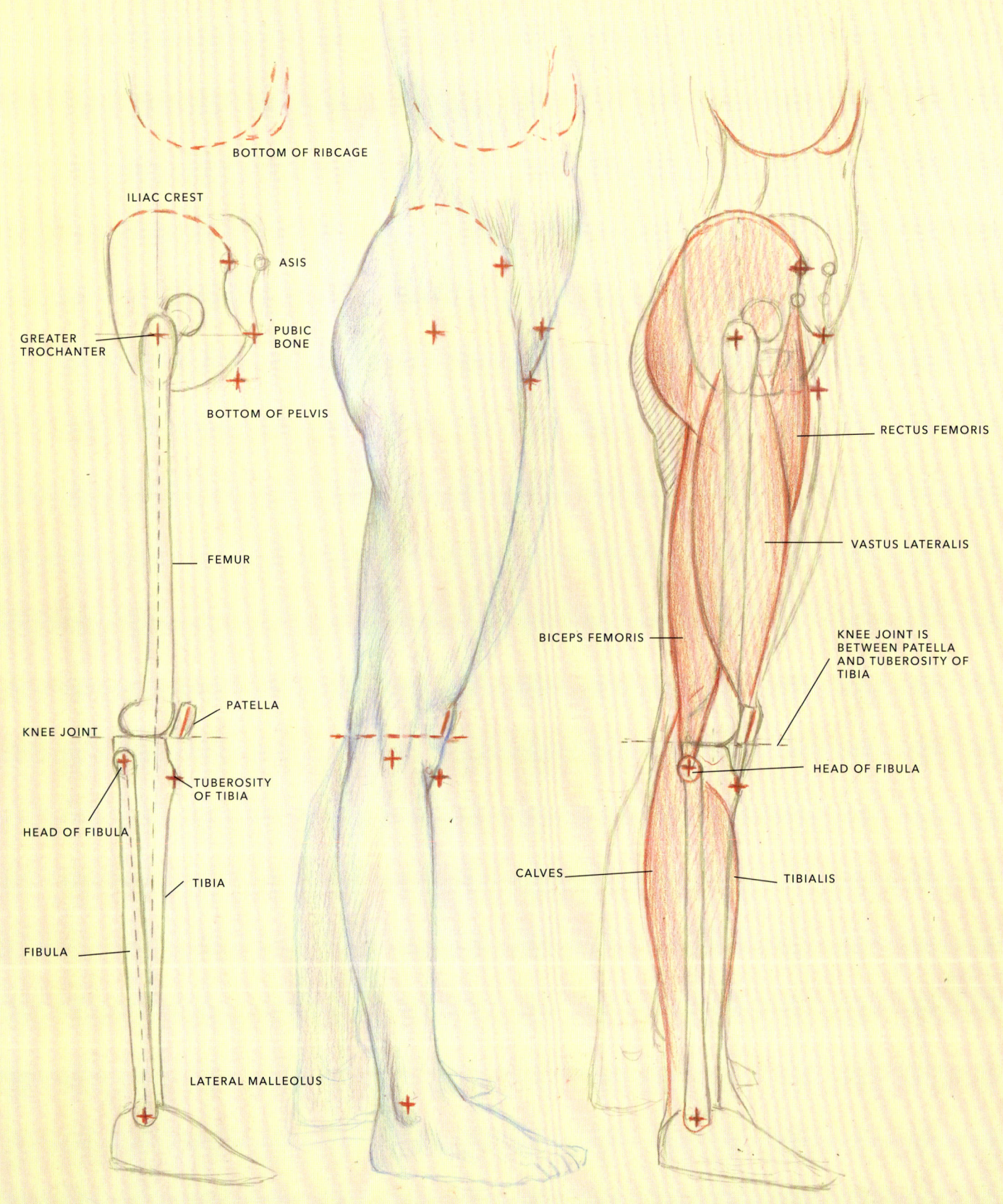

BOTTOM OF RIBCAGE

ILIAC CREST

ASIS

GREATER
TROCHANTER

PUBIC
BONE

BOTTOM OF PELVIS

RECTUS FEMORIS

FEMUR

VASTUS LATERALIS

PATELLA

KNEE JOINT

BICEPS FEMORIS

KNEE JOINT IS
BETWEEN PATELLA
AND TUBEROSITY OF
TIBIA

TUBEROSITY
OF TIBIA

HEAD OF FIBULA

HEAD OF FIBULA

TIBIA

CALVES

TIBIALIS

FIBULA

LATERAL MALLEOLUS

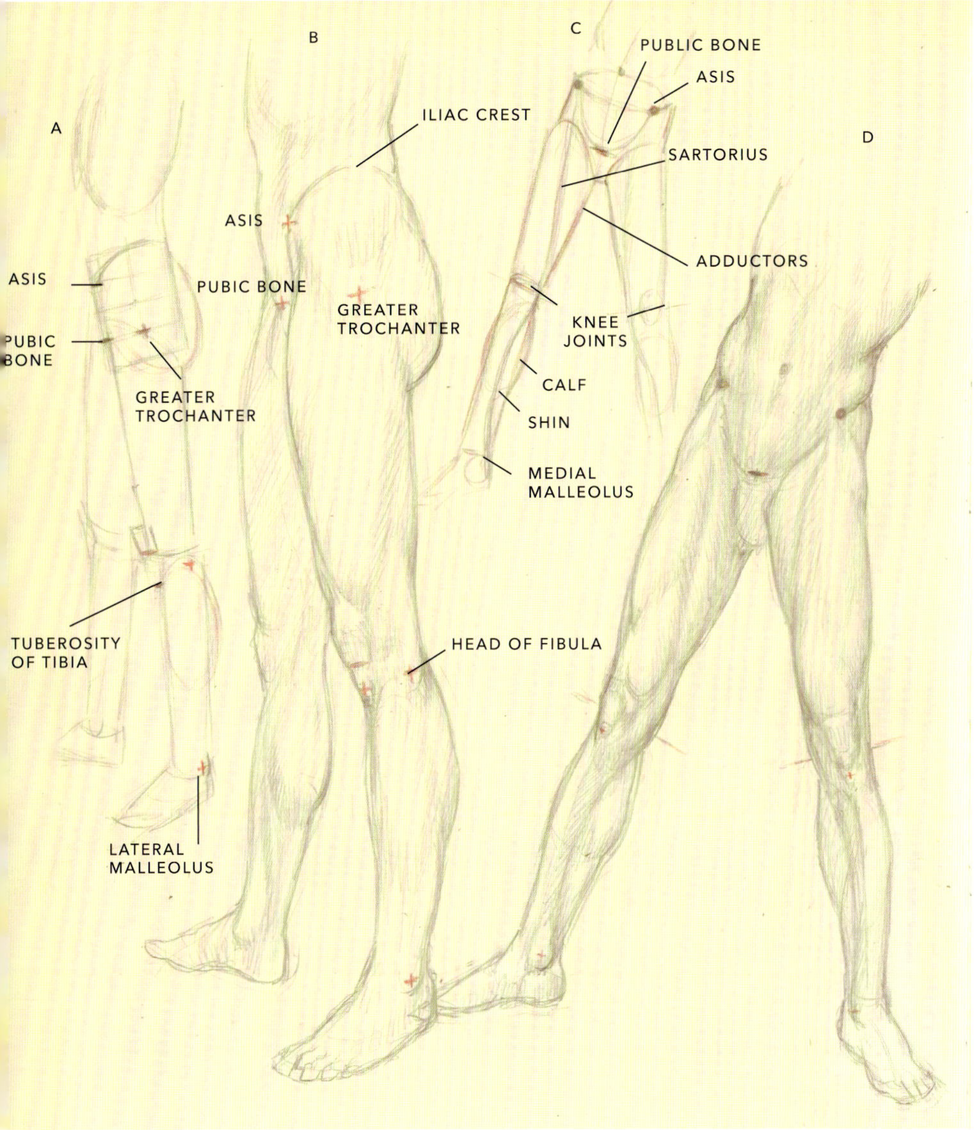

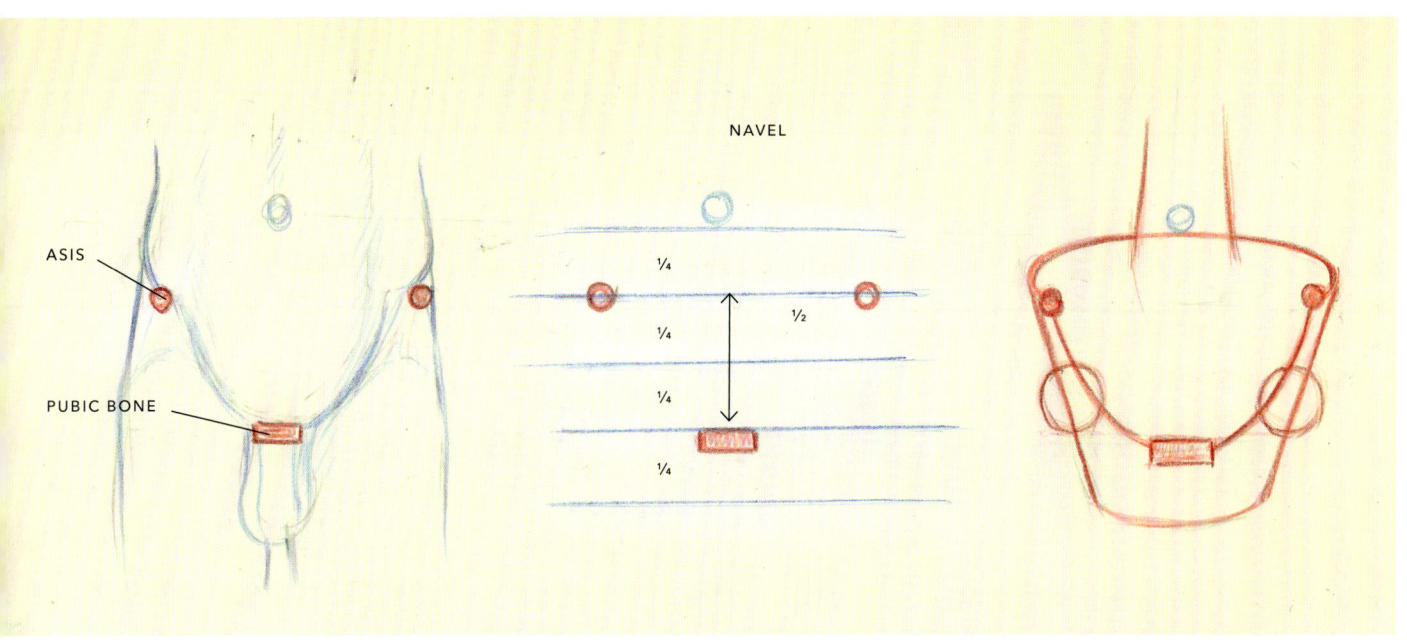

A B C D

PUBLIC BONE
ASIS
ILIAC CREST
SARTORIUS
ASIS
PUBIC BONE
ADDUCTORS
GREATER TROCHANTER
KNEE JOINTS
ASIS
PUBIC BONE
CALF
GREATER TROCHANTER
SHIN
MEDIAL MALLEOLUS
TUBEROSITY OF TIBIA
HEAD OF FIBULA
LATERAL MALLEOLUS

OPPOSITE: Reconstructing the skeleton and muscles of the pelvis and leg using the landmarks, lateral view

Imagine that the central drawing here is the model posing and that you have to extrapolate the skeleton and the muscles from the surface forms. To do so, find the landmarks (red dots and dotted lines) and use them to re-create an essential rendering of the skeleton (left). Then complete the analysis of the pose by adding the muscular forms. (You can use the chart "Positioning the muscles over the skeleton, lateral view," page 136, as a reference.)

LEFT: Using the landmarks and basic volumes to draw the legs

Starting from a stereometric rendering of the volumes of the leg and locating the main landmarks (A and C) is of great help in capturing the pose, the angles of the volumes of the body, and the proportional relationships. With the next step, the organic forms are developed (B and D).

BELOW: Extrapolating the pelvis

The size and position of the pelvis can be extrapolated using the anterior superior iliac spines (ASIS's) and the pubic bone. The height of the pelvis is about the same as the height of the head. The space between the iliac spines and the pubic bone is about one-half the measure of the head. The top and the bottom of the pelvis can be visualized by adding a measure of one-quarter of one head above the pubic bone and below the iliac spines.

ASIS
PUBIC BONE

NAVEL
¼
¼
½
¼
¼

FROM SKELETON TO MUSCLES TO EXTERNAL FORMS

You can understand the human figure more completely by employing various methods of analysis. You can start from the external forms and gradually "dissect" your way to the skeleton, as described by the images on pages 140–143, which showed the external forms of the figure and the extrapolation of the skeleton, or you can use the "additive" approach described in this sequence. In this analysis, you start from a visualization of the skeleton and gradually add muscles and external forms.

1

The sequence starts from the skeleton; some of the main muscular volumes are indicated as arrows connecting segments of the skeleton.

2

This image visualizes the superficial muscles, which can be used to identify the muscular volumes perceived under the skin in the next image.

3

Here is the finished figure, showing the surface forms.

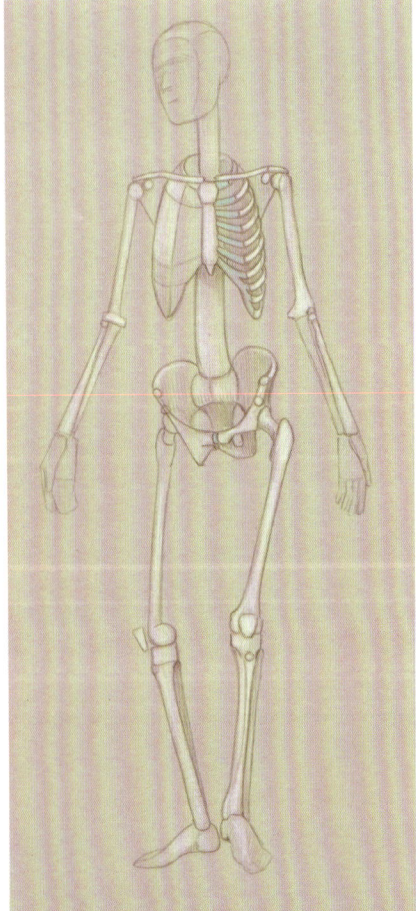
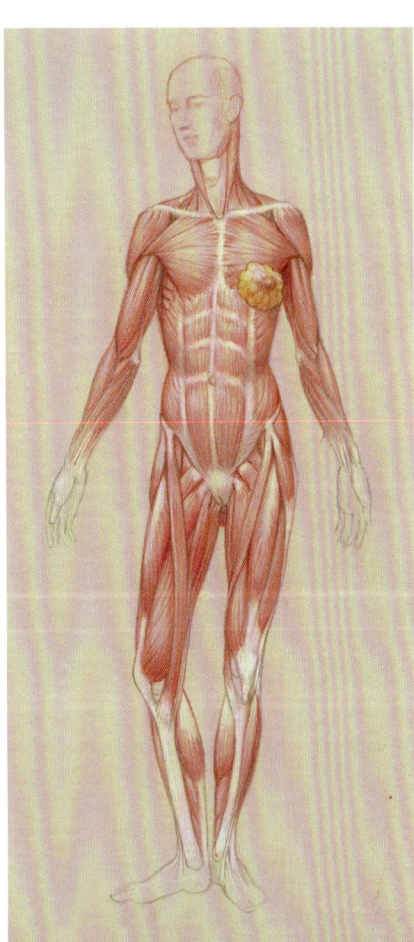
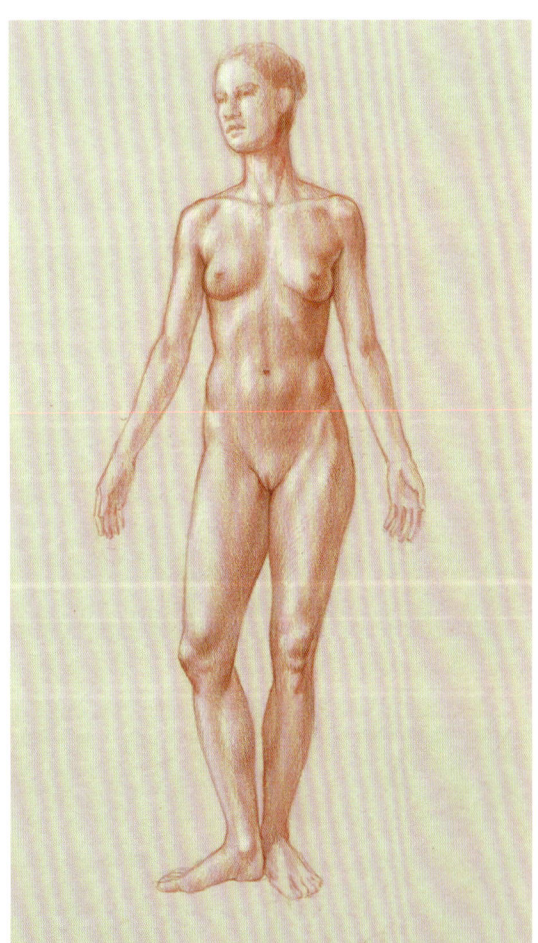

USING LANDMARKS TO VISUALIZE GEOMETRIC PATTERNS

The drawings here show a few possible geometric patterns created by connecting the landmarks of the torso. Reducing the body's complex organic forms to straight lines or geometric shapes makes it easier to read the forms of the body more objectively and precisely, especially when drawing foreshortened figures. In the case shown below, as the body changes position, the triangle created by connecting the nipples and jugular fossa changes from an equilateral to an isosceles triangle, and then, in a foreshortened view, to a scalene triangle. The types of triangles obtained by connecting the various landmarks will vary acccording to the specific proportions of the model.

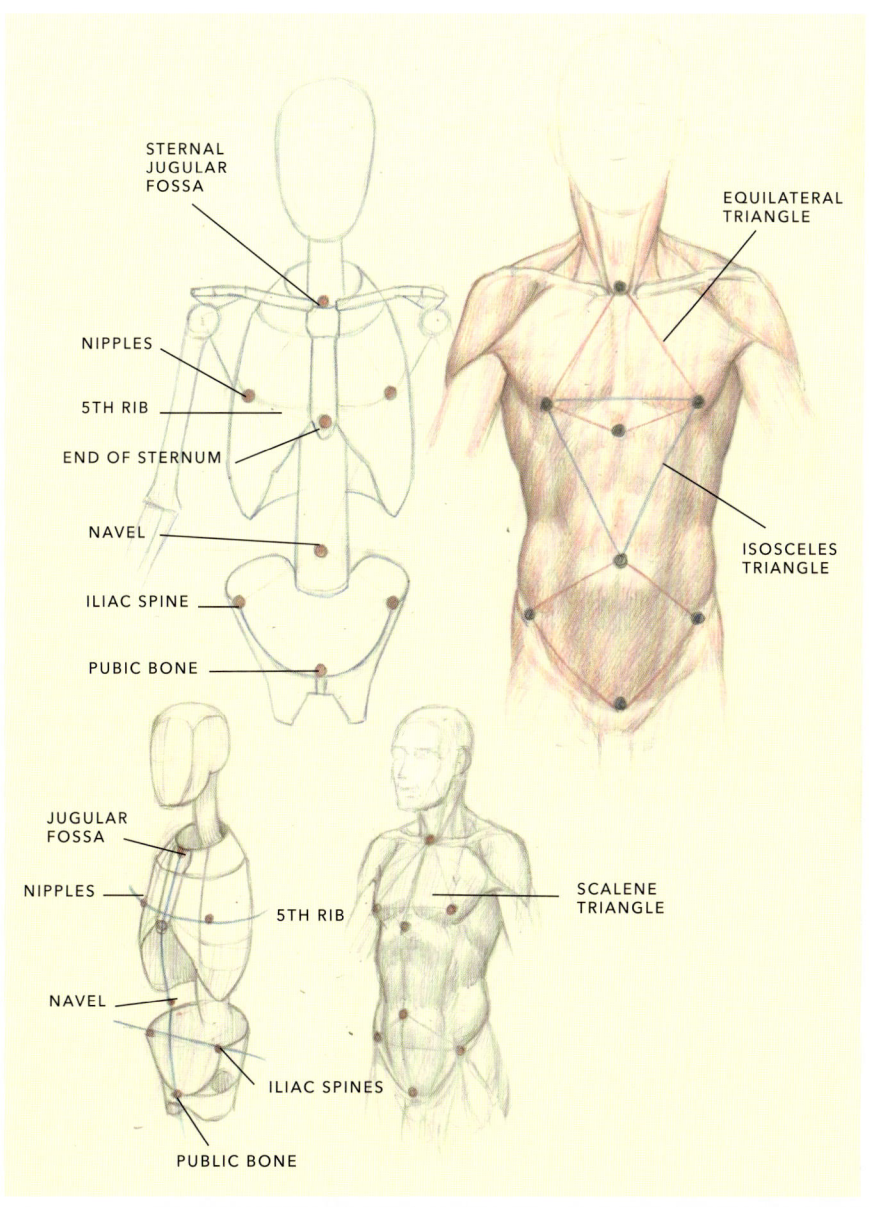

STERNAL JUGULAR FOSSA

NIPPLES

5TH RIB

END OF STERNUM

NAVEL

ILIAC SPINE

PUBIC BONE

EQUILATERAL TRIANGLE

ISOSCELES TRIANGLE

JUGULAR FOSSA

NIPPLES

NAVEL

5TH RIB

SCALENE TRIANGLE

ILIAC SPINES

PUBLIC BONE

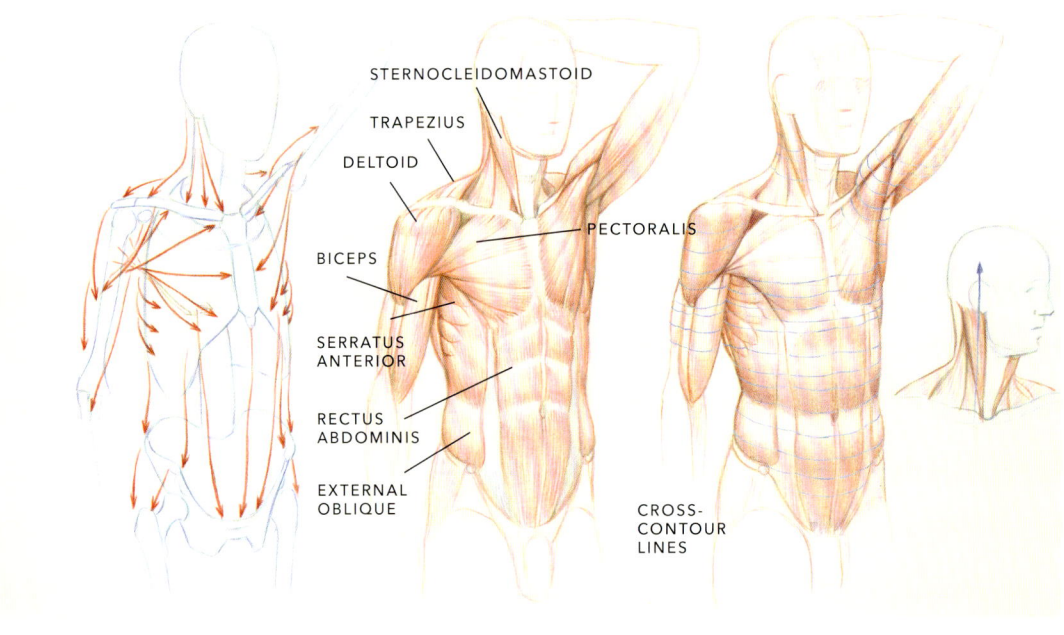

STERNOCLEIDOMASTOID

TRAPEZIUS

DELTOID

BICEPS

PECTORALIS

SERRATUS
ANTERIOR

RECTUS
ABDOMINIS

EXTERNAL
OBLIQUE

CROSS-
CONTOUR
LINES

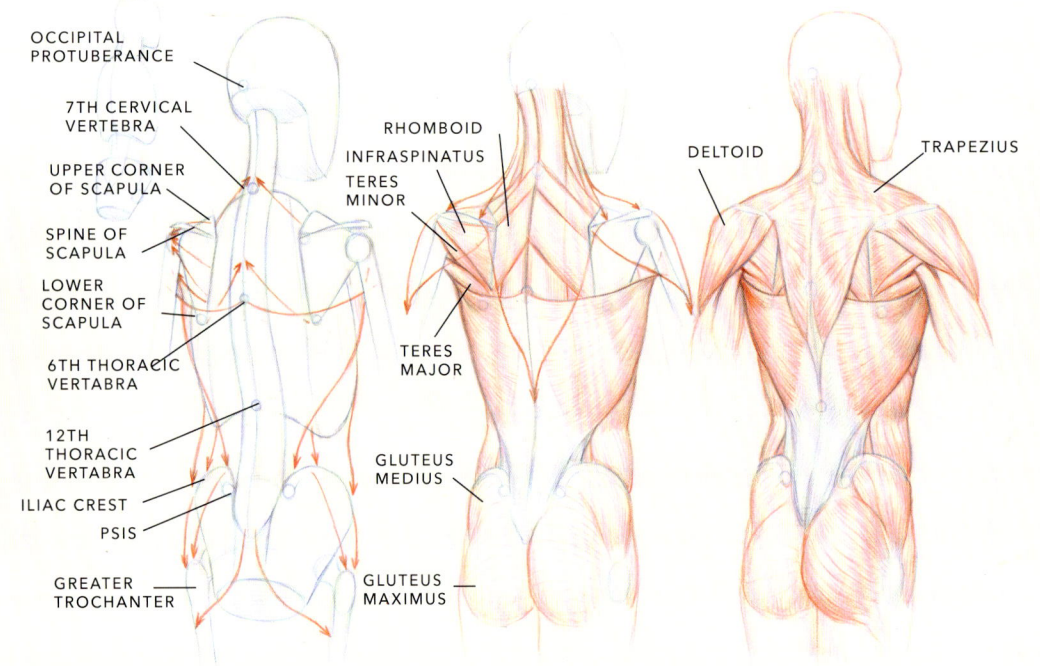

OCCIPITAL
PROTUBERANCE

7TH CERVICAL
VERTEBRA

UPPER CORNER
OF SCAPULA

SPINE OF
SCAPULA

LOWER
CORNER OF
SCAPULA

6TH THORACIC
VERTABRA

12TH
THORACIC
VERTABRA

ILIAC CREST

PSIS

GREATER
TROCHANTER

RHOMBOID

INFRASPINATUS

TERES
MINOR

TERES
MAJOR

GLUTEUS
MEDIUS

GLUTEUS
MAXIMUS

DELTOID

TRAPEZIUS

TOP: Muscular-skeletal connections of head and torso, three-quarters anterior view

This sequence shows how to connect the muscles and skeleton of the front of the neck, ribcage, and pelvis. At left, the red arrows show how to position the muscles over the skeleton of the torso and neck. (Please note that these arrows do not necessarily follow the direction from origin to insertion.) The figure at center shows the superficial muscle layer. When drawing the muscles, you must always consider how a muscular volume will be affected when positioned over the skeleton or wrapped around it. The semi-schematic rendering of the muscles in the figure

at right shows how to use vertical and horizontal sections for a better understanding of the volumetric characteristics of the form. The tonal development of your drawing should not be obtained by imitating the values you see on your subject but by understanding the effects of light on the forms of the body.

ABOVE: Muscular-skeletal connections of head and torso, three-quarters posterior view

This sequence, similar to that in the previous image, shows how to connect the muscles of the back of the torso and head to the skeleton.

THE WHOLE FIGURE

Now all the methods of analyzing the human figure can be applied to the whole figure. The sequence of the female figure, below, reviews the various levels of conceptualization we have seen so far. The large crouching male figure on the following page shows how to extract clues from the external forms to identify the skeleton, and the sequence of the sitting female figure, page 149, shows the method to follow to reconstruct the skeleton starting from the landmarks and then to layer the muscles over it.

BELOW: Review of the whole figure from the lateral view

This sequence reviews the whole figure— the landmarks, skeleton, external forms, and muscles—from the side view. Starting with the stereometric volumes of the figure (A), we move to the skeleton and landmarks (B). The external forms (C) are largely shaped by the superficial muscles (D). Your drawing skills will improve as your knowledge of the body increases. Copy the sequence as a practice exercise.

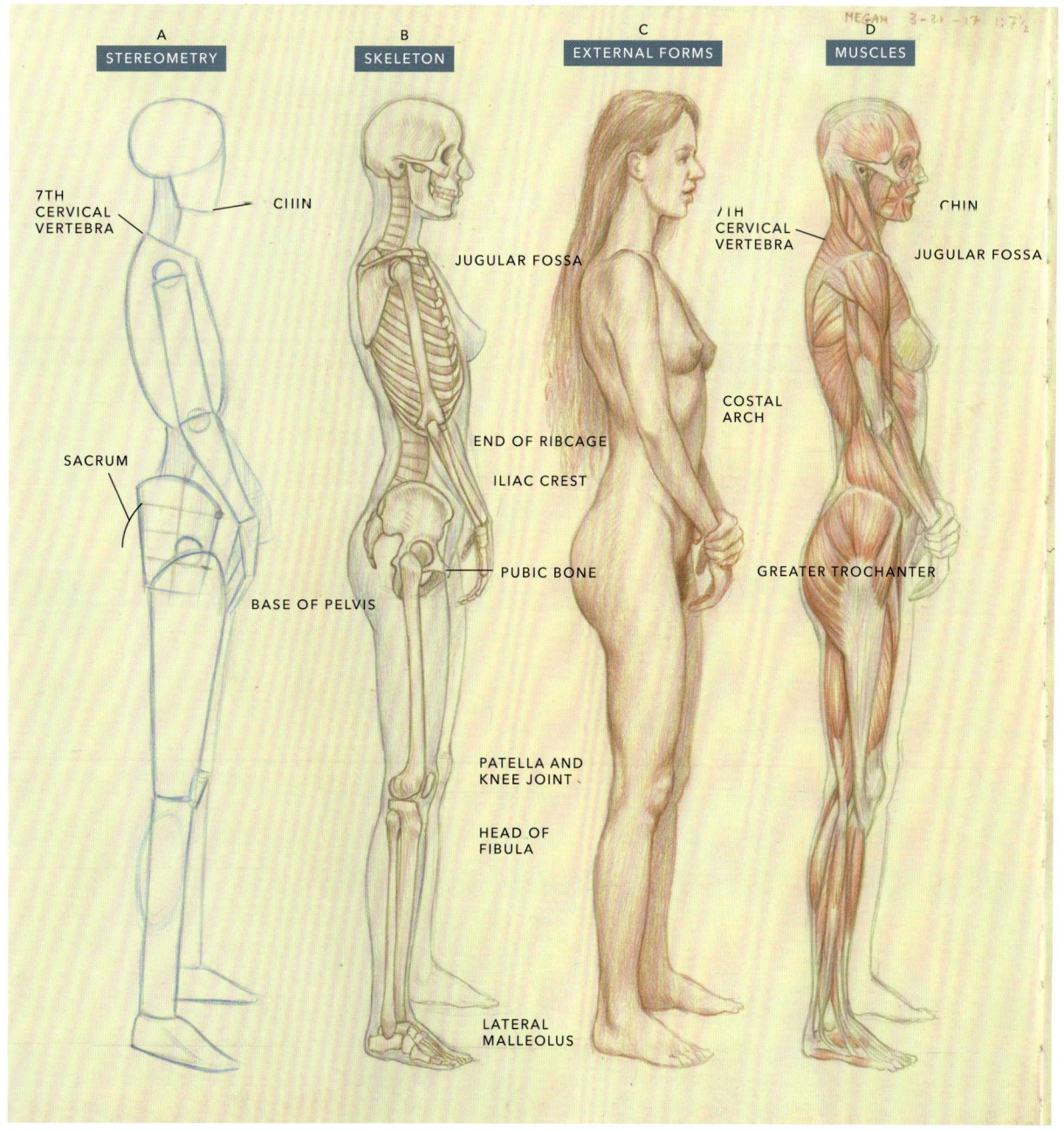

A — STEREOMETRY

7TH CERVICAL VERTEBRA

CHIN

SACRUM

B — SKELETON

JUGULAR FOSSA

END OF RIBCAGE

ILIAC CREST

PUBIC BONE

BASE OF PELVIS

PATELLA AND KNEE JOINT

HEAD OF FIBULA

LATERAL MALLEOLUS

C — EXTERNAL FORMS

COSTAL ARCH

D — MUSCLES

7TH CERVICAL VERTEBRA

CHIN

JUGULAR FOSSA

GREATER TROCHANTER

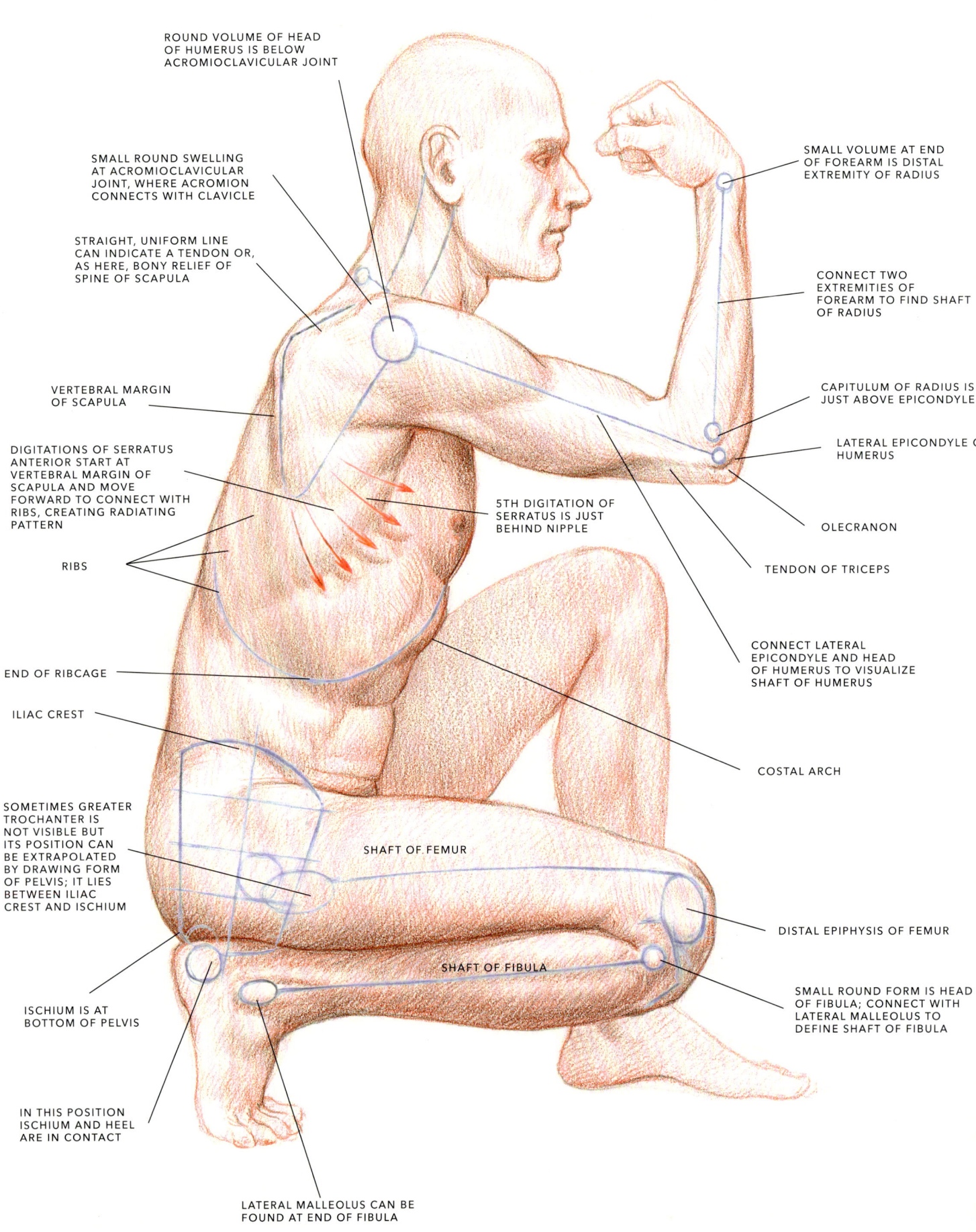

ROUND VOLUME OF HEAD
OF HUMERUS IS BELOW
ACROMIOCLAVICULAR JOINT

SMALL ROUND SWELLING
AT ACROMIOCLAVICULAR
JOINT, WHERE ACROMION
CONNECTS WITH CLAVICLE

STRAIGHT, UNIFORM LINE
CAN INDICATE A TENDON OR,
AS HERE, BONY RELIEF OF
SPINE OF SCAPULA

VERTEBRAL MARGIN
OF SCAPULA

DIGITATIONS OF SERRATUS
ANTERIOR START AT
VERTEBRAL MARGIN OF
SCAPULA AND MOVE
FORWARD TO CONNECT WITH
RIBS, CREATING RADIATING
PATTERN

RIBS

END OF RIBCAGE

ILIAC CREST

SOMETIMES GREATER
TROCHANTER IS
NOT VISIBLE BUT
ITS POSITION CAN
BE EXTRAPOLATED
BY DRAWING FORM
OF PELVIS; IT LIES
BETWEEN ILIAC
CREST AND ISCHIUM

ISCHIUM IS AT
BOTTOM OF PELVIS

IN THIS POSITION
ISCHIUM AND HEEL
ARE IN CONTACT

LATERAL MALLEOLUS CAN BE
FOUND AT END OF FIBULA

SMALL VOLUME AT END
OF FOREARM IS DISTAL
EXTREMITY OF RADIUS

CONNECT TWO
EXTREMITIES OF
FOREARM TO FIND SHAFT
OF RADIUS

CAPITULUM OF RADIUS IS
JUST ABOVE EPICONDYLE

LATERAL EPICONDYLE (
HUMERUS

OLECRANON

TENDON OF TRICEPS

CONNECT LATERAL
EPICONDYLE AND HEAD
OF HUMERUS TO VISUALIZE
SHAFT OF HUMERUS

COSTAL ARCH

5TH DIGITATION OF
SERRATUS IS JUST
BEHIND NIPPLE

SHAFT OF FEMUR

DISTAL EPIPHYSIS OF FEMUR

SHAFT OF FIBULA

SMALL ROUND FORM IS HEAD
OF FIBULA; CONNECT WITH
LATERAL MALLEOLUS TO
DEFINE SHAFT OF FIBULA

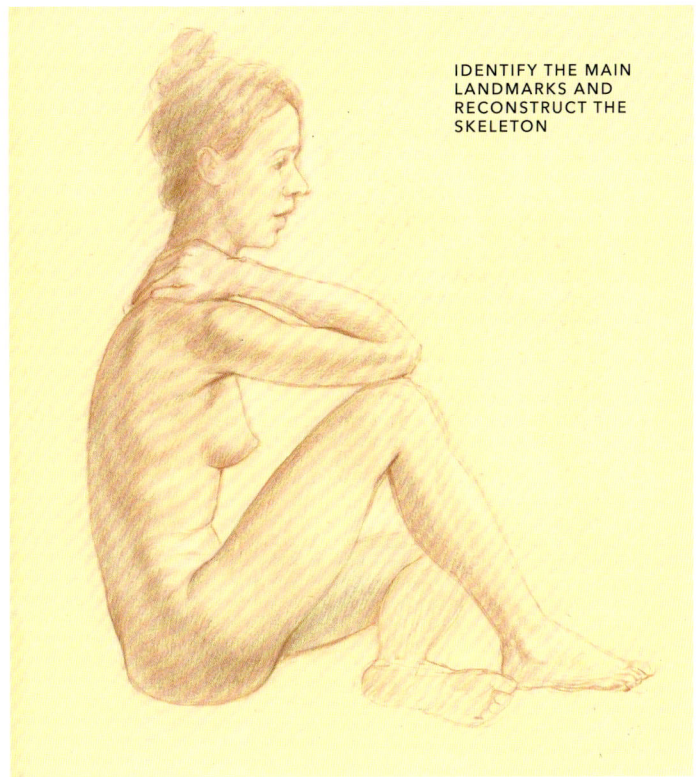

IDENTIFY THE MAIN
LANDMARKS AND
RECONSTRUCT THE
SKELETON

OPPOSITE: "Reading" proportions, landmarks, and muscular volumes of a posing model

This image exemplifies how we can look at a posing model and read the proportions, landmarks, and muscular volumes, then use these clues to construct an anatomically correct, structurally sound, and harmonious depiction of the figure.

LEFT AND BELOW: Reconstruction of the skeleton and muscular volumes using landmarks

This sequence provides another example of how to extrapolate the skeletal structure from an analysis of the external forms and then how to begin layering the muscles over it.

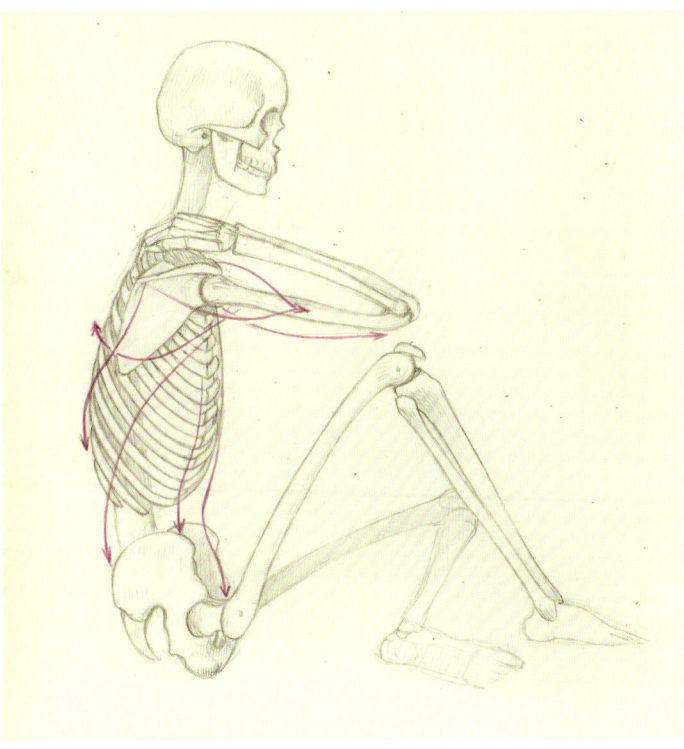

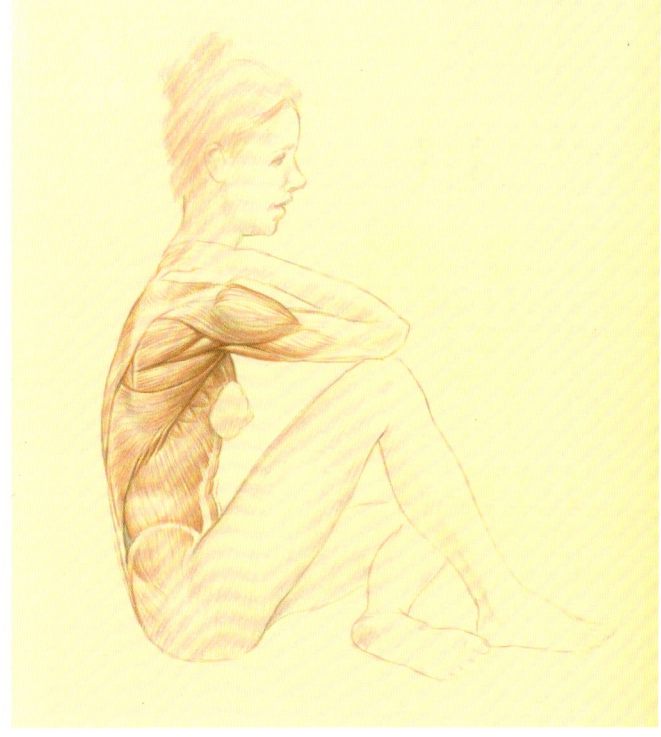

FROM ESSENTIAL VOLUMES TO FULLY RENDERED FIGURE

First, block in the essential volumes of the skeleton of the head and torso, marking the main landmarks as shown in image 1. Next, mark the directions of the muscles that connect these segments of the skeleton, considering their origins and insertions (image 2). Note that the upper origin of the rectus abdominis and external oblique is at the level of the fifth rib, a little above the costal arch. Then, add the more superficial muscles (image 3) over the previous deeper layer. Finally, finish rendering the figure as in image 4. If you continue to practice this method of layering muscles over the skeleton, you'll eventually be able to perform sequences like this from memory or imagination.

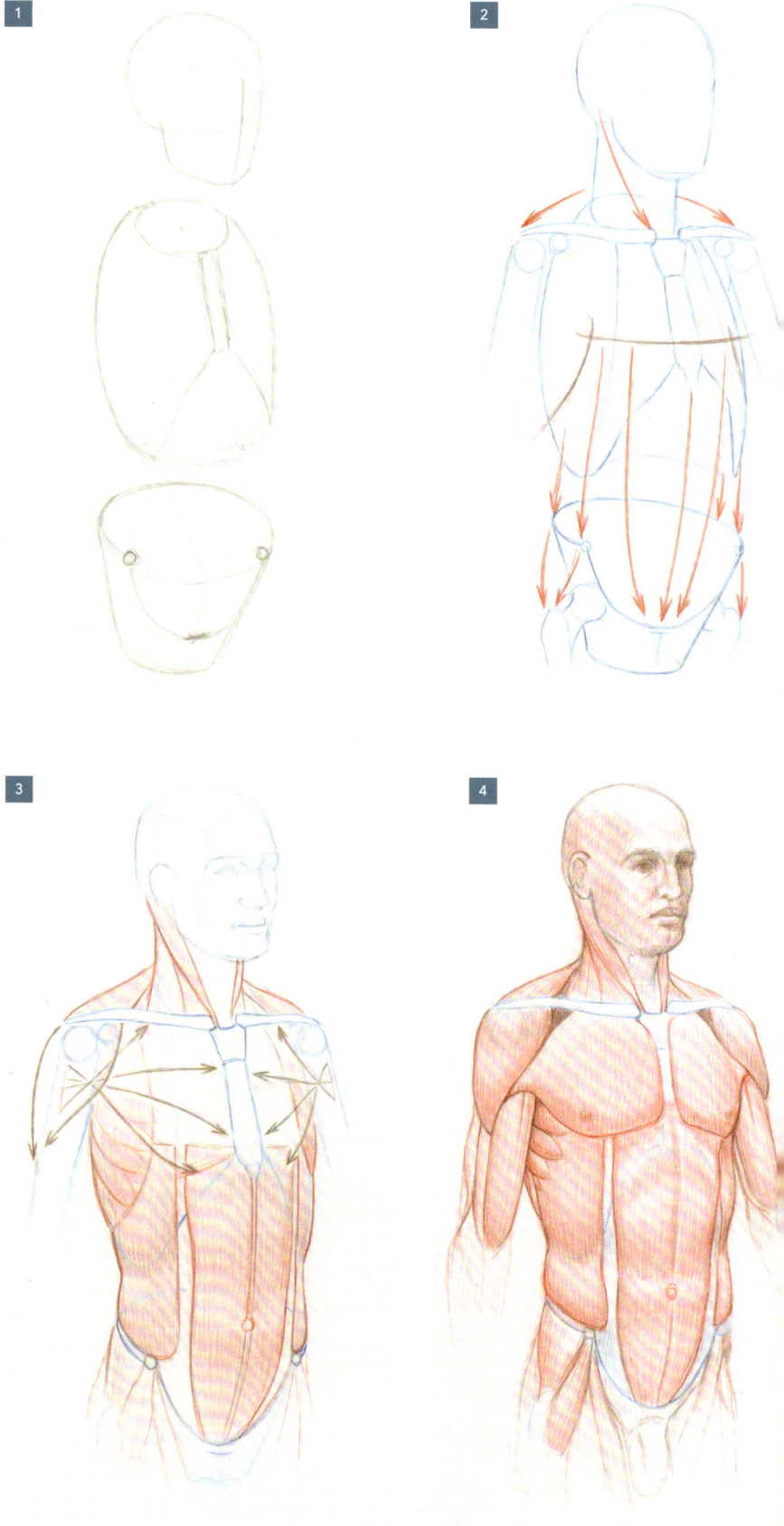

EXERCISE

In this exercise, you'll be using a reference pose to reconstruct a posed figure. To begin, trace the figure in the reference pose, top, using a sheet of tracing paper.

Then, using the stereometric image, center, as your guide, identify the landmarks and joints, establish the lengths of the limbs that connect them and check how they relate to each other proportionally (as shown by the blue lines), then render the main volumes of the body stereometrically.

Then, referring to the image at bottom showing the main forms being defined, draw the main external forms over the previous layer. (You can partly erase that layer so that it's just visible enough to guide your hand.) Finally, render the figure realistically, gradually adding more details and tonal development.

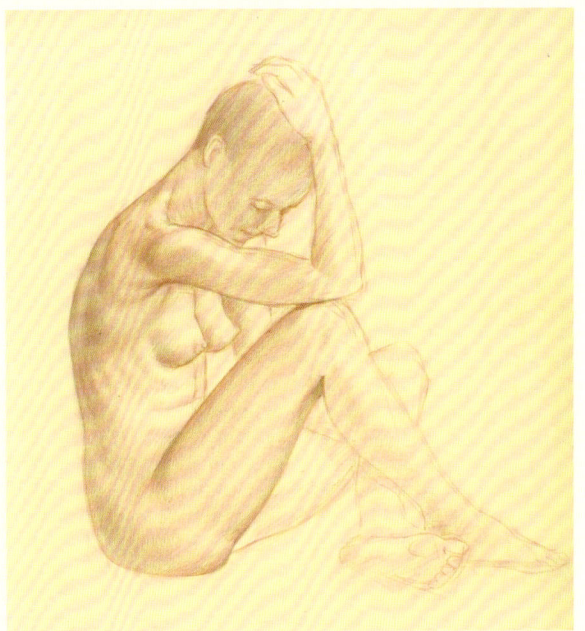

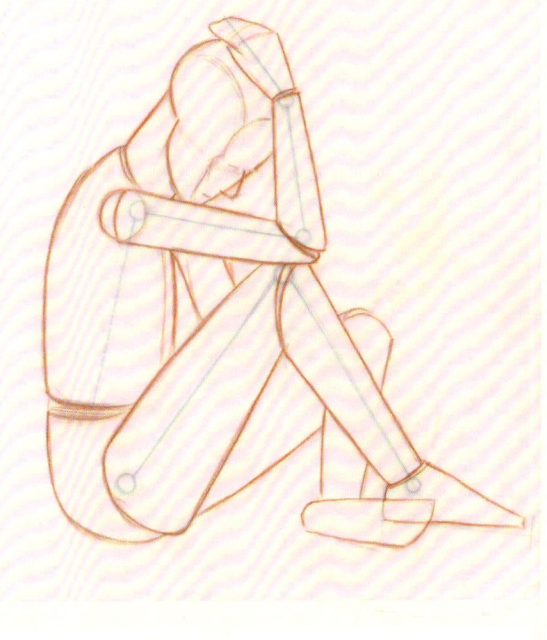

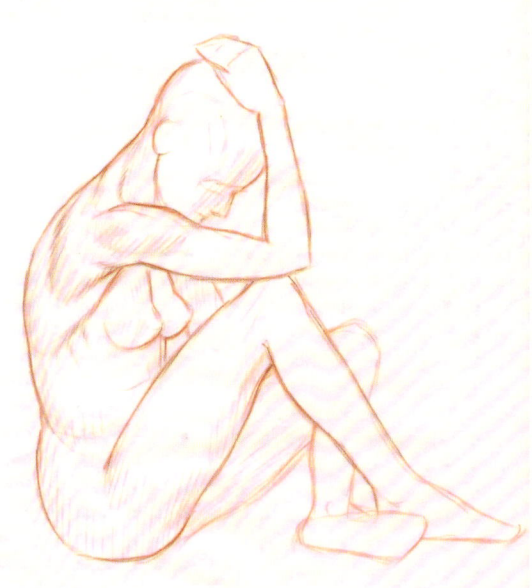

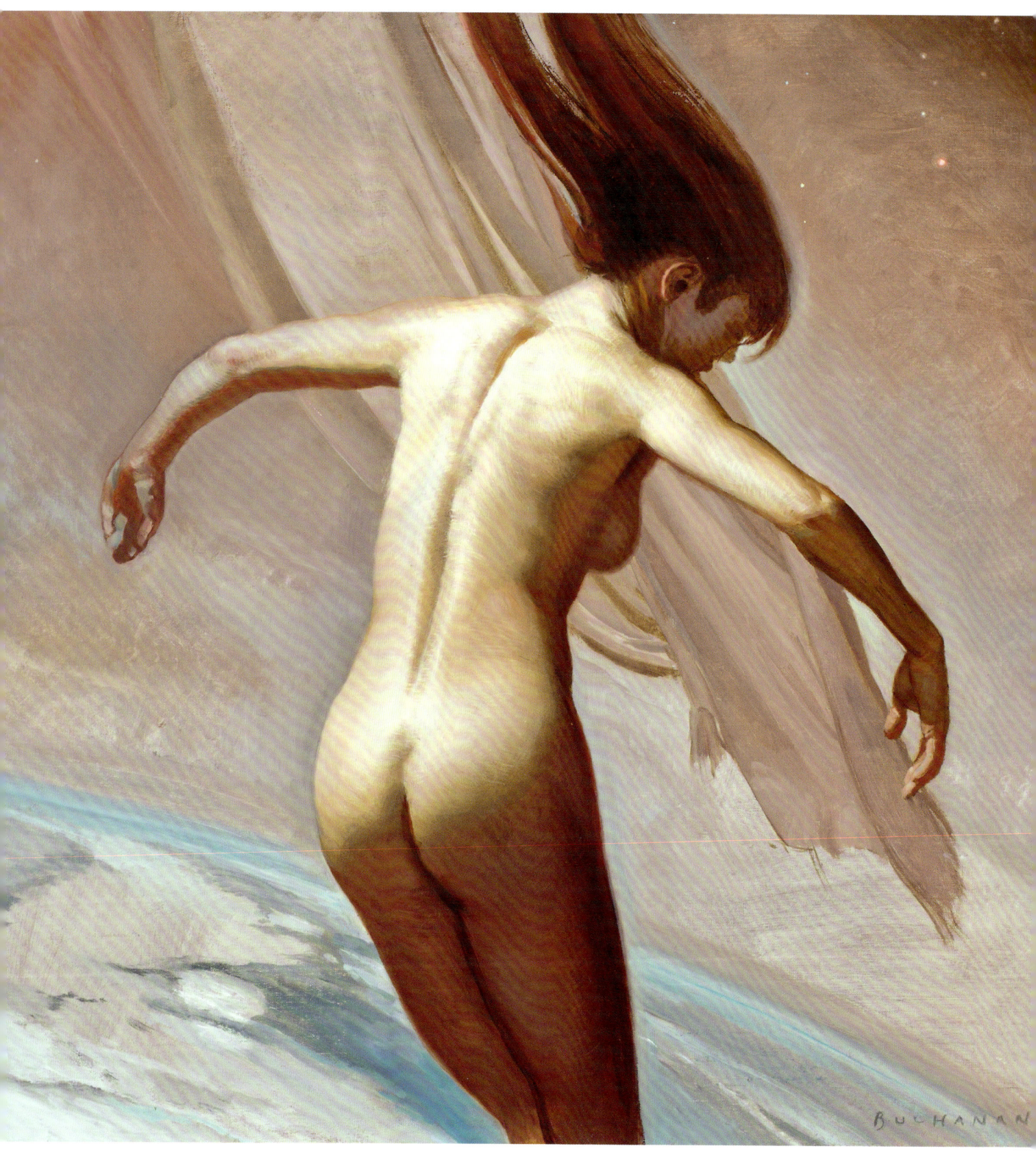

CHAPTER 5

FLOWS & RHYTHMS OF THE FIGURE

Depending on our intent, we see different things when we look at the body. Scientists and artists have both dissected the body for centuries, but with different intentions and different ends. Physicians and other medical professionals study anatomy for healing purposes; artists study anatomy with an aesthetic intention. When Leonardo or Michelangelo took bodies apart, they later put them back together again through their art, elevating the body beyond its material state.

OPPOSITE: Noah Buchanan, *Venus Descending,* 2018, oil on linen, 46 × 46 inches (116.84 × 116.84 cm). Courtesy of the artist.

Studying anatomy
with an aesthetic
intention

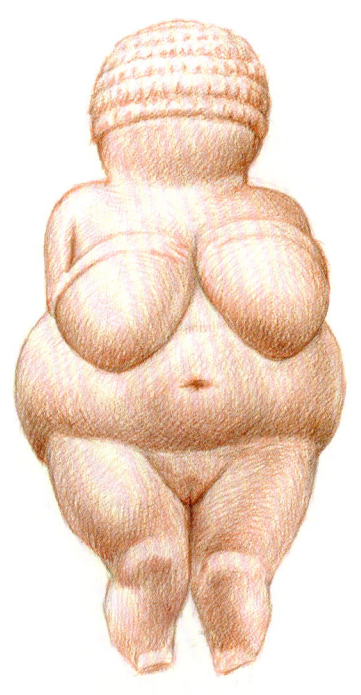

When artists study the body through dissection, by preparing an écorché (flayed model), or by examining a textbook, they become acquainted with the body's parts, what they look like, their locations, and what they are called. But after taking the body apart, artists must also put it back together through an artwork, adding an aesthetic component and giving it "cultural life." This indispensable operation transforms the human body into a signifier, a vehicle for the transmission of cultural values. The drawing by Leonardo opposite shows this process of transcendence: the legs in this small masterpiece are anatomically correct—all the muscles are accounted for—but that is secondary to the pose, the stance, and sense of life that these powerful legs convey.

The biological forms of the body have been culturally interpreted through art for millennia. One of the earliest examples of the inextricable connection between culture and biology is the Willendorf Venus, a small sculpture that may date back as far as 30,000 years ago. This figurine of a naked woman fits in the palm of a hand, making it easy to transport—an important consideration for a band of hunter-gatherers always on the move. Her obesity symbolizes abundance and fertility—beautiful because it meant survival to the Paleolithic people who created her.

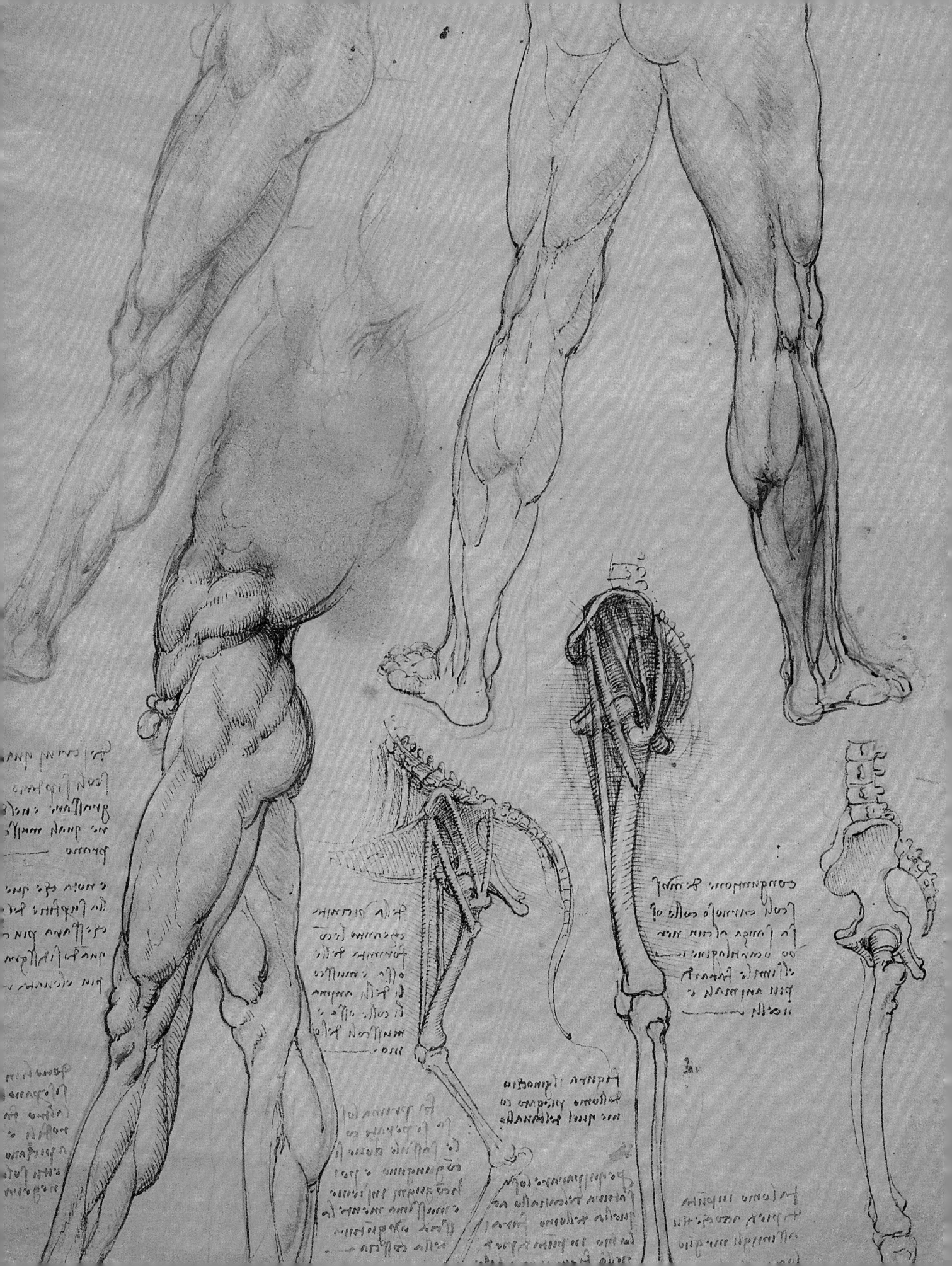

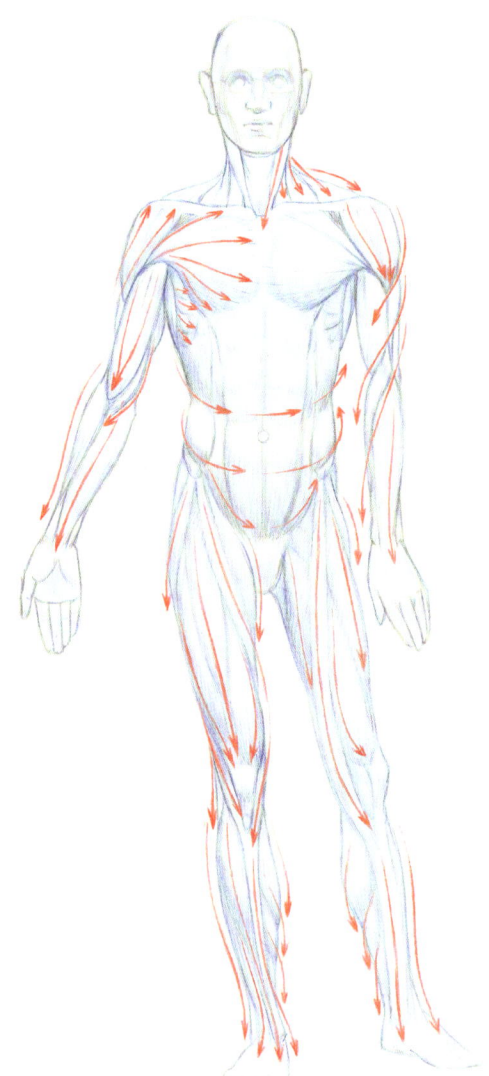

The body as
a vehicle for
cultural values

FLOWS, RHYTHMS, AND MOVEMENT

Look at the body with an open mind, and you'll be amazed by the things you'll see. There are hundreds of muscles in the body, and more than one muscle is involved in almost every movement. For example, there are three different flexors of the forearm: the biceps brachii, brachialis, and brachioradialis. They all flex the forearm but from slightly different angles, and when one of them is working, the other two contribute to the flexion to differing degrees, creating specific patterns on the external forms of the body. Another type of connection is that a muscle group may be antagonist with another muscle group—for example, one group may extend a part of the body while another group flexes it.

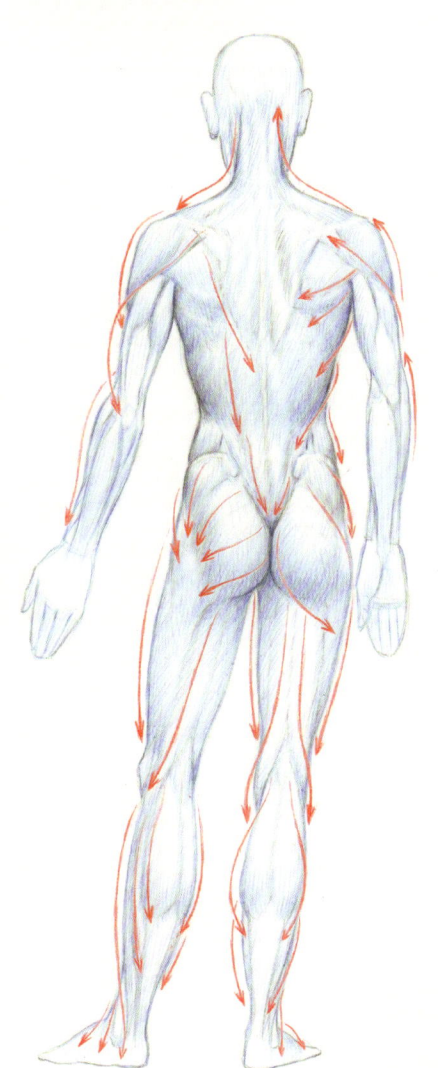

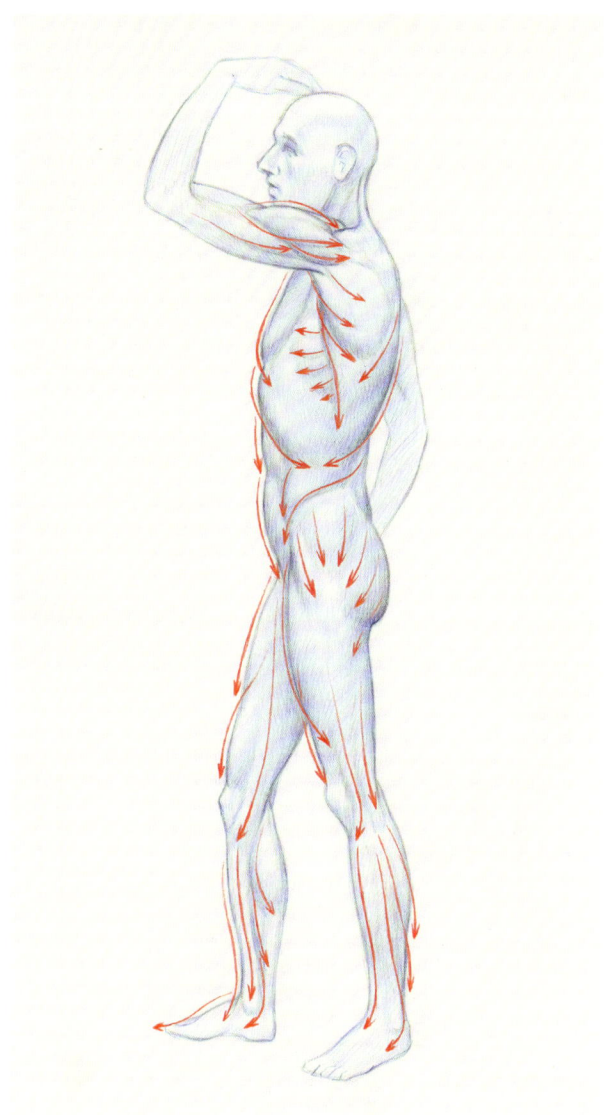

These interactions between muscles and between muscles and skeleton create lines of flow—pathways, patterns, and harmonious connections that are typical of the human body and that, although explicable structurally, also possess and express aesthetics. If the muscles and skeleton are the alphabet, these rhythms are the poetry created by the human figure. Learning to recognize them permits you to "read" the aesthetics of the human body and to speak them through your art.

The charts here show the main pathways of the flows created by the interaction of the volumes of the body. In this chapter, I bring attention to the flows that connect and harmonize the various parts of the human figure and the aesthetic that they create. These are the flows that I call *inherent*—meaning that they are typical of the body *as a biological structure*. The following chapter will explore the rhythms and lines of action created by the body in movement.

The poetry created by the human figure

FLOWS OF THE TORSO

Let's begin looking at specific parts of the human figure from a variety of angles and in a variety of poses to see how to apply the concept of anatomical harmonies to the practice of figure drawing. The images here show the beautiful aesthetic patterns created by the muscles of the raised arm in continuity with the muscles of the side of the ribcage.

RIGHT: Lateral view of male torso with raised arm, tonal rendering

When you render the figure tonally, having a good understanding of the anatomical forms and their aesthetic harmonies will help you describe the figure correctly and in detail. This image visualizes the areas of light mass and shadow mass, divided by the shadow core. As you can see, the line of the core follows the peaks of the various muscular volumes, helping you identify them and read the body forms more completely.

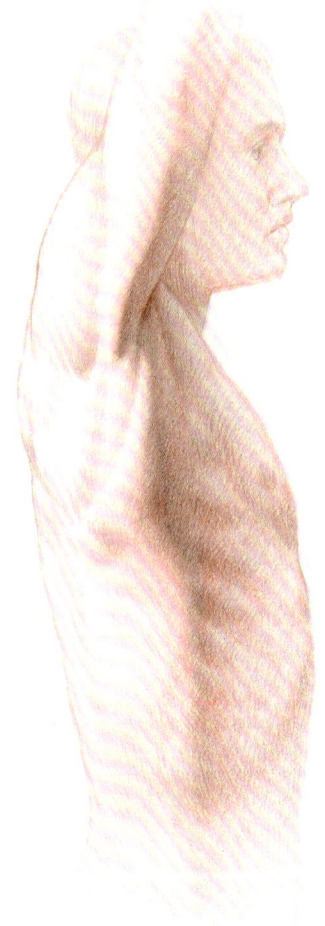

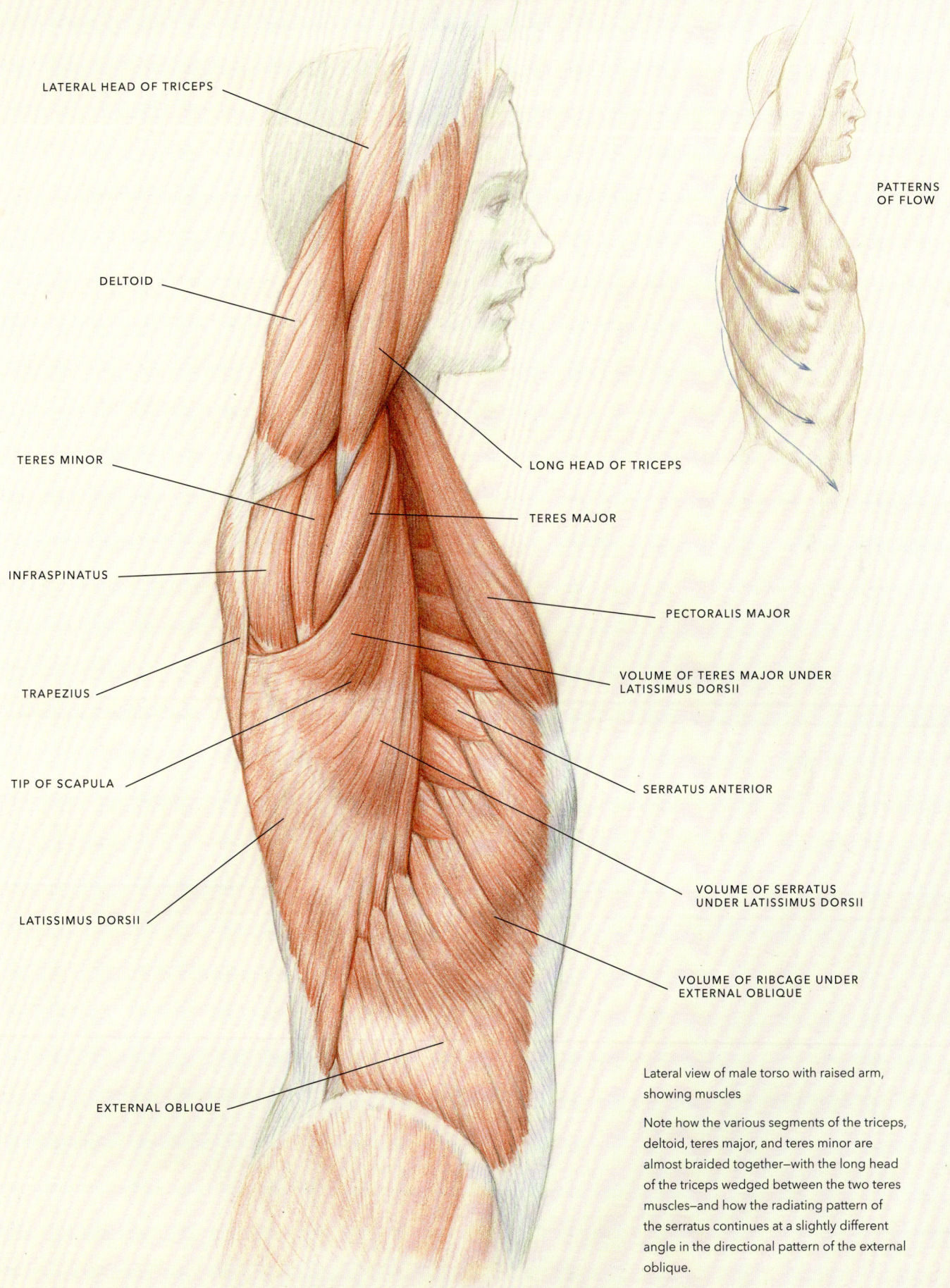

LATERAL HEAD OF TRICEPS

DELTOID

TERES MINOR

INFRASPINATUS

TRAPEZIUS

TIP OF SCAPULA

LATISSIMUS DORSII

EXTERNAL OBLIQUE

PATTERNS
OF FLOW

LONG HEAD OF TRICEPS

TERES MAJOR

PECTORALIS MAJOR

VOLUME OF TERES MAJOR UNDER
LATISSIMUS DORSII

SERRATUS ANTERIOR

VOLUME OF SERRATUS
UNDER LATISSIMUS DORSII

VOLUME OF RIBCAGE UNDER
EXTERNAL OBLIQUE

Lateral view of male torso with raised arm,
showing muscles

Note how the various segments of the triceps,
deltoid, teres major, and teres minor are
almost braided together—with the long head
of the triceps wedged between the two teres
muscles—and how the radiating pattern of
the serratus continues at a slightly different
angle in the directional pattern of the external
oblique.

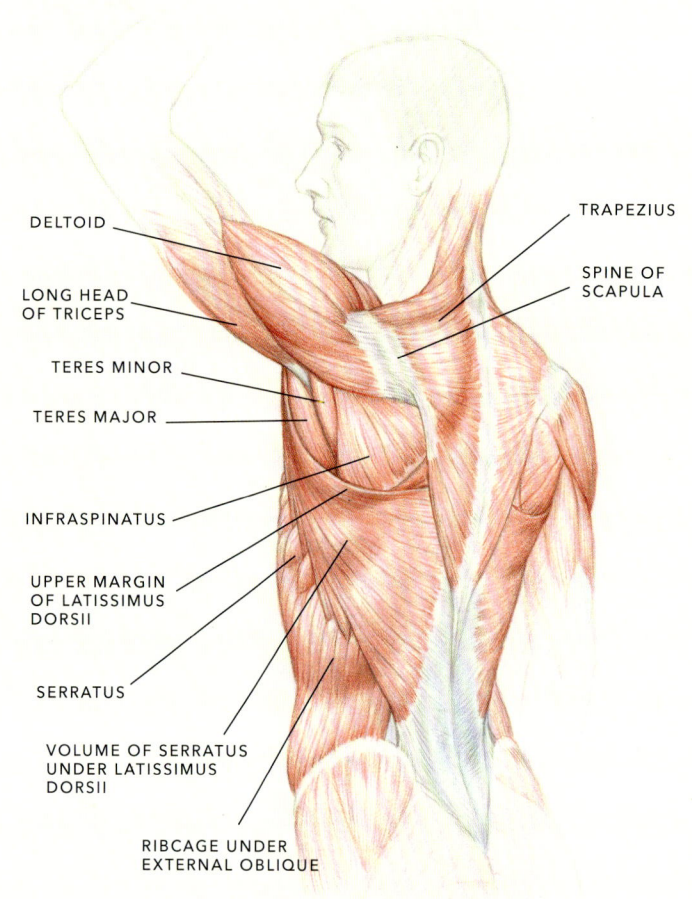

DELTOID

LONG HEAD
OF TRICEPS

TERES MINOR

TERES MAJOR

INFRASPINATUS

UPPER MARGIN
OF LATISSIMUS
DORSII

SERRATUS

VOLUME OF SERRATUS
UNDER LATISSIMUS
DORSII

RIBCAGE UNDER
EXTERNAL OBLIQUE

TRAPEZIUS

SPINE OF
SCAPULA

ABOVE AND RIGHT: Underlying muscles and lines of flow, three-quarters posterior view of torso with raised arm

Here's a slightly different pose from a different angle. Again, the underlying musculature determines the main lines of flow.

OPPOSITE: Main volumes and flows of the female torso

In this drawing I have visualized some of the main pathways of flow of the torso's external forms created by the muscles, by the passage from the muscles to the breasts, and by the ribcage, iliac crest, inguinal ligament, and genitals.

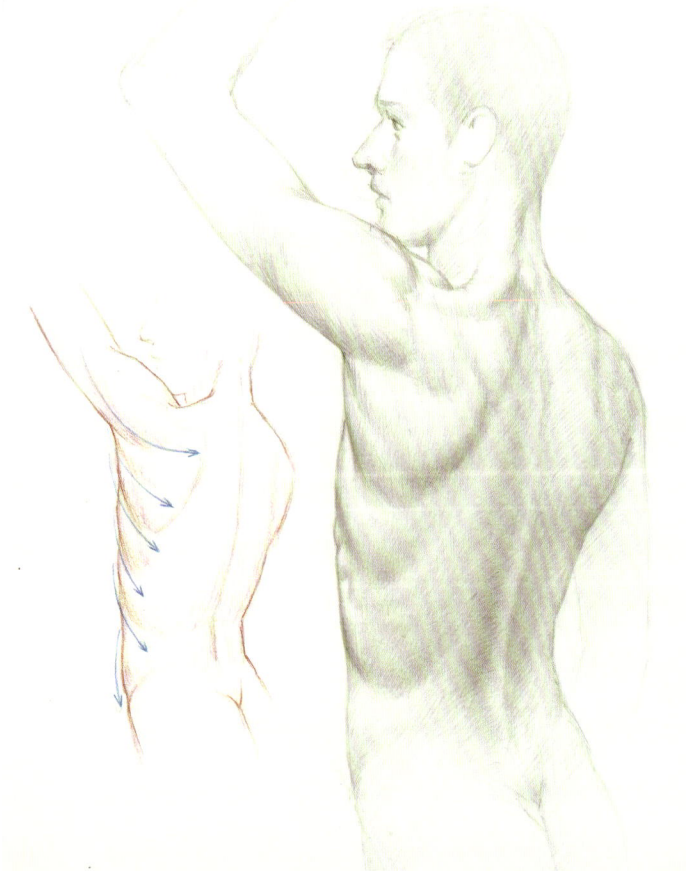

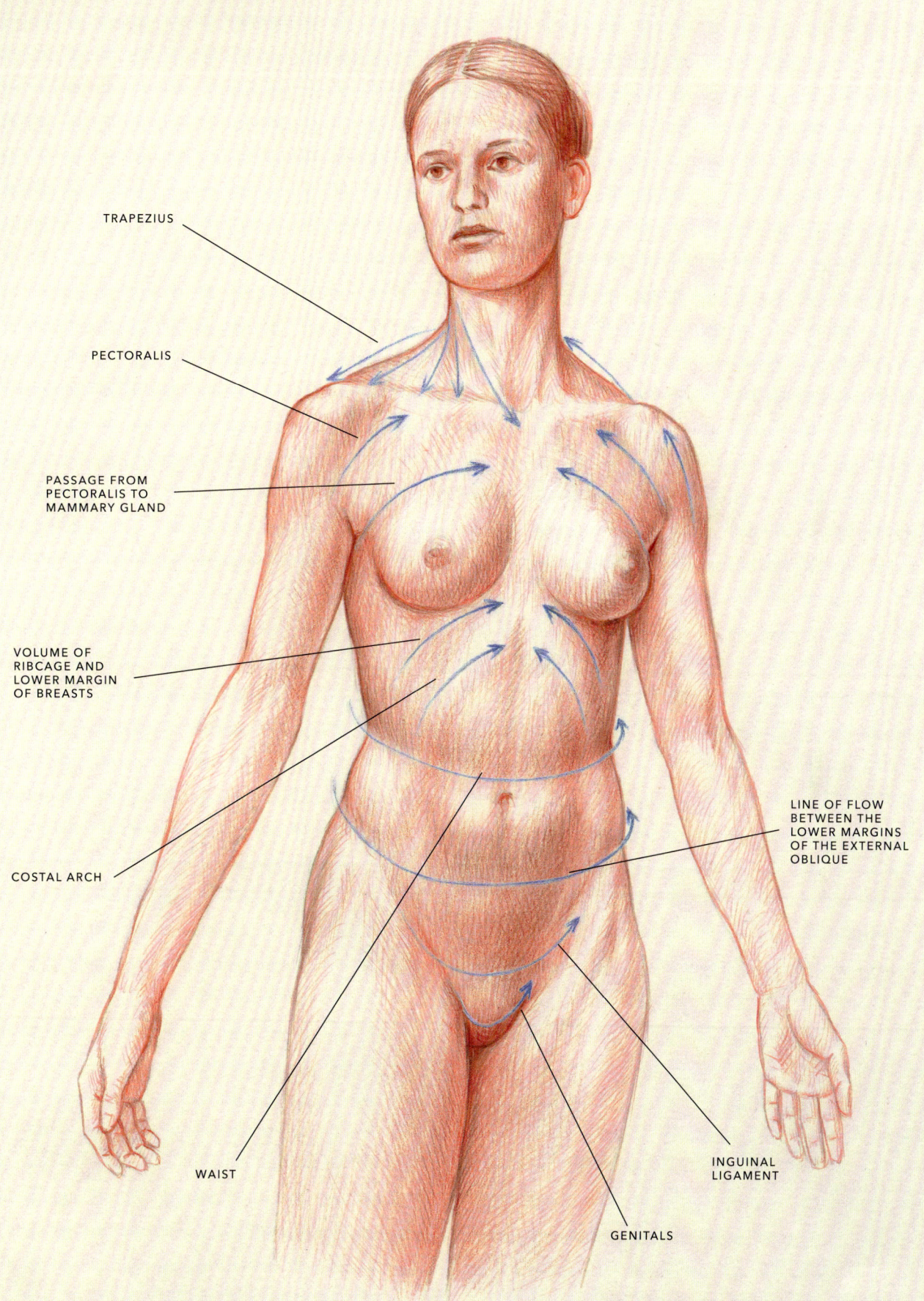

TRAPEZIUS

PECTORALIS

PASSAGE FROM
PECTORALIS TO
MAMMARY GLAND

VOLUME OF
RIBCAGE AND
LOWER MARGIN
OF BREASTS

COSTAL ARCH

LINE OF FLOW
BETWEEN THE
LOWER MARGINS
OF THE EXTERNAL
OBLIQUE

WAIST

INGUINAL
LIGAMENT

GENITALS

FLOWS OF THE ARM

The high degree of mobility of the arm and its many muscles create great dynamism and innumerable lines of flow. The images in this section show the forms and flows of the arm in various positions and from various angles. The scope of this thorough, but not exhaustive, exploration is to point out how many aesthetic pathways the human figure can create, depending on pose, movement, and point of view.

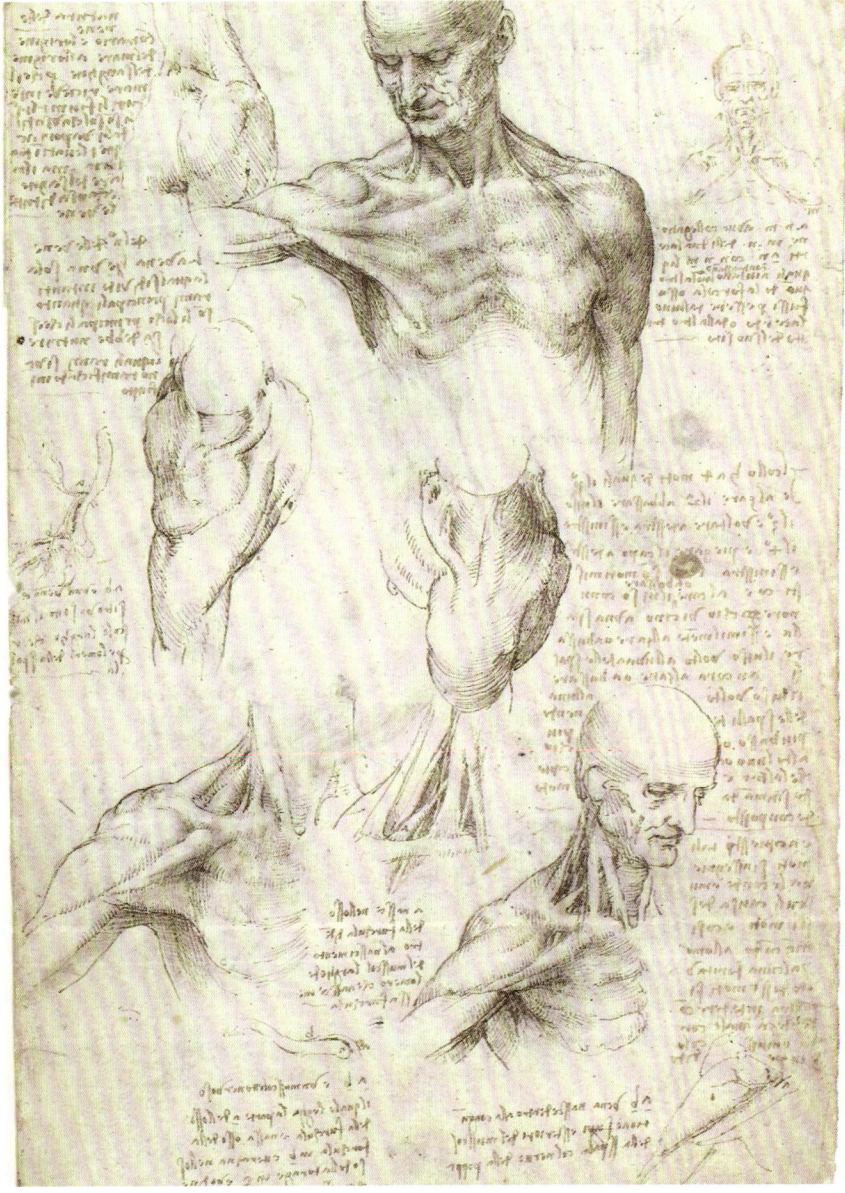

LEFT: Leonardo da Vinci, anatomical studies of the shoulder, 1510–11, black chalk and ink on paper, 11⅜ × 7¹³⁄₁₆ inches (28.9 × 19.9 cm). Royal Library, Windsor, United Kingdom.

Leonardo da Vinci invented an incredibly efficient method of visualizing the muscles, reducing them to lines to see their paths more clearly and to focus on their function.

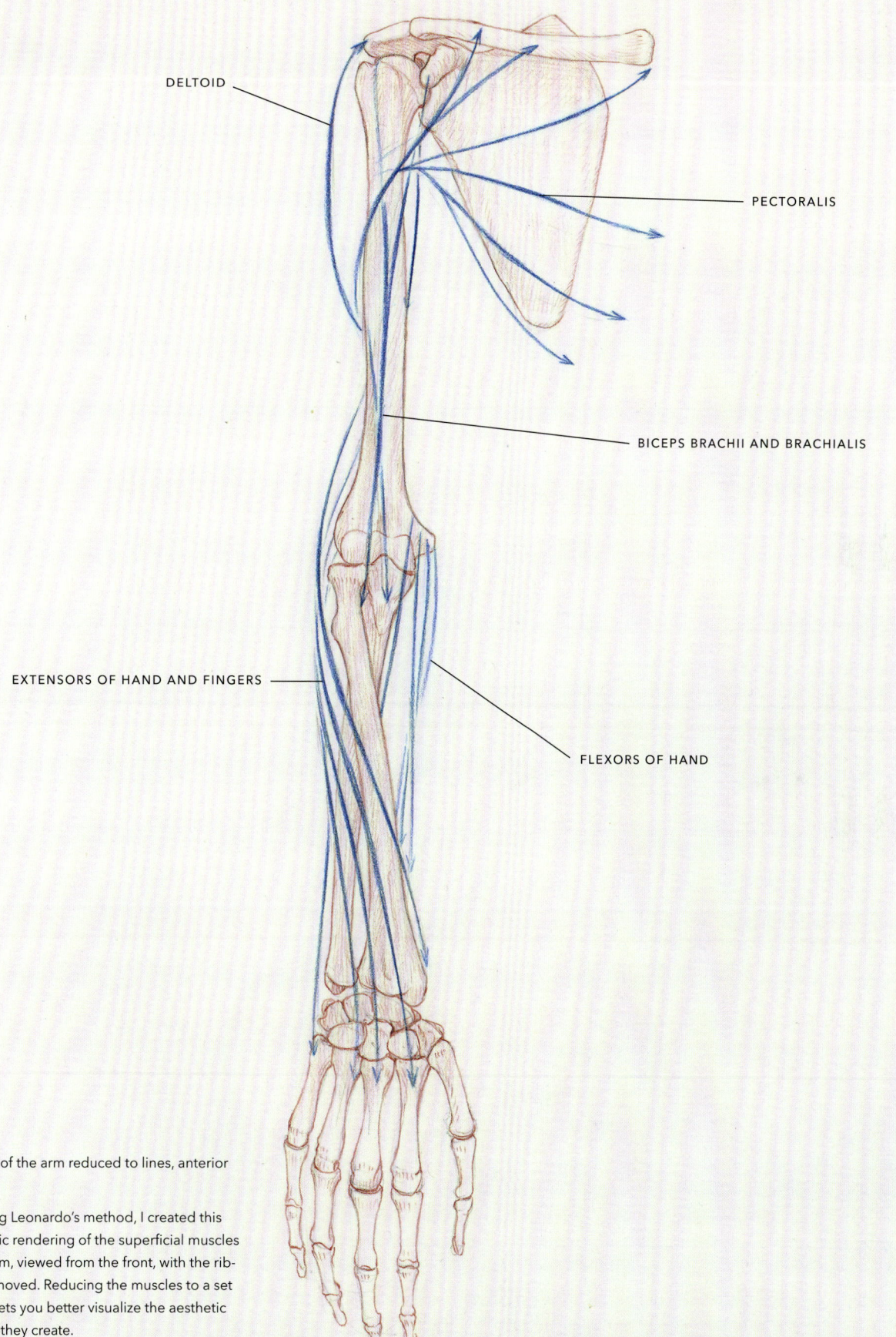

DELTOID

PECTORALIS

BICEPS BRACHII AND BRACHIALIS

EXTENSORS OF HAND AND FINGERS

FLEXORS OF HAND

Muscles of the arm reduced to lines, anterior view

Following Leonardo's method, I created this schematic rendering of the superficial muscles of the arm, viewed from the front, with the ribcage removed. Reducing the muscles to a set of lines lets you better visualize the aesthetic patterns they create.

LINES OF FLOW VERSUS LINES OF ACTION

In this book, I distinguish between lines of flow and lines of action. The images here are examples of the pathways of lines of flow created by the interaction of muscular volumes. Lines of action are discussed in the next chapter, on movement.

RIGHT: Flows of the arm, two views

Different angles and different poses produce different flows and aesthetic pathways.

OPPOSITE, TOP AND BOTTOM LEFT: Flows of the muscular and external forms of the arm in supination

These three images show a direct comparison between muscular forms, superficial forms, and the flows they create. The drawing at top right visualizes two types of flow patterns: the blue arrows show flows of the muscle groups and their reciprocal interaction, and the spiraling red arrow shows an overall flow based more on aesthetics than on structure.

OPPOSITE BOTTOM RIGHT: Schematization of the main muscular groups of the arm

The muscles can also be lumped together in main groups to facilitate the identification of the pathways. This schematization of the main muscular groups of the arm makes it easier to see the lines of flow. The cross-contour lines make the volumes of the arm clearer.

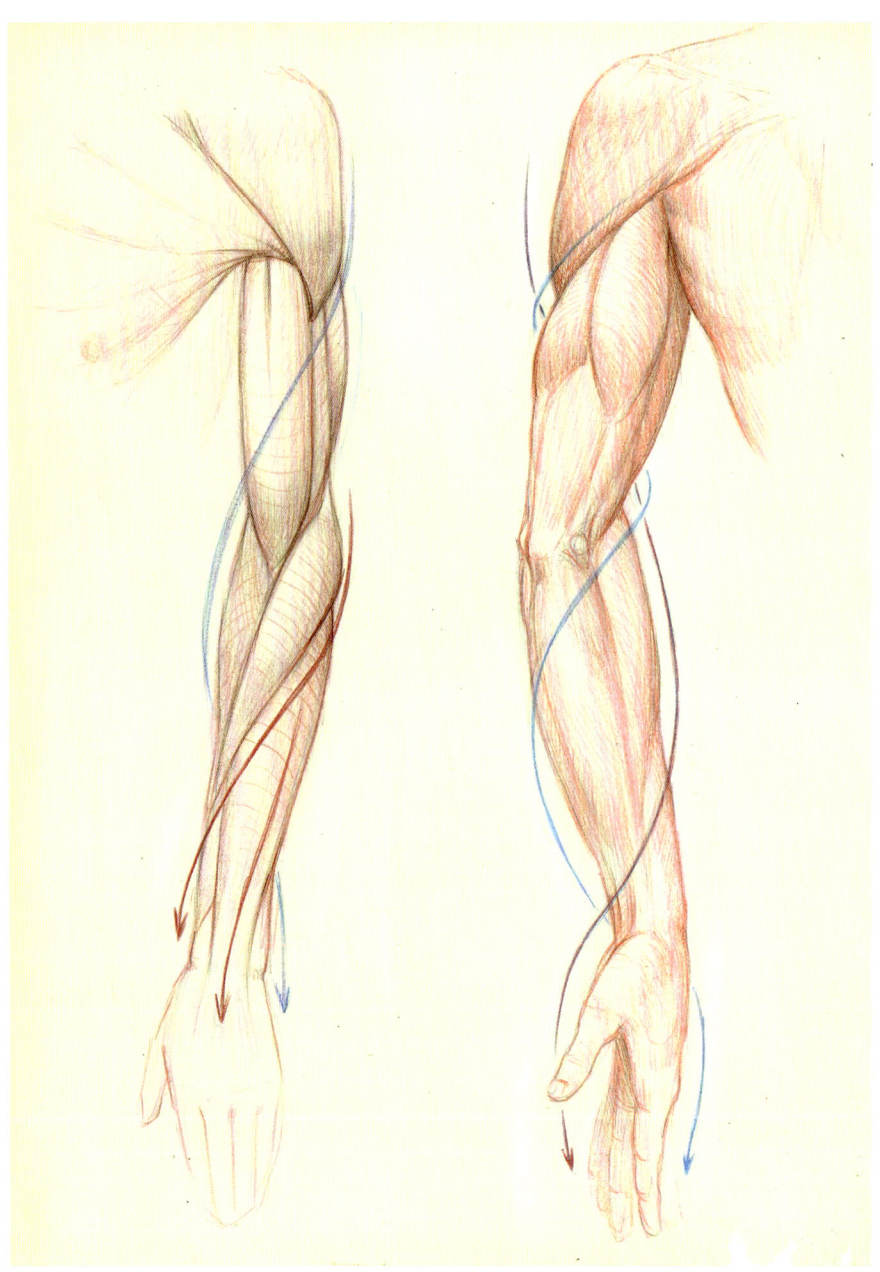

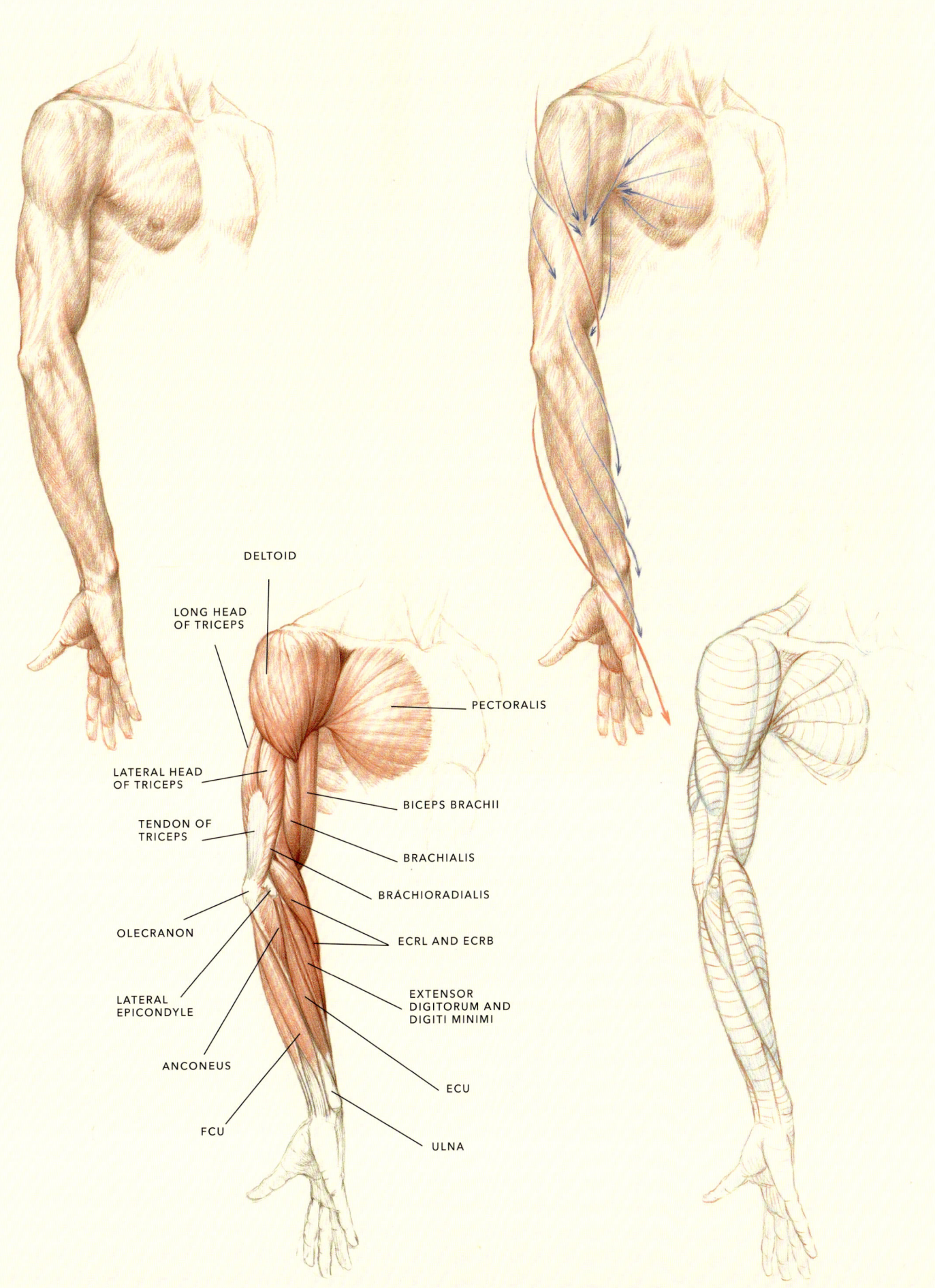

DELTOID

LONG HEAD
OF TRICEPS

PECTORALIS

LATERAL HEAD
OF TRICEPS

BICEPS BRACHII

TENDON OF
TRICEPS

BRACHIALIS

BRACHIORADIALIS

OLECRANON

ECRL AND ECRB

LATERAL
EPICONDYLE

EXTENSOR
DIGITORUM AND
DIGITI MINIMI

ANCONEUS

ECU

FCU

ULNA

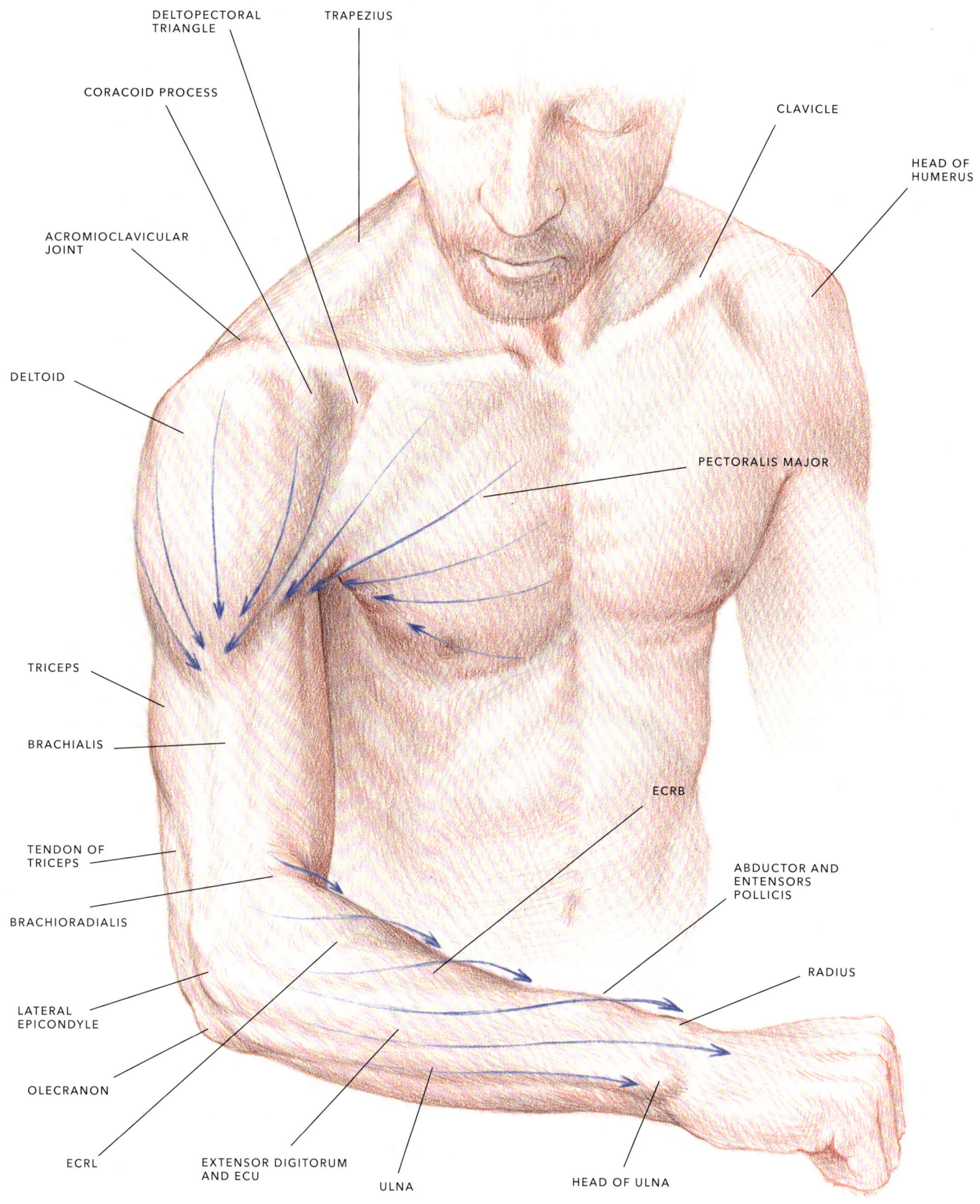

DELTOPECTORAL
TRIANGLE

TRAPEZIUS

CORACOID PROCESS

CLAVICLE

HEAD OF
HUMERUS

ACROMIOCLAVICULAR
JOINT

DELTOID

PECTORALIS MAJOR

TRICEPS

BRACHIALIS

ECRB

TENDON OF
TRICEPS

ABDUCTOR AND
ENTENSORS
POLLICIS

BRACHIORADIALIS

RADIUS

LATERAL
EPICONDYLE

OLECRANON

ECRL

EXTENSOR DIGITORUM
AND ECU

ULNA

HEAD OF ULNA

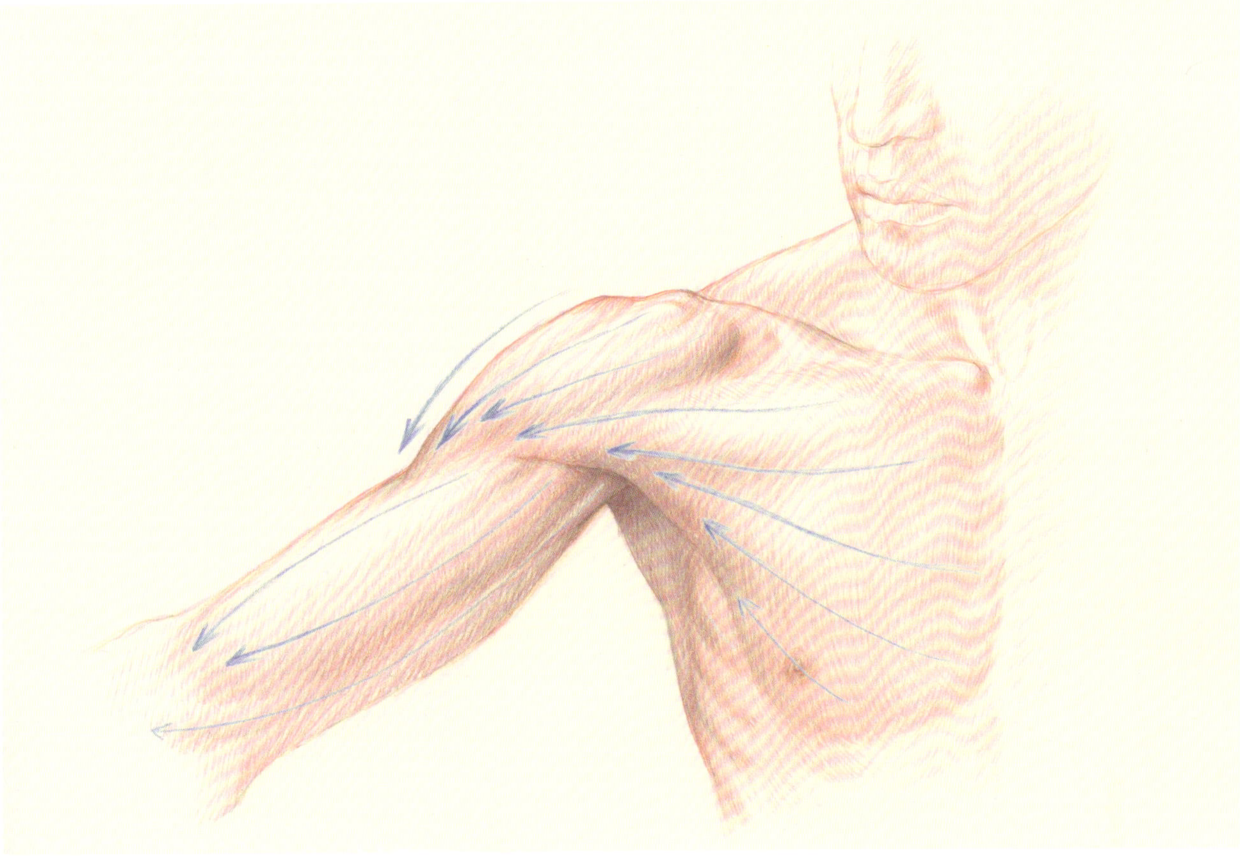

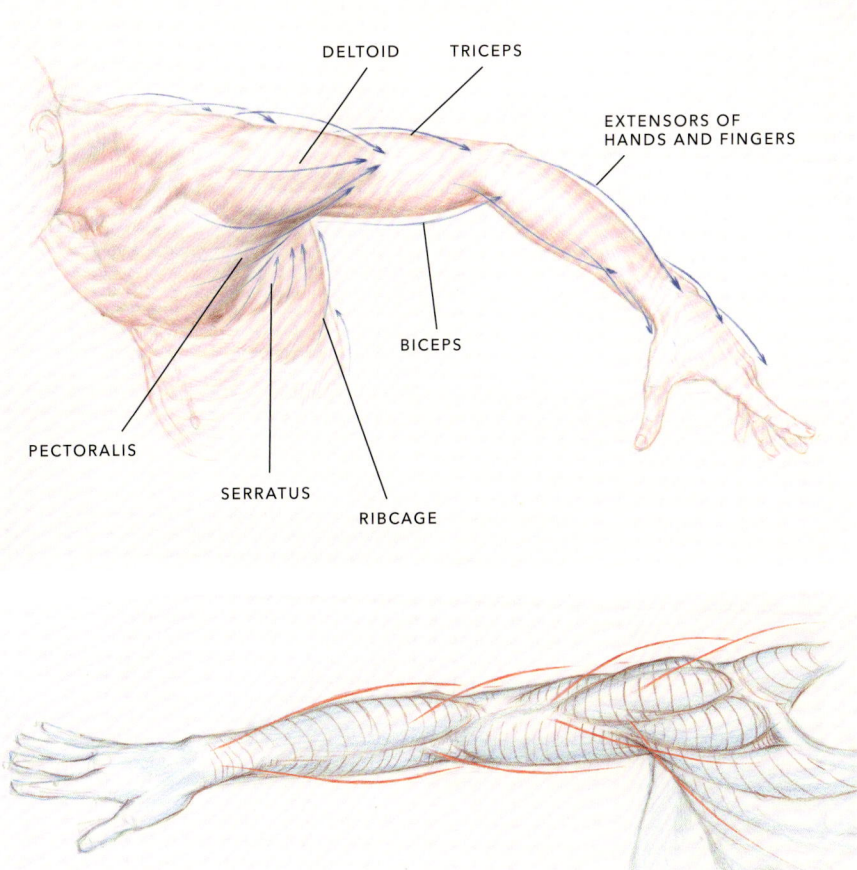

DELTOID   TRICEPS

EXTENSORS OF
HANDS AND FINGERS

BICEPS

PECTORALIS

SERRATUS

RIBCAGE

OPPOSITE: Muscular flows from upper torso to forearm

This drawing, which you have already encountered in chapter 3 (page 102), can also be analyzed for muscular flows. Note how the extensors wrap around the forearm, as well as how the converging fascicles of the pectoralis go under the deltoid.

TOP: Continuity and convergence of the fibers of the pectoralis and deltoid

CENTER: Flows of the shoulder and arm, superior view, example 1

This and the following figures offer yet more examples of flows of the arm from different points of view. As you can imagine, there really are infinite possible visualizations of these patterns.

BOTTOM: Flows of the shoulder and arm, superior view, example 2

This view of a slightly different pose seen from a different angle shows analogies to the flows and volumes of the previous view.

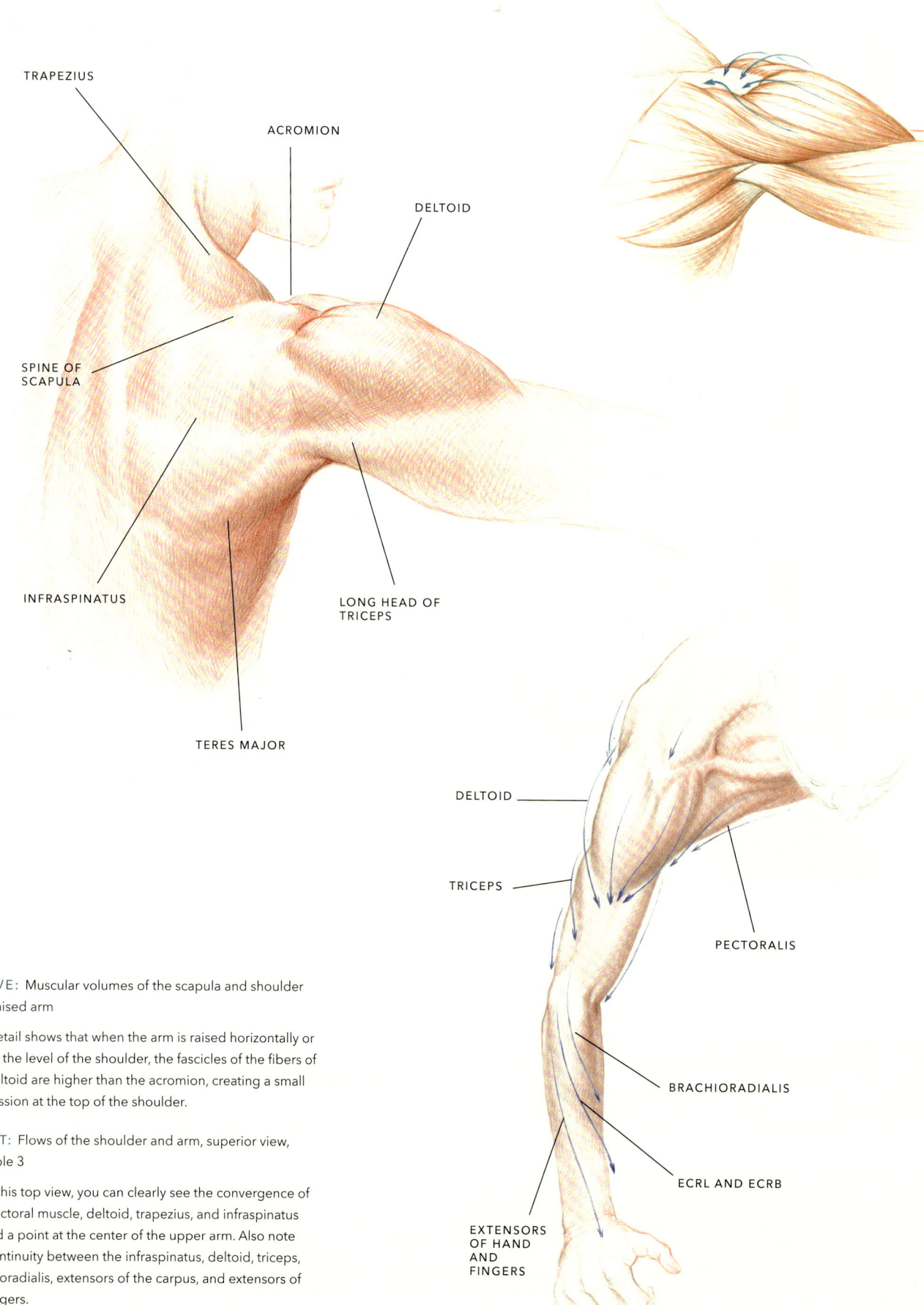

TRAPEZIUS

ACROMION

DELTOID

SPINE OF
SCAPULA

INFRASPINATUS

LONG HEAD OF
TRICEPS

TERES MAJOR

DELTOID

TRICEPS

PECTORALIS

BRACHIORADIALIS

ECRL AND ECRB

EXTENSORS
OF HAND
AND
FINGERS

ABOVE: Muscular volumes of the scapula and shoulder
with raised arm

The detail shows that when the arm is raised horizontally or
above the level of the shoulder, the fascicles of the fibers of
the deltoid are higher than the acromion, creating a small
depression at the top of the shoulder.

RIGHT: Flows of the shoulder and arm, superior view,
example 3

From this top view, you can clearly see the convergence of
the pectoral muscle, deltoid, trapezius, and infraspinatus
toward a point at the center of the upper arm. Also note
the continuity between the infraspinatus, deltoid, triceps,
brachioradialis, extensors of the carpus, and extensors of
the fingers.

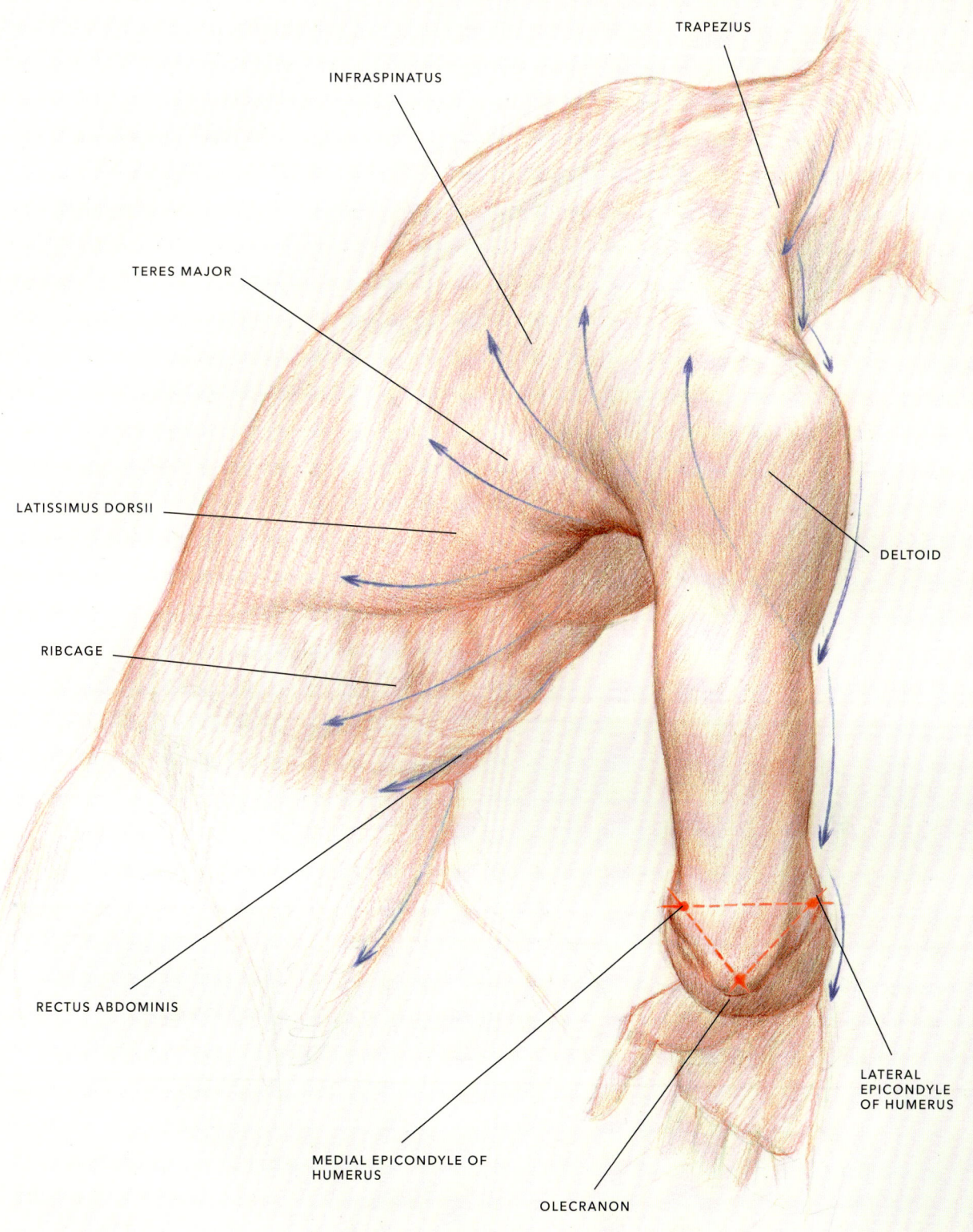

TRAPEZIUS

INFRASPINATUS

TERES MAJOR

LATISSIMUS DORSII

RIBCAGE

RECTUS ABDOMINIS

DELTOID

MEDIAL EPICONDYLE OF
HUMERUS

OLECRANON

LATERAL
EPICONDYLE
OF HUMERUS

A different pose or different angle creates
different pathways. In addition to the flows
created by the muscles, also note the *V* pattern
created by the alignment of the epicondyles of
the humerus with the olecranon.

FLOWS OF THE LEG

There are many ways to interpret the harmonious connections between the muscular and skeletal structures of the leg. The flows visualized in the drawings here result from the interaction of muscle groups and the skeleton. Some of the leg's flows, however, are purely aesthetic, not necessarily directly connected with the structure or function of the leg. Because of this, visualizing these flows can be more intuitive and based on individual opinion.

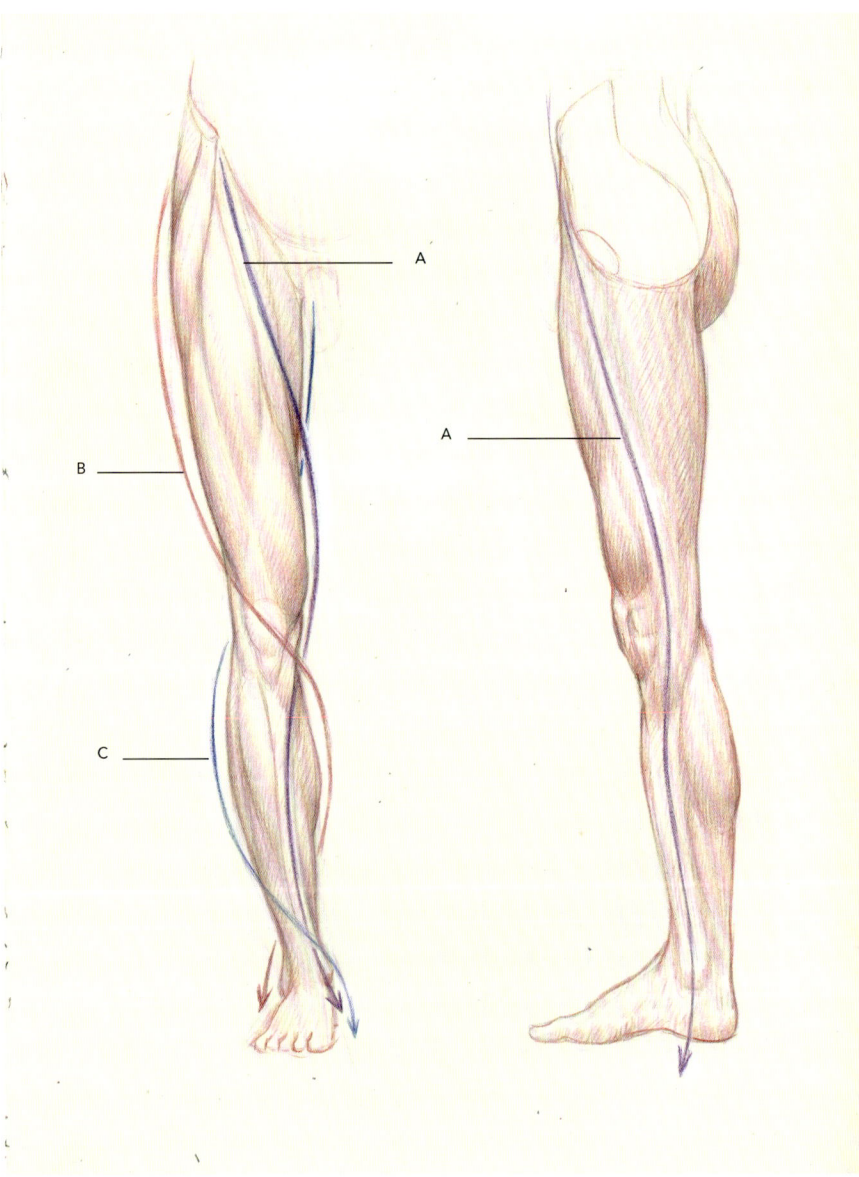

RIGHT: Flows of the leg

Some of the flows of the leg are created by a structural continuity, as shown, for example, by the purple line *(A)* that goes from the iliac spine to the sartorius, knee, tibia, and malleolus. This line is known as Cupid's Bow, a perfect balance between structural and anatomical flows. The red *(B)* and blue *(C)* flows that spiral along the leg, following muscle volumes or running between muscles groups, are obtained more objectively and instead describe an aesthetic continuity between forms.

CUPID'S BOW

It was my former teacher and now friend and colleague John Horn who introduced me to the pattern visible in the image here. Created by the sartorius and the tibia, it starts from the ASIS and runs all the way down to the medial malleolus. During the Italian Renaissance, this pattern was named Cupid's Bow—a beautiful example of the humanistic approach to anatomy, which finds aesthetics in biology. The details of the knee show how its forms alter when the knee is flexed and extended. When the knee is extended *(A)*, the sartorius is over the posterior half of the knee; in the flexed knee *(B)*, the sartorius slides off the posterior half of the knee, making the profile of the knee wider.

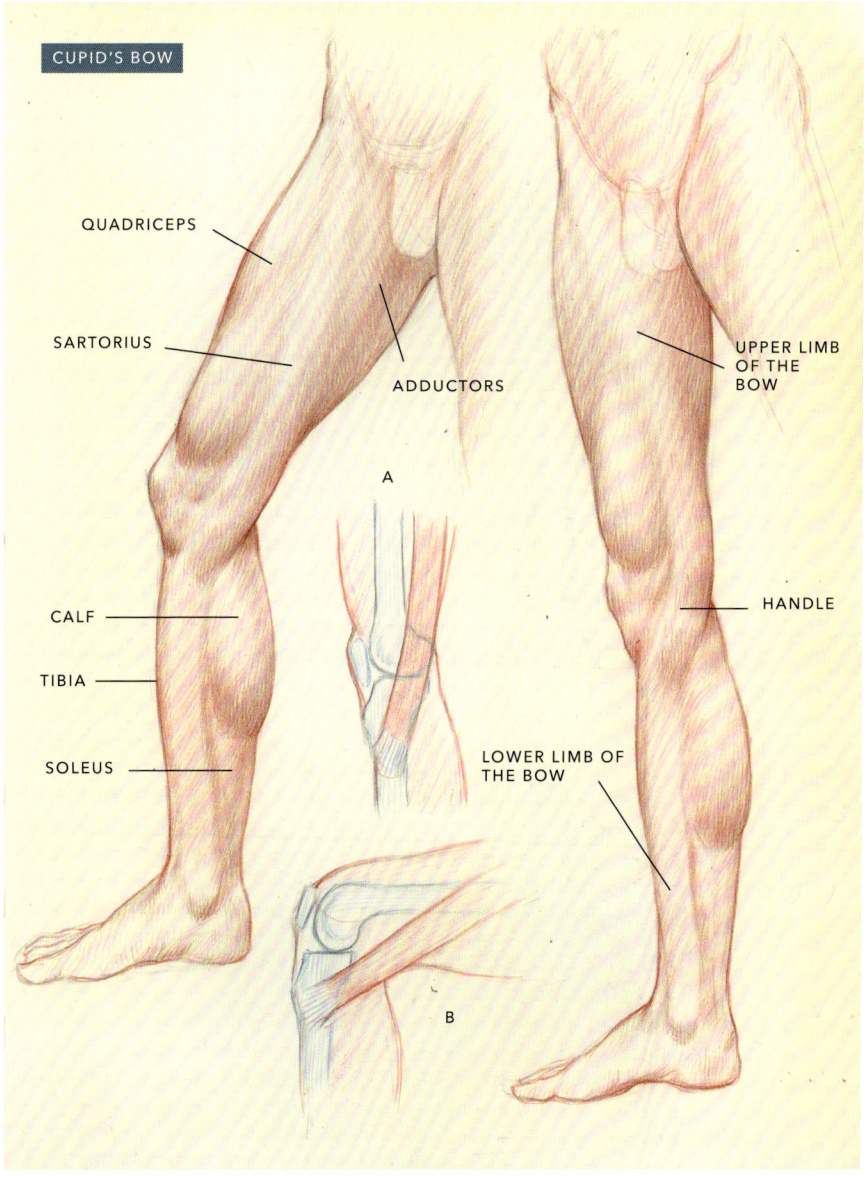

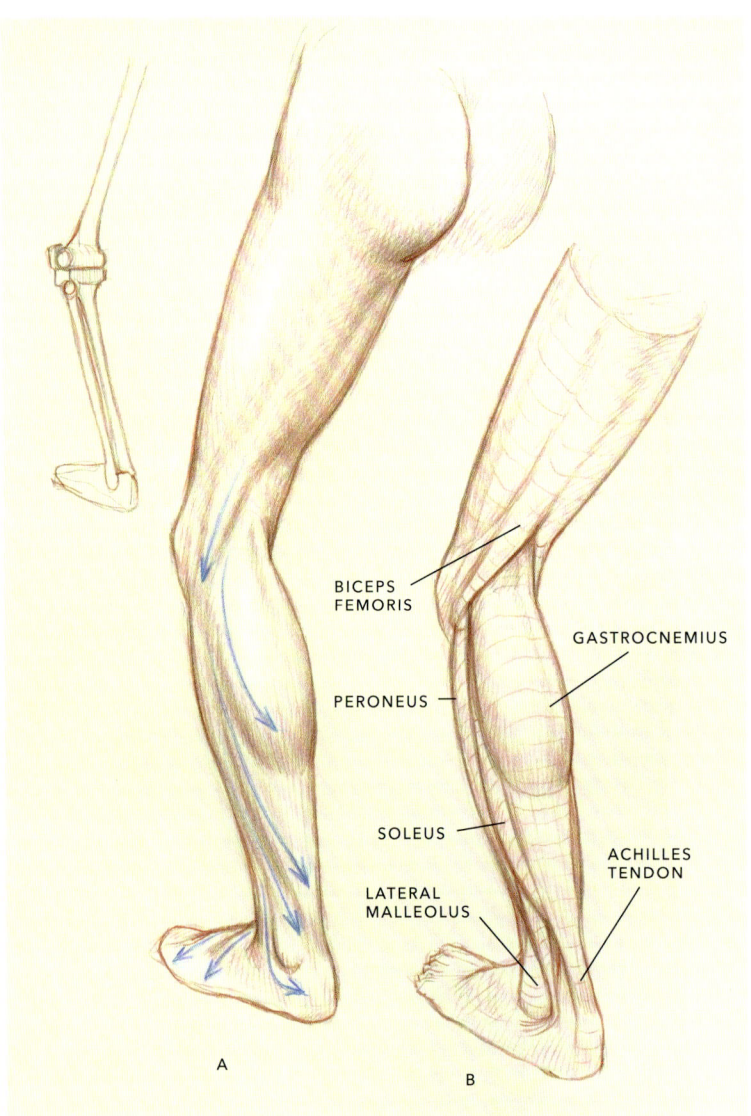

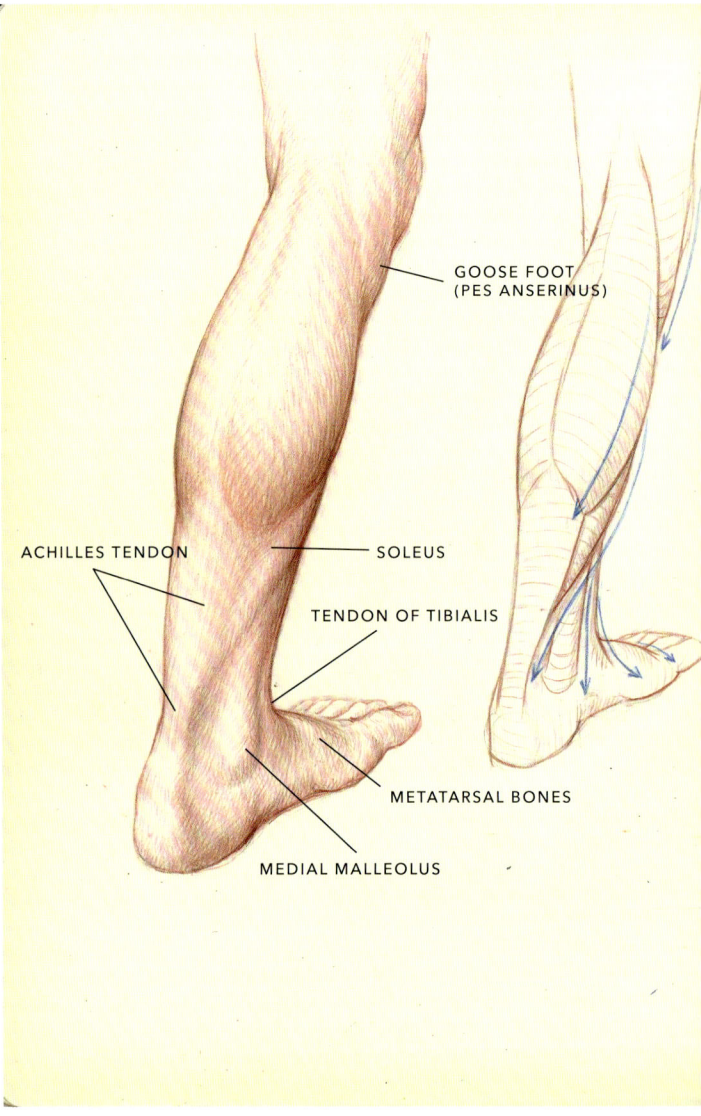

BICEPS
FEMORIS

GASTROCNEMIUS

PERONEUS

SOLEUS

LATERAL
MALLEOLUS

ACHILLES
TENDON

A

B

GOOSE FOOT
(PES ANSERINUS)

ACHILLES TENDON

SOLEUS

TENDON OF TIBIALIS

METATARSAL BONES

MEDIAL MALLEOLUS

ABOVE LEFT: Lower leg, posterior view with arrows

Many interconnected lines of flow run along the leg. Here are those that are visible on the lateral view *(A)*. The flayed leg *(B)* shows the muscular forms that produce the flows in more detail.

ABOVE RIGHT: Detail of the flows of the leg, posterior medial three-quarters view

This posterior medial view of the leg completes the analysis of the flows of the leg created by the muscular and skeletal structures. For a model, I used the cast of a Classical sculpture we have at the New York Academy of Art. Such casts are a fantastic resource because their anatomy is idealized and therefore easier to understand than the anatomy of a live model.

DRAWING FROM PLASTER CASTS

Every art school used to have a beautiful collection of plaster casts of sculptures from various periods that students could use for drawing practice. But during the "Cultural Revolution" purge that swept the art academies during the last few decades of the twentieth century, many of these collections were disposed of. If, however, you're lucky enough to attend a school that still has its casts, you can use them to study anatomy.

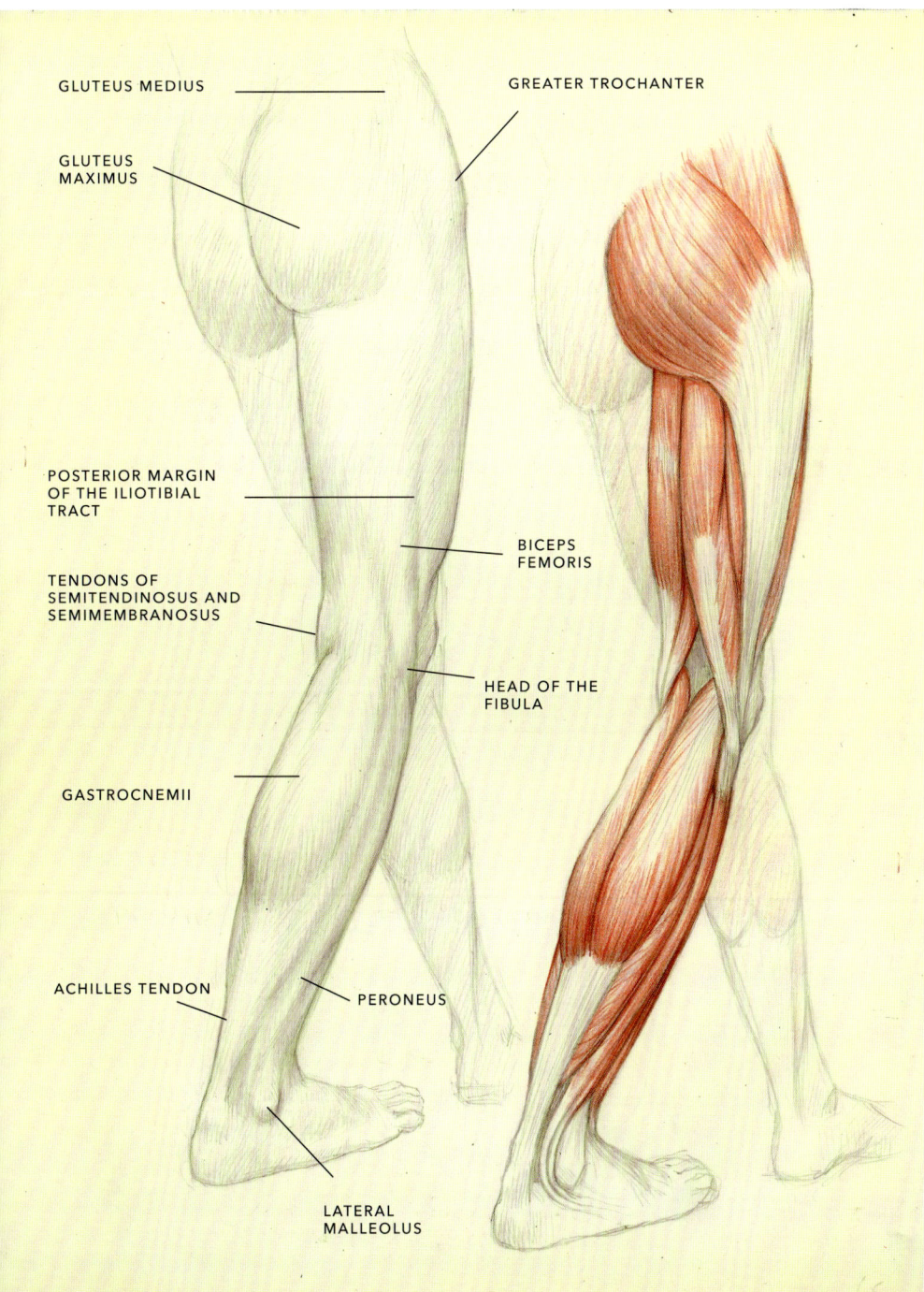

GLUTEUS MEDIUS

GREATER TROCHANTER

GLUTEUS MAXIMUS

POSTERIOR MARGIN OF THE ILIOTIBIAL TRACT

BICEPS FEMORIS

TENDONS OF SEMITENDINOSUS AND SEMIMEMBRANOSUS

HEAD OF THE FIBULA

GASTROCNEMII

ACHILLES TENDON

PERONEUS

LATERAL MALLEOLUS

LEFT: Cast drawing of *Silenus Holding the Infant Dionysus*

I based the drawing on the left on the New York Academy of Art's cast of the early Hellenistic Greek sculpture *Silenus Holding the Infant Dionysus*. I then created the drawing of the flayed legs on the right. The anatomy of Classical and Hellenistic sculptures is very accurate, but it is also idealized, making it easier for students to identify the muscles, landmarks, and flows and patterns of the body. Looking at the drawing of the cast, you can see how easy it is to recognize the muscular forms and landmarks.

FLOWS OF THE WHOLE BODY

So far we have analyzed the dynamic and aesthetic pathways of specific segments of the figure: torso, arms, and legs. Now it's now time to progress to the whole figure. The next drawings address the more complex but always beautiful interactions among the muscular forms of the entire body.

Correspondence between flows and superficial muscles, lateral view of crouching figure

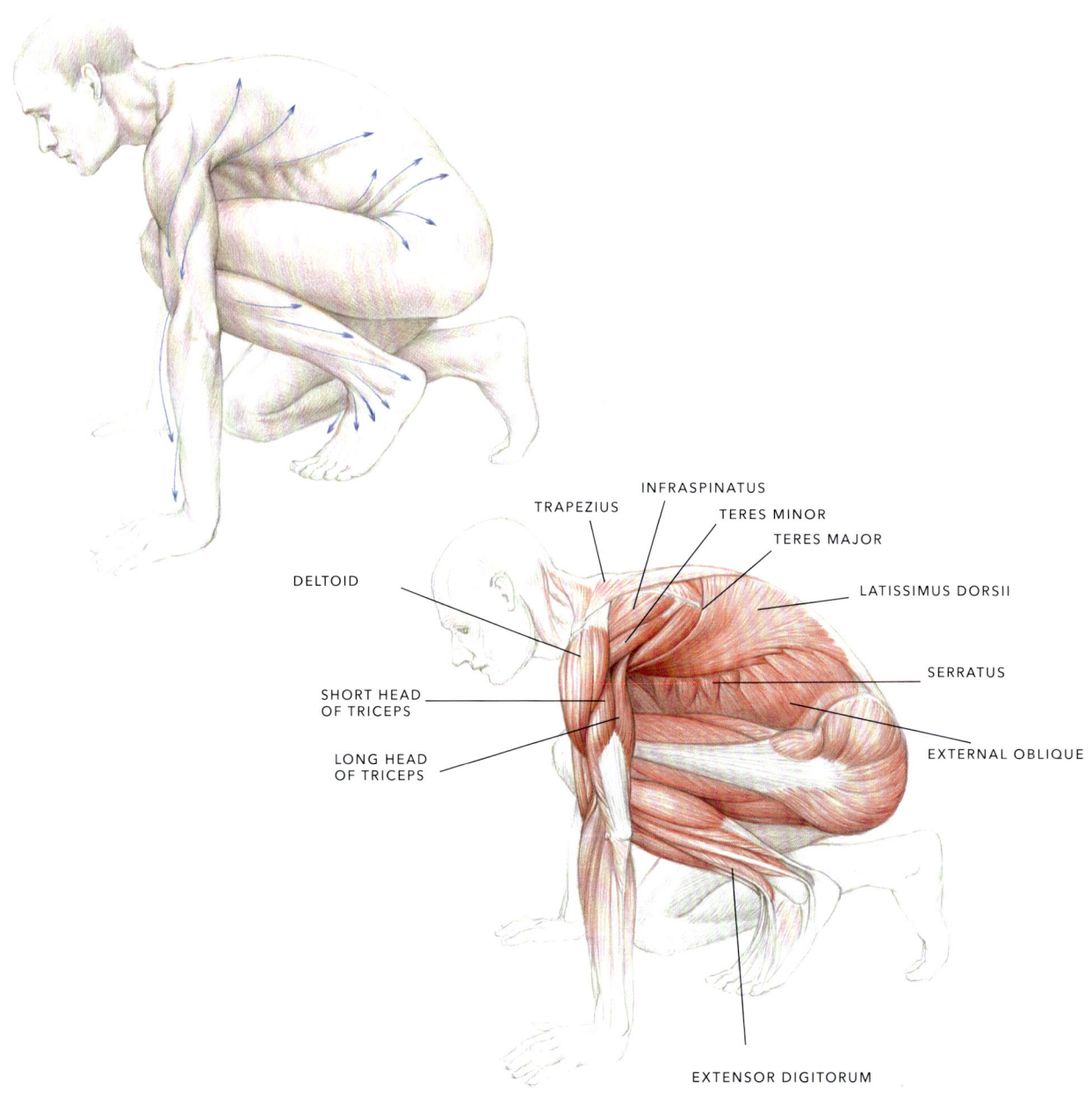

TRAPEZIUS

INFRASPINATUS

TERES MINOR

TERES MAJOR

DELTOID

LATISSIMUS DORSII

SERRATUS

SHORT HEAD OF TRICEPS

EXTERNAL OBLIQUE

LONG HEAD OF TRICEPS

EXTENSOR DIGITORUM

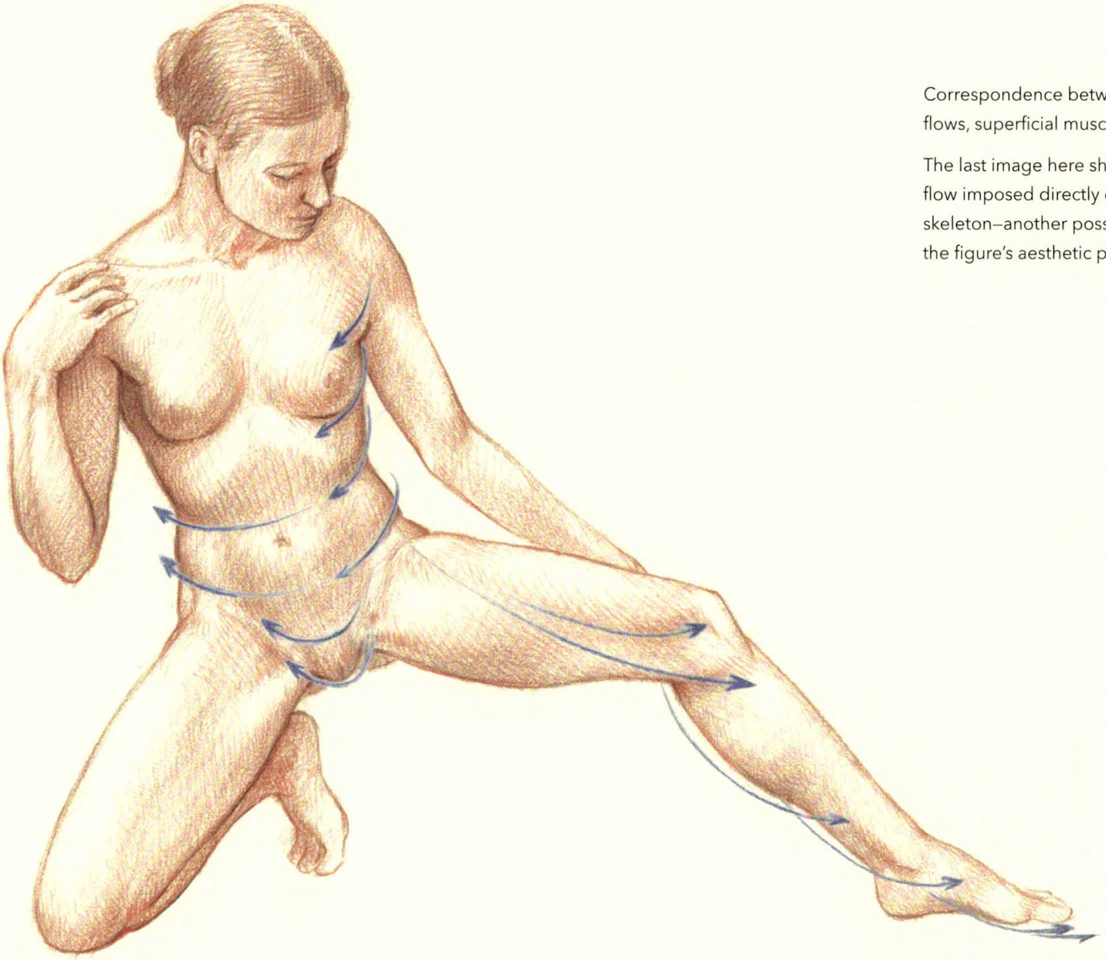

Correspondence between external flows, superficial muscles, and skeleton

The last image here shows the lines of flow imposed directly on a schematic skeleton—another possible way to read the figure's aesthetic pathways.

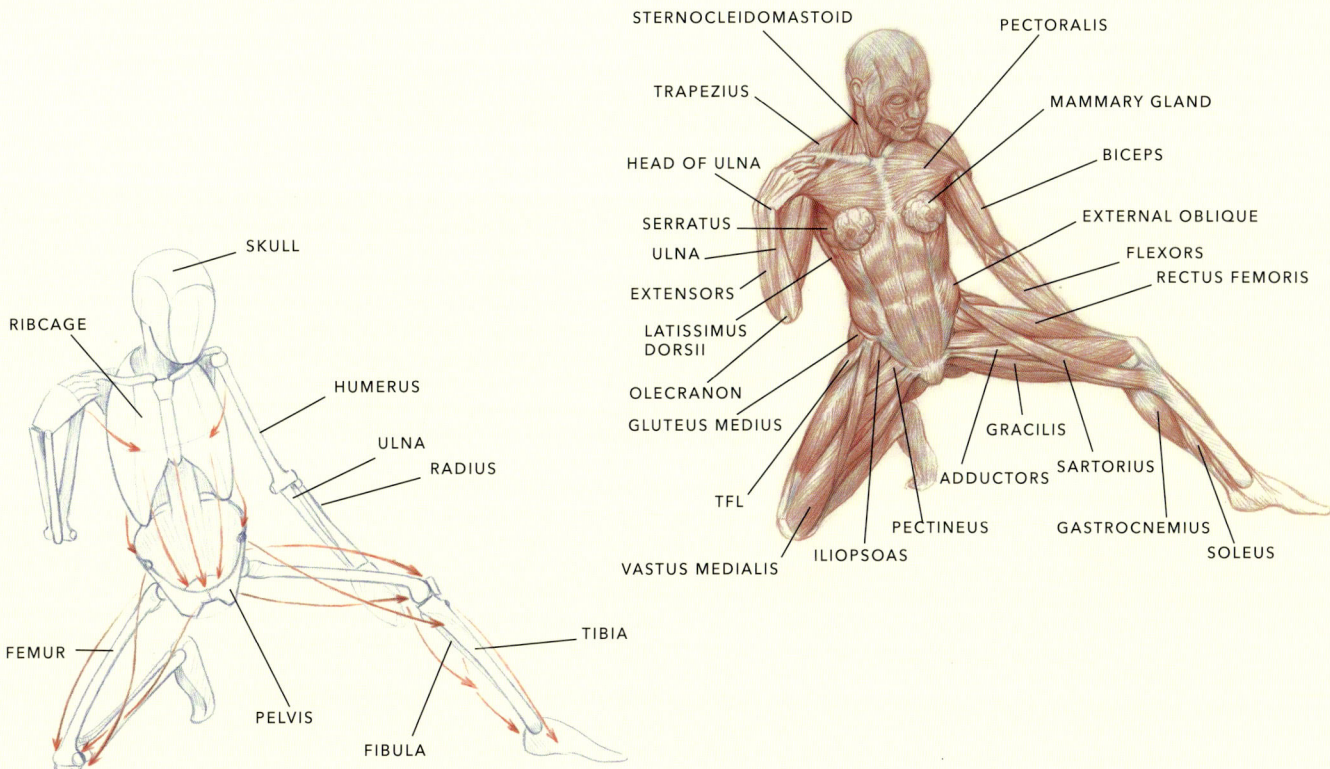

SKULL

RIBCAGE

HUMERUS

ULNA
RADIUS

FEMUR

PELVIS

TIBIA

FIBULA

STERNOCLEIDOMASTOID

PECTORALIS

TRAPEZIUS

MAMMARY GLAND

HEAD OF ULNA

BICEPS

SERRATUS

EXTERNAL OBLIQUE

ULNA

FLEXORS

EXTENSORS

RECTUS FEMORIS

LATISSIMUS DORSII

OLECRANON

GLUTEUS MEDIUS

GRACILIS

TFL

ADDUCTORS

SARTORIUS

VASTUS MEDIALIS

PECTINEUS

GASTROCNEMIUS

ILIOPSOAS

SOLEUS

USING FLOWS IN FIGURE DRAWING

When drawing the figure in a long or challenging pose it is always a good idea to create sketches for studying details of the various parts of the figure, the muscular forms, the pathways, and the effect of the light on the form. The images here exemplify this approach.

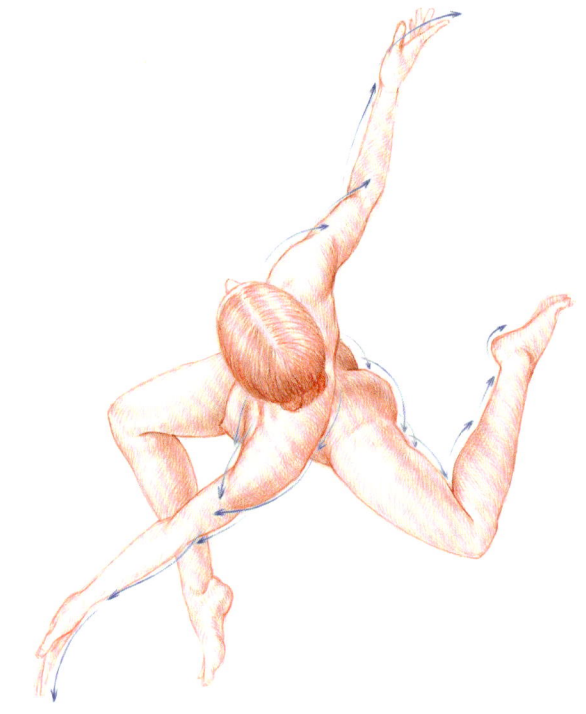

ABOVE RIGHT: Muscular flows on a female figure seen from above

I climbed a ladder to get this unusual view of my model Megan's pose. The arrows show some of the flows created by the muscular volumes. Noticing these pathways is very helpful when drawing the figure, especially from a challenging point of view such as this.

BELOW RIGHT: Patterns of flow of various parts of the body of a standing figure leaning forward.

BELOW: Flows of the whole body, sitting figure

Here is yet another example of the aesthetic pathways created by the muscles of the whole body, this time in a figure sitting on the ground.

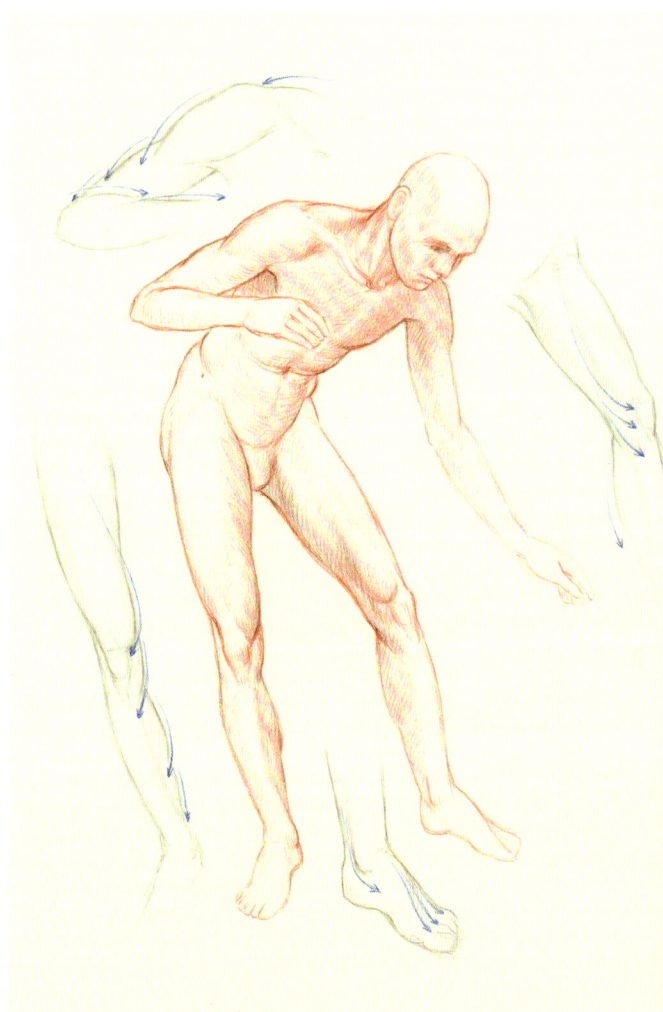

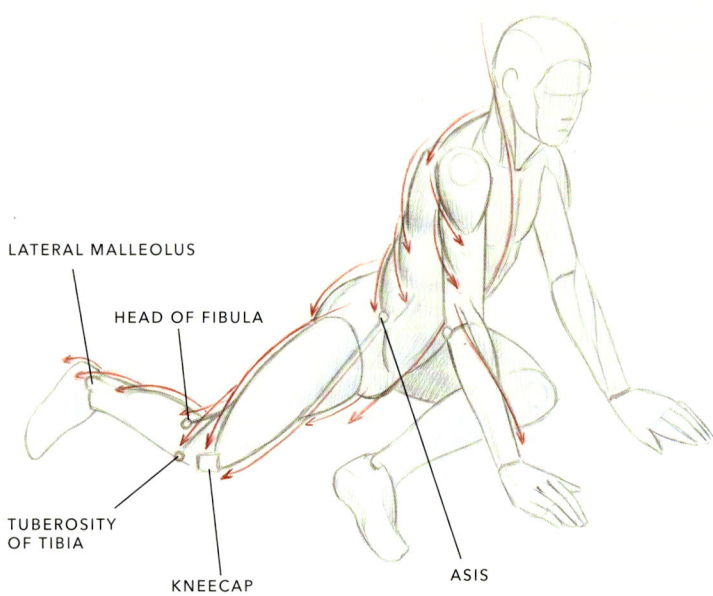

LATERAL MALLEOLUS

HEAD OF FIBULA

TUBEROSITY OF TIBIA

KNEECAP

ASIS

EXERCISE

Photocopy these three images and draw the lines of flow over them.

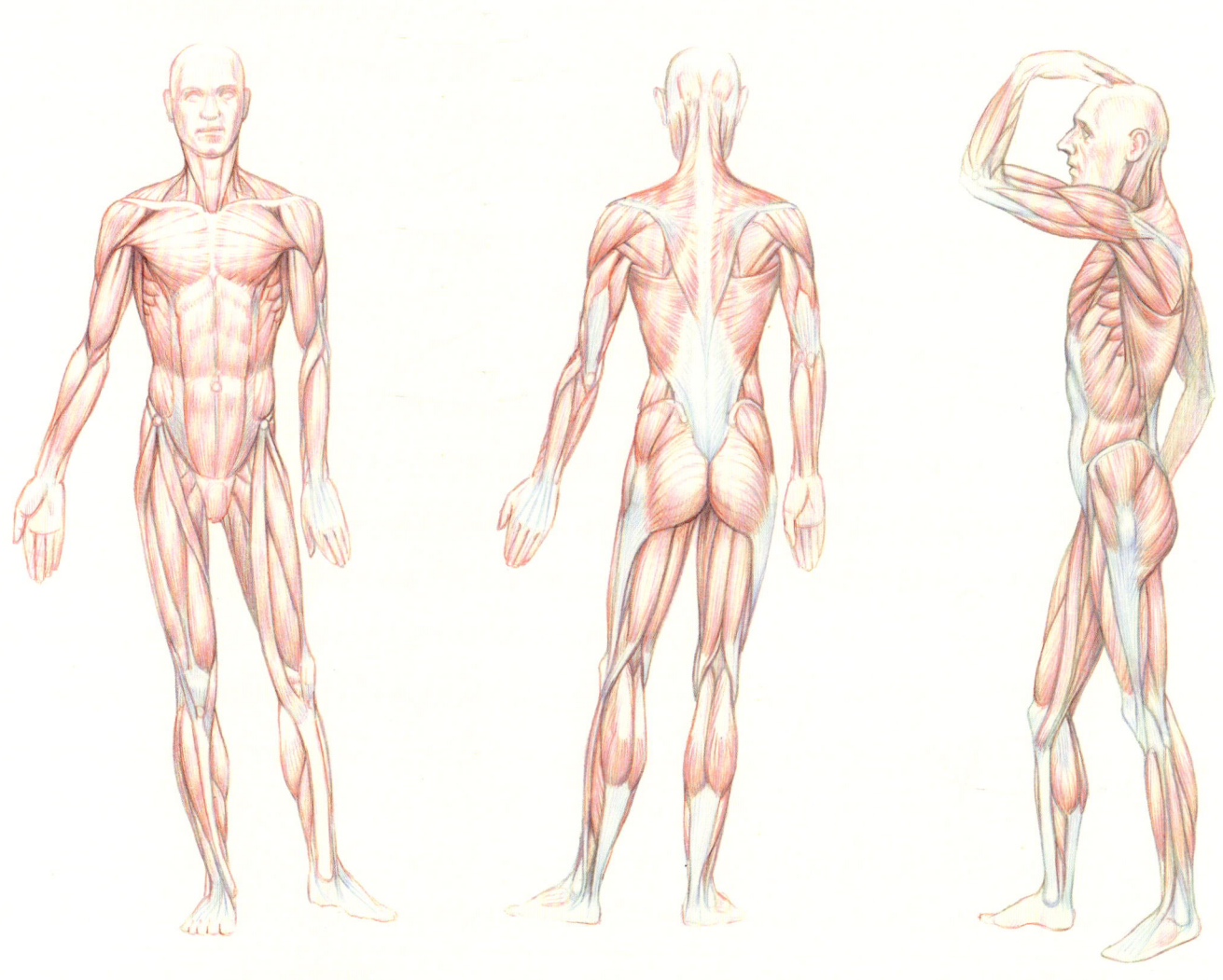

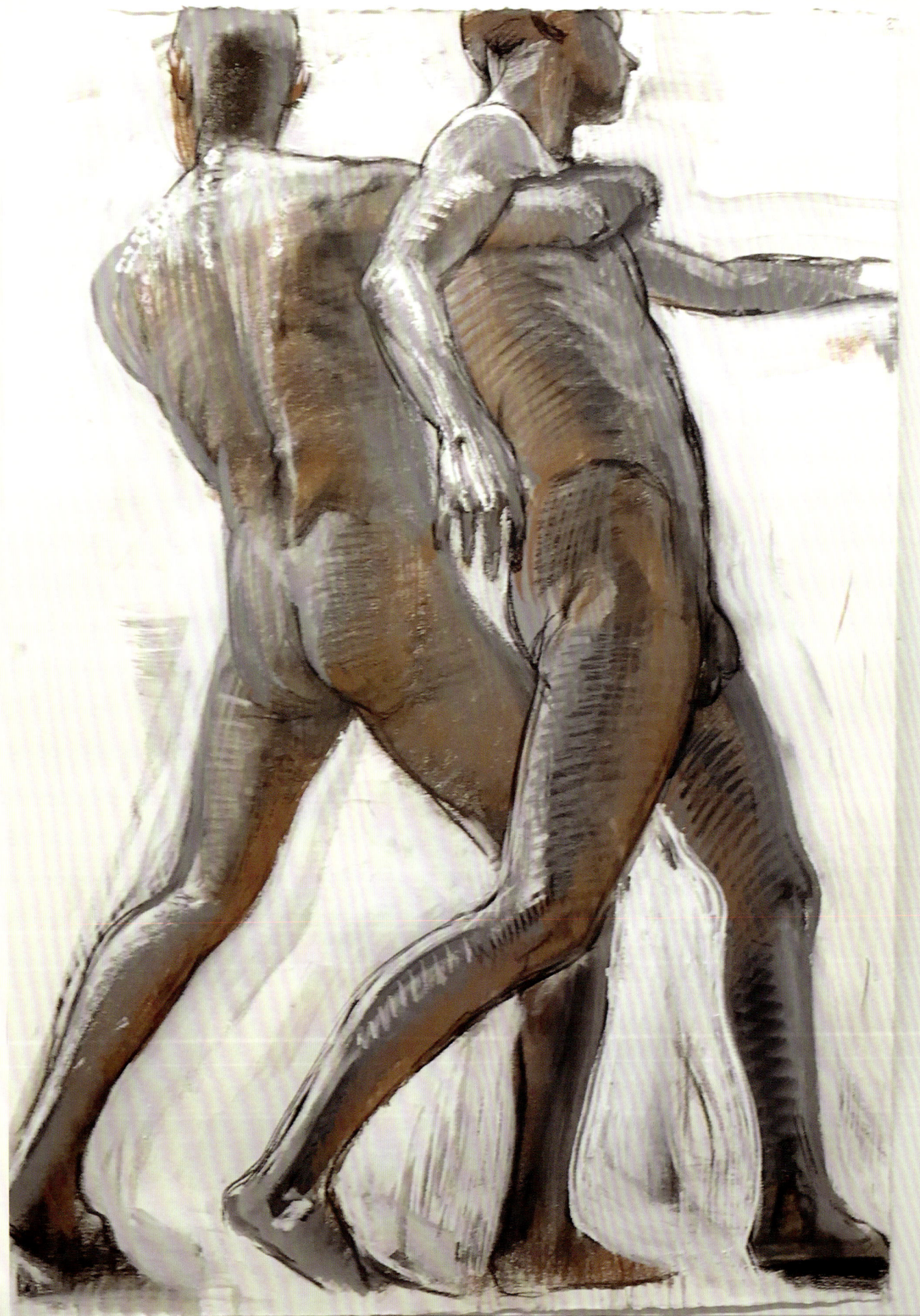

CHAPTER 6

MOVEMENT

In this chapter, I first look at how the sense of movement was developed in art over a span of about two thousand years, from the Archaic, Classical, and Hellenistic periods of ancient Greece through the Renaissance and Baroque periods in Italy. This analysis focuses on the stylistic aspects of movement and the dynamism of the pose. In the latter part of the chapter I discuss the movement of the human body from a mechanical–physiological point of view.

Here you will also find diagrams and demonstrations that flesh out the ideas explored in previous chapters, including structure, identification of landmarks, and muscular flows. These will help you achieve convincing dynamism and expressive qualities in your figurative art.

OPPOSITE: Scott Noel, *Wrestling Figures,* 2020, pastel, acrylic, and oil on paper, 42 × 30 inches (106.68 × 76.20 cm). Courtesy of the artist.

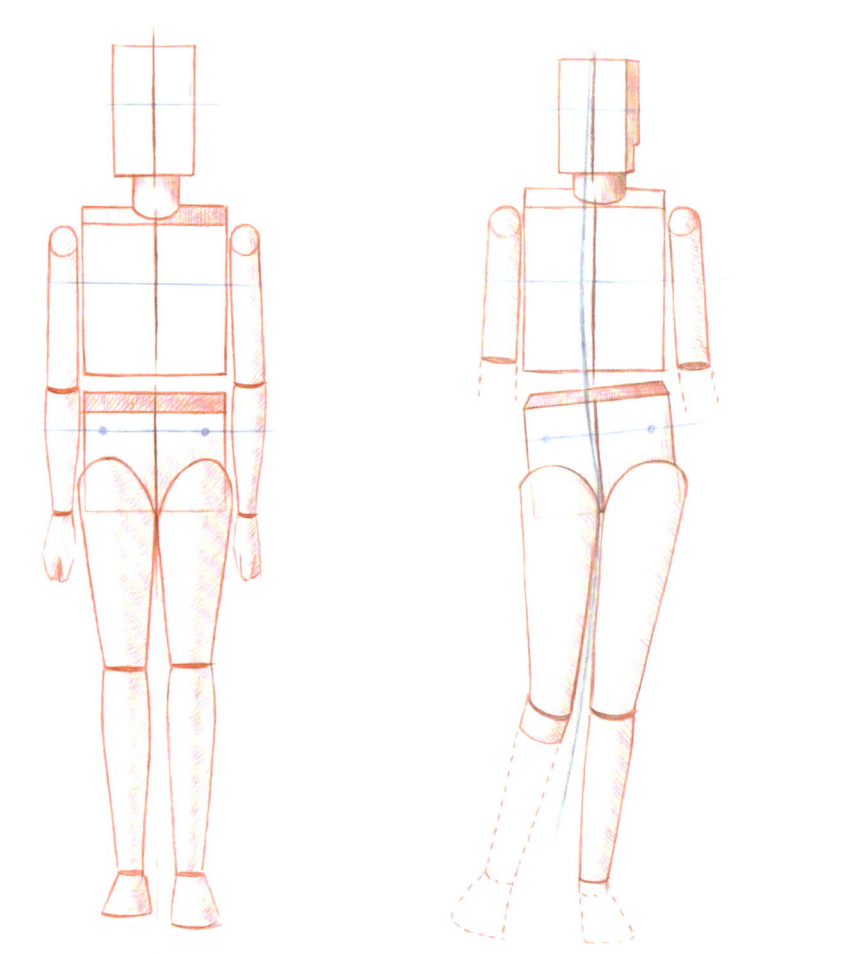
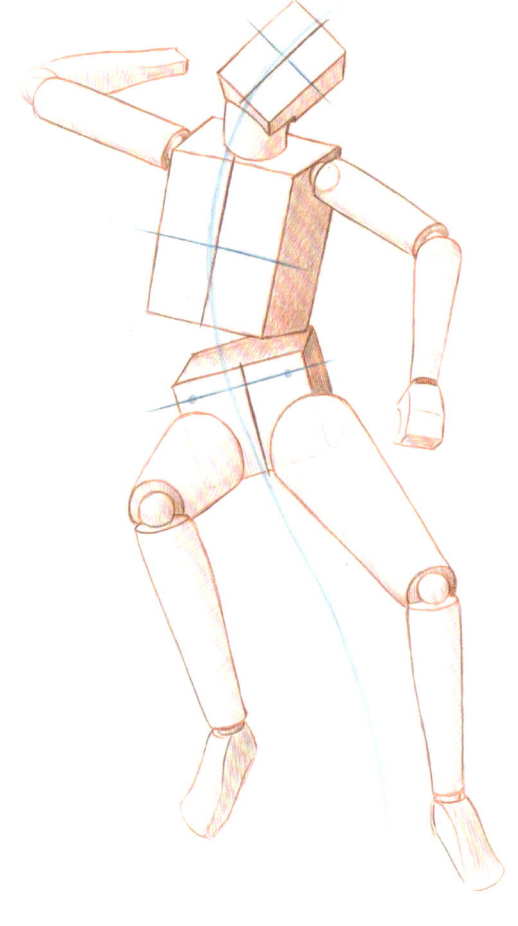

ABOVE: Progression of movement: Kouros, Kritios Boy, Laocoön

From the Archaic through the Hellenistic period, movement progressed through three basic patterns: in the Archaic kouros, the head, torso, and legs are aligned along a straight central axis; in the Kritios Boy, the head and torso segments are slightly tilted at different angles aligned along a sinuous axis; finally, the Laocoön's flailing limbs, arched torso, and tilted head create a dramatic spiraling, centrifugal effect.

THE ORIGINS OF MOVEMENT IN ART

The sense of movement that Greek sculptors imparted to their works developed over the course of centuries, becoming gradually more realistic and giving their art an increasingly convincing sense of life. One great innovation of the Archaic period is the freestanding, life-size sculpture. These sculptures have a fairly rigid pose, and the sense of life is achieved by what's called the "Archaic smile." (Originally, the surfaces of the sculptures were also realistically painted, although the paint has mostly worn off over time.)

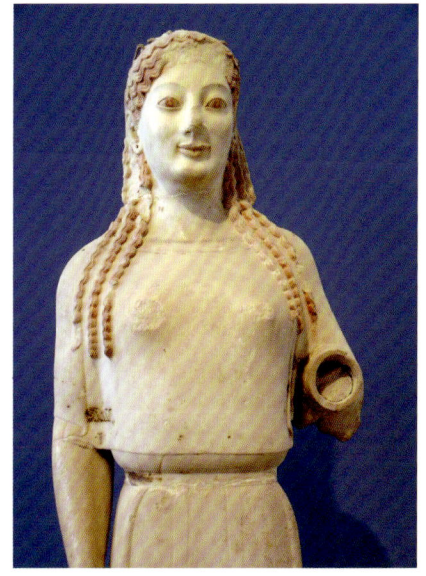

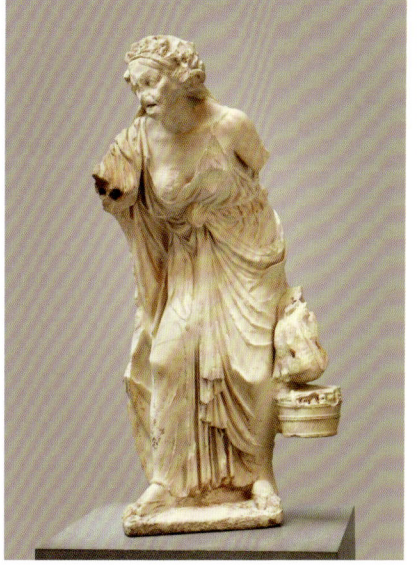

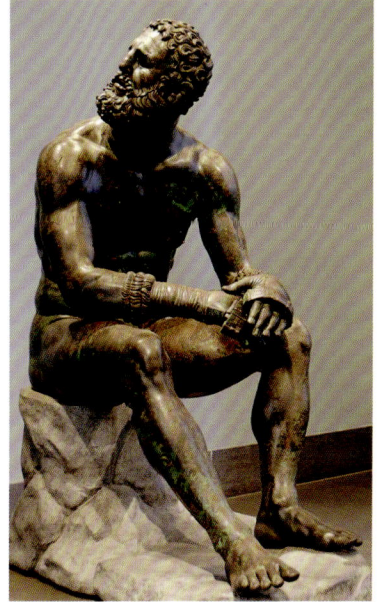

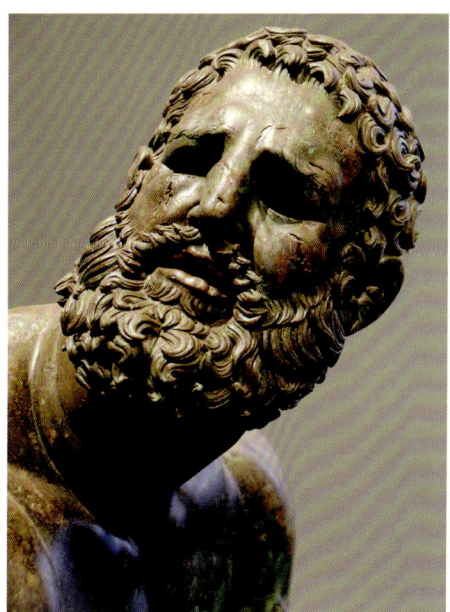

During the Classical period, a lifelike effect was obtained with realistic, dynamic poses; increasingly accurate anatomy; and the innovation known as *contrapposto* (see following page). The poses and anatomical forms of Classical sculptures are usually controlled and elegant. During the Hellenistic period the sense of movement, both physical and psychological, became much more forceful, culminating in artworks like the powerful Laocoön Group, which is animated by an intense emotional writhing, and the statue of an old woman, top right, an extremely realistic depiction of someone straining under the weight of a heavy basket. But even when the subjects of Hellenistic sculptures are at rest, they exude an emotional intensity and impending sense of movement, like the Thermae Boxer, above, who seems ready to stand up and walk away at any moment.

TOP LEFT Peplos Kore, 530 BCE, Parian marble, height 47¼ inches (119.88 cm). Acropolis Museum, Athens. Photo credit: Marsyas.

The facial expression known as the "Archaic smile" is typical of sculptures of the Archaic period.

TOP RIGHT Marble statue of an old woman, c. 14–68 CE, Roman copy of Greek original of second century BCE, height 49⅝ inches (125.98 cm). Metropolitan Museum of Art, New York, Rogers Fund, 1909.

BOTTOM LEFT Thermae Boxer, 3rd-2nd century BCE, bronze, height 47 inches (119 cm). Palazzo Massimo alle Terme, National Museum of Rome. Photographer: Marie-Lan Nguyen.

BOTTOM RIGHT: Detail of Thermae Boxer

CONTRAPPOSTO

A sense of elegance and emotional life

The term *contrapposto* (Italian for "counterpoise") describes a pose in which the various segments of the body are counterposed: the head, ribcage, and pelvis are tilted in opposite directions and aligned along a slightly *S*-curved line. The earliest known example of contrapposto is the Kritios Boy, opposite, sculpted in about 480 BCE. This pose conveys a sense of elegance, emotional life, and the psychology of the subject portrayed. To better understand contrapposto, it can be very useful to analyze a pose that is *not* contrapposto.

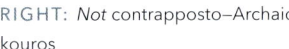

RIGHT: *Not* contrapposto—Archaic kouros

The pose is stiff and rigid, and the alignment of the iliac spines is perpendicular to the vertical axis.

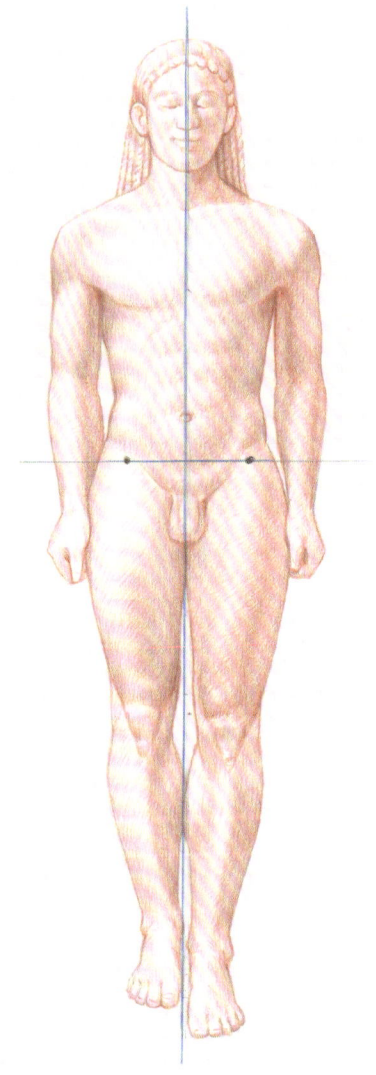

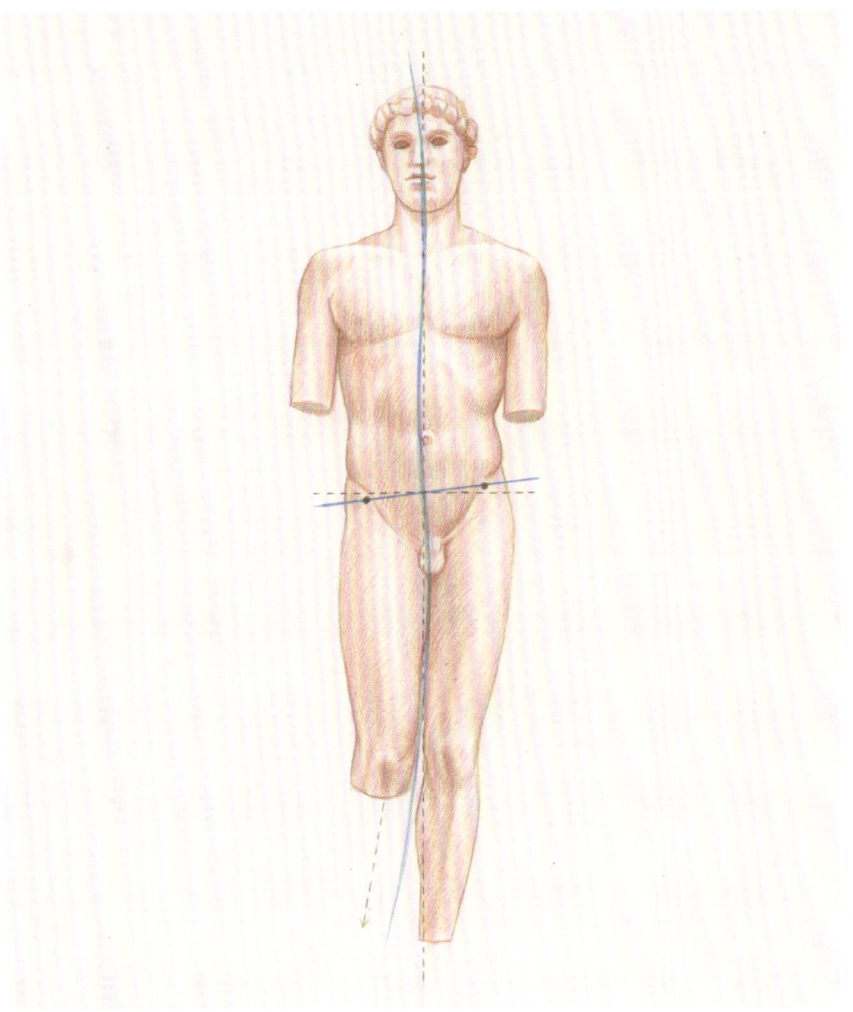

The sixth-century BCE Archaic kouros opposite is definitely *not* contrapposto. Evidently derived from Egyptian sculpture, its pose is fairly rigid and static, and the head, ribcage, and pelvis are aligned along a straight vertical axis. The horizontal axis, visualized by the alignment of the anterior superior iliac spines of the pelvis, is oriented perpendicularly to the vertical axis. The weight of the body is equally distributed on both legs, which are held rigidly straight; the arms are equally straight and held parallel to the sides of the body. The sculpture is freestanding and the face has the so-called Archaic smile.

With the Kritios Boy, the stiffness of the Archaic kouros is replaced by a delicate, expressive pose that conveys the impression that the boy, now at rest, could start moving at any moment. His head, chest and pelvis are slightly tilted at different angles and aligned along a gently curved central *S*-line that extends to the legs. The line connecting the iliac spines is not completely horizontal, showing a slight tilt of the pelvis. The legs, even if partly missing, show another typical characteristic of contrapposto: one leg is slightly bent and mostly free of the body's weight, which is instead concentrated on the straight and engaged leg.

ABOVE: Contrapposto–Kritios Boy

The alignment of the iliac spines shows a slight tilt. The segments of the body are aligned along a sinuous central line.

A revival of Classical ideals

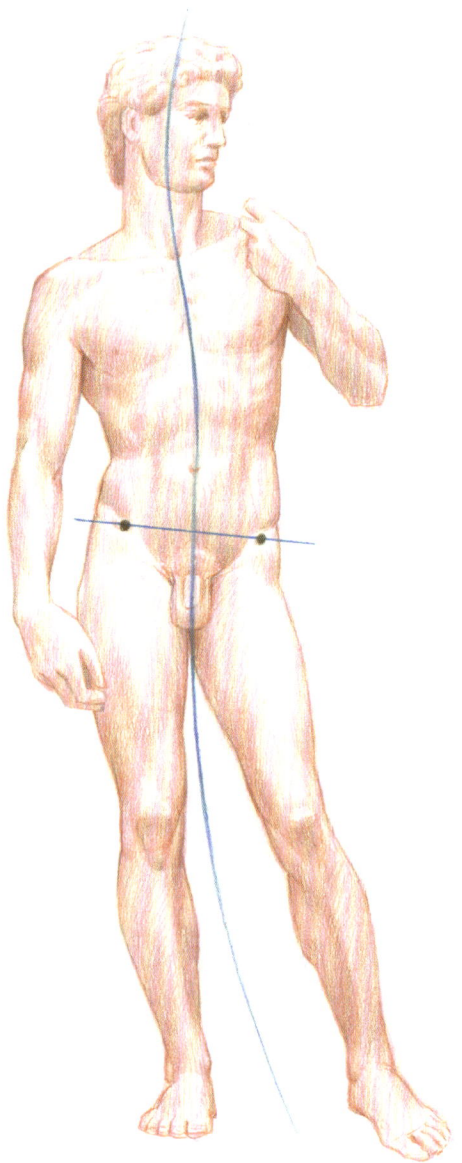

The Classical ideals of ancient Greece and Rome—including contrapposto—
were revived during the Italian Renaissance. In Michelangelo's *David*, the various
segments of the body are aligned along a gently curved central *S*-line. The head is
slightly tilted to the viewer's right and turned to a three-quarters view; the ribcage
is tilted to the viewer's left and faces front; and the pelvis is tilted to the viewer's
right, as visualized by the alignment of the iliac spines. The leg to our left is straight
and engaged, meaning that most of the body weight is leaning on it, while the leg
to our right is slightly flexed and free, meaning that the leg provides stability but
carries very little of the weight of the body. The arms are also counterposed in relation to each other: the arm on our left is straight and relaxed, while the arm on our
right, holding the fatal sling, is flexed.

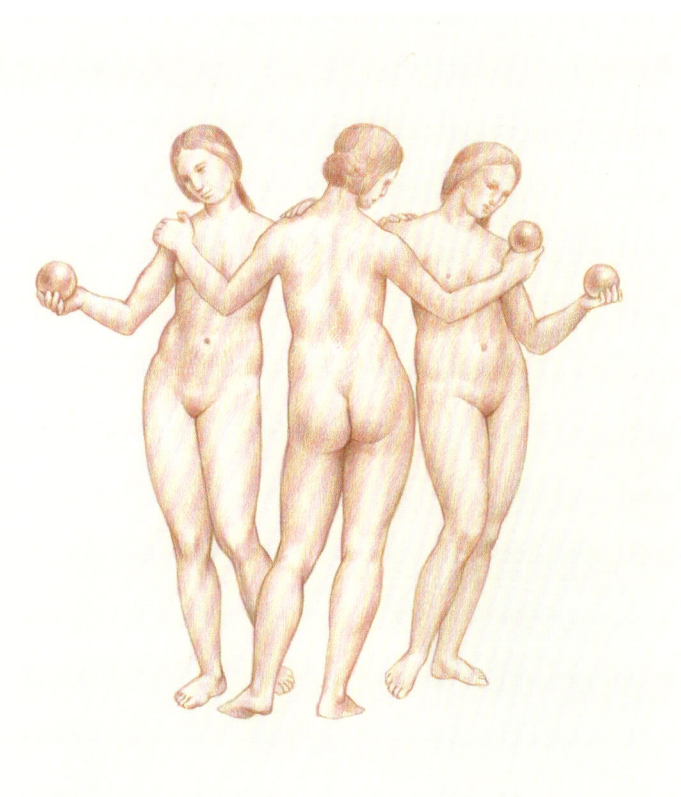

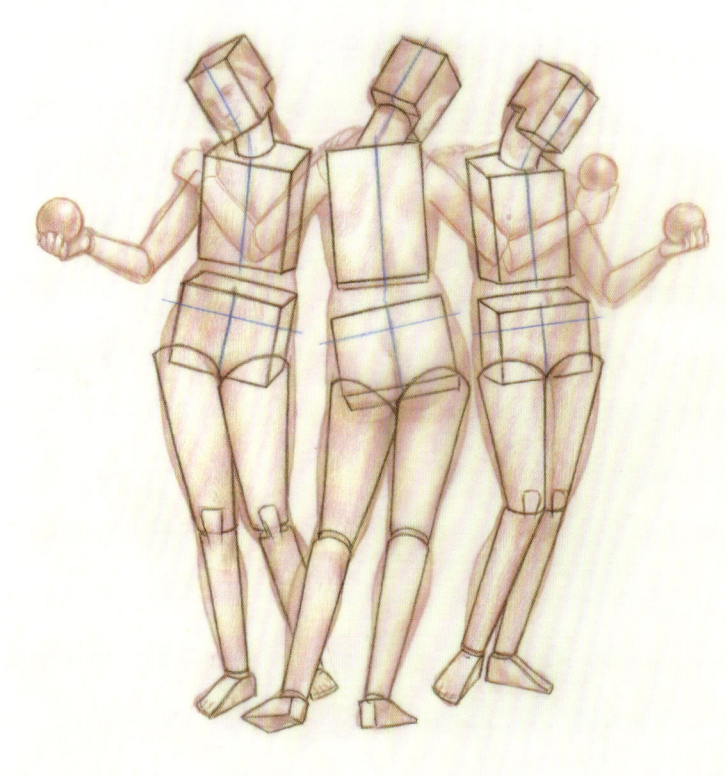

Contrapposto was also used in paintings to create complex compositions, as demonstrated by the schematic rendering of Raphael's *The Three Graces*. In this painting, created during the first decade of the sixteenth century, the bodies of all three female figures are aligned along *S*-curved lines. Each figure's head, chest, and pelvis are oriented at different angles, as shown by the curved lines and alignments of the iliac spines. The legs alternate between engaged and free and straight and slightly flexed; the arms create a zigzagging up-and-down pattern; and the figures are alternately oriented toward the front, the back, and then the front again.

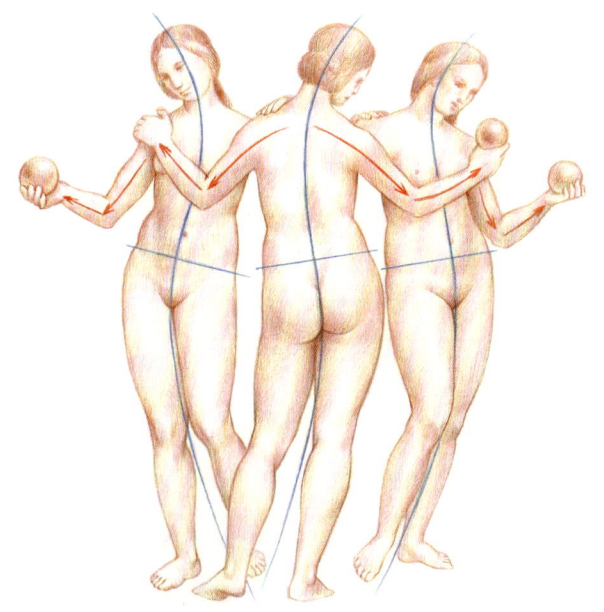

The Graces' *S*-curves also alternate: the curves of the first and third figures turn, respectively, to the left and right, and although the curves of the second and third figures are both oriented to the right, the figures themselves are counterposed, in that they face in different directions.

DYNAMIC FLOWS

BELOW LEFT: Barberini Faun, dynamic flows

BELOW RIGHT: Wounded Niobid (Greek original c. 440 BCE), dynamic flows

This section focuses on what I call *dynamic flows*. Dynamic flows can be created, for example, by deliberately positioning a figure's torso and limbs in a specific pattern—as can be seen, for example, in the Hellenistic Barberini Faun and the fifth-century BCE Classical sculpture known as the Wounded Niobid. Although the poses are somewhat different, in both cases movement is signaled by bent arms, legs spiraling outward from a slightly curved torso, and a head thrown back and turning.

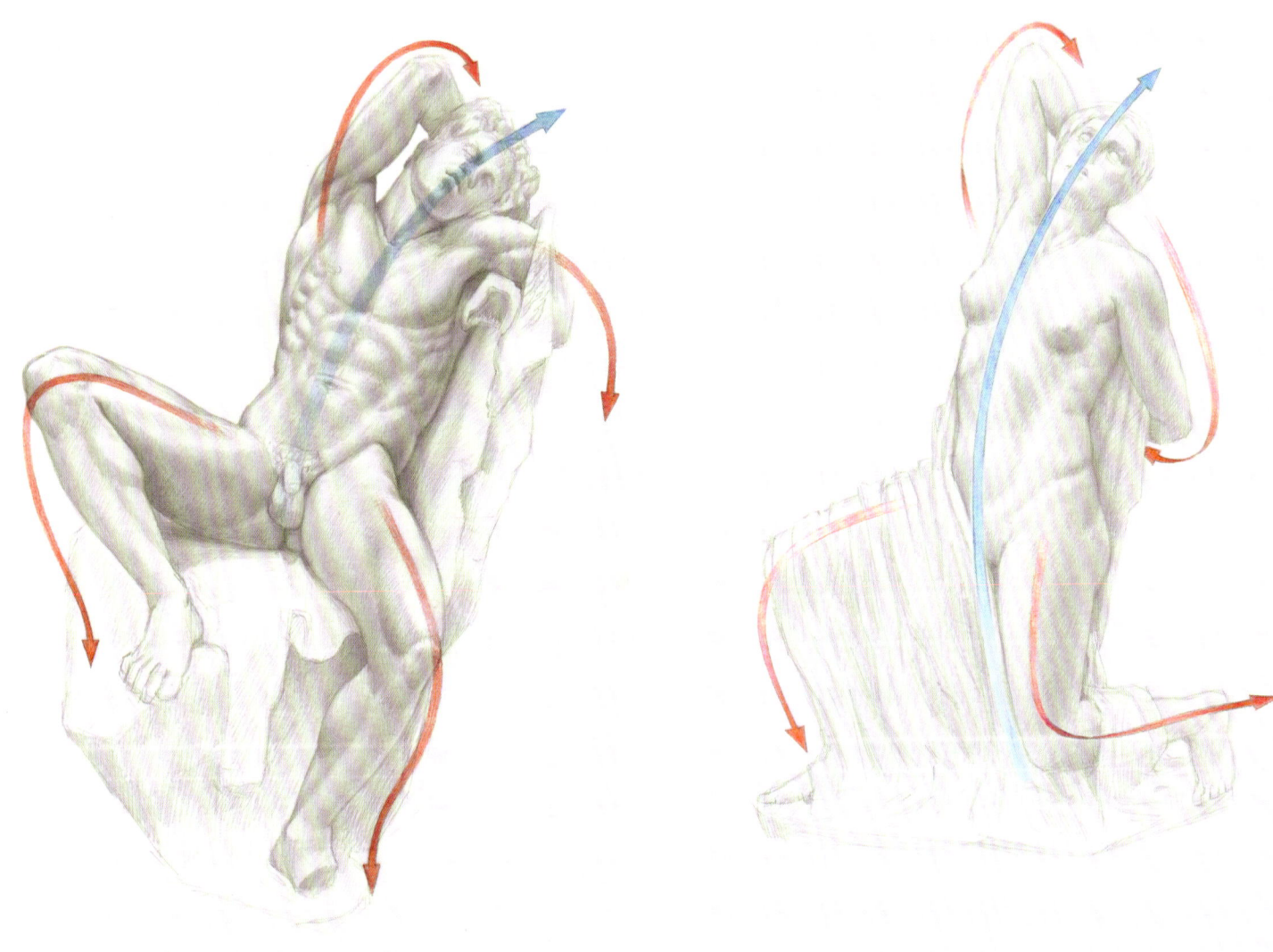

Many Hellenistic works, including the Laocoön, are based on this type of pose, which is also characteristic of the figure of Christ in Michelangelo's *Last Judgment*. The analysis of the Laocoön's dynamic flows using a stereometric rendition of the main volumes of the body reveals even more clearly how its powerful dynamism was obtained by stringing up the massive body's volumes on the sinuous central axis.

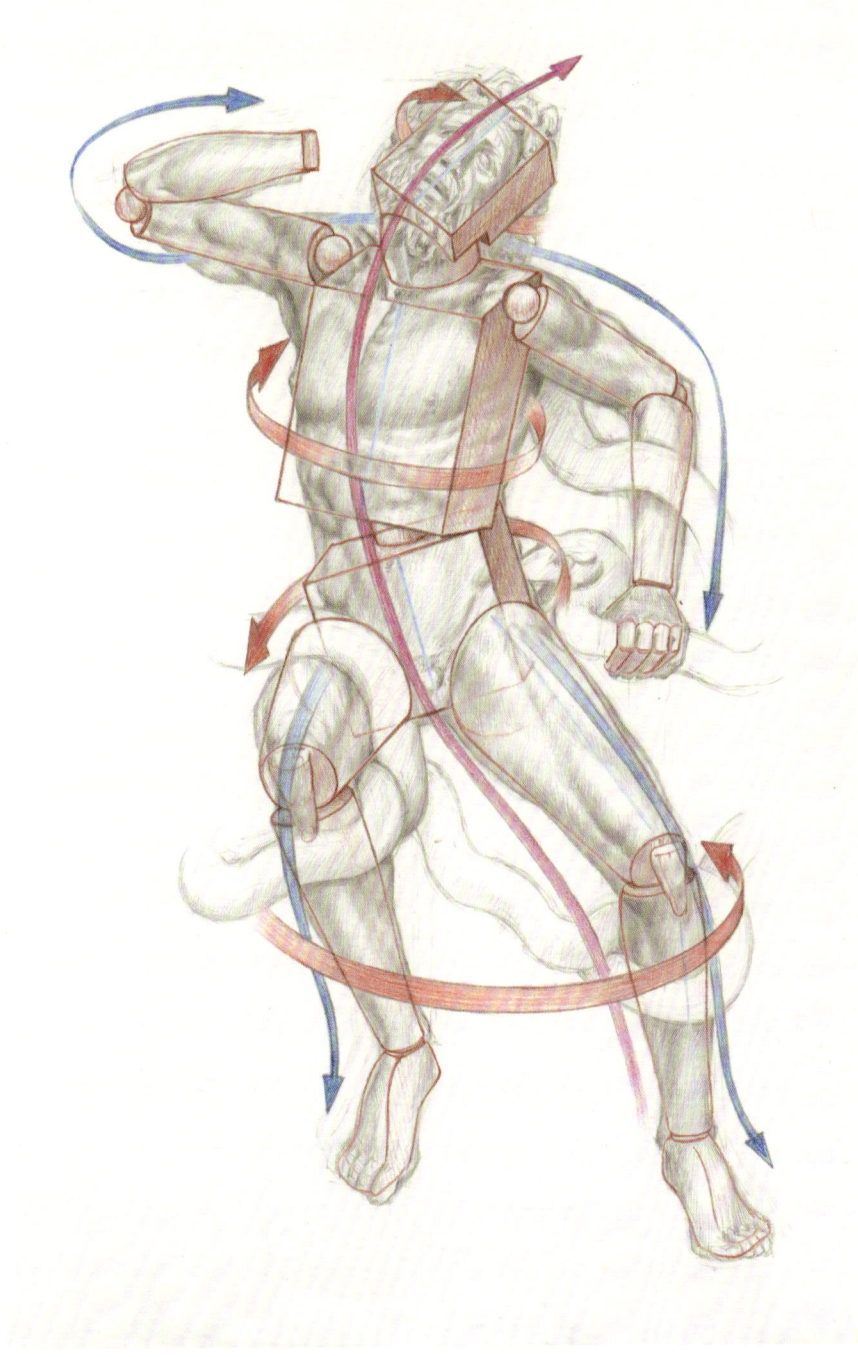

LEFT: Laocoön, stereometric rendering with dynamic flows

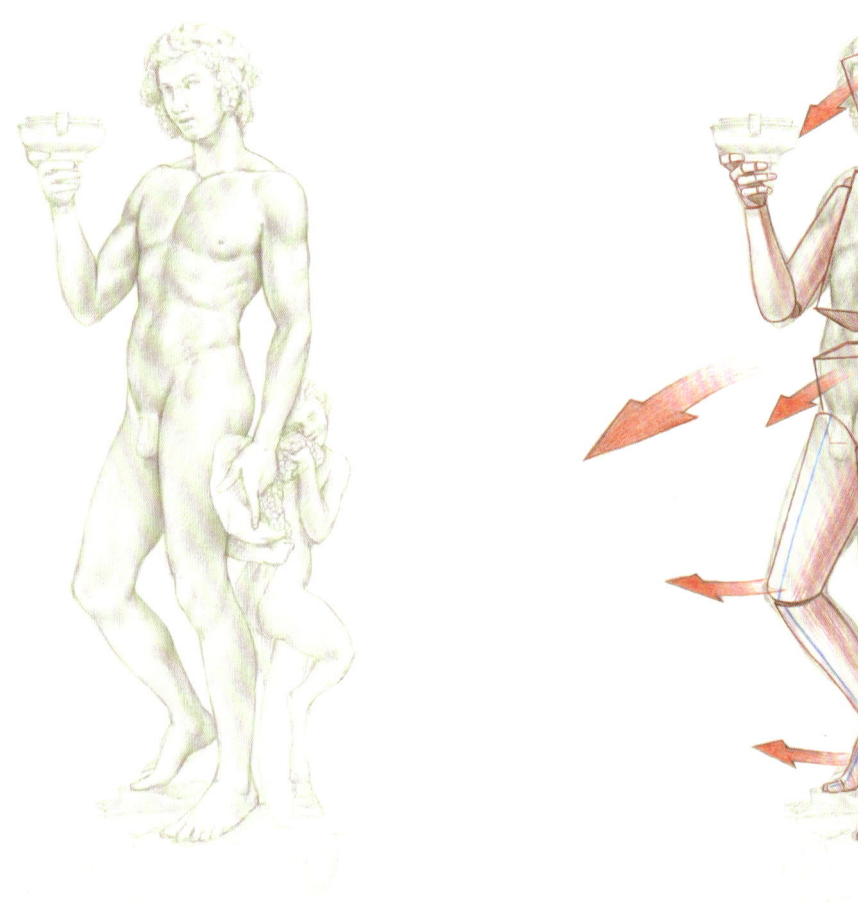

Masterfully messing with Classical conventions

ABOVE: Michelangelo's *Bacchus* (1496–97), rendering and stereometric rendering showing directions of movement

Even though Bacchus's ribcage, pelvis, and left leg are aligned along a backward-arching line (red arrow at the back of the shoulders), the whole body is stumbling forward because of his drunkenness.

DRUNKEN OR UNCONTROLLED MOVEMENT

Now let's fast-forward a millennium and a half to examine a couple of works by Michelangelo and analyze his development of the Classical and Hellenistic paradigms. In *Bacchus,* which Michelangelo completed at the incredibly young age of twenty-two, the center of gravity is offset, creating a sense of imbalance. The straight leg, which in classic contrapposto is engaged and therefore provides support to the body, is in this case unstable. The "free" leg, which in classic contrapposto is typically bent and passive, is active, catching up with Bacchus's body as it tips forward and trying to prevent him from falling.

In *Bacchus,* the alternating tilt of the various segments of the body does not signal a controlled and elegant pose but rather uncontrolled, drunken movement. Michelangelo is masterfully messing with the Classical conventions of harmony, balance, and self-control.

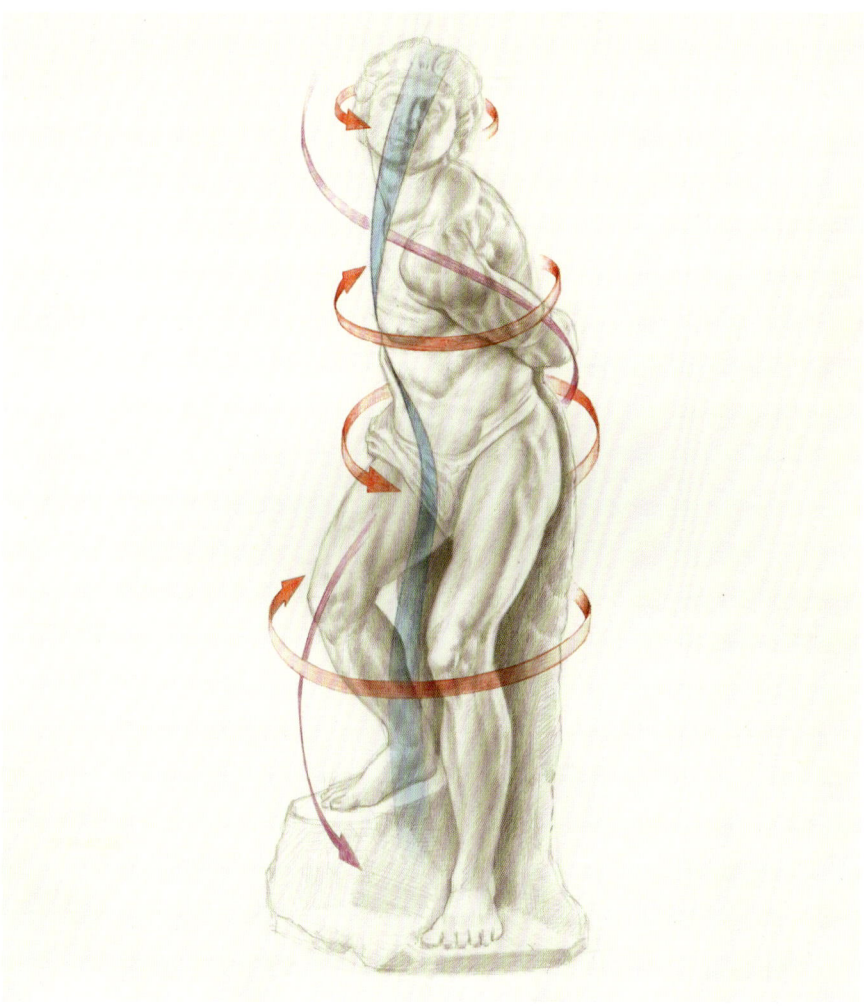

TENSION AND STRUGGLE

The psychological tension visualized by the swelling muscles of Michelangelo's *Rebel Slave* was probably inspired by the torsions of the Laocoön Group, which Michelangelo had seen just a few years before creating his own masterpiece. *Rebel Slave* is a masterful fusion of Florentine composition, which can be summarized as a spiraling action developing around a central axis, and the Hellenistic conventions recalled by the figure's bent and twisted body. The sculpture is a spiral around a spiral. In the central spiral of the body (the blue line in the image above) the head turns to the front, the ribcage toward the back, and the pelvis toward the front again while the legs appear to change direction, twisting one more time toward the back (red arrows). A second spiral, concentric to the central one (purple arrow), starts from the left of the head, following down the upper arm, wrapping around the back, and continuing down along the thigh.

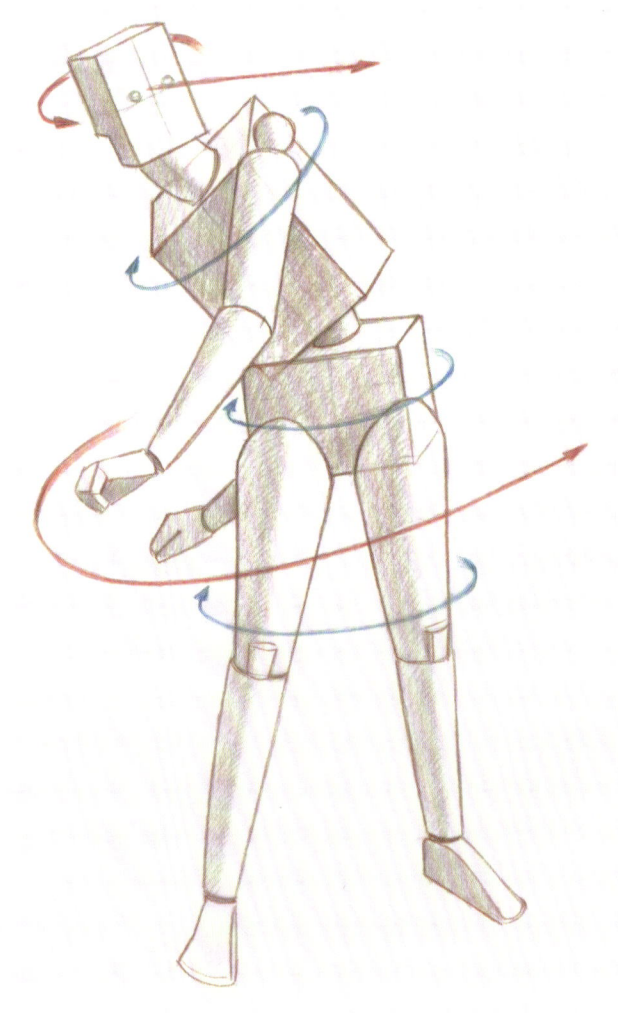

Theatricality
and spatial
interpenetration

PROJECTING NARRATIVE

As Bernini's *David* illustrates so well, theatricality and spatial interpenetration are prominent aspects of Baroque art. The human figure is now a device for the delivery of a narrative that is not self-contained in the artwork but is instead evoked in the mind of the viewer. The statue's gaze anticipates the trajectory of the stone and Goliath's fate, and the strain of head and chest turning toward opposite directions creates a sense of physical and psychological tension. As in Michelangelo's *Rebel Slave,* the compositional structure of Bernini's sculpture is based on two concentric coils, but here one coil describes the torsion of the body, an action that has already happened, while the other suggests an action that is about to happen—the uncoiling of the body and the release of the stone.

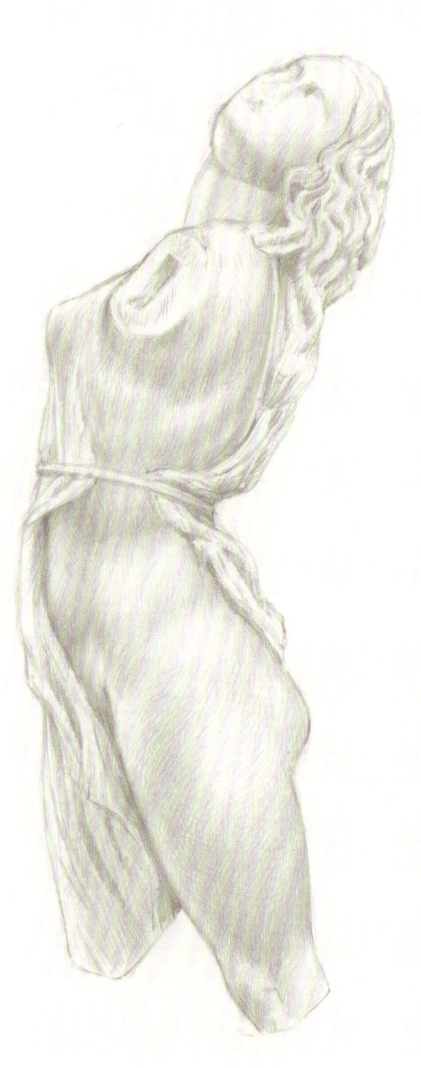
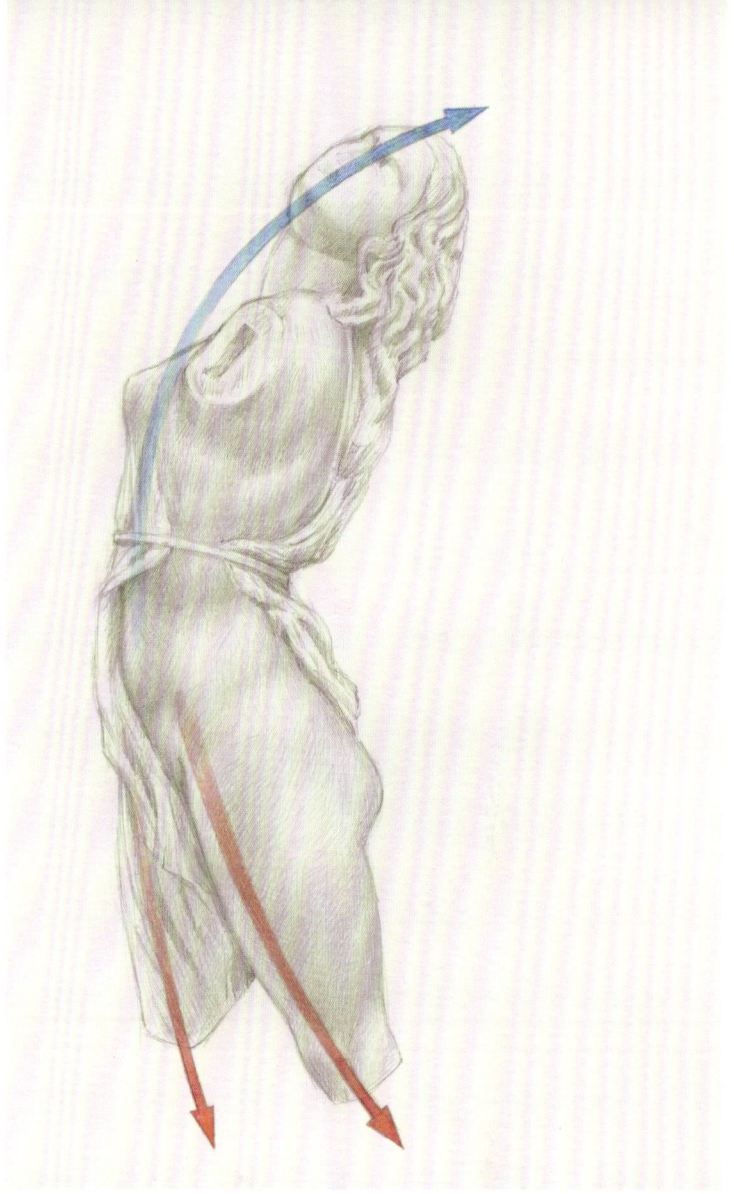

ECSTASY

In Greek mythology, the Maenads were the female followers of Dionysos. The sculpture known as the Raging Maenad—a Roman copy of an original of the Hellenistic Greek sculptor Skopas—depicts one of these women in the arched-back pose typically used to evoke ecstasy. Bernini's interpretation of this pose is visible in his *Ecstasy of Saint Teresa* (following page). Saint Teresa of Ávila is also arching back, but the eroticism of the scantily dressed Maenad is not present because of the concealing clothing of the chaste saint. In fact, the heavy habit denies Saint Teresa's physicality and enhances her spirituality by visualizing the mystical experience through the turmoil of her robe.

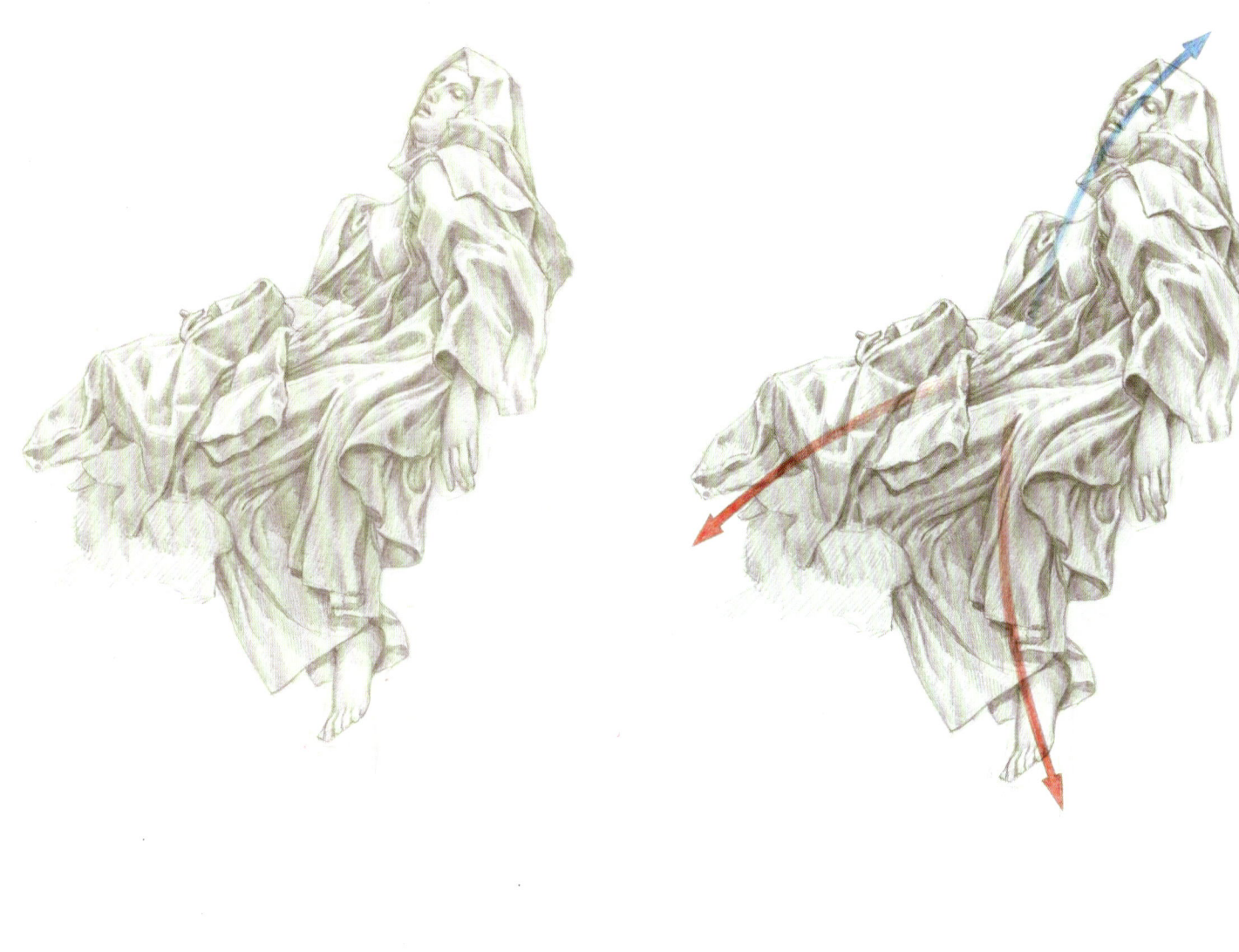

ABOVE: Bernini's *Ecstasy of Saint Teresa* (1647–52), showing dynamic flows at right

MUYBRIDGE'S STUDIES OF MOVEMENT

The work of English-American photographer Eadweard Muybridge (1830–1904) shed a bright and revealing light on the secrets of human and animal motion. The more than 100,000 images he created, beginning in 1877, document the mechanics and details of all types of movement: walking, running, dancing, bending, wrestling, turning, climbing, and so on. These instant-by-instant stop-action images remain an invaluable reference for artists.

TOP: Eadweard Muybridge, *Running at a Half-Mile Gait,* plate 60 from *Animal Locomotion: An Electro-Photographic Investigation of Consecutive Phases of Animal Movements* (1887).

BOTTOM: Eadweard Muybridge, *Woman Dancing (Fancy),* plate 187 from *Animal Locomotion.*

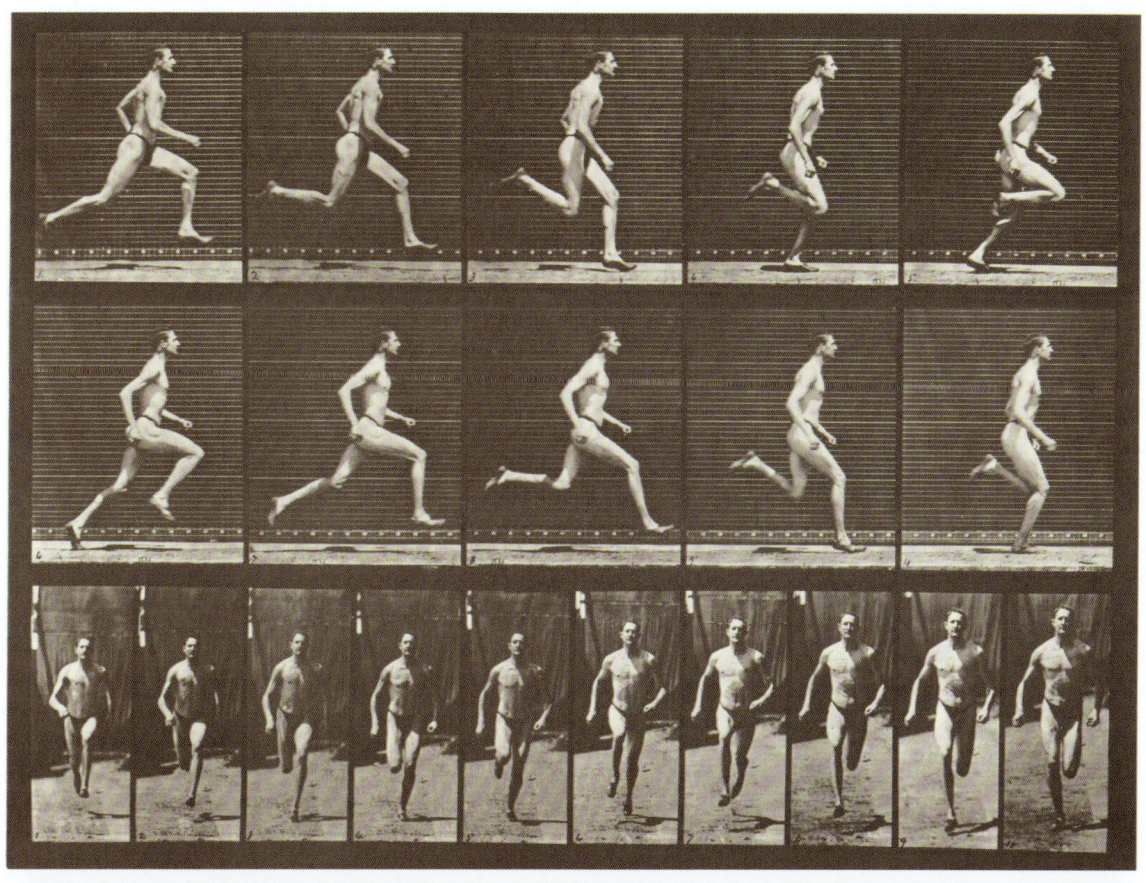

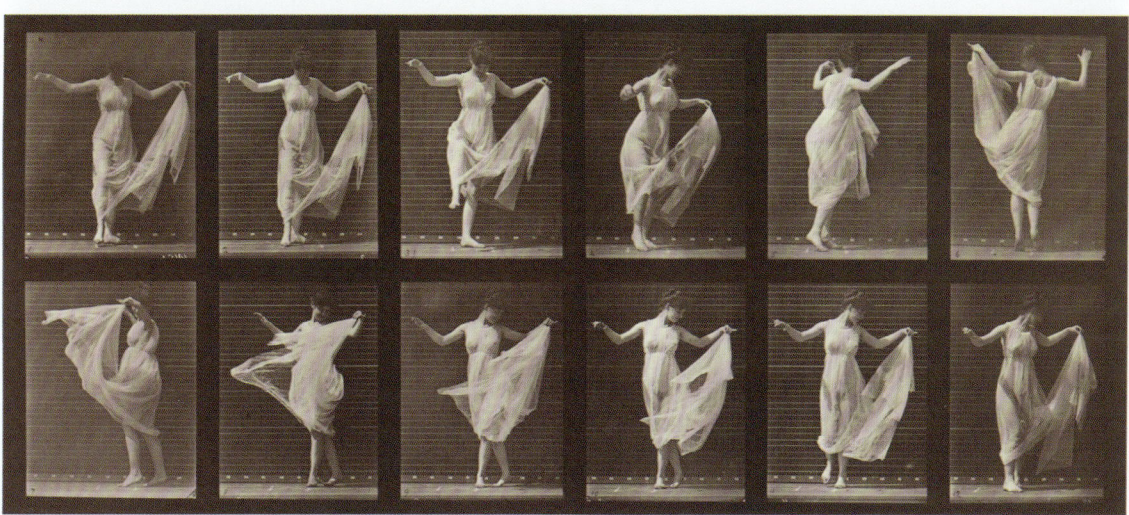

THE MOVEMENTS OF THE BODY

The images in the charts below and opposite bring together the main volumes, proportions, and joints of the male and female figures. These are three of the four essential elements to be considered when drawing the figure in movement. (The fourth is the center line of gravity, discussed later in this chapter.) We have already looked at the proportional relationships of the various segments of the body (for example, the segments of the arm and hand). Now we examine how the various segments are connected to each other as well as the positions of the main joints to better understand—and draw—figures in movement.

RIGHT: Male proportions and joints

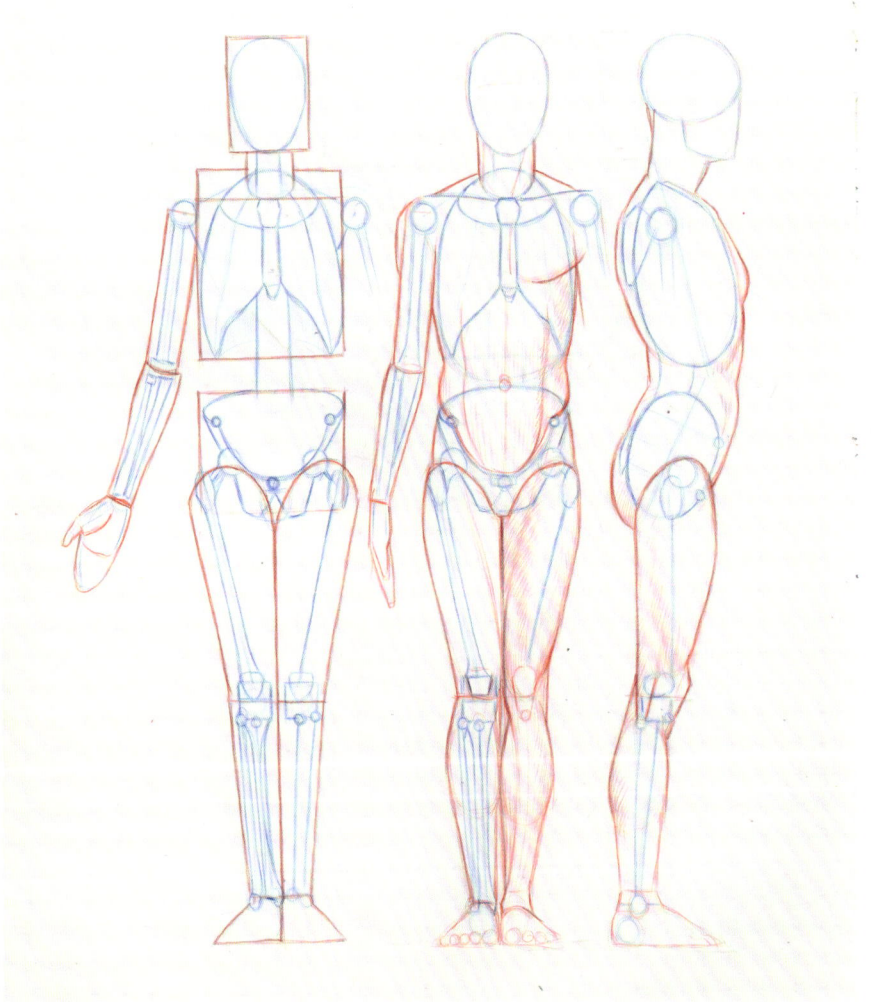

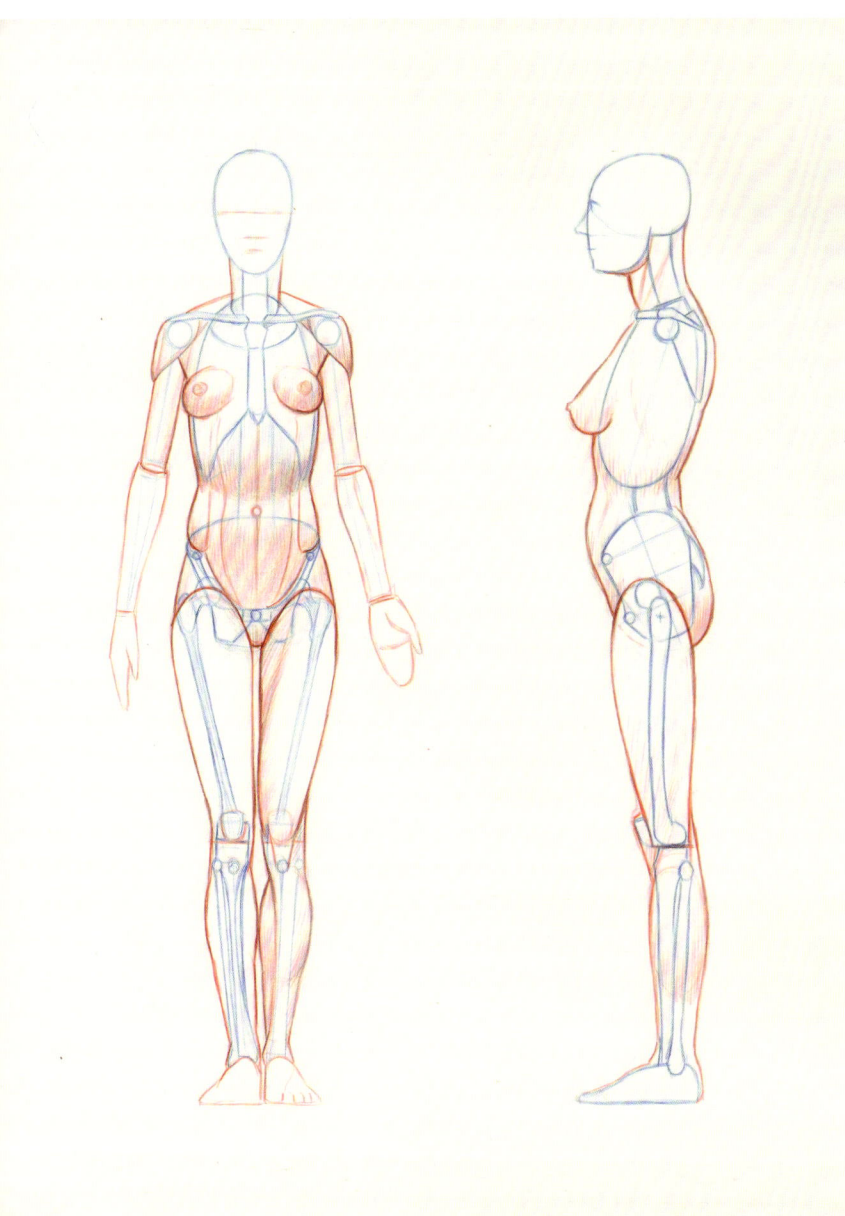

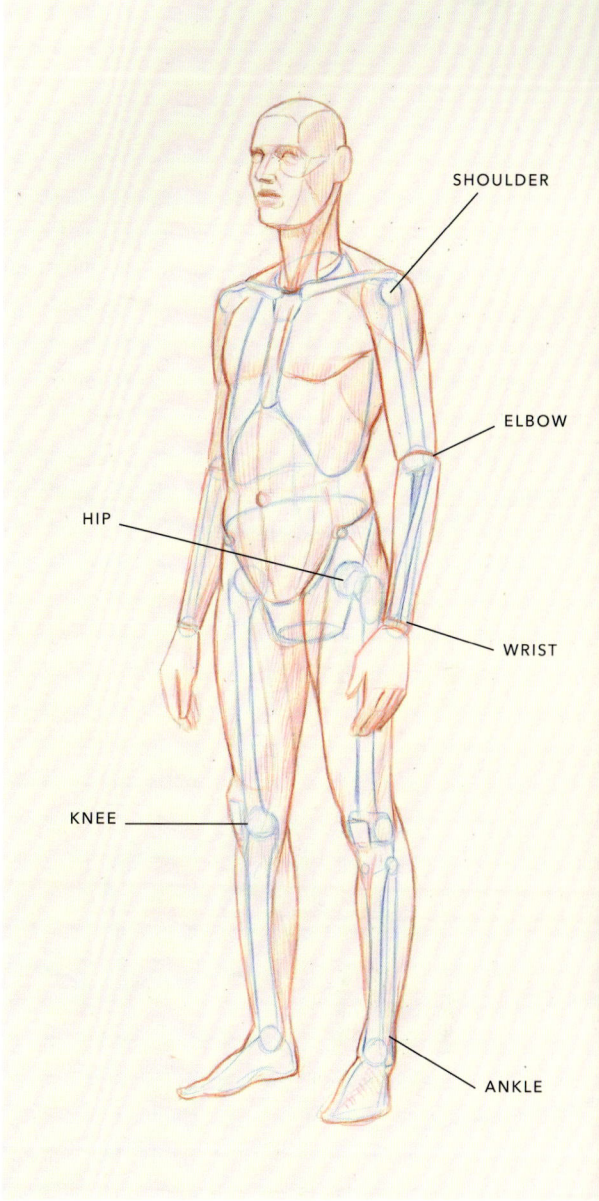

SHOULDER

ELBOW

HIP

WRIST

KNEE

ANKLE

The three diagrams on pages 196–98 display the main movements of the human body. Of course there are many other types of movement, but these are the most essential.

ABOVE LEFT: Female proportions and joints

ABOVE RIGHT: Male proportions and joints, three-quarters anterior view

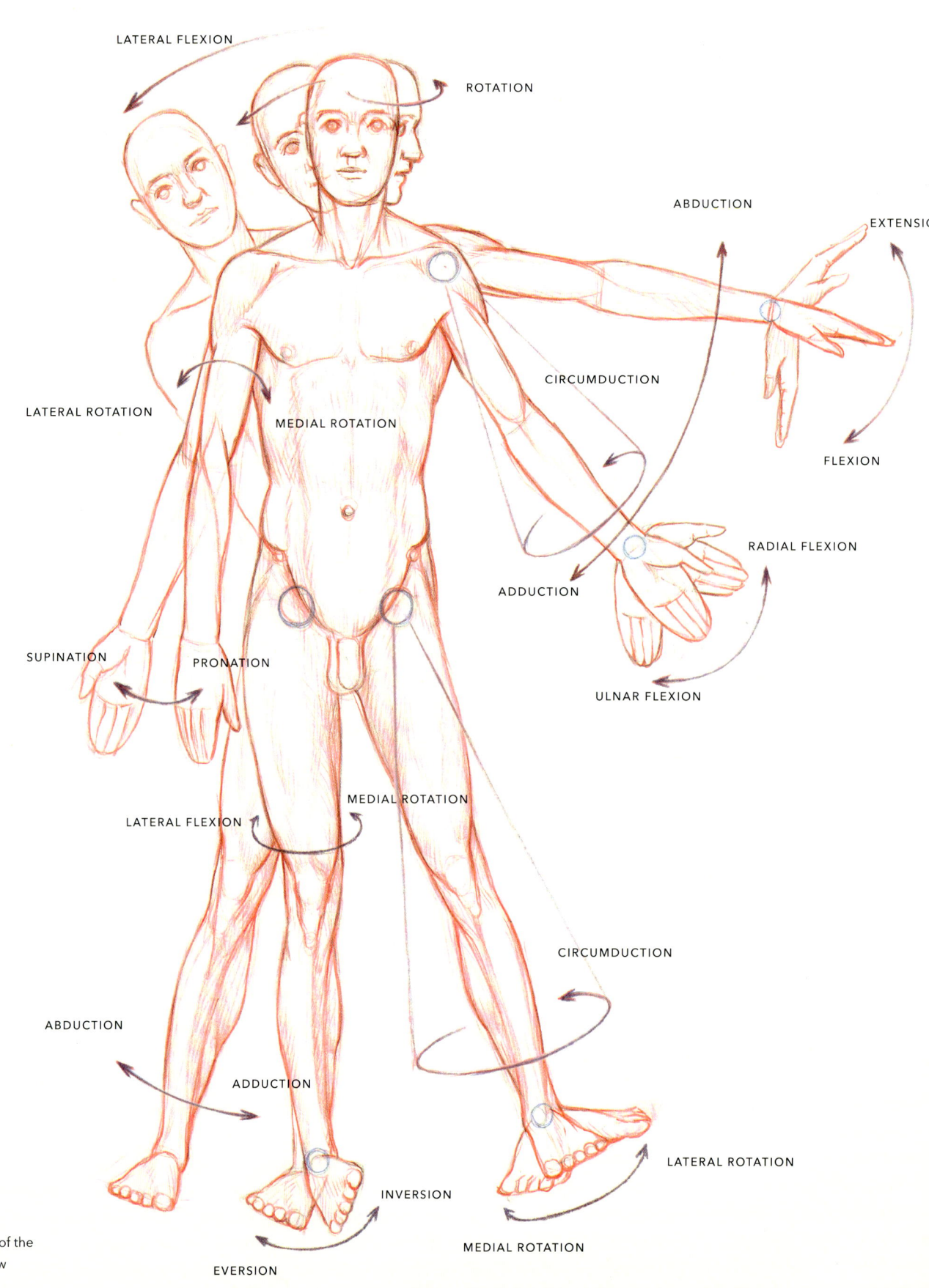

LATERAL FLEXION

ROTATION

ABDUCTION

EXTENSION

LATERAL ROTATION

MEDIAL ROTATION

CIRCUMDUCTION

FLEXION

RADIAL FLEXION

SUPINATION

PRONATION

ADDUCTION

ULNAR FLEXION

LATERAL FLEXION

MEDIAL ROTATION

CIRCUMDUCTION

ABDUCTION

ADDUCTION

LATERAL ROTATION

INVERSION

MEDIAL ROTATION

EVERSION

Main movements of the
body, anterior view

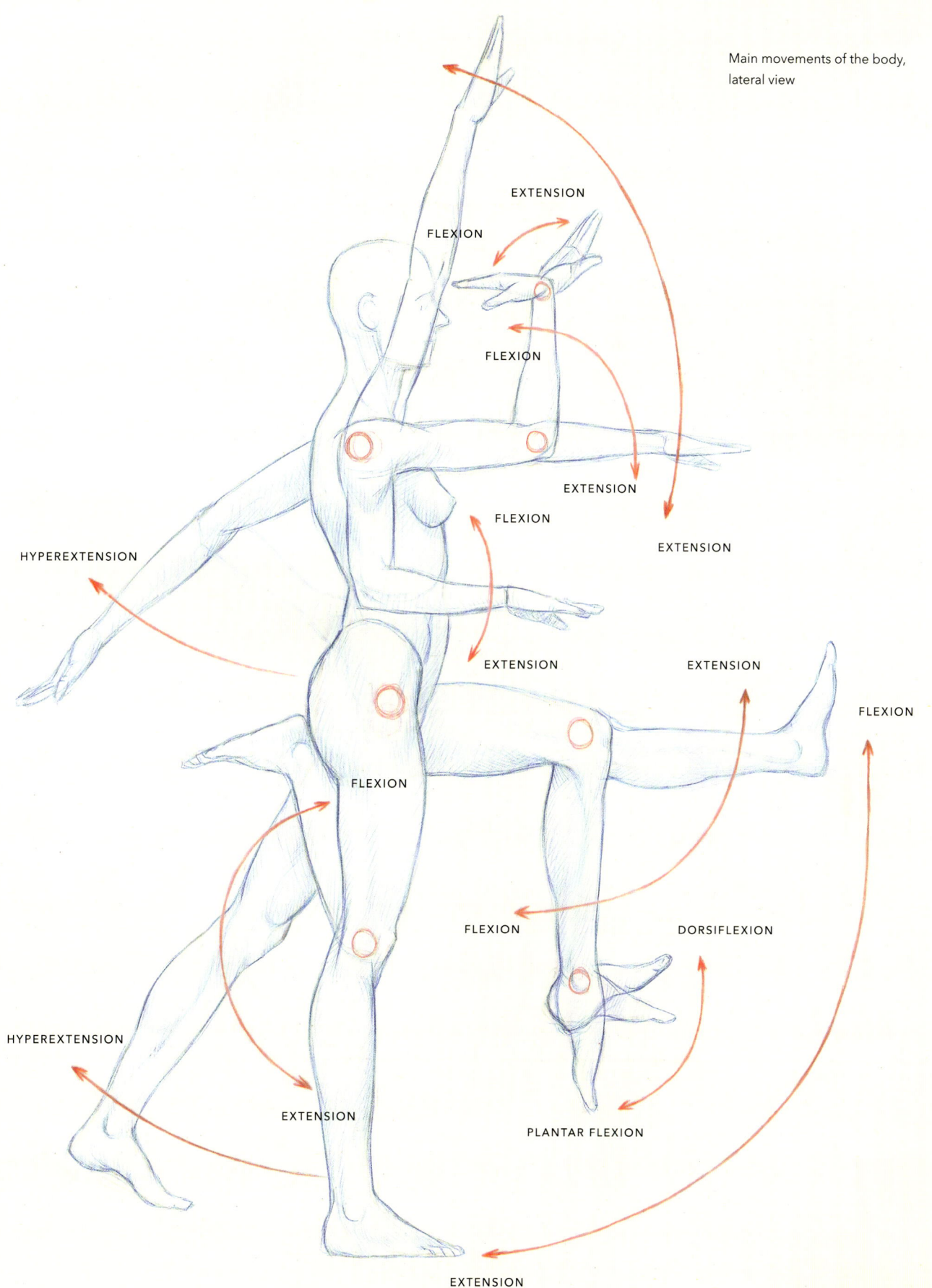

Main movements of the body, lateral view

EXTENSION

FLEXION

FLEXION

EXTENSION

EXTENSION

HYPEREXTENSION

FLEXION

EXTENSION

EXTENSION

FLEXION

FLEXION

FLEXION

DORSIFLEXION

HYPEREXTENSION

EXTENSION

PLANTAR FLEXION

EXTENSION

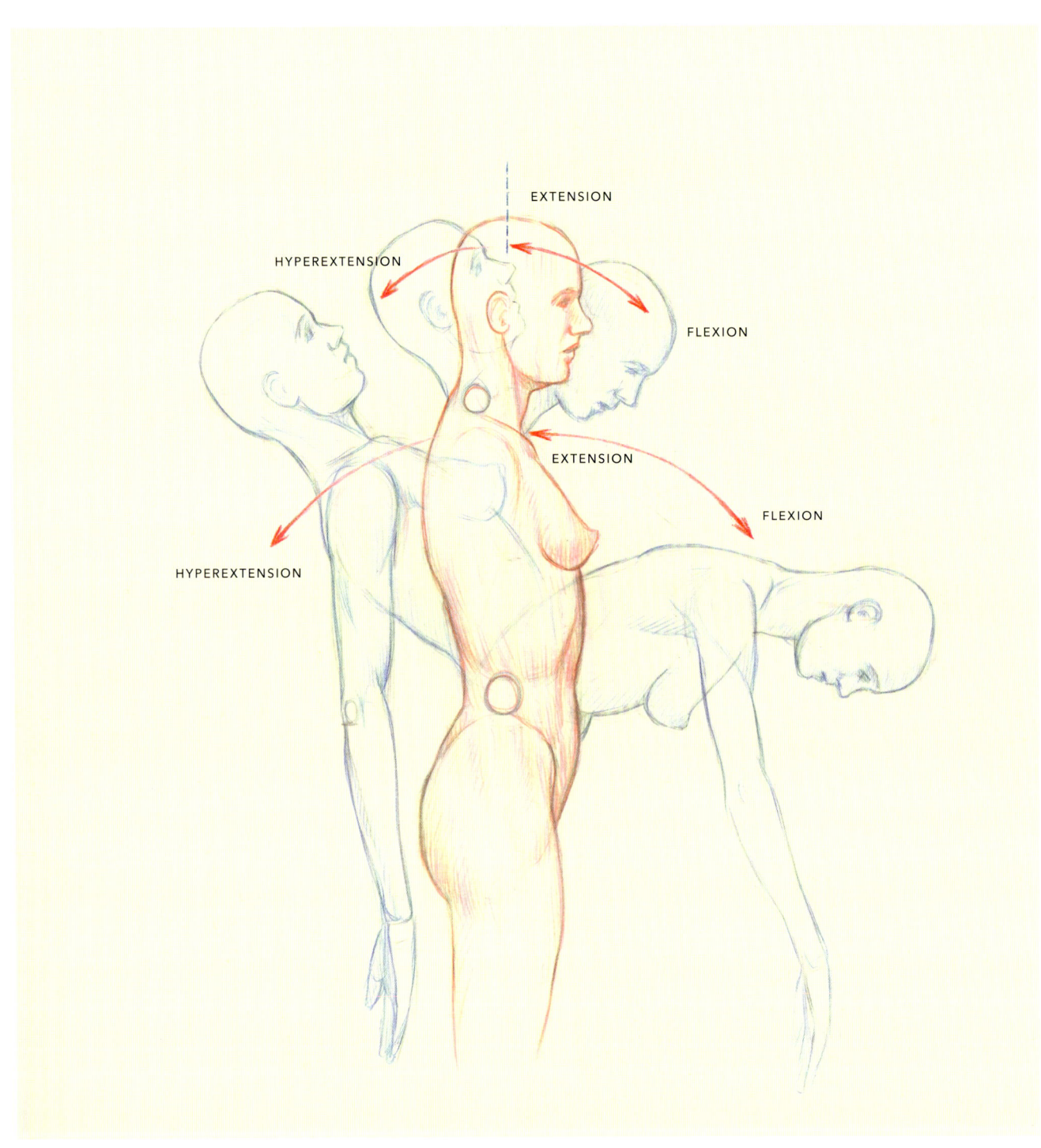

EXTENSION

HYPEREXTENSION

FLEXION

EXTENSION

FLEXION

HYPEREXTENSION

ABOVE: Movements of the torso and
head, lateral view

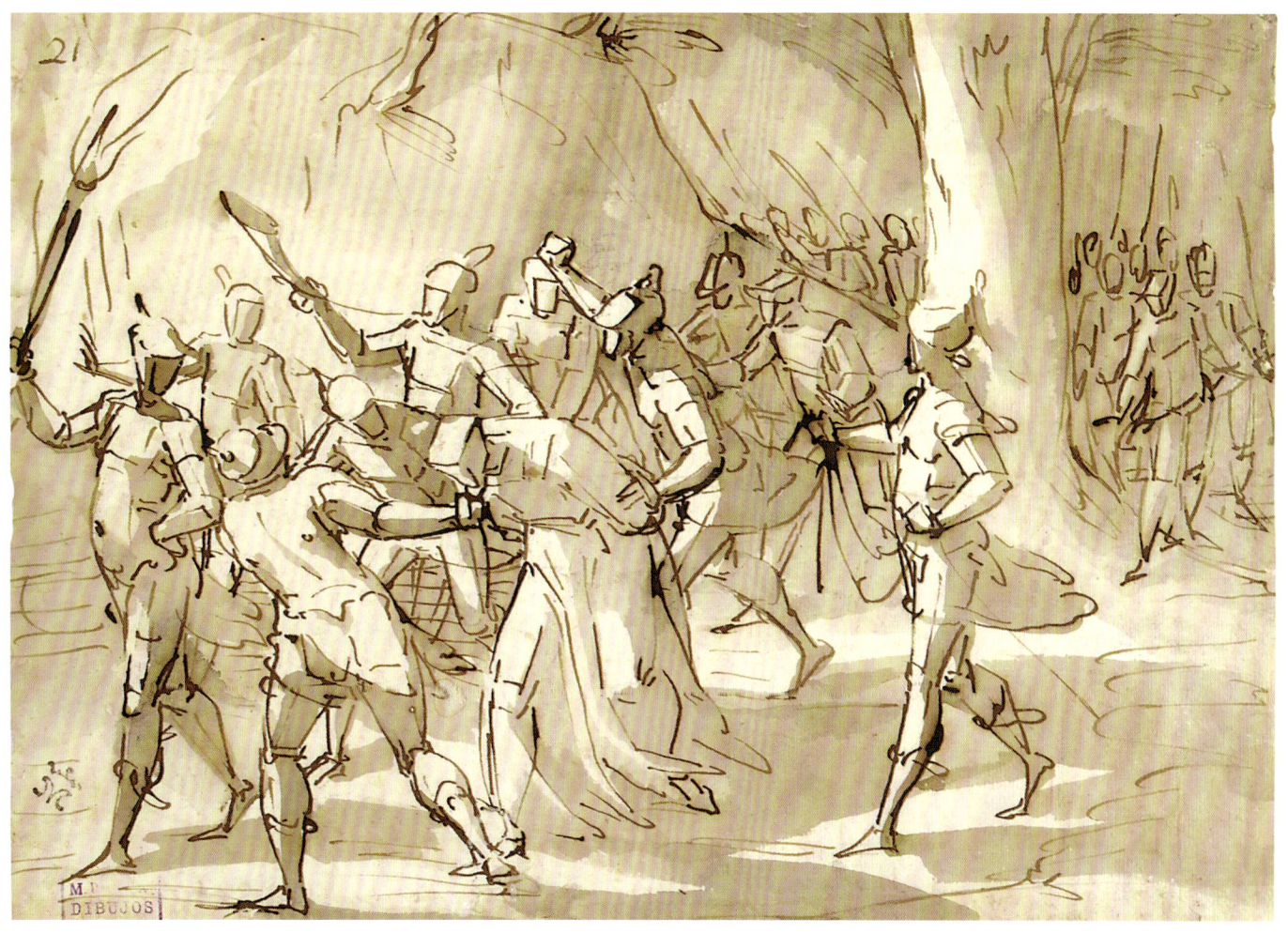

MOVEMENT AND STEREOMETRIC VOLUMES

It's easier to understand the movement of the figure and its three-dimensional characteristics if we think of the body as an assemblage of separate parts. Stereometric rendering of the figure can be of great help in this, since it allows you to start with the essential volumes of the body and to see how they are articulated, focusing only on the movement and excluding the organic anatomical detail that for now could be confusing. The blocky figures in the quick sketch by the sixteenth-century painter Luca Cambiaso above illustrate how artists have long been using this method for studying composition, movement, and the effect of light on the figure.

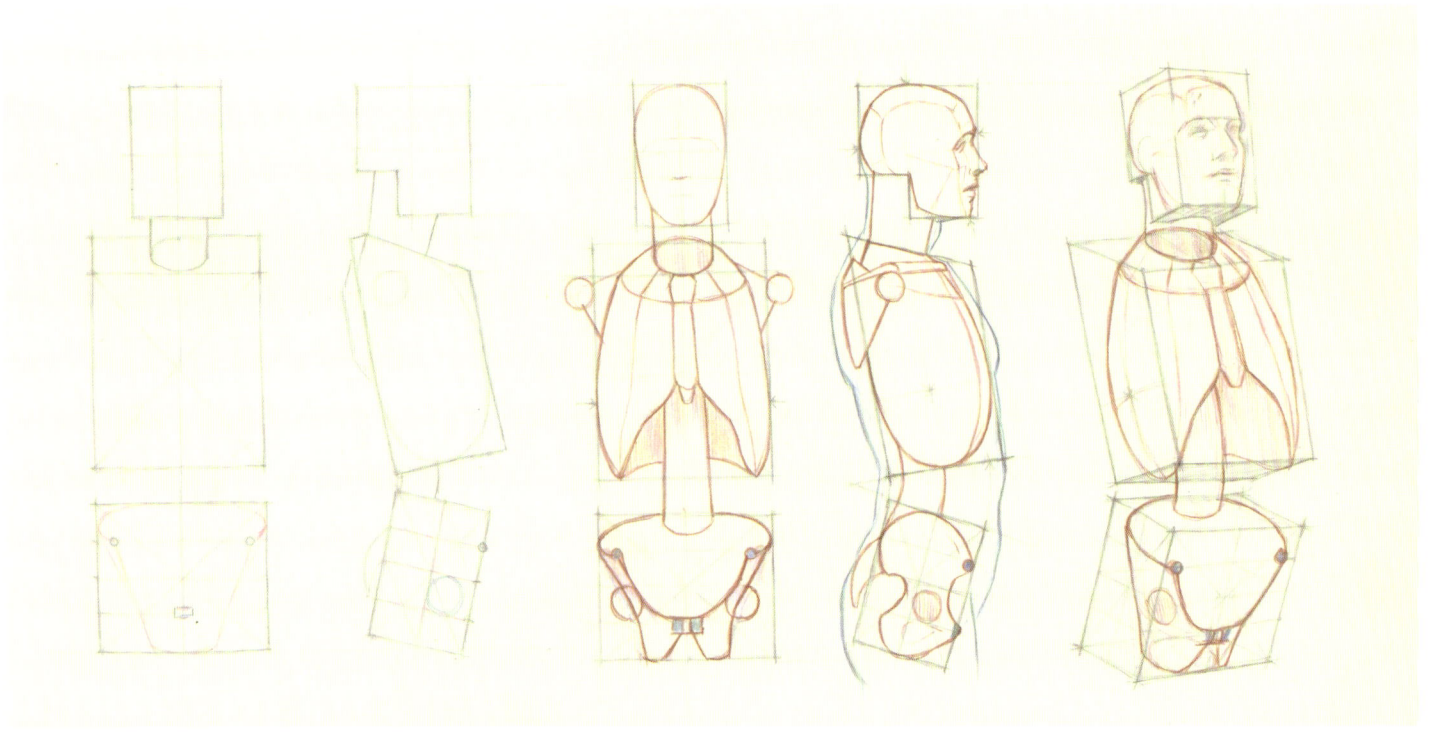

TOP ROW: Stereometric rendering of the torso and head, male proportions

Note the different angles of orientation between the various segments of the axial skeleton (head, ribcage, and pelvis) in the side view.

RIGHT: Stereometric rendering of the torso and head, female proportions

A structural rendering of the skeleton can be fit inside the stereometric volumes.

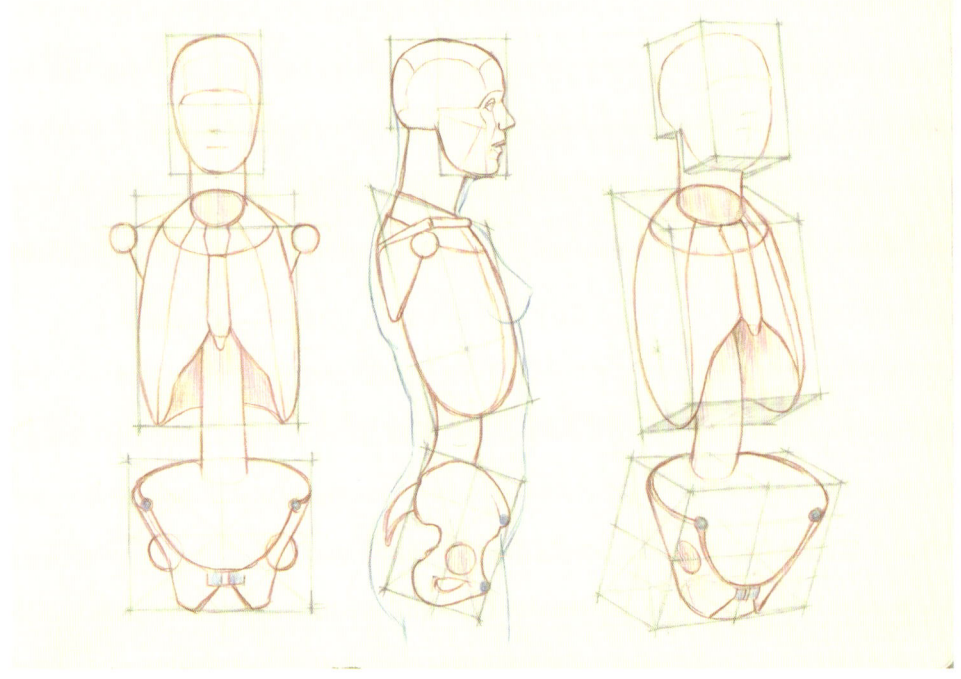

The images above compare stereometric renderings of male and female torsos. Two main differences: (1) The male ribcage and pelvis have the same width, while the female ribcage is slightly narrower than the pelvis. (2) In the side view, the tilt between the pelvis and ribcage tends to be more pronounced in women than in men.

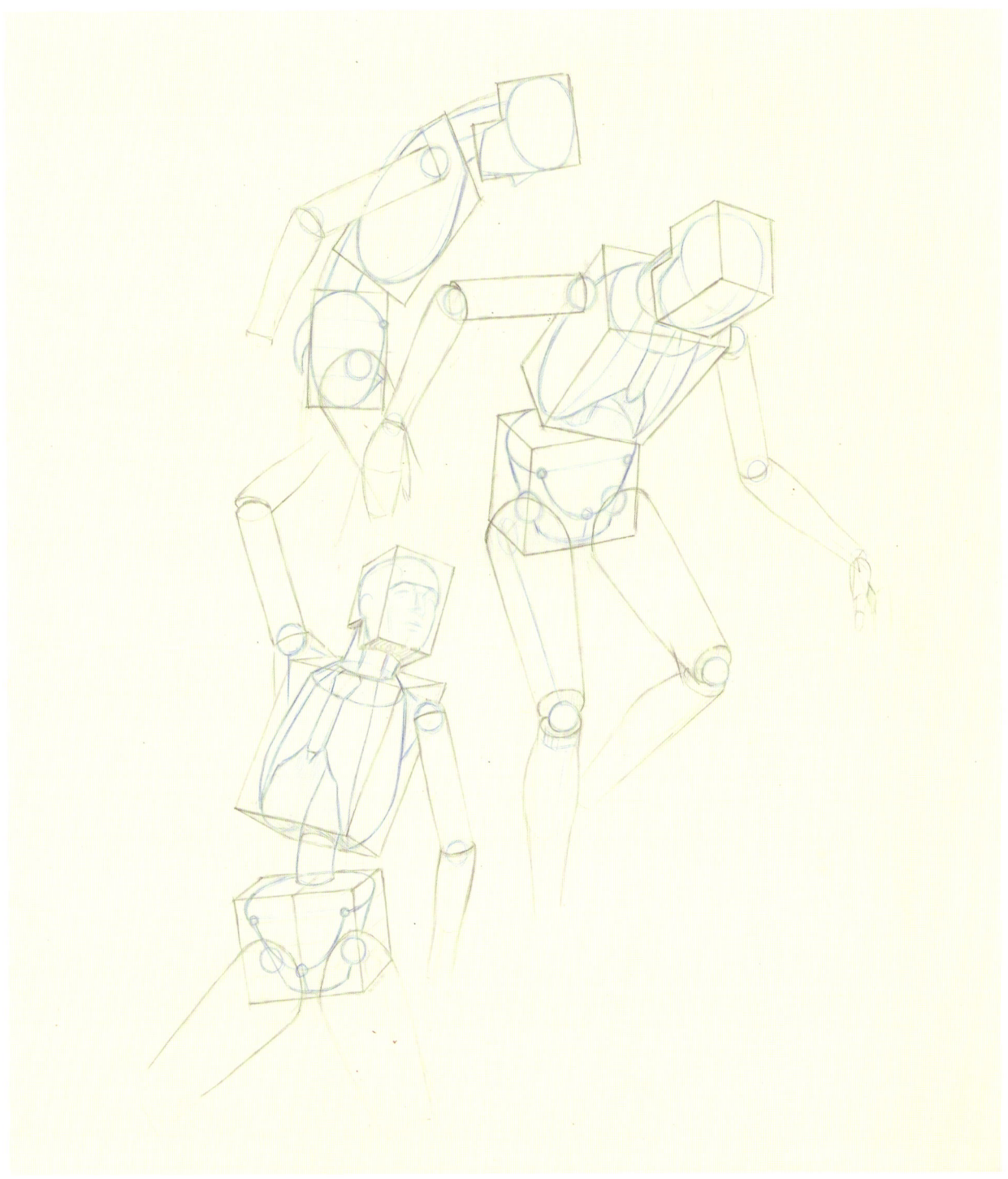

You should practice moving the axial segments of the figure—head, ribcage, and pelvis—before moving to the full body. Start by copying the examples in the image above and then try on your own from memory or imagination or by reducing a realistic rendering of the figure to its basic volumes.

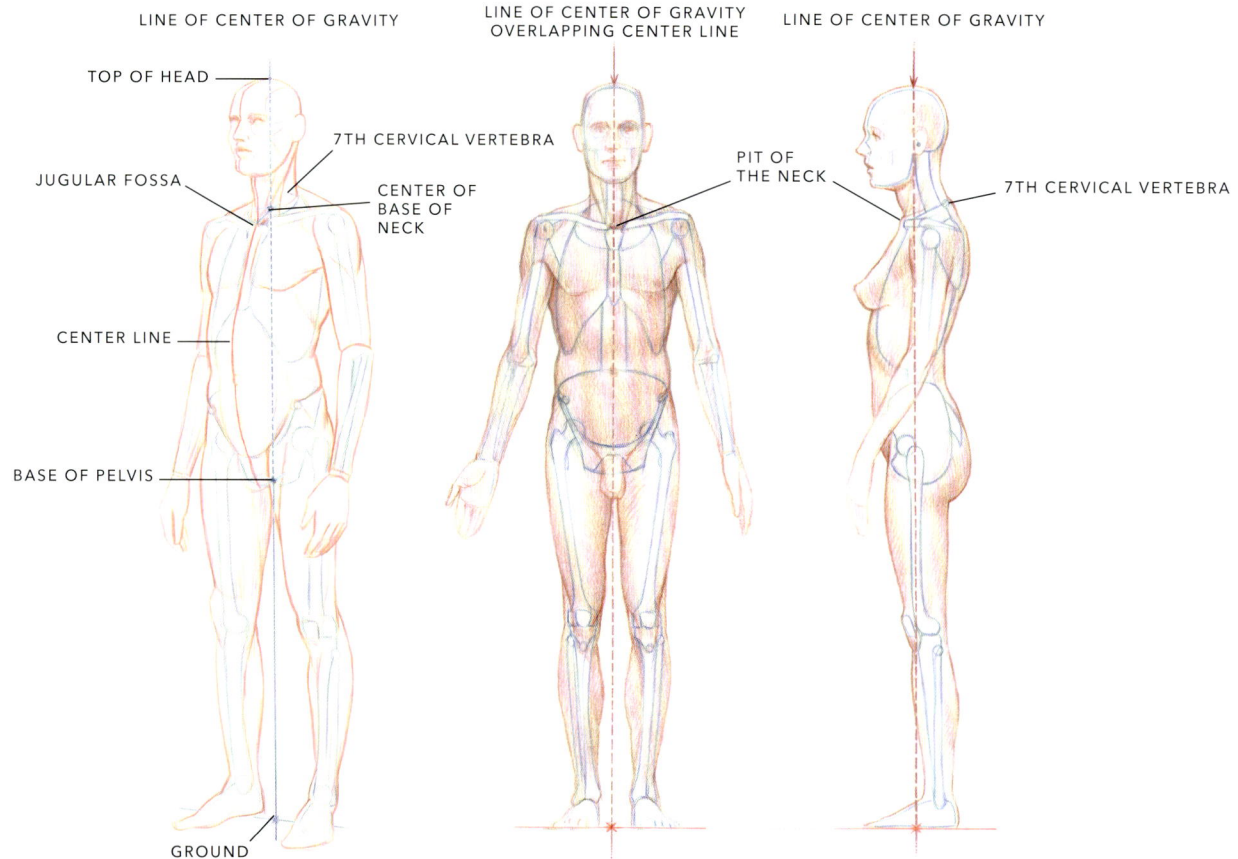

LINE OF CENTER OF GRAVITY

TOP OF HEAD

JUGULAR FOSSA

CENTER LINE

BASE OF PELVIS

GROUND

7TH CERVICAL VERTEBRA

CENTER OF
BASE OF
NECK

LINE OF CENTER OF GRAVITY
OVERLAPPING CENTER LINE

PIT OF
THE NECK

LINE OF CENTER OF GRAVITY

7TH CERVICAL VERTEBRA

Indispensable
for capturing balance
and posture

THE CENTER LINE AND THE LINE OF THE CENTER OF GRAVITY

ABOVE: The center line and the line of the center of gravity

The figure at left shows the line of the center of gravity (blue) and the center line (red) in a three-quarters-view standing figure. In the front view, the center line and LCG overlap, and in the side view figure only the LCG is visible.

The *line of the center of gravity* (LCG; also called the center line of gravity) is an imaginary line that, starting from the top of the head, goes down through the body and ends between the feet. Even though the LCG starts at the top of the head, it is easier to use the pit of the neck (on the front of the body) and the prominent seventh cervical vertebra (on the back) when visualizing the movements of the body in relation to this line. Understanding this alignment is indispensable for capturing the balance and posture of the subject and the structural and harmonious coherence between the parts of the figure.

By contrast, the *center line* is an imaginary line that follows the external profile of the body, dividing it vertically in two halves. In a straight-on front view, the center line overlaps the LCG; in a three-quarters view, the center line is not straight

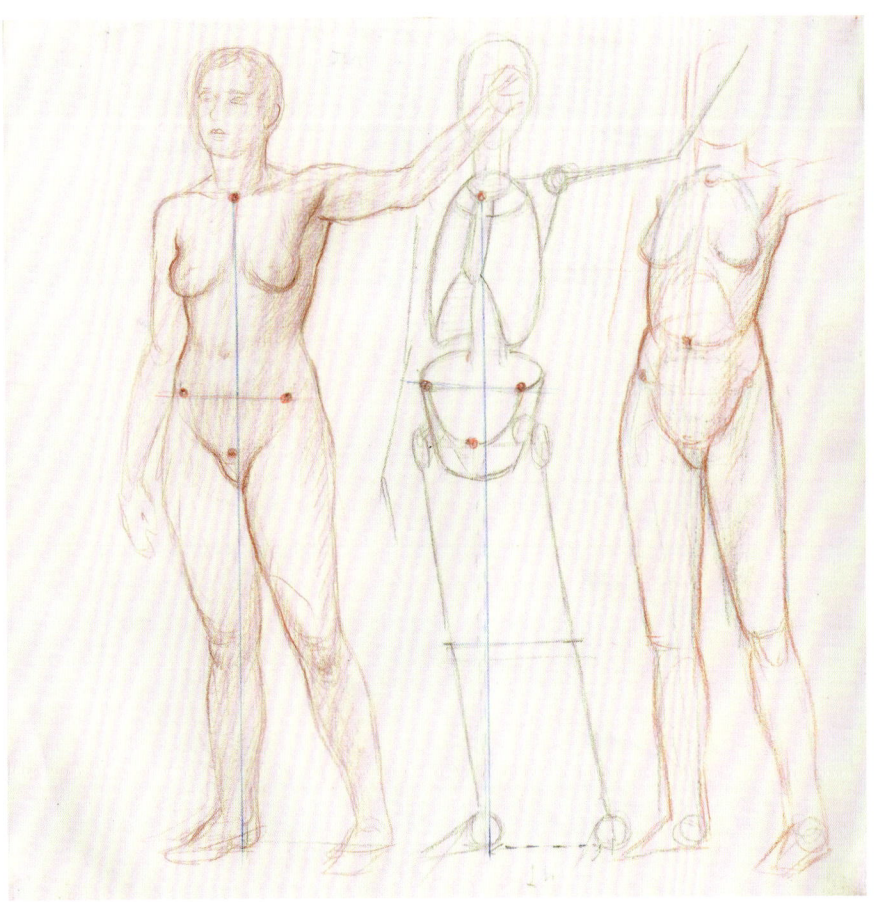

because it follows the surface of the figure and reveals its relief, dividing the torso and head into two unequal parts that can be compared for accuracy when drawing.

The three-step sequence in the diagram above shows how to use the LCG. The figure at left represents the model, and the four dots on her torso visualize the jugular fossa, the two anterior superior iliac spines, and the pubic bone. The LCG is visualized as the thin blue line that starts at the jugular fossa and cuts vertically through her body, running through the sternum, to the right of the pubic bone, and ending at the heel. The artist obtains it by holding a plumb line in front of the model. A plumb line consists of a string to which a brass weight has been tied; invented by masons to make sure the walls they built were perfectly vertical and straight, it is also a very useful tool also for artists. The figure at center shows the re-creation of the skeleton based on the landmarks. Here, the blue line serves as a guide replicating the alignment of the landmarks on the model. Now that the structural and proportional aspects of the model are resolved, you can render the forms of the body, as shown in the figure at right.

ABOVE: Using the line of the center of gravity in the practice of drawing

MOVING THE FIGURE

The two figures in the image below show how to gradually impart a sense of movement to your drawing while considering its structural aspects. Start drawing the axial skeleton and then attach the limbs after having established the shoulders and hip joints. The movement in the figure on the left is minimal: the axis of head, torso, and hips is a straight line, one of the arms is in supination, and one of the legs is slightly bent. The movement in the figure on the right is greater: note that the axes (red lines) of the head, torso, and hips are all at angles in relation to each other, the movements of the limbs are more pronounced, and the whole figure is turned slightly to the left.

RIGHT: Imparting movement to your drawing

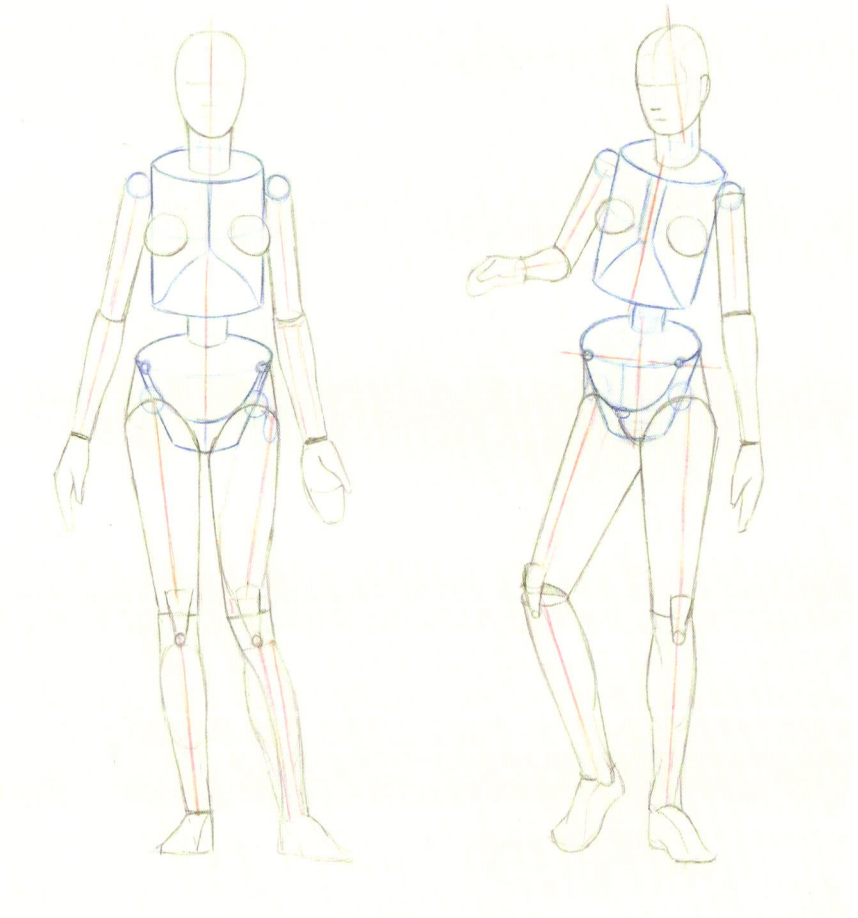

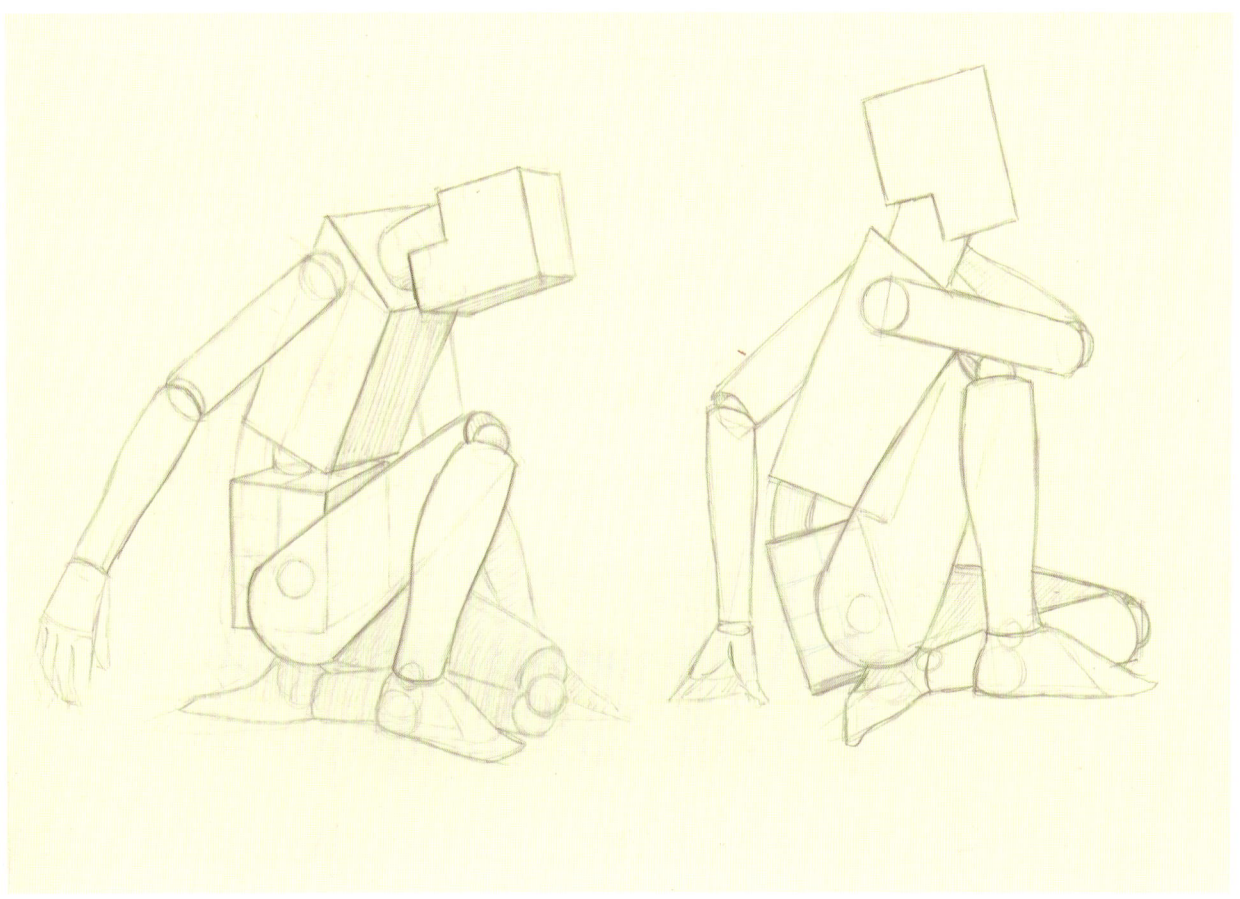

When drawing the figure in more dynamic poses it is easier, in the beginning, to use the essential stereometric rendering of the volumes of the body as shown in the two crouching figures in the image above. Later you can move on to a more rounded, organic rendering of the volumes of the body and (with the help of a plumb line) include the line of the center of gravity, as shown in images on the following pages. Starting from the pit of the neck (jugular fossa) if the figure is being viewed from the front or from the seventh cervical vertebra if from the back, drop the LCG vertically to the ground to relate the upper body's position to that of the lower body and to capture the sense of stability and balance—or the lack thereof—of the pose. Also note how the LCG relates to the various parts of the body as it moves from the top of the torso down to the ground.

ABOVE: Stereometric rendering in dynamic poses

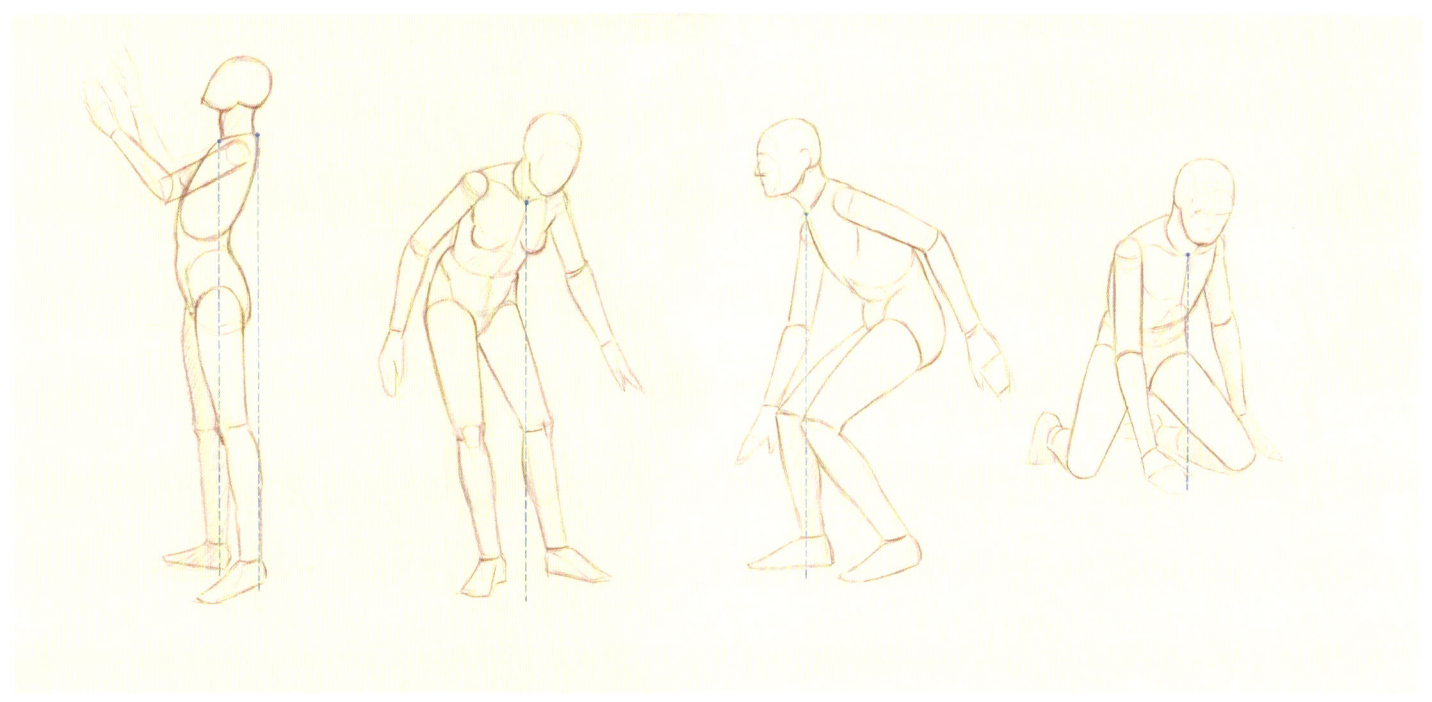

ABOVE: Dynamic poses with the line of the center of gravity

In the figure at far left, the LCG can be visualized from both the front and the back of the figure. The LCG that starts from the back of the torso is tangent to the glutei and the calf, eventually barely cutting through the heel while the LCG that starts from the jugular fossa cuts through the center of the body, emerges at the knee, and hits the middle of the foot. In the figure second from left, the LCG starts at the jugular fossa, cuts diagonally through the thigh, shaves the calf, and connects with the ground between the feet. As you can see in these and the other two figures, the LCG can give you great accuracy when assessing the pose.

RIGHT: An unbalanced pose with the line of the center of gravity

The line of the center of gravity can also be very useful when drawing an unbalanced or very complex pose where the LCG falls completely outside the body.

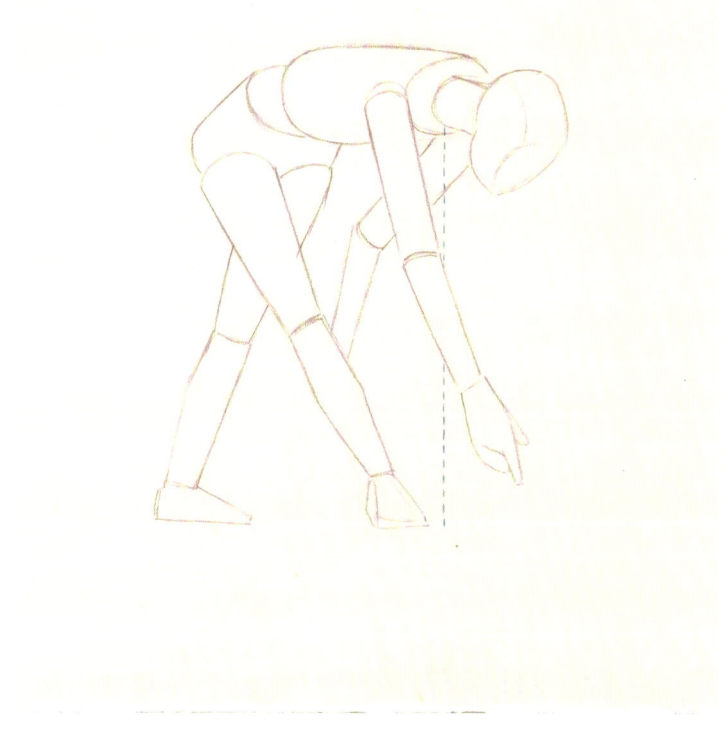

DEL SARTO'S STRUCTURAL APPROACH

In this detail from an engraving after a work by Andrea del Sarto, one of my favorite High Renaissance artists, it is evident that the figure was constructed using a structural approach that resembles the one I recommend. Del Sarto has described a few main muscular volumes, and these essential volumes are barely disguised by the figure's clothing.

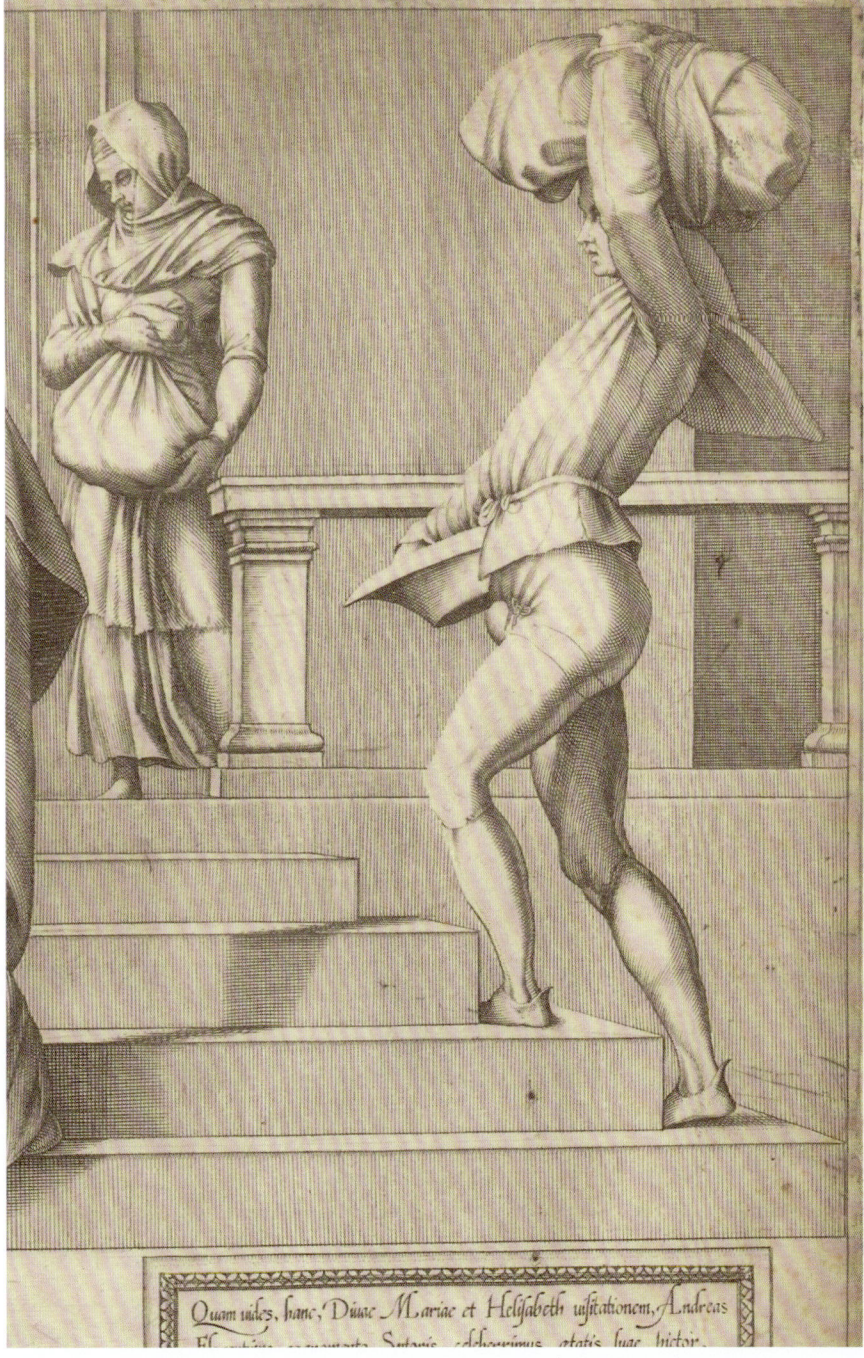

LEFT: Enea Vico, Antonio Salamanca, and Antonio Lafrere, after Andrea del Sarto, *The Visitation* (detail), 1561, engraving, whole sheet 11 13/16 × 16 5/16 inches (30 × 41.4 cm). Metropolitan Museum of Art, New York.

A FIGURE RISES

This sequence brings together all the concepts discussed so far: the basic volumes of the skeleton, the joints, proportional relationships, main external volumes, and the center line of gravity. To create this sequence I took photos of Joseph, one of my favorite models, as he moved from a recumbent position to a standing one. I then identified the main landmarks and joints on the photos and reconstructed the skeleton and external forms. You can create your own version of this sequence by taking photos of a model or a friend in movement.

1

Layering a sheet of tracing paper over each photo in the sequence, I marked the main joints and the landmarks of the pelvis to re-create an essential skeletal structure. Then I added the main volumes of the body to obtain a more organic figure. I repeated this process for each of the stages of movement.

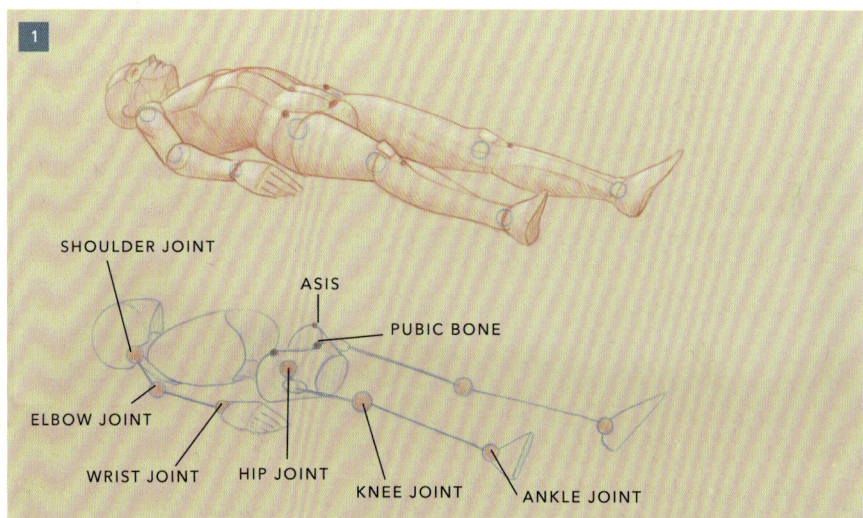

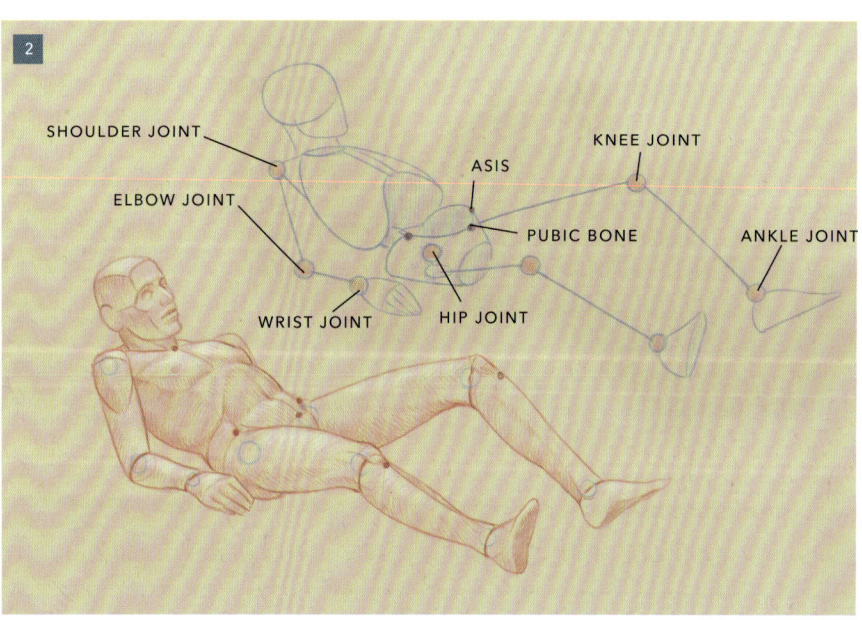

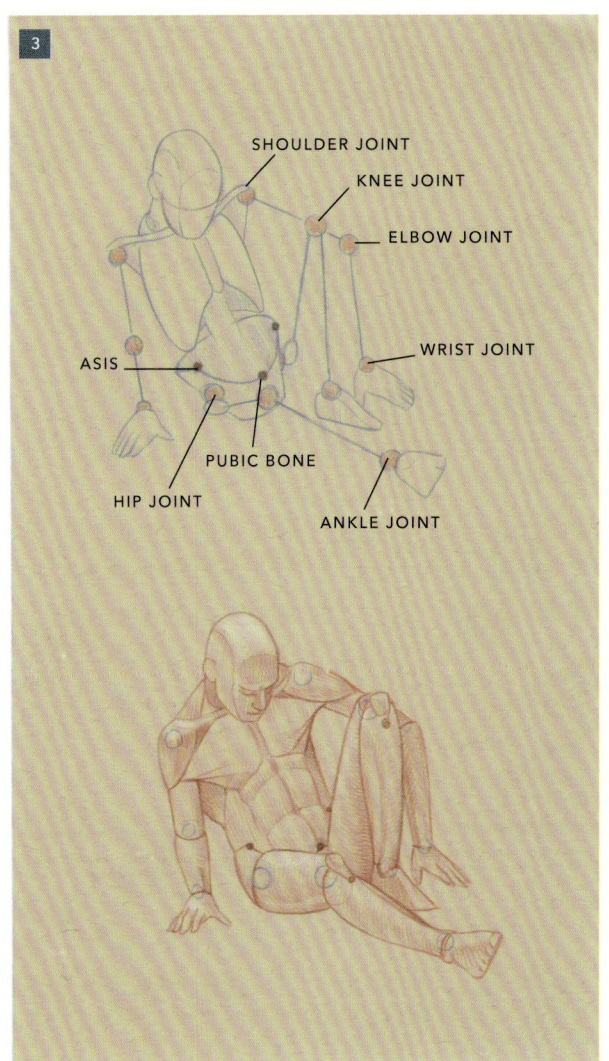

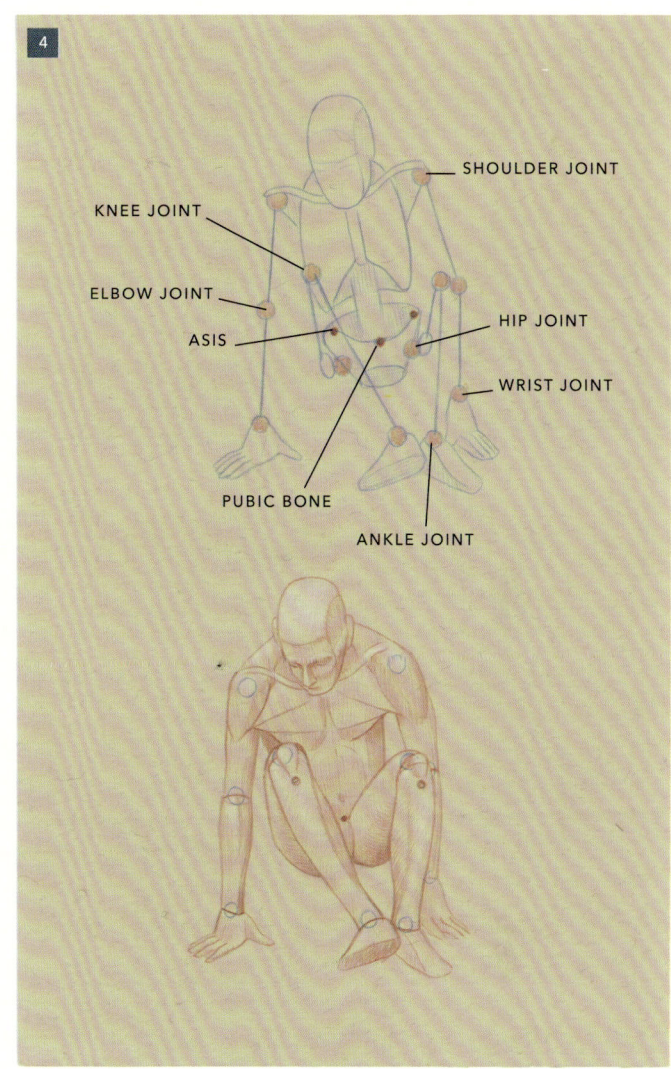

SHOULDER JOINT
KNEE JOINT
ELBOW JOINT
WRIST JOINT
ASIS
PUBIC BONE
HIP JOINT
ANKLE JOINT

KNEE JOINT
SHOULDER JOINT
ELBOW JOINT
ASIS
HIP JOINT
WRIST JOINT
PUBIC BONE
ANKLE JOINT

5

The red dotted
line added to
this figure shows
the center line
of gravity.

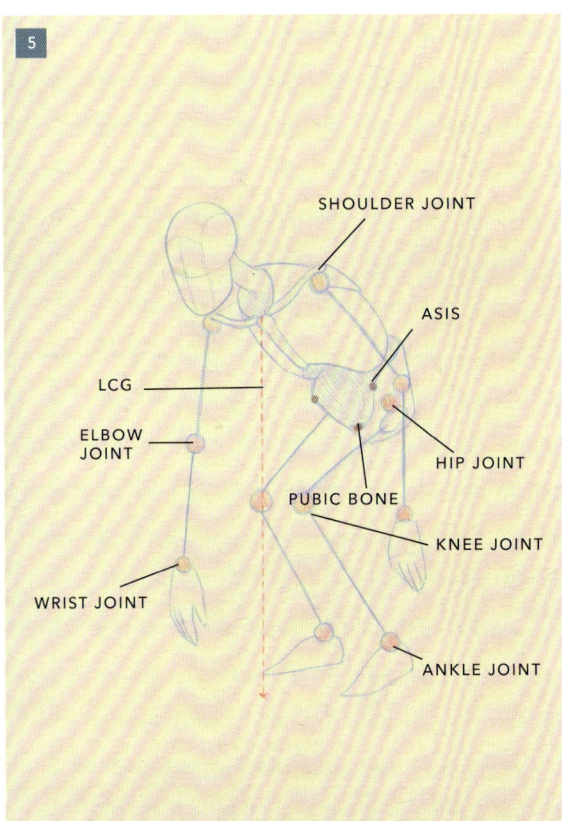

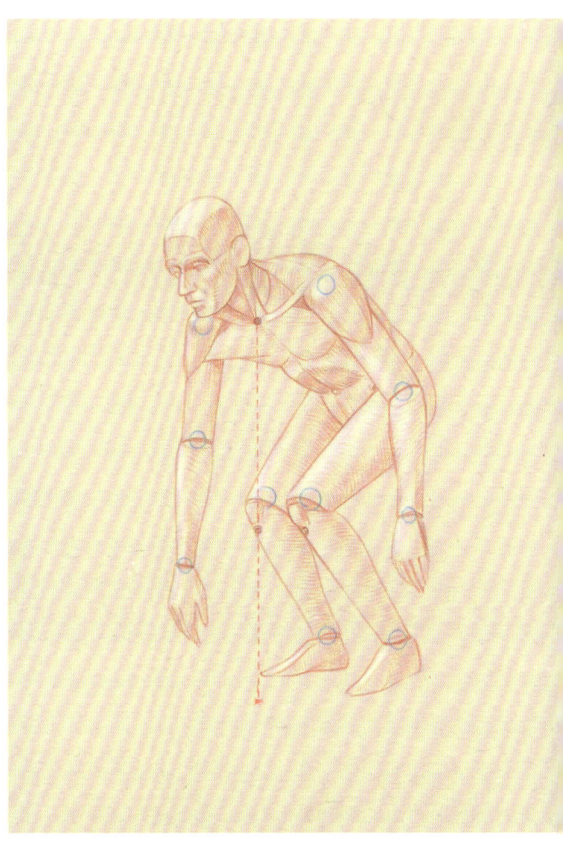

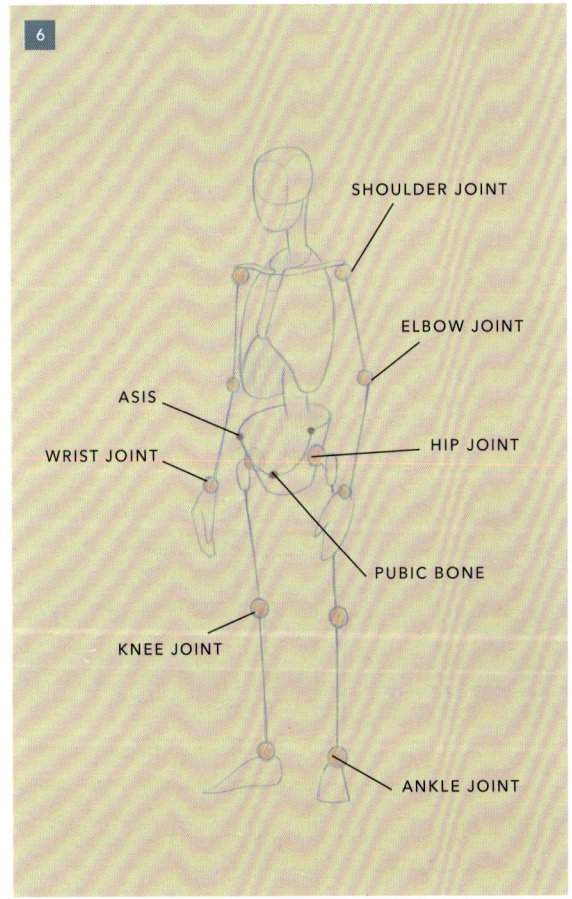

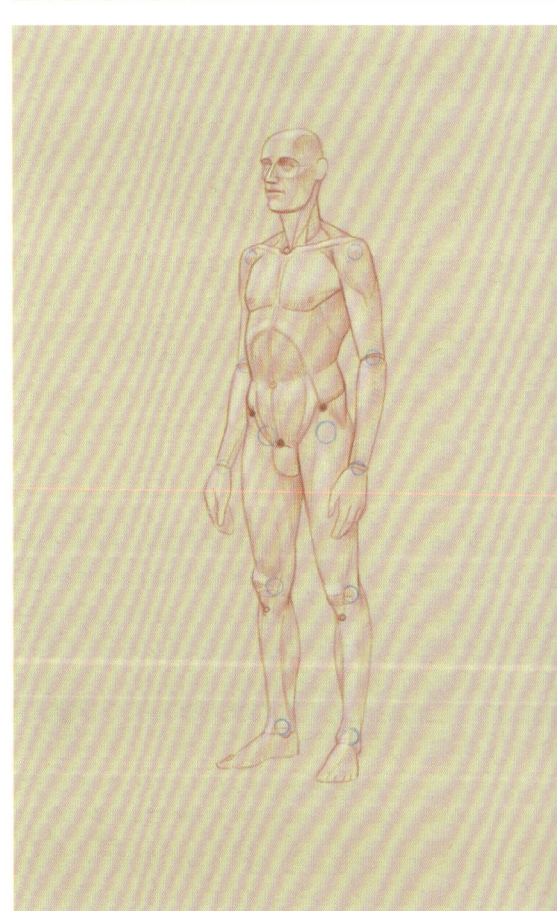

FROM STEREOMETRIC TO ORGANIC FORM

The images here demonstrate how to apply muscular forms to structural renderings of the figure. Starting from a schematic stereometric visualization, gradually move toward a more realistic rendering of the human figure by adding the main muscular volumes while considering proportional relationships and dynamic flows. After taking the human figure apart with virtual dissection and conceptualization, we put it back together, adding aesthetics and dynamism.

BELOW: From schematic to realistic rendering

This image summarizes the steps of a gradual passage from stereometric to more rounded volumes and, finally, to organic forms.

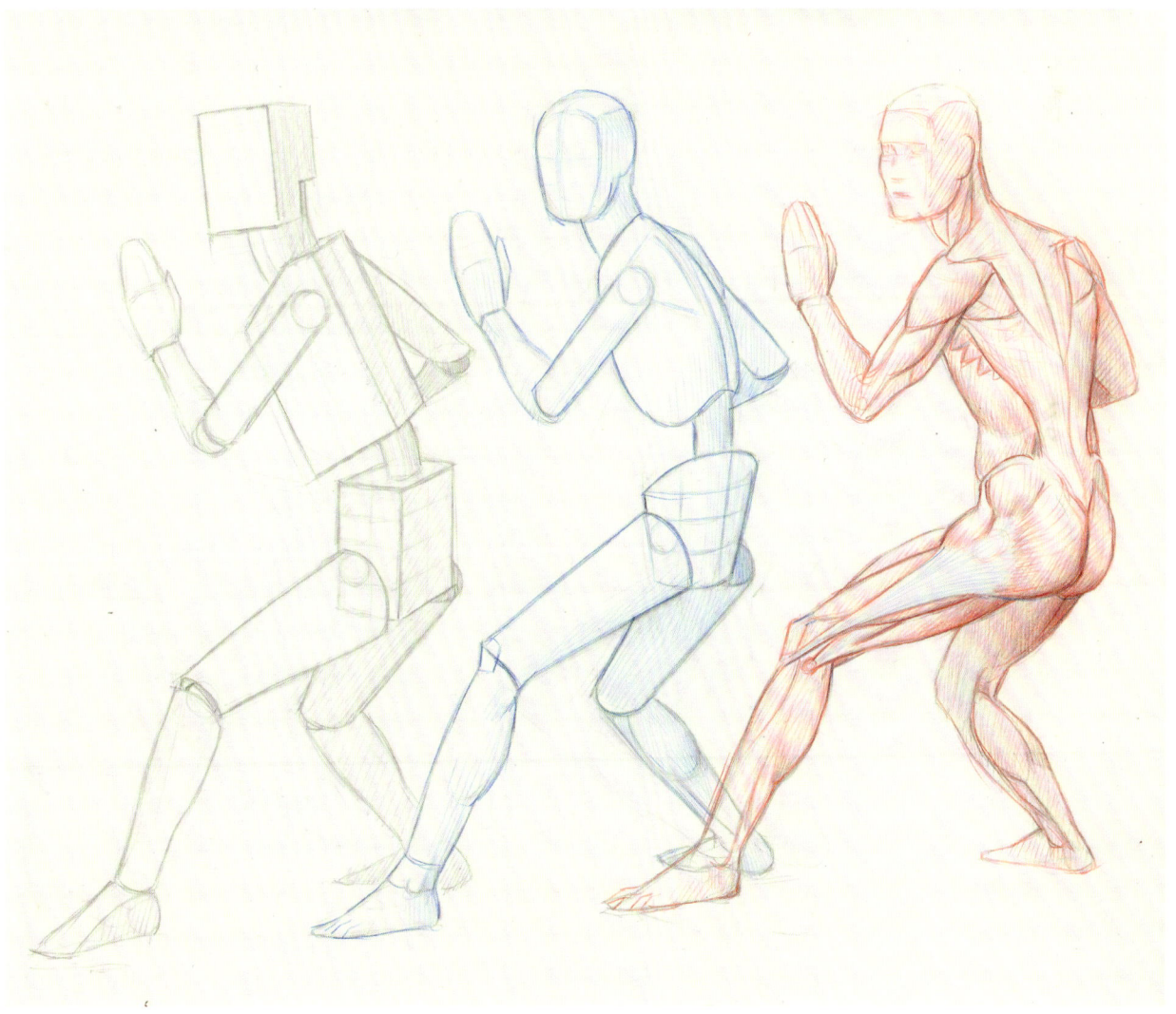

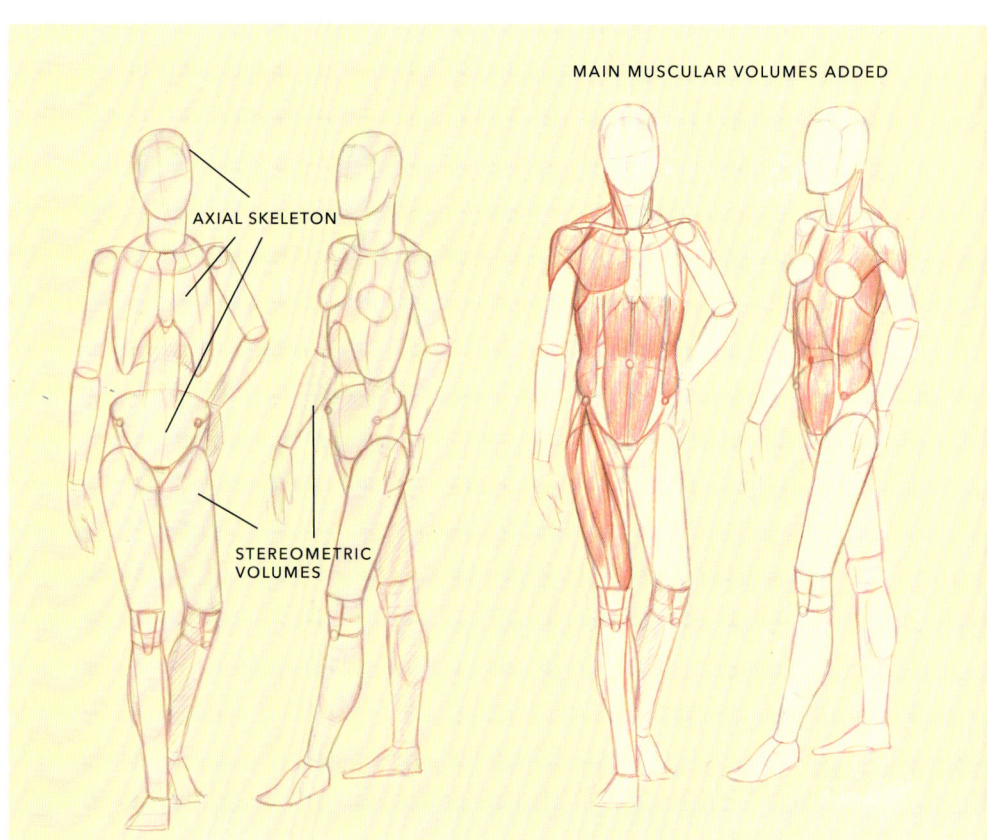

MAIN MUSCULAR VOLUMES ADDED

AXIAL SKELETON

STEREOMETRIC
VOLUMES

TOP: In this sequence, the male and female figures on the left are rendered very schematically. I have added some of the main muscle groups to the figures on the right.

BOTTOM: Muscles on dynamic poses

Here are two more examples showing how to position muscles over the skeleton in a dynamic pose.

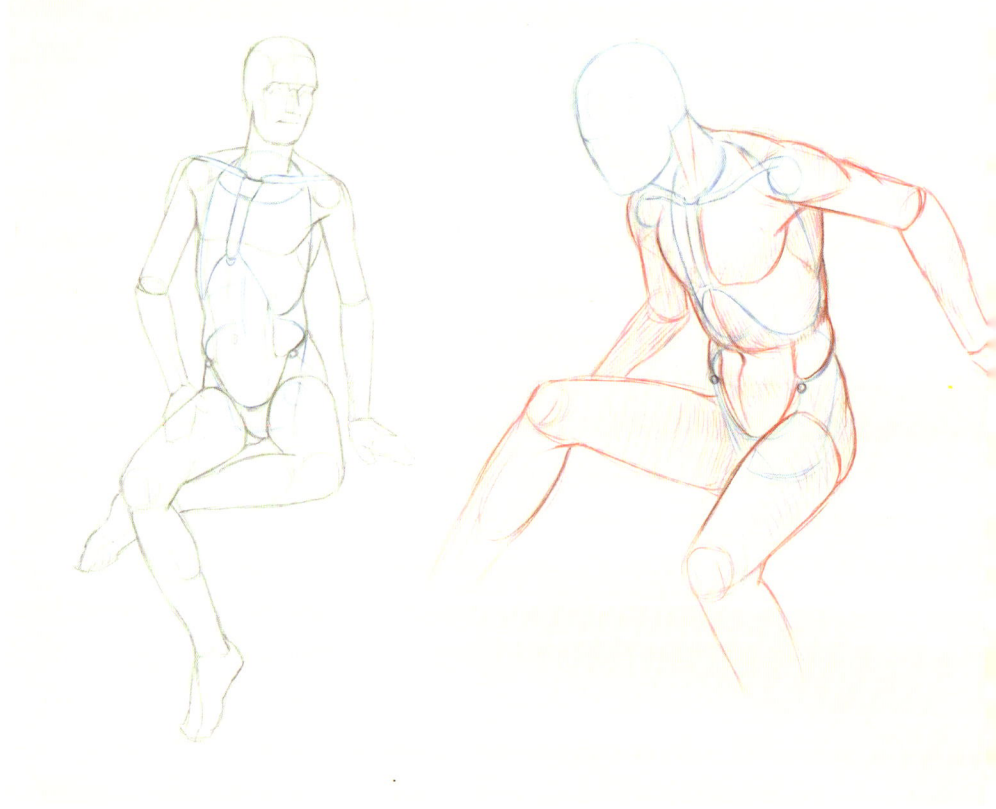

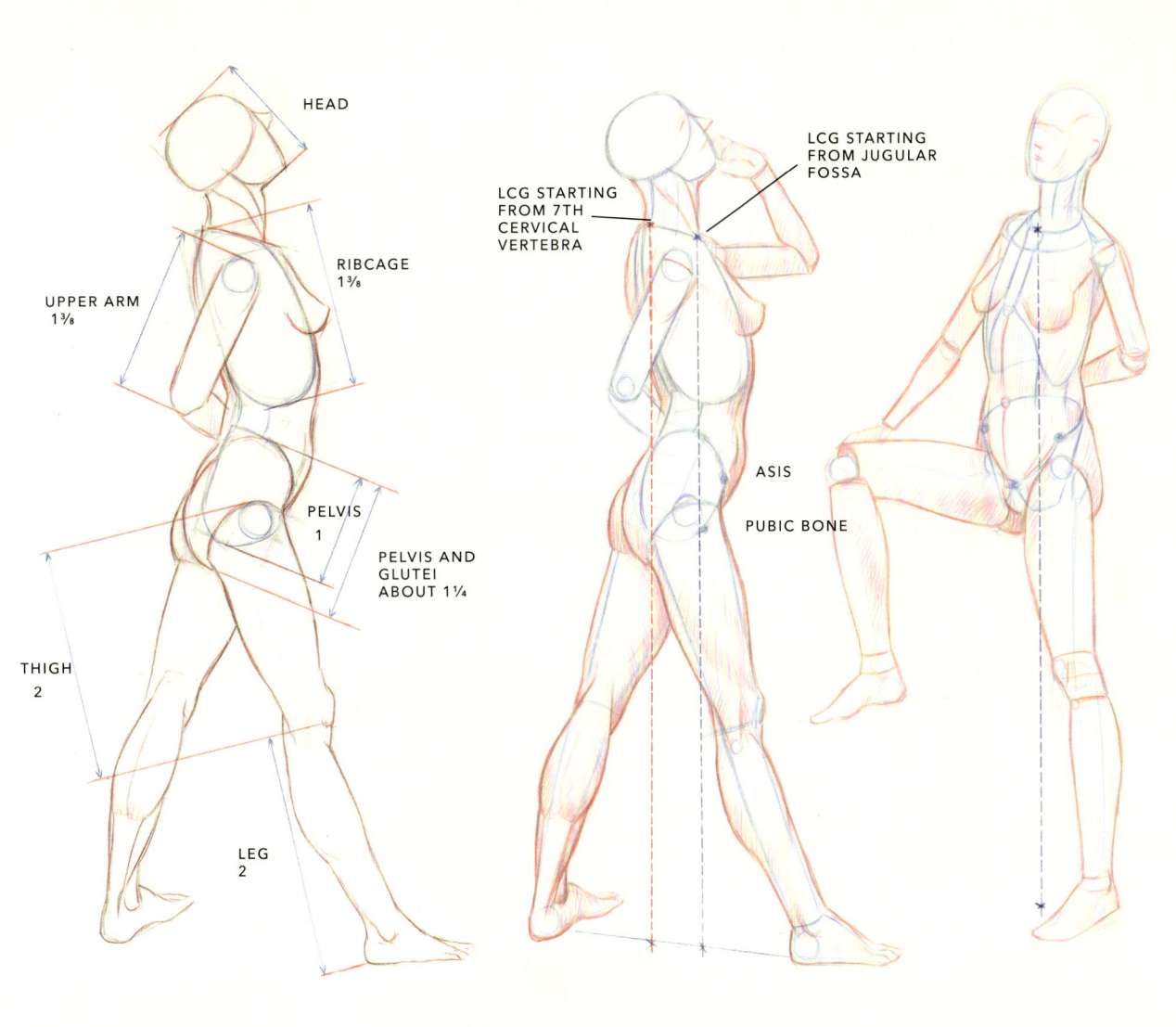

HEAD

RIBCAGE
1 ³/₈

UPPER ARM
1 ³/₈

PELVIS
1

PELVIS AND
GLUTEI
ABOUT 1 ¼

THIGH
2

LEG
2

LCG STARTING
FROM JUGULAR
FOSSA

LCG STARTING
FROM 7TH
CERVICAL
VERTEBRA

ASIS

PUBIC BONE

ABOVE: Using proportions and LCG to capture a pose

The drawing at left shows how to measure the various segments of the figure using the height of the head (1) as the unit of measure to maintain the correct proportional relationships. The drawing at center shows how the segments of the body can be lined up with the help of the line of the center of gravity. In this side-view pose, either the jugular fossa or the seventh cervical vertebra can be used as the starting point of the LCG. The figure at right is another example of how the LCG can be used; in this case, the LCG starts from the jugular fossa, cuts between the ASIS and the pubic bone, and ends next to the big toe.

FROM AXIAL SKELETON TO MUSCULATURE

The images in this demonstration are drawn from imagination to exemplify how a good understanding of the human body can give us the freedom to draw poses even without a model—a very important skill when brainstorming or creating a composition from memory or imagination. In this sequence, a figure moves from a sitting to a standing position. In each step, the figure is first visualized as just an axial skeleton, which is then developed by adding the limbs. Each step shows a figure onto which the muscles have been added.

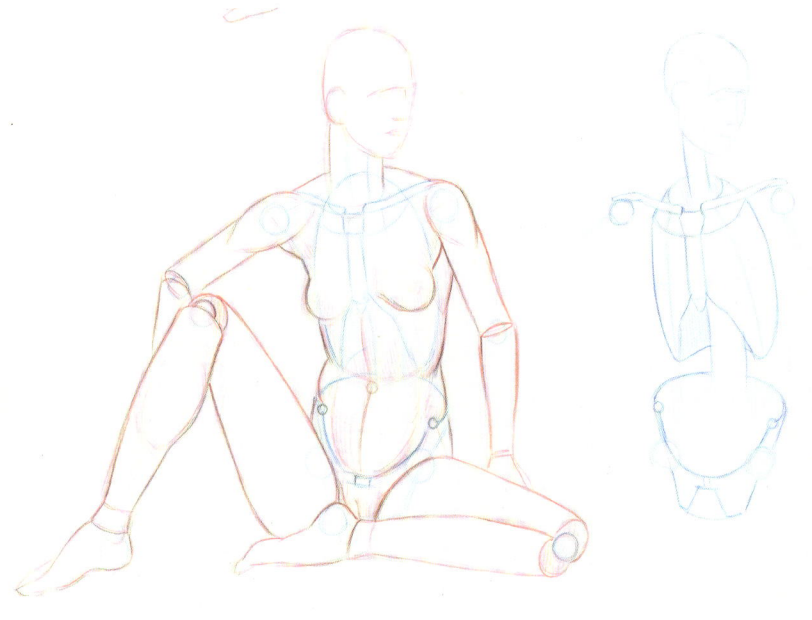

1
We begin with the sitting figure.

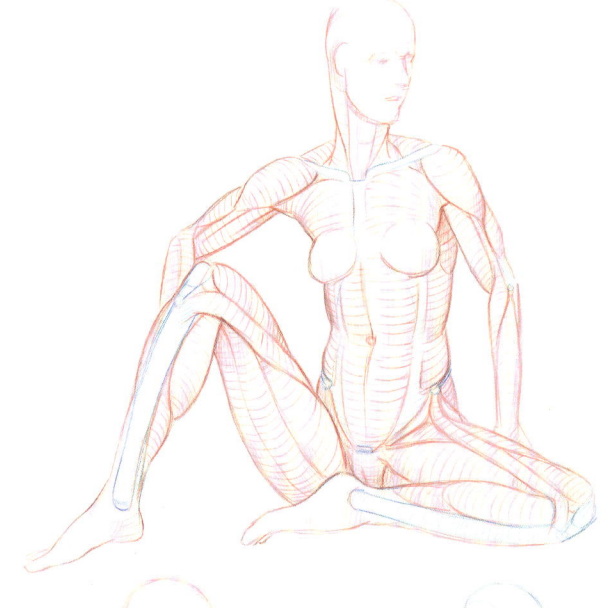

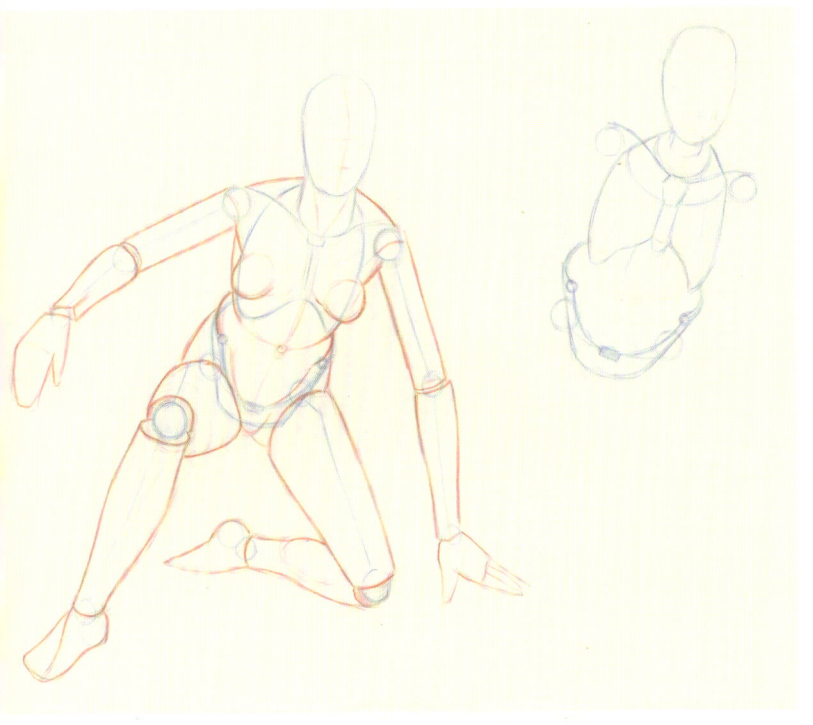

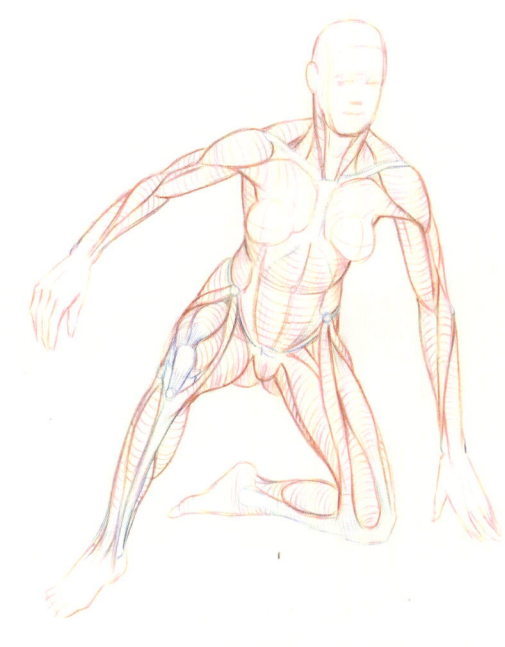

2 (above)
In this intermediate stage, the figure has risen to a crouching position.

3 (below)
Finally, the figure approaches a standing position.

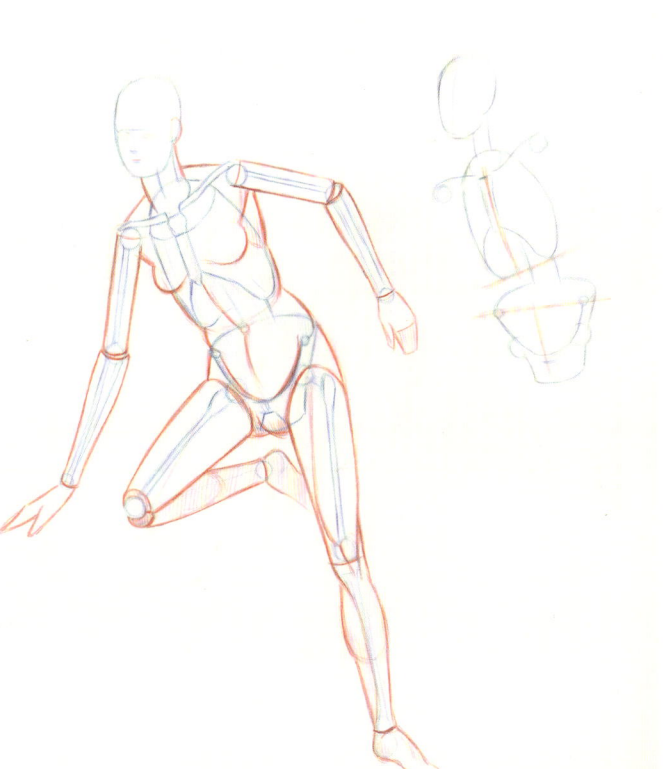

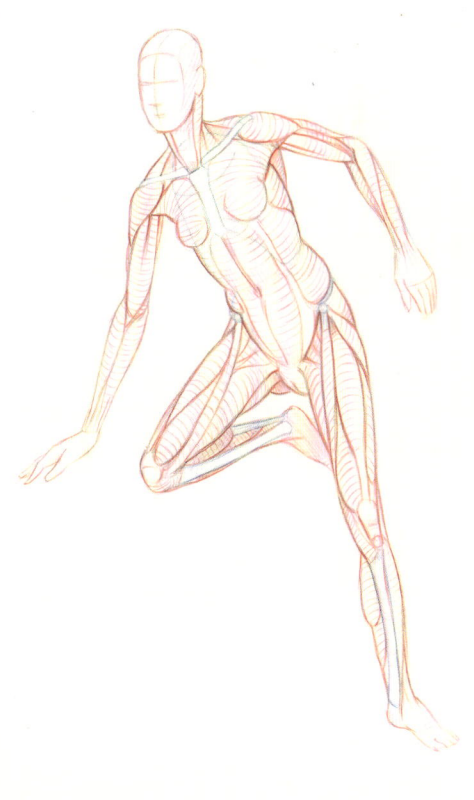

MUSCLES IN ACTION

The muscles in movement and at rest exhibit specific structural characteristics that are very often subtle and can be easy to overlook. As a general rule, the muscles (like all the forms of the body with the exception of the face) are not symmetrical. Drawing a symmetrical muscle will create an unnatural form that appears to be inflated from the inside. Both at rest and in movement, asymmetries are present in single muscles, in muscle groups, and between groups of antagonist muscles. These asymmetries become even more evident where the muscle peaks at its maximum width. So, for example, identifying the peaks of the muscle group on the inside of the leg and the peak of the muscles on the outside of the leg is essential for properly positioning these two opposite forms in relation to each other. The peaks of these two muscular groups are always at an angle in relation to the main axis of the limb they belong to.

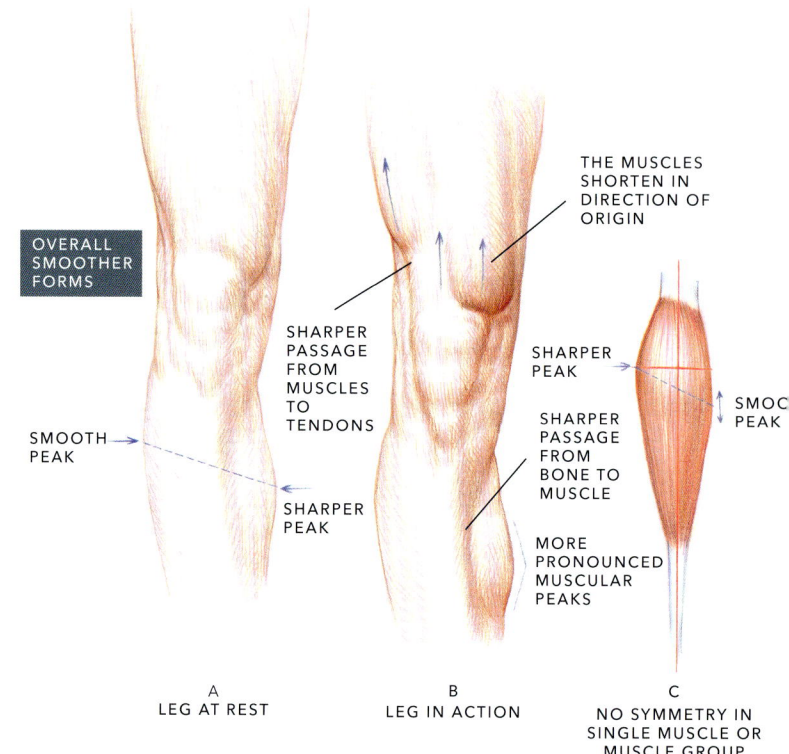

OVERALL SMOOTHER FORMS

SMOOTH PEAK

SHARPER PEAK

SHARPER PASSAGE FROM MUSCLES TO TENDONS

THE MUSCLES SHORTEN IN DIRECTION OF ORIGIN

SHARPER PEAK

SHARPER PASSAGE FROM BONE TO MUSCLE

MORE PRONOUNCED MUSCULAR PEAKS

SMOC PEAK

A
LEG AT REST

B
LEG IN ACTION

C
NO SYMMETRY IN SINGLE MUSCLE OR MUSCLE GROUP

TOP: Muscles of the leg at rest and in action

There is no symmetry in muscular forms. The alignment of the peaks of a muscle or muscle group is never oriented perpendicularly to the muscle's main axis. Very commonly, the peak of one side of the muscle or muscle group is smoother and more difficult to locate with precision than the opposite peak, which is more angular and evident. The drawing at left (A) shows the overall smoother forms of a leg at rest; the passages from muscles to tendons and bones to muscles are more gradual. Notice that the peaks of the muscles of the medial and lateral sides of the lower leg do not align perpendicularly to its main vertical axis. In this case, the lateral peak is higher and less pronounced than the medial peak. In the drawing at center (B), the muscles of the leg are moving in the direction of origin, lifting the patella upward. The muscular forms become bulgier and more angular, creating sharper distinctions between muscles, tendons, and bones. The inset detail at right (C) describes some of the structural characteristics of a fusiform muscle.

RIGHT: Upper arm muscles in action

This drawing shows the changes in form and in the orientation of the peaks of the muscles of the upper arm at rest and when contracted.

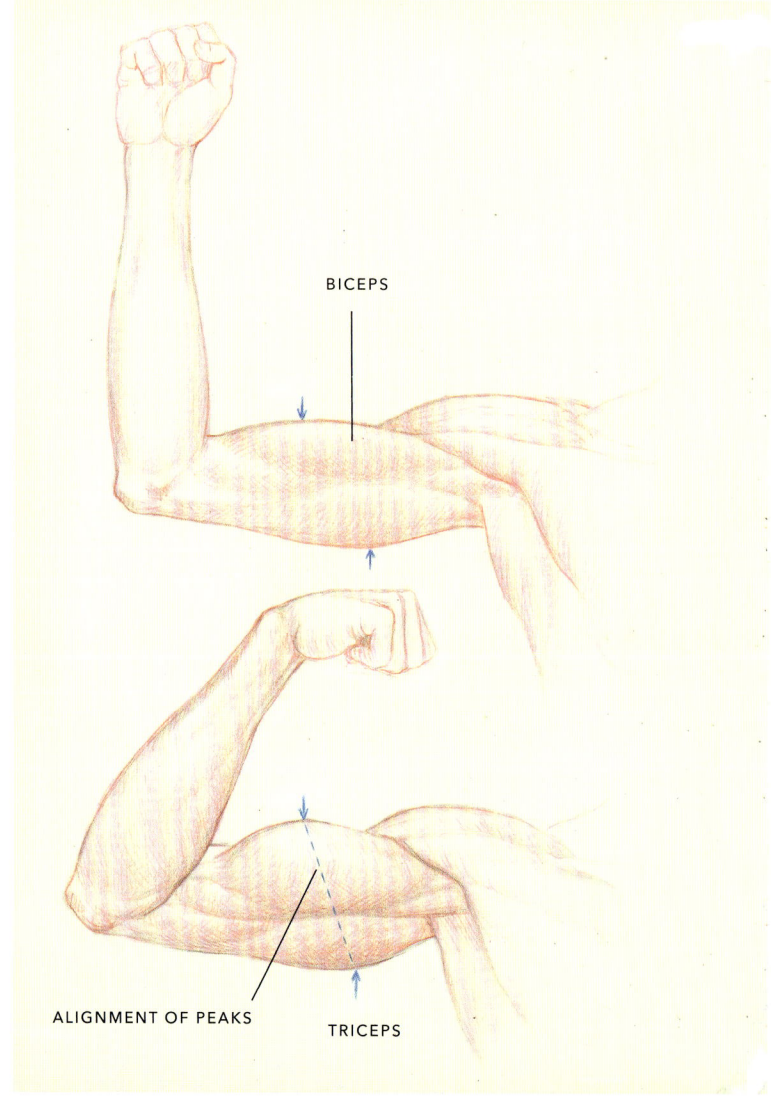

BICEPS

ALIGNMENT OF PEAKS

TRICEPS

MUSCULAR–SKELETAL CONNECTIONS IN DETAIL

The next images further describe the muscular and skeletal connections, introducing specific realistic details. These studies show the effects that torsion, flexion, and extension have on the muscular forms and how to render them correctly. Using these examples as references, try drawing the torso in various positions or actions starting from an essential rendering of the skeleton and then adding the muscles over it.

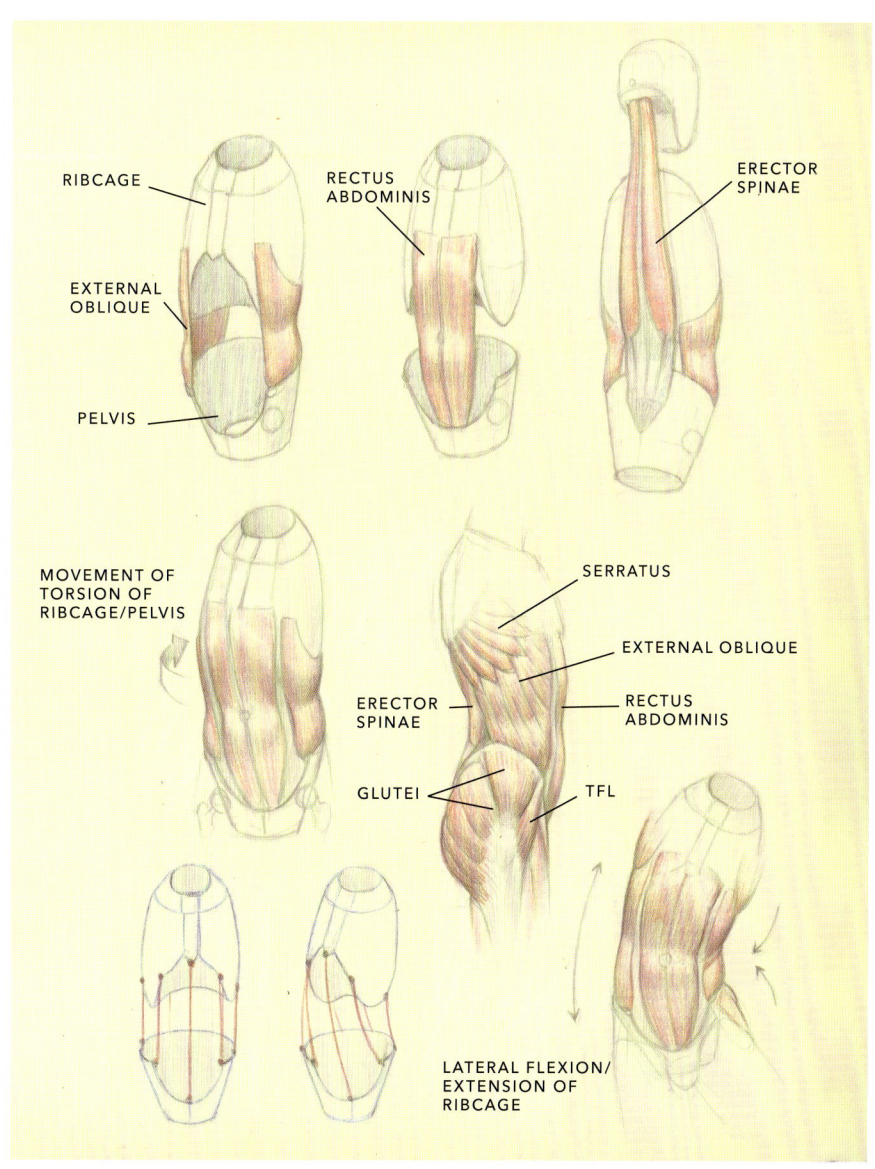

RIBCAGE

RECTUS ABDOMINIS

ERECTOR SPINAE

EXTERNAL OBLIQUE

PELVIS

MOVEMENT OF TORSION OF RIBCAGE/PELVIS

SERRATUS

EXTERNAL OBLIQUE

ERECTOR SPINAE

RECTUS ABDOMINIS

GLUTEI

TFL

LATERAL FLEXION/ EXTENSION OF RIBCAGE

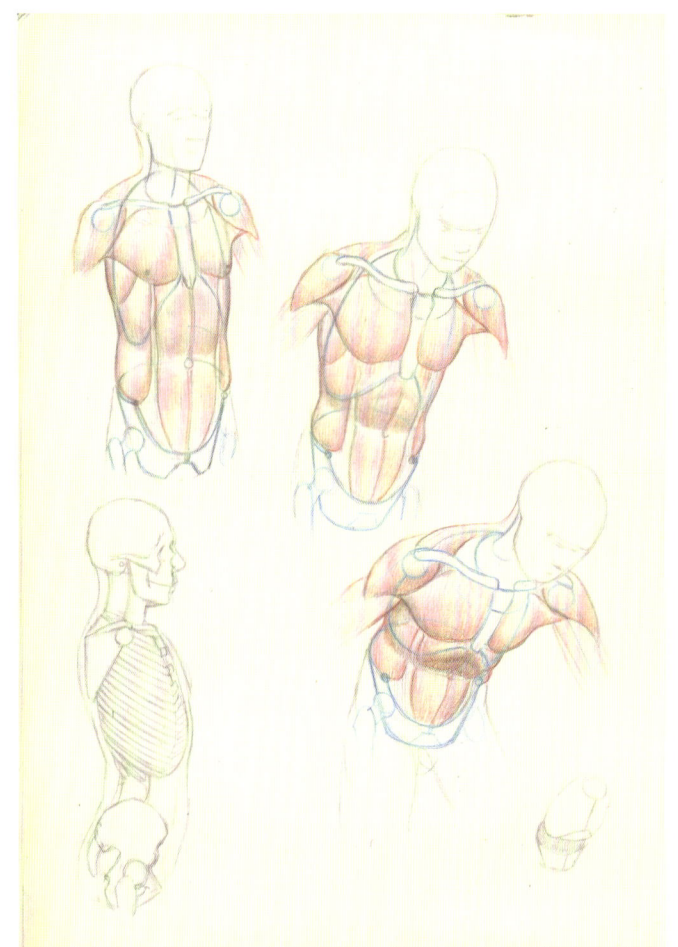

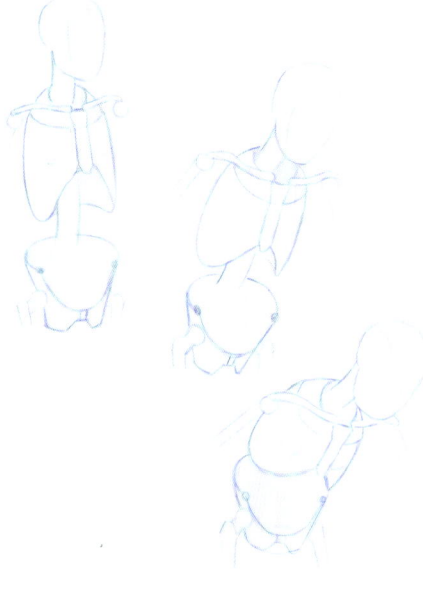

TOP: Flexion sequence, torso

When drawing a movement of the torso such as this flexion sequence, start with the ribcage. This will allow you to accurately add the muscles over the skeleton. Consider the overlapping, foreshortening, and compression of the muscular volumes as the torso is flexed.

BOTTOM: Lateral flexion and hyperextension, torso

Considering the skeletal structure (A) when drawing the figure in movement is helpful in understanding the modifications of the form created by compression and (lateral) flexion (B) and extension (C) or foreshortening (D). You can study a foreshortened pose (D) by first drawing it from an angle that does not have overlapping forms (C). It is often easiest to start from the skeleton and then to add the muscular forms, eventually projecting these measures on the foreshortened pose.

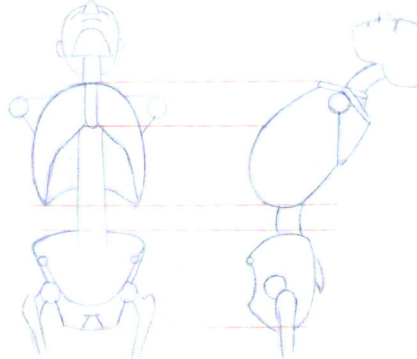

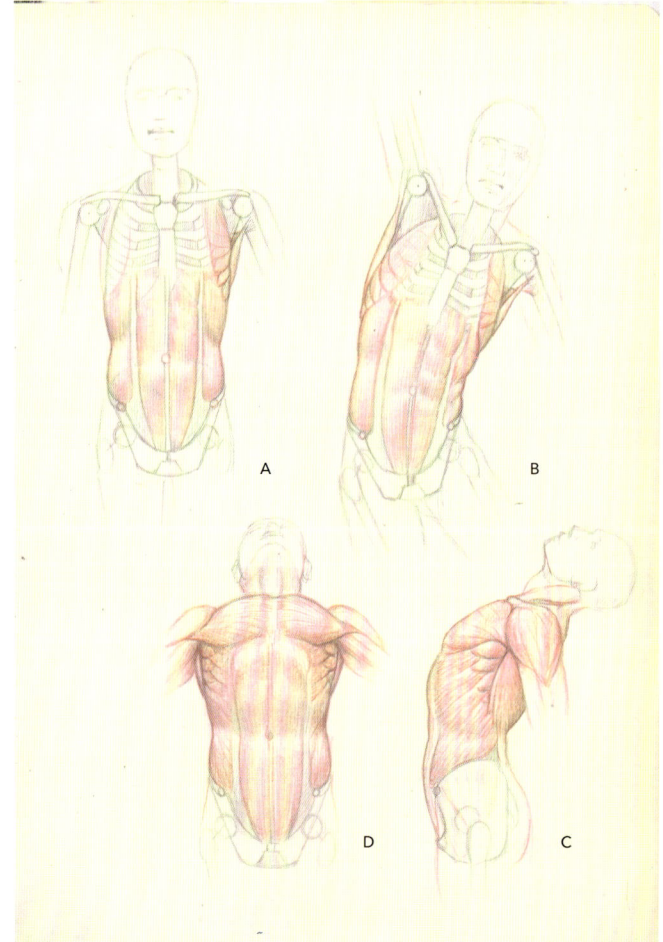

A

B

D

C

DYNAMISM, MOVEMENT, AND FLOWS IN THE WHOLE FIGURE

Now let's practice applying movement to the whole figure, considering the effect that the position of the skeleton has on the main muscular groups. To do this, first block-in a schematic rendering of the skeleton, then apply the muscular volumes.

OPPOSITE: Studying movement using stereometry

The figure study on the left shows skeletal and muscular structures together. The stereometric rendering on the right is a study of the orientation of the planes and volumes of the figure and their alignment along a curved axis. Studies like these are very useful in preparation for a long-pose drawing.

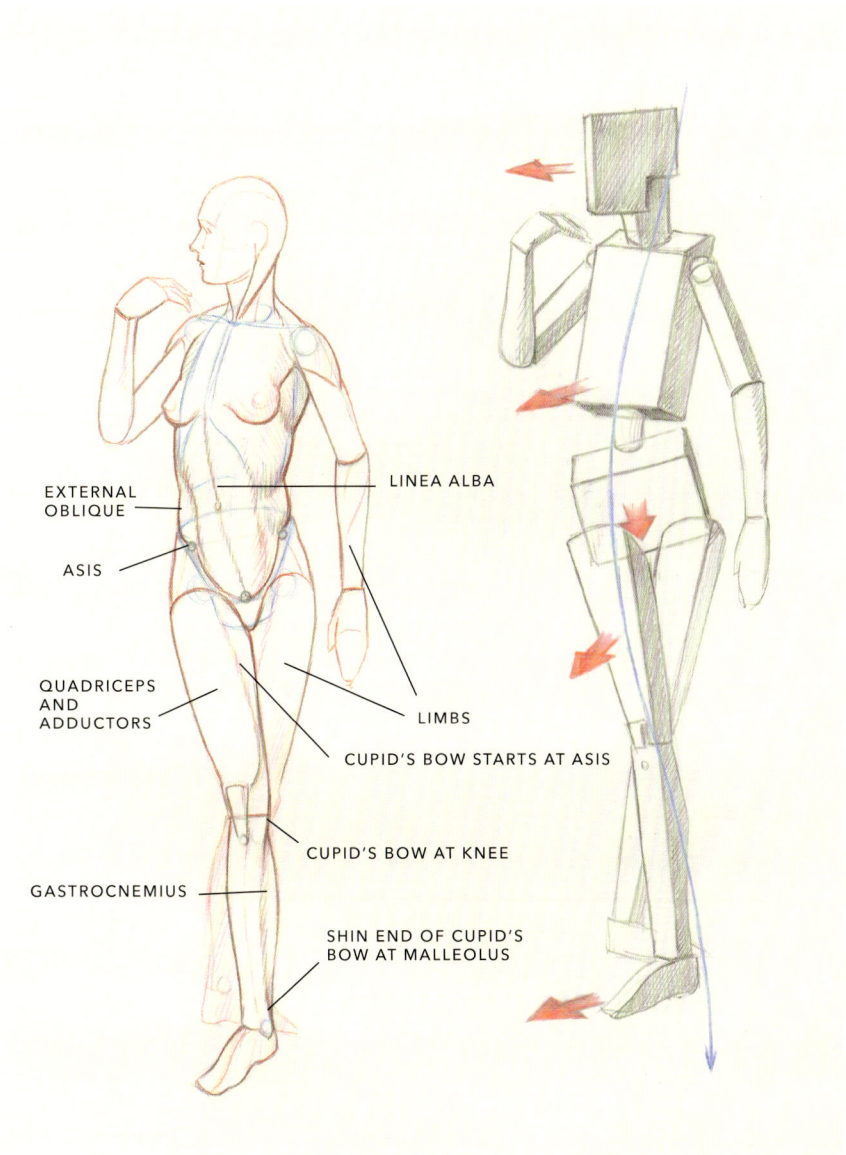

EXTERNAL OBLIQUE

LINEA ALBA

ASIS

QUADRICEPS AND ADDUCTORS

LIMBS

CUPID'S BOW STARTS AT ASIS

CUPID'S BOW AT KNEE

GASTROCNEMIUS

SHIN END OF CUPID'S BOW AT MALLEOLUS

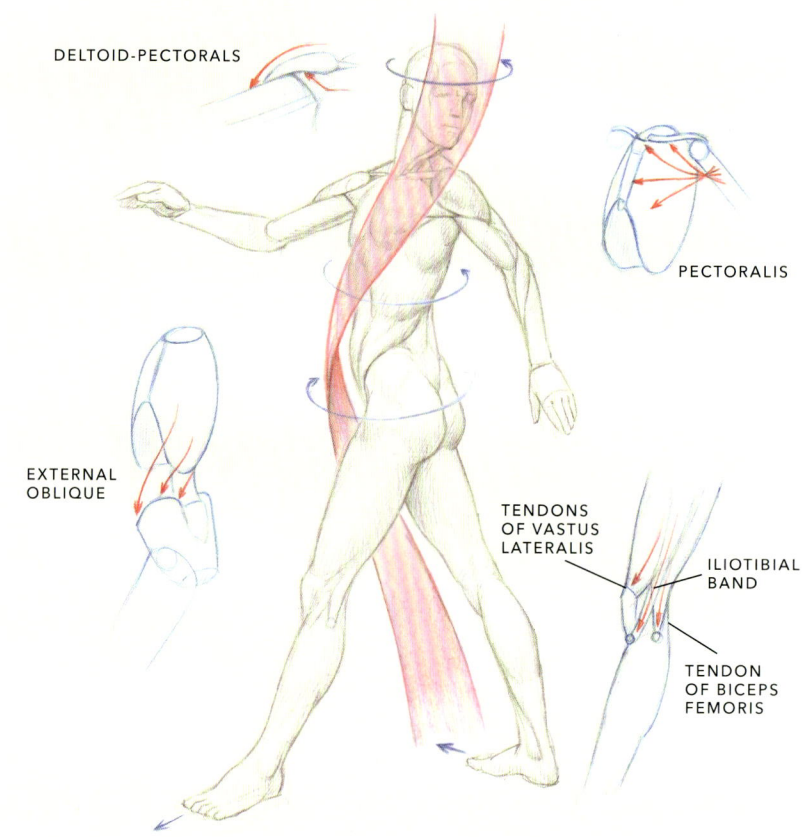

DELTOID-PECTORALS

PECTORALIS

EXTERNAL
OBLIQUE

TENDONS
OF VASTUS
LATERALIS

ILIOTIBIAL
BAND

TENDON
OF BICEPS
FEMORIS

RIGHT: Flows and dynamism of the figure in movement

BELOW: Structure, flows, and movement

These drawings show the progressive layering of the muscles over the skeleton of a figure in movement.

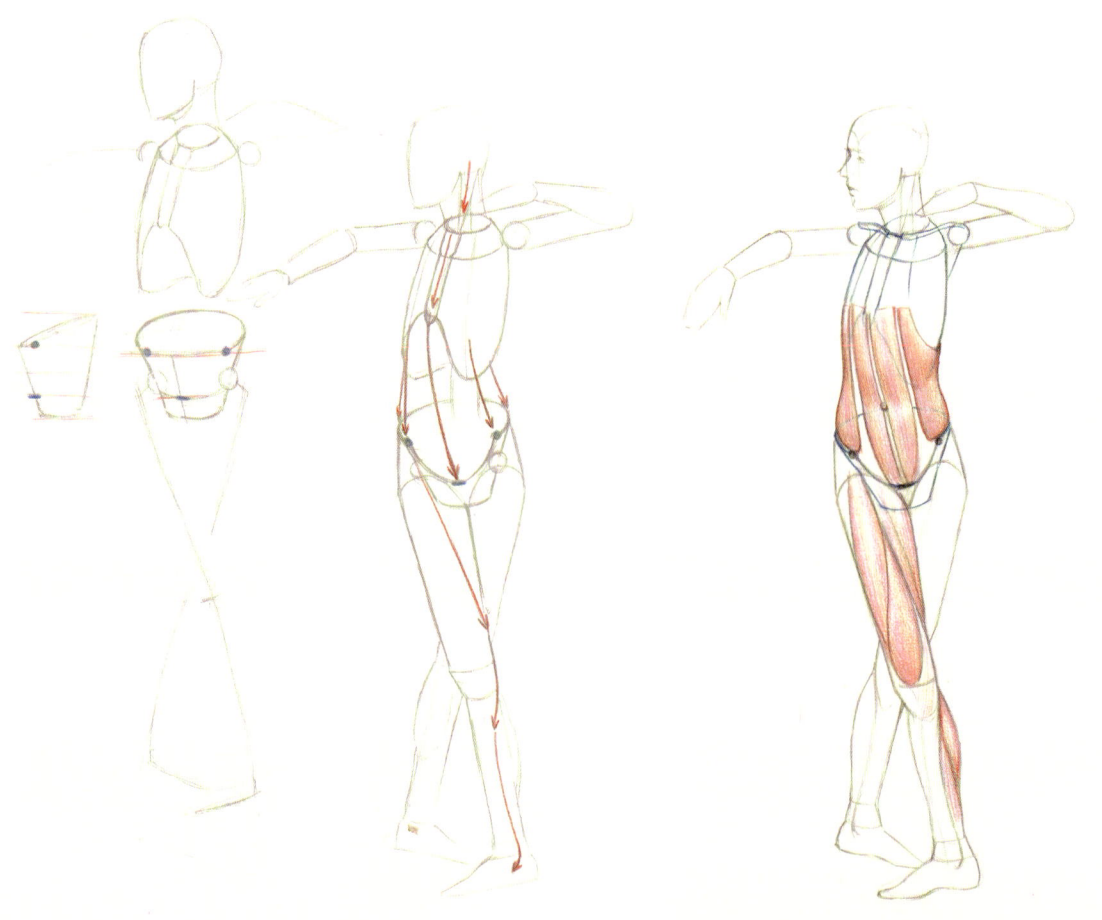

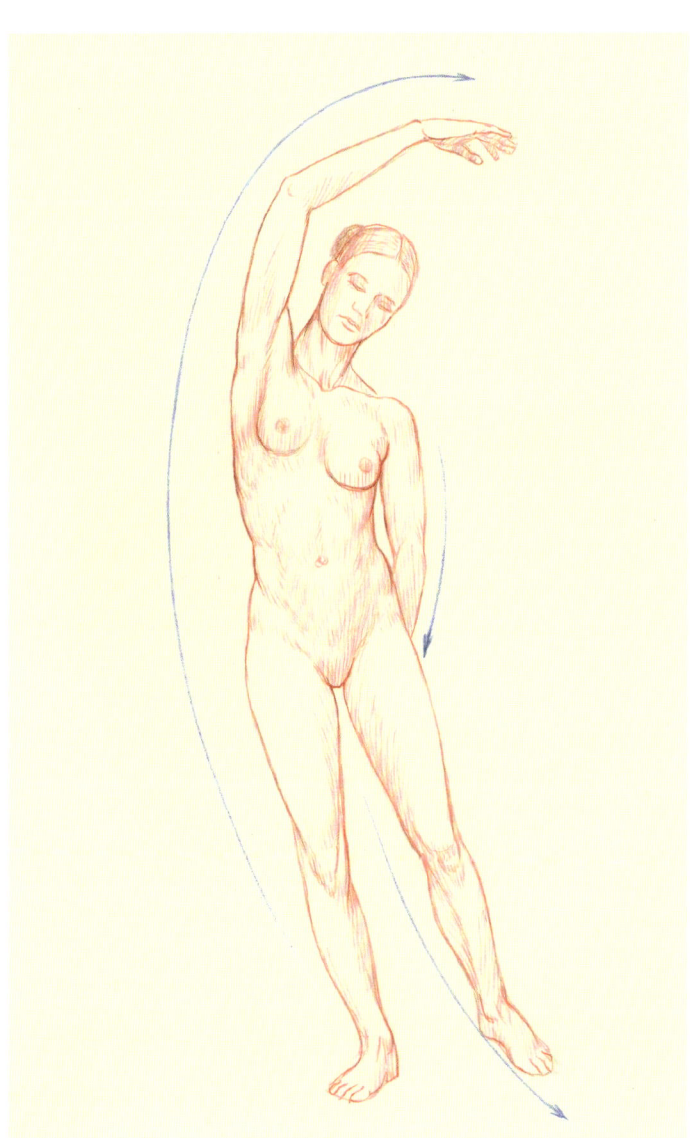

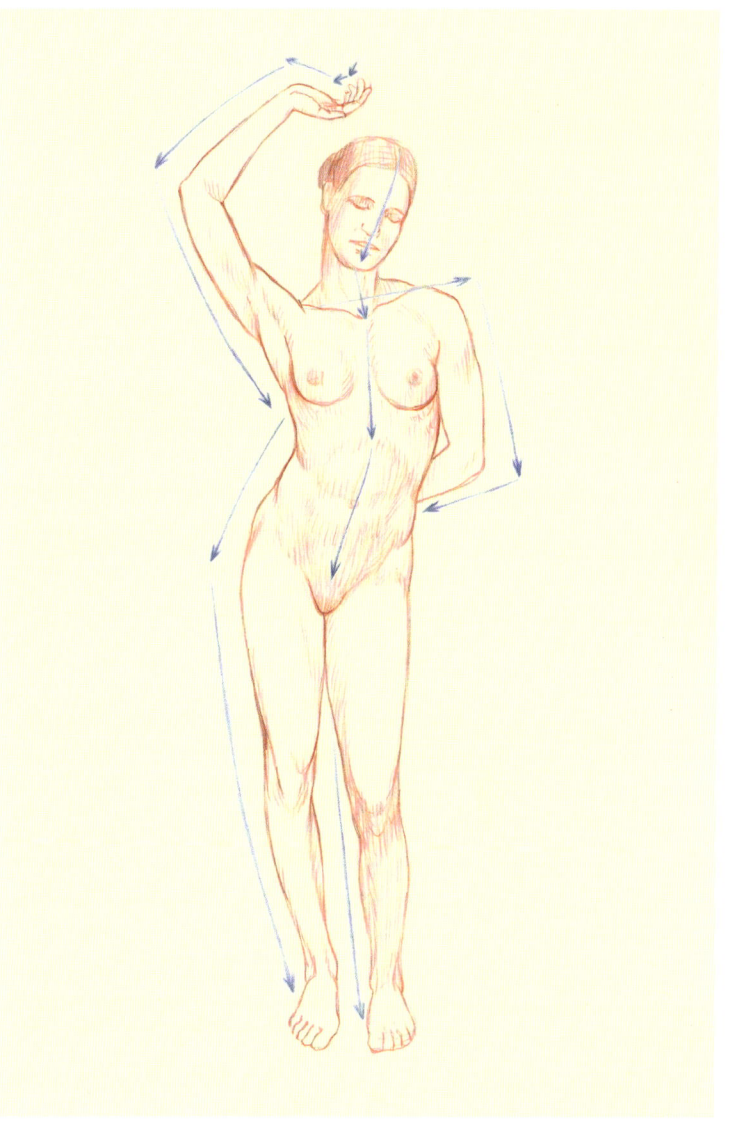

I conclude this section with the gorgeous and lively sketch by Raphael on the following page, which perfectly summarizes all the aspects of the figure in movement we have seen so far. The proportions, landmarks, muscular volumes, lines of flow, and movement all come together in a beautiful composition.

ABOVE: Dynamic and aesthetic aspects of a pose

The lines of action in the figure at left visualize the aesthetics and dynamism of its movement. By contrast, the figure on the right is in a static pose denoting a deliberate and controlled positioning of the limbs. This could be described as a contrapposto pose arranged with aesthetic intent.

OVERLEAF: Raphael, *Fighting Men*, 1510–11, red chalk over leadpoint, 15 × 11⅛ inches (37.89 × 28.09 cm). Ashmolean Museum, Oxford.

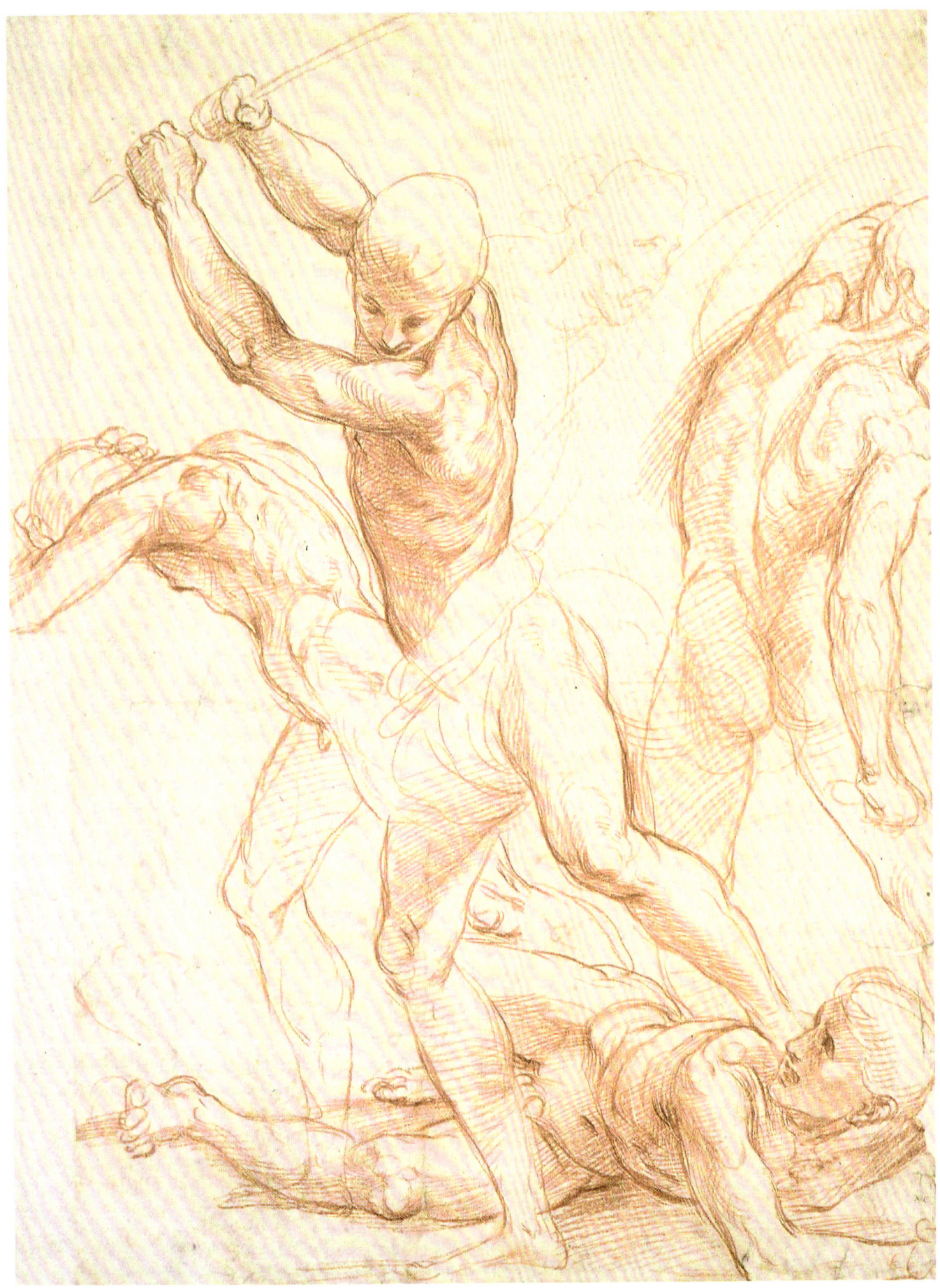

A CONTEMPORARY MASTER OF ANATOMICAL FORM

BELOW: Brian Booth Craig, *Jess,* 2015, bronze, 34 ×10 × 8 inches (86 × 25 × 20 cm). Courtesy of the artist.

This work by Brian Booth Craig is a perfect example of mastery of anatomical forms in movement. In *Jess,* the structural, anatomical, and dynamic aspects of the human body are captured and synthetized in a beautiful, elegant pose. Viewing the sculpture from the back, we can appreciate the graceful torsion of the erector spinae muscles as they stem from the sacrum and are directed toward the back of the head. In the front view, the iliac spine, the tensor fascia latae, the beginning of the sartorius, and the rectus femoris are clearly distinguishable at the level of the pelvis. In fact, all the muscles in this artwork are perfectly positioned, but the anatomical aspect of this work is secondary to the dynamism and aesthetic of the figure, which is the real subject of the artwork.

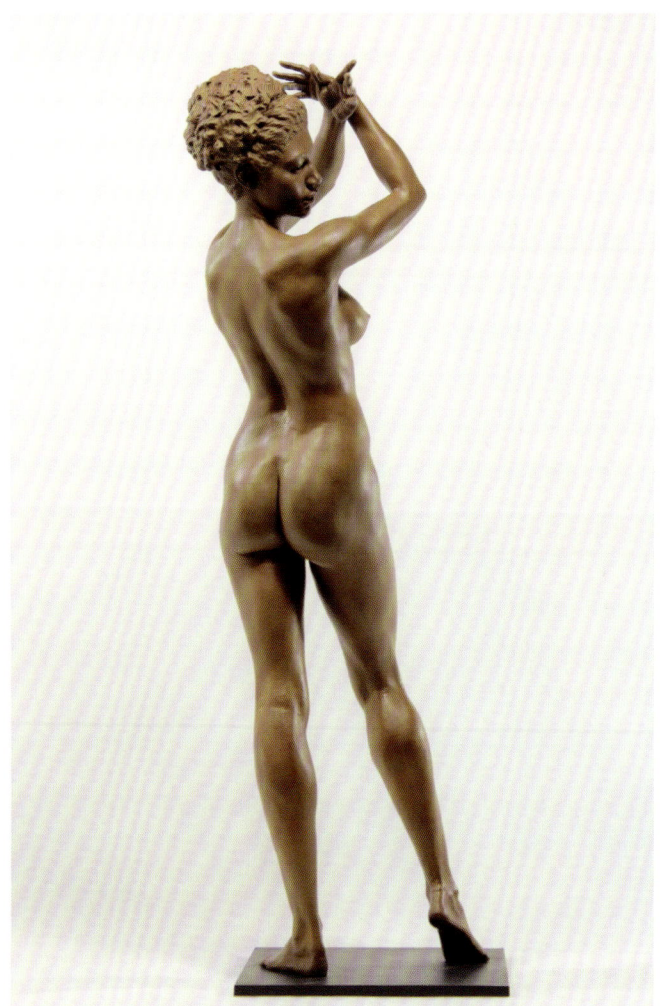
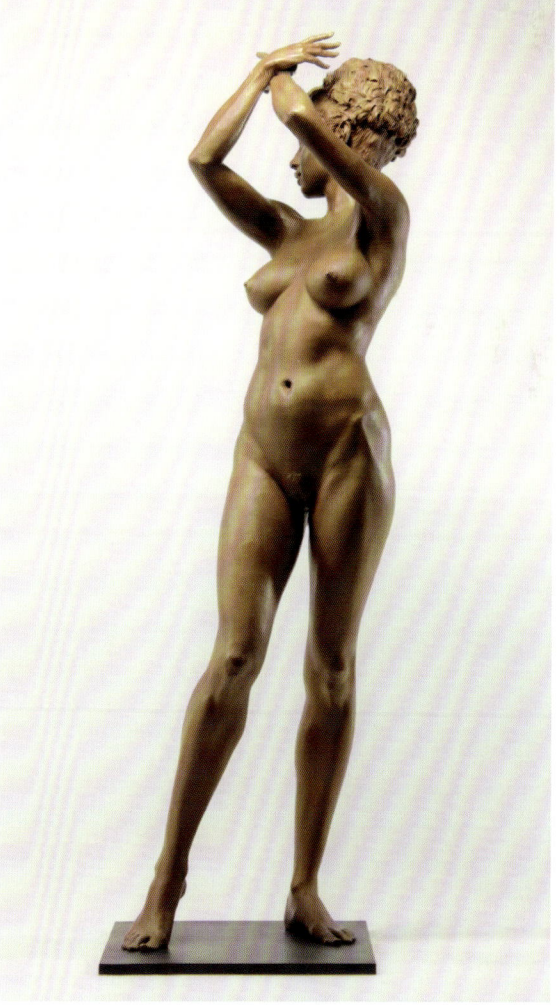

FROM STATIC POSE TO MOVEMENT

Each step is analyzed from several points of view: first the skeleton with the lines of flow created by the muscular volumes, then the superficial anatomy, and finally the external forms. The intent is to capture the aesthetic and elegance of the pose—the final goal of the study of anatomy for an artist.

1

The red arrows in the first of these figures show some muscular-skeletal connections and the pathways they produce. Compare these lines of flow with those of the following images to see how movement can affect the aesthetics of the body in various poses and actions. The center figure is a complete analysis of the superficial muscles, which that can be useful in understanding the superficial forms of the last image of this sequence. The last figure demonstrates how even a static pose can express a certain dynamism as shown by the long sweeping line of action (red). The shorter blue lines describe the flows of the external forms created by the superficial muscular volumes.

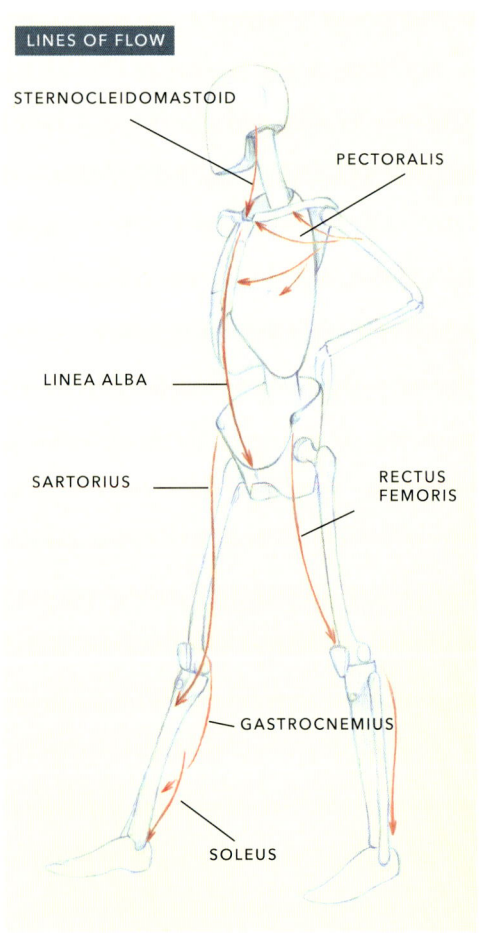

LINES OF FLOW

STERNOCLEIDOMASTOID

PECTORALIS

LINEA ALBA

SARTORIUS

RECTUS FEMORIS

GASTROCNEMIUS

SOLEUS

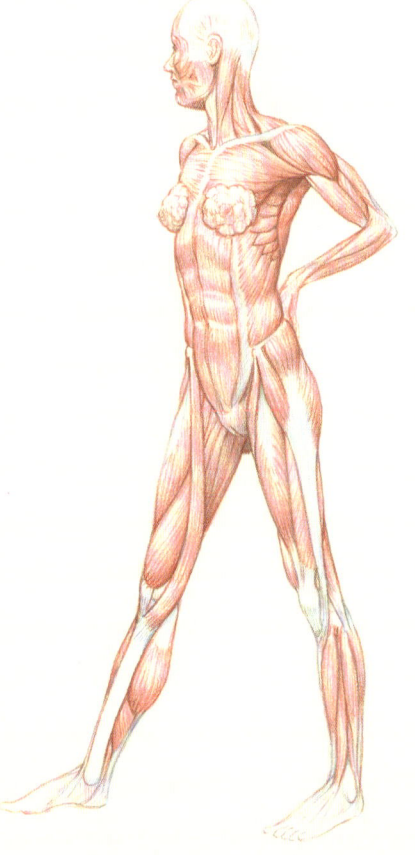

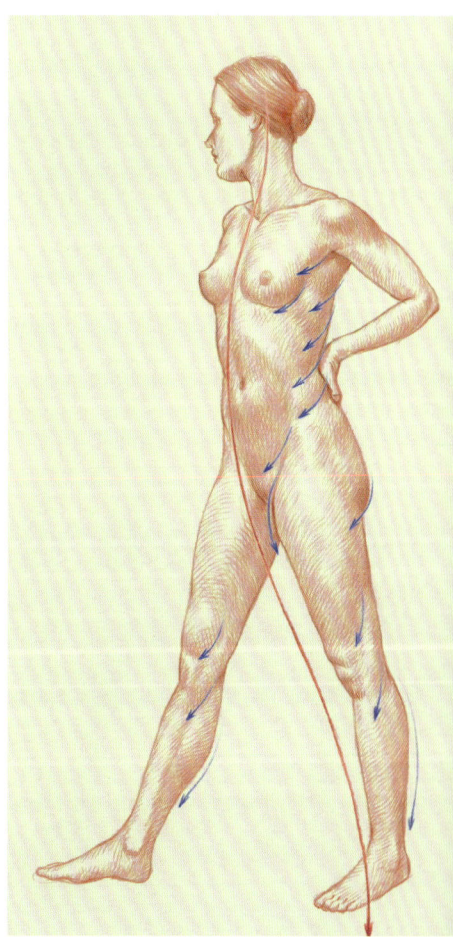

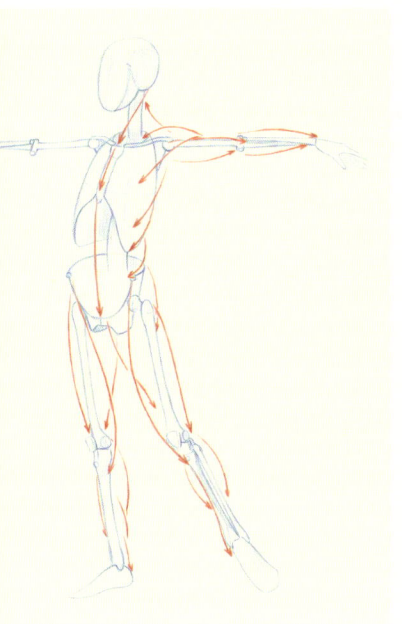
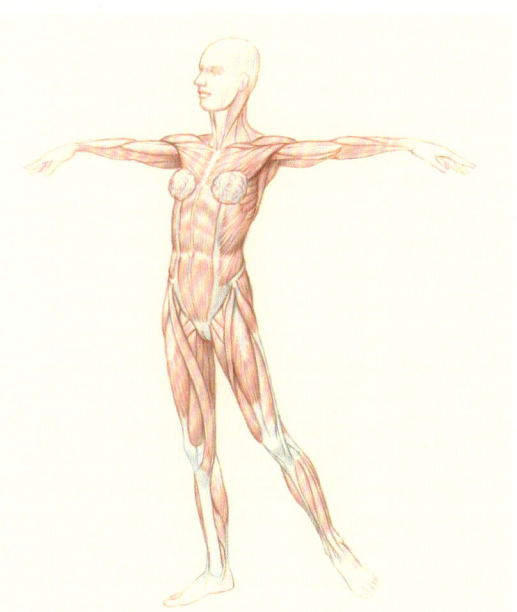
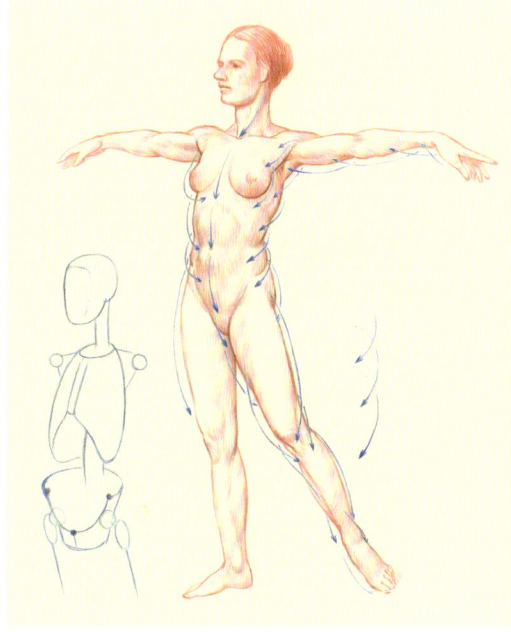

2 (above)

This second sequence shows the figure in slight hyperextension of one leg and with lifted arms (abduction). The initial figure, synthetizes the flows of the direction of the muscles; the second is a study of the superficial muscles; and the third figure shows the effect that the superficial muscles have on the external forms.

3 (below)

These three images conclude the series. The figure is now arched back in a powerful and elegant movement reminiscent of the ecstatic pose of a Hellenistic maenad. As in the previous sequences, the first figure displays patterns of flow that synthetize the paths of the main muscular forms; the second shows all the superficial muscles; and the third figure allows us to appreciate the elegance of the external forms. The long curving line sweeping down in front of the figure is the line of action.

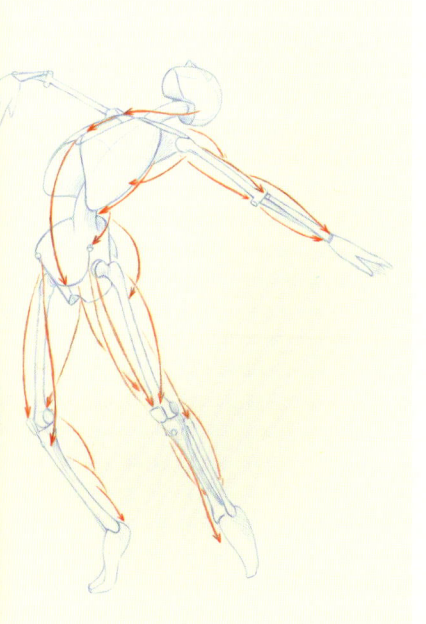
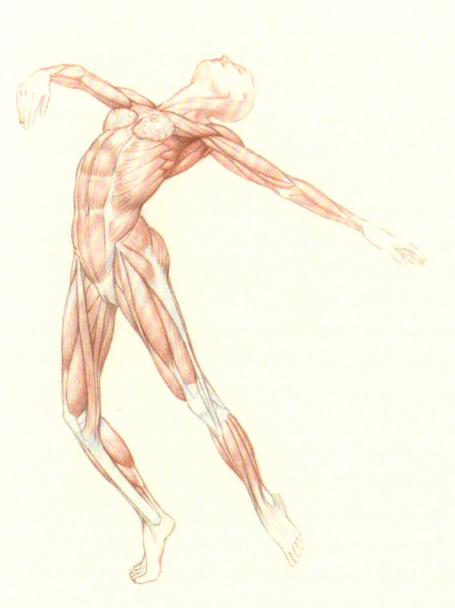
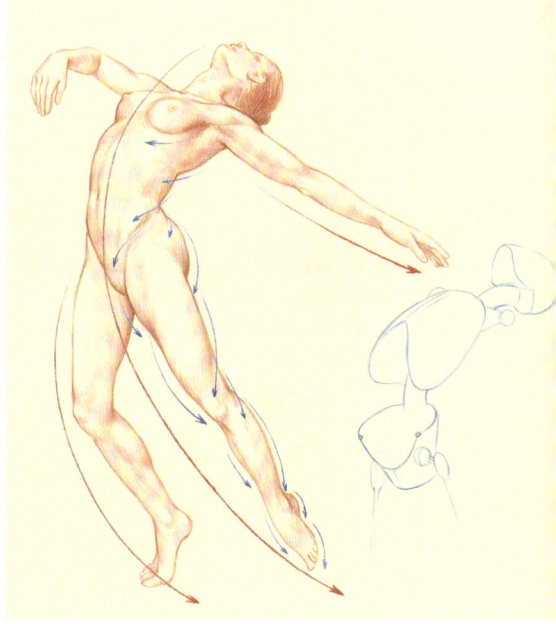

ANALYZING FIGURES IN MOVEMENT—THREE SEQUENCES

The sequences in this section show how a figure in movement can be studied using different methods of visualization: stereometric, anatomical (skeleton or superficial muscles), and realistic renderings. Analyzing and depicting the figure using *different methods in different orders* heightens your observational skills. You can use any of the sequences in this section as an exercise by copying the steps.

SEQUENCE 1—FROM STEREOMETRY TO MUSCLES TO SURFACE FORMS

BELOW LEFT: Starting with a stereometric rendering

This first sequence begins with a stereometric rendering of a figure in action. I worked from a photograph of a ballerina.

BELOW RIGHT: Superimposing the muscles

Next I added the muscles to the stereometric structure.

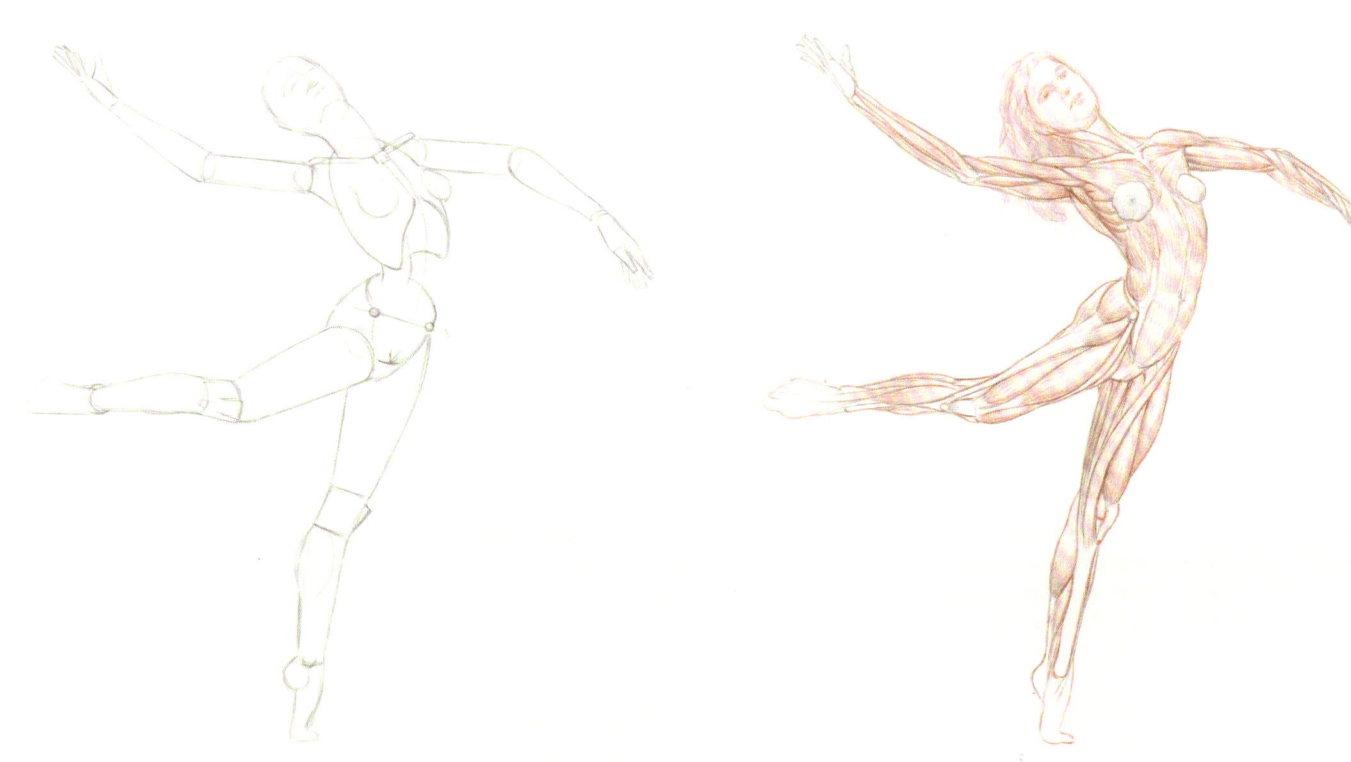

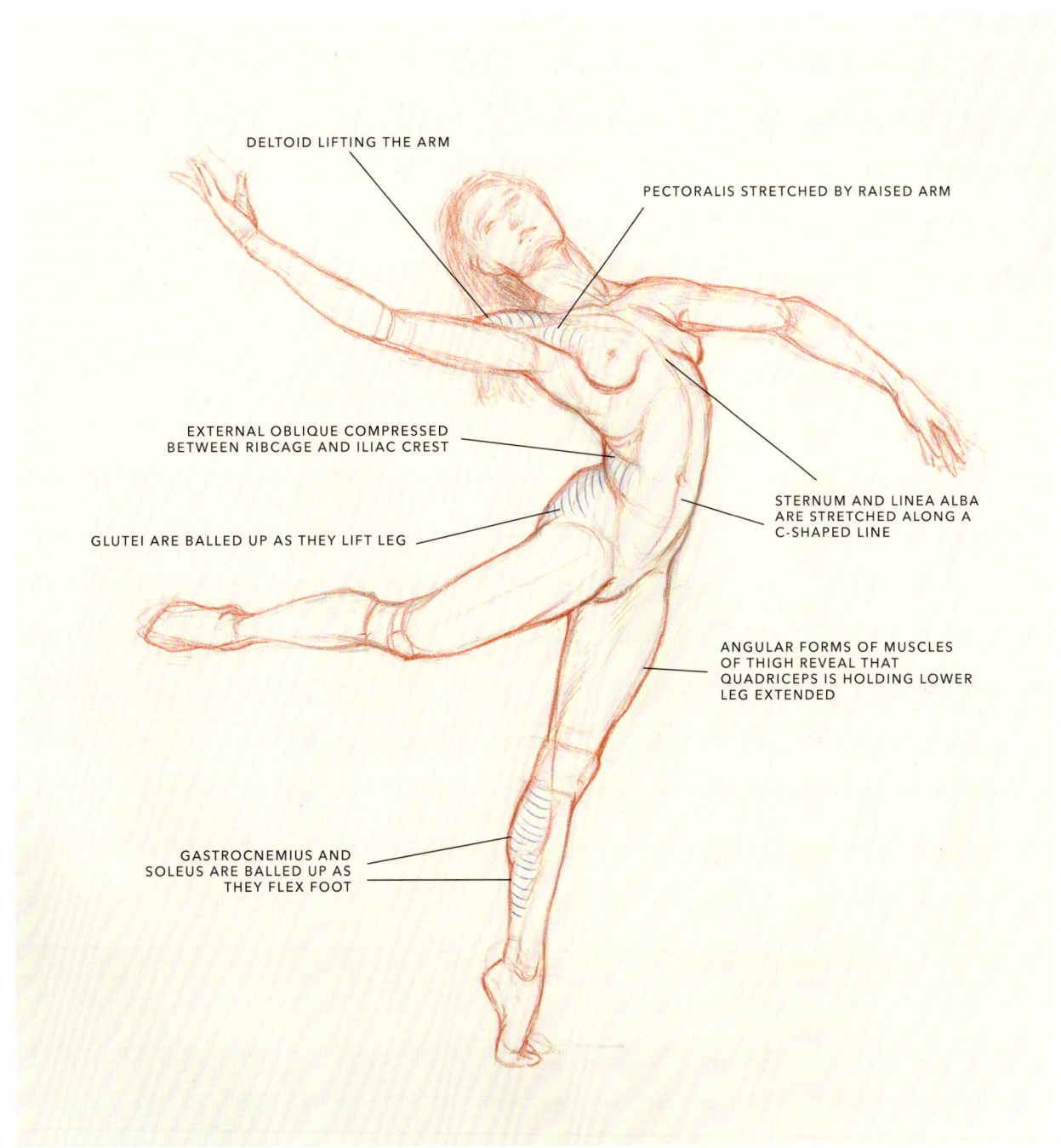

DELTOID LIFTING THE ARM

PECTORALIS STRETCHED BY RAISED ARM

EXTERNAL OBLIQUE COMPRESSED
BETWEEN RIBCAGE AND ILIAC CREST

STERNUM AND LINEA ALBA
ARE STRETCHED ALONG A
C-SHAPED LINE

GLUTEI ARE BALLED UP AS THEY LIFT LEG

ANGULAR FORMS OF MUSCLES
OF THIGH REVEAL THAT
QUADRICEPS IS HOLDING LOWER
LEG EXTENDED

GASTROCNEMIUS AND
SOLEUS ARE BALLED UP AS
THEY FLEX FOOT

ABOVE: Developing the external forms

In this final image of the sequence, I added the external forms, exploring the changes of the muscular volumes in movement as visualized by the cross-contour lines.

SEQUENCE 2—FROM SURFACE FORMS TO SKELETON

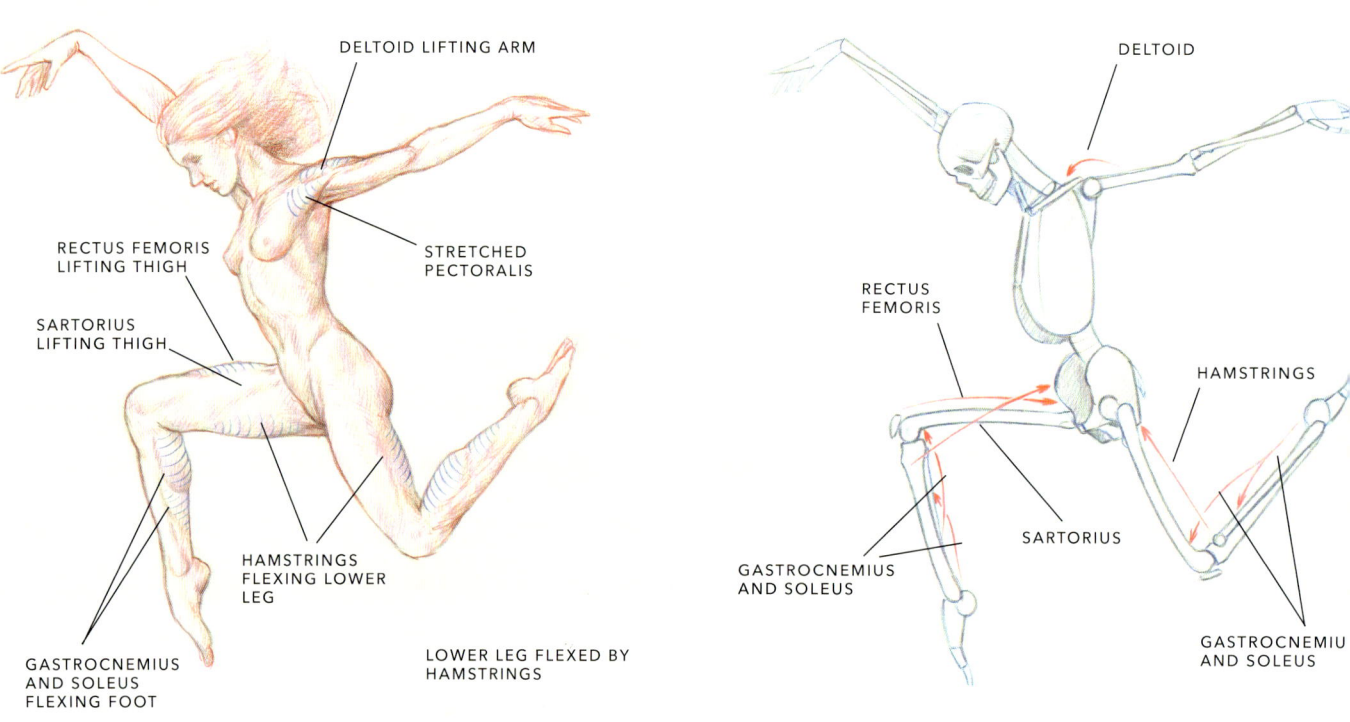

DELTOID LIFTING ARM

RECTUS FEMORIS
LIFTING THIGH

SARTORIUS
LIFTING THIGH

STRETCHED
PECTORALIS

HAMSTRINGS
FLEXING LOWER
LEG

LOWER LEG FLEXED BY
HAMSTRINGS

GASTROCNEMIUS
AND SOLEUS
FLEXING FOOT

DELTOID

RECTUS
FEMORIS

HAMSTRINGS

SARTORIUS

GASTROCNEMIUS
AND SOLEUS

GASTROCNEMIU
AND SOLEUS

ABOVE LEFT: Starting with the external forms

Now we work "from the outside in," beginning with the external forms. I based this image on a photo, and, as for the previous sequence, I analyzed the movements of the figure by drawing cross-contour lines over the muscles involved in the action.

ABOVE RIGHT: Visualizing the skeleton

After identifying the landmarks in the previous figure, I was able to re-create its skeletal structure. The actions of the muscles used in the pose are synthetized in this image with red arrows.

SEQUENCE 3—FROM REALISTIC TO SCHEMATIC

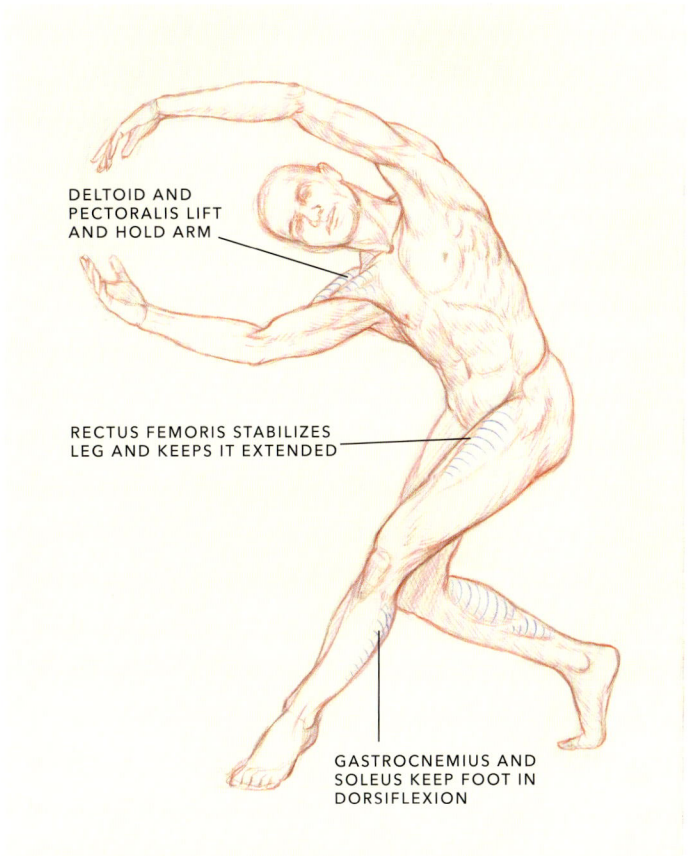

DELTOID AND
PECTORALIS LIFT
AND HOLD ARM

RECTUS FEMORIS STABILIZES
LEG AND KEEPS IT EXTENDED

GASTROCNEMIUS AND
SOLEUS KEEP FOOT IN
DORSIFLEXION

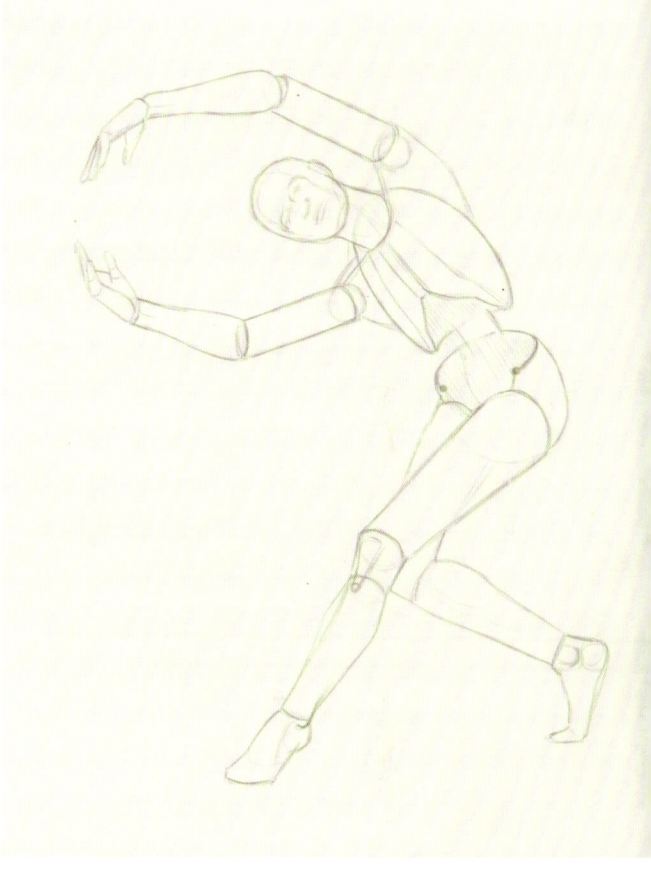

ABOVE LEFT: Starting with a realistic rendering

This final sequence starts with a realistic rendering of the figure, which I then analyzed to identify which muscles are involved in the movement.

ABOVE RIGHT: Synthesizing the stereometric forms

This final drawing is obtained by synthesizing the organic forms into stereometric volumes.

The arm and
forearm have
twenty-four muscles

BELOW: Blocking in the main volumes
Start simple. Always consider the
segments of the arm—or of any other
part of the body—as separate volumes
joined together. This will help you draw
the body part more correctly and create
a credible sense of movement.

MOVING THE ARMS

The arms contain many muscles and are capable of a great range of different move-ments, making them a complex subject. This section looks specifically at the arm and its structural, anatomical, and dynamic characteristics.

There are twenty-four muscles in the arm and forearm combined, and it can be daunting to try to understand the effects of movement on the arm if these muscles are considered individually. In the images in this section, it is not my intention to describe all the possible combinations of movements of the arm—flexion, exten-sion, pronation, supination—from all possible angles but instead to show how to approach reading a position of the arm, even one of the more complicated ones, and to draw it properly. In the images opposite, I grouped the muscles of the fore-arm in three main volumes to show more clearly the change in the forms of the forearm during various actions.

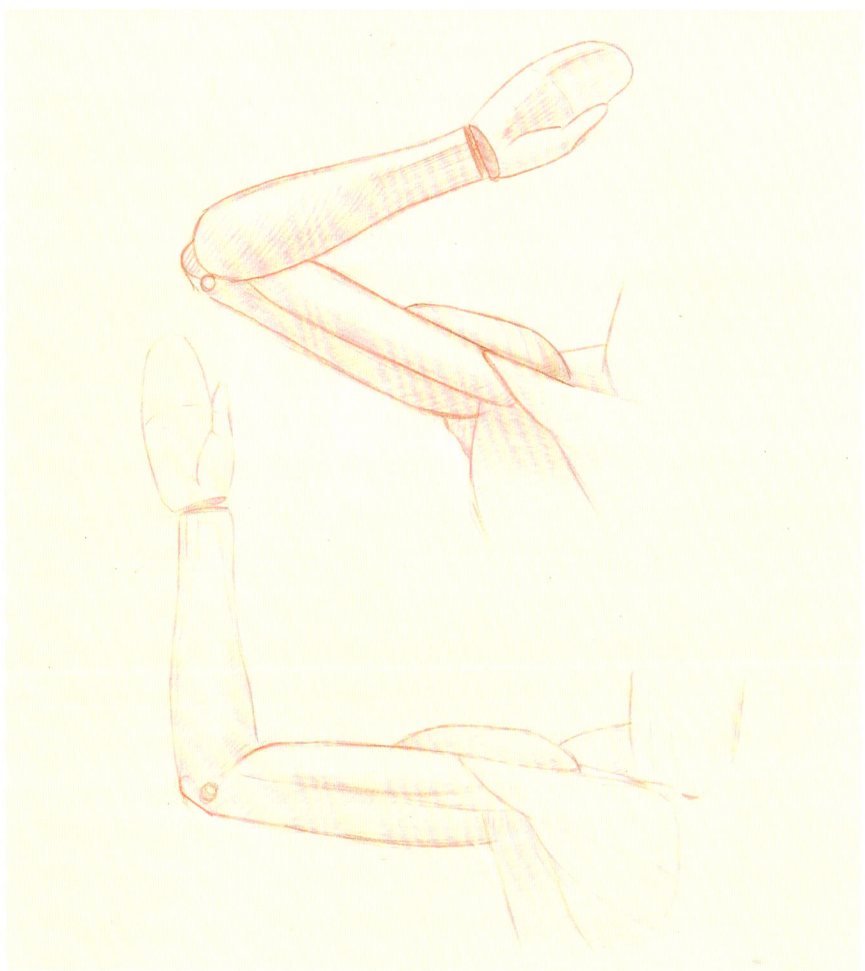

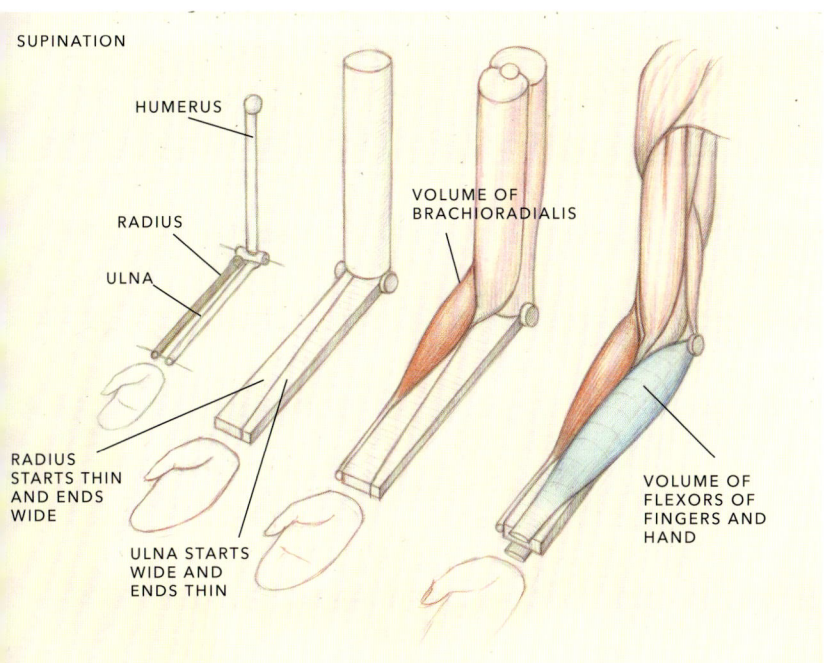

HUMERUS

RADIUS

ULNA

VOLUME OF
BRACHIORADIALIS

RADIUS
STARTS THIN
AND ENDS
WIDE

ULNA STARTS
WIDE AND
ENDS THIN

VOLUME OF
FLEXORS OF
FINGERS AND
HAND

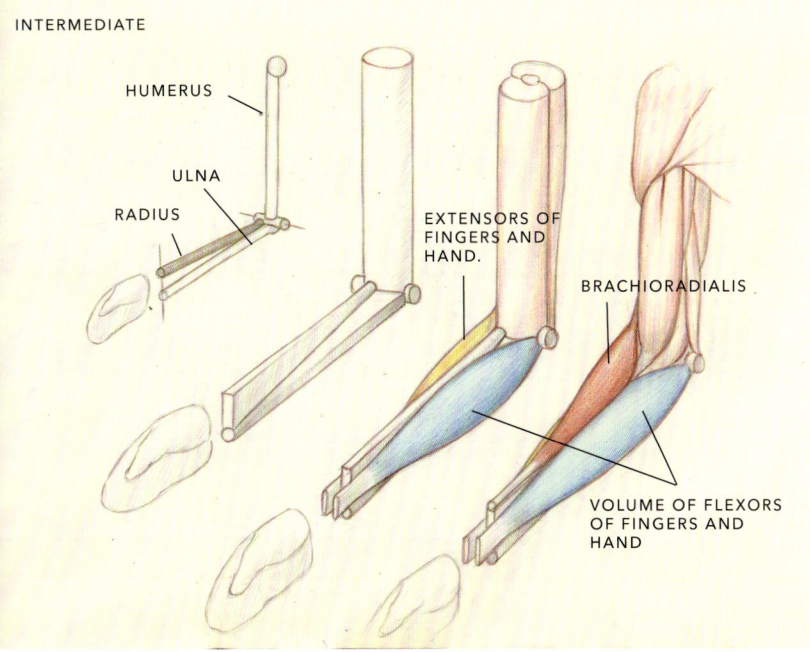

INTERMEDIATE

HUMERUS

ULNA

RADIUS

EXTENSORS OF
FINGERS AND
HAND.

BRACHIORADIALIS

VOLUME OF FLEXORS
OF FINGERS AND
HAND

LEFT: From supination to pronation of the flexed arm

These three sequences show the arm turning from supination, top, through an intermediate position, to pronation. In the sequences, the muscles of forearm are grouped together in three main volumes: in red are the brachioradialis, ECRL, and ECRB; in blue are the flexors of the hand and fingers; in yellow are the extensors of the hand and fingers (excluding the ECRL and ECRB). The sequences start with the skeleton to make evident the effect that movement has on the muscular and skeletal structures. To figure out the relative positions of radius and ulna, remember this: The thumb is on the radius side and the little finger on the ulna side, so if you just follow the thumb you'll know where the two bones are. In supination, with the palm facing forward, the thumb is on the outside and radius and ulna are parallel. In pronation, the thumb is on the inside and radius and ulna are crossed.

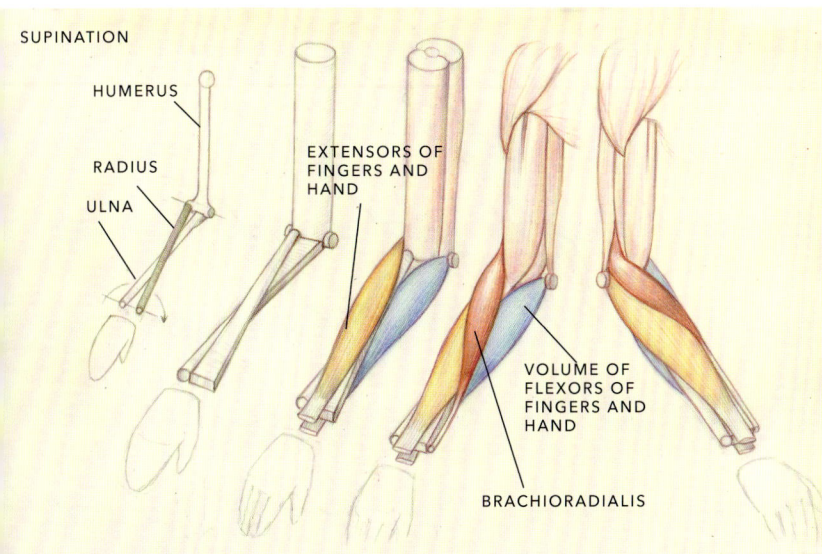

SUPINATION

HUMERUS

RADIUS

ULNA

EXTENSORS OF
FINGERS AND
HAND

VOLUME OF
FLEXORS OF
FINGERS AND
HAND

BRACHIORADIALIS

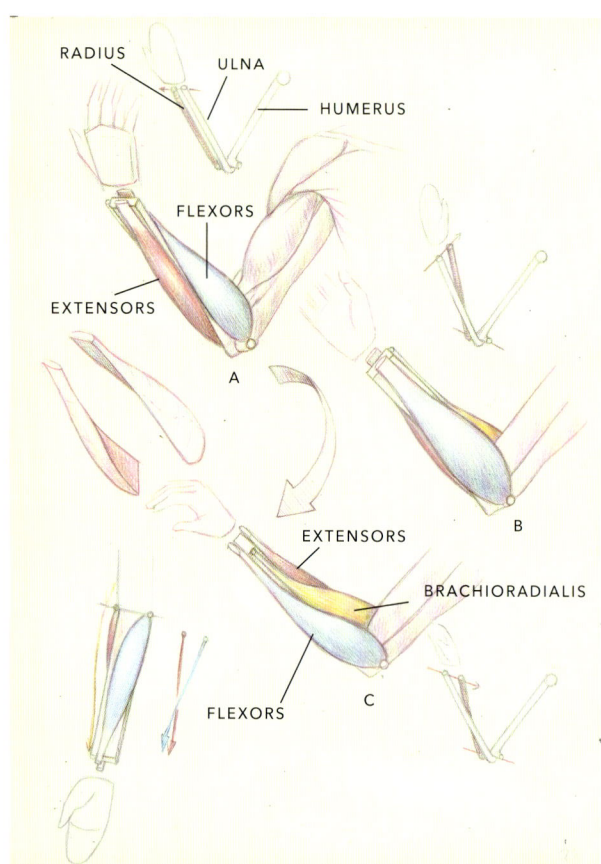

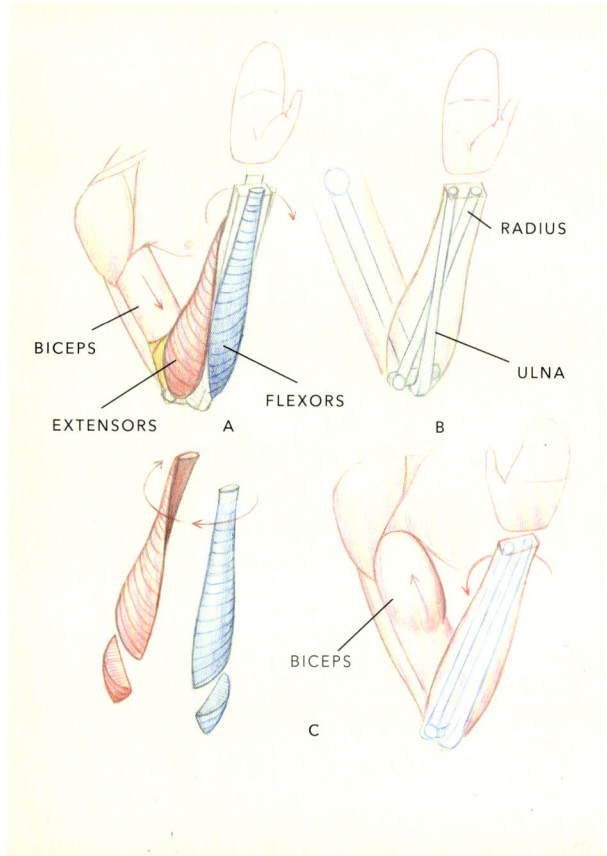

ABOVE LEFT: From supination to pronation, flexed arm

This three-step sequence shows the correspondence between the movement of the skeleton and the external muscles. With the arm flexed and in supination *(A)*, radius and ulna are parallel, the wrist joint is also parallel to the elbow joint, the biceps is balled up, and the flexors (blue) and extensors (red) are twisted around the skeletal axis (as is also visualized in the small detail below this first diagram). With the arm halfway between supination and pronation *(B)*, the volumes of flexors and extensors "untwist" and are parallel to each other, and the radius moves above the ulna at the wrist, which is now perpendicular to the elbow joint. When the arm is in pronation *(C)*, the flexor and extensor groups twist again, but now the brachioradialis muscle (yellow) becomes visible between them; the wrist joint is again parallel to the elbow joint, but the radius and ulna are now crossed. The small detail at the bottom of the sequence shows how the flexors and extensors, as groups, start on opposite sides of the elbow joint and on opposite epicondyles and move toward the center of the wrist, where the two groups overlap. To figure out the position of radius and ulna at the wrist remember that the radius is on the side of the thumb.

ABOVE RIGHT: From pronation to supination, flexed arm—another view from a different angle and the opposite direction of movement

Try this at home: hold your arm flexed as you see in the first image,

looking at the back of your hand *(A)*. In this position, the ulna and humerus are crossed as you can see in *B*. Drawing *c* shows how the flexors (blue) and extensors (red) of the hand and fingers wrap around the forearm with the hand in pronation and the biceps relaxed and elongated. Now, turn the hand in supination with the palm facing you: the biceps balls up, the radius and ulna are now parallel, and the muscles of the forearm twist in the opposite direction. When the thumb is on the inside, radius and ulna are crossed, when the thumb is on the outside, they are parallel.

OPPOSITE: Abduction of the arm and movement of the scapula

This three-step sequence shows the correspondence between the movement of the scapula and the arm as it is raised laterally. Compare the two drawings of each set to see the effect that the movement of the skeleton has on the external forms. At the starting point, with the arm resting along the side, the shaft of the humerus is parallel to the vertebral margin of the scapula. As the arm is abducted (second set of drawings), the scapula follows, sliding on the ribcage laterally and pivoting on its upper corner so that its vertebral margin is at a slight angle. Finally, when the arm is raised close to the head, the scapula slides farther out, and its tip reaches the lateral margin of the ribcage. With the arm in this position, the shaft of the humerus becomes perpendicular to the vertebral margin of the scapula.

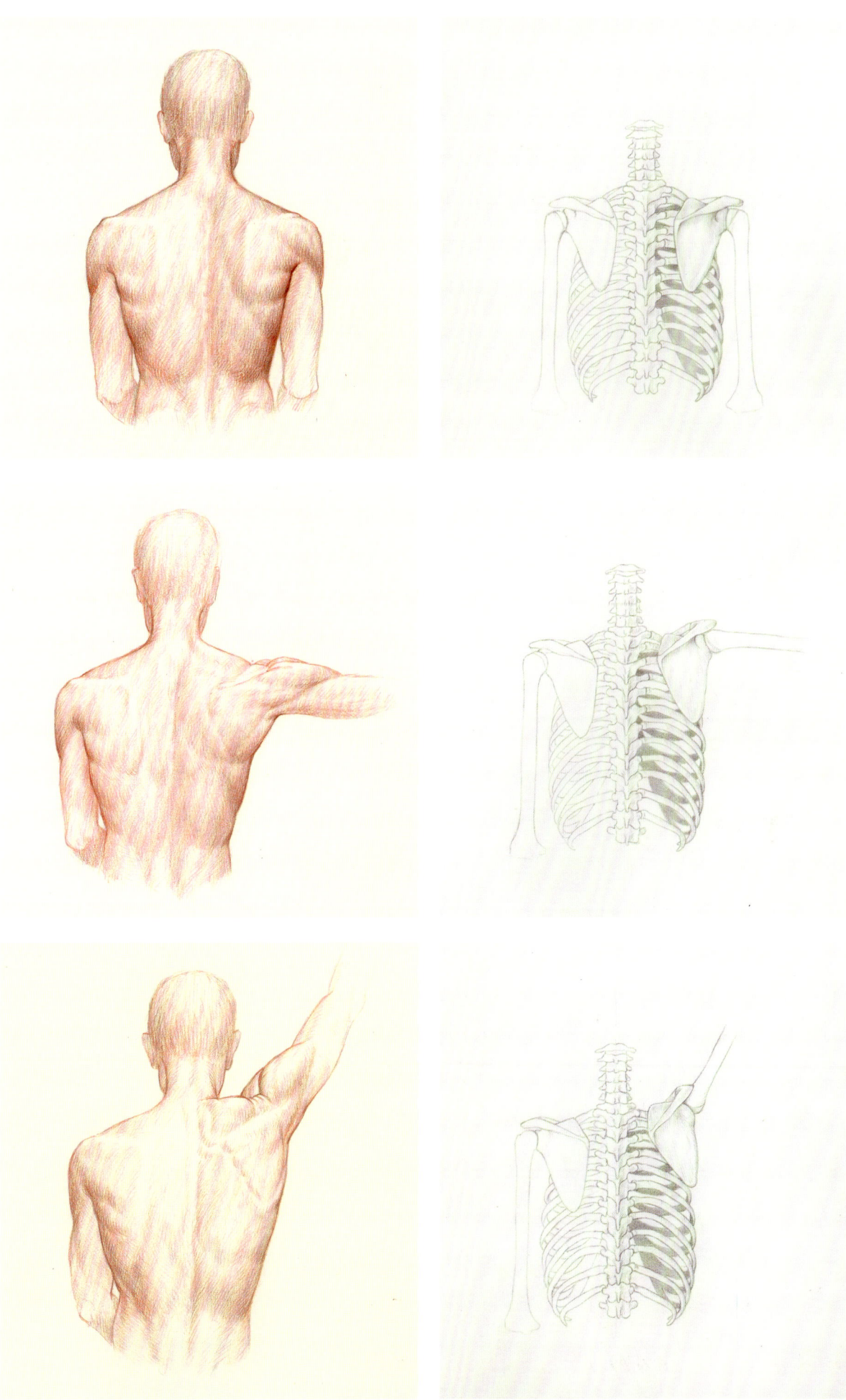

MOVEMENT AND FLOWS OF THE ARM

This sequence brings together the downward movement of an arm with the visualization of the changing muscle flows as the arm goes from supination to pronation.

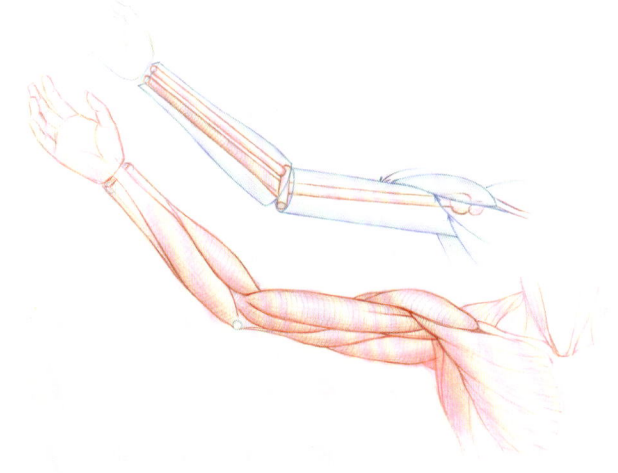

1

In the starting position (supination), the arm is raised and the hand faces forward. The radius and ulna are parallel.

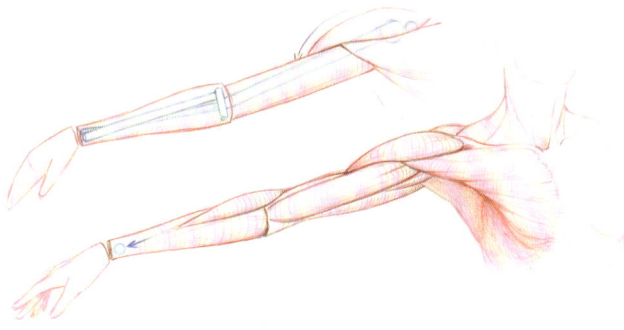

2

In the intermediate position, the arm is lowered and the hand rotated. Now the radius and ulna overlap.

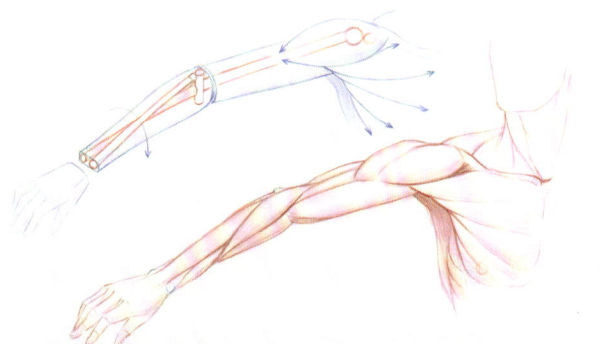

3

In the final position (pronation), the hand is rotated facing downward. Now the ulna and radius are crossed.

EXERCISE

Starting from a photo or a cast of a sculpture depicting a dynamic pose, find the landmarks, reconstruct the skeleton, and block in the muscular volumes, as in this series of images. As an example, I've used Bernini's *David* (for a rendering of the statue, see page 12), but you may work from any sculpture you wish.

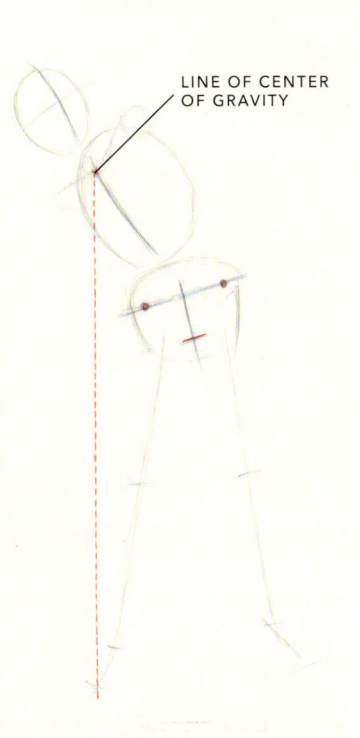

LINE OF CENTER OF GRAVITY

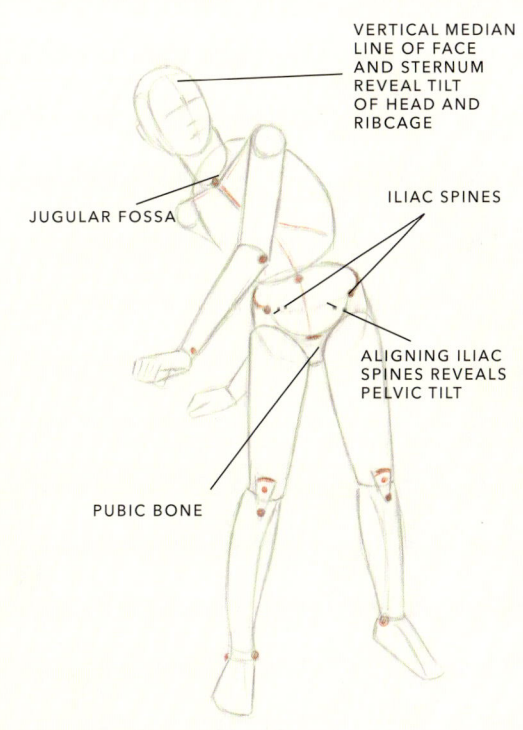

VERTICAL MEDIAN LINE OF FACE AND STERNUM REVEAL TILT OF HEAD AND RIBCAGE

JUGULAR FOSSA

ILIAC SPINES

ALIGNING ILIAC SPINES REVEALS PELVIC TILT

PUBIC BONE

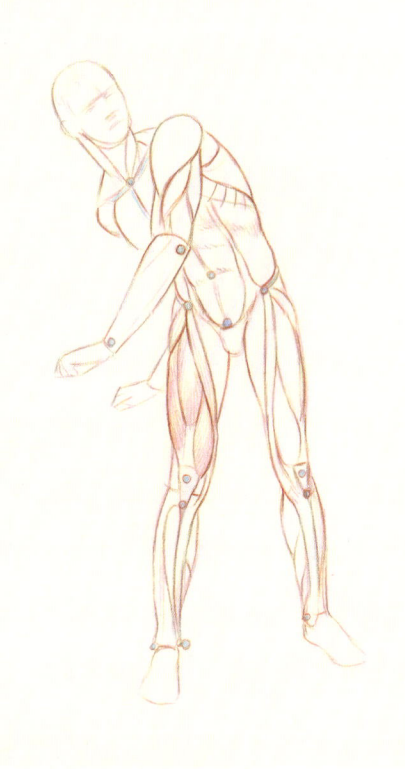

1

Visualize the skeleton. First, study the landmarks of the figure depicted in the cast or photo, and visualize the skeleton based on those landmarks. Block in the volumes of the head, ribcage, and pelvis, making sure the proportional relationships are correct. In this case, the height of the ribcage approximately corresponds to the height of one and one-half heads, and the pelvis is about one head high. Next, draw the axis of the legs to establish the proportional relationships between head, torso, and legs and the subject's contact with the ground. Draw the arms last, considering how they overlap and relate to the dominant form of the ribcage.

2

Add volumes of arms and legs. Refine the drawing by adding the volumes of arms and legs, in addition to more landmarks that will help to position the muscles in the next step.

3

Define the muscular forms. Gradually move from a schematic rendering to a more organic and realistic one. Try labeling the muscles to help you memorize their names and positions. Practice copying these steps, then try from memory. Eventually, repeat this progression using a different photo or any other sculpture you might like.

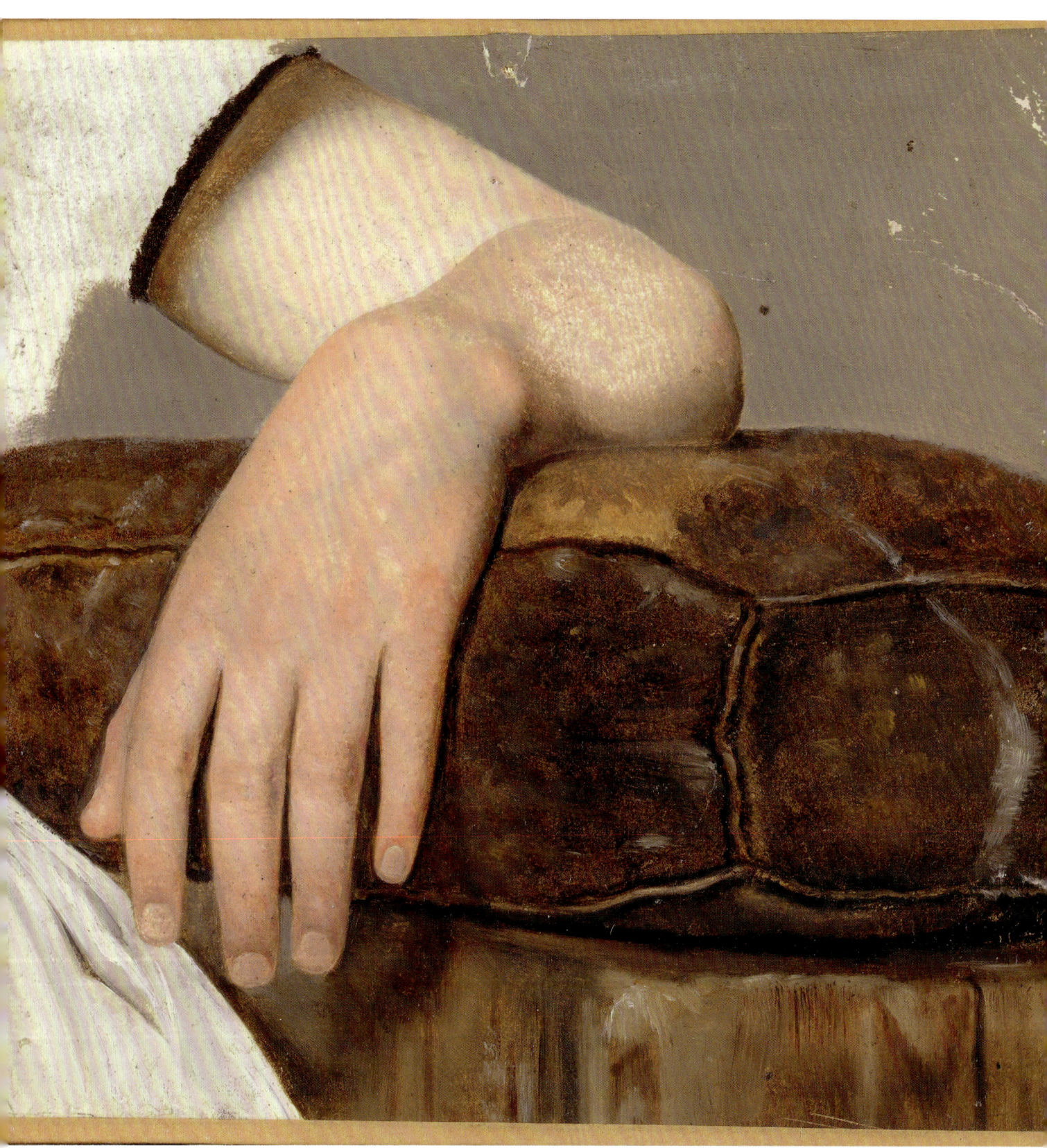

CHAPTER 7

THE HANDS

The hand is a marvelous combination of functionality and aesthetics. The complexity of its forms and its great mobility make it a challenging shape-shifter and irresistible subject for artists.

Throughout this book I've stressed that the secret to drawing the human form correctly is to understand it first: drawing is an intellectual act, an operation of synthesis in which a mobile, colored, three-dimensional object with no uniform lines is transformed in a static, monochromatic, two-dimensional shape rendered with lines on a piece of paper. That's quite a metamorphosis!

The same approach I've used for the human figure in previous chapters will now be applied to the hand, focusing on only a few of its essential characteristics at a time to limit its complexity. You need to observe the hand carefully to create sound, convincing depictions of the wide range of poses created by its many moving parts.

OPPOSITE: Adolph Tidemand, *A Woman's Arm,* 19th century, oil on paper glued to board, 8¼ × 8½ inches (21 × 21.5 cm). National Gallery of Norway.

A challenging shape-shifter and irresistible subject

SKELETAL STRUCTURE OF THE HAND

Let's start by taking a look at the hand's skeletal structure. Each hand is composed of twenty-seven bones, including

- Eight carpal bones, making up the wrist
- Five metacarpal bones, making up the body of the hand
- Fourteen phalanges (sing., phalanx), constituting the fingers (note that the thumb has only two phalanges)

BELOW LEFT: Side view of hand

BELOW RIGHT: Dorsal view of the hand and its skeleton

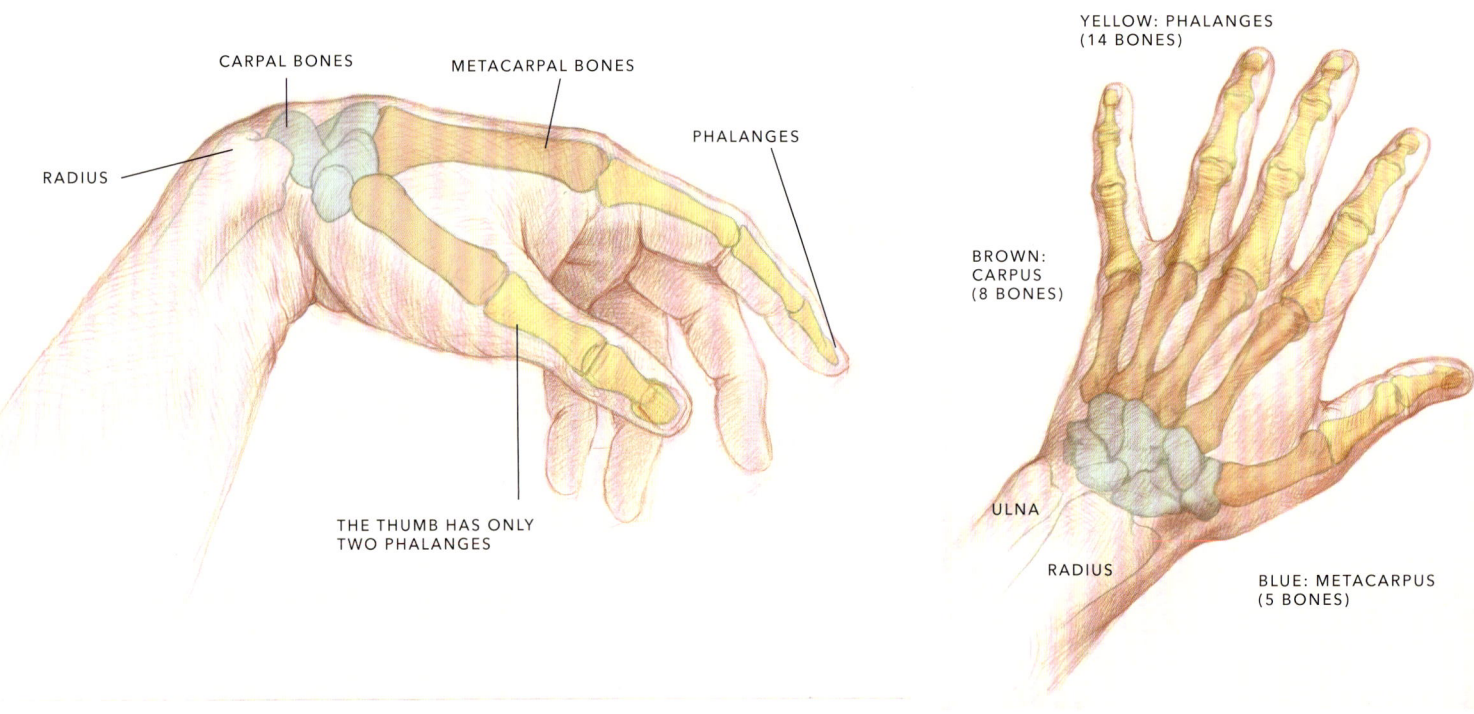

CARPAL BONES

METACARPAL BONES

PHALANGES

RADIUS

THE THUMB HAS ONLY TWO PHALANGES

YELLOW: PHALANGES (14 BONES)

BROWN: CARPUS (8 BONES)

ULNA

RADIUS

BLUE: METACARPUS (5 BONES)

STEREOMETRIC RENDERING OF THE HAND

An assemblage of basic solid shapes

The hand can be conceptualized by rendering it in essential volumes obtained using the maximum height, width, and depth of its various parts. Visualizing the hand as an assemblage of basic solid shapes without considering the organic details makes drawing it much easier, especially when dealing with complex or dynamic poses.

The demonstrations and other illustrations in this section are not meant to be the sole method you use for drawing the hand (or the human figure generally); rather, they show a process for analyzing the human form. It is important to practice drawing human forms as stereometric volumes in order to understand the proportional and three-dimensional characteristics of the body, but keep in mind that these are finally just exercises to help you visualize your analytical process.

BELOW: Proportional relationships of the hand, palmar and side views

The hand's width-to-height ratio is about 1:2, meaning that the height is twice the measure of the width (A). Note how the fingers appear to be shorter on the palmar side than the dorsal side. Measuring the segments of the fingers from the dorsal side shows that the measure of the distal and medial phalanges together is the same as the measure of the proximal phalanx (B).

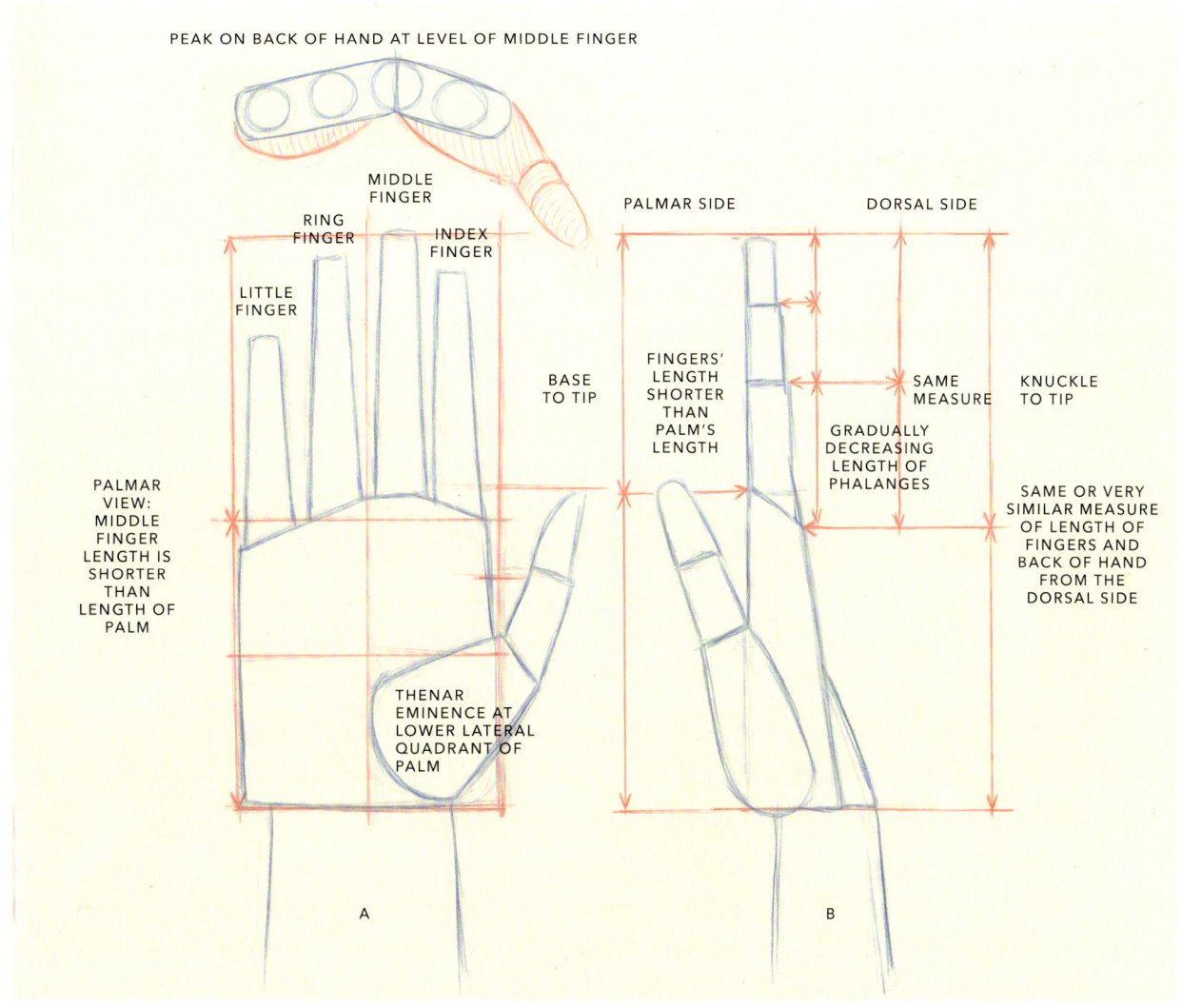

PEAK ON BACK OF HAND AT LEVEL OF MIDDLE FINGER

MIDDLE FINGER

RING FINGER

INDEX FINGER

LITTLE FINGER

BASE TO TIP

PALMAR SIDE

DORSAL SIDE

FINGERS' LENGTH SHORTER THAN PALM'S LENGTH

SAME MEASURE

KNUCKLE TO TIP

GRADUALLY DECREASING LENGTH OF PHALANGES

PALMAR VIEW: MIDDLE FINGER LENGTH IS SHORTER THAN LENGTH OF PALM

SAME OR VERY SIMILAR MEASURE OF LENGTH OF FINGERS AND BACK OF HAND FROM THE DORSAL SIDE

THENAR EMINENCE AT LOWER LATERAL QUADRANT OF PALM

A

B

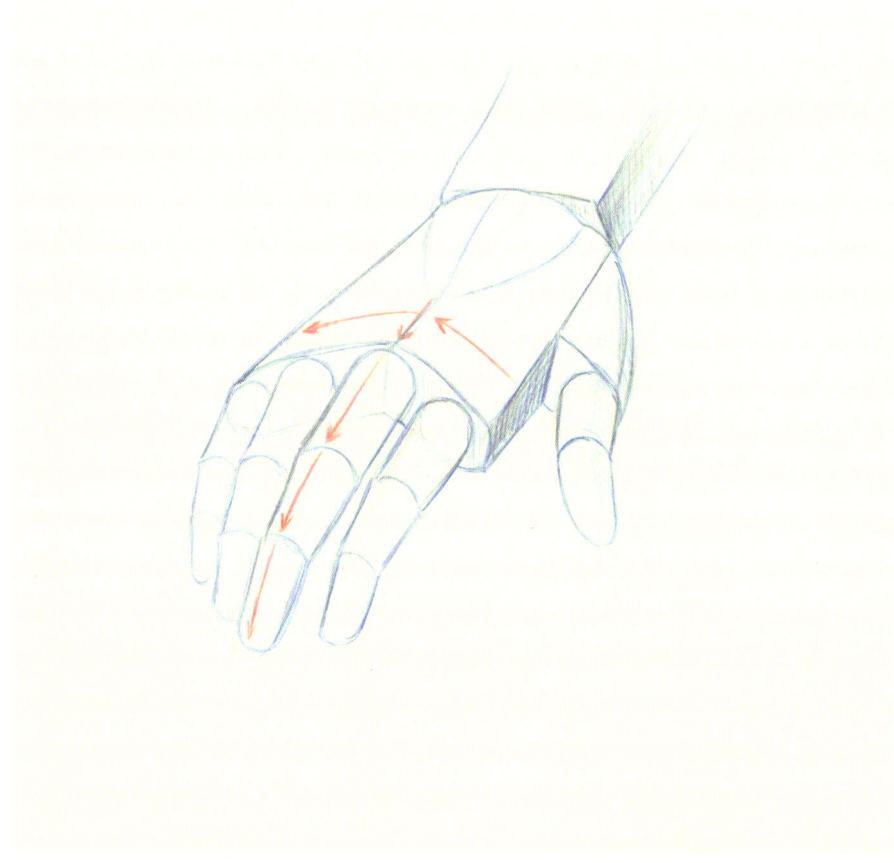

TOP: Stereometric rendering of the hand, three-quarters dorsal view

Note that the middle finger is aligned with the peak of the back of the hand.

BOTTOM: Stereometric renderings of the hand, side view

Here, I started by drawing the volumes of hand and fingers *(A),* considering the progressive tapering and shortening of the segments as they move away from the arm. I then added more detail *(B),* including the fleshy volume between the thumb and the hand, as well as the rest of the fingers. At this point, you can also start thinking about the effect of the light on the hand.

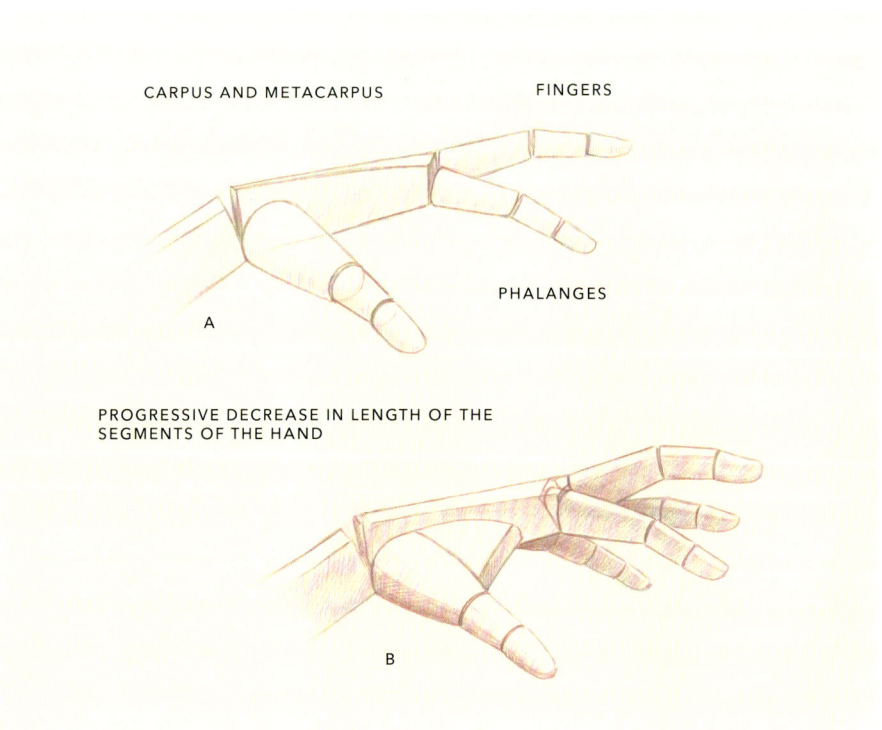

CARPUS AND METACARPUS   FINGERS

PHALANGES

A

PROGRESSIVE DECREASE IN LENGTH OF THE
SEGMENTS OF THE HAND

B

In the images here, I draw the hand in various poses using the stereometric approach. It's easiest to start with a side view, bottom opposite, and then move on to more challenging poses. If you replicate these drawings, imagine you have an actual 3-D hand model and are moving its parts.

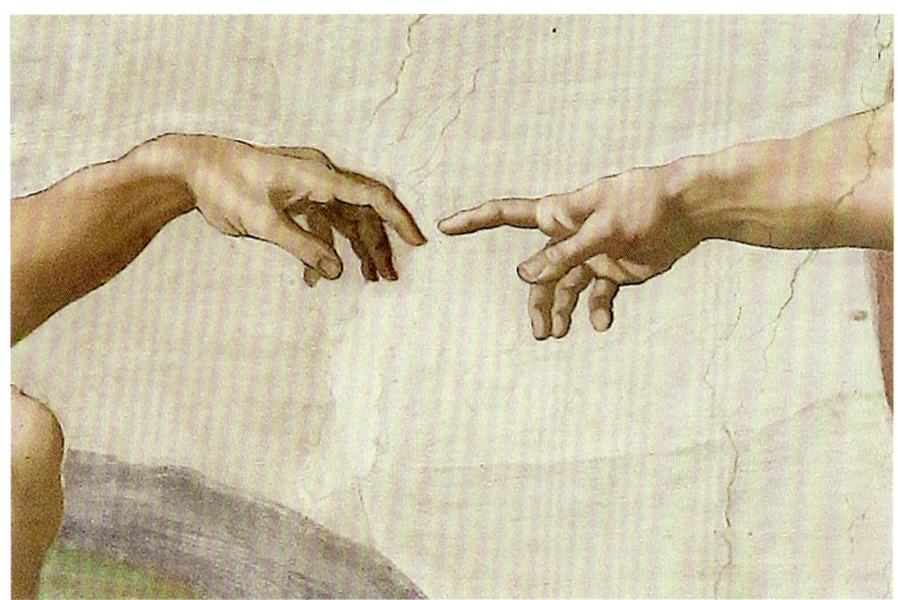

The hands of God and Adam as depicted by Michelangelo in this famous detail from the Sistine Chapel ceiling provide a perfect example of the sense of volume and solidity that can be obtained with anatomical knowledge and a structural approach.

BOTTOM: Stereometric rendering of the hand, another three-quarters dorsal view

You can practice drawing a stereometric rendering in a three-quarters view by looking at your own hand. Try posing the fingers at various angles and levels of flexion. First, block-in the wrist and body of the hand (A). Add the base of the thumb and then the fingers—at first as lines to quickly visualize the pose or direction (B). Next, render the fingers as cylinders whose lengths decrease as they move away from the hand (C). Note that I also added the volume of the first dorsal interosseous muscle, which is the fleshy volume between the base of the thumb and the hand.

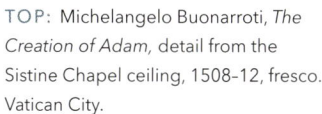

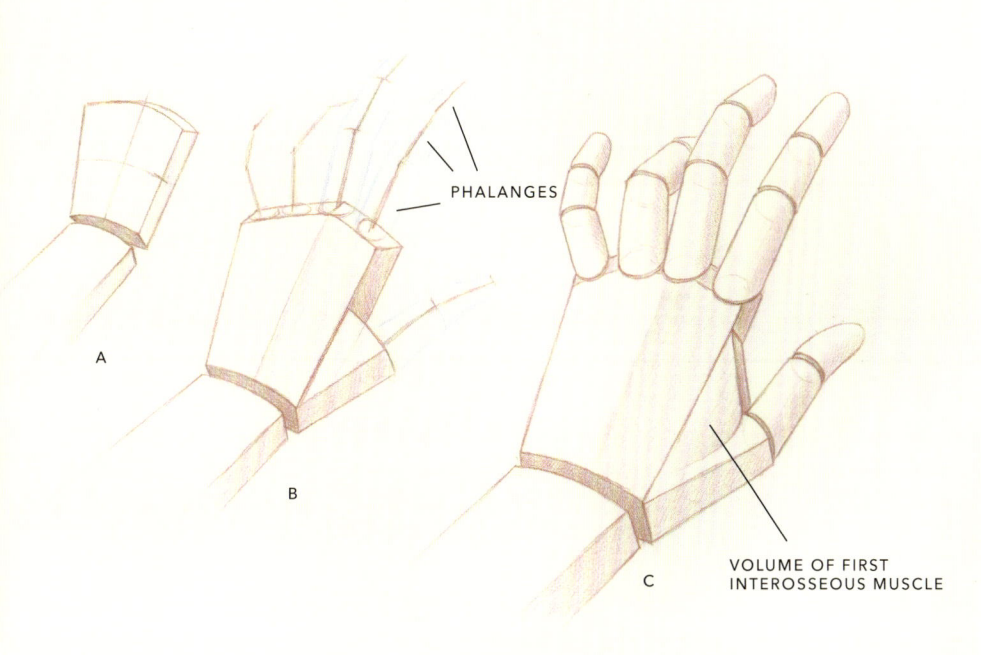

PHALANGES

VOLUME OF FIRST
INTEROSSEOUS MUSCLE

A

B

C

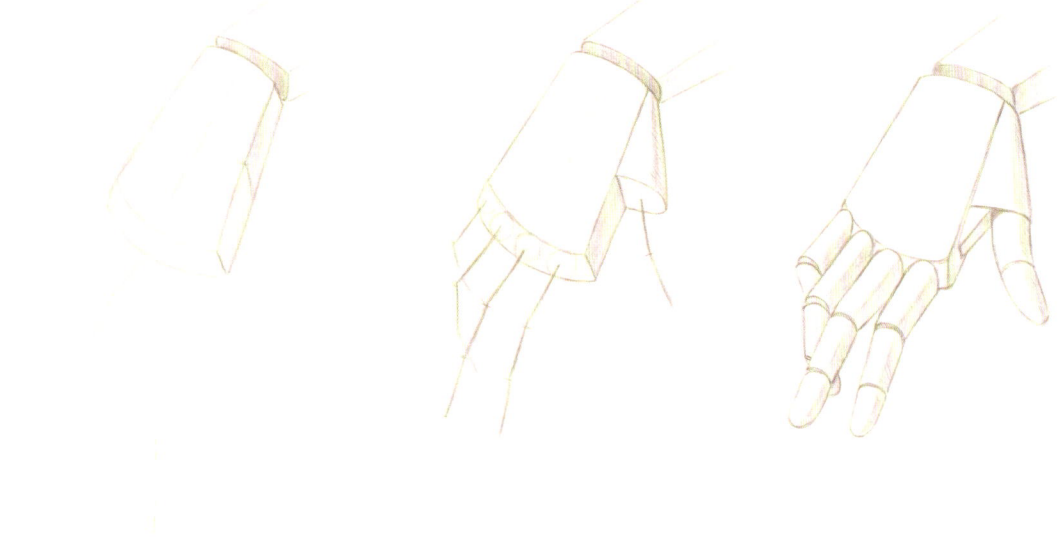

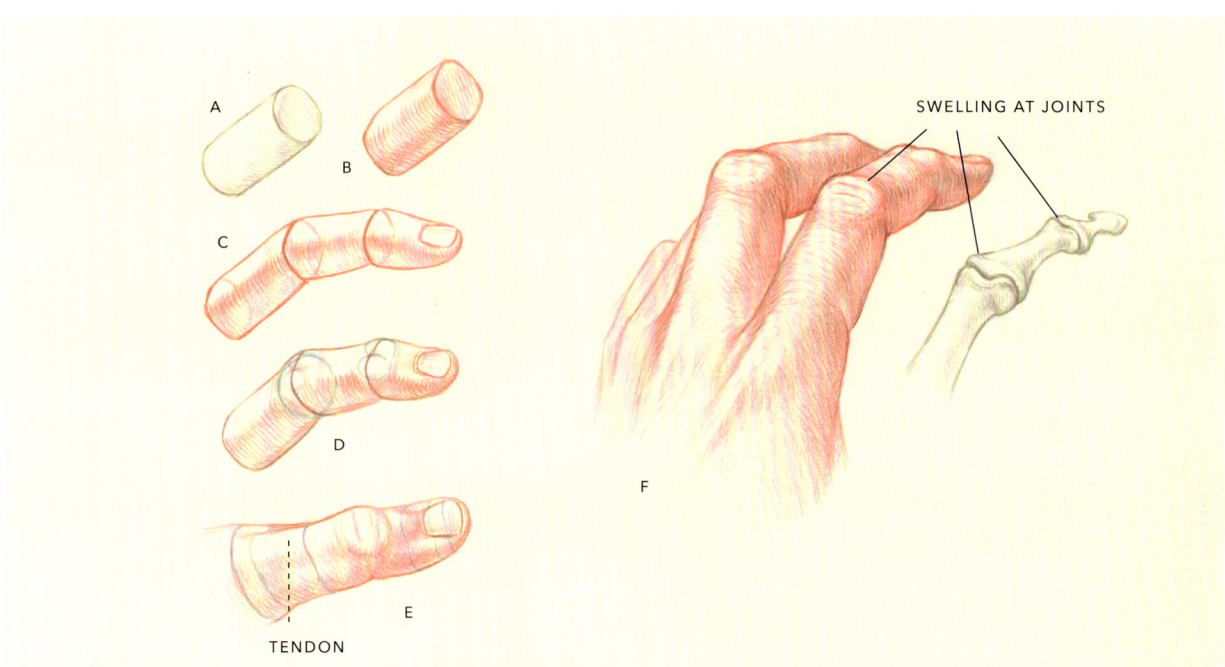

SWELLING AT JOINTS

TENDON

A

B

C

D

E

F

TOP: Stereometric rendering of the hand, another three-quarters dorsal view

Here's yet another stereometric rendering of the hand, viewed from a different angle. The steps are the same as in the previous drawing. You can try this yourself, using another person's hand or your own hand seen in a mirror as your model.

BOTTOM: Drawing the fingers, from stereometry to realistic rendering

Drawing the segments of the fingers first as cylinders (A) is fast and easy and lets you focus only their length and circumference. Once those measures are established you can start refining the fingers by adding more details. A section of the finger is closer to a square (B) than a circle (A); this translates into somewhat defined planes (C). Eventually, you can add the swellings at the joints (D) and the forms of the tendons on the back of the hand and at the base of the fingers (E) to finally achieve a convincing realistic effect. The last detail (F) shows how the thickening of the bones at the joints is responsible for the external swelling at the joints of the fingers.

STUDYING AND DRAWING THE HAND

The first image in this sequence shows you how to *look* at the hand, studying it before beginning the process of drawing described in the subsequent images. You can also perform an exercise like this by measuring and using the proportions of your own or a friend's hand. Doing so will give you a better idea of hands' variations and individual characteristics.

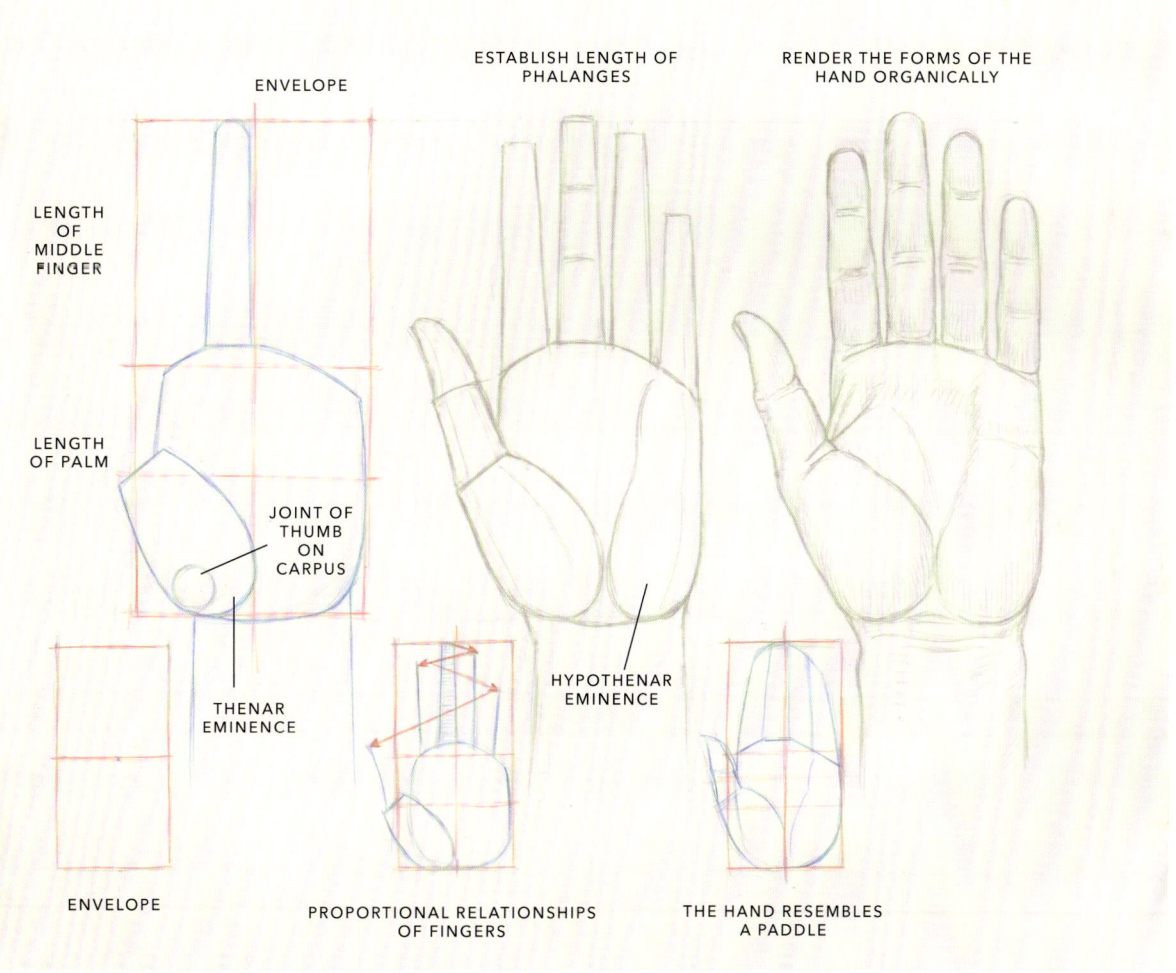

ENVELOPE

ESTABLISH LENGTH OF PHALANGES

RENDER THE FORMS OF THE HAND ORGANICALLY

LENGTH OF MIDDLE FINGER

LENGTH OF PALM

JOINT OF THUMB ON CARPUS

THENAR EMINENCE

HYPOTHENAR EMINENCE

ENVELOPE

PROPORTIONAL RELATIONSHIPS OF FINGERS

THE HAND RESEMBLES A PADDLE

1

Study the hand to capture the proportional relationships between its various parts. Think of this as developing a plan of action before starting to draw.

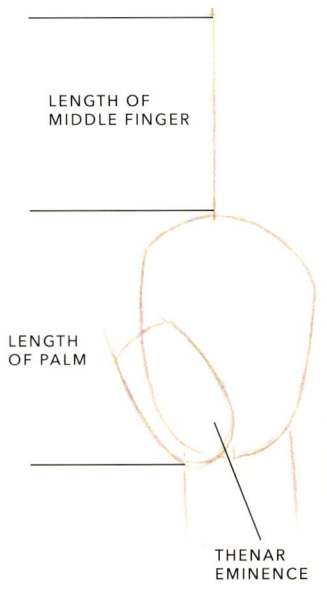

LENGTH OF
MIDDLE FINGER

LENGTH
OF PALM

THENAR
EMINENCE

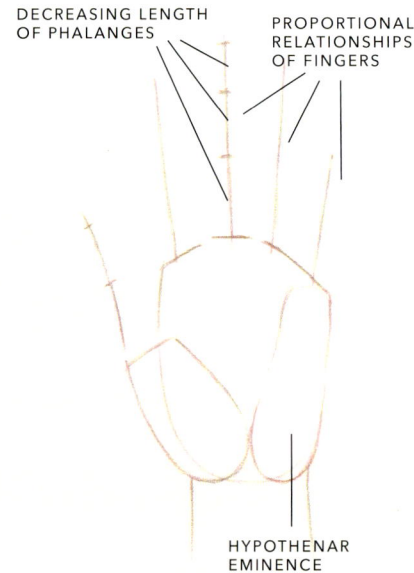

DECREASING LENGTH
OF PHALANGES

PROPORTIONAL
RELATIONSHIPS
OF FINGERS

HYPOTHENAR
EMINENCE

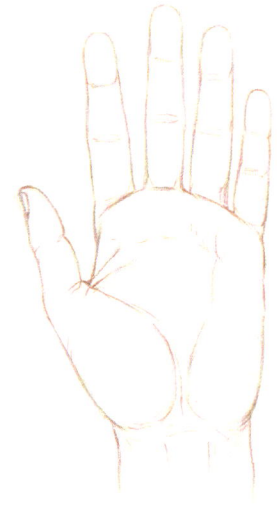

2

Now begin to draw. Block in the volume of the palm and establish the length of the middle finger, which, from the palmar view, should be slightly shorter than the length of the palm. The thenar eminence (the base of the thumb) is located at the lower lateral quadrant of the palm.

3

Now, add the other fingers, making sure they have the correct proportional relationships to each other, and subdivide the fingers into segments of decreasing length as they move away from the palm. Add the hypothenar eminence (the volume at the base of the little finger).

4

Finish by adding the organic forms, rendering the forms of the hand realistically.

CROSS-CONTOUR LINES

These are *cross-contour drawings*. Imagine a CT scan slicing through the hand or another part of the body. The cross-contour lines visualize these sections, revealing the relief of the volumes. Drawing such section lines cutting through the forms of the hand is a fun and compelling exercise that will give you a better understanding of the hand's three-dimensional characteristics. You can do this over any of your drawings or on tracing paper placed over a finished drawing from this chapter.

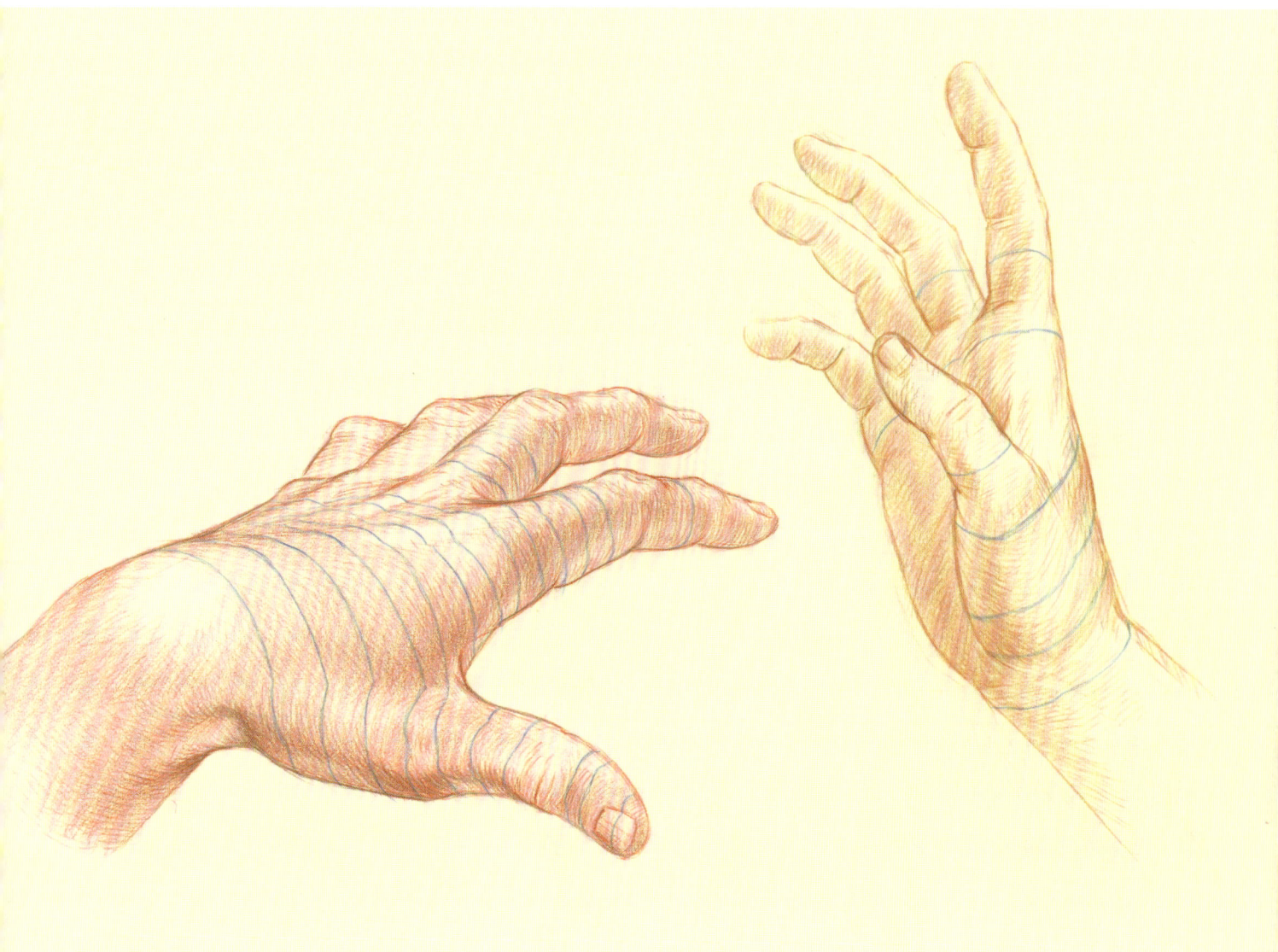

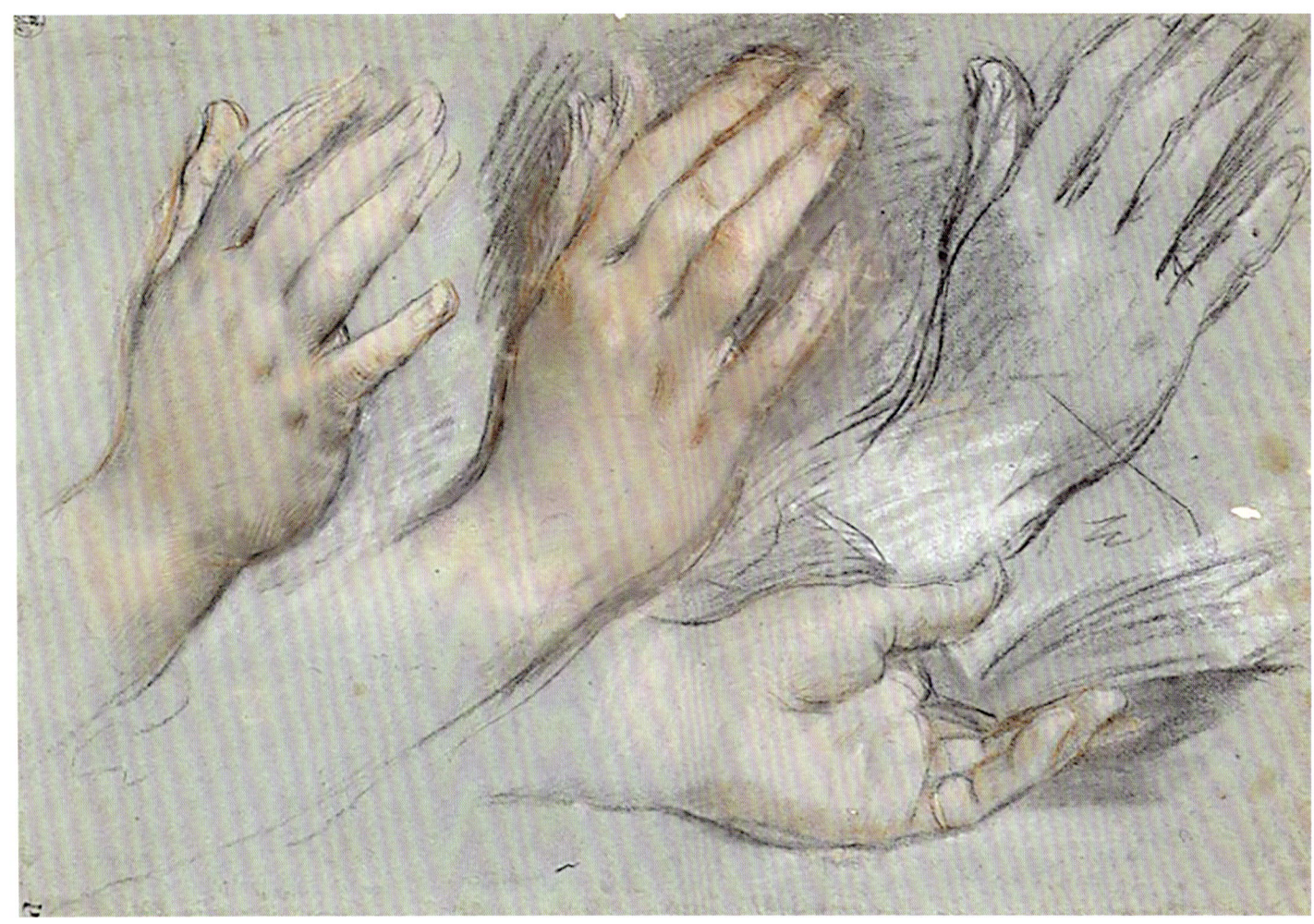

A FREER APPROACH TO DRAWING THE HAND

Once you internalize the stereometric approach you won't need to keep drawing those geometric forms anymore. The image left opposite shows a freer approach to drawing the hand—but one that is still informed by the proportional relationships and volumetric characteristics described so far. The measuring lines or "searching lines" of this first stage will have to disappear as the drawing progresses. Remember: keep your searching lines at a minimum and very light. A light searching line will be easier to overrule with more precise ones in case you change your mind, and it will minimize the visual noise.

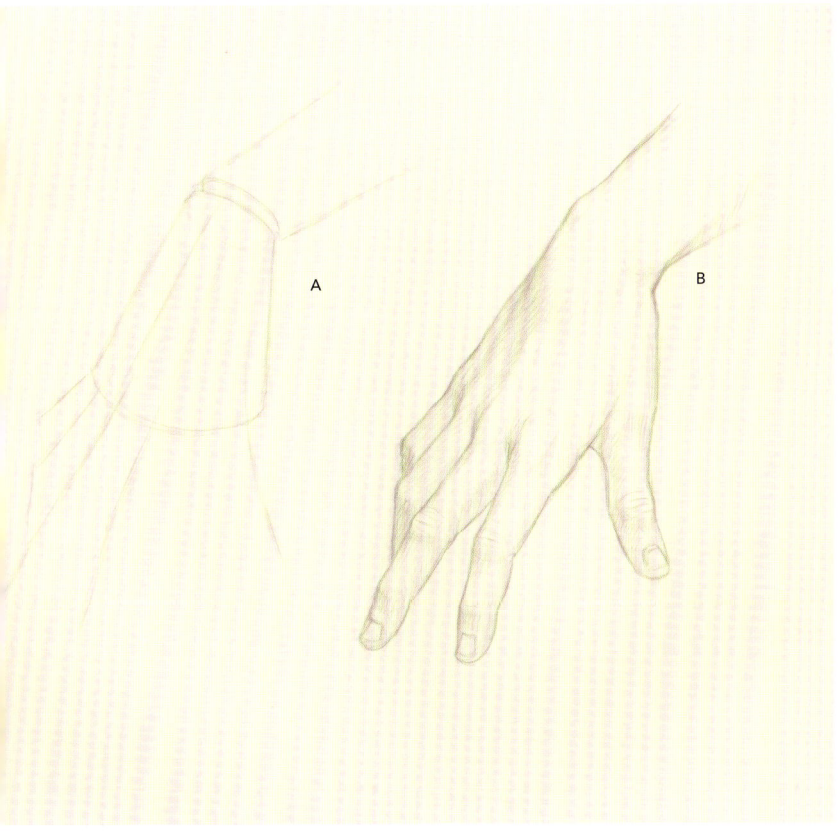

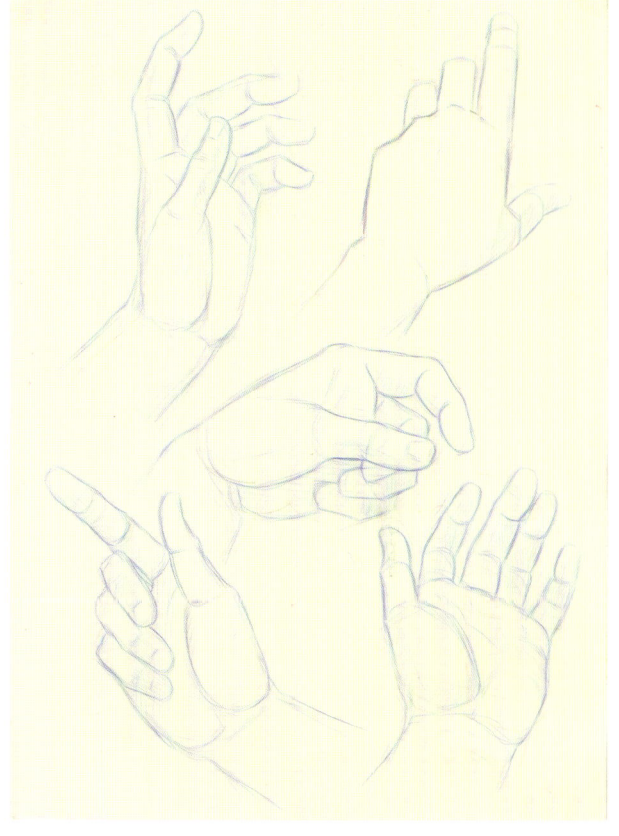

Using this freer approach, you can practice drawing the hands in a more sketchy way and at various levels of schematization, as in the images above right. Do a few pages of quick studies in your sketchbook—and try to have fun with it! You don't need to do beautiful renditions of the hands right away. Give yourself some time to practice and internalize the method.

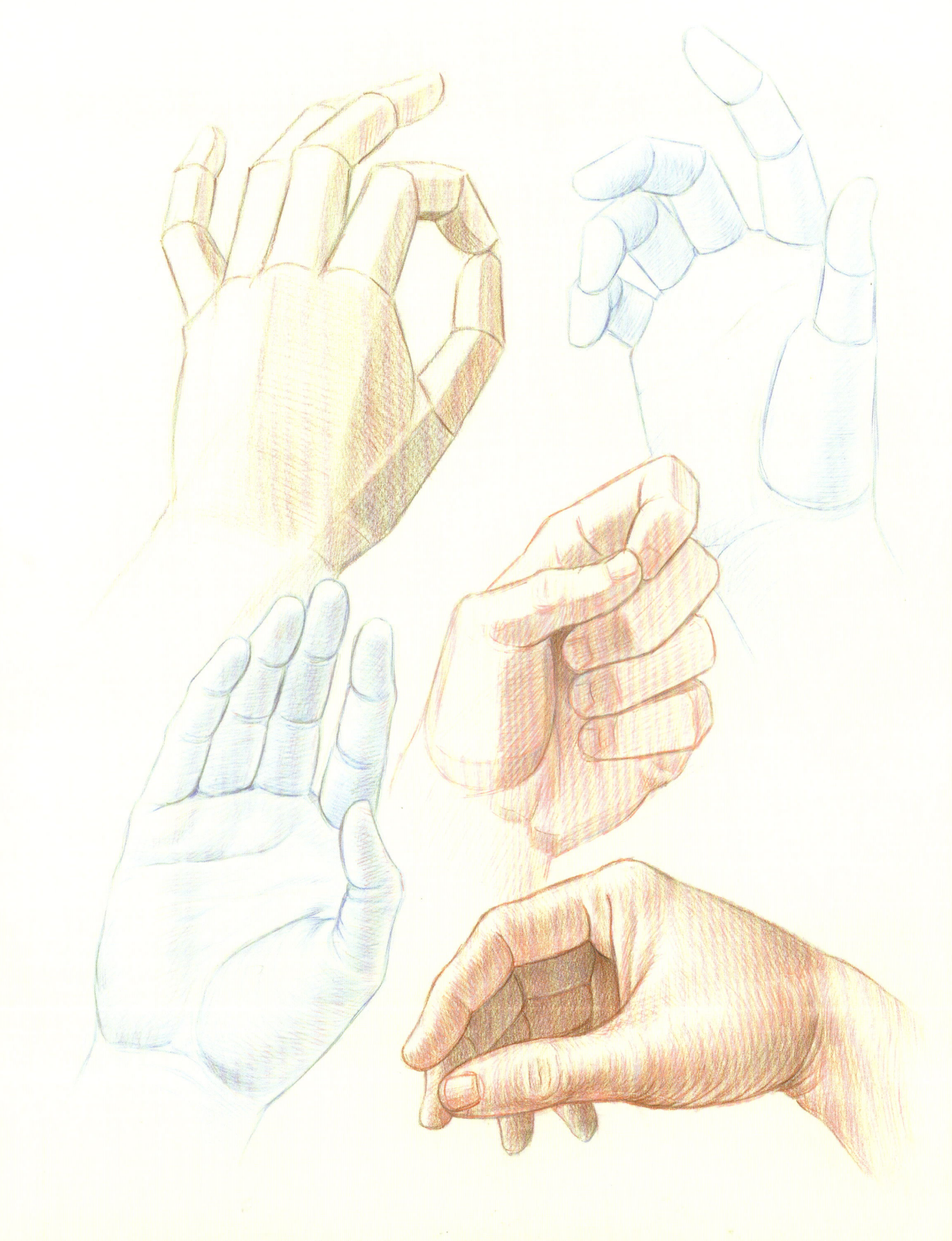

LIGHT ON FORM

The knowledge obtained by analyzing the hand and synthetizing its organic forms in essential volumes is very helpful when developing the drawing tonally. You always want to consider the angle and distance of the light from your subject: the brightest highlights on the subject are where the light source is closest and most perpendicular to the form.

Don't just copy the chiaroscuro (light and shadow) effect on the subject or evaluate it only on the basis of a tonal scale that goes from 1 to 10—or even 1 to 200, for that matter. That's a very imitative and passive approach. Consider instead the direct connection between the value on the form and its angle and distance from the light source: the value reveals the three-dimensional characteristics of the subject. In other words, try to understand why you find a specific value in a certain spot—the *local value*—and what produced it.

The local value is explained by the distance of the light source from the form and the orientation of the planes of the form in relation to the light source. As you can see in the images here, stereometric renditions make it easier to understand the effects of light on the hand.

Always consider the light's angle and distance

BELOW LEFT: Light on the hand–stereometric and tonal renderings, example 1

BELOW RIGHT: Light on the hand–stereometric and tonal renderings, example 2

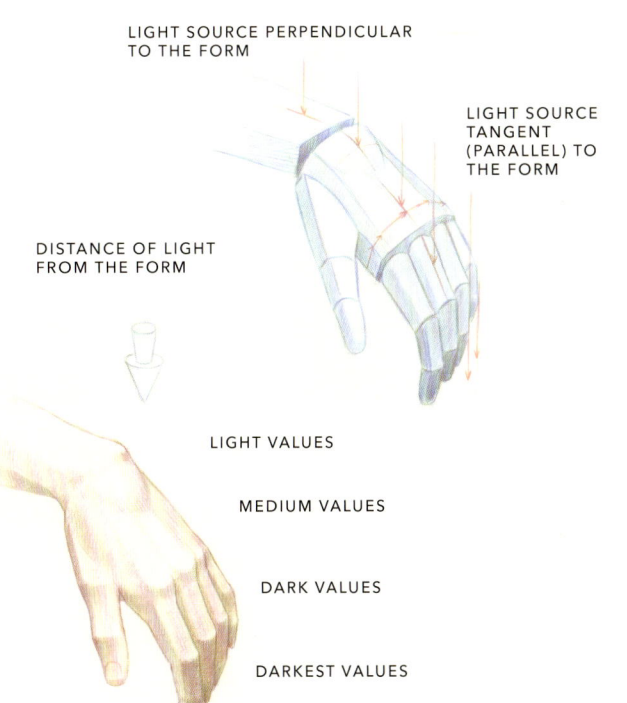

LIGHT SOURCE PERPENDICULAR TO THE FORM

LIGHT SOURCE TANGENT (PARALLEL) TO THE FORM

DISTANCE OF LIGHT FROM THE FORM

LIGHT VALUES

MEDIUM VALUES

DARK VALUES

DARKEST VALUES

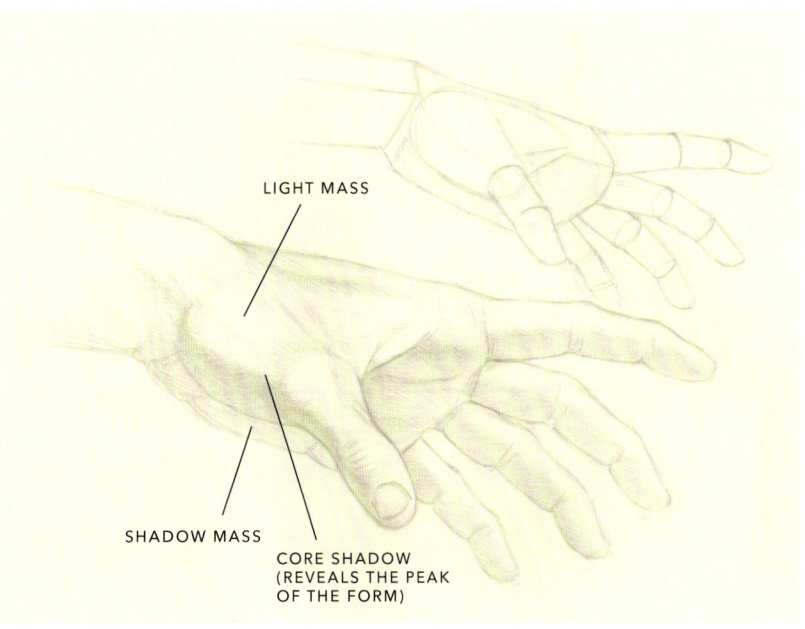

LIGHT MASS

SHADOW MASS

CORE SHADOW (REVEALS THE PEAK OF THE FORM)

A CONTEMPORARY MASTER OF LIGHT ON FORM

Haley Manchon is a talented, prolific artist. In this detail of her colored pencil and pastel drawing *Illuminated,* she plays with light that is taking over the form. The elegant pose of the hand is supported by a strong anatomical structure.

BELOW: Haley Manchon, *Illuminated* (detail), 2019, colored pencil and pastel, 8 × 8 inches (20.32 × 20.32 cm). Courtesy of the artist.

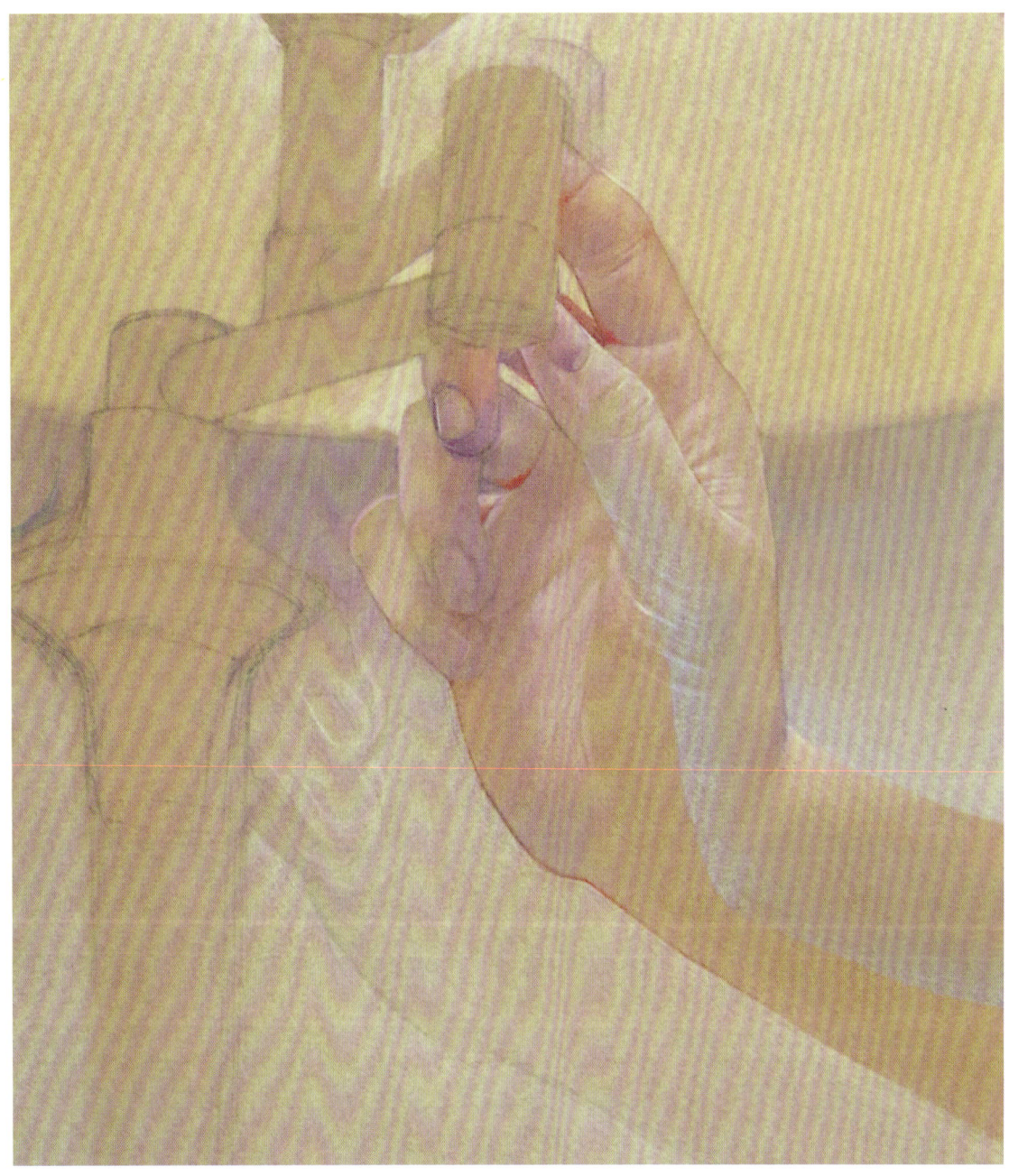

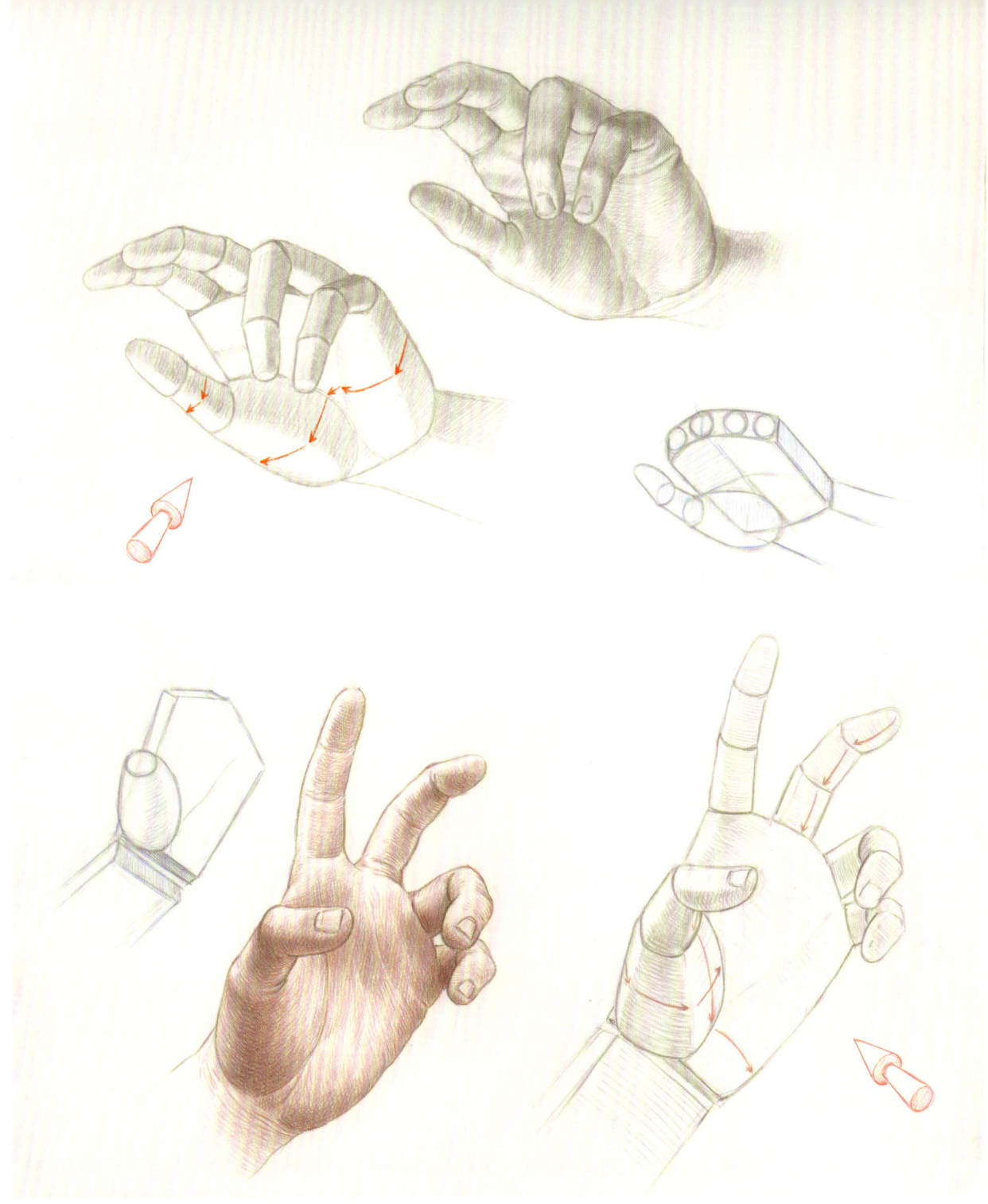

The images here offer further examples of light's effect on form. As mentioned earlier, the brightest highlights on a form will occur where the light source is closest and most perpendicular to the form. Conversely, values grow darker as the form recedes from the light source or the form is gradually less perpendicular in relation to the light source. The arrows in the images reveal this connection by visualizing the orientation of the planes and the corresponding changes of value.

TOP: Light on the hand—stereometric and tonal renderings, example 3

BOTTOM: Light on the hand—stereometric and tonal renderings, example 4

Practice drawing the hand in various positions. Start by copying images from this chapter, and then draw hands from life using the approaches discussed. You can use a mirror to view your hand from a wide range of angles or take photos of your own or others' hands in poses that are too hard to hold for very long.

TOP: Opposition of thumb and little finger—stereometric rendering

Start the sequence by first rendering the hand as basic volumes (left); the pearlike volume of the thenar eminence is added *over* the flat form of the palm and hinged at the lower corner of the hand. Then start moving the thumb, making it pivot toward the center of the palm (center); simultaneously, start moving the little finger and ring finger toward the thumb. In the final step, the thumb and little finger touch (right). Drawing the fingers transparently makes it easier to consider the overlapping of the forms.

BOTTOM: Opposition of thumb and little finger—line drawing to tonal rendering

Now try drawing the hand realistically as it does the same movement sequence. Copying your own hand, start drawing very lightly, using only essential or "searching" lines (left). Superimpose the organic forms on that base drawing. Once you have developed the structure of the hand, you can move on to the tonal rendering.

THE HAND IN DYNAMIC POSES

Now let's start to explore the various movements of the hand and fingers. The images below focus on one simple movement: the opposition of the thumb and little finger. You can copy the steps from the images and then try doing the exercise from memory or imagination.

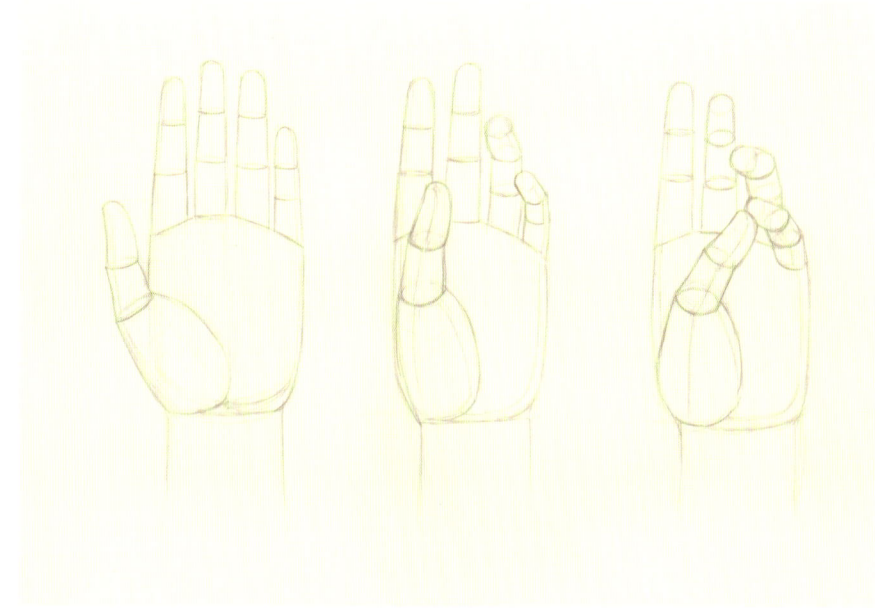

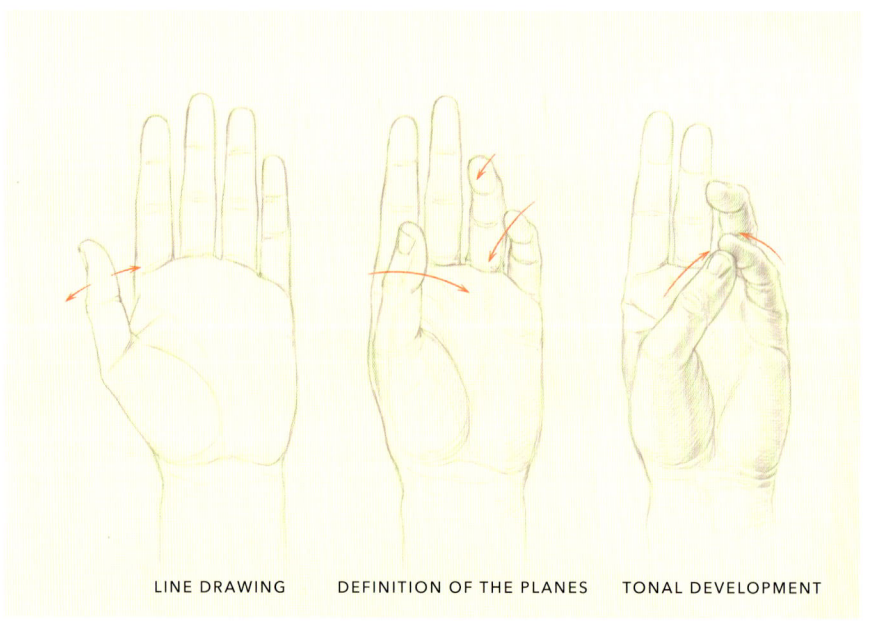

LINE DRAWING   DEFINITION OF THE PLANES   TONAL DEVELOPMENT

LIGHT ON FORM

Copy the following sequence to practice rendering the effects of light on form.

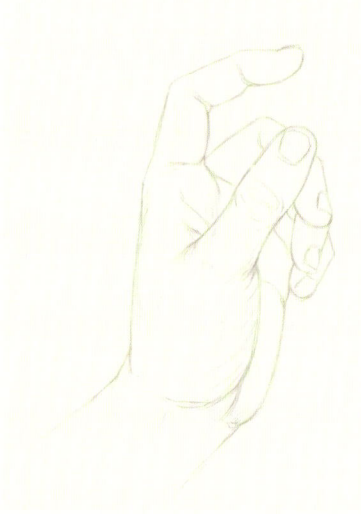

1

This line drawing of a hand is the reference image—the hand you'll use as the model for this sequence.

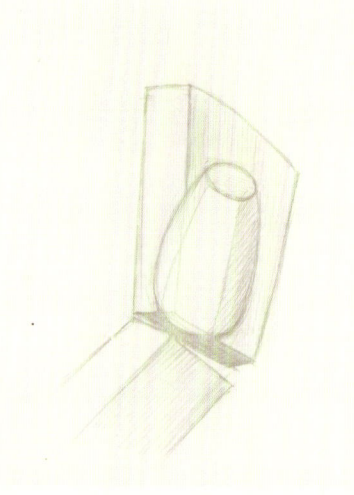

2

Start by blocking-in the basic volumes of the palm and the base of the thumb.

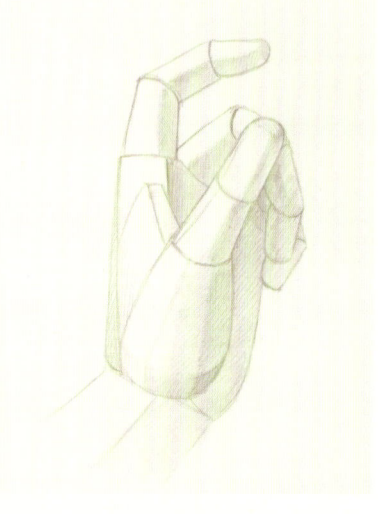

3

Now add the volumes of the fingers, considering how they overlap.

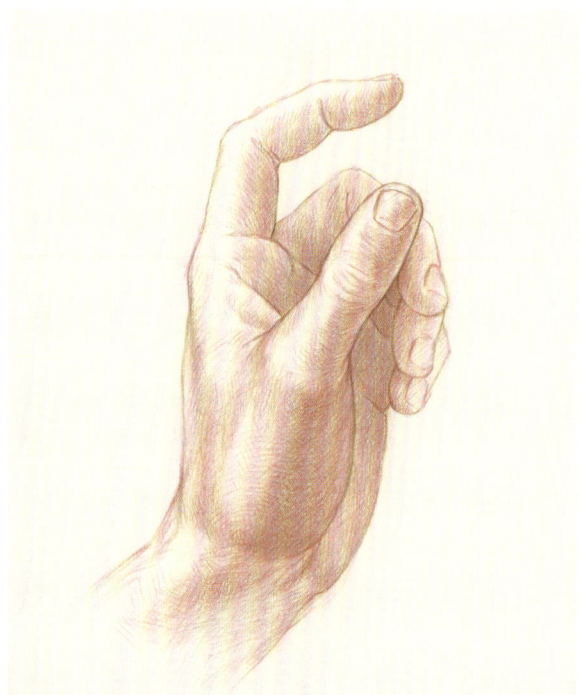

4

Finish with the organic forms and tonal rendering. Consider the effect of the light on the hand to render its forms more realistically and obtain a convincing three-dimensional effect.

USING THE ENVELOPE METHOD TO DRAW THE HAND

The so-called envelope method probably originated in the nineteenth-century academy, but it was just one aspect of an artist's training, which also included the study of anatomy. Today, this method has been revived and is taught in many ateliers and art schools, but many of these schools do not teach anatomy, believing, I suppose, that the envelope method is all an artist needs.

The advantage of the envelope approach is that it allows you to draw the figure—or any part of the figure—by reducing it to measures and angles and disregarding its anatomical characteristics. But that's the drawback, too: a great many of the specific anatomical aspects of the subject tend to get ignored.

This can lead to a slick but less than complete drawing. For example, knowing which muscles create certain forms on the surface or the influence that skeletal structure can have on the superficial muscular and external forms helps you to capture the organic and functional components of the human figure. These forms and interconnections may be difficult to identify on your subject if you don't know they exist. You see what you know, and you draw what you see; therefore, the more you know, the more you'll see, and the more complete and informed your drawing will be. In my opinion, only artists who have a good knowledge of anatomy and the structure of the body can use the envelope technique successfully.

A FEW WORDS ABOUT TECHNIQUES

It's always a good idea to practice a variety of techniques. Each technique is a specific method of analysis that requires you to look at a subject with a specific end result in mind. One technique might focus on structure or color or the tonal aspects; another may concentrate on the expressive qualities or essential dynamism of the figure. The technique used for a short gestural pose differs from one employed for a long pose, and so on.

My personal approach is fundamentally based on the structural-anatomical method developed during the Italian Renaissance, but I like to hybridize it with other helpful methods, like the "envelope" method discussed in the sidebar opposite.

USING A SINGLE ENVELOPE

This three-step sequence shows you how to proceed using increasingly accurate measurements of the subject.

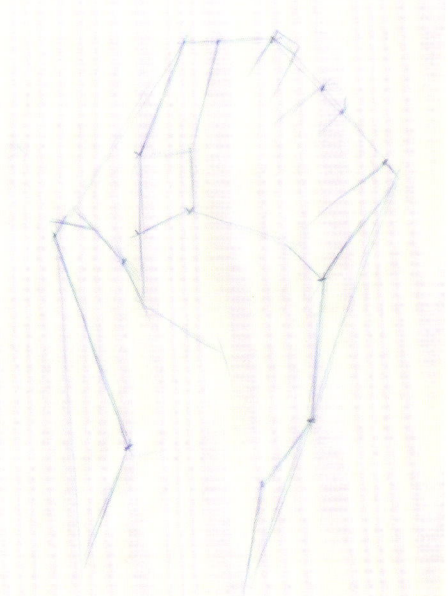

1

Start by drawing the envelope—an outline that essentially defines the space occupied by the figure.

2

Gradually establish more measurements, increasing the level of detail.

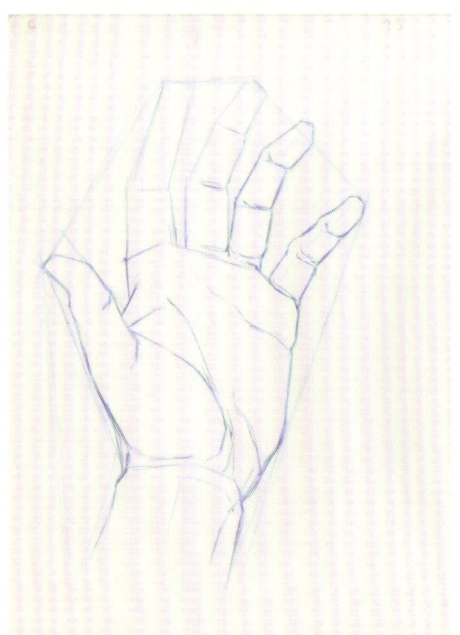

3

Eventually, you'll approach a fine level of detail. At this point you can start with the tonal rendering.

USING MULTIPLE ENVELOPES

In the following sequence—for a hand doing the "Number One!" gesture—I drew not just one envelope containing the whole subject but several separate envelopes.

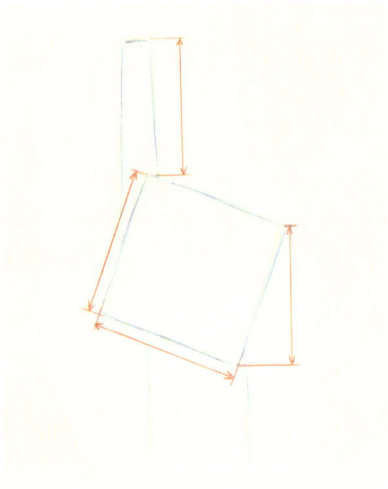

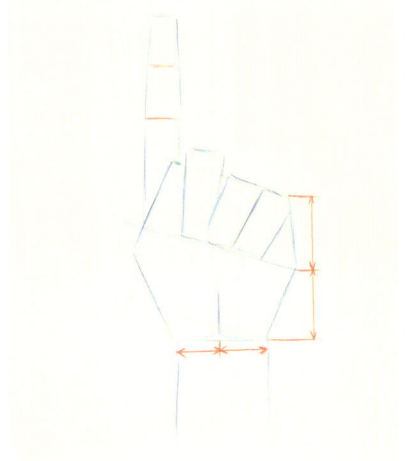

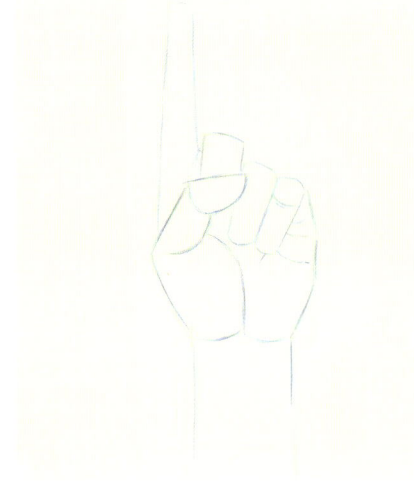

1

I began with three envelopes: one for the fist, one for the raised index finger, and one for the forearm/wrist. Doing so let me focus on the proportional relationships between these three parts, as visualized by the arrows.

2

Next, I drew gradually smaller envelopes for the other fingers, always keeping an eye on the proportional relationships. The envelopes overlap, establishing what's in front and what's behind.

3

After using envelopes to define all the parts of the hand as flat shapes, I started defining the three-dimensional forms.

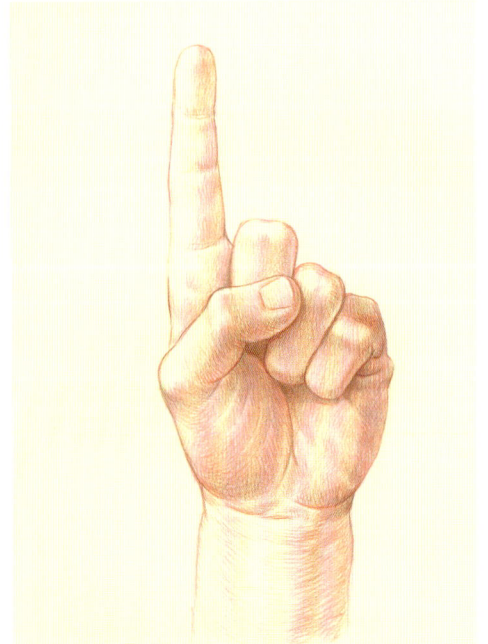

4

Here's the fully rendered hand in the "Number One!" gesture.

OVERLAPPING, FORESHORTENING, MOVEMENT

Study the forms of the hand, rendering them first as basic volumes to better understand their proportional relationships and the overlapping of the smaller volumes of the fingers over the larger ones of the body of the hand. The time you spend getting to know your subject will pay off in terms of accuracy and structural soundness of the drawing. Practice copying the examples here and on the following page, then draw your own hands or a friend's from life.

BELOW: Thenar and hypothenar eminences in relation to the palm

The schematic details here are preparatory studies that helped me in creating a realistic drawing of the hand. The small drawing of the section of the palm (B) was useful in visualizing the positions of the volumes of the thenar and hypothenar eminences. With another sketch (C), I studied the position of the thenar eminence on the palm from a different angle. In a further step (D), I started attaching the fingers to the main volume of the hand, beginning with the index finger and gradually overlapping the other fingers over one another. This approach resulted in a more volumetric effect in the final drawing (A).

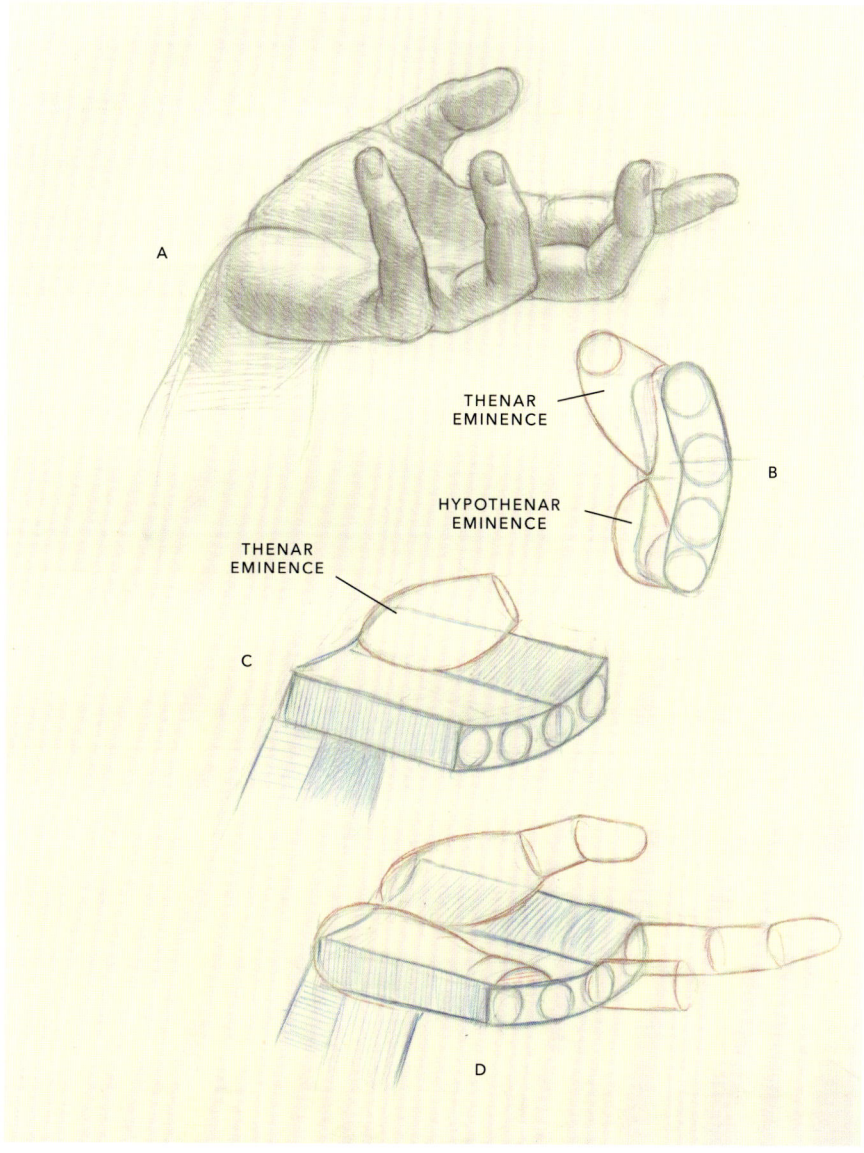

A

THENAR
EMINENCE

HYPOTHENAR
EMINENCE

THENAR
EMINENCE

B

C

D

TOP: Using different conceptualizations

Here, I tried three different approaches to capturing the hand's action: a conical volume *(A)*, flat shapes *(B)*, and a parallelepiped with cylinders for the fingers *(C)*. The more visualizations you use, the more complex and interesting your work will be.

BOTTOM: A strongly foreshortened view of the hand

Preparing stereometric studies in which the parts of the hand are transparent is very useful when drawing a strongly foreshortened pose like this one.

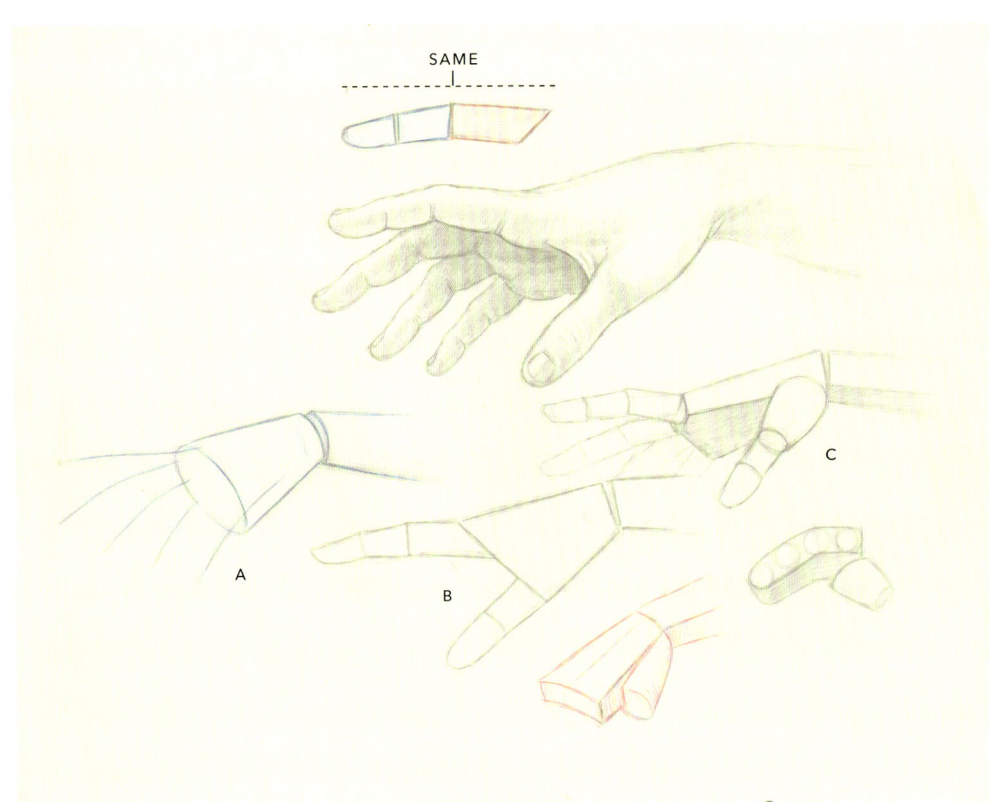

SAME

A

B

C

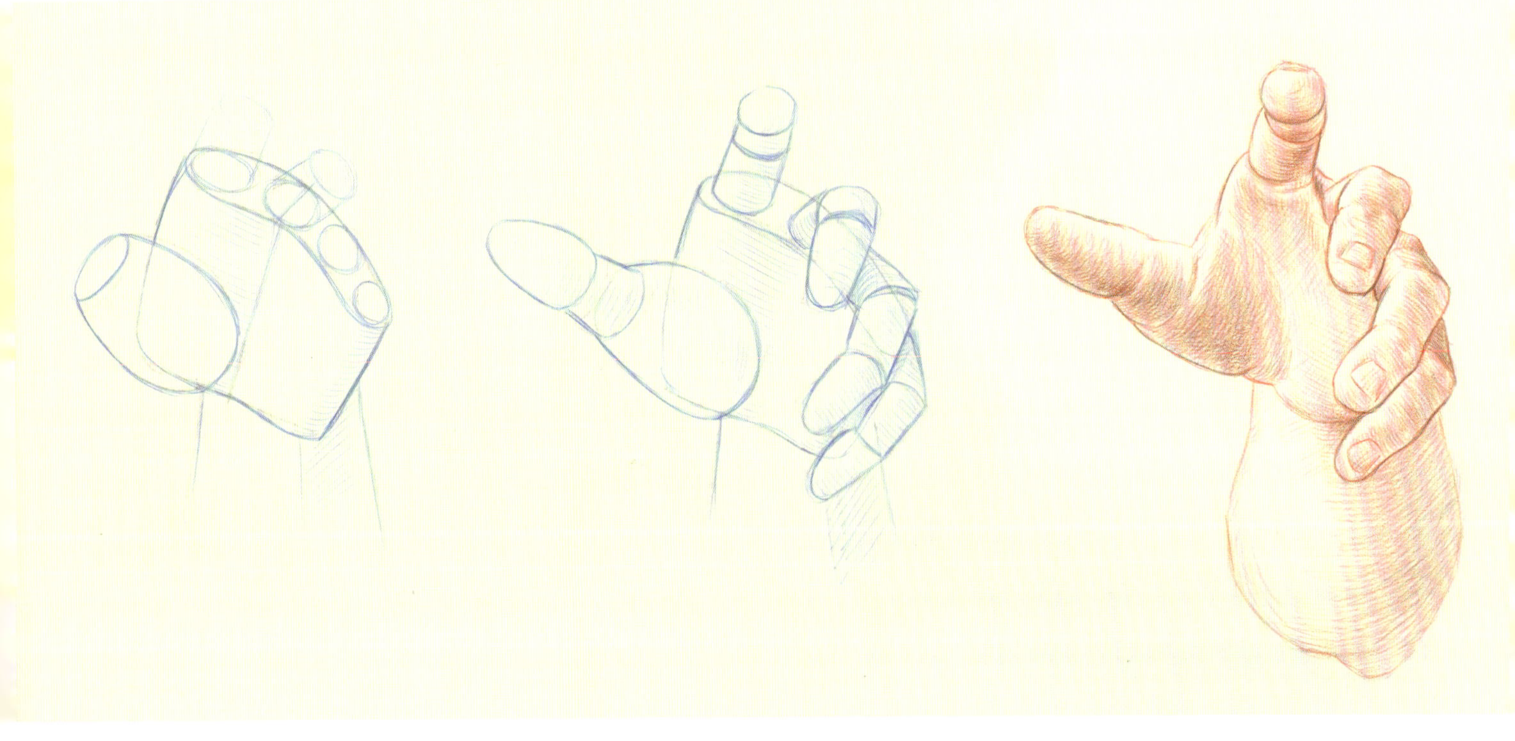

THE HAND IN ACTION

The movements of the hand are easier to understand now that we have examined its structure in depth. When drawing the hand in action, imagine that you are moving the parts of a three-dimensional model.

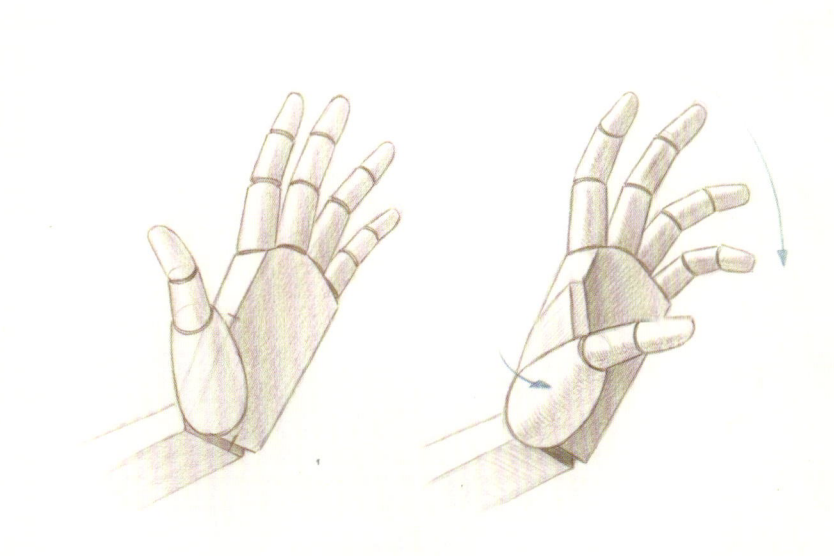

Here, the fingers are moving forward in a grabbing motion and the thumb is also moving forward, pivoting at the base of the palm.

BOTTOM: Palmar abduction and flexion, example 2

This diagram shows the flexion of the fingers and abduction of the thumb from the side view.

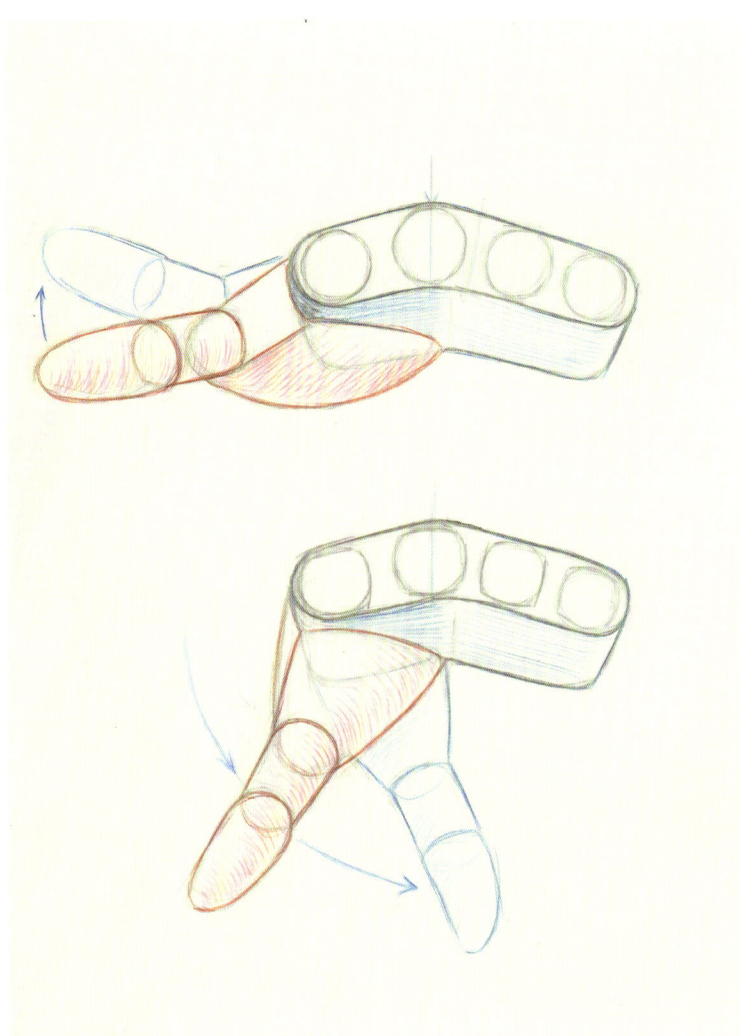

TOP: Retroposition and anteposition of the thumb

These two cross-section sketches show the thumb moving toward the back of the hand (retroposition) and toward the palm (anteposition) with the fulcrum at the base of the thumb.

BOTTOM: Establishing the dominant forms of the hand

In this sketch I first established the dominant form of the palm and forearm and then the thenar eminence. Finally, I added the fingers, thinking of the pinching movement of index finger and thumb (red arrows) and of how the tips of the other fingers would line up (blue arrow).

OPPOSITE: A summary of movements of the fingers

Creating a page of sketches of hands in movement is a good exercise to help you better understand the hand's range of movements and expressive qualities.

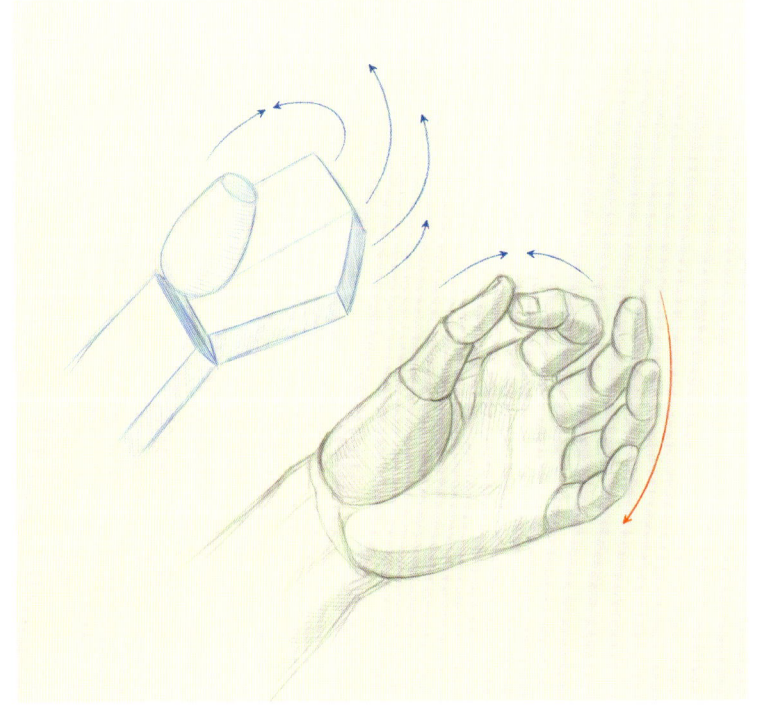

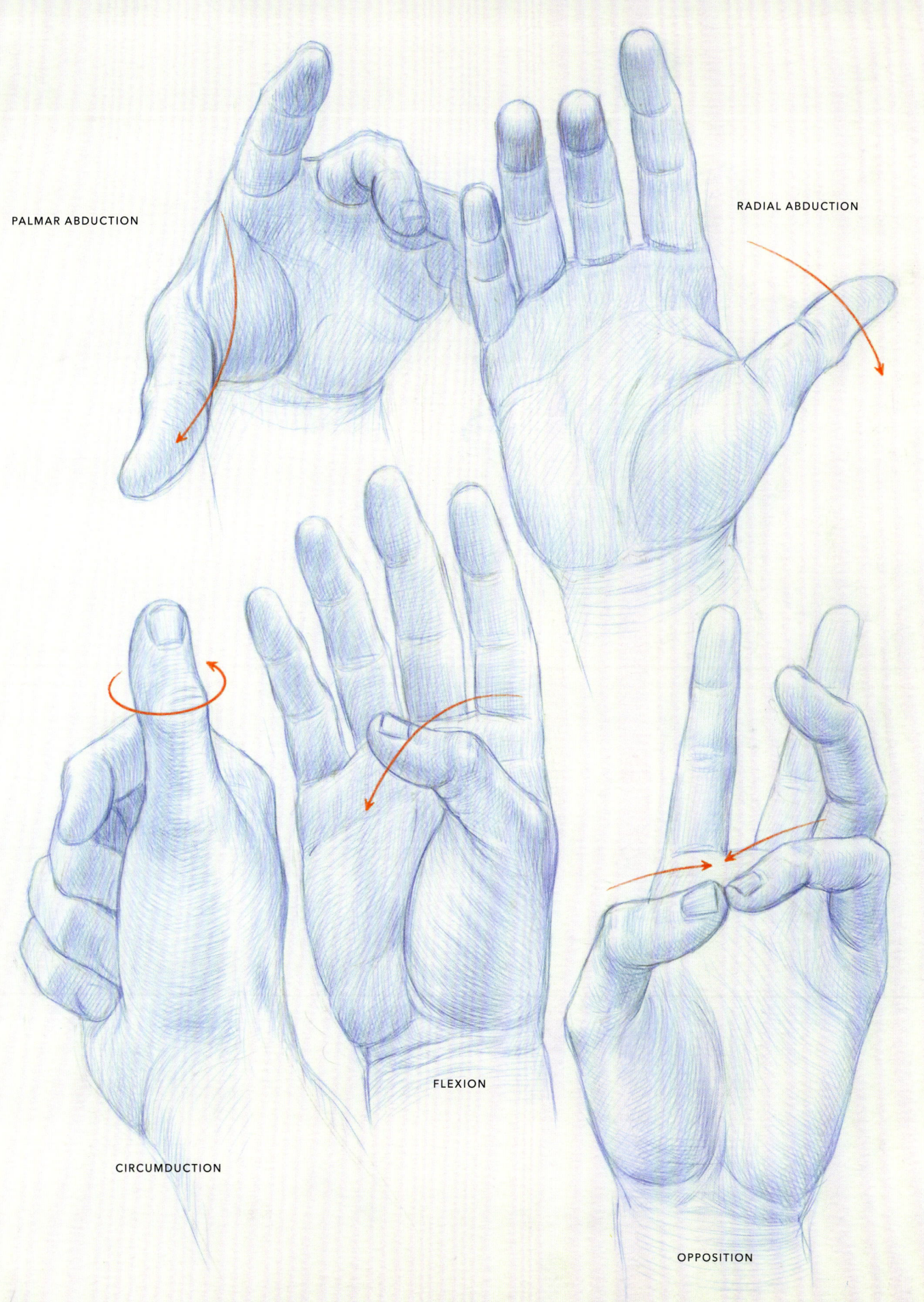

PALMAR ABDUCTION

RADIAL ABDUCTION

CIRCUMDUCTION

FLEXION

OPPOSITION

SKETCHING HANDS

The more hands you draw, the better you'll get at drawing hands. Fill a few pages of your sketchbook now by drawing hands performing a variety of movements in different conceptualizations, as shown here. Some of your drawings can be quick sketches, others longer studies. Start by drawing a hand in one position and then impart a sense of movement by moving the fingers or lowering, raising, and/or turning the hand. Always consider the overlapping of volumes when drawing a foreshortened pose.

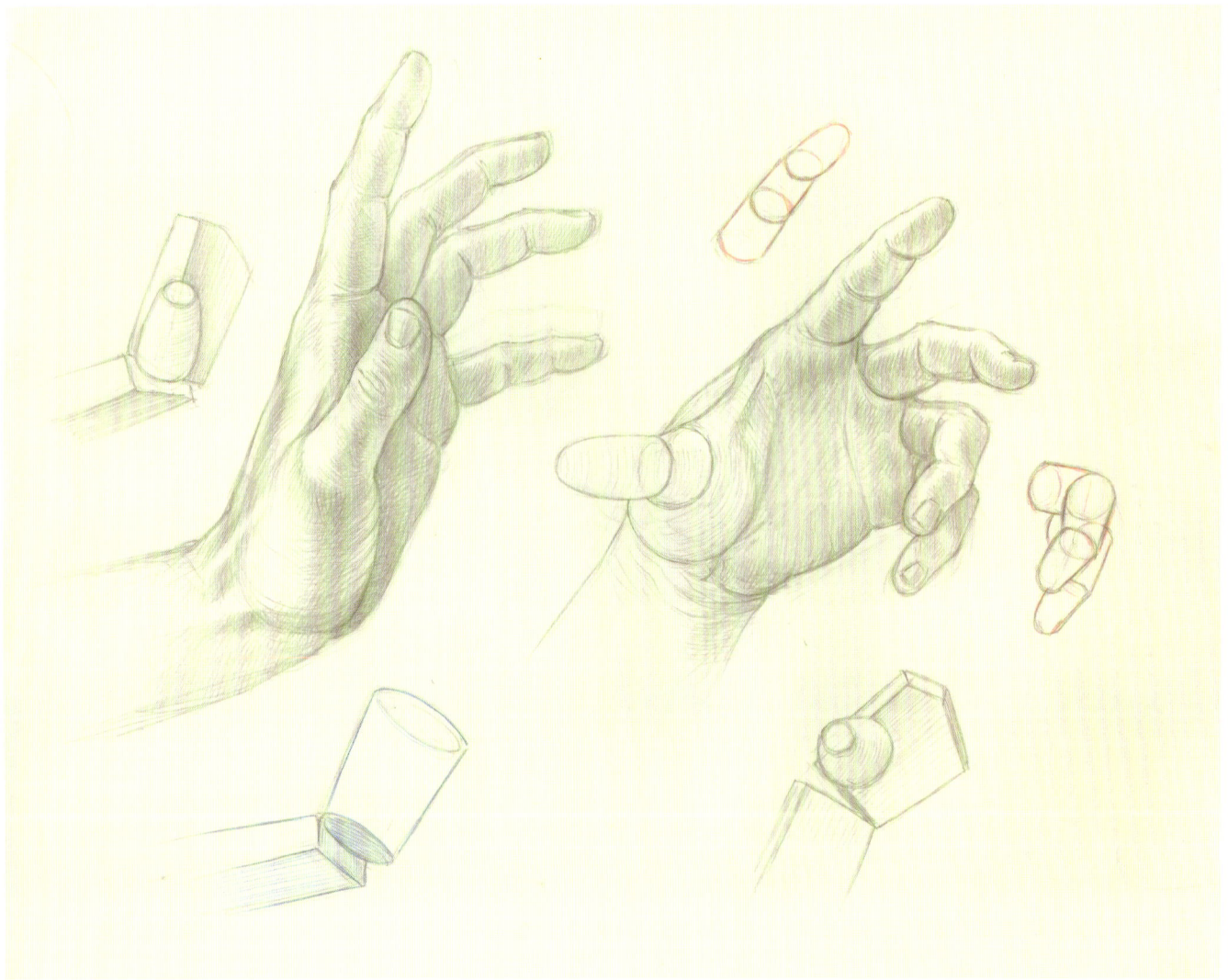

HOLDING OBJECTS

Drawing a foreshortened hand—or, in fact, any hand—with a convincing sense of three-dimensionality, strength, and movement becomes much easier as you master its structure and anatomy. The next step is to draw hands holding or interacting with objects, which increases the level of difficulty while heightening the sense of action and the expressiveness of the artwork. You can start by copying the examples in this section and then drawing your own or another person's hand holding various objects. Eventually, draw from imagination or memory.

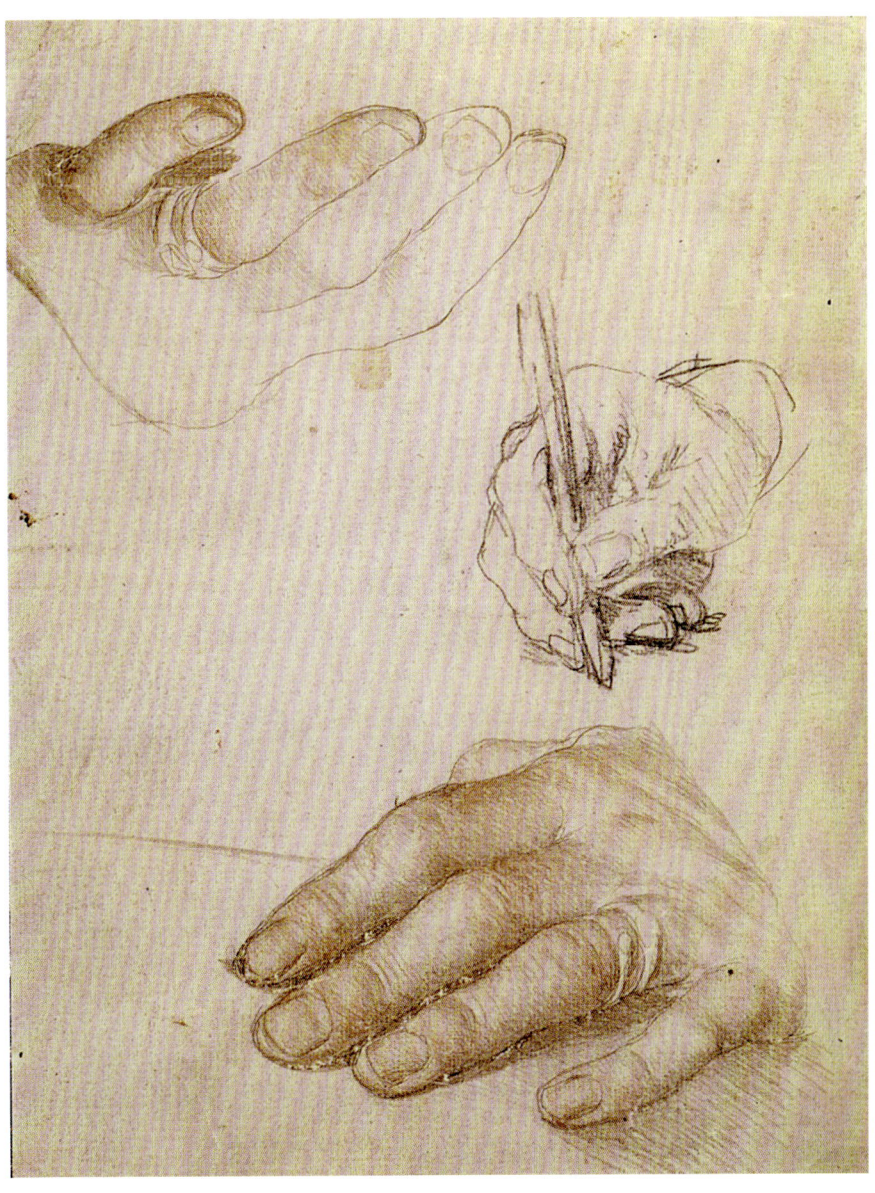

BELOW: Hans Holbein the Younger, *Two Studies of the Left Hand of Erasmus of Rotterdam; Study of the Right Hand Writing*, c. 1523, silverpoint, black crayon and red chalk on gray-primed paper, 8⅛ × 6¹⁄₃₂ inches (20.6 × 15.3 cm). Louvre, Paris.

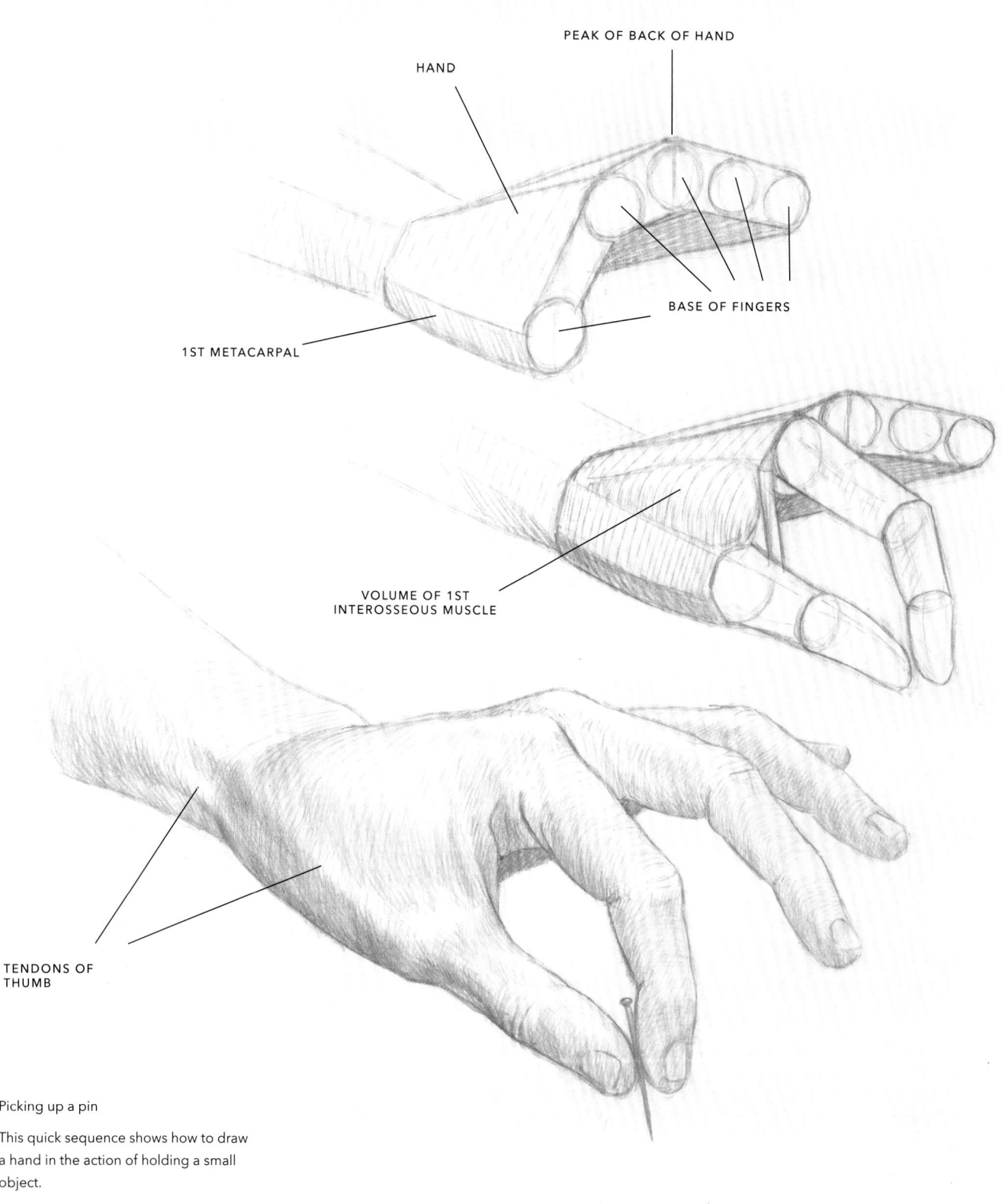

PEAK OF BACK OF HAND

HAND

BASE OF FINGERS

1ST METACARPAL

VOLUME OF 1ST
INTEROSSEOUS MUSCLE

TENDONS OF
THUMB

Picking up a pin

This quick sequence shows how to draw
a hand in the action of holding a small
object.

A MIXED APPROACH TO DRAWING THE HAND

In this mixed approach, you start with an envelope (the main volume), move quickly to boxes representing the forms, and from there to the line drawing and tonal rendering.

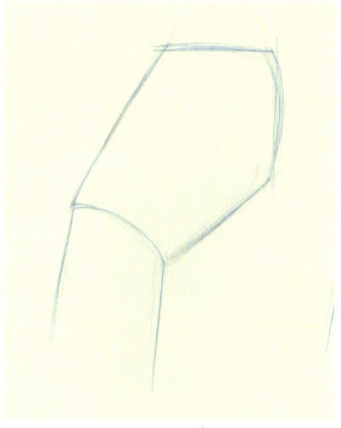

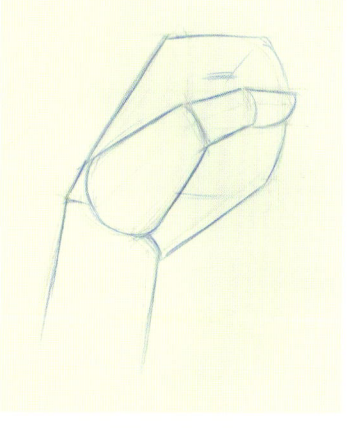

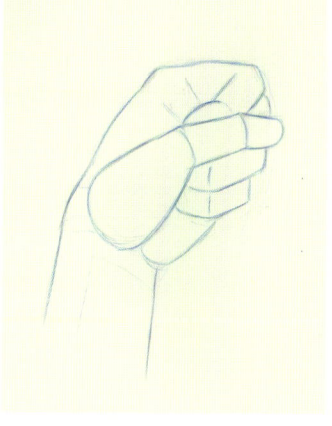

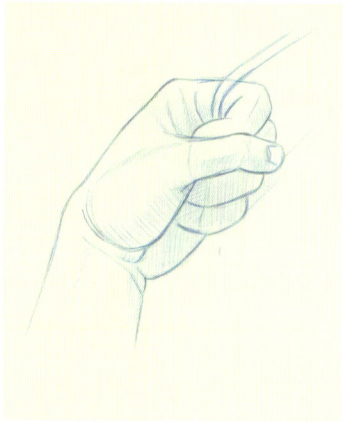

1
Draw the main volumes with envelopes.

2
Add the volumes of the thumb, and compare measures.

3
Rough-in the line drawing.

4
Refine the line drawing and start the tonal rendering.

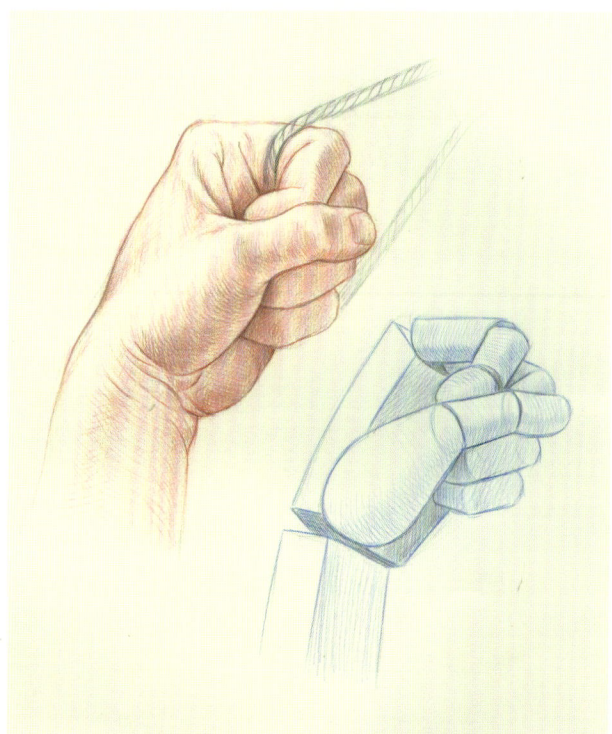

5
Here is the fully developed drawing (left) along with a stereometric study. The stereometric study need not be part of your sequence, but it can be very useful in revealing the effect of the light on the form before rendering the hand tonally.

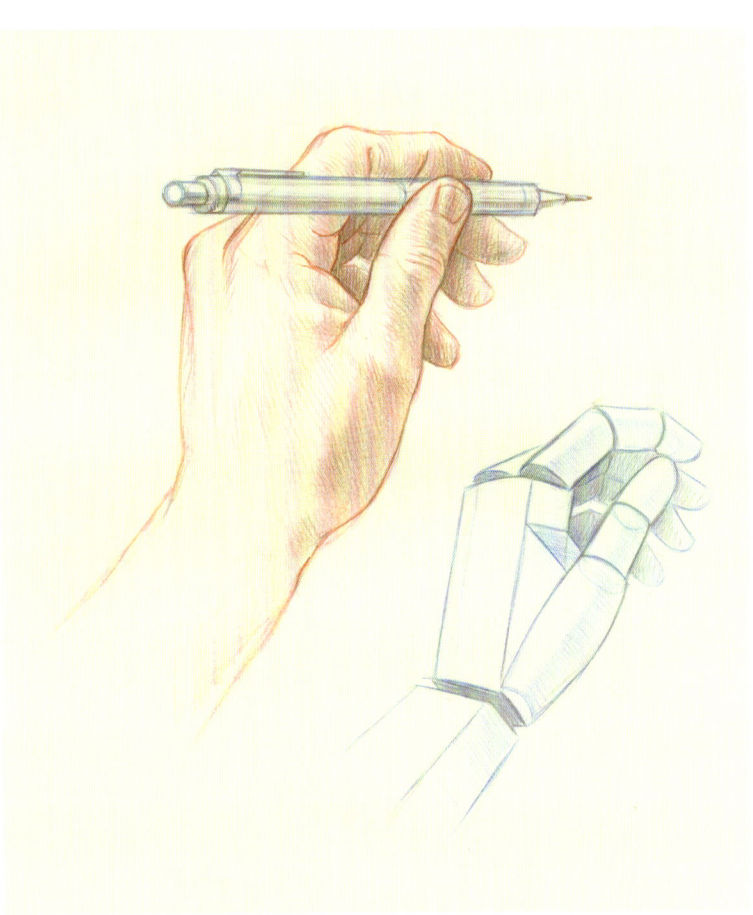

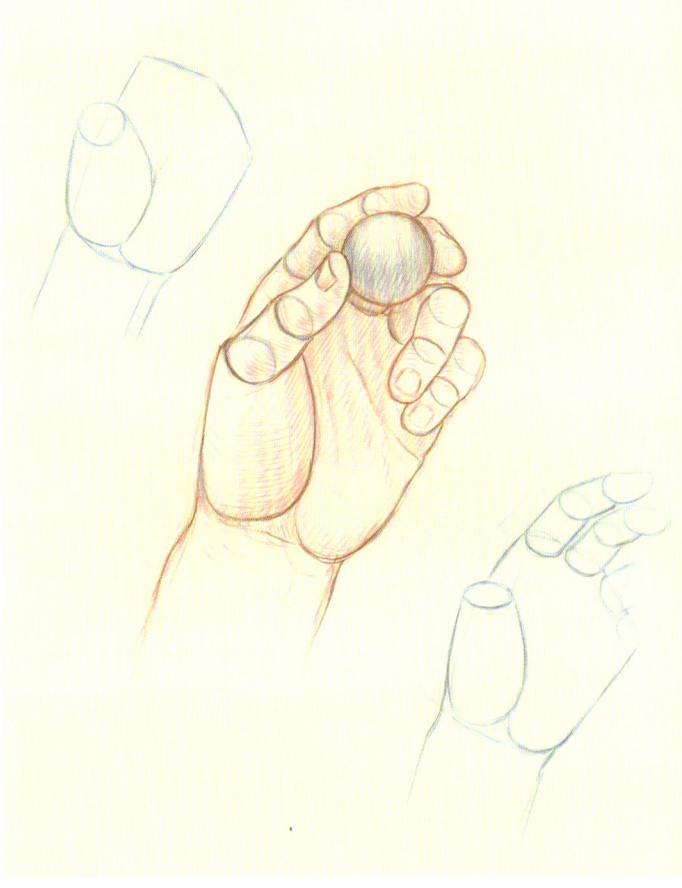

ABOVE LEFT: Writing with a mechanical pencil

In this case, the stereometric study is used to study both the pose of the hand and the effect of the light on it.

ABOVE RIGHT: Holding a ball

In a pose like this, where the fingers are hiding a good part of the hand, start by drawing the palm, because it is the dominant structure. This will make it easier to correctly connect the fingers to the hand.

RIGHT: Holding a piece of cloth

When the hand is partially hidden by an object, as with the piece of cloth shown here, it is best to draw the hand in its entirety first and then drape the cloth over it.

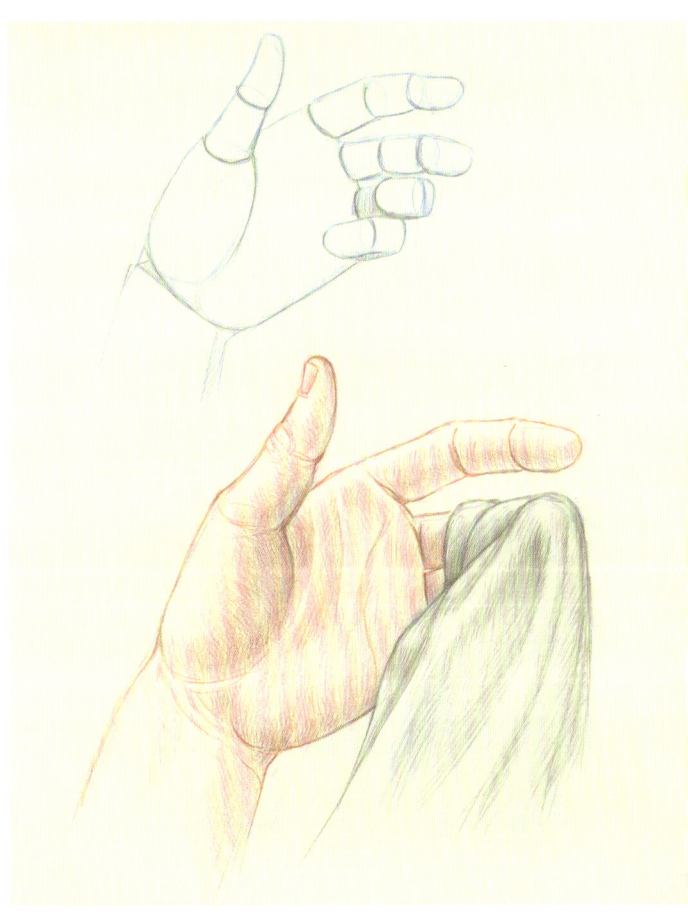

VISUALIZING FLOWS AND RHYTHMS

Once you've acquired a solid understanding of the structure of the hand, you can start focusing on aspects that are not purely anatomical but more aesthetic and dynamic. The following sequences visualize lines of flow created by gestures of the hands—specifically, of two hands holding each other in two different ways.

STUDY OF CLASPED HANDS

For this pose I asked the patient collaboration of a former graduate student of mine, Bernard Garcia. You can ask a friend to do so, too, or work from a photo if the pose proves too hard to hold.

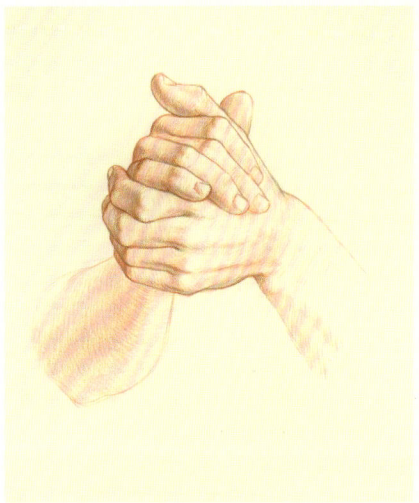

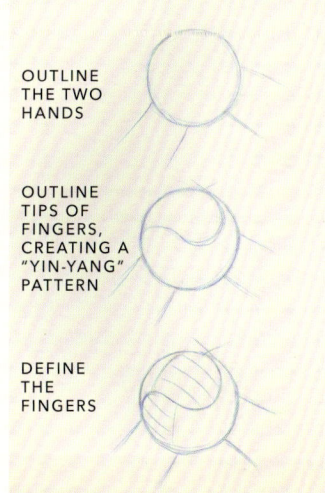

OUTLINE THE TWO HANDS

OUTLINE TIPS OF FINGERS, CREATING A "YIN-YANG" PATTERN

DEFINE THE FINGERS

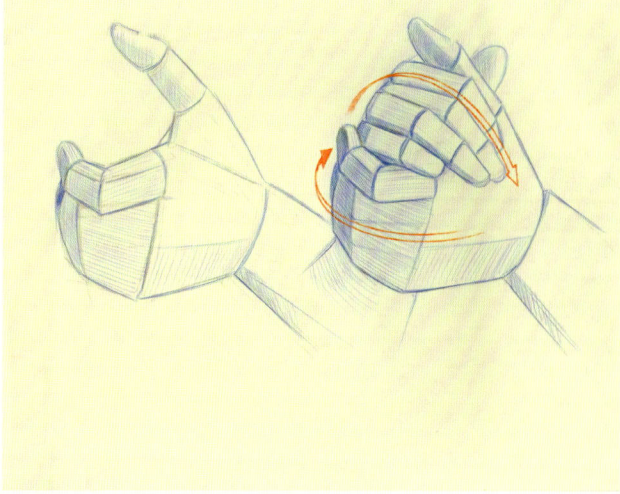

1

This is the reference image. The next steps discuss two possible ways to read this pose of hand holding hand.

2

In this little sequence, I focus on the "yin-yang" pattern produced by the outlines of the tips of the fingers.

3

Here, the focus is on the structural, three-dimensional aspects of the hands. This approach makes it easier to consider the volumetric aspect of the subject, facilitating tonal development and resulting in a more three-dimensional artwork. In creating this sequence, I first drew the dominant hand—the one you see more of. At first, I also drew the portion of the hand that would not be visible when hidden under the fingers of the other hand. I then wrapped the second hand around the first.

STUDY OF INTERLOCKED FINGERS

Drawing interlocked fingers always causes panic among artists. To overcome the anxiety, observe the pose for a few moments before you start to draw and try to extrapolate patterns and flows, as I did for this sequence.

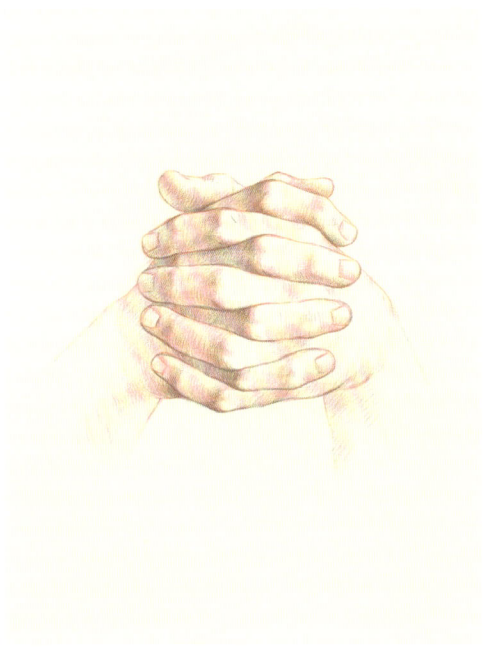

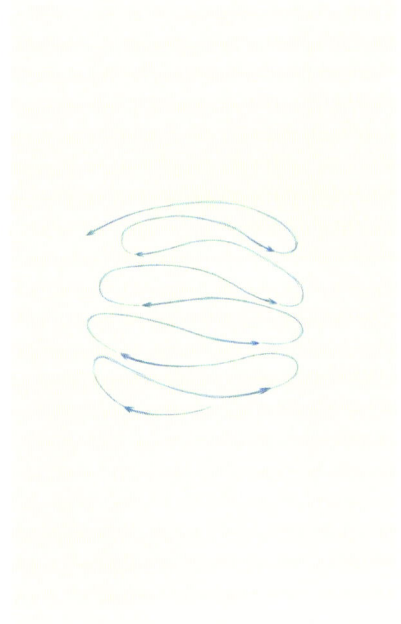

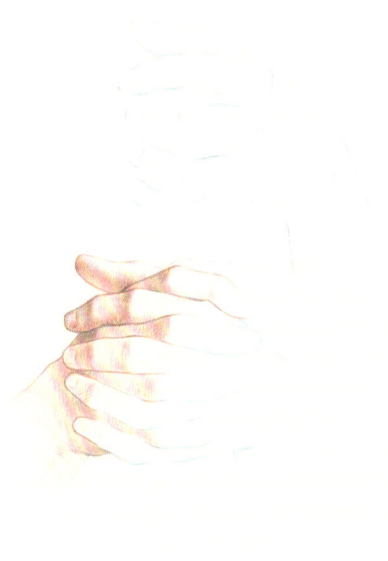

1
This is the reference image for the study.

2
Here, you see the interesting, meandering aesthetic flow created by the interlocked fingers.

3
This image shows the progression from the initial sketch to the tonal rendering. Make sure that the initial "searching lines" are very light, so they disappear as the drawing is developed tonally.

A CONTEMPORARY MASTER
OF ANATOMICAL FORM

Harry He (He Lihuay) is a Chinese artist living and working in Beijing. This beautiful painting of hands demonstrates a perfect synthesis of the structural/anatomical aspects of the hand and a perfect painting technique rooted in the academic tradition.

BELOW: He Lihuai, "Hand", 2017, oil on linen, 23¼ x 15¾ inches (59 x 40 cm). Courtesy of the artist.

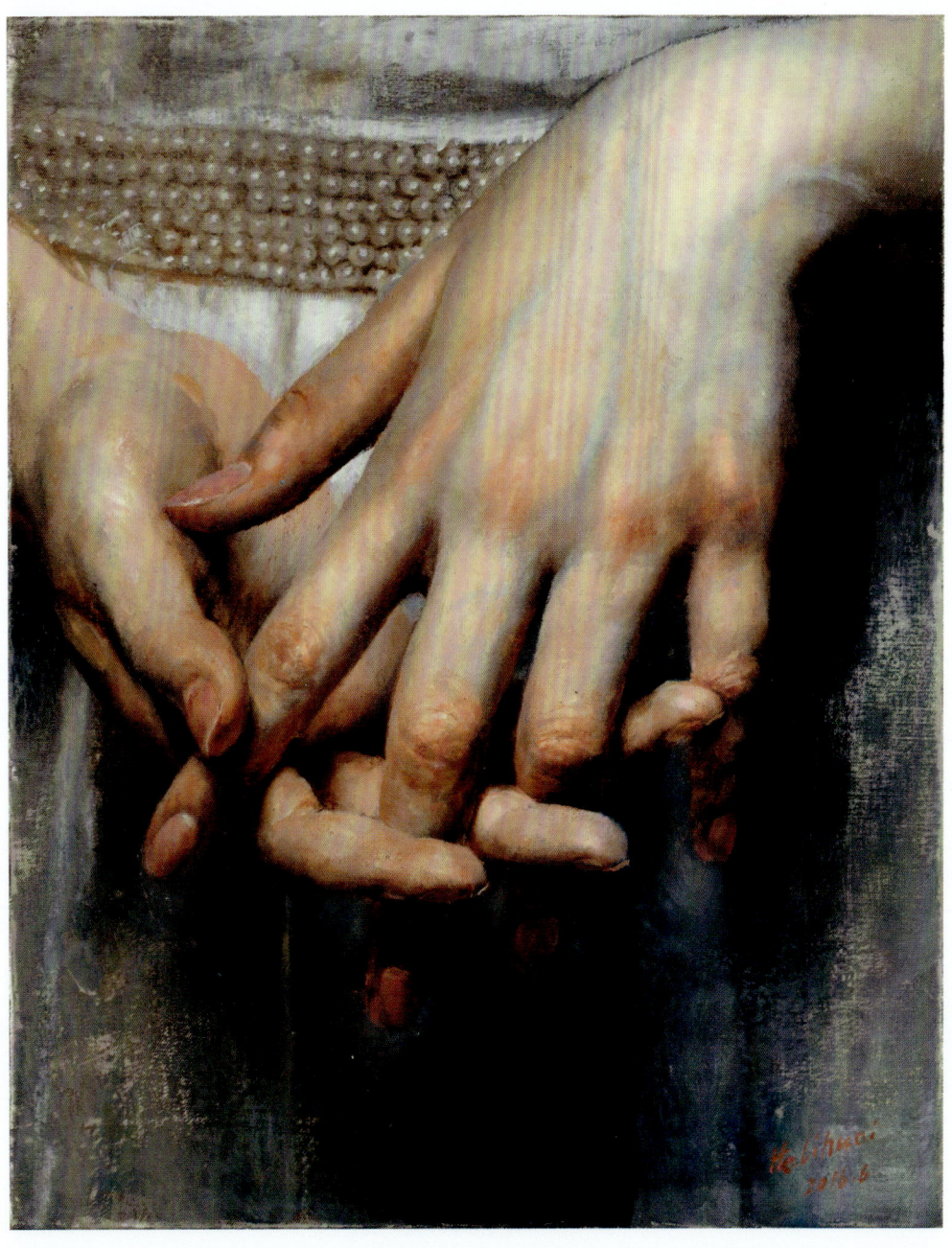

EXERCISES

Here are two quick exercises based on material covered in this chapter. The second one brings together stereometry, organic forms, light and shadow, and movement.

EXERCISE 1

Start by drawing the proportional relationships of the hand *(A)*; keep this step light and essential. Then create a hybrid version of the hand halfway between stereometric and realistic *(B)*, in which the various segments are still distinct, but neither as rigid and mechanical as in the first step nor as fully organic as they will be in the last step *(C)*.

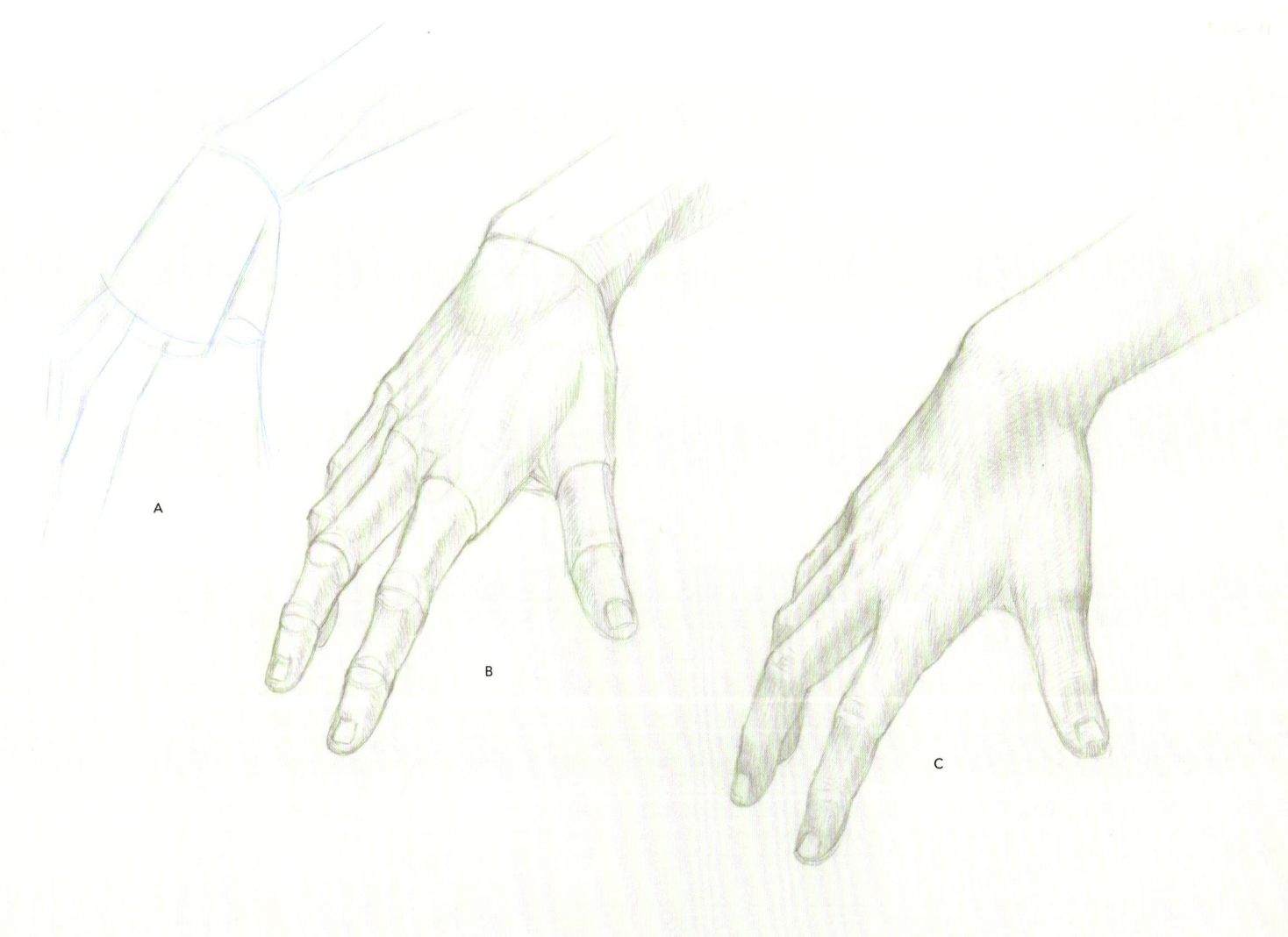

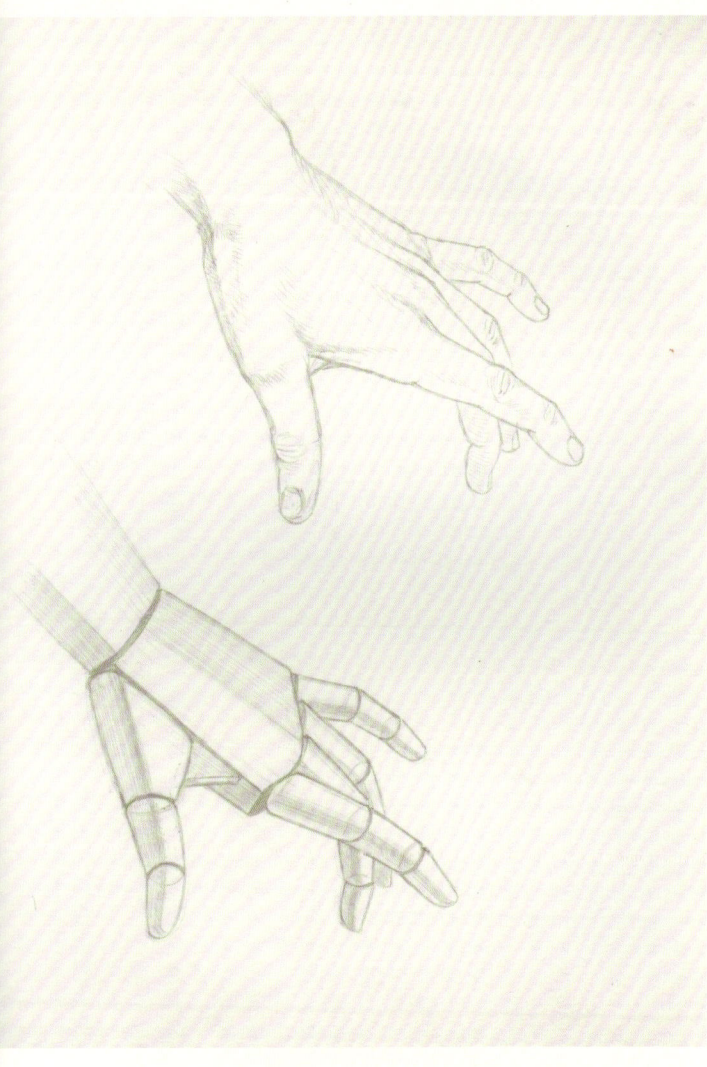

EXERCISE 2

Follow this step-by-step sequence to further capturing the structural, dynamic, and tonal aspects of the hand.

1

The realistic drawing at top in the image at left serves as your starting point. Remember that when drawing the human form, you are always "deconstructing" an observed reality and then reconstructing it. Here, the first step in that reconstruction is the stereometric rendition.

2

Next (below left), start developing the organic forms of the hand, which is now somewhere between schematic and realistic.

3

In the final step (below), devote more attention to the chiaroscuro (light and shadow) effects and realistic rendering.

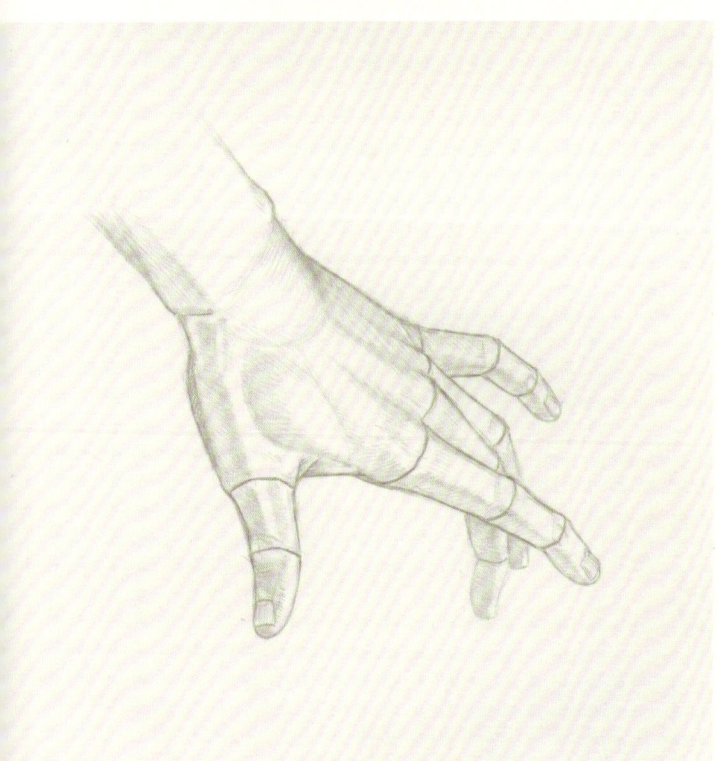

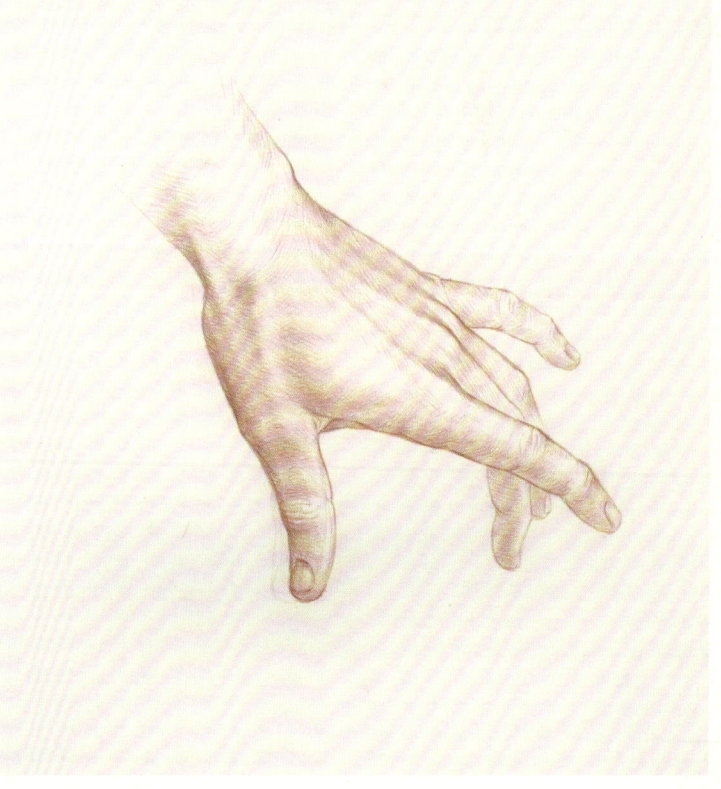

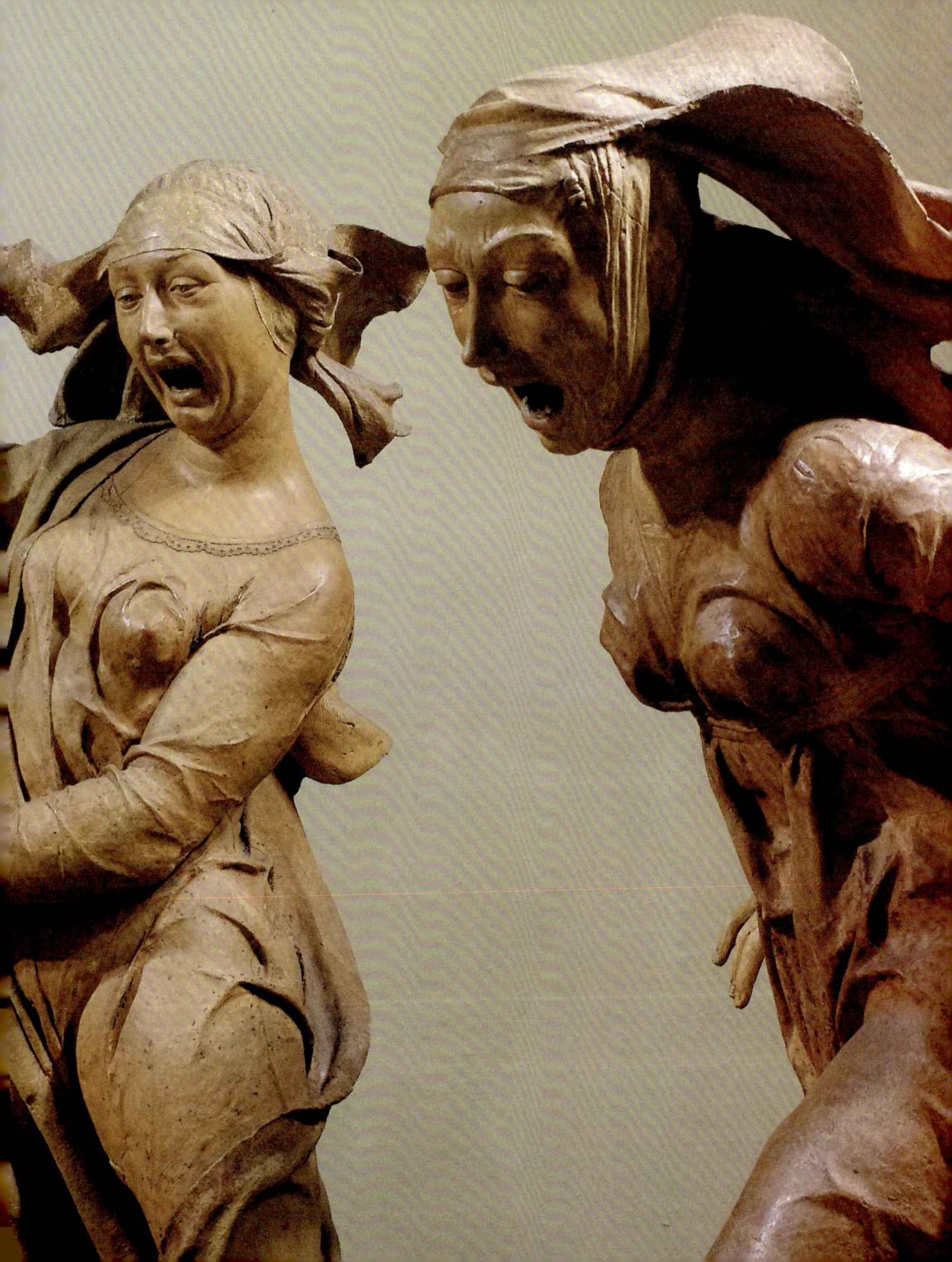

CHAPTER 8

THE FACE & FACIAL EXPRESSIONS

A good understanding of human anatomy was conducive to the creation of increasingly more realistic and expressive depictions of the human figure during the Greek Classical period. But the height of expressivity, both of the body and the face, was reached in antiquity with Hellenistic works like, for example, the Laocoön and the Barberini Fawn. The works of this period probably also reflect the Hellenistic theater; the artists who created these masterpieces charged them with incredible theatricality and evoked intense emotions.

OPPOSITE: Niccolò dell'Arca, *Lamentation over the Dead Christ* (detail), c. 1485, terra cotta. Sanctuary of Santa Maria della Vita, Bologna, Italy. Photo by Paolo Villa.

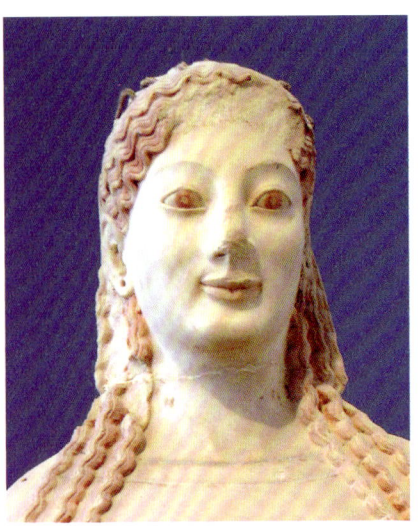 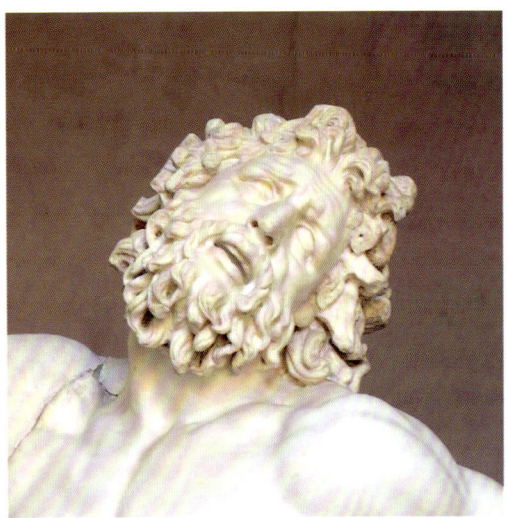 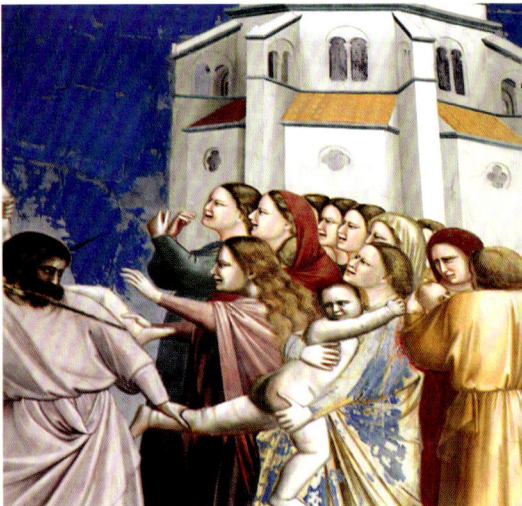

The same progression can be seen in Europe between the fourteenth and seventeenth centuries, prompted by renewed interest in the classics and the revival of the study of anatomy by scientists and artists. The late medieval Gothic style art is already characterized by highly expressive, naturalistic artworks like the frescoes that Giotto, who is considered a precursor of the Italian Renaissance, painted in Padua's Scrovegni Chapel in the early fourteenth century.

The life-size, terra cotta sculptural group *Lamentation over the Dead Christ* (c. 1485) by the late Gothic artist Niccolò dell'Arca—a detail from which opens this chapter displays an incredibly accurate and sophisticated representation of grief, desperation, and sadness, convincingly evoking the emotions of the people who took care of the body of Christ after it was taken down from the cross.

But it was during the Renaissance proper that artists started to study the expressive aspects of the human face consistently and systematically and to apply mathematics, geometry, anatomy, and perspective to the practice of art. Classical texts, translated by scholars, were increasingly available to intellectuals, who now included artists among their ranks.

The systematic study
of the expressive
aspects of the face

RENAISSANCE FACES

The early Renaissance painter Piero della Francesca applied geometry and mathematics to the study and depiction of the human form, as you can see in the image below, showing the measurements and coordinates of the head, which permitted the artist to render a human head in perspective.

Later, the Renaissance genius Leonardo da Vinci created detailed anatomical studies of facial expressions in preparation for his never-finished and now lost fresco *Battle of Anghiari* (c. 1505). And in preparation for his famous fresco *The Last Supper* (1490s), he studied people's facial expressions by creating many sketches from life of people on the streets and squares of Florence. After Leonardo, beautifully expressive artworks were created by the likes of Michelangelo, Caravaggio, Bernini, Le Brun, Greuze, Hals, and many others.

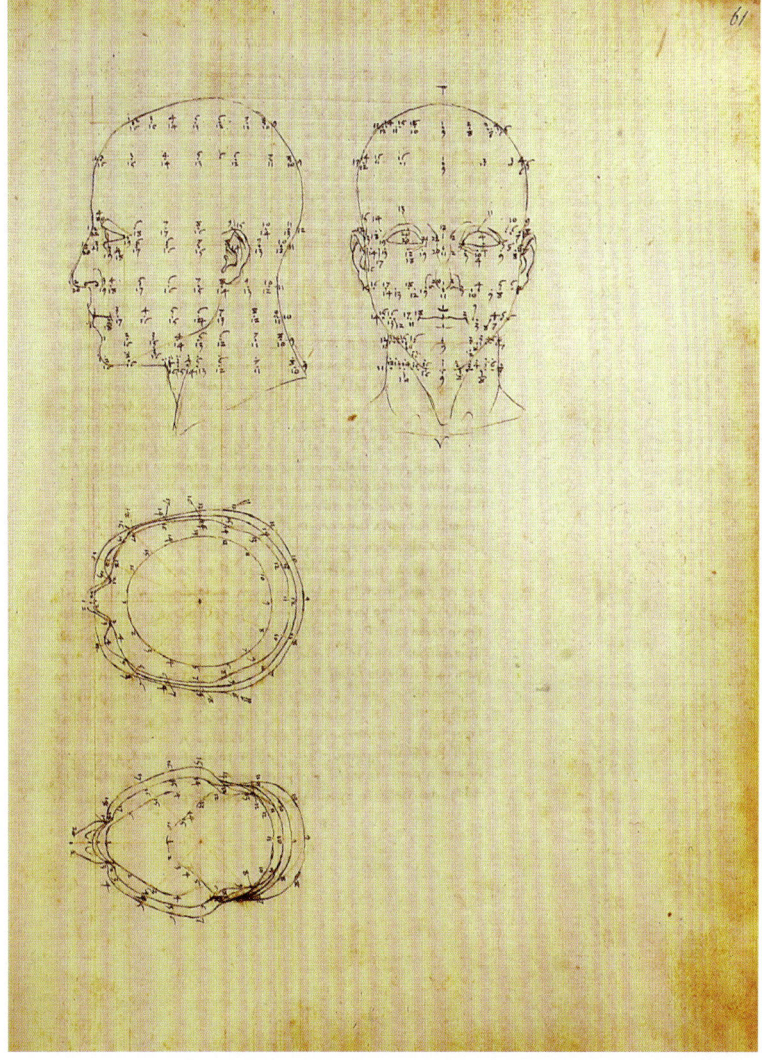

LEFT: Piero della Francesca, projections of a foreshortened head, illustration from Piero's *On the Perspective of Painting,* before 1482. Ambrosian Library, Milan.

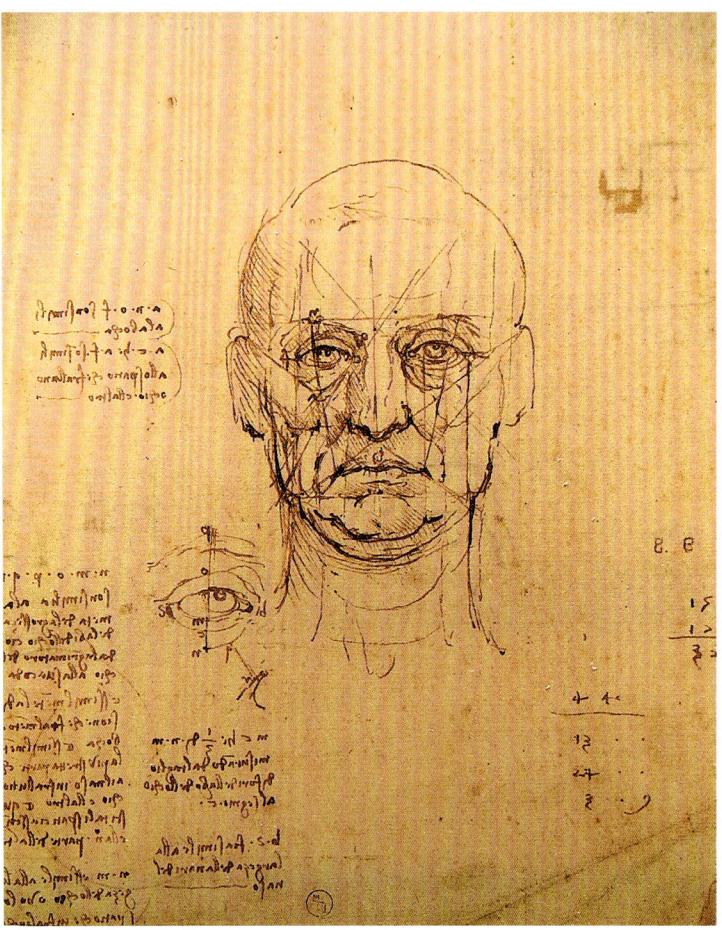

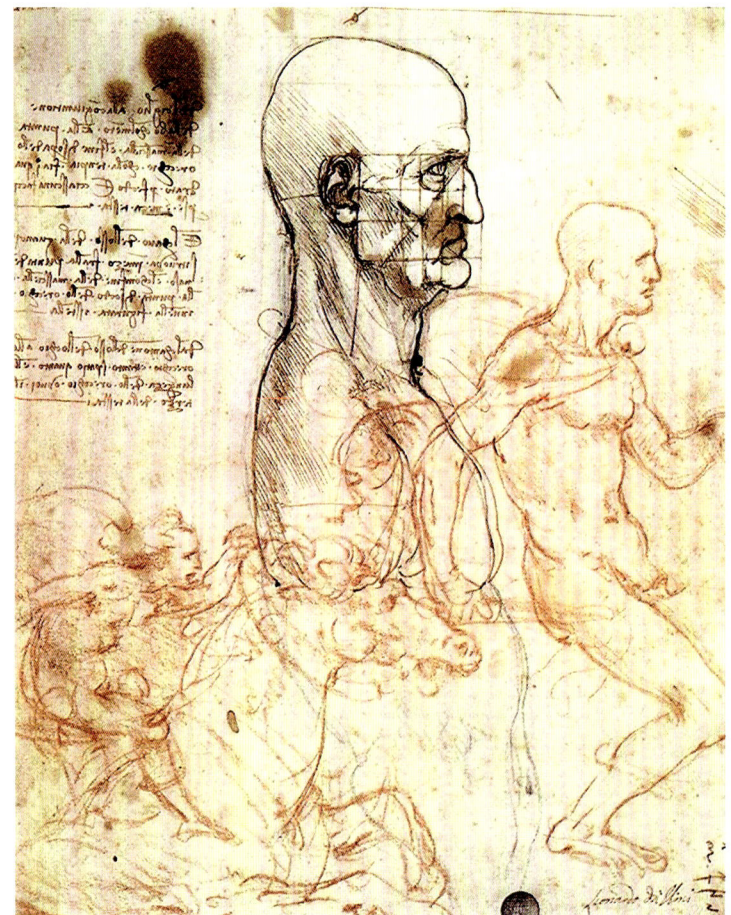

TOP: Leonardo da Vinci, *Study of Facial Proportions*, 1489–90, metalpoint, 7¾ × 6¼ inches (19.70 × 16 cm). Royal Library of Turin. Photo by Luc Viatour/https://Lucnix.be.

RIGHT: Leonardo da Vinci, *Profile of a Man and Study of Two Riders*, 1490 and 1504, red chalk and pen and ink on paper, 11 × 8¾ inches (27.89 × 22.28 cm). Gallerie dell'Accademia, Venice.

Leonardo studied the typical proportions of the head in depth, as these images of gridded faces show.

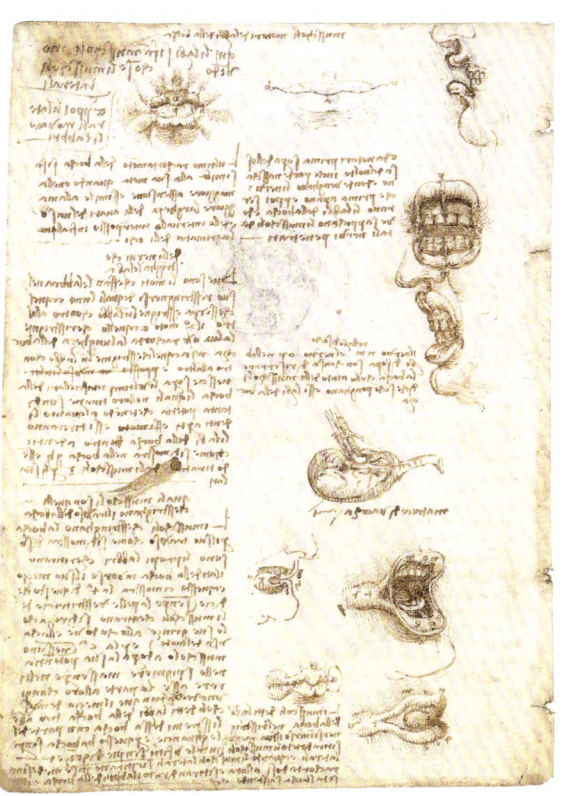

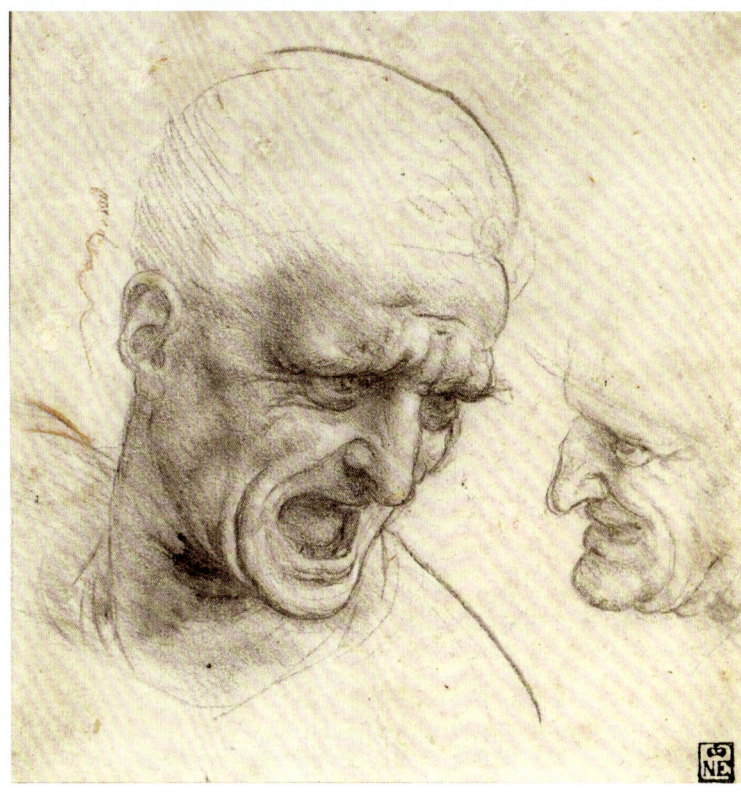

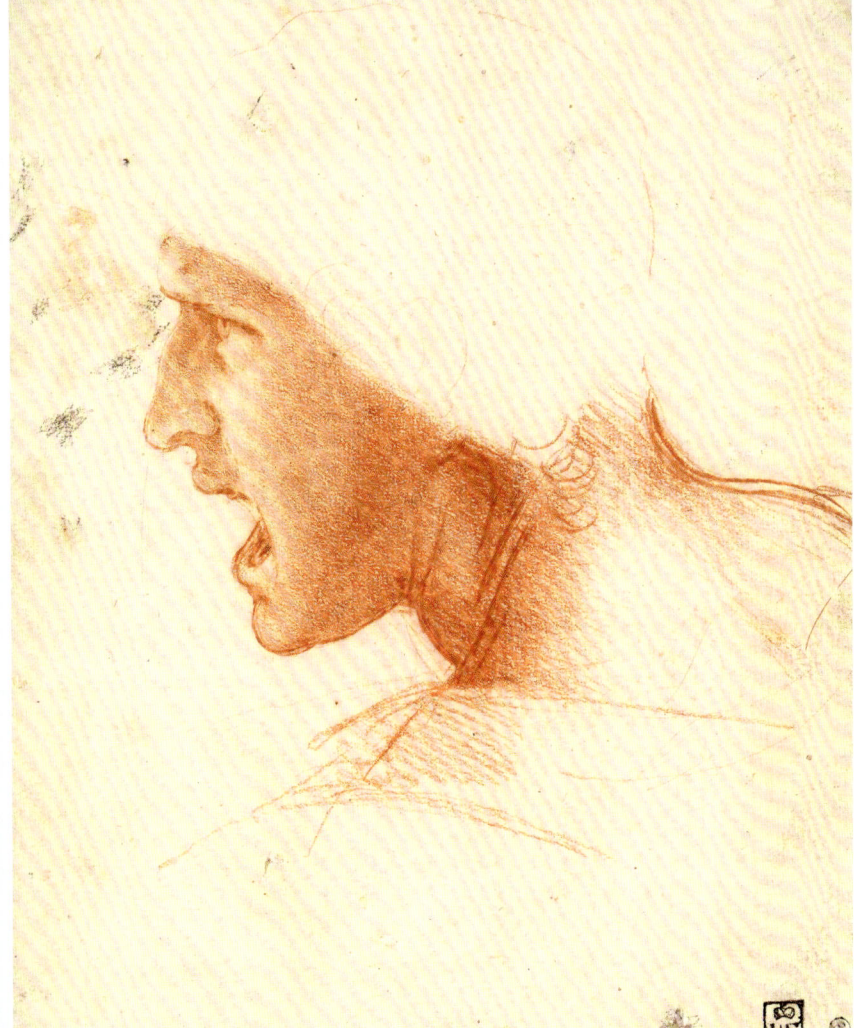

Leonardo systematically applied anatomy to the preparation of his art to achieve more realistic and expressive human figures and facial expressions, as we can see in his sketches for *The Battle of Anghiari.*

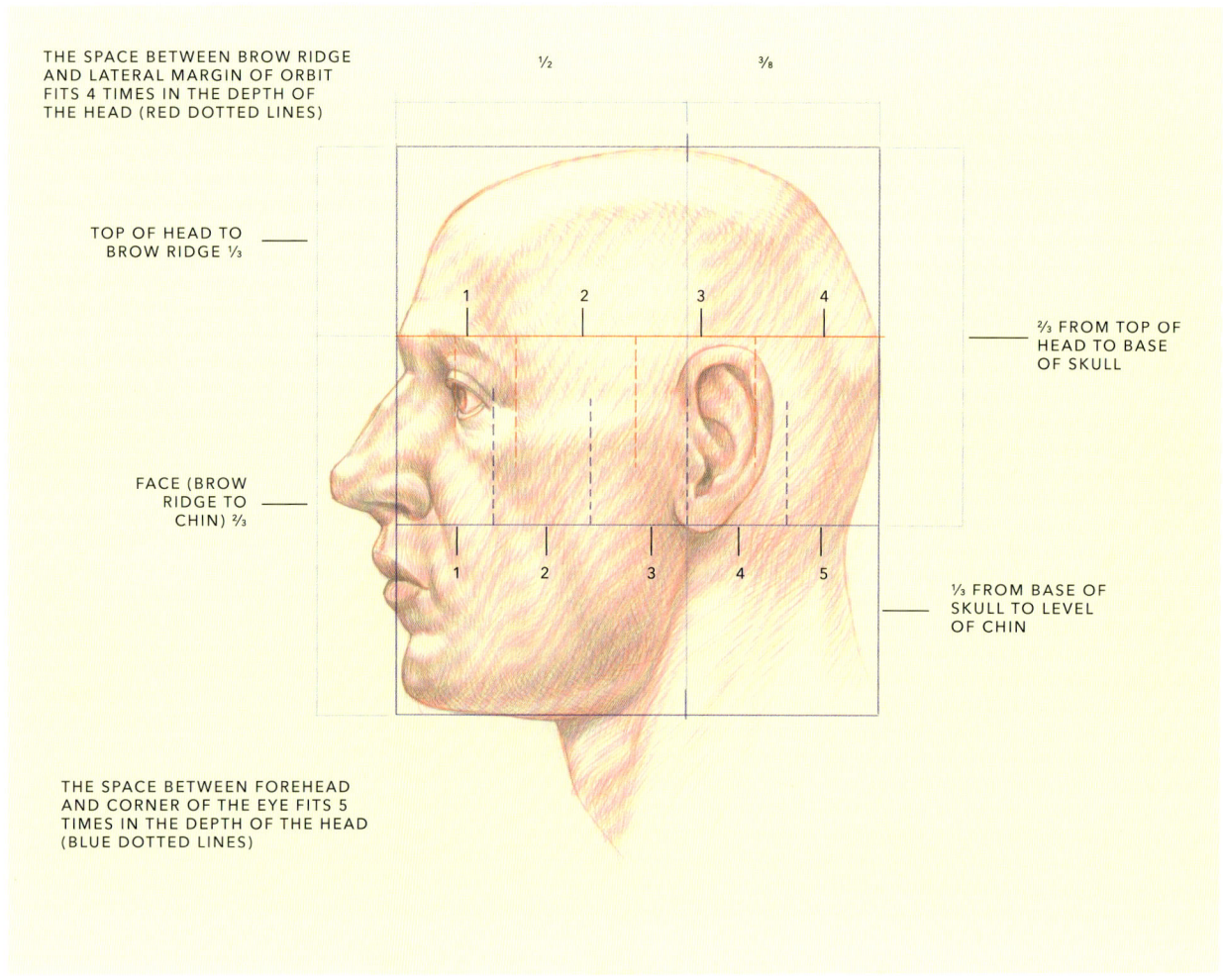

THE SPACE BETWEEN BROW RIDGE AND LATERAL MARGIN OF ORBIT FITS 4 TIMES IN THE DEPTH OF THE HEAD (RED DOTTED LINES)

½   ⅜

TOP OF HEAD TO BROW RIDGE ⅓

FACE (BROW RIDGE TO CHIN) ⅔

⅔ FROM TOP OF HEAD TO BASE OF SKULL

⅓ FROM BASE OF SKULL TO LEVEL OF CHIN

THE SPACE BETWEEN FOREHEAD AND CORNER OF THE EYE FITS 5 TIMES IN THE DEPTH OF THE HEAD (BLUE DOTTED LINES)

ABOVE: Typical proportions of face, profile view

OPPOSITE: Typical proportions of face, front view

THE STRUCTURE OF THE HEAD

Now let's turn to the essential structure of the head, its typical proportions, the planes of the head, and the positions and characteristics of the facial features. The demonstrations in this and the following sections will help you to practice and better understand these concepts. The charts here show the typical proportions. Following these proportions will help you position the main landmarks of the face when drawing a portrait; these typical measures can then be adjusted based on the specific measures of your subject.

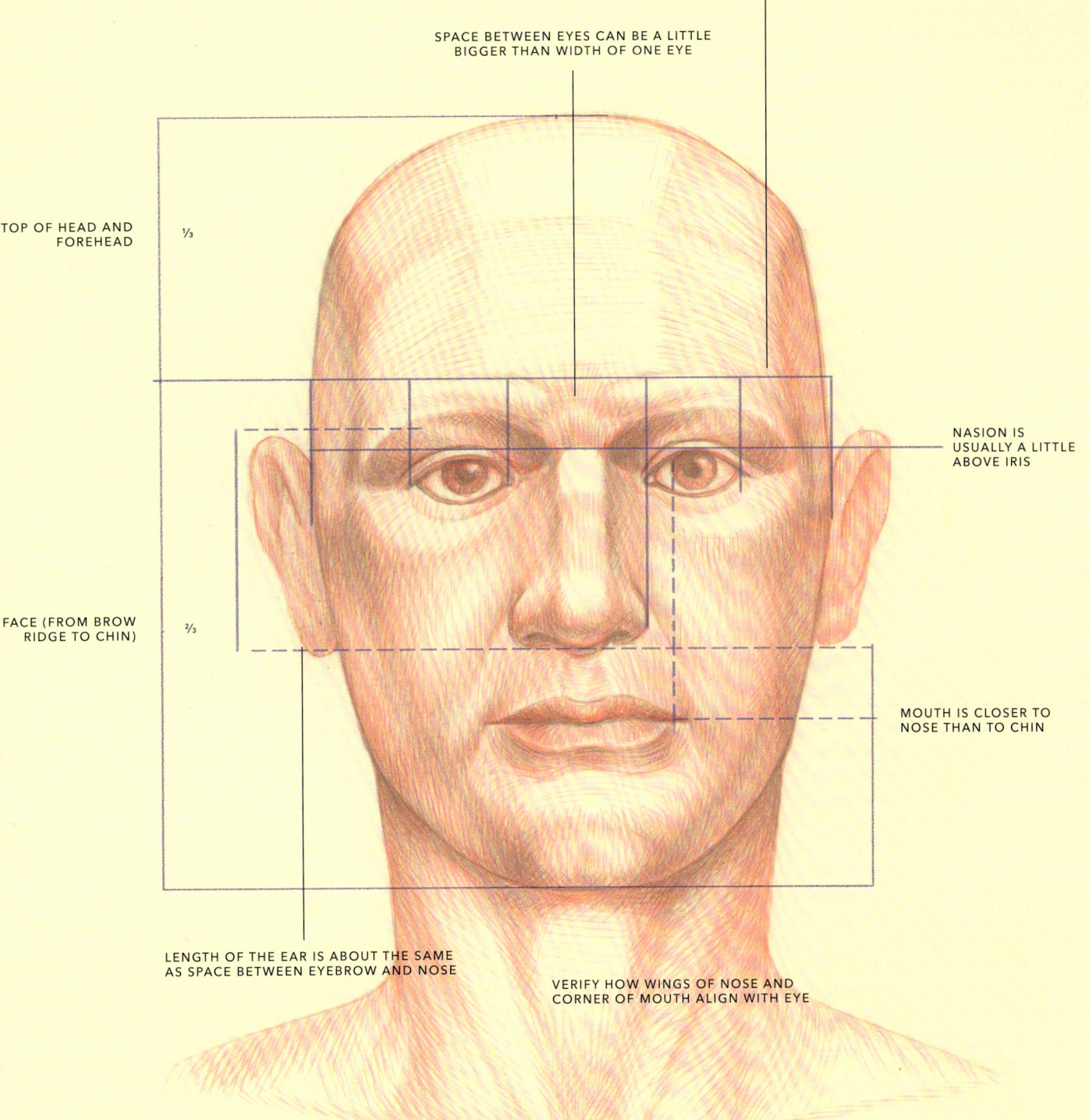

WIDTH OF FACE AT ZYGOMATIC BONE IS
ABOUT THE SAME AS WIDTH OF FIVE EYES

SPACE BETWEEN EYES CAN BE A LITTLE
BIGGER THAN WIDTH OF ONE EYE

TOP OF HEAD AND
FOREHEAD

⅓

NASION IS
USUALLY A LITTLE
ABOVE IRIS

FACE (FROM BROW
RIDGE TO CHIN)

⅔

MOUTH IS CLOSER TO
NOSE THAN TO CHIN

LENGTH OF THE EAR IS ABOUT THE SAME
AS SPACE BETWEEN EYEBROW AND NOSE

VERIFY HOW WINGS OF NOSE AND
CORNER OF MOUTH ALIGN WITH EYE

THE BASIC MEASURES OF THE HEAD

This quick demonstration shows how to approach drawing the head starting from its two main volumes: the cranial volume (blue lines) and the facial volume, or face mask (red lines). After these two volumes are established, you can proceed to position the nose and the mouth and then all the other facial features.

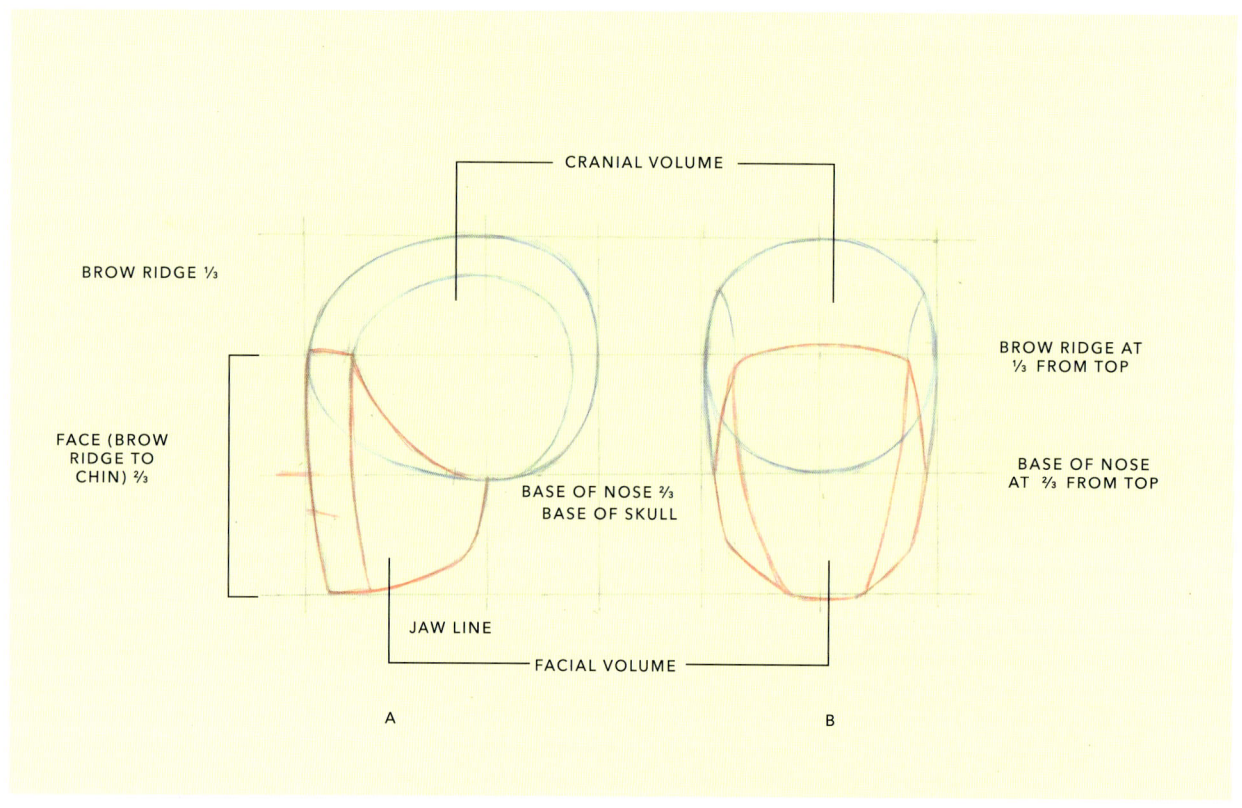

CRANIAL VOLUME

BROW RIDGE ⅓

BROW RIDGE AT ⅓ FROM TOP

FACE (BROW RIDGE TO CHIN) ⅔

BASE OF NOSE ⅔
BASE OF SKULL

BASE OF NOSE AT ⅔ FROM TOP

JAW LINE

FACIAL VOLUME

A

B

1

Start with the big volumes: first draw the cranial mass (blue lines) and face mask (red lines) following the proportions described here. Seen from the side (A), the cranial volume can be schematized as an egg; from the front (B) it looks like a sphere. The facial volume can be synthesized as a mask. The height of the face is two-thirds of the total height of the head. From the side, the width of the face (red mask) is a little more than half the width of the head (blue ovoid). The base of the nose and the base of the skull are at the same level, as is visible from the side. Seen from the front, the width of the head is commonly between two-thirds and three-quarters of its height, in this diagram I used the two-thirds ratio (front view).

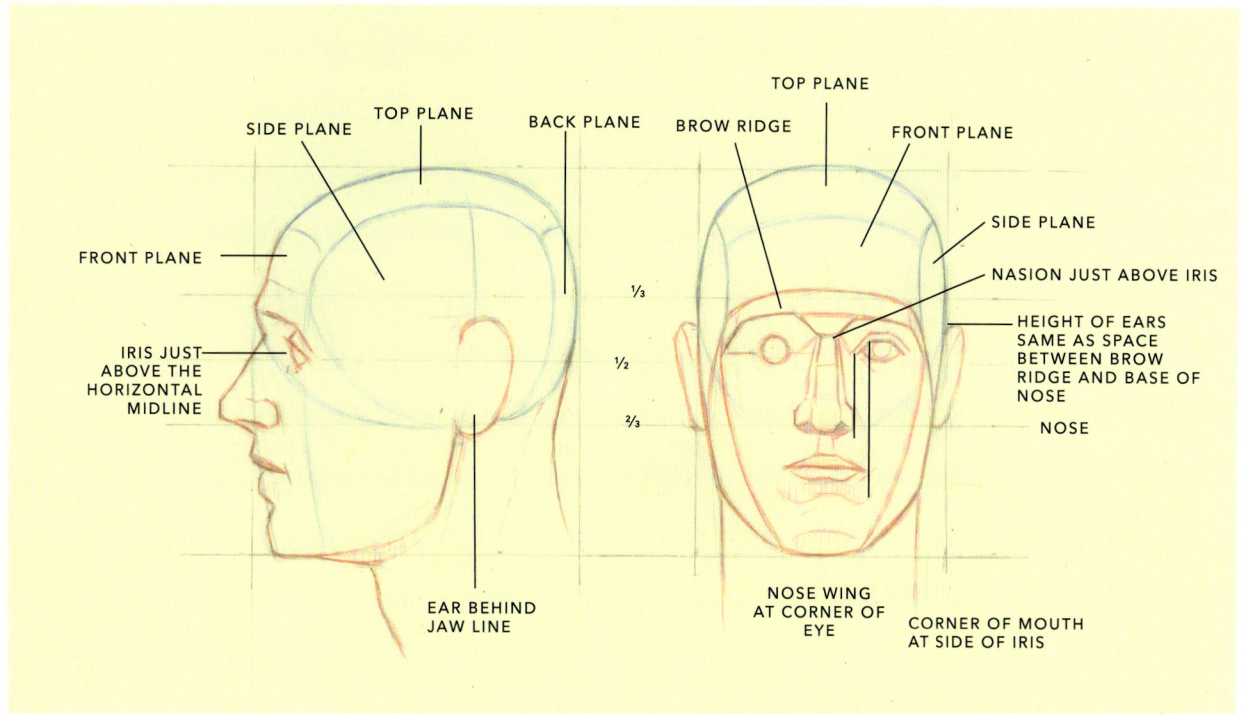

FRONT PLANE

SIDE PLANE TOP PLANE BACK PLANE

TOP PLANE

BROW RIDGE FRONT PLANE

SIDE PLANE

NASION JUST ABOVE IRIS

IRIS JUST ABOVE THE HORIZONTAL MIDLINE

HEIGHT OF EARS SAME AS SPACE BETWEEN BROW RIDGE AND BASE OF NOSE

NOSE

⅓

½

⅔

EAR BEHIND JAW LINE

NOSE WING AT CORNER OF EYE

CORNER OF MOUTH AT SIDE OF IRIS

2

Next, add the main facial features. The brow ridge, starting at the upper third of the measure of the head, defines the top of the face. Block in the nose, which starts a little bit below the brow ridge and ends at the lower third of the height of the head. The jaw line is in line with the ears, and the line of the center of gravity runs between the two. The mouth is between the nose and chin but always closer to the nose; the measure of the ears is equivalent to the space between the brow ridge and the bottom of the nose.

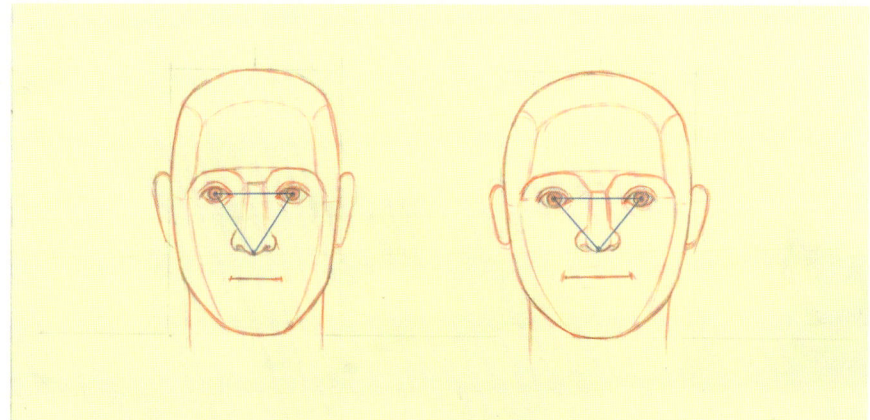

3

When drawing a face, focus first on the essential proportional characteristics of your subject: Is the head rounder or more elongated? Is the nose longer or shorter? Connecting the eyes and nose with a triangle helps you visualize the distance between the eyes and between the eyes and the nose. As a general rule, it is easier to appreciate the measures of the body by using geometric patterns or straight lines rather than organic forms.

THE PARTS OF THE FACE

The two semi-schematic drawings here acquaint you with the various parts of the face and the basic anatomical nomenclature.

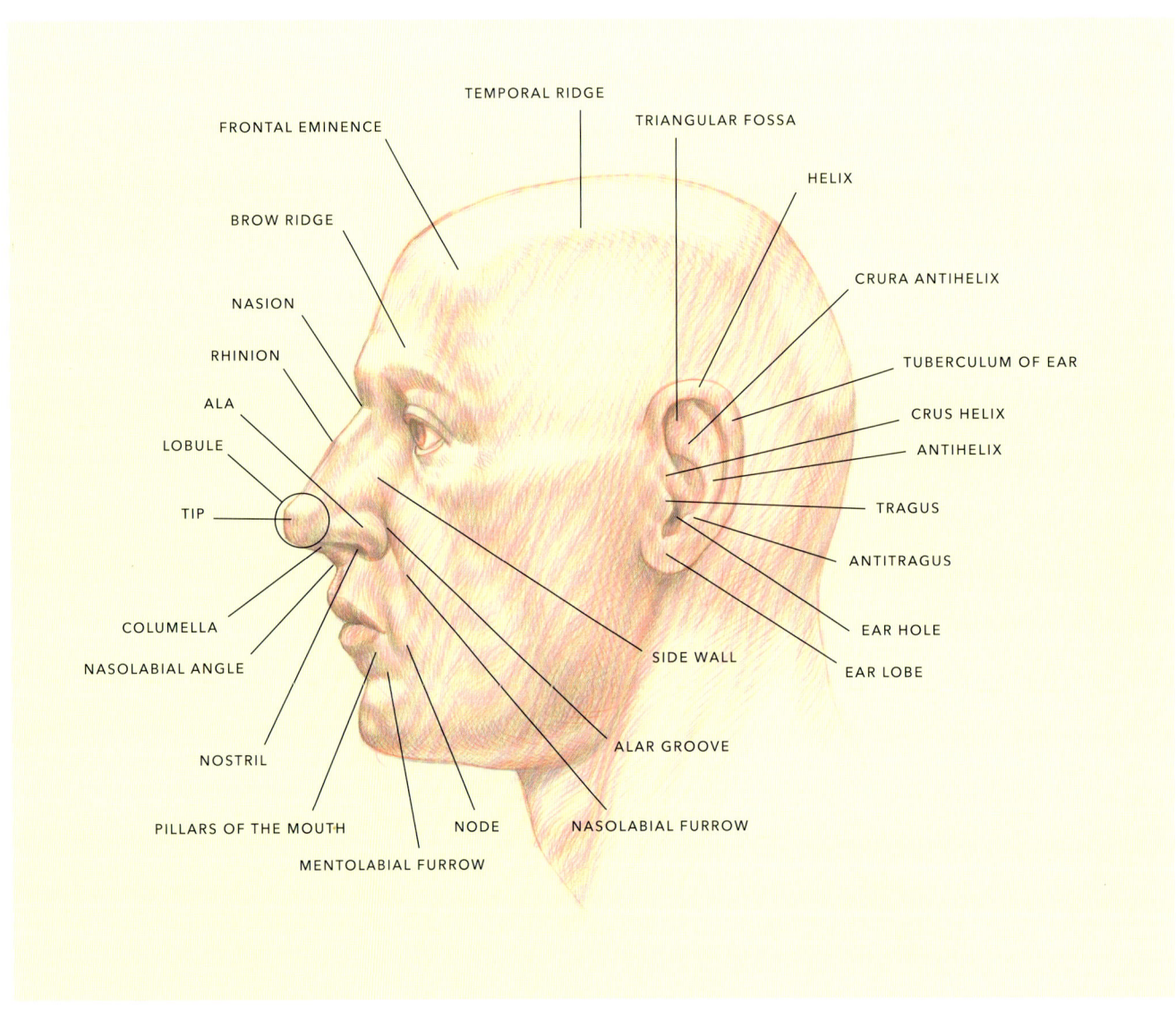

TEMPORAL RIDGE

FRONTAL EMINENCE

TRIANGULAR FOSSA

HELIX

BROW RIDGE

CRURA ANTIHELIX

NASION

TUBERCULUM OF EAR

RHINION

CRUS HELIX

ALA

ANTIHELIX

LOBULE

TRAGUS

TIP

ANTITRAGUS

EAR HOLE

EAR LOBE

COLUMELLA

SIDE WALL

NASOLABIAL ANGLE

NOSTRIL

ALAR GROOVE

PILLARS OF THE MOUTH

NODE

NASOLABIAL FURROW

MENTOLABIAL FURROW

ABOVE: Side view of the face

OPPOSITE: Front view of face

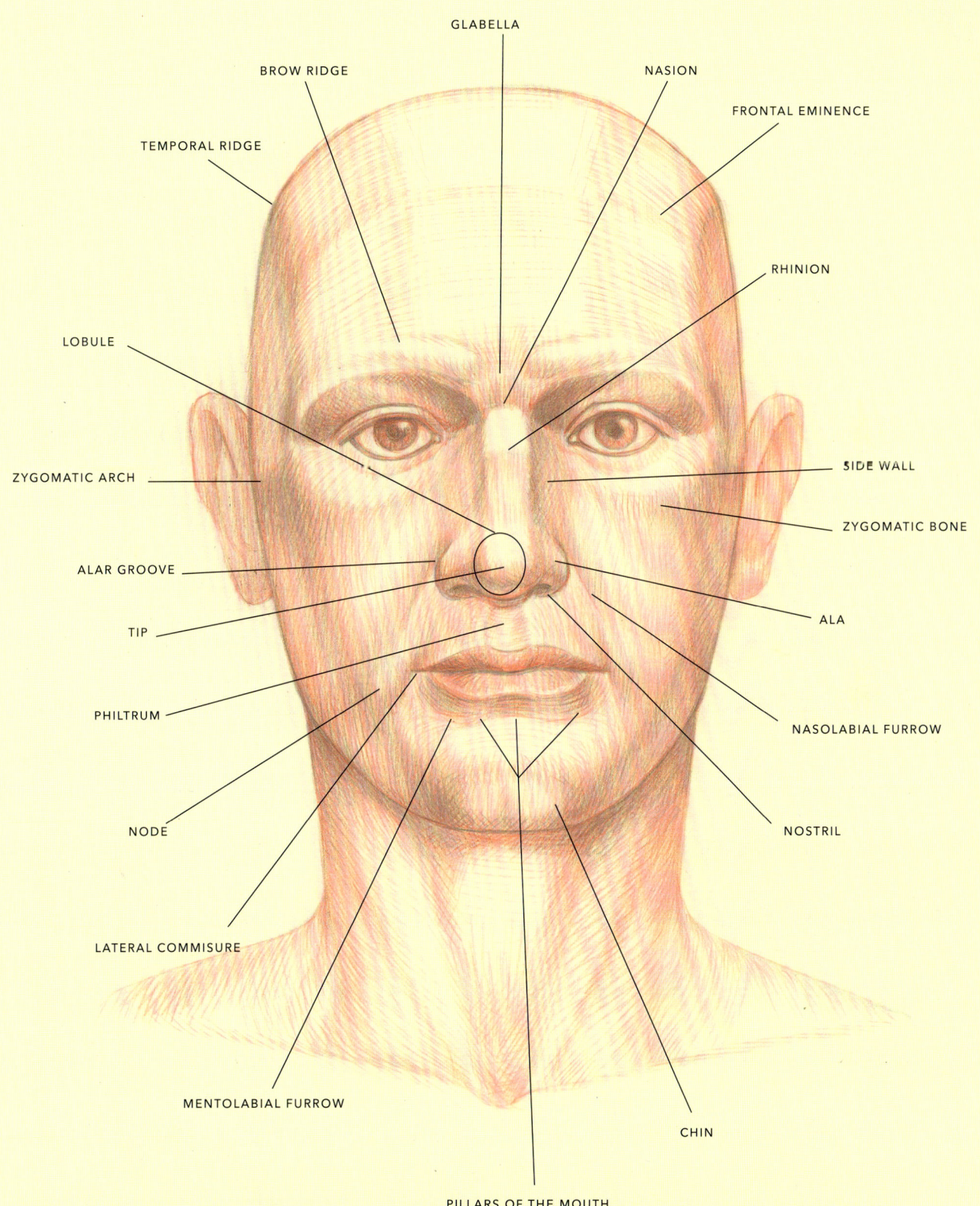

GLABELLA

BROW RIDGE

NASION

FRONTAL EMINENCE

TEMPORAL RIDGE

RHINION

LOBULE

ZYGOMATIC ARCH

SIDE WALL

ZYGOMATIC BONE

ALAR GROOVE

TIP

ALA

PHILTRUM

NASOLABIAL FURROW

NODE

NOSTRIL

LATERAL COMMISURE

MENTOLABIAL FURROW

CHIN

PILLARS OF THE MOUTH

THE PLANES OF THE HEAD

For this demonstration, I used a portrait of Frank, a fantastic model with whom I frequently work. The demonstration is designed to help you to identify the planes of the head and to develop a good idea of its three-dimensional characteristics. The back, or posterior, plane is not included in this view.

1

This finished portrait of Frank serves as the reference image. To practice, you can use any image of a human head—drawing, painting, or photo. Begin by placing a sheet of tracing paper over the image.

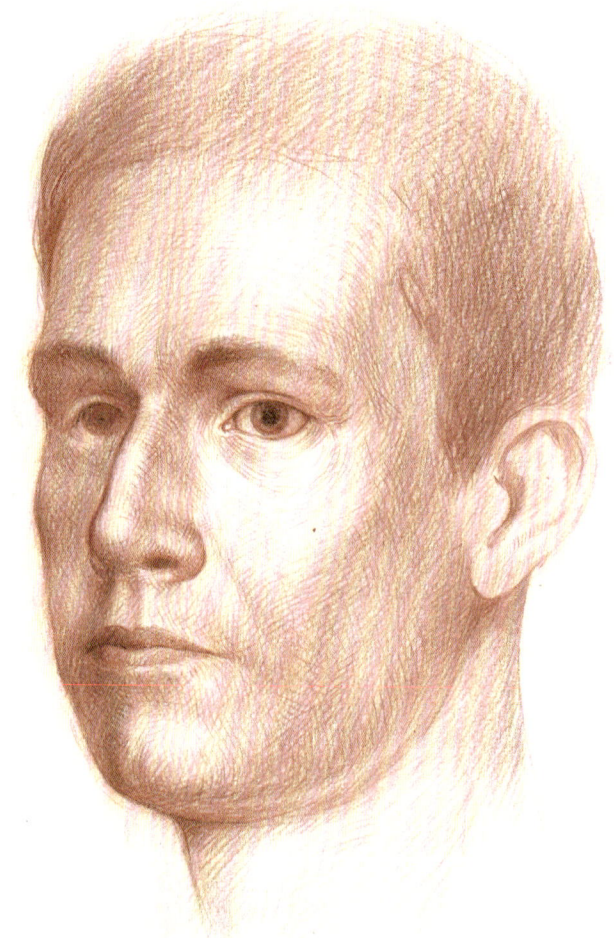

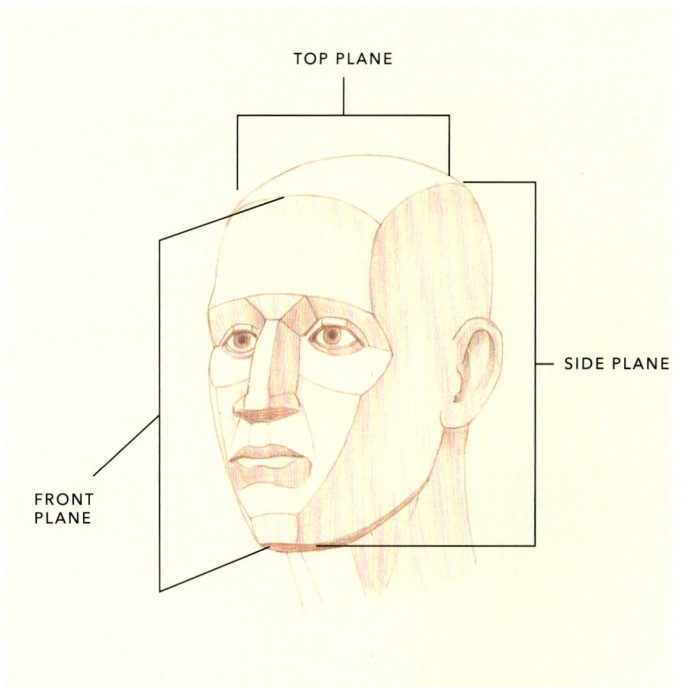

TOP PLANE

SIDE PLANE

FRONT PLANE

2

First, find the main planes, as shown here. You can add some shade to define the planes more clearly.

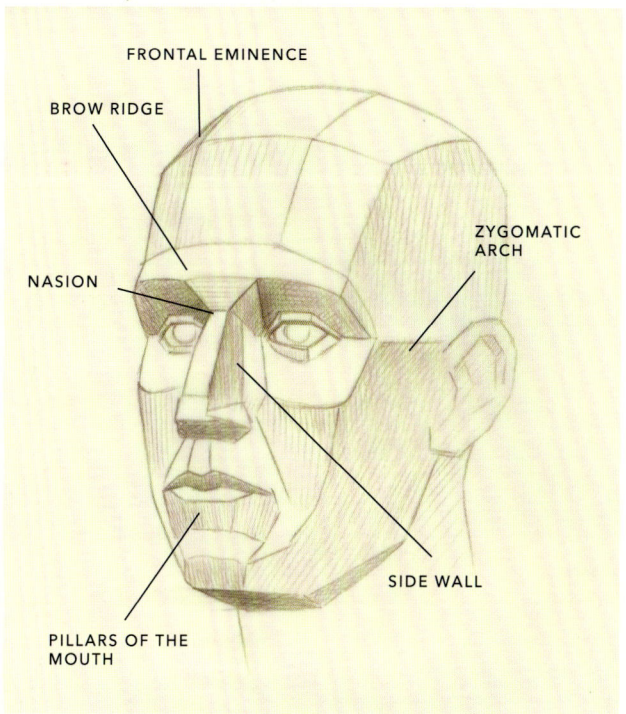

FRONTAL EMINENCE

BROW RIDGE

ZYGOMATIC ARCH

NASION

PILLARS OF THE MOUTH

SIDE WALL

3

Gradually develop the drawing on the tracing paper, subdividing the main planes into smaller and smaller ones.

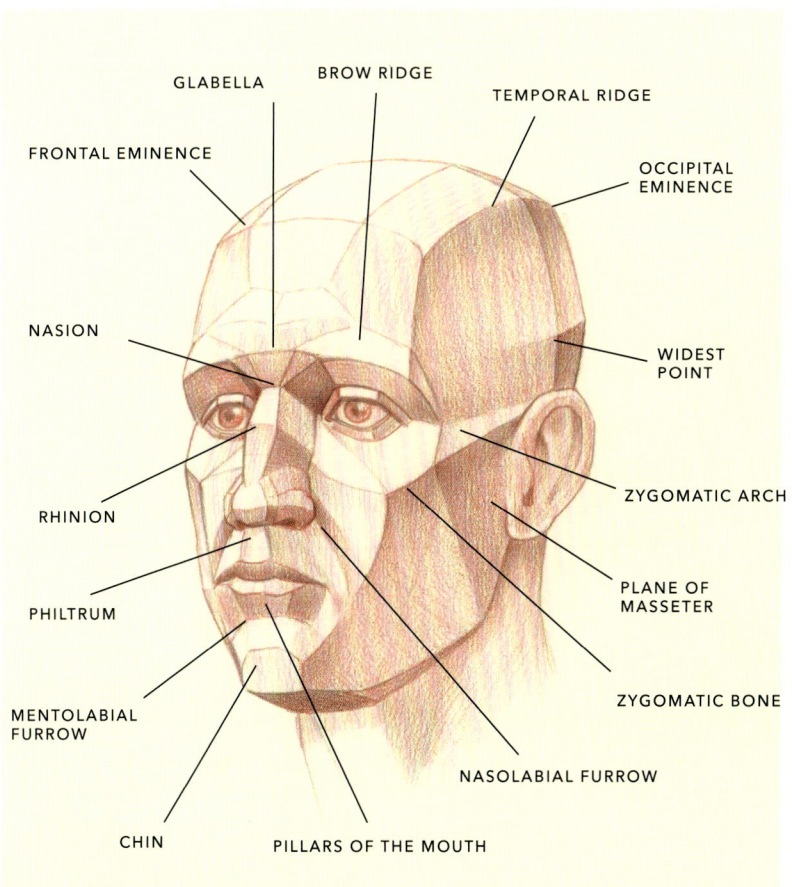

GLABELLA

BROW RIDGE

TEMPORAL RIDGE

FRONTAL EMINENCE

OCCIPITAL EMINENCE

NASION

WIDEST POINT

RHINION

ZYGOMATIC ARCH

PHILTRUM

PLANE OF MASSETER

MENTOLABIAL FURROW

ZYGOMATIC BONE

NASOLABIAL FURROW

CHIN

PILLARS OF THE MOUTH

4

As you draw more and more planes, you'll obtain an increasingly realistic portrait.

PLANES OF THE SKULL

You can utilize the method described in the demonstration on the previous pages to draw the planes of the skull. Start by copying a skull from life or from a photo, then draw the main planes on a sheet of tracing paper laid over the image. Keep finding more and more planes, as you did when drawing the planes of the head.

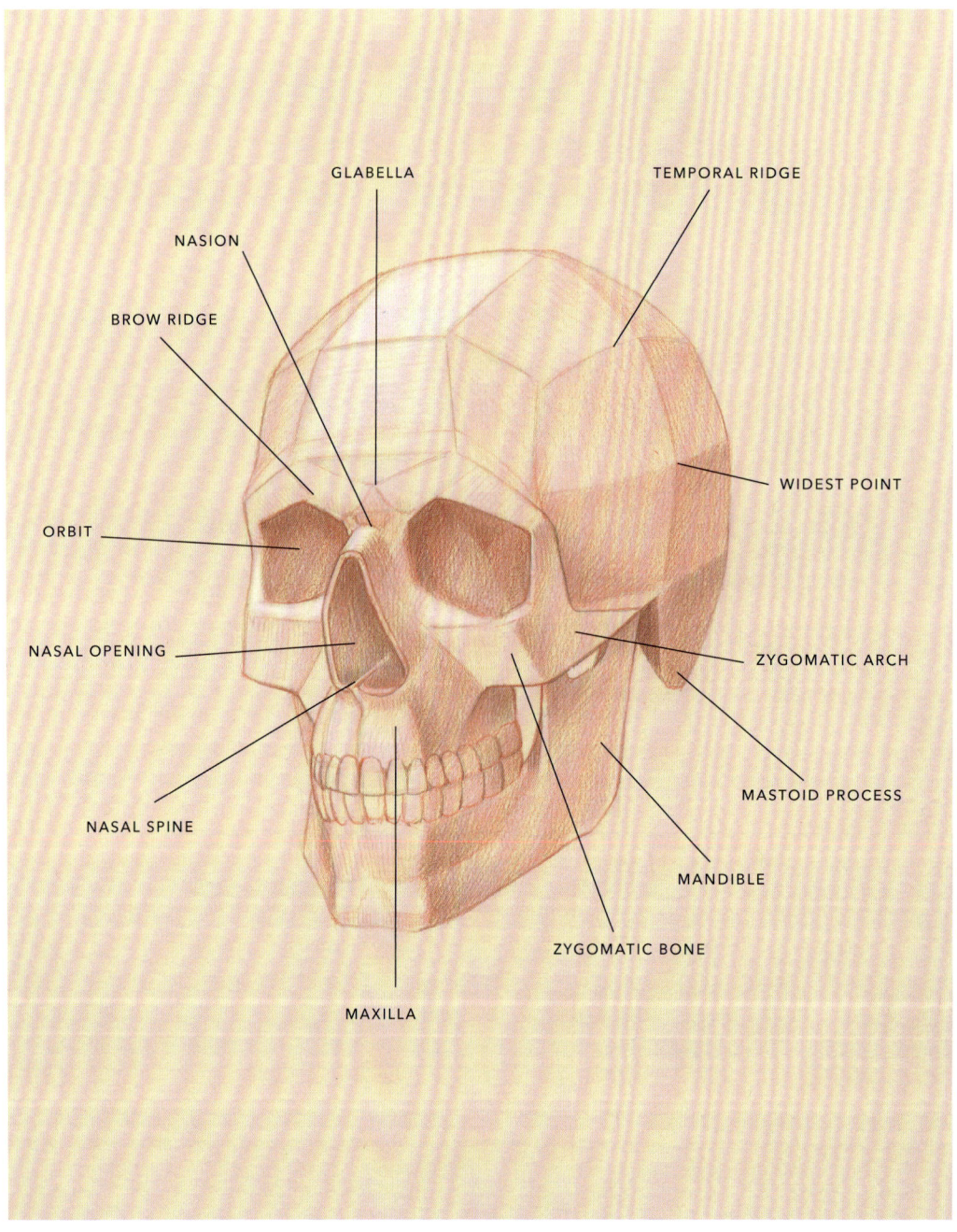

GLABELLA

TEMPORAL RIDGE

NASION

BROW RIDGE

WIDEST POINT

ORBIT

NASAL OPENING

ZYGOMATIC ARCH

MASTOID PROCESS

NASAL SPINE

MANDIBLE

ZYGOMATIC BONE

MAXILLA

FACIAL FEATURES

This section describes the structural and anatomical characteristics of the facial features and introduces you to the basic nomenclature. The role of the features in facial expressions is discussed later in the chapter.

THE EYE

The famous phrase "The eyes are the window to the soul" has been attributed to many sources—the Bible, Leonardo da Vinci, and Shakespeare, to name a few. There are innumerable variations on the proverb, but the meaning is always the same: the eyes are highly revealing of a person's emotions, feelings, and intentions. Exactly because they are so expressive, eyes are notoriously difficult to capture in a drawing or painting. The images here present some of the essential anatomical and structural characteristics of the eye.

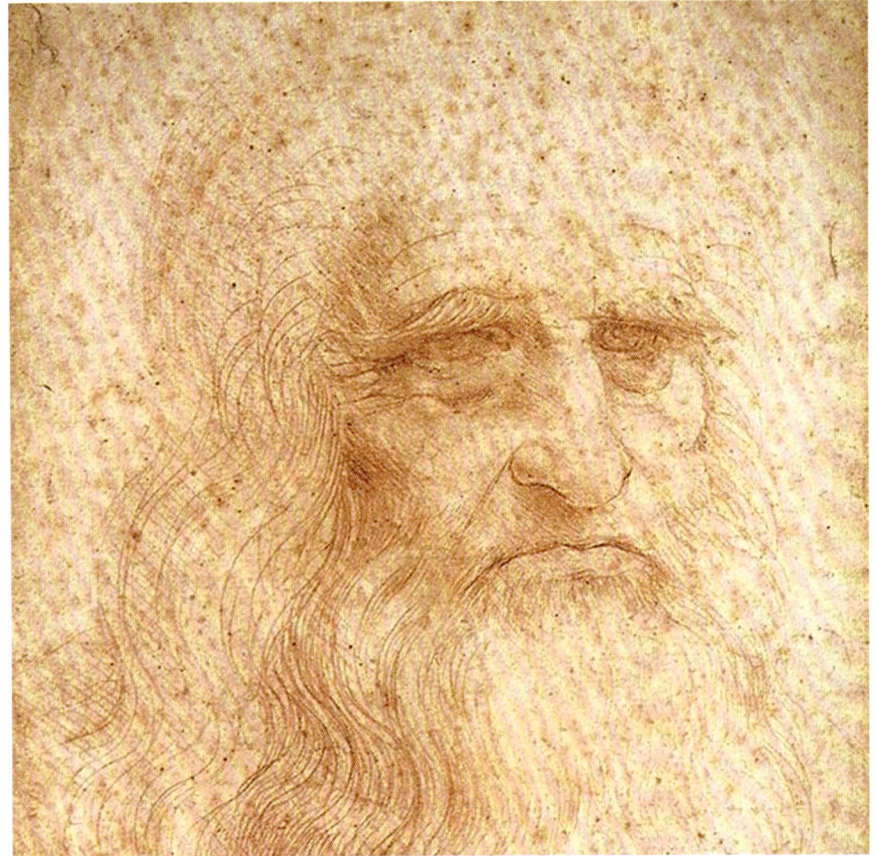

LEFT: Leonardo da Vinci, presumed self-portrait (detail), c. 1512, red chalk on paper, 13⅛ × 8⅜ inches (33.29 × 21.28 cm). Royal Library of Turin.

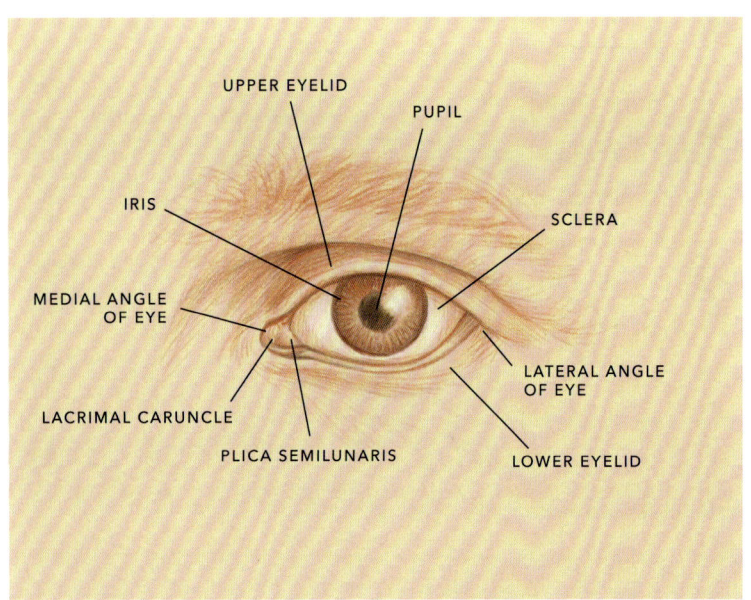

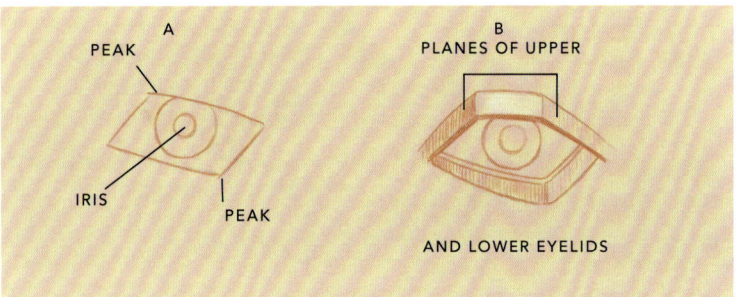

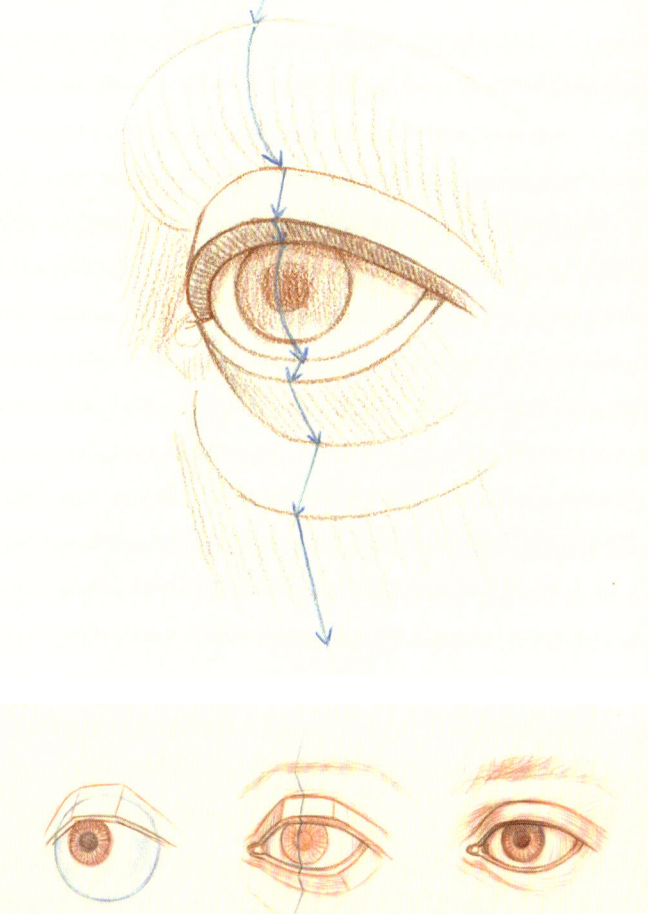

TOP LEFT: The external parts of the eye

BOTTOM LEFT: Structural analysis of the eye

The eyelids are not symmetrical, either as single structures or in relation to each other. The medial margin of the upper eyelid is shorter and steeper than the lateral one while the lateral margin is longer and curves more gradually. The same pattern can be found in the lower eyelid, but reversed (A). The schematic three-dimensional rendering (B) breaks the upper eyelid into three segments and the lower into two. Because these segments have different spatial orientations, they also have different tonal characteristics.

TOP RIGHT: Schematic three-quarters view of the external eye

This image shows more completely the planes that surround the eye: the brow ridge, the eyelids, the curvature of the eye, and the upper margin of the zygomatic bone. This more detailed structural analysis reveals how the various segments of the eyelids wrap around the sphere of the eyeball, producing specific planes to be considered when working on the tonal development of the face.

BOTTOM RIGHT: Drawing the eye in three steps

When drawing the eyelids, consider how they wrap around the spherical volume of the eyeball.

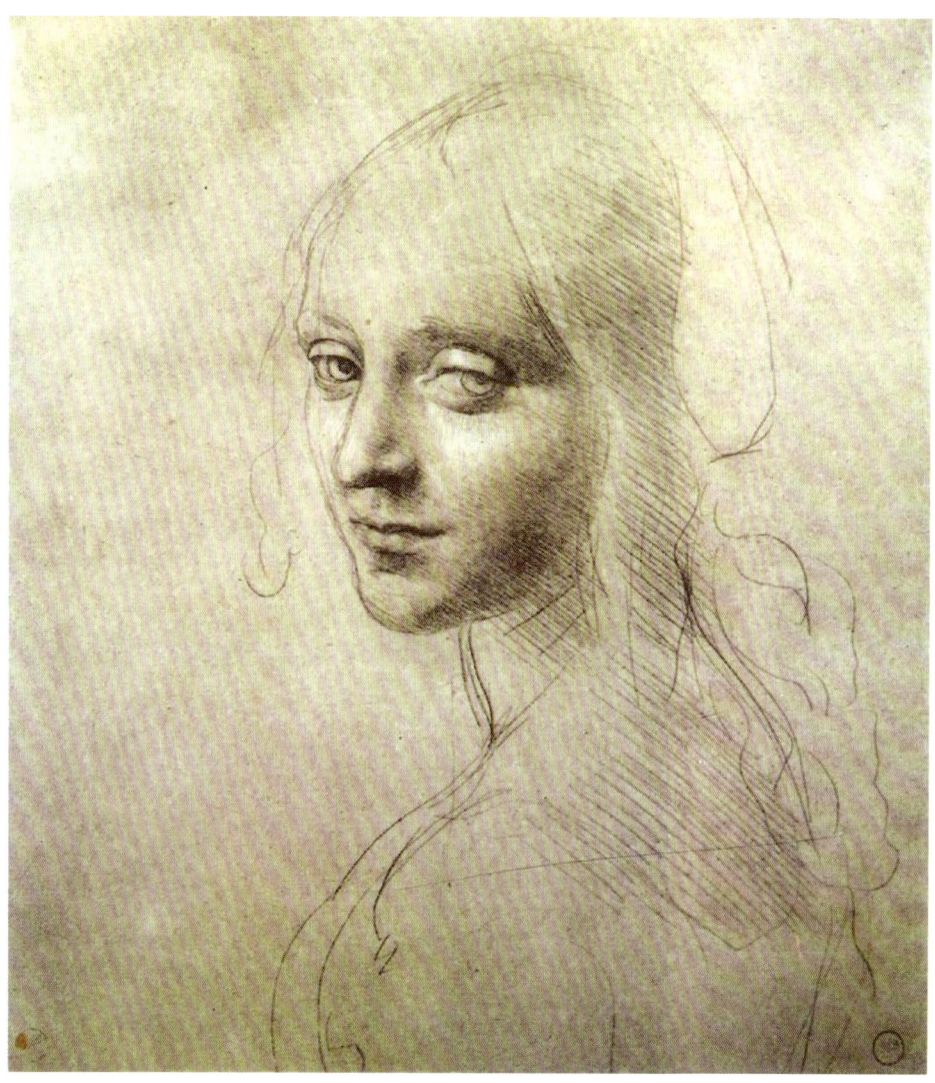

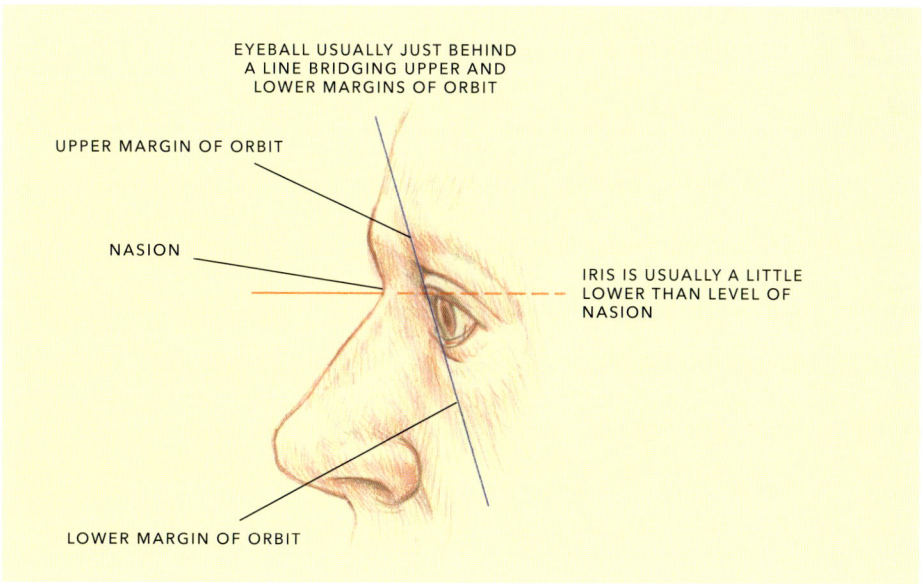

EYEBALL USUALLY JUST BEHIND
A LINE BRIDGING UPPER AND
LOWER MARGINS OF ORBIT

UPPER MARGIN OF ORBIT

NASION

IRIS IS USUALLY A LITTLE
LOWER THAN LEVEL OF
NASION

LOWER MARGIN OF ORBIT

TOP: Leonardo da Vinci, *Head of a Girl* (detail), c. 1483, silverpoint and white highlights on prepared paper, full drawing: 7⅛ × 6¼ inches (18.10 × 15.90 cm). Royal Library of Turin.

This beautiful little sketch by Leonardo shows the importance of understanding the essential structure of the parts of the body. With just a few essential lines, he was able to convey a very convincing and expressive depiction of the eye.

BOTTOM: The eye is usually positioned behind the alignment of the upper and lower margins of the orbits, as shown here by the blue line bridging the two orbital margins. In people of European descent, the iris is below the level of the nasion. In people of other ethnicities, the nasion may be positioned differently in relation to the iris, so you should pay attention to specific physiognomic characteristics of your subject to determine the starting point of the nose.

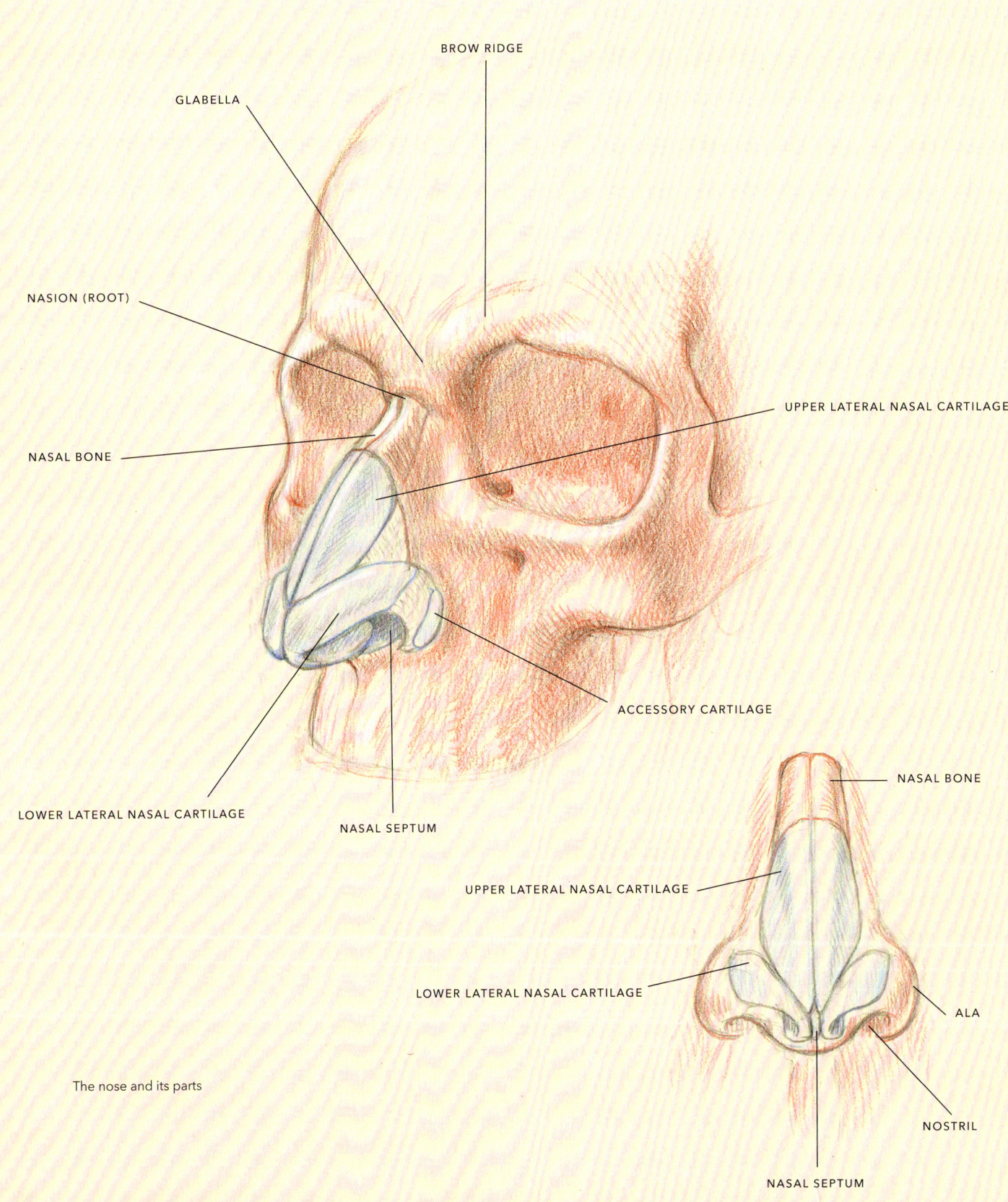

BROW RIDGE

GLABELLA

NASION (ROOT)

NASAL BONE

UPPER LATERAL NASAL CARTILAGE

ACCESSORY CARTILAGE

LOWER LATERAL NASAL CARTILAGE

NASAL SEPTUM

NASAL BONE

UPPER LATERAL NASAL CARTILAGE

LOWER LATERAL NASAL CARTILAGE

ALA

NOSTRIL

NASAL SEPTUM

The nose and its parts

THE NOSE

Noses come in a nearly infinite range of sizes and shapes. Leonardo da Vinci tried to systematize the variety by creating a "classification" of types of noses he observed on his fellow Florentines: noses with a big hump or a small one, pointy or bulbous noses, crooked or straight noses, and so on.

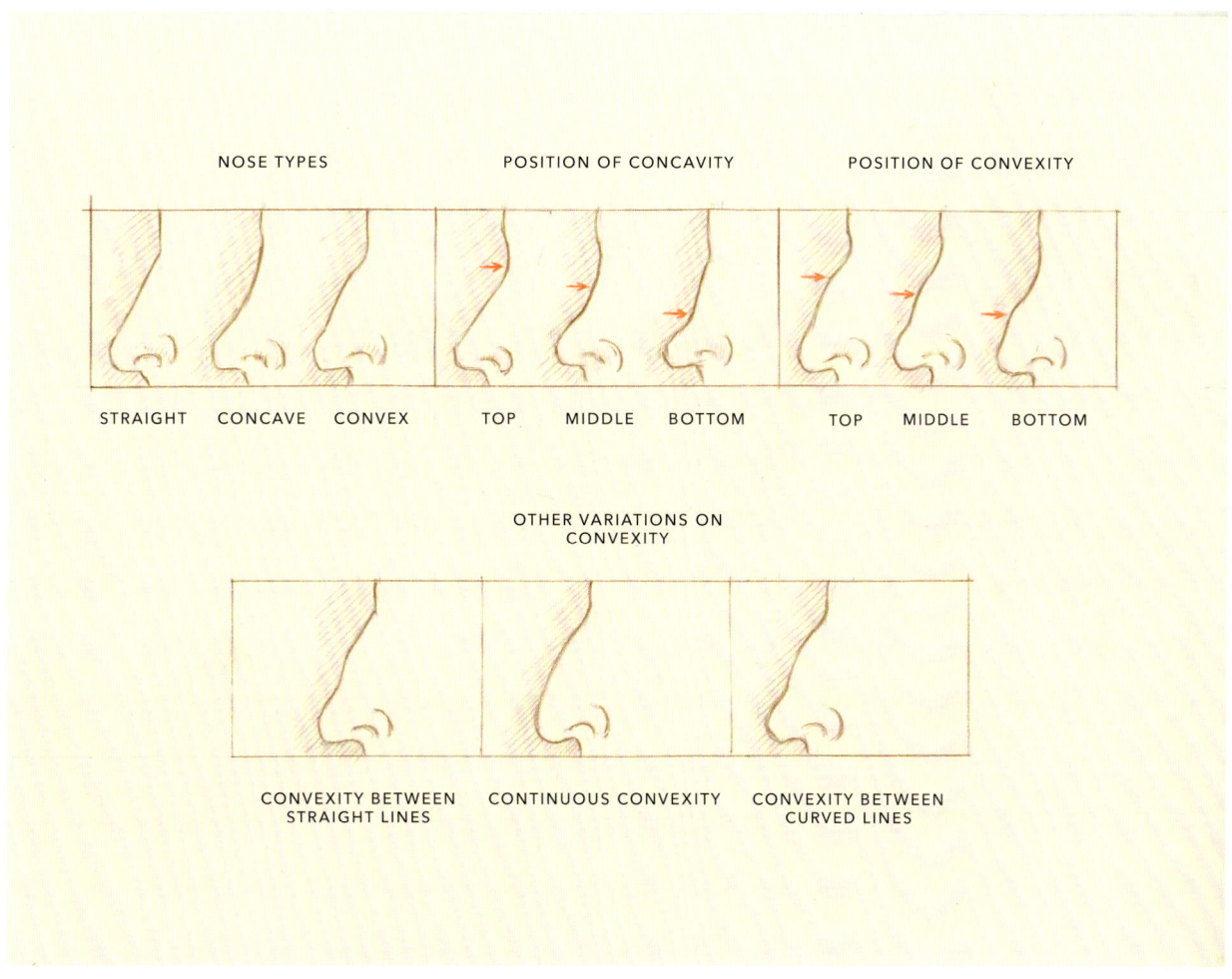

NOSE TYPES

STRAIGHT   CONCAVE   CONVEX

POSITION OF CONCAVITY

TOP   MIDDLE   BOTTOM

POSITION OF CONVEXITY

TOP   MIDDLE   BOTTOM

OTHER VARIATIONS ON CONVEXITY

CONVEXITY BETWEEN STRAIGHT LINES

CONTINUOUS CONVEXITY

CONVEXITY BETWEEN CURVED LINES

ABOVE: Leonardo's noses

This drawing is my copy of a copy of a lost Leonardo manuscript. The sketches reveal Leonardo's methodical analysis and classification.

A fleeting
movement of the
mouth can betray
an emotion

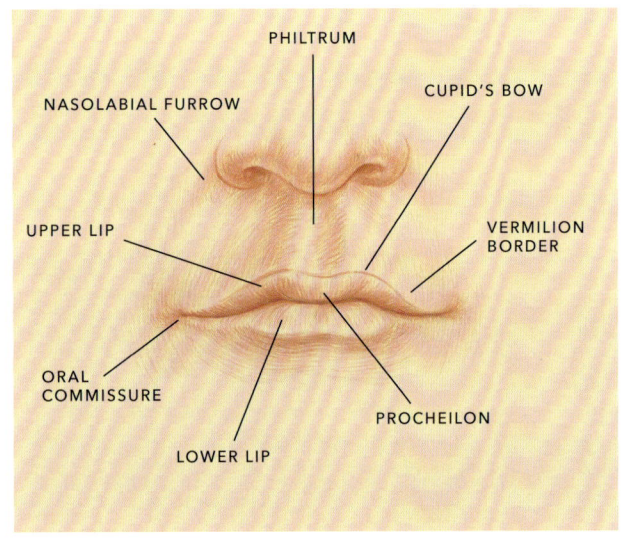

PHILTRUM

CUPID'S BOW

NASOLABIAL FURROW

UPPER LIP

VERMILION
BORDER

ORAL
COMMISSURE

PROCHEILON

LOWER LIP

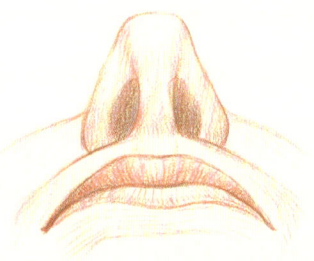

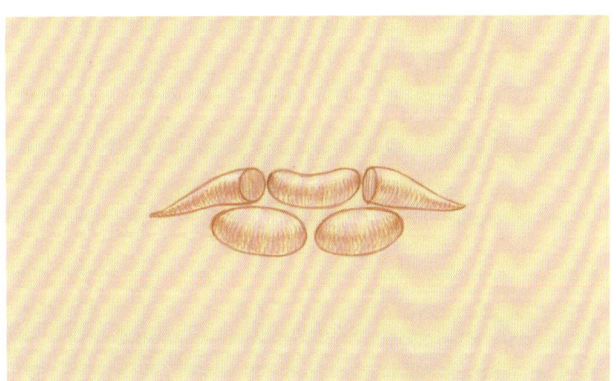

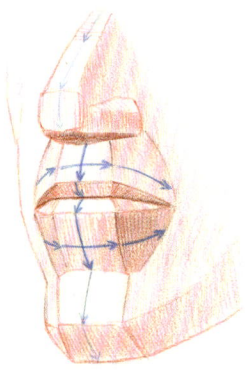

TOP LEFT: The mouth and its parts

BOTTOM LEFT: The volumes of the mouth

The pink portion of the lips can be seen as composed of five segments: at the center of the upper lip is the beanlike form of the procheilon, with two side "horns" directed slightly downward and back; the lower lip has two forms shaped like jelly beans. Thinking of the lips (or any other part of the body) as a set of geometric volumes helps you draw them more accurately and three-dimensionally.

TOP RIGHT: Curvature of the lips, view from below

BOTTOM RIGHT: Planes of the mouth and tonal rendering

Always remember that a change of plane corresponds a change of tone or value.

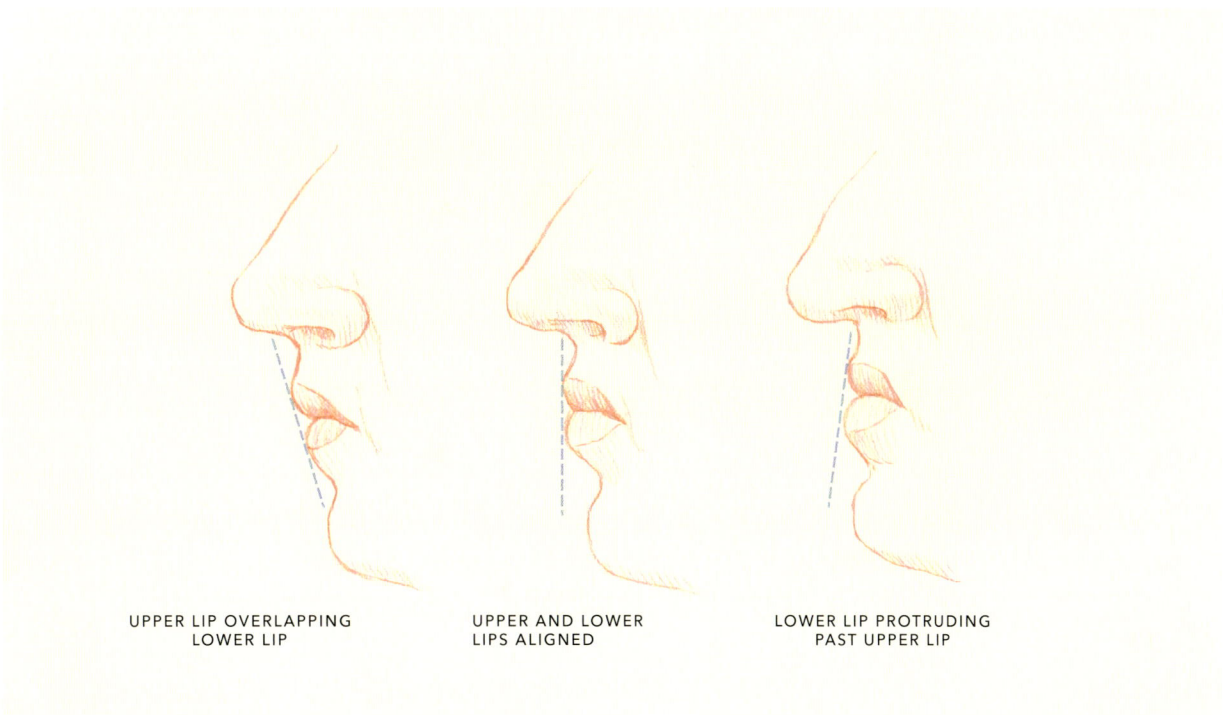

UPPER LIP OVERLAPPING
LOWER LIP

UPPER AND LOWER
LIPS ALIGNED

LOWER LIP PROTRUDING
PAST UPPER LIP

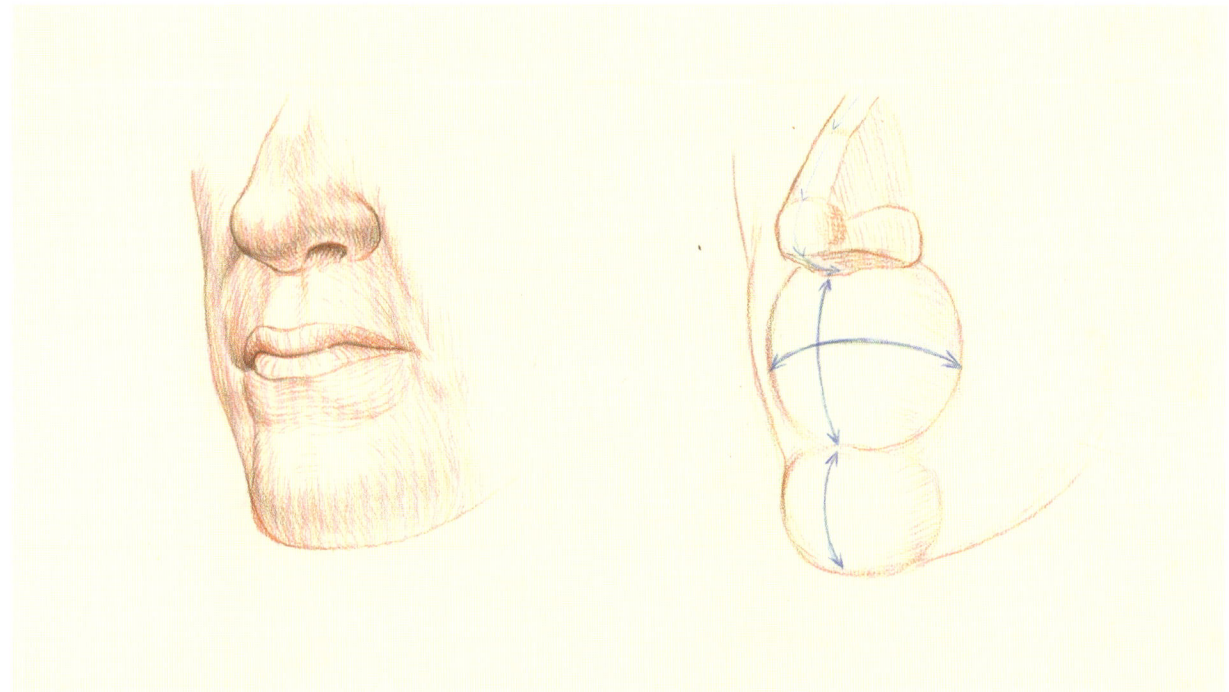

The lips "wrap" over the curved profile of the teeth so that the front of the mouth is farther forward than the corners of the mouth. Vertically, the upper lip is angled slightly upward and the lower lip slightly downward. The analysis is helpful in visualizing the planes of the mouth—an important prerequisite for accurate tonal rendering.

TOP: The mouth in profile

When drawing a profile, pay attention to the distinct physiognomies created by the alignment of the upper and lower lip.

BOTTOM: Curvature of the lips, anterior three-quarters view

THE EAR

Ears can be cute or funny or ugly, but you can't really say that they're expressive. We can barely move them because our ear muscles are pretty much vestigial. But the forms of the ear are very complicated, and a badly drawn ear can ruin an otherwise fine artwork.

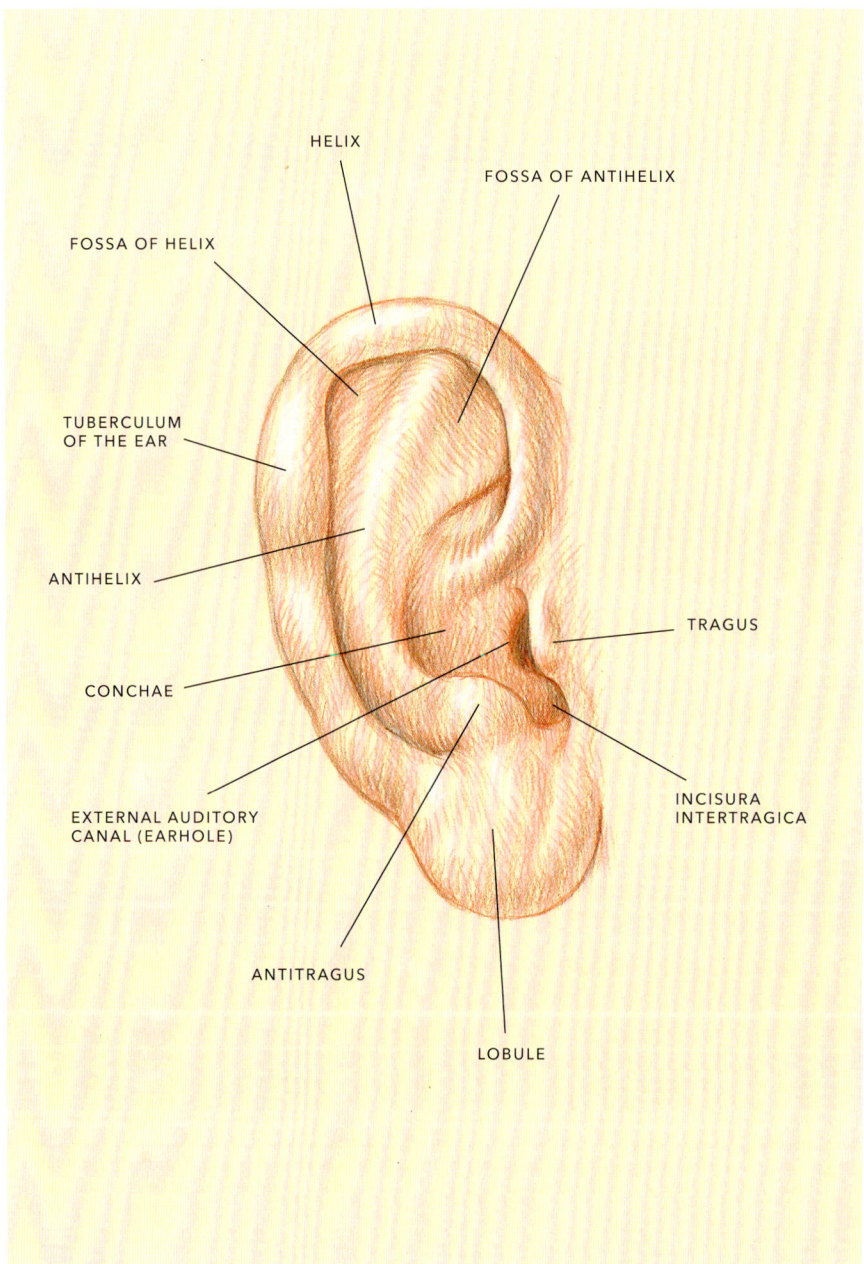

HELIX

FOSSA OF ANTIHELIX

FOSSA OF HELIX

TUBERCULUM
OF THE EAR

ANTIHELIX

TRAGUS

CONCHAE

EXTERNAL AUDITORY
CANAL (EARHOLE)

INCISURA
INTERTRAGICA

ANTITRAGUS

LOBULE

THE CURVATURES OF THE FACE

The view of the face from below, as seen here, shows its many curvatures and how the forehead, the nose, the alignment of the eyes, the zygomatic bones, the lips, and the chin all have specific radiuses. Consider this structural aspect of the face to achieve better volumetric effects and more accurate tonal rendering

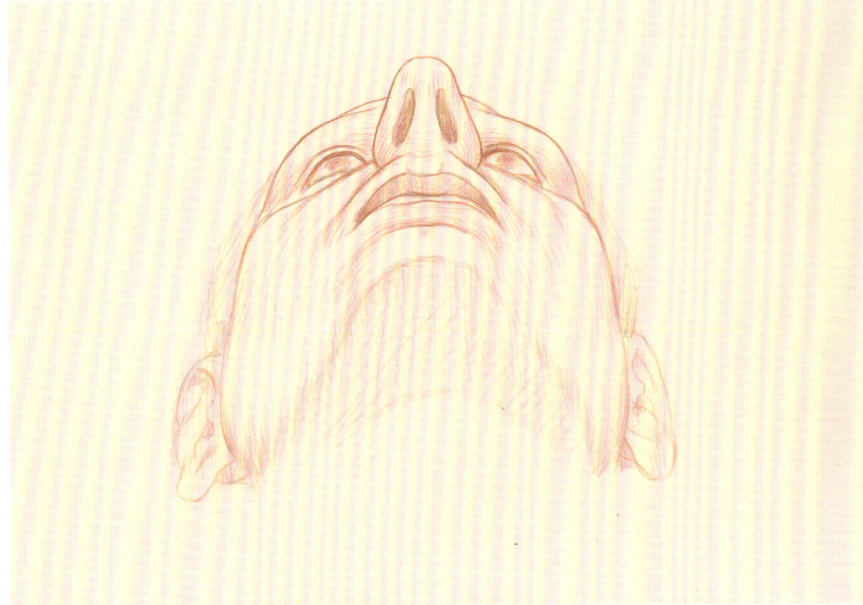

LEFT: Curvatures of the face, seen from below

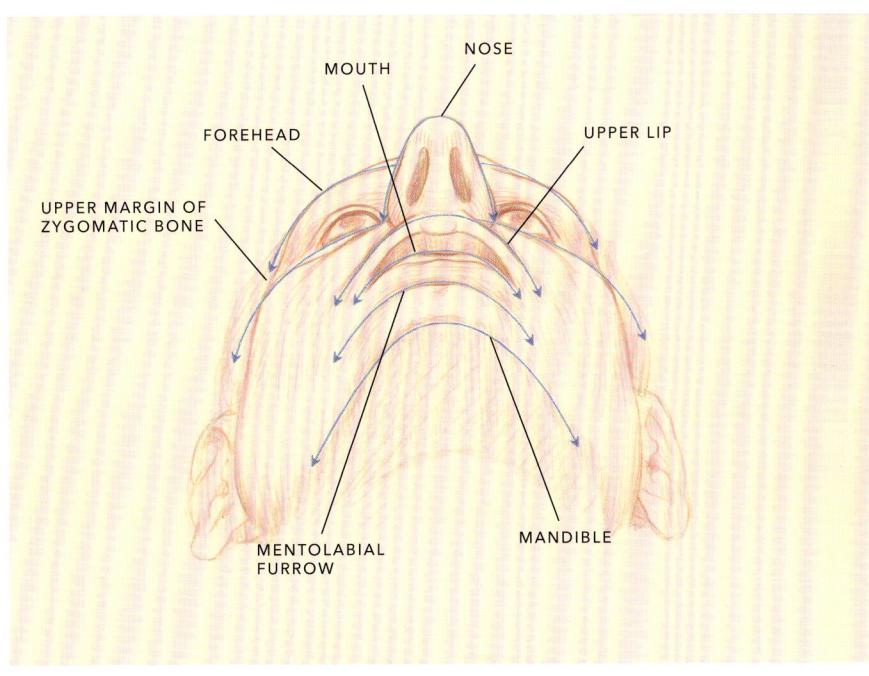

MOUTH

NOSE

FOREHEAD

UPPER LIP

UPPER MARGIN OF
ZYGOMATIC BONE

MENTOLABIAL
FURROW

MANDIBLE

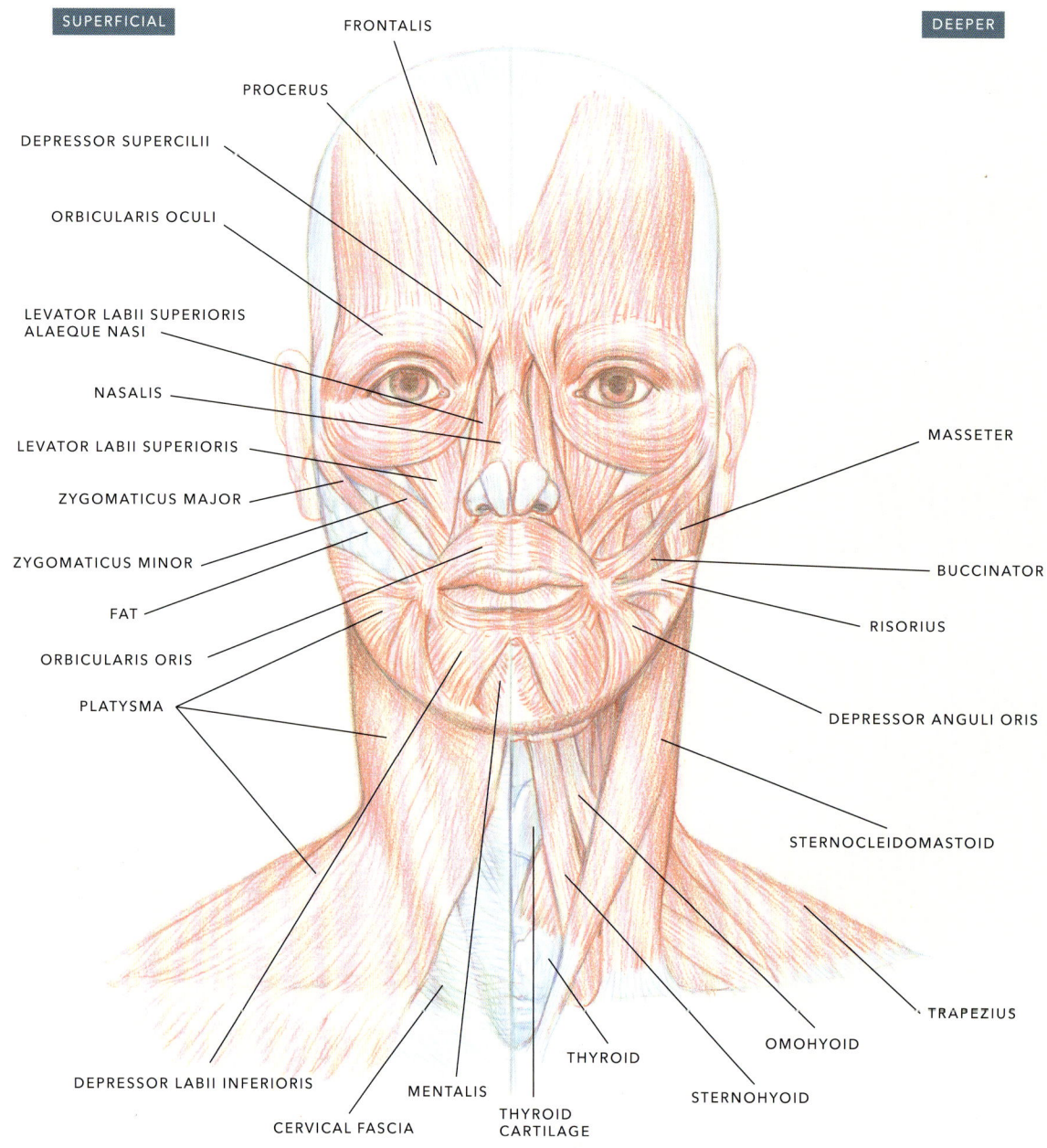

FRONTALIS

PROCERUS

DEPRESSOR SUPERCILII

ORBICULARIS OCULI

LEVATOR LABII SUPERIORIS
ALAEQUE NASI

NASALIS

LEVATOR LABII SUPERIORIS

ZYGOMATICUS MAJOR

ZYGOMATICUS MINOR

FAT

ORBICULARIS ORIS

PLATYSMA

MASSETER

BUCCINATOR

RISORIUS

DEPRESSOR ANGULI ORIS

STERNOCLEIDOMASTOID

TRAPEZIUS

DEPRESSOR LABII INFERIORIS

CERVICAL FASCIA

MENTALIS

THYROID
CARTILAGE

THYROID

STERNOHYOID

OMOHYOID

ABOVE: Muscles of the face—two layers

This chart shows two muscle layers: On the left is the most superficial layer, including the platysma muscle as well as the fat that fills in the cheeks and hides some of the deeper muscles. On the right side of the diagram, the platysma muscle has been removed to show the underlying muscles.

THE MUSCLES OF THE FACE

To better understand facial expressions, you need to become acquainted with the muscles that produce them. The two charts here depict the layers of muscles of the face.

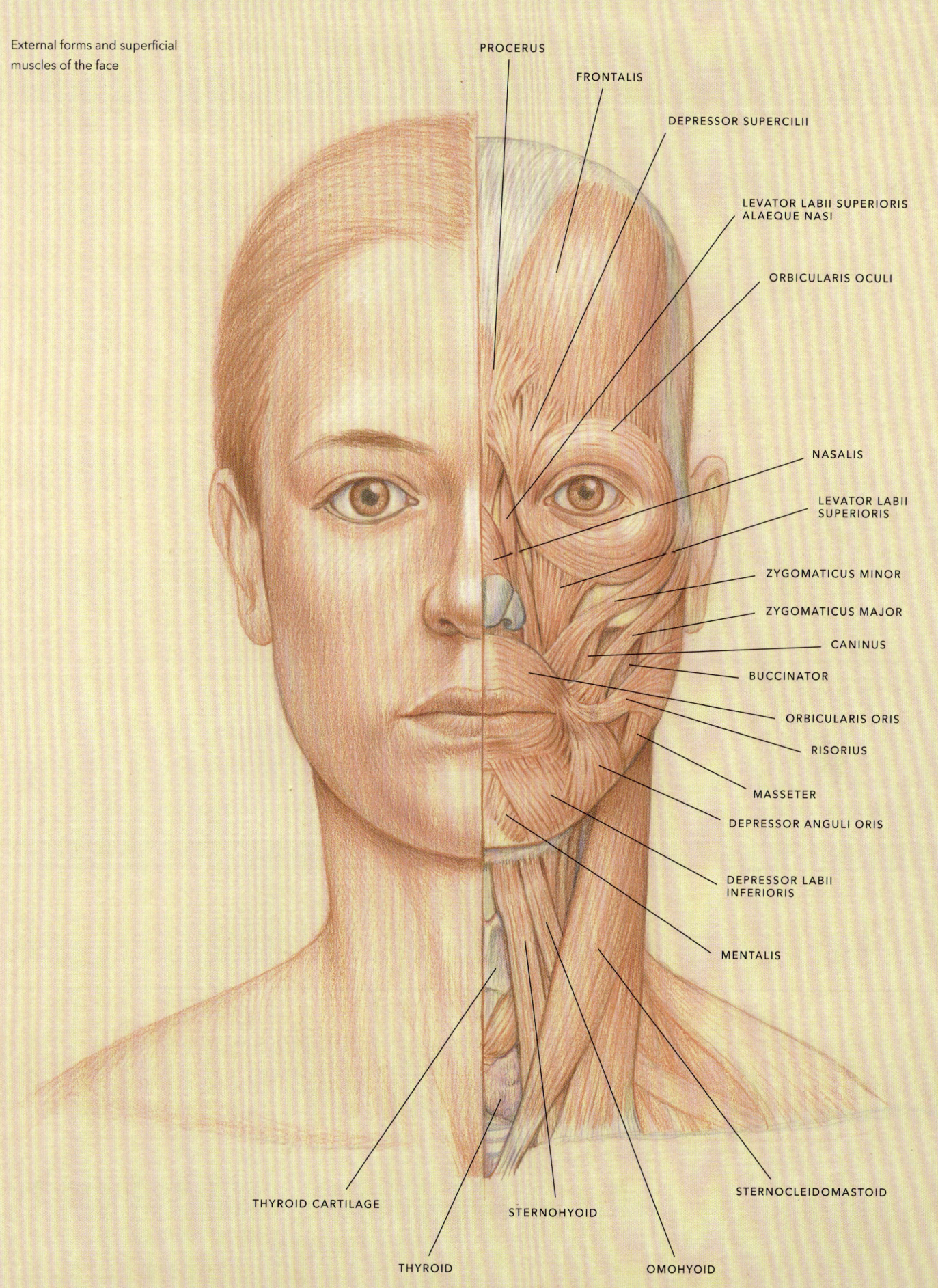

External forms and superficial
muscles of the face

PROCERUS

FRONTALIS

DEPRESSOR SUPERCILII

LEVATOR LABII SUPERIORIS
ALAEQUE NASI

ORBICULARIS OCULI

NASALIS

LEVATOR LABII
SUPERIORIS

ZYGOMATICUS MINOR

ZYGOMATICUS MAJOR

CANINUS

BUCCINATOR

ORBICULARIS ORIS

RISORIUS

MASSETER

DEPRESSOR ANGULI ORIS

DEPRESSOR LABII
INFERIORIS

MENTALIS

STERNOCLEIDOMASTOID

THYROID CARTILAGE

STERNOHYOID

THYROID

OMOHYOID

FACIAL EXPRESSIONS

As social animals, we use facial expressions to communicate an incredibly wide range of emotions, feelings, intentions, and shades of meaning. For example, we can express genuine emotions or fake them; we can demonstrate real happiness or pretend to be happy; we can be sarcastically happy or ironically sad. This detailed exploration of components of the head, facial proportions, facial features, and facial muscles will, I hope, make the following discussion of the complexity of facial expressions easier to grasp.

EXPRESSIONS OF THE EYES

Even a barely perceptible movement of the eyes and eyelids can reveal a great deal about a person's thoughts or mood. How many times, for example, have you seen the eyelids of someone you're talking with drop slightly for just a millisecond—indicating boredom during a conversation *you* thought was incredibly fascinating and engaging! The images here show how miniscule movements of the eyelids can make a big difference in facial expression.

RIGHT: Gustave Courbet, *The Desperate Man*, 1843–45, oil on canvas, 17¾ × 21¼ inches (45 × 54 cm). Private collection.

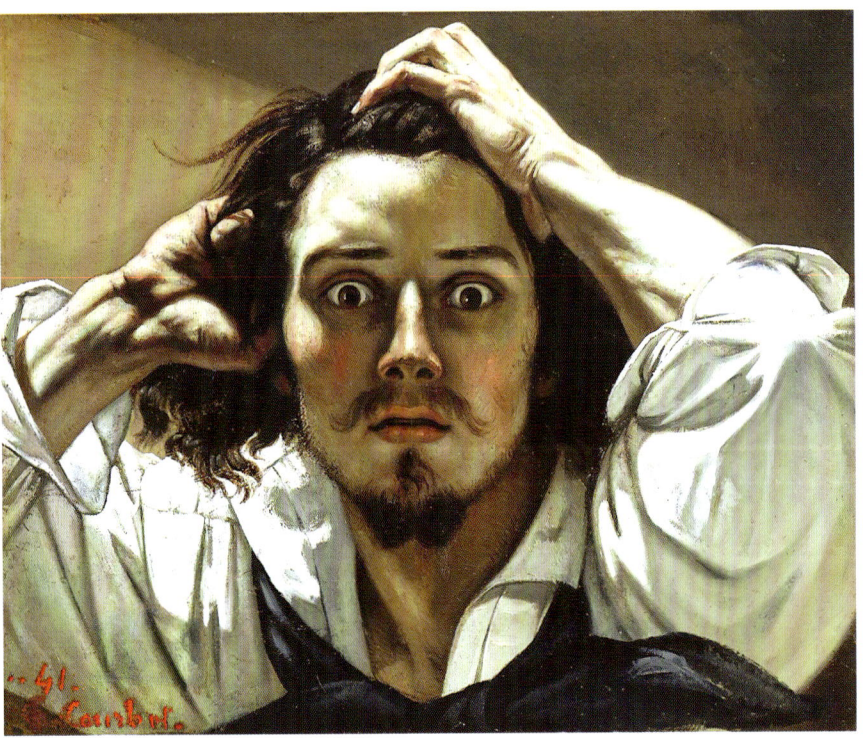

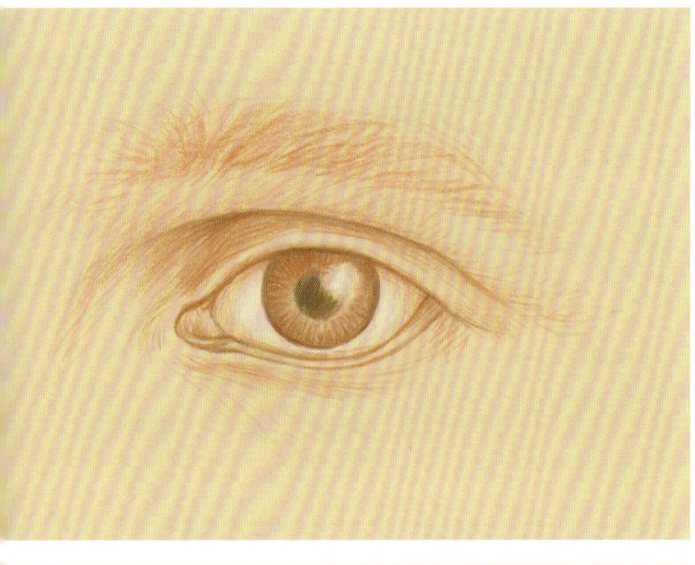

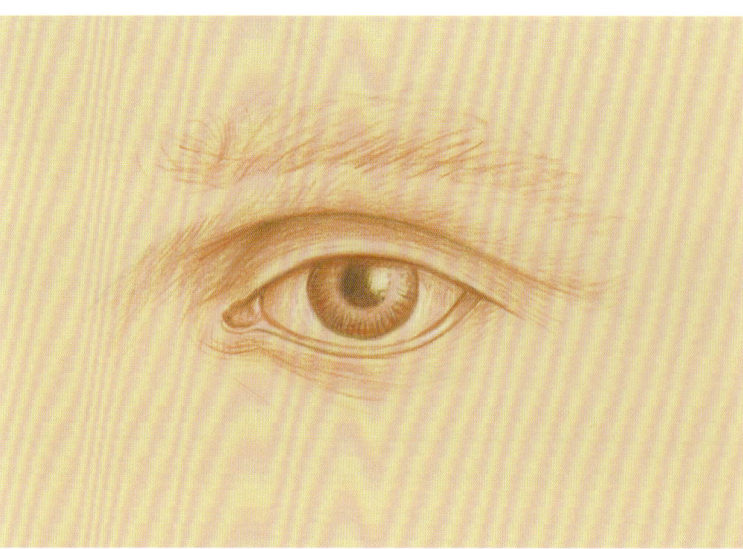

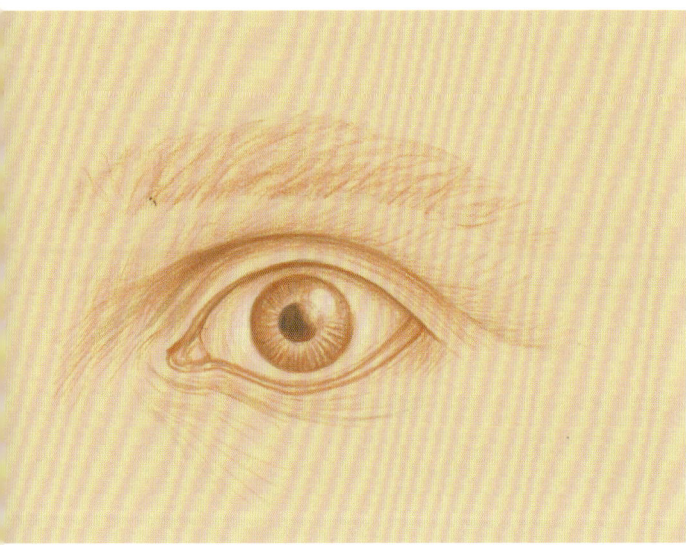

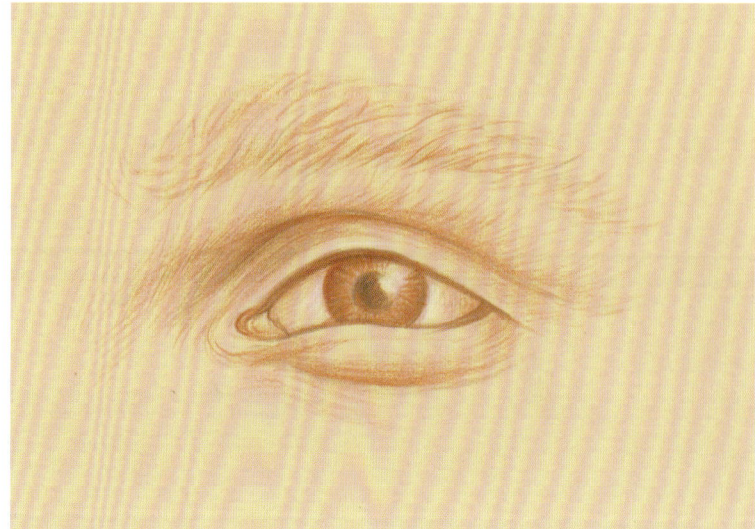

TOP LEFT: A normal, relaxed expression

The iris is barely covered by the upper eyelid, and the sclera is barely visible below the iris.

BOTTOM LEFT: Alert!

In an alert eye, the eyelid is lifted and the sclera is visible above and below the iris.

TOP RIGHT: Tired or bored

When the iris is just a little bit more covered by the eyelid, the eye conveys a tired, bored, or sleepy look.

BOTTOM RIGHT: "Squinty" eye

The "squinty" eye, in which the lower eyelid covers the lower margin of the iris, can accompany a smile—but it can also indicate disgust or even rage.

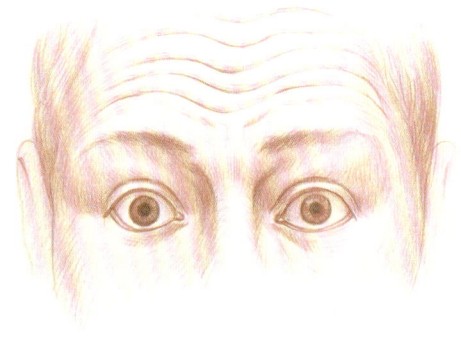

A

FRONTALIS LIFTS SKIN OF FOREHEAD (AND
INCIDENTALLY THE EYELIDS), CREATING AN
ALERT EXPRESSION

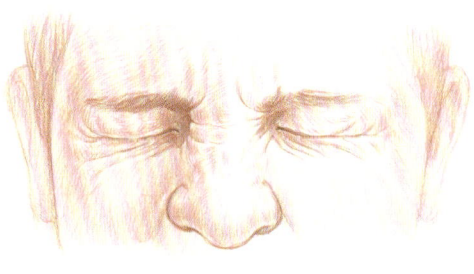

B

CONCENTRIC FIBERS OF ORBICULARIS OCULI
SHUT EYES TIGHT

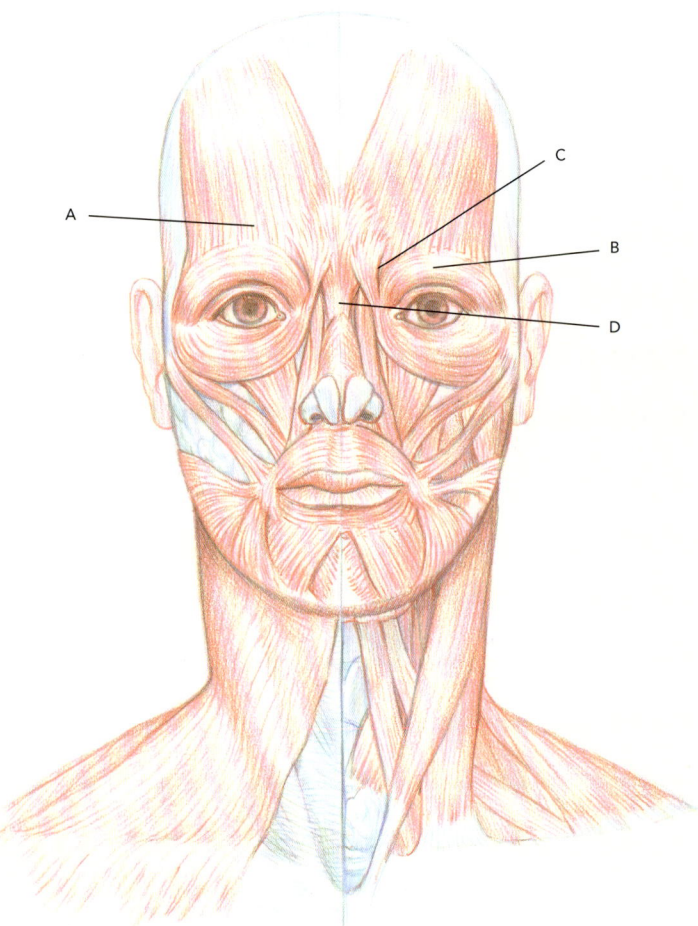

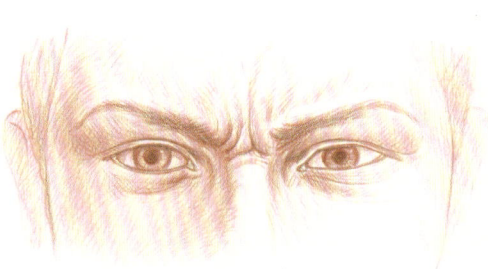

C–D

PROCERUS AND DEPRESSOR SUPERCILII ARE
RESPONSIBLE FOR THIS UPSET OR ANGRY
EXPRESSION

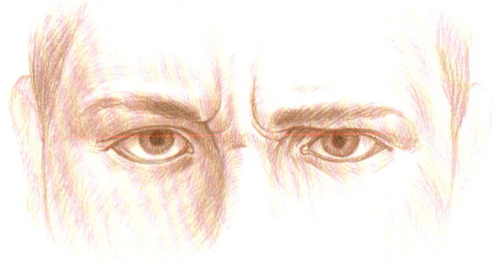

D

DEPRESSOR SUPERCILII BRINGS DOWN
EYEBROWS, PRODUCING A SERIOUS,
DISAPPROVING, OR UPSET LOOK

Actions of muscles surrounding the eyes and their effects

The muscles around the eyes—the orbicularis oculi, frontalis, procerus, and depressor supercilii—are responsible for the expressions illustrated here. The deeper
corrugator muscle, also involved in some of these expressions, is discussed later.

EXPRESSIONS OF THE MOUTH

Many more muscles are responsible for the movements of the mouth than for the eyes' movements. The charts on the following pages show the effect that single muscles have on the mouth.

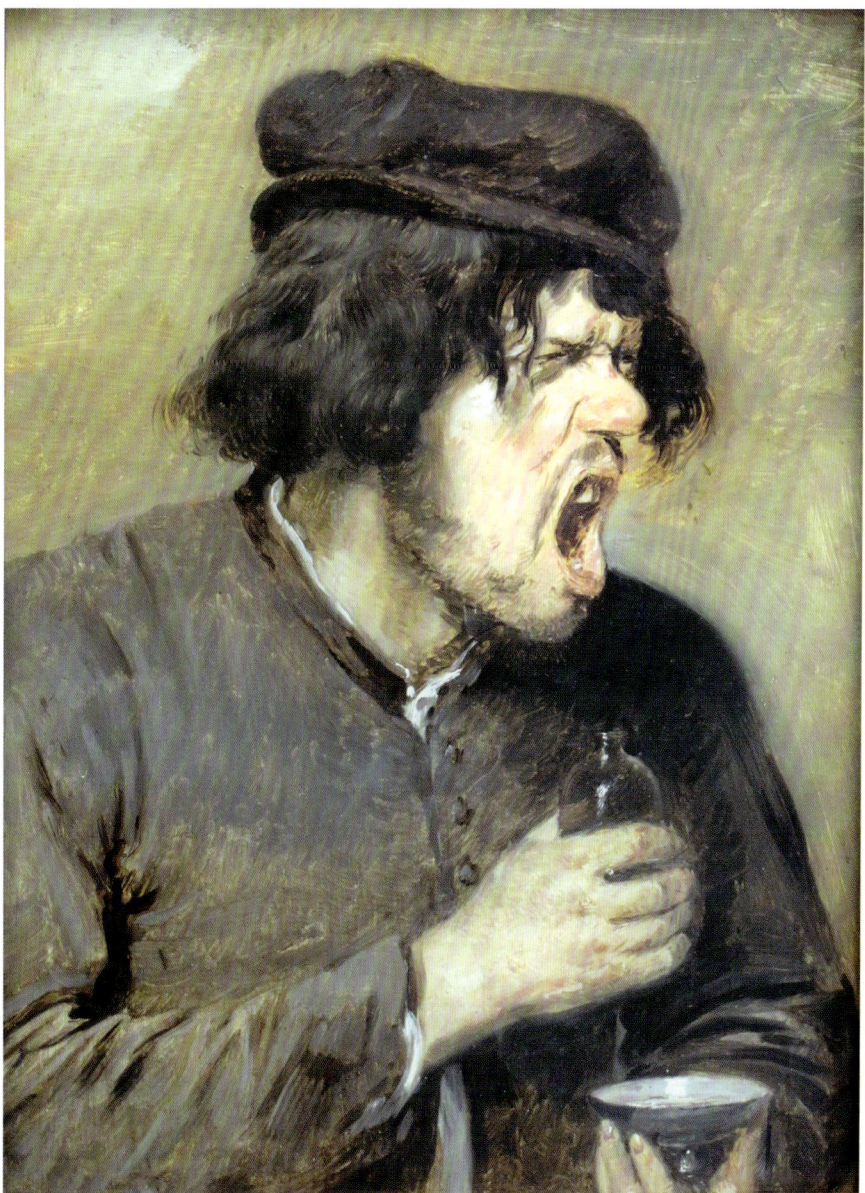

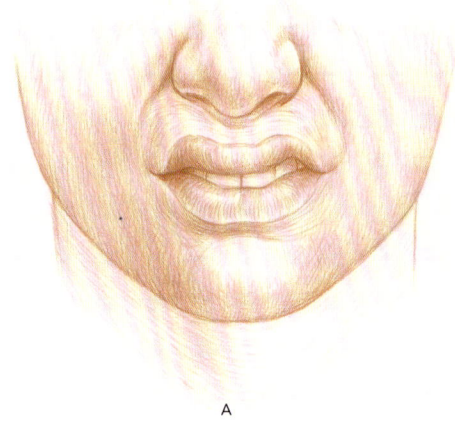

A

LEVATOR LABII SUPERIORIS LIFTS UPPER
LIPS IN DISGUST OR CONTEMPT

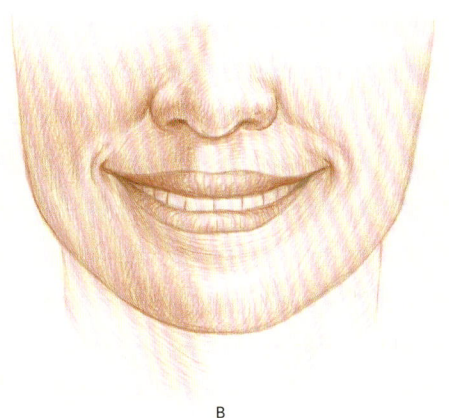

B

ZYGOMATICUS MAJOR WIDENS
THE LIPS IN A SMILE

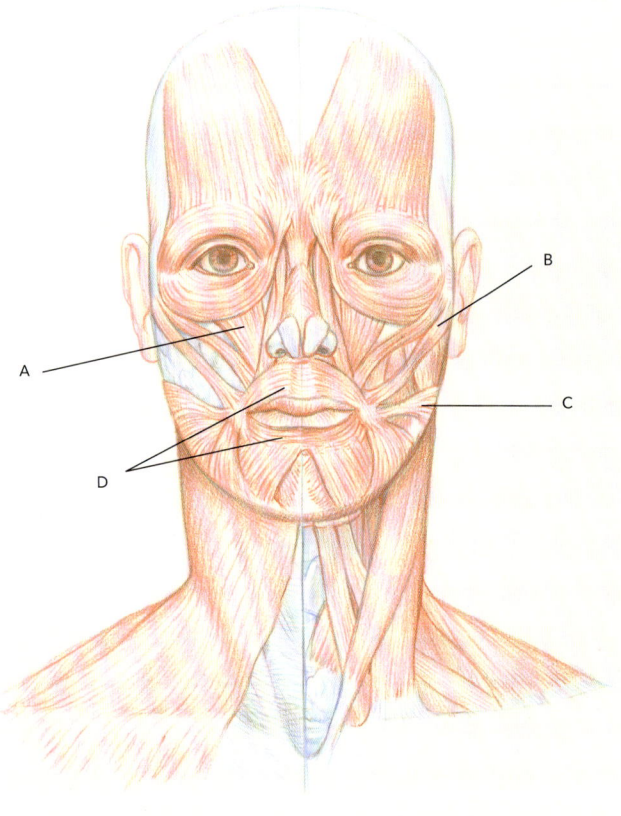

Actions of muscles of the mouth and their effects, part 1

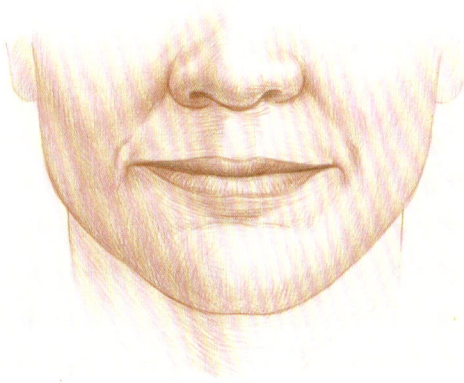

C

RISORIUS PULLS THE CORNERS OF THE
MOUTH INTO A HORIZONTAL SMILE

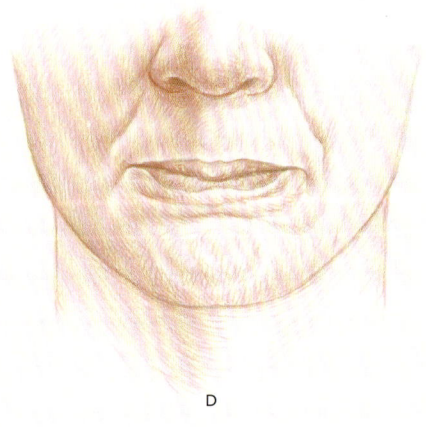

D

ORBICULARIS ORIS SHUTS THE LIPS TIGHT

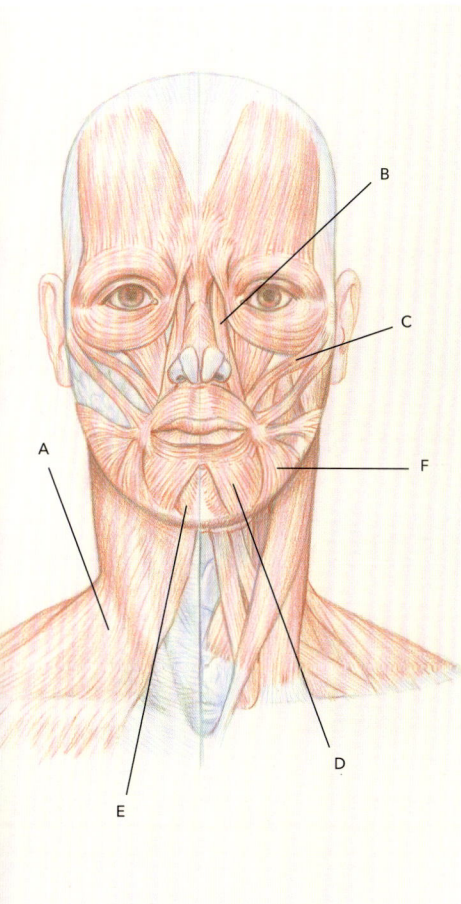

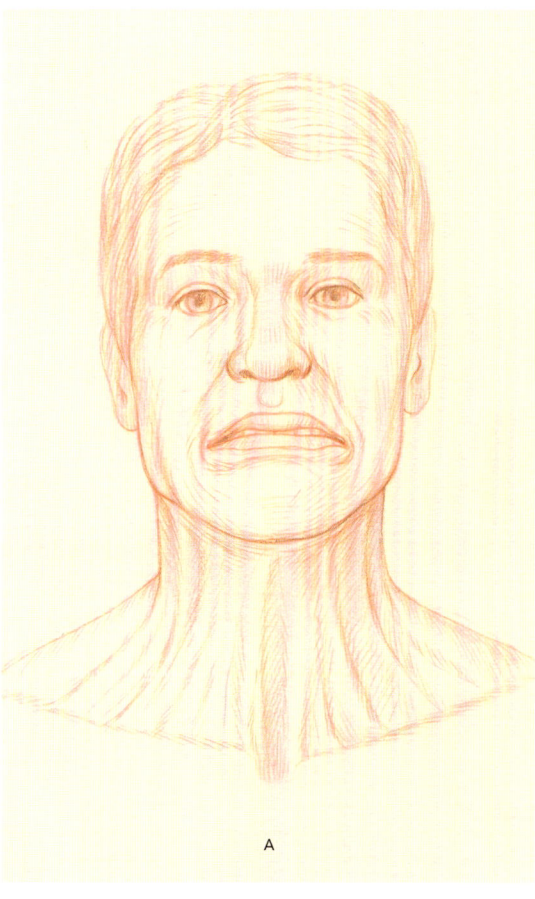

A

PLATYSMA, A VERY THIN MUSCLE COVERING
NECK, IS VISIBLE ONLY WITH EXTREME
FACIAL EXPRESSIONS SUCH AS THIS

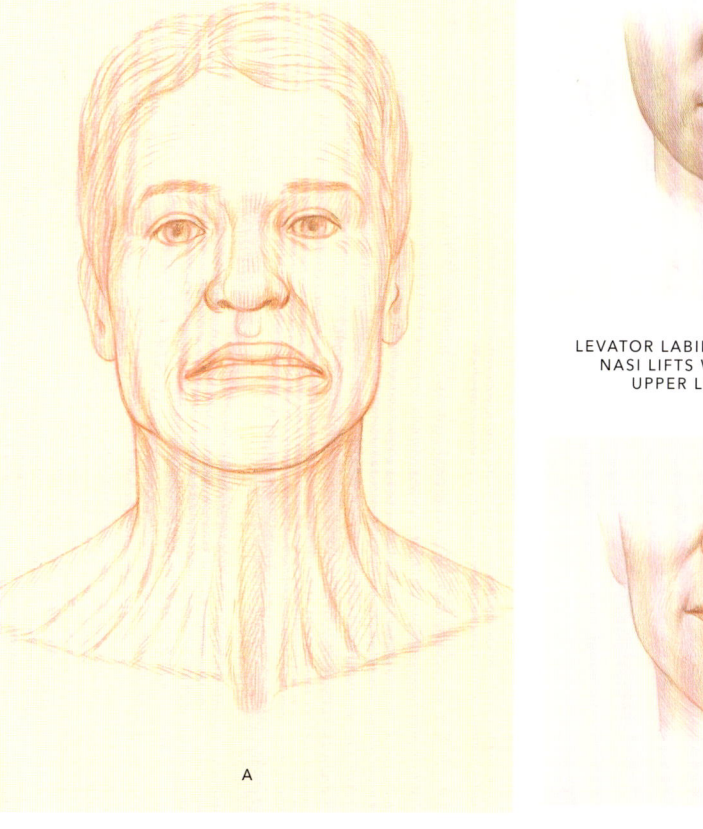

B

LEVATOR LABII SUPERIORIS ALAEQUE
NASI LIFTS WING OF NOSE AND
UPPER LIP IN CONTEMPT

C

ZYGOMATICUS MINOR LIFTS UPPER LIPS
AS WHEN ABOUT TO CRY

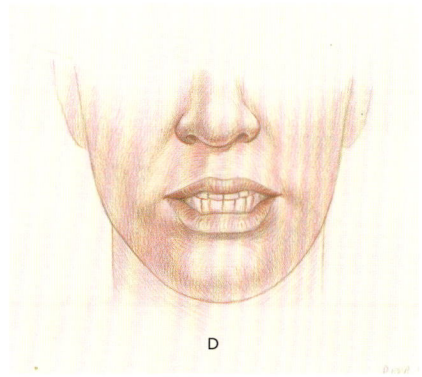

D

DEPRESSOR LABII INFERIORIS
LOWERS THE LOWER LIP

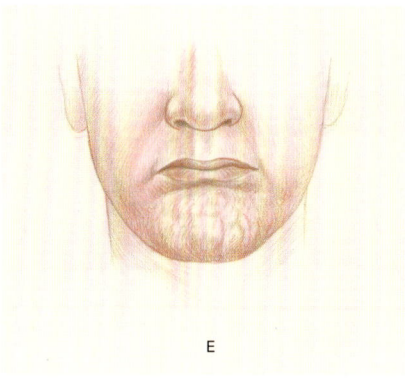

E

MENTALIS CORRUGATES THE CHIN IN
DISAPPOINTMENT OR SADNESS

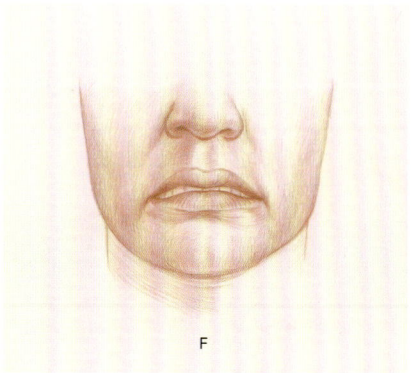

F

DEPRESSOR ANGULI ORIS LOWERS CORNERS
OF MOUTH IN FEAR OR SADNESS

Actions of muscles of the mouth and
their effects, part 2

EXPRESSIONS CAUSED BY DEEPER MUSCLES

The expressions depicted here are created by muscles below the superficial layer.

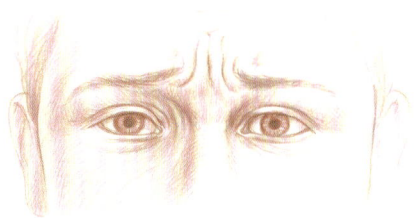

A

CORRUGATOR CREATES VERTICAL WRINKLES
IN MIDDLE OF FOREHEAD

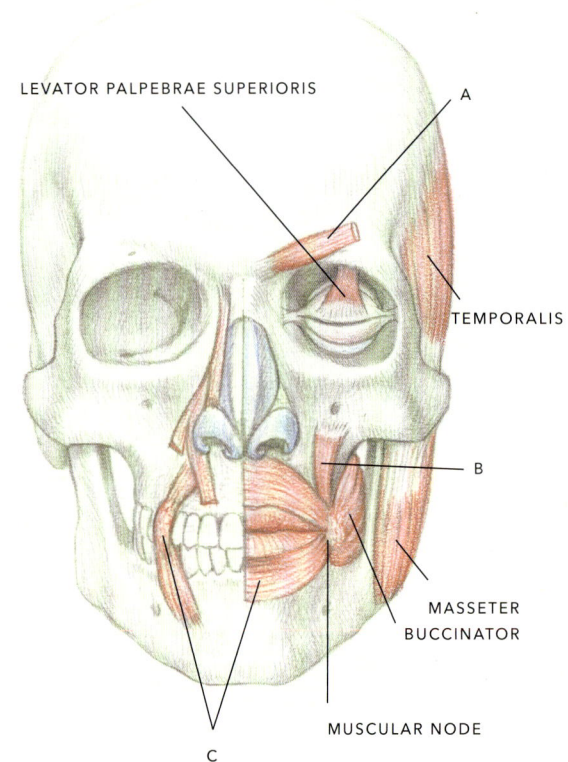

LEVATOR PALPEBRAE SUPERIORIS

A

TEMPORALIS

B

MASSETER
BUCCINATOR

MUSCULAR NODE

C

Actions of deeper muscles and their effects

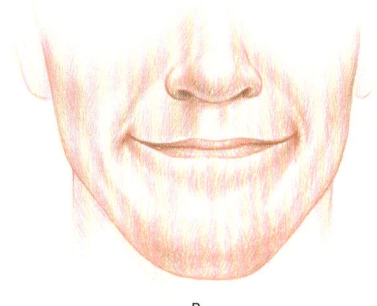

B

LEVATOR ANGULI ORIS LIFTS UPPER CORNERS
OF LIPS IN A FORCED SMILE

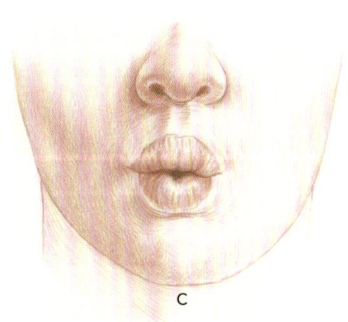

C

ORBICULARIS ORIS TOGETHER WITH
THE INCISIVUS LABII SUPERIORIS AND
INFERIORIS PUCKER LIPS AS WHEN
WHISTLING OR GENTLY BLOWING AIR

SIX BASIC FACIAL EXPRESSIONS

About six facial expressions convey the main human emotions. Each emotion can be expressed in various ways and with different degrees of intensity. A facial expression can also convey a number of emotions at the same time, as in Caravaggio's painting *Judith Beheading Holofernes,* below. The face of Holofernes (which is a self-portrait of Caravaggio!) shows surprise, horror, and pain, while Judith's shows hate but mostly determination. The old lady, probably Judith's mother, seems to be thinking, "He's getting what he deserves!"

The six basic facial expressions shown here are instinctual—they express reactions to emotional situations or are manifestations of moods. But facial expressions can also be intentionally produced, faked, or charged with specific meaning: think of a sarcastic smile, an ironic frown, or a fake expression of happiness.

BELOW: Caravaggio (Michelangelo Merisi), *Judith Beheading Holofernes,* c. 1598-99 or 1602, oil on canvas, 57 × 77 inches (145 × 195 cm). Galleria Nazionale d'Arte Antica, Palazzo Barberini, Rome.

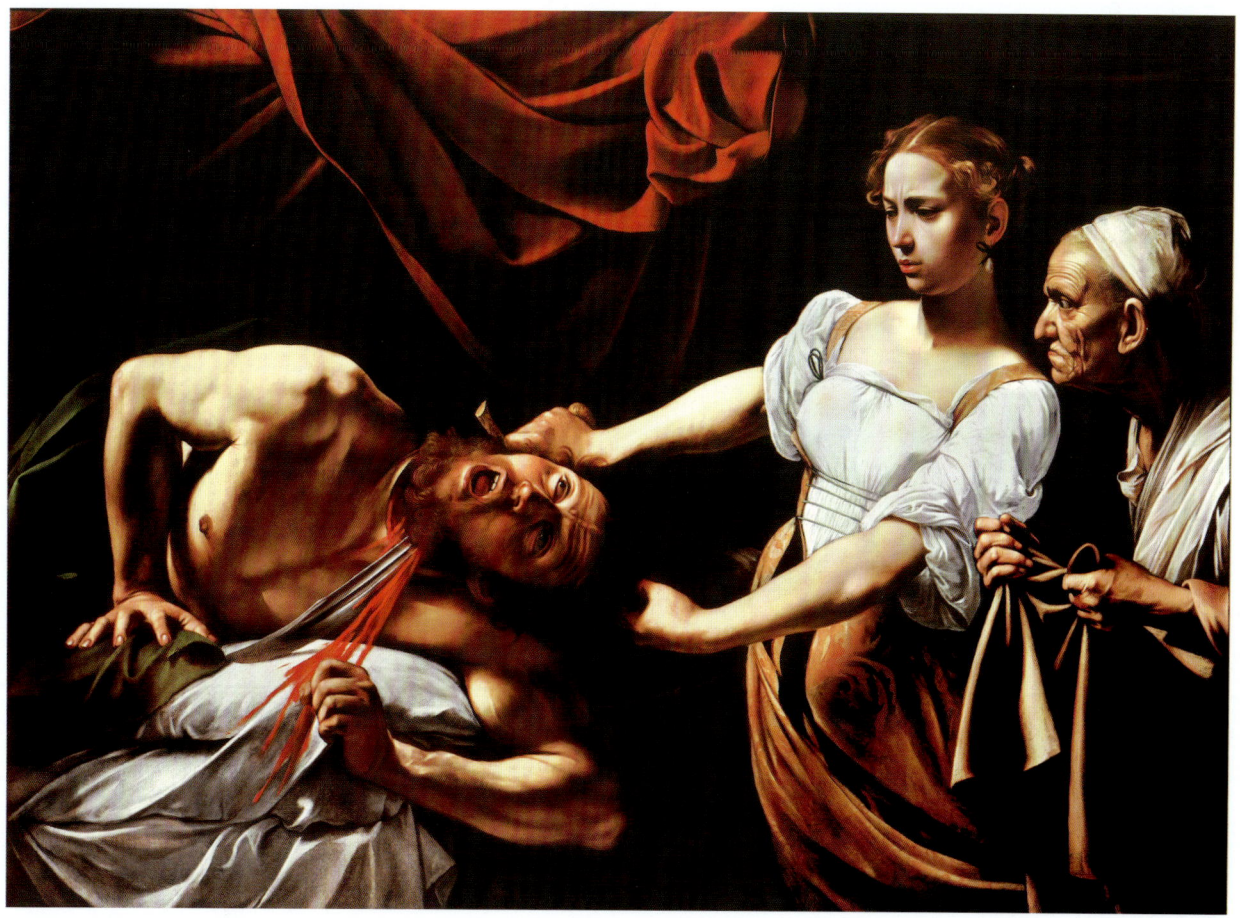

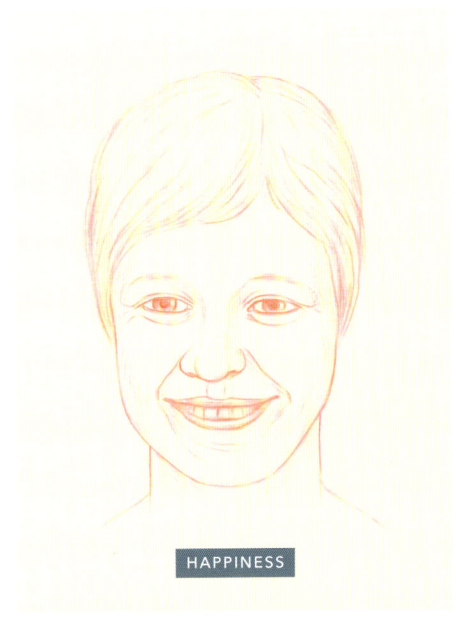

HAPPINESS

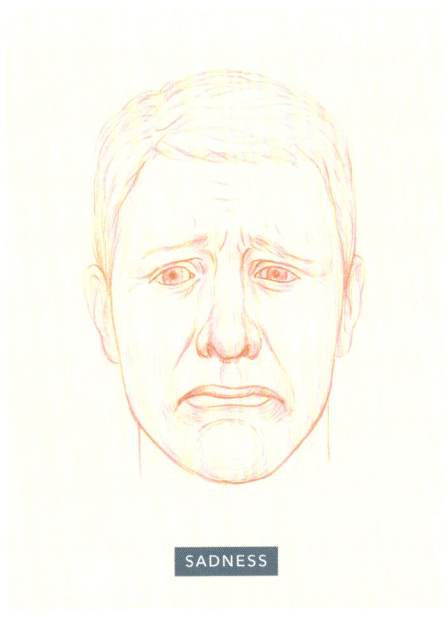

SADNESS

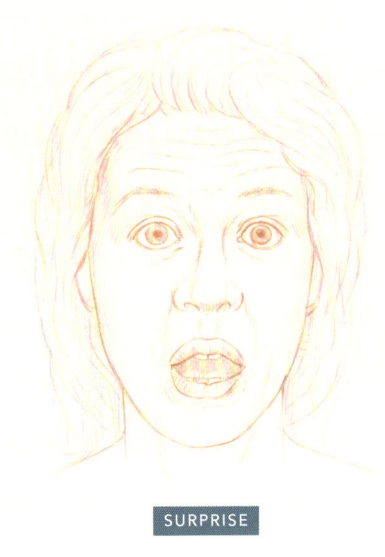

SURPRISE

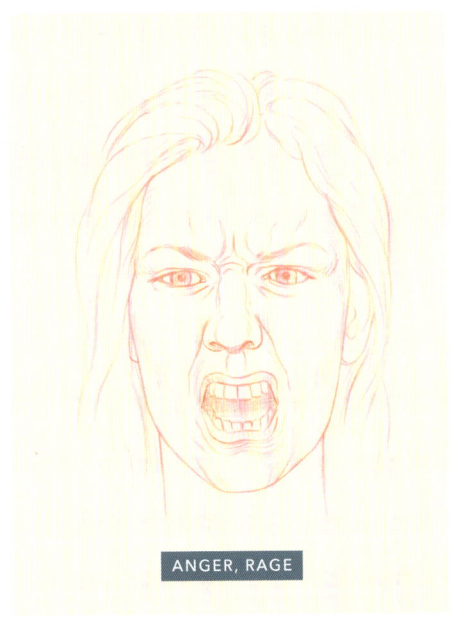

ANGER, RAGE

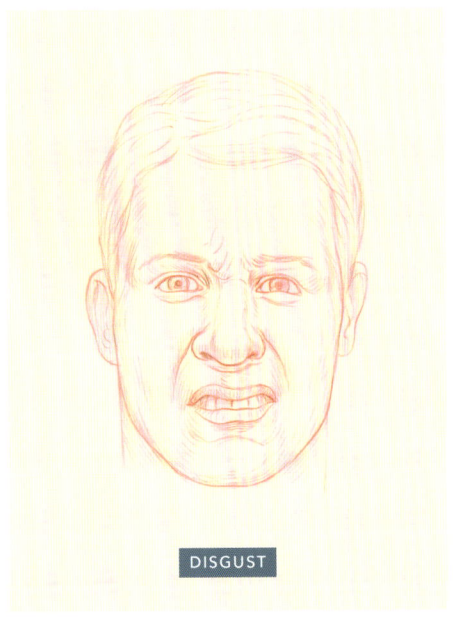

DISGUST

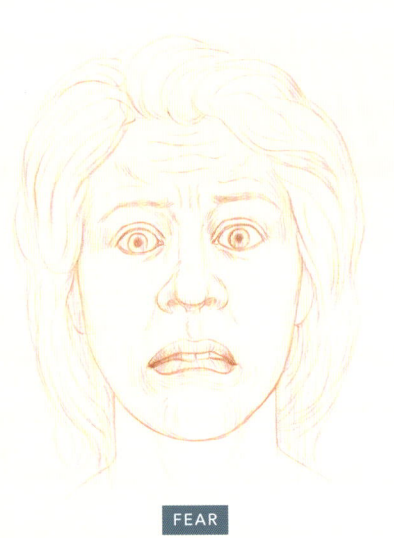

FEAR

ANALYZING COMPLEX FACIAL EXPRESSIONS

Most facial expressions are produced not by just one muscle but by the interaction of two, three, or more muscles. Now let's look at expressions created by several muscles working simultaneously. To study these expressions on your own, take pictures of yourself or friends making faces or faking expressions and draw arrows on printouts of the photos showing the directions in which the muscles are moving—just like you see in the images on the following pages. Keep in mind that the directions of the wrinkles that appear during facial expressions are perpendicular to the directions of the muscular fibers.

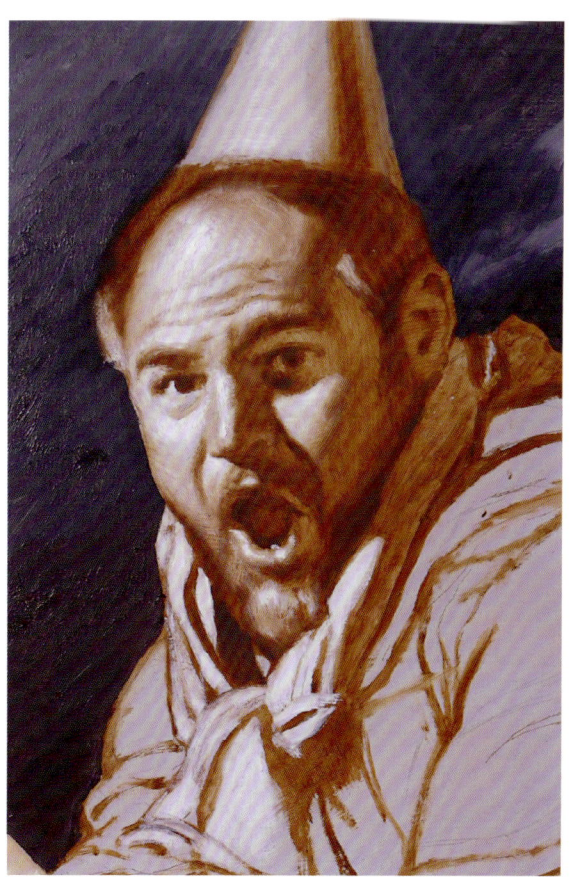

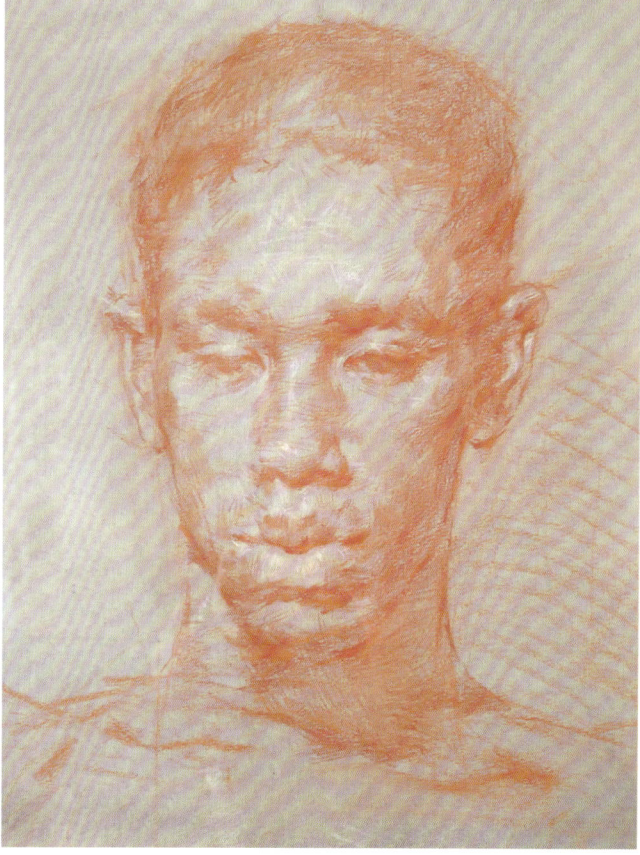

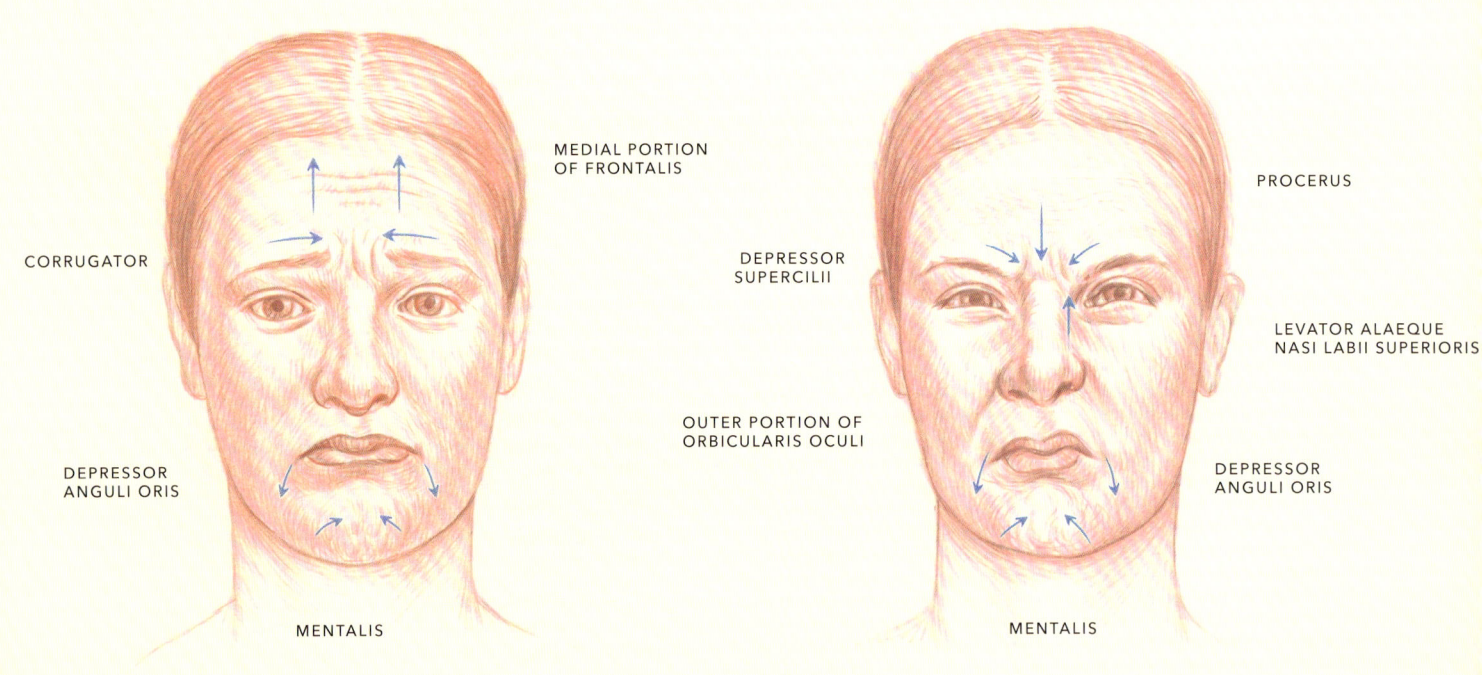

CORRUGATOR

MEDIAL PORTION
OF FRONTALIS

DEPRESSOR
ANGULI ORIS

MENTALIS

DEPRESSOR
SUPERCILII

OUTER PORTION OF
ORBICULARIS OCULI

MENTALIS

PROCERUS

LEVATOR ALAEQUE
NASI LABII SUPERIORIS

DEPRESSOR
ANGULI ORIS

ABOVE: Complex facial expressions

RIGHT: Giacomo Trecourt, *Self Portrait in Oriental Costume,* 1840s, oil on canvas, 25 × 32 inches (63.50 × 81.28 cm). Civic Museums of Pavia, Italy.

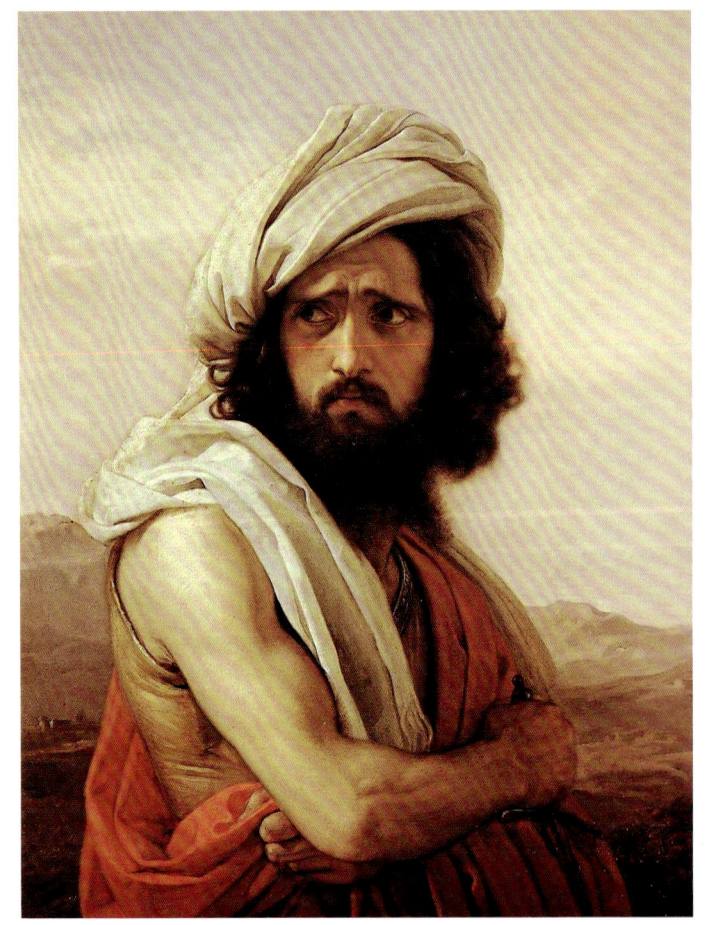

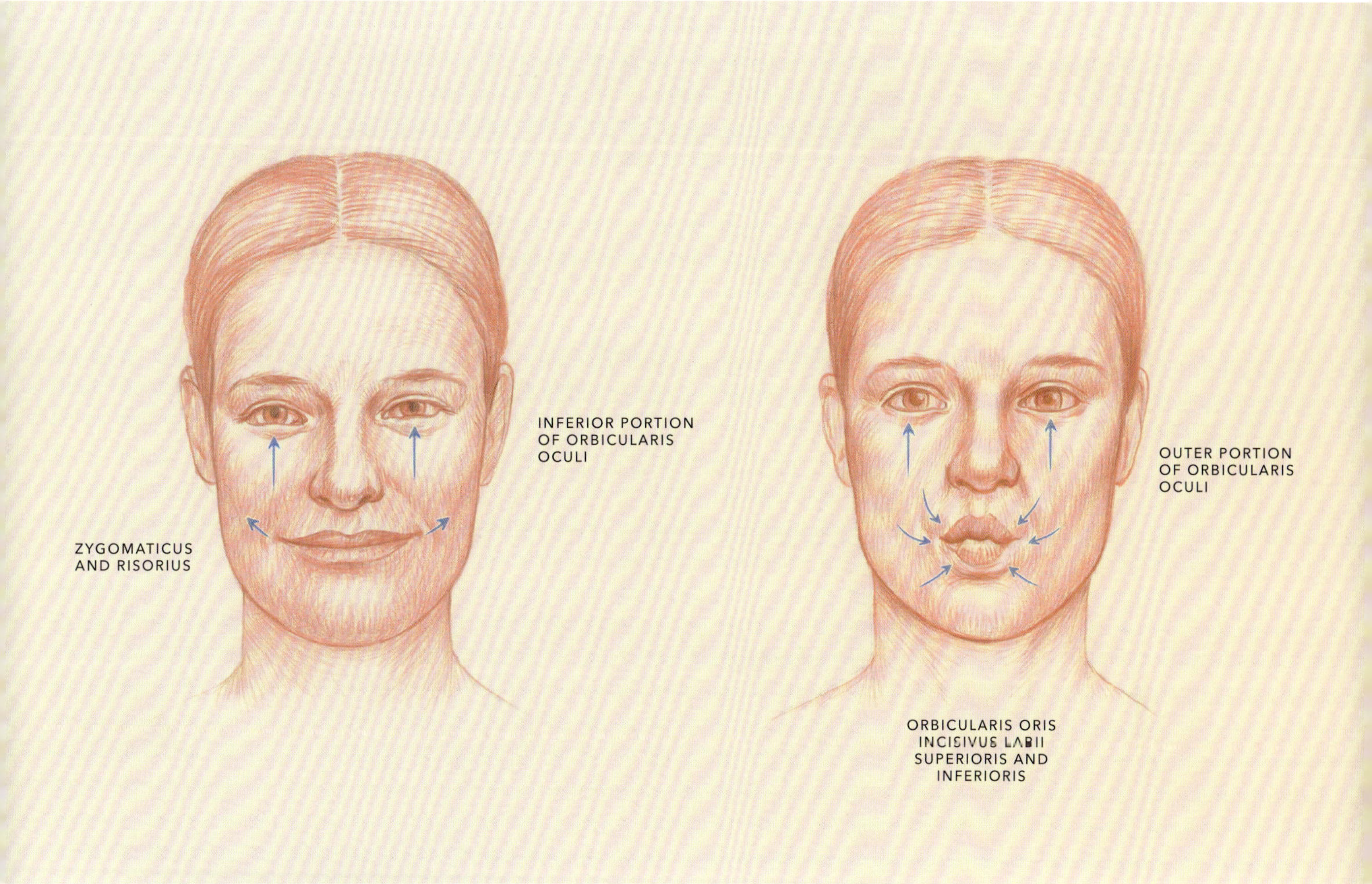

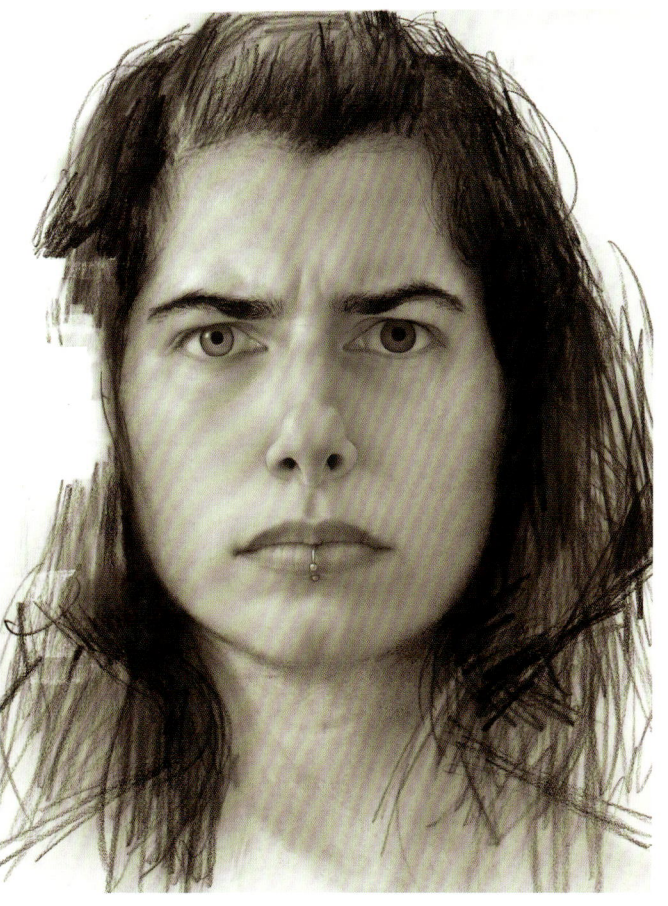

INFERIOR PORTION
OF ORBICULARIS
OCULI

ZYGOMATICUS
AND RISORIUS

OUTER PORTION
OF ORBICULARIS
OCULI

ORBICULARIS ORIS
INCISIVUS LABII
SUPERIORIS AND
INFERIORIS

ABOVE: Complex facial expressions, continued

LEFT: Gabriela Handal, *Self-Portrait at an Age,* 2018, charcoal on Fabriano Artistico paper, 19.25 ×14.75 inches (48.89 × 37.46 cm). Courtesy of the artist.

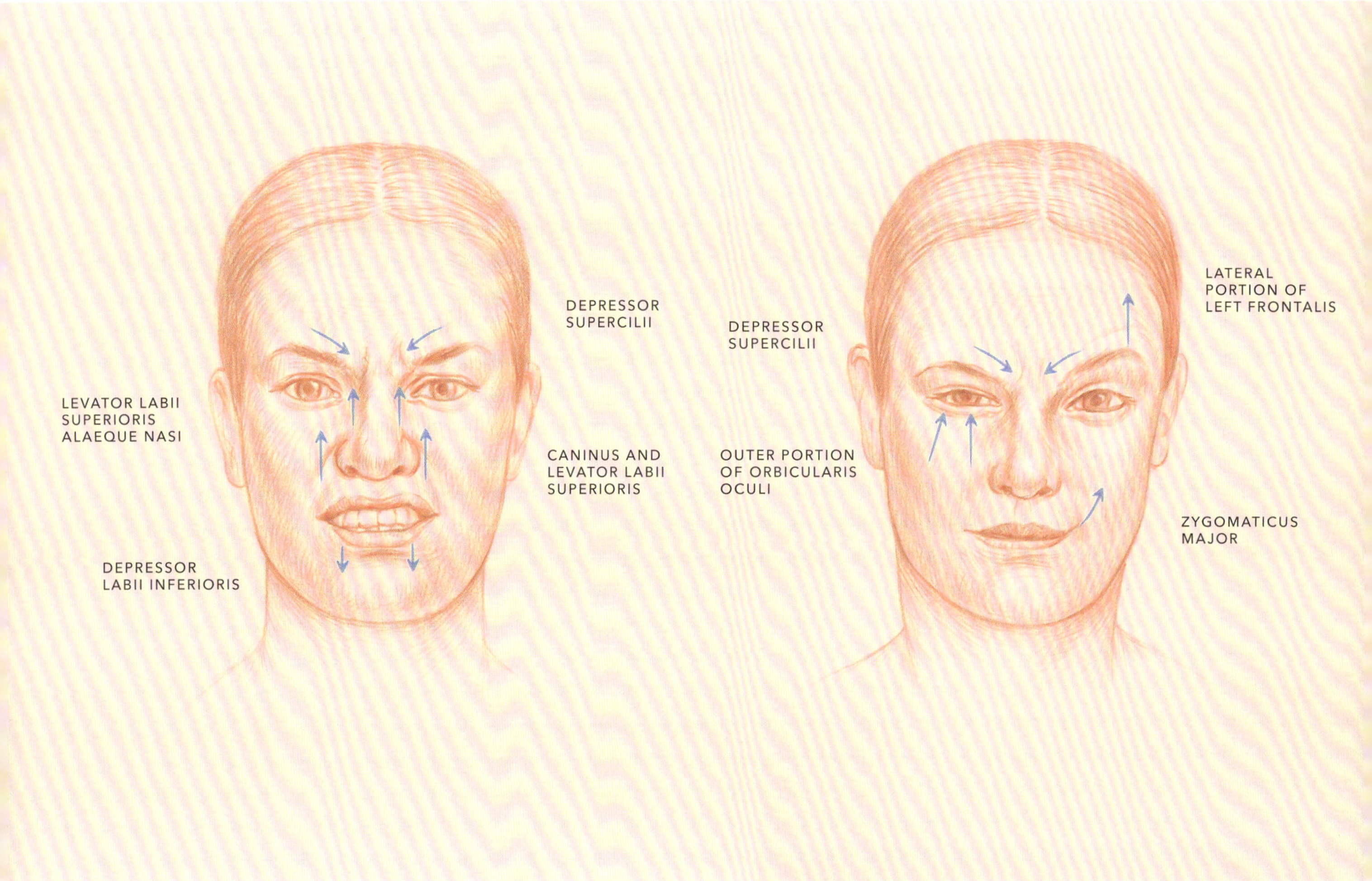

DEPRESSOR
SUPERCILII

LEVATOR LABII
SUPERIORIS
ALAEQUE NASI

CANINUS AND
LEVATOR LABII
SUPERIORIS

DEPRESSOR
LABII INFERIORIS

DEPRESSOR
SUPERCILII

LATERAL
PORTION OF
LEFT FRONTALIS

OUTER PORTION
OF ORBICULARIS
OCULI

ZYGOMATICUS
MAJOR

TOP: Complex facial expressions, continued

BOTTOM: Franz Xaver Messerschmidt, *Simplicity in the Highest Degree,*
number 9 of the "Character Heads," after 1770, alabaster. Vienna Museum
Karlsplatz.

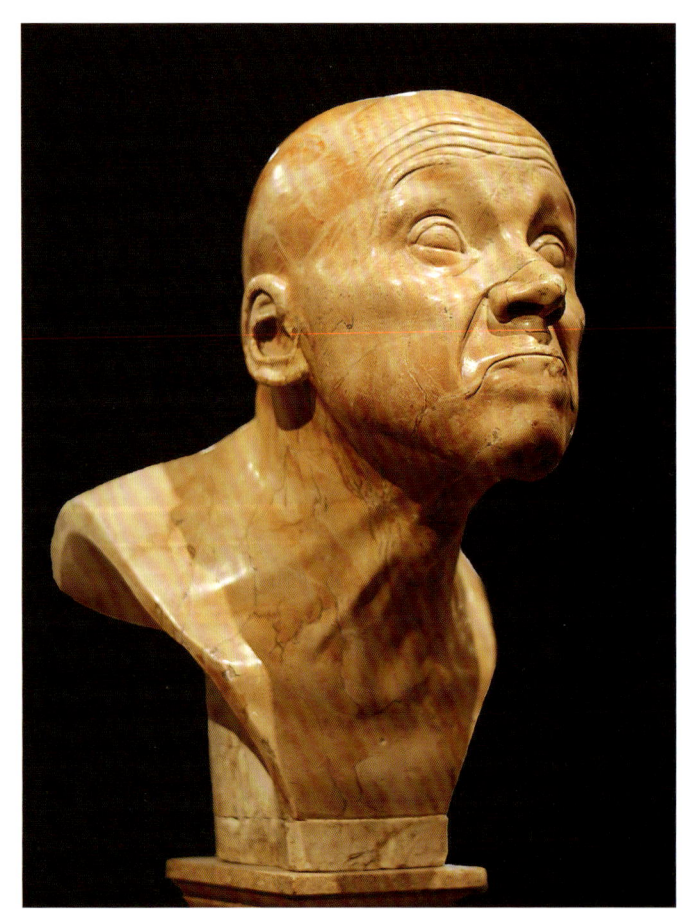

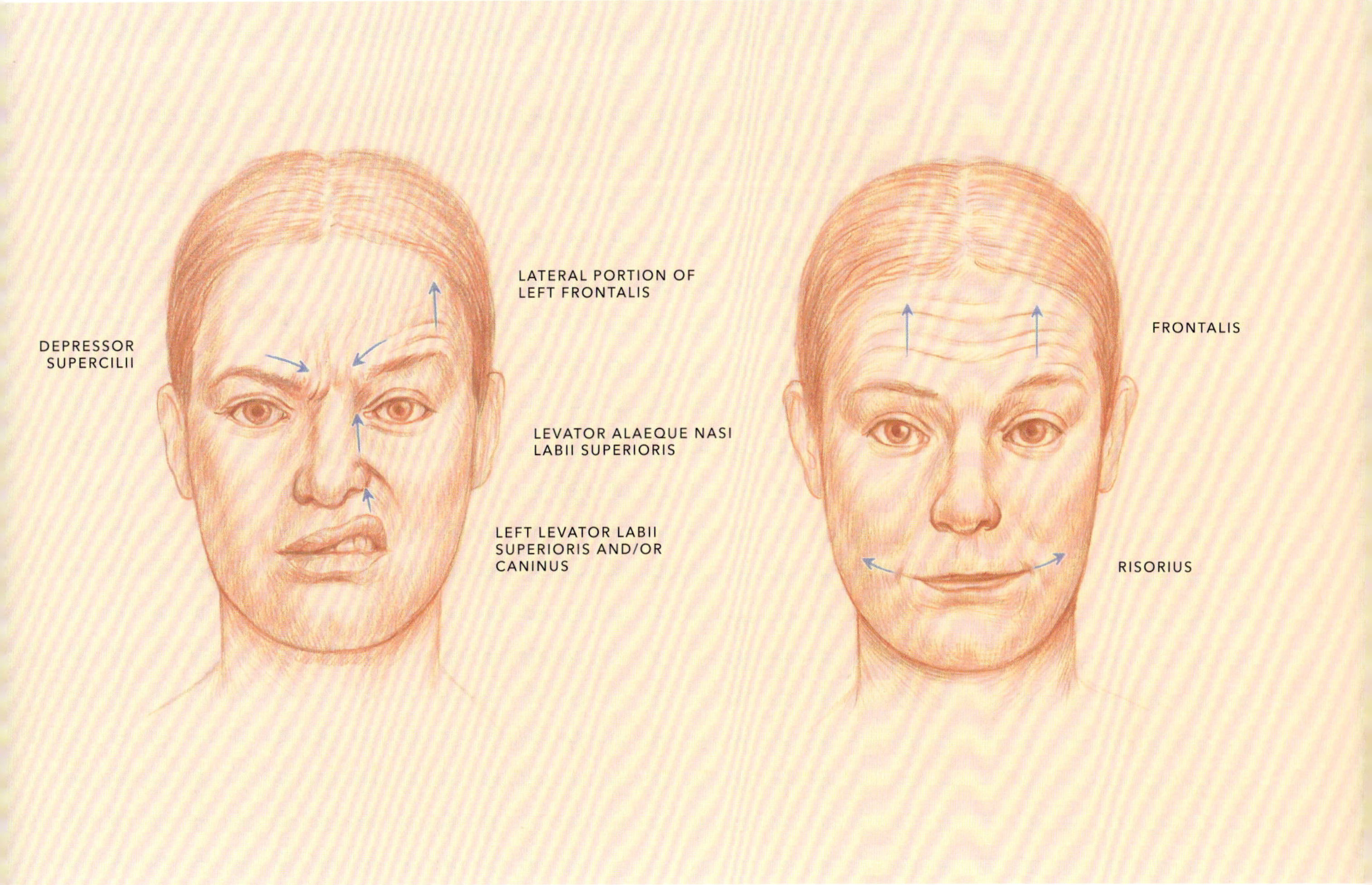

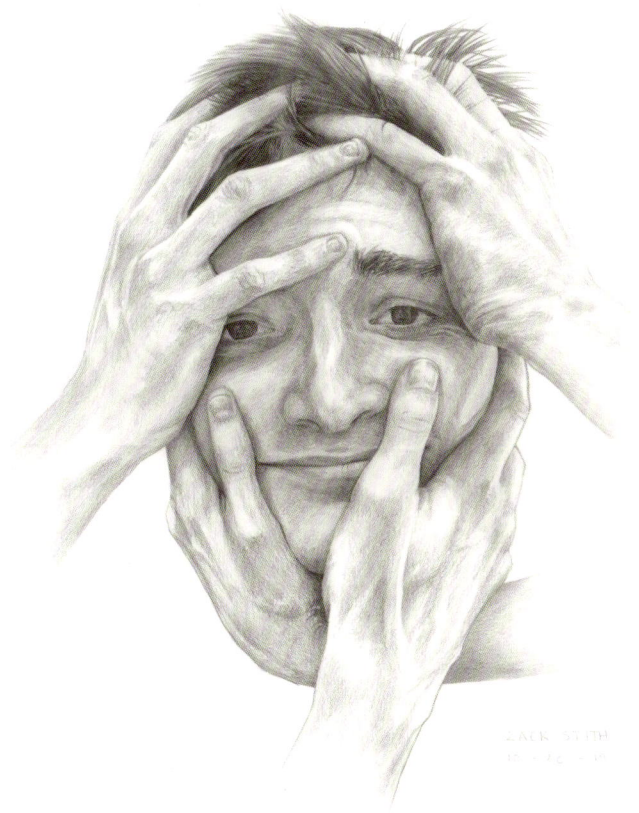

DEPRESSOR
SUPERCILII

LATERAL PORTION OF
LEFT FRONTALIS

LEVATOR ALAEQUE NASI
LABII SUPERIORIS

LEFT LEVATOR LABII
SUPERIORIS AND/OR
CANINUS

FRONTALIS

RISORIUS

TOP: Complex facial expressions, continued

BOTTOM: Zachary Stith, *Head in Hands,* 2019, graphite on paper, sheet 20 x 16 (cm). Courtesy of the artist.

This wonderful drawing, done by a student of mine as a class assignment, shows how creativity can be enhanced by mastering the two most difficult parts of the body—face and hands.

EXERCISES

EXERCISE 1

Practice drawing the volumes of the head from various angles both from imagination and from snapshots of the heads of your friends. Create about thirty quick sketches like those you see here.

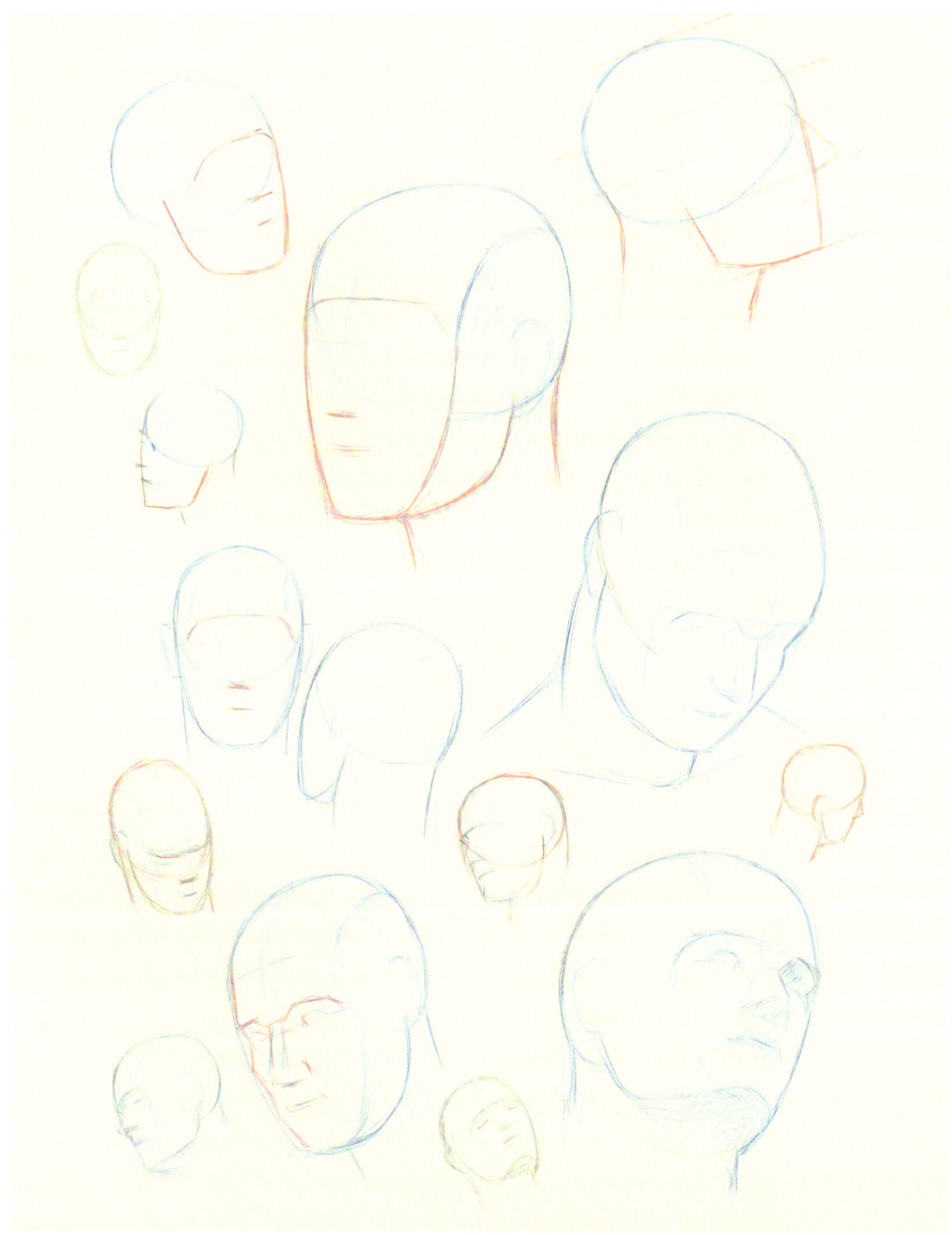

EXERCISE 2

Looking in a mirror, practice drawing your own eye in a normal, relaxed expression. It will probably be too hard for you to hold a more active expression for an extended period of time, so move on to copying eyes in various expressions and from various angles using photographs.

EXERCISE 3

Take pictures of yourself or your friends expressing the six basic emotions: happiness, sadness, surprise, anger, disgust, fear. Working from the photos, render the faces in line drawings, which will permit you to focus on the essential aspects of each expression.

EXERCISE 4

Take photos of four or five of your typical facial expressions and make detailed tonal drawings of each. Working for a longer amount of time will make you more aware of subtleties of facial expressions that you might not usually notice.

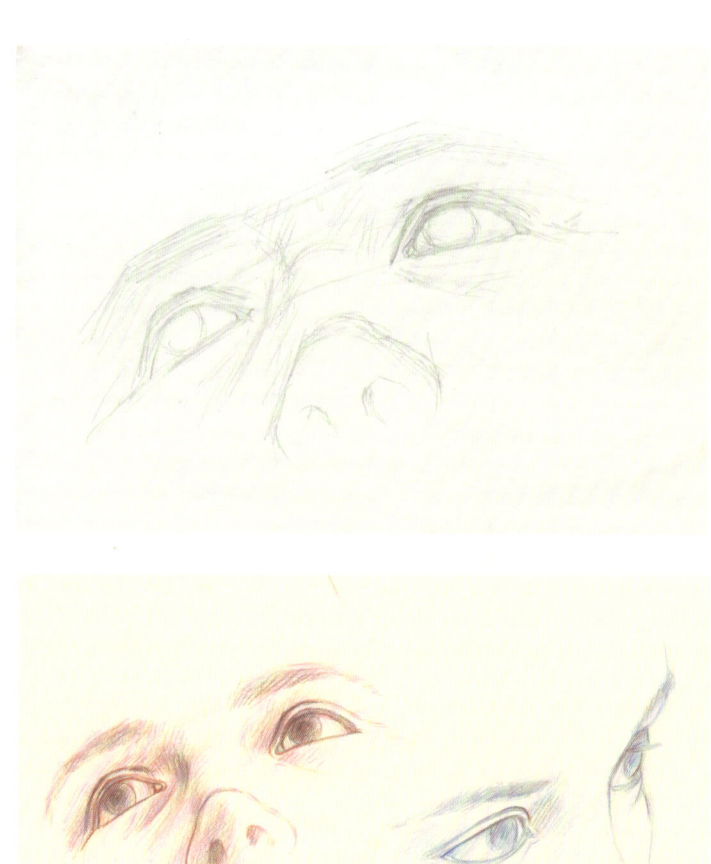

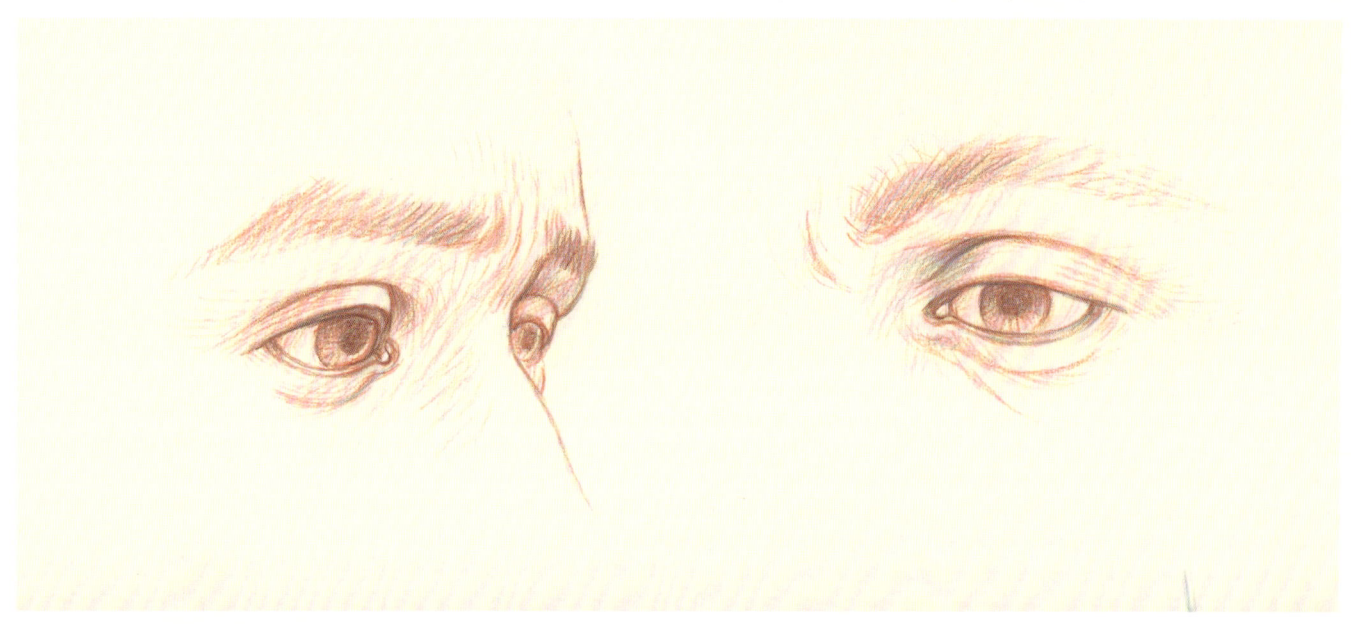

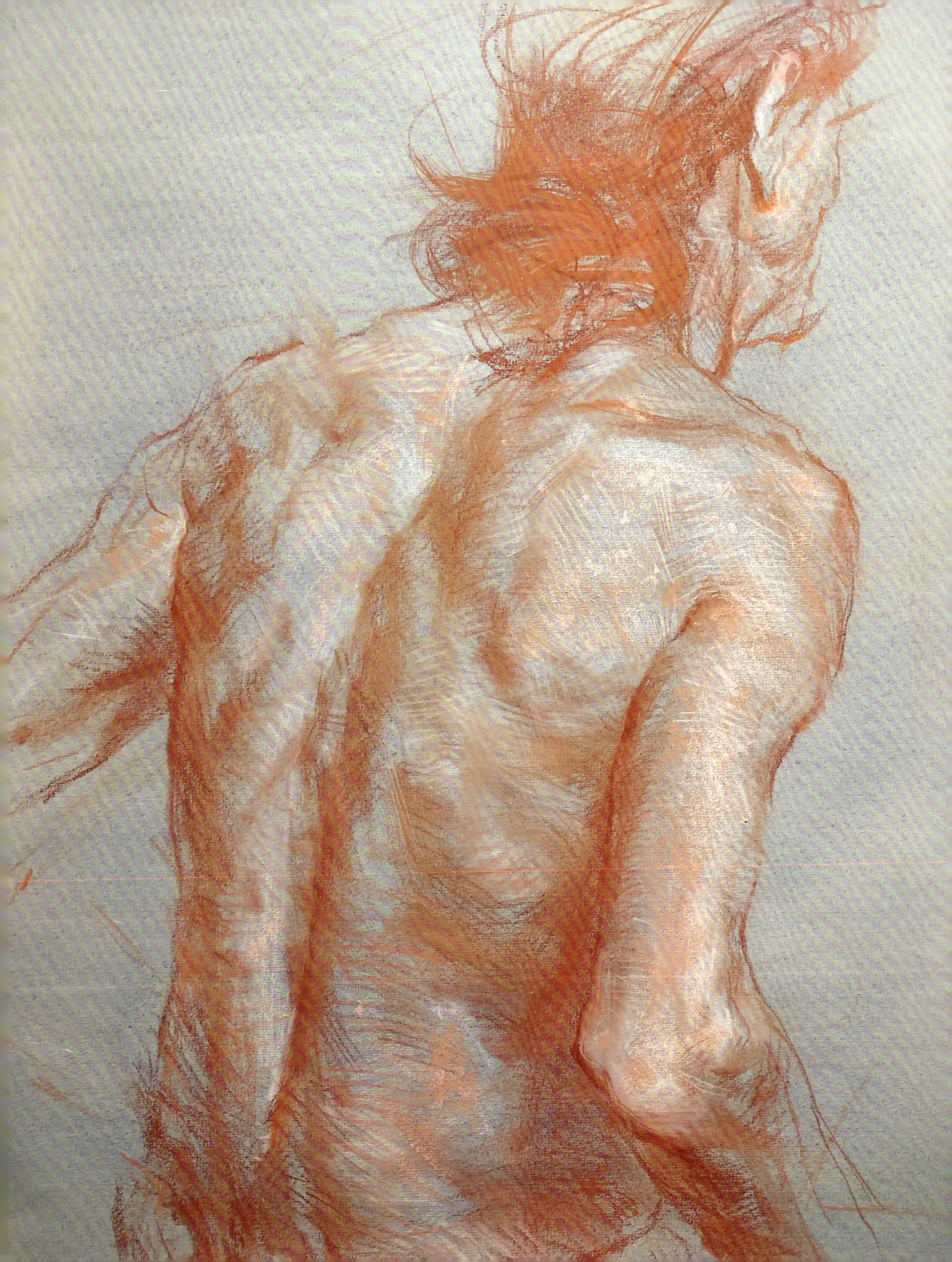

CHAPTER 9

MEASURING & DRAWING TECHNIQUES

I close this book with an examination of a few essential measuring and drawing techniques traditionally associated with figure drawing. By now you have a solid understanding of how important anatomical knowledge is for creating a good figure drawing. An artist who is well trained in anatomy can read a model's body and pose in great detail and with a high degree of accuracy, and the resulting artwork will be more aesthetically complex, expressive, and realistic.

For much of the twentieth century and up until fairly recently, the theoretical aspect of art and art-making was considered to be the most important. The technical part was dismissed, with few exceptions, as "craft" or as showing-off on the part of the artist. The result was a great loss of expressive possibility and a limitation of creativity. But it's also true that an excessive or exclusive focus on the technical aspect of art to the detriment of the conceptual can be equally deleterious, causing a work of art to become just a narcissistic display of technical prowess. The almost alchemical interaction between the technical and the conceptual marries theory and practice and generates creativity, diversity, and innovation.

OPPOSITE: Dan Thompson, *The Runner*, 2017, red and white chalk on paper, 20 × 15 inches (50.80 × 38.10 cm). Courtesy of the artist.

The importance of technical execution is exemplified by the great stylistic and compositional diversity achieved during the Renaissance: the styles of Raphael, Pontormo, Leonardo, Rosso Fiorentino, Michelangelo, Andrea del Sarto—to name just a few—are their immediately recognizable artistic identities. Technical and conceptual development in art has been a constant through the millenniums, a product of the socioeconomic, cultural, and historical events of the various historic periods. During the Renaissance, for example, the emerging merchant class and the revival of humanistic ideals were paired with technical innovations in architecture, sculpture, and painting, including the study of anatomy and the invention of perspective. Leonardo's studies of anatomy were revolutionary, and the technical accuracy of his drawings was fundamental for describing his acute scientific observations. The depiction of the human figure during the Renaissance in sculpture and painting is based on a good, sometimes excellent understanding of human anatomy. The Reformation and Counter-Reformation dictated the theological content of art, which became an important tool for the propagation of religious doctrines; the accurate depiction of the human form remained indispensable, though not to glorify the body as a reflection of the divine but rather to exalt the sacrifice of martyrs convincingly depicted in graphic, realistic paintings. In the first half of the nineteenth century, Johann Wolfgang von Goethe's *Theory of Colors* had a great influence in the work of J. M. W. Turner and other artists. The Impressionists took advantage of the new, intense colors developed during the industrial revolution and inspired a technical and conceptual revolution that spawned a great number of artistic movements, each with its defining characteristics—think, for example, of Pointillism, Expressionism, Fauvism, or the Nabis. The quantum mechanics theories developed between the 1890s and 1920s were misunderstood by artists but nevertheless contributed to opening the path to abstraction. In so many cases, an artwork's technical component is essential to the expression of its narrative or conceptual content

In what follows, I first discuss measuring methods. I then turn to four figure-drawing techniques, each of which focuses on an essential element of drawing.

1. *Structural drawing.* This technique privileges the description of the structural and three-dimensional aspects of a subject. I like to refer to structural drawing as a rendering of the forms using "framing" lines—lines that describe the volumetric characteristics of the subject using a cross-contour hatching technique. The drawing by Jean-Baptiste Greuze opposite exemplifies this approach; note, for example, how

The technical component is essential to expression

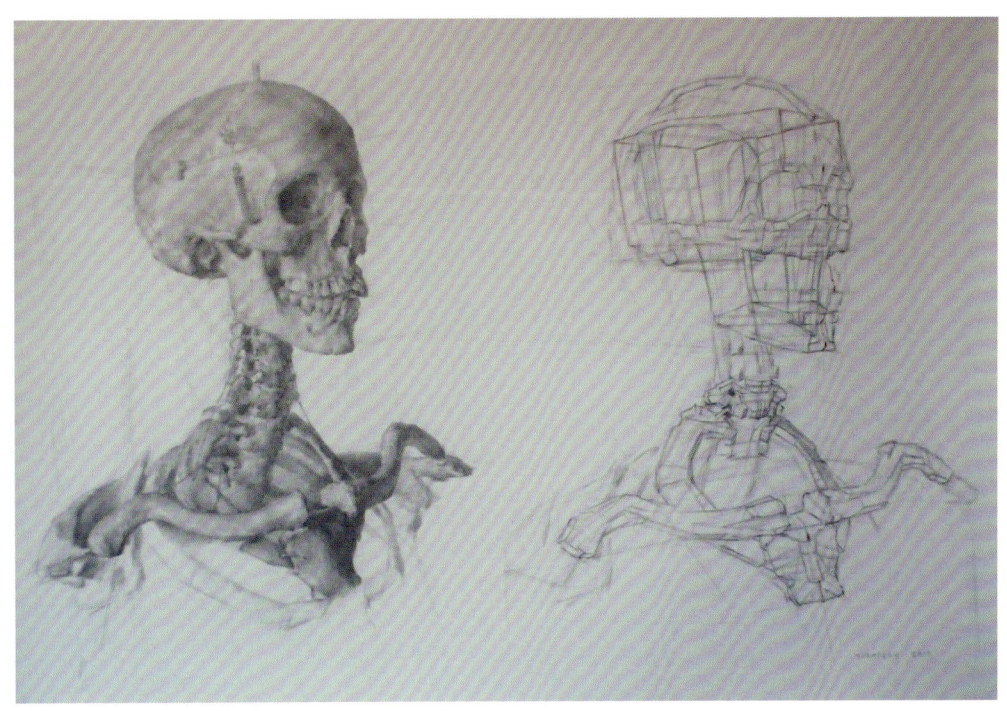

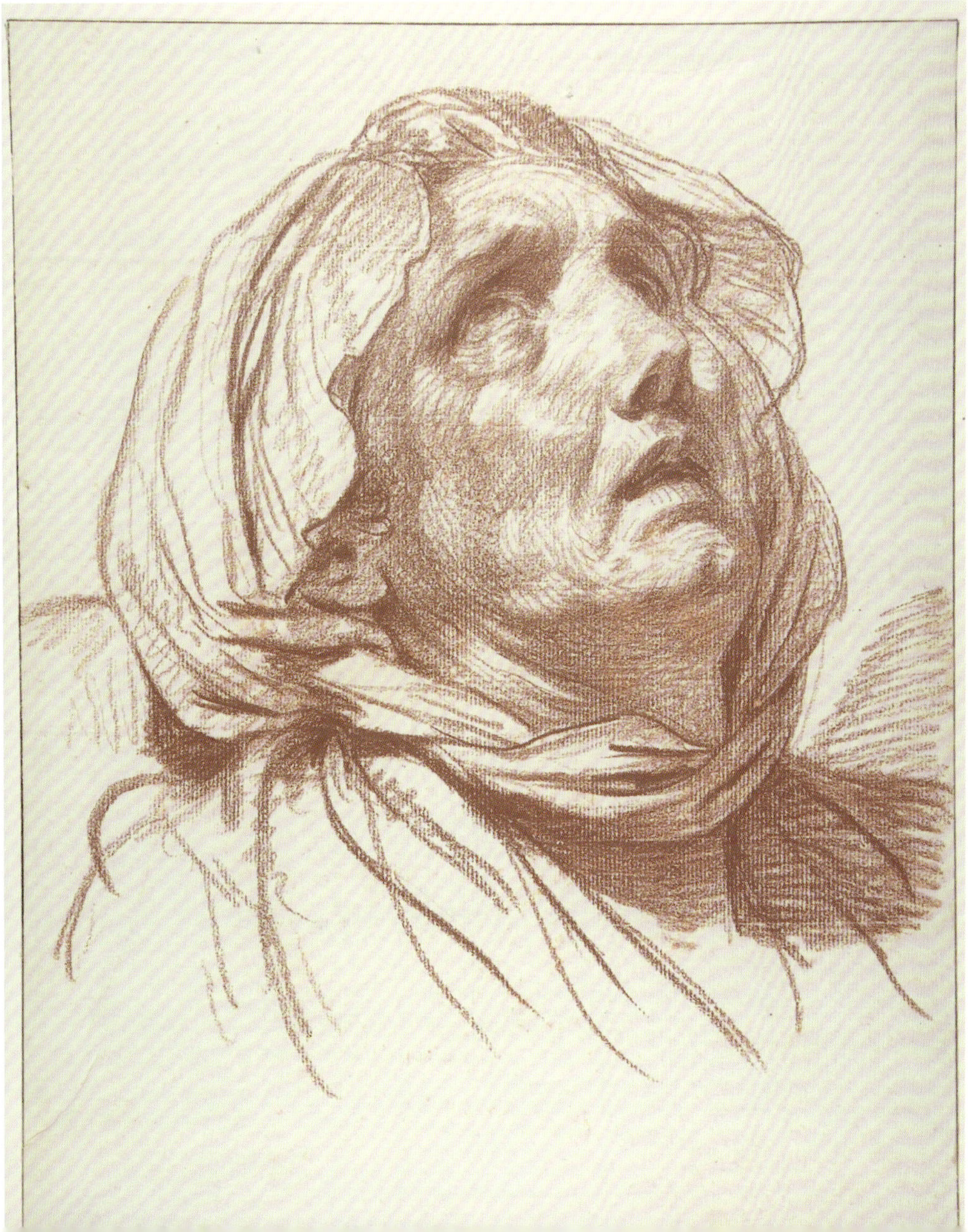

TOP: Dan Thompson, anatomical plate for Grand Central Academy, 2009, graphite on paper, 15 × 20 inches (38.10 × 50.80 cm). Courtesy of the artist.

These two renderings by Dan Thompson provide an excellent example of structural analysis of a subject. The drawing on the right is used as a preparatory drawing to inform the more realistic rendering of the skull and upper portion of the torso visible on the left.

BOTTOM: Jean-Baptiste Greuze, *Head of an Old Woman Looking Up,* c. 1763, red chalk, framing lines in pen and brown ink, 16¼ × 12⅞ inches (41.27 × 32.70 cm). Metropolitan Museum of Art, New York, Rogers Fund, 1949.

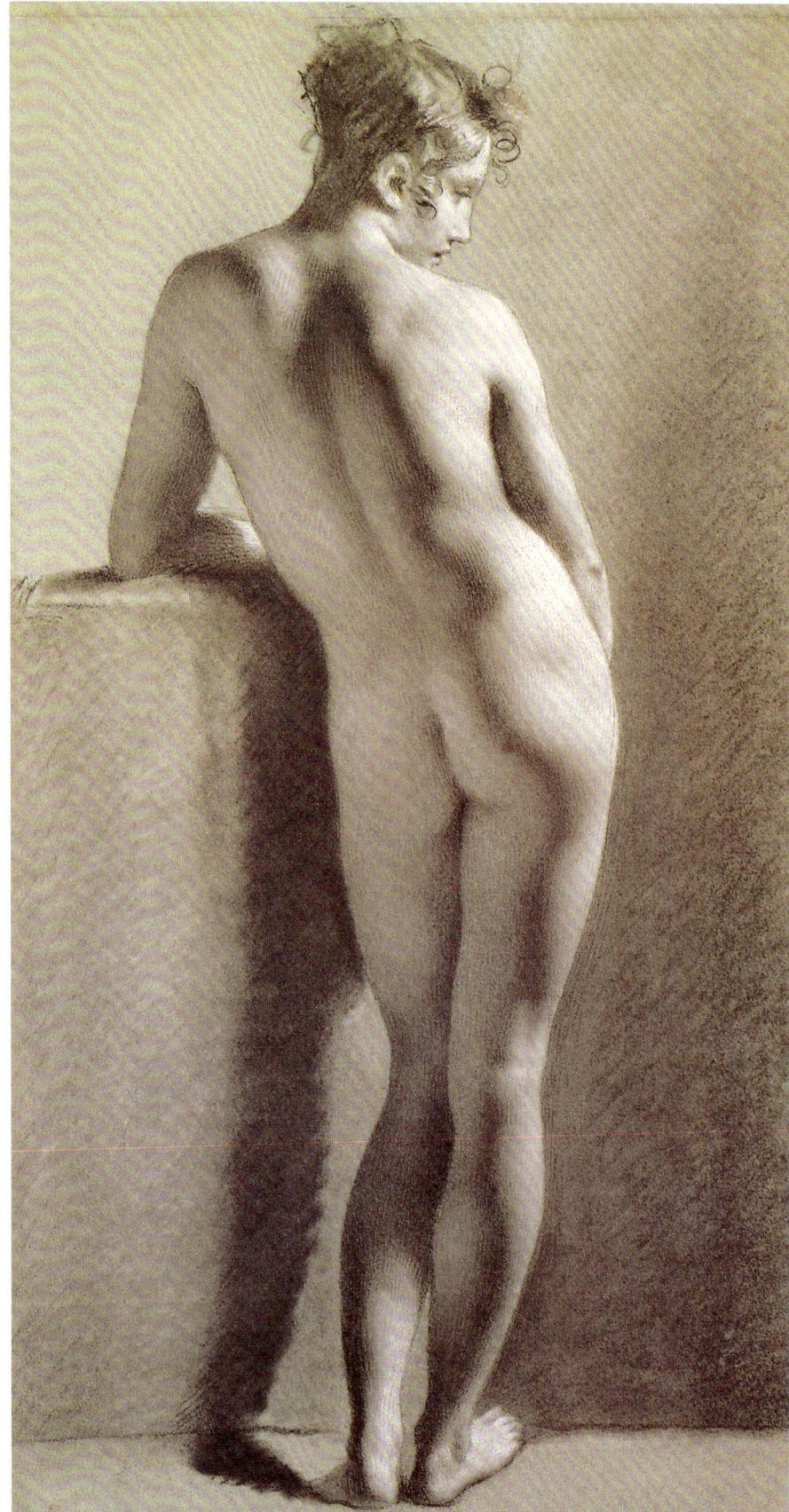

RIGHT: Pierre-Paul Prud'hon, *Standing Female Nude Seen From the Back*, 1810.

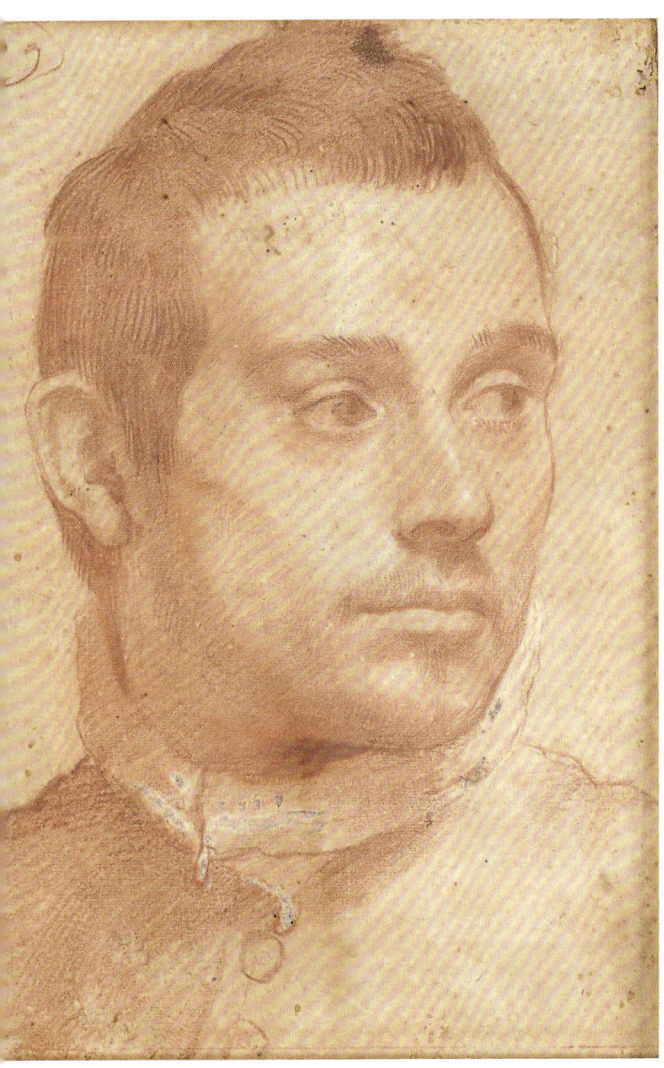

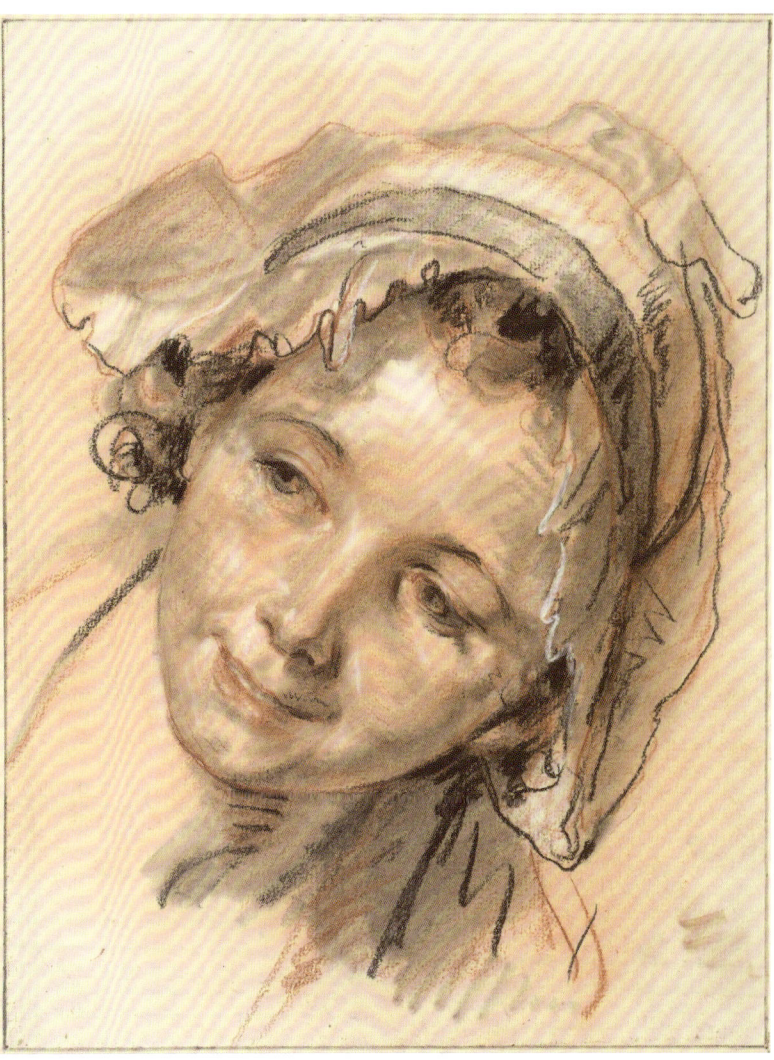

efficiently the relief of the face of the old woman is described using structural lines. More modern examples are drawings by American artist Paul Cadmus (1904–99), who beautifully mastered this technique.

2. Tonal drawing. This method focuses primarily on the tonal aspects of a subject—lightness and darkness—to reproduce its volumes, relying on areas of value rather than on lines. The drawing by Pierre-Paul Prud'hon, right, is a sublime example of tonal drawing.

3. Trois crayons. This technique gets its French name from its use of three different-colored chalks, or crayons: red, black, and white. It focuses on color temperature, chroma, opacity, and transparency. This technique is essential because it teaches the fundamental elements of color mixing and color manipulation using only three colors. The portraits by Annibale Carracci and Jean-Baptiste Greuze above are fine examples of *trois crayons* technique.

ABOVE LEFT: Annibale Carracci, *Portrait of a Man (a member of the Mascheroni family?)*, c. 1580-90, sanguine on paper, 14½ × 10½ inches (37 × 26.8 cm). Museu Nacional de Belas Artes, Rio de Janeiro, Brazil.

ABOVE RIGHT: Jean-Baptiste Greuze, *Head of a Smiling Girl*, c. 1765, white and black pastel, red chalk, ground partly stumped with red chalk. Albertina Museum, Vienna.

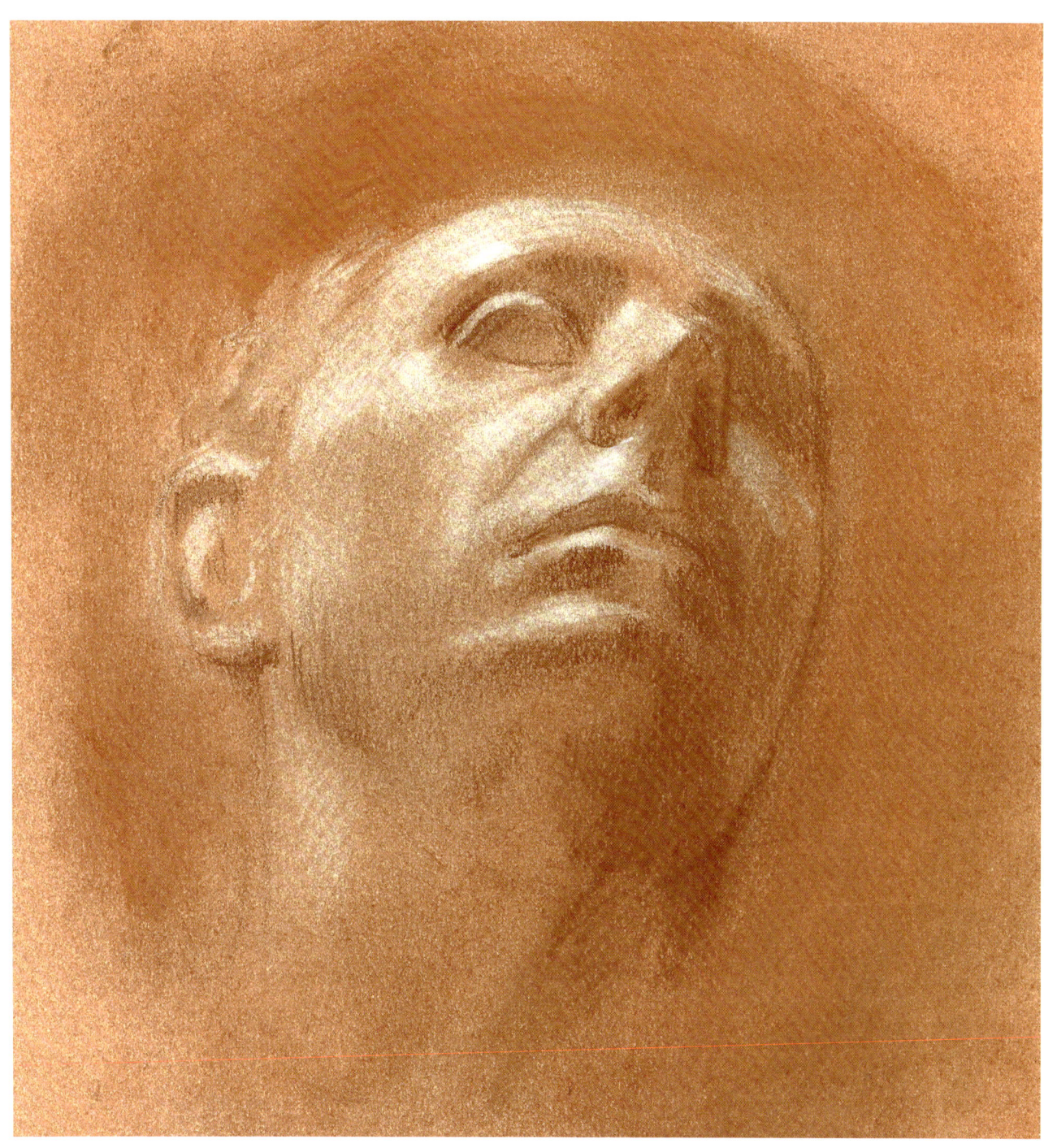

4. *Reduction technique*. This method, also called subtractive technique, requires the toning of the paper with a dry medium, such as charcoal dust or, as in my drawing above, conté sepia powder pigment. The pigment is then gradually removed to obtain tonal effects. With this technique, the focus is on light; form is defined not with outlines but by areas of value.

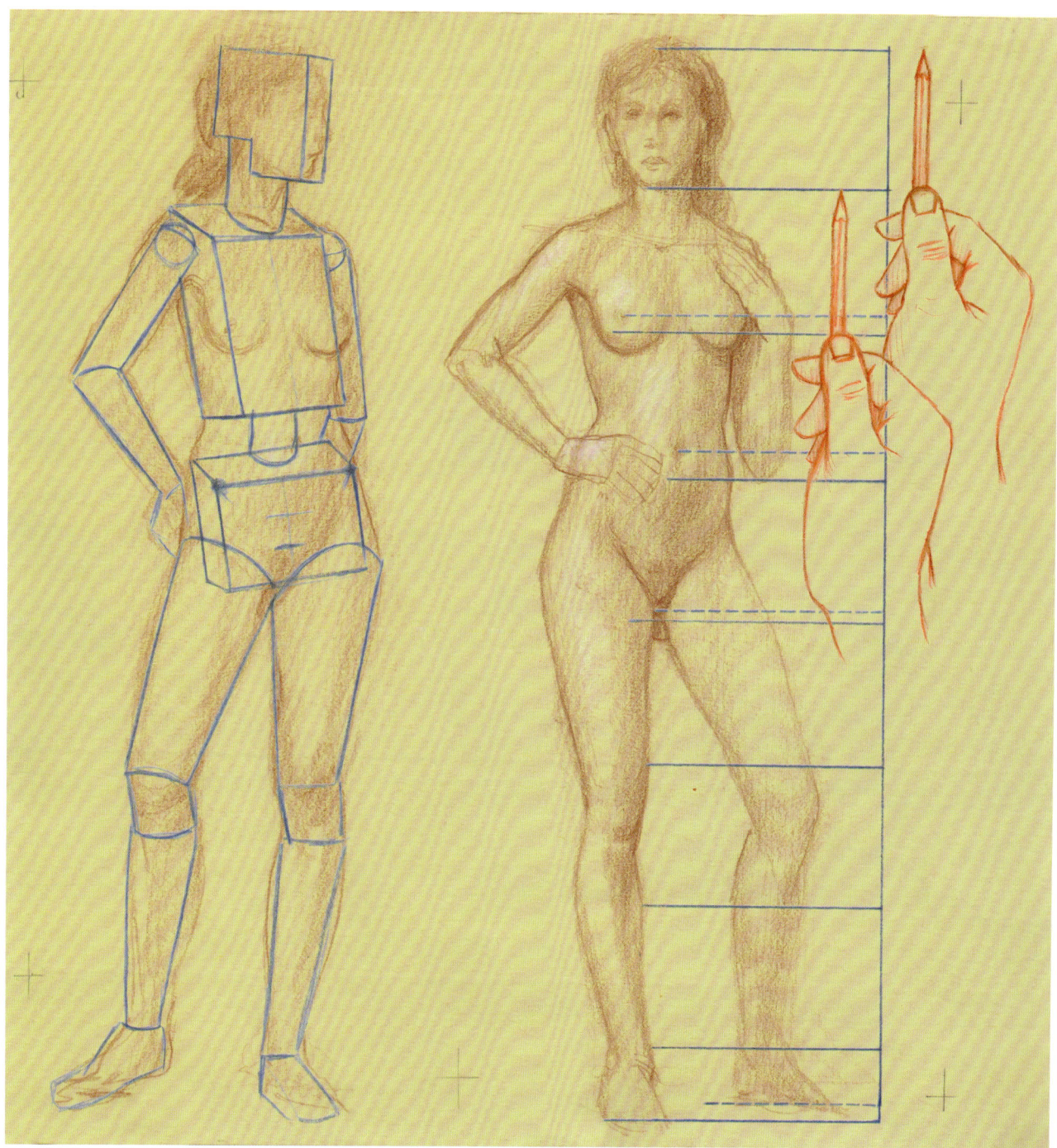

MEASURING YOUR SUBJECT

ABOVE: The sighting method

No matter which drawing technique you use, you must first properly measure the proportions of your subject. There are several measuring techniques, and each can have variations and personal interpretations. Here, I discuss two principal measuring techniques that will greatly increase your drawings' accuracy: the *sighting technique* and the *envelope technique*. Both are based on sighting the subject, but they differ in how the measurements obtained are then utilized for drawing the figure.

THE SIGHTING METHOD

The drawing on the previous page summarizes the sighting method. Holding the pencil upright, line up its tip with the top of the model's head, then slide your thumbnail down the pencil until it lines up with the measurement you want to obtain—in this case, from the top of the head to the chin. (Note: Although in this case I'm using the head as the unit of measurement to which other parts of the body will be compared, any other segment of the body can be used, depending on the pose.) Now that you've obtained the measurement of the head, you can use it as a unit of measure. Holding this measurement with your thumb on the pencil, slowly lower your hand vertically until the tip of the pencil is aligned with the chin. Now check where the top of your thumbnail aligns with the body. In this case, the measure of one head down corresponds approximately to the bottom of the breasts. The level of the nipples, marked in this diagram with the dotted line, is slightly above this measure. Proceed downward, finding more measurements: the navel is a little above the measure of the third head down; the bottom of the genitals is about at the same level as the measure of the fourth head down.

THE ENVELOPE TECHNIQUE

As I mentioned above, each measuring technique can be interpreted personally, so let me tell you how I use the envelope technique. I start by finding the subject's height-to-width ratio by measuring the maximum width of the subject and then checking how many times the width fits into the height. With this ratio, I create an envelope that contains the subject. This envelope is then gradually refined with further measurements to describe the outline of the subject more and more precisely until I achieve the level of definition I require. The images opposite summarize the process.

OPPOSITE, TOP LEFT: Measuring a standing pose with the envelope method—the model posing

The figure drawing represents the model posing and visualizes the envelope that contains it.

OPPOSITE, TOP RIGHT: Envelope method, step 1

Find the points of the figure's maximum height and maximum width and create an envelope that contains the figure. In this case, the maximum width is the measurement from one elbow to the other, which fits into the maximum height about two and a half times.

OPPOSITE, BOTTOM LEFT: Envelope method, step 2

Continue measuring, finding more and more point-to-point measurements that gradually define the figure. This figure shows this progression with the gray, blue, and red lines.

OPPOSITE, BOTTOM RIGHT: Envelope method, step 3

Eventually you will obtain a precise line drawing. From here you can proceed to fully render the figure.

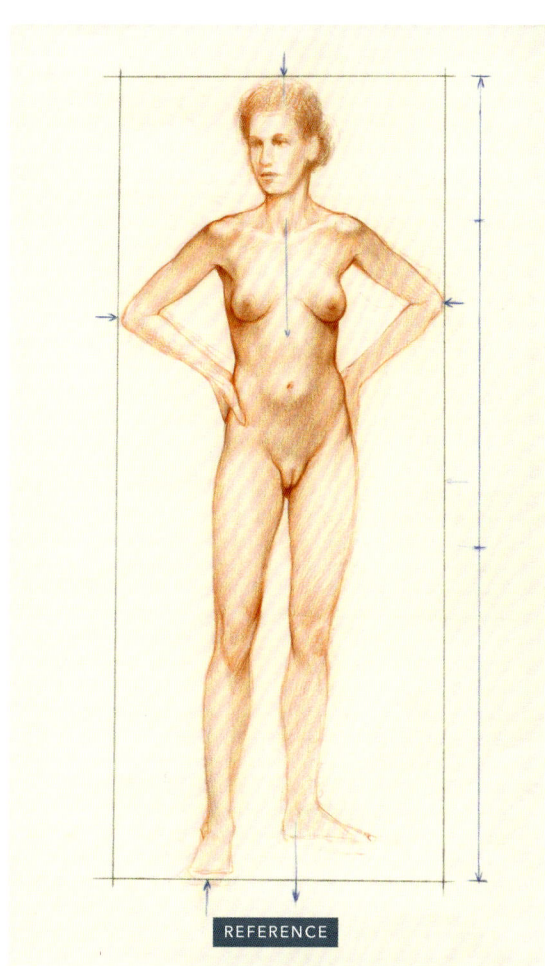

REFERENCE

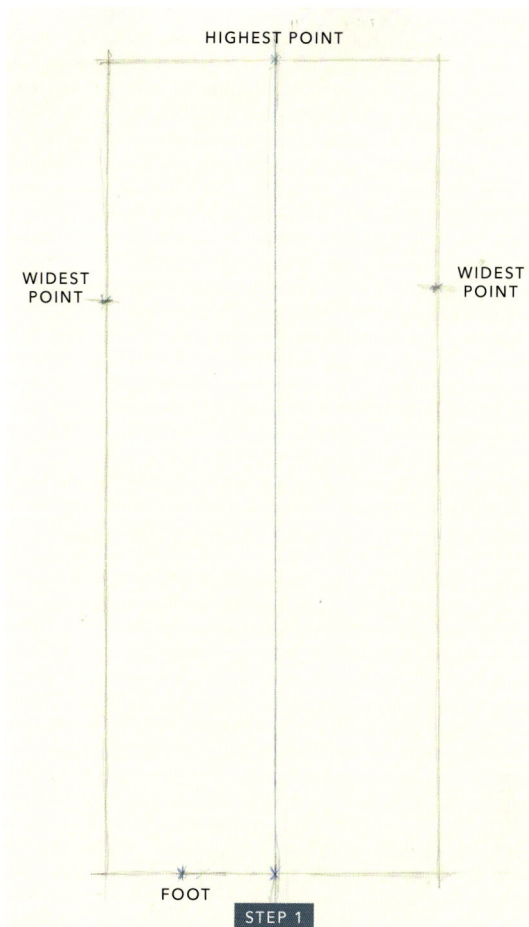

HIGHEST POINT

WIDEST POINT

WIDEST POINT

FOOT

STEP 1

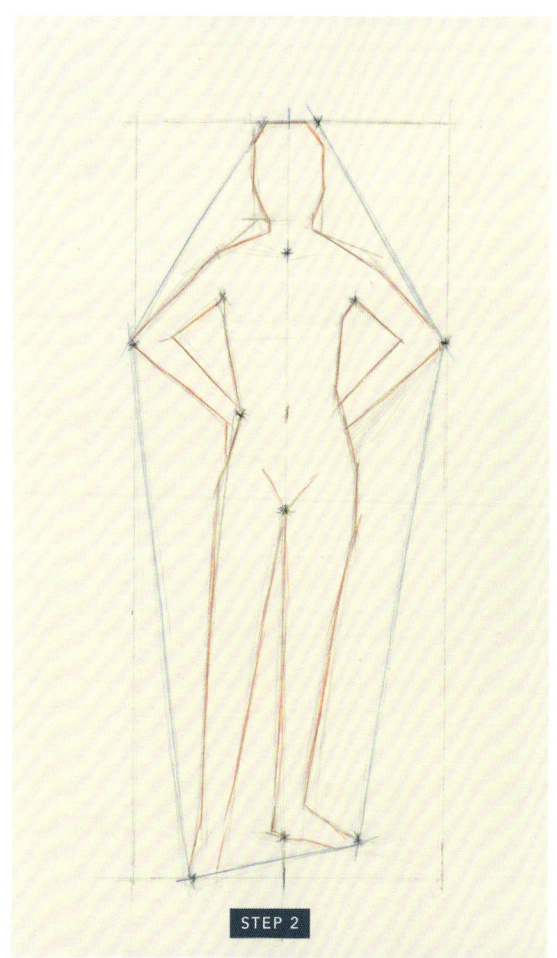

STEP 2

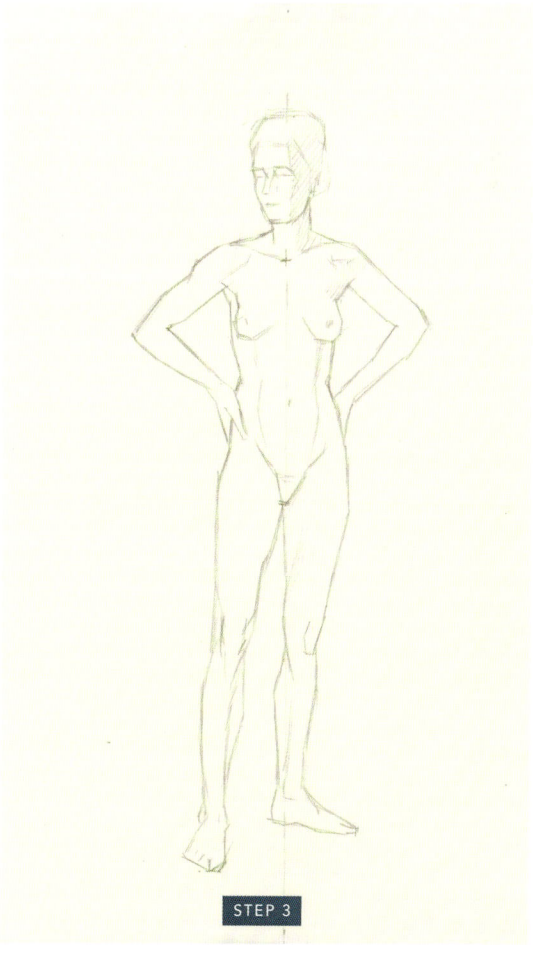

STEP 3

MEASURING A COMPLEX POSE WITH THE ENVELOPE METHOD

It is somewhat easier to draw a standing figure than one in a different kind of pose because the proportions, proportional relationships, and landmarks are clearly iden-tifiable. This sequence shows how to measure and draw using the envelope method when the model is in a more complex and foreshortened pose.

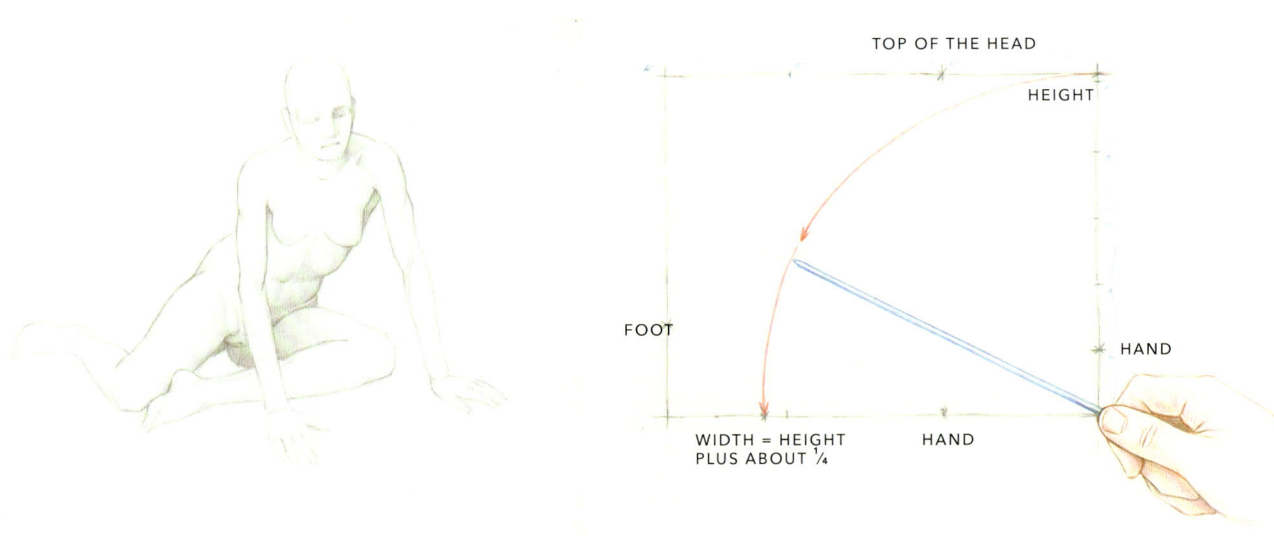

1

First, find the height-to-width ratio of the pose by measuring the maximum height (in this case, from the top of the model's head to her front hand) and the maximum width of the figure (from her foot on the left to her hand on the right). In this pose, the max-imum width is about one-quarter longer than the measure of the height. With these two measures, you can mark the envelope that contains the figure. Next, find more measurements to gradually "tighten" the envelope, marking the positions of the land-marks used to determine height and width on the sides of the envelope. The measure of the position of the hand on the right, is at about one-fifth of the total height of the side of the envelope. The position of the head is at about one-third of the total width of the box starting from the right. Proceeding with this method, find the position of the front hand on the lower margin of the envelop and the foot on the right margin of the envelope.

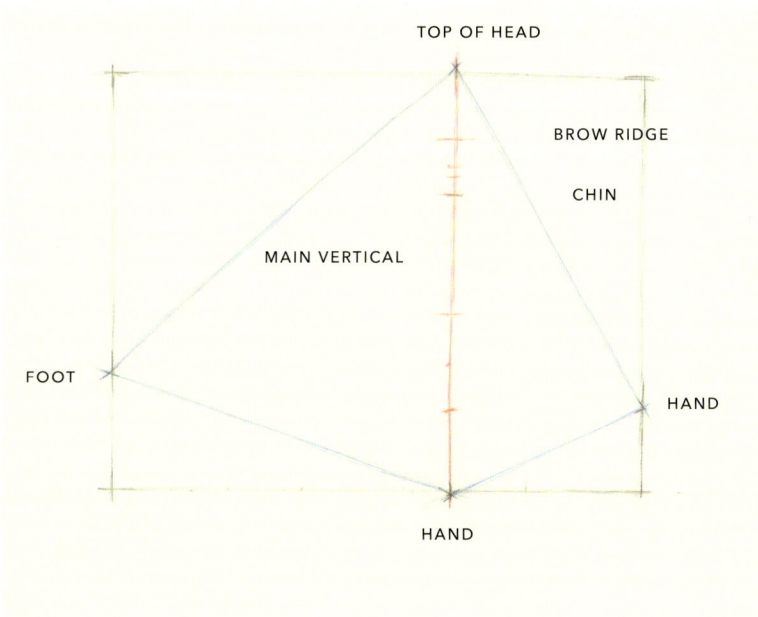

TOP OF HEAD

BROW RIDGE

CHIN

MAIN VERTICAL

FOOT

HAND

HAND

2

Next, define a more precise outline of the space occupied by the figure by connecting these four points. Then find the main vertical—a line along which three or four other landmarks are aligned. In this case, the main vertical goes from the top of the head through the chin and the angle between the waist and thigh and ends at the front hand. Note that the main vertical will not always correspond to the maximum height of the envelope, as it does in this pose.

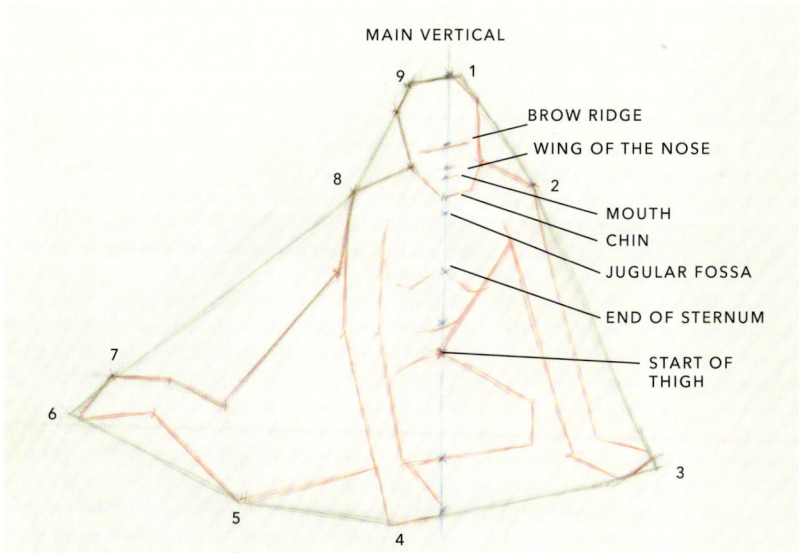

MAIN VERTICAL

BROW RIDGE
WING OF THE NOSE
MOUTH
CHIN
JUGULAR FOSSA
END OF STERNUM
START OF THIGH

3

Now refine the outline of the figure by finding more angles established by more measurements. This image summarizes two stages of measurement: the gray lines show the initial measurement and the red lines a more complete one. Find more landmarks and measuring points along the main vertical.

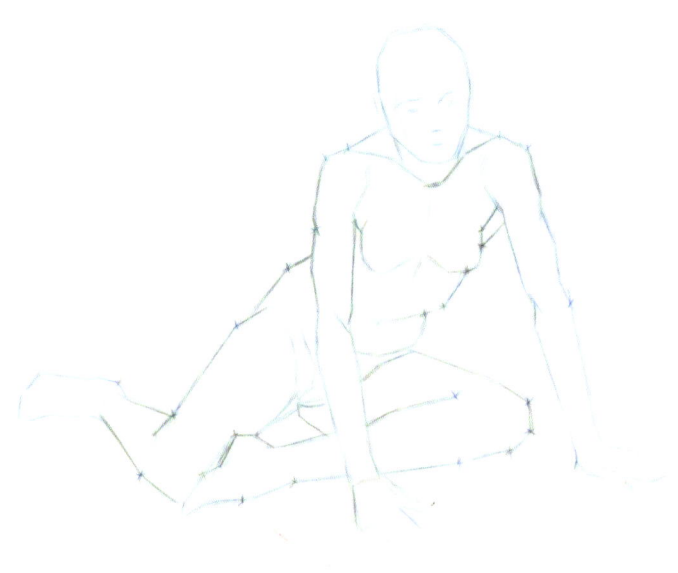

4

Continue to refine the figure, finding more and more measuring points. At this point, you can start erasing the envelope and measuring lines.

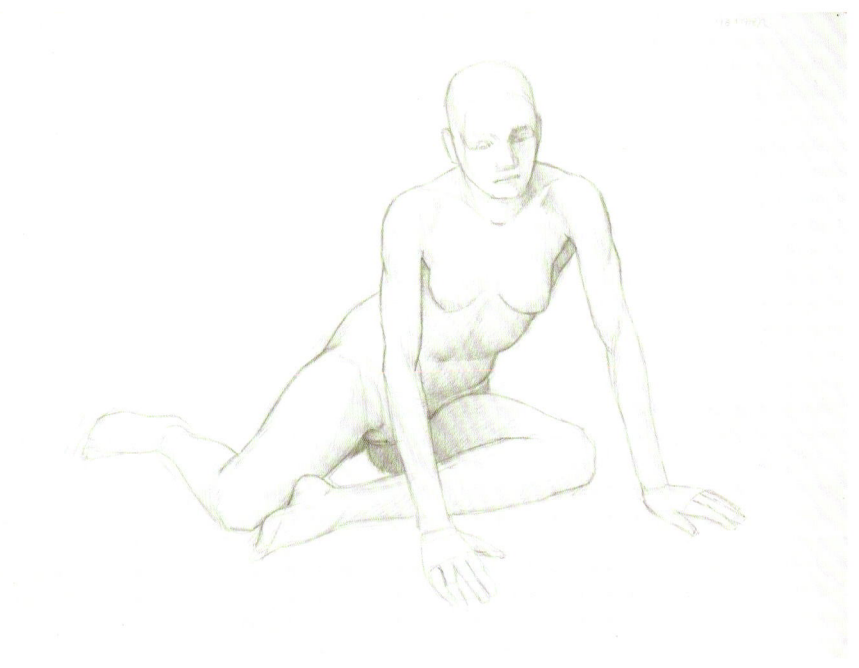

5

Refine the line drawing further to render the figure more realistically, then proceed with either a tonal or a structural rendering.

SIGHTING TECHNIQUE FOR A FORESHORTENED FIGURE

Measuring the figure in foreshortened poses is less complicated than you might think. Just take objective measurements to first create a solid, synthetic version of your subject onto which you can then superimpose the organic forms. For example, when drawing the reclining figure depicted in the sequence below, I decided to use the thigh as the starting point because it was central and easy to measure. The positions of the ribcage, pelvis, and pubic bone were obtained by measuring where their points of contact with the thigh were.

Using a knitting needle (any thin, straight object can be used), I found how the main landmarks of the torso– the top of the chest, the line of the belly that leads to the navel, the pubic bone (A)–lined up on the thigh. I used the thigh simply because it was comparable to a ruler along which I could easily locate the positions of the landmarks. The top of the ribcage (1) was conveniently at mid-thigh, and from there, by approximation, I found the spots where the bottom (2) and top (3) of the pelvis lined up on the thigh. I then drew an approximation of the volume of the thigh, trying to replicate its angle, and marked the positions of the segments of the body lined up behind it (B). Next, I reconstructed the volumes of the head, chest, and pelvis as basic volumes (C). Finally, always using the knitting needle held horizontally (blue lines represent the horizontal alignments), I found more measurements that helped me to refine my drawing, gradually blocking in the whole figure rendered in essential volumes (D). More measurements along vertical lines can be found with the help of a plumb line or by holding the knitting needle vertically, as visualized by the red line in D.

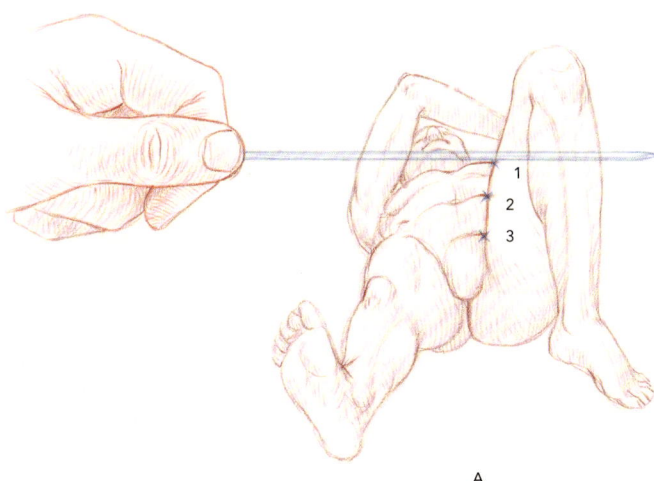

A

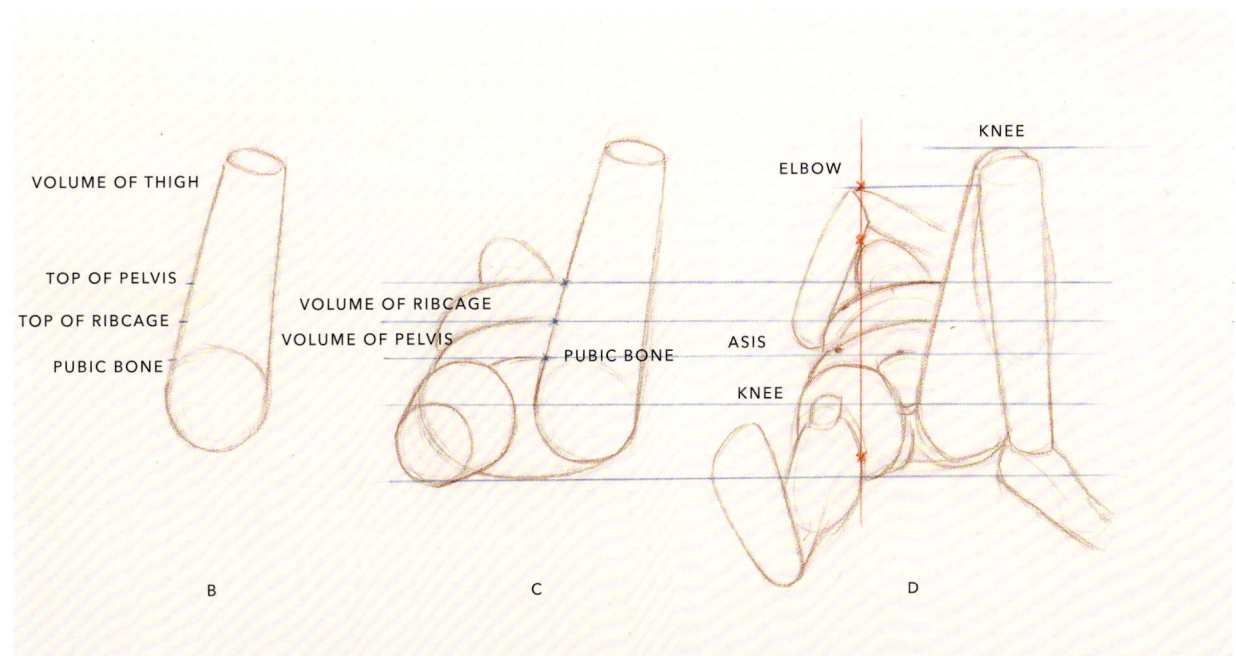

B   C   D

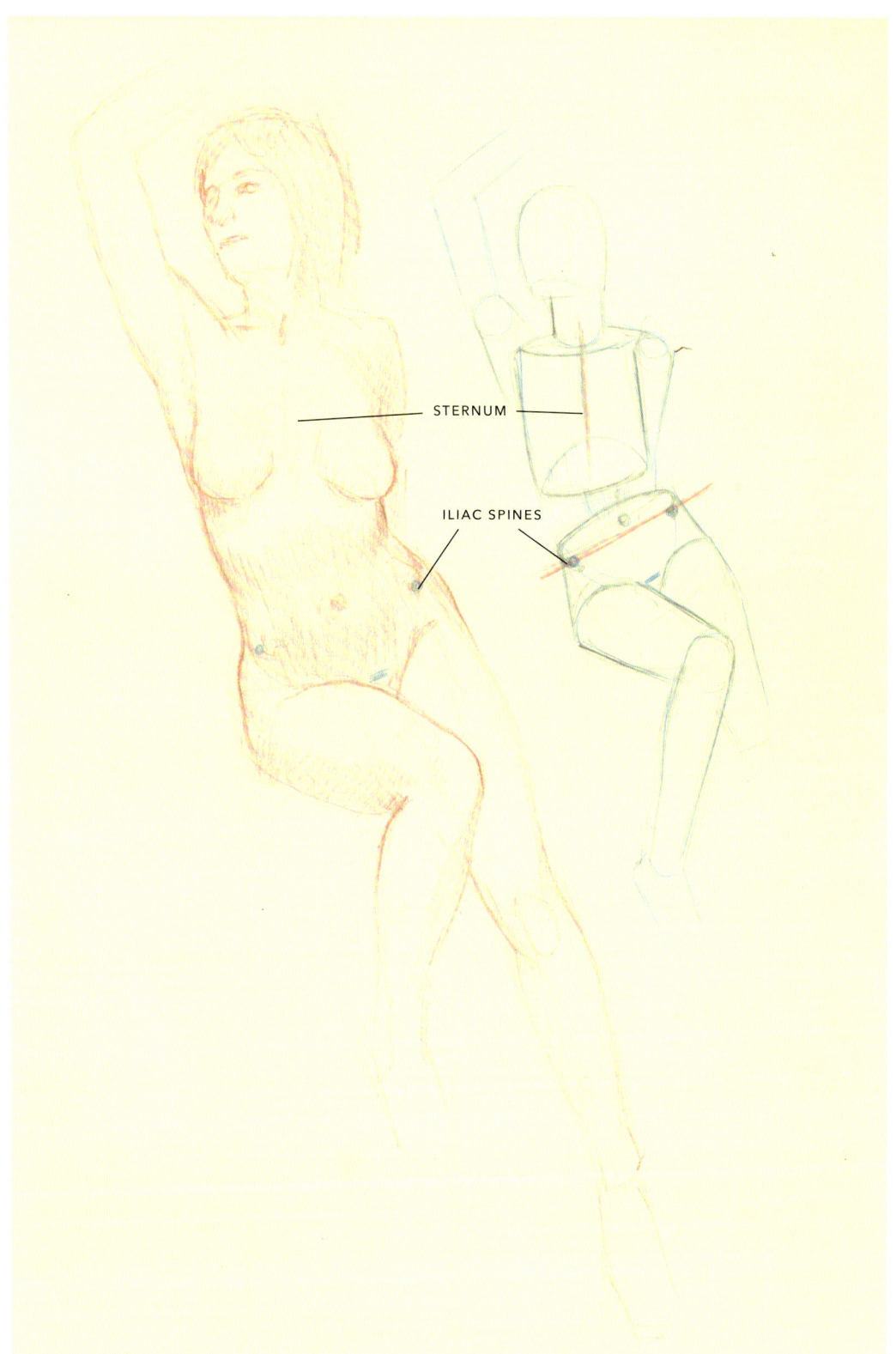

STERNUM

ILIAC SPINES

RIGHT: Drawing a sitting figure with overlapping forms

Use landmarks to identify and draw the main volumes of the torso, head, and limbs and to see how they overlap. Here, identifying the sternum and iliac spines enables you to find the tilts of the ribcage and pelvis.

STRUCTURAL DRAWING

I use the term *structural drawing* to refer to techniques that use line and hatching to describe the structure and volume of the subject. There are a number of such techniques, but here I focus on three: cross-contour, cross-contour hatching, and tonal cross-contour hatching. (These are my definitions; elsewhere you may find different definitions.) The image below summarizes the three techniques.

Structural drawing permits you to describe the planes and volumes of the body accurately. It requires a good working knowledge of human anatomy bur also enables you to refine your knowledge as you draw.

BELOW: Hatching

In cross-contour technique, the line describes a section line of the form that is usually horizontal or vertical *(A)*. In cross-contour hatching *(B)*, the line still follows a cross-section of the form, but the lines overlap at points where there is a change of plane, creating a sense of turning of the volume. In tonal cross-hatching *(C)*, the hatching network is more developed to obtain a tonal as well as structural rendering of the form.

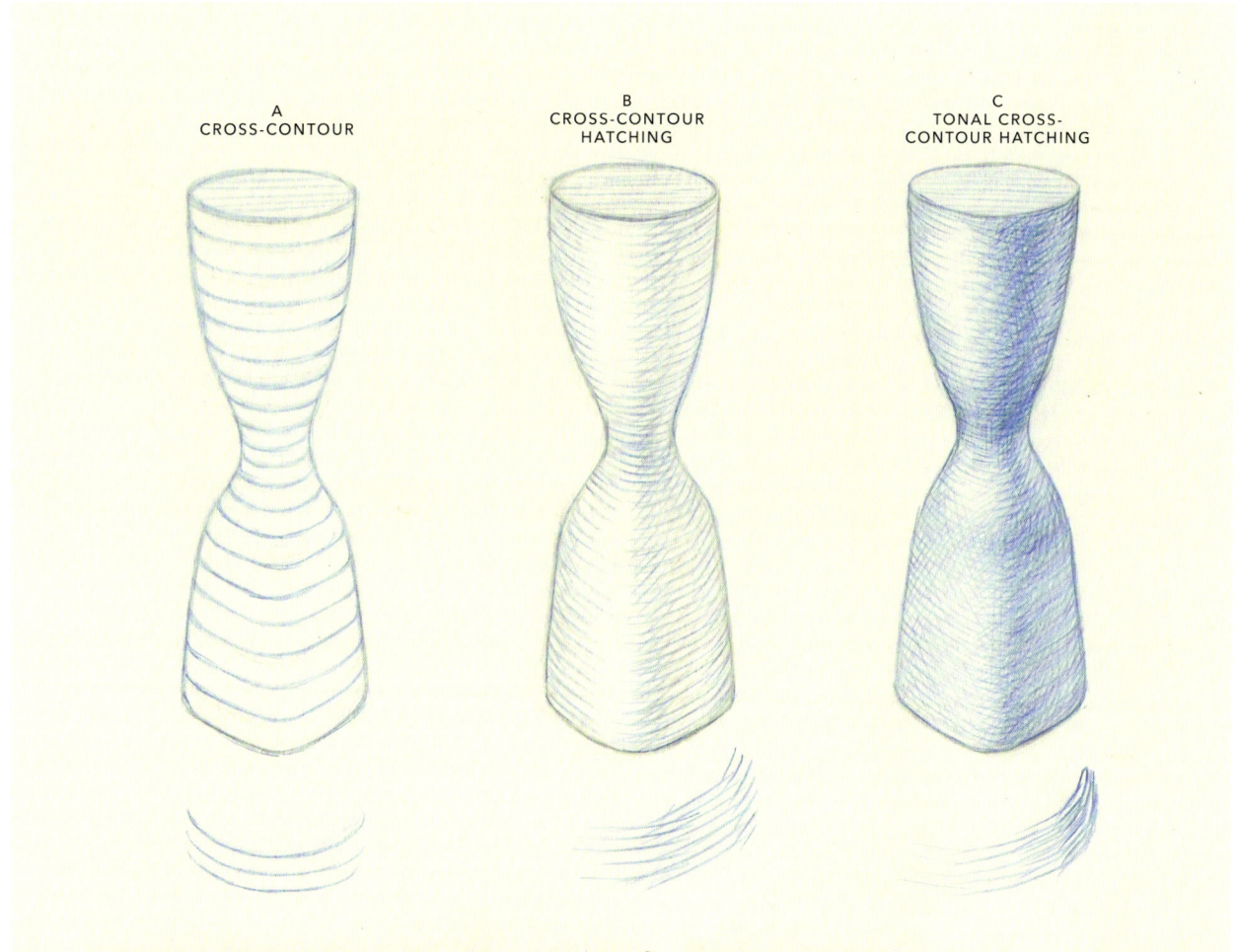

A
CROSS-CONTOUR

B
CROSS-CONTOUR
HATCHING

C
TONAL CROSS-
CONTOUR HATCHING

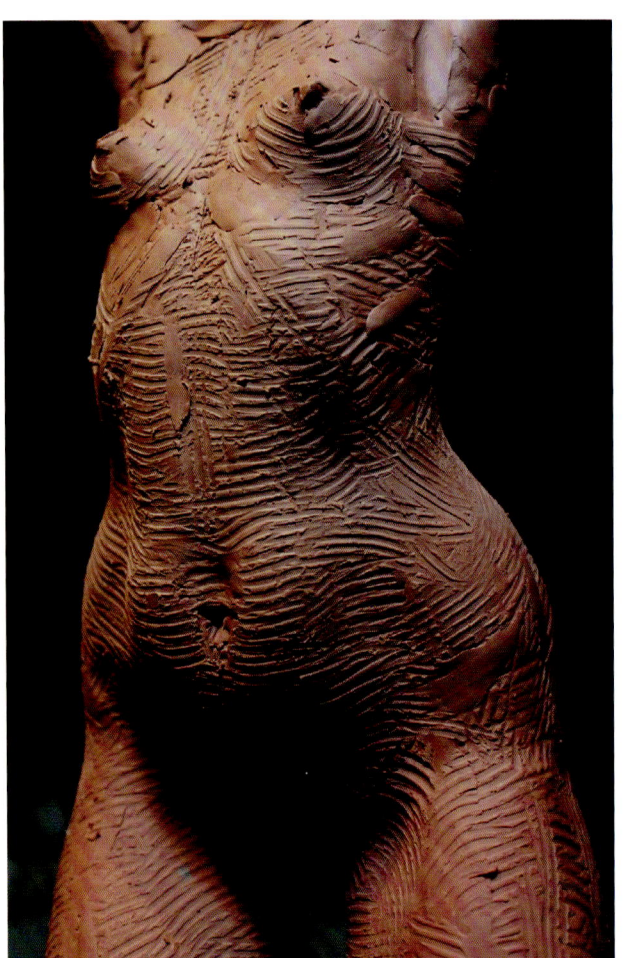
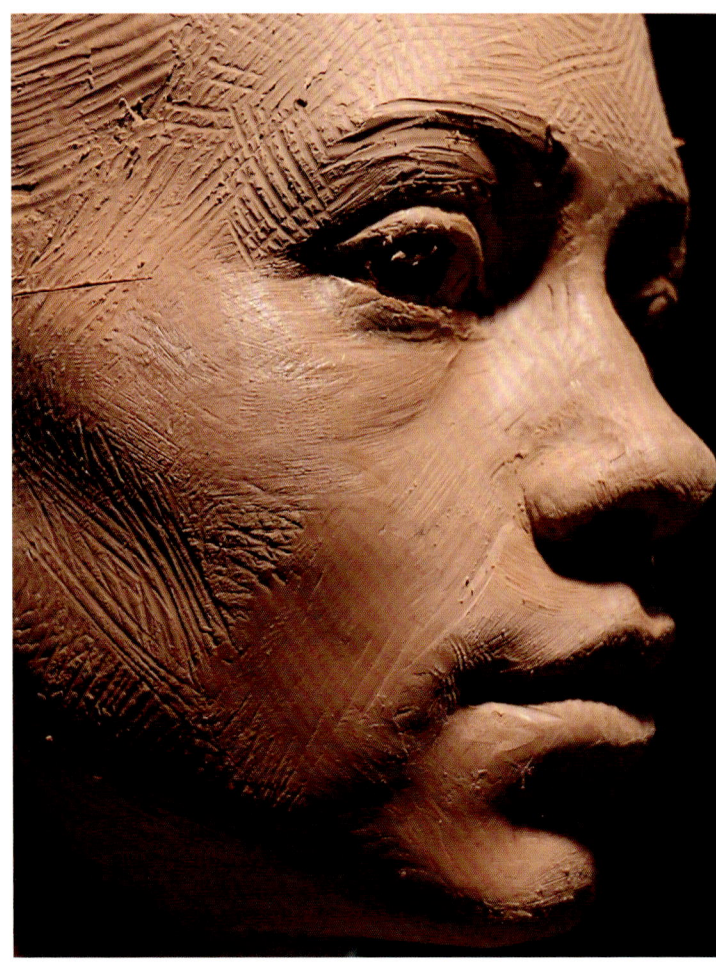

These two examples of works in progress by Brian Booth Craig show the equivalent of the structural drawing method in sculpture. The cross-hatched lines on the face and the body of the sculptures are obtained with a serrated modeling tool. These lines describe much the same kinds of hatching patterns seen in Old Master drawings like those by Michelangelo and Carracci.

When you draw using this method, you start thinking like a sculptor who has to physically re-create a volume. Like the lines of a topographic map, the lines of a structural drawing describe the movement of volumes and the direction of planes.

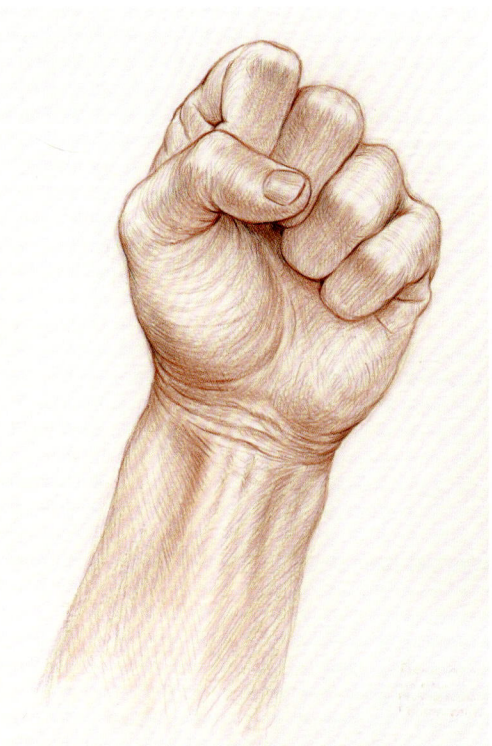

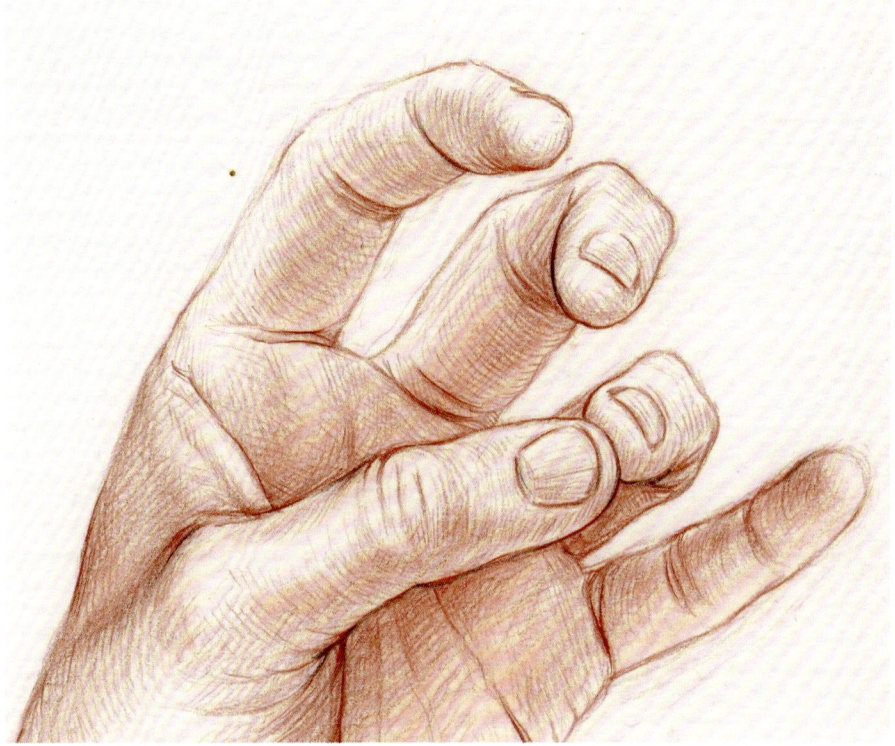

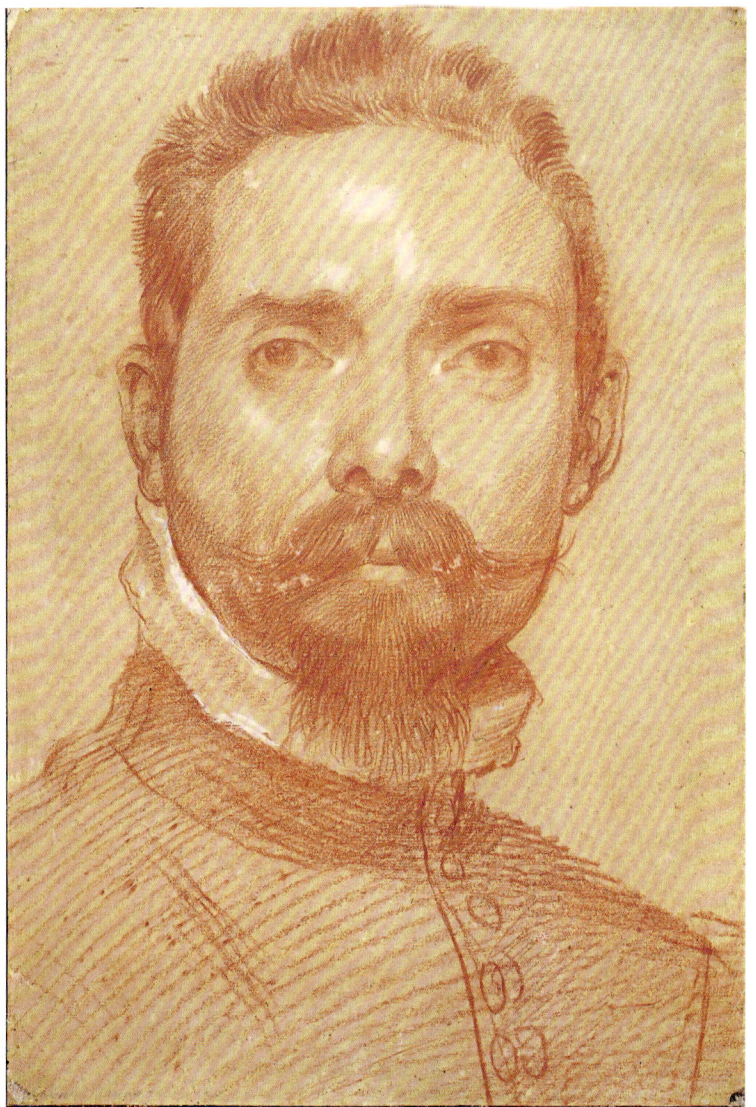

ABOVE: Structural drawings of hands

These two drawings show how I use this technique. The network of lines is more easily visible in the drawing at right.

LEFT: Annibale Carracci, *Male Portrait (The Lutenist Mascheroni),* c. 1593–94, red chalk heightened with white chalk on reddish brown paper. Albertina, Vienna, Austria.

Annibale Carracci, a noted painter from my hometown of Bologna, Italy, produced a great number of very expressive portraits. Note the delicate structural cross-hatching in this drawing done with red chalk on toned paper with white chalk highlights.

MICHELANGELO'S DRAWING TECHNIQUE

Many of Michelangelo's drawings are executed with the structural cross-hatching method, though these drawings are often polished to a smooth finish. The artist's drawings always express a very strong sense of volume informed by a thorough knowledge of anatomy and a masterful drawing technique.

RIGHT: Michelangelo Buonarroti, *Studies for the Libyan Sibyl,* 1510-11, red chalk, with small accents of white chalk on the left shoulder of the figure in the main study, sheet: 11⅜ × 8⁷⁄₁₆ inches (28.9 × 21.4 cm). Metropolitan Museum, New York, purchase, Joseph Pulitzer Bequest, 1924.

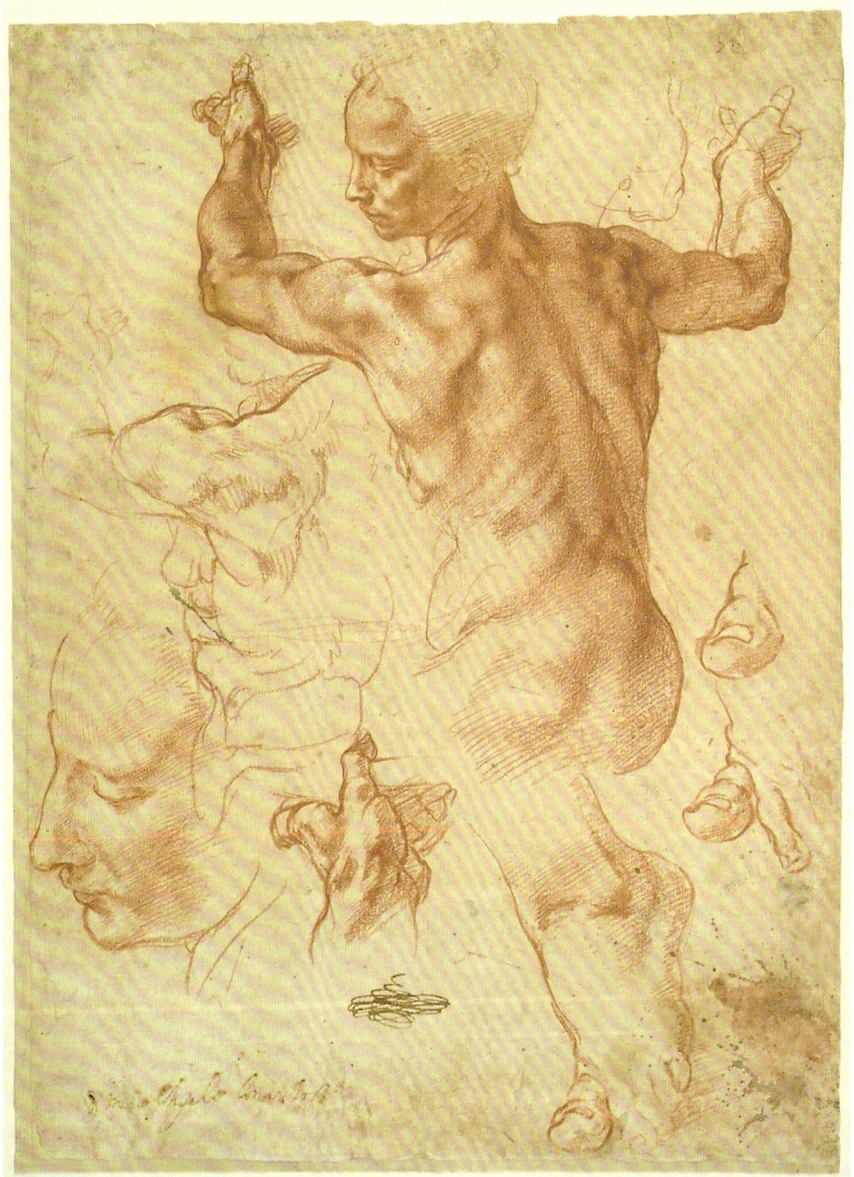

TONAL DRAWING

The drawings of the French Romantic artist Pierre-Paul Prud'hon (1758–1823) are excellent examples of tonal development, as these images demonstrate. In the image below right, you can actually see the various stages of drawing that characterized his technique. First, Prud'hon sketched-in the general outlines of the figure with charcoal. (This first stage remains visible at the level of the feet and lower legs.) Prud'hon then defined the three dominant values: for the light mass he used white chalk; for the shadow mass he used charcoal; and he left untouched the mid-value areas that corresponded to the value of the toned paper. He then started extending the tonal scale a few values at a time, gradually blending the values. The upper part of drawing shows the final stage, with extended tonal development and blending. Prud'hon worked on toned paper, but you can also use this technique on white paper.

BELOW LEFT: Pierre-Paul Prud'hon, *Study of a Man*, c. 1810-20, black and white chalk on blue paper, 22¾ × 13¼ inches (57.79 × 33.66 cm). Los Angeles County Museum of Art.

BELOW RIGHT: Pierre-Paul Prud'hon, *Standing Nude*, 1806 or 1807, black and white chalk and black crayon on paper, sheet: 18¼ x 10 inches (46.4 x 25.4 cm). Detroit Institute of the Arts, Bequest of John S. Newberry.

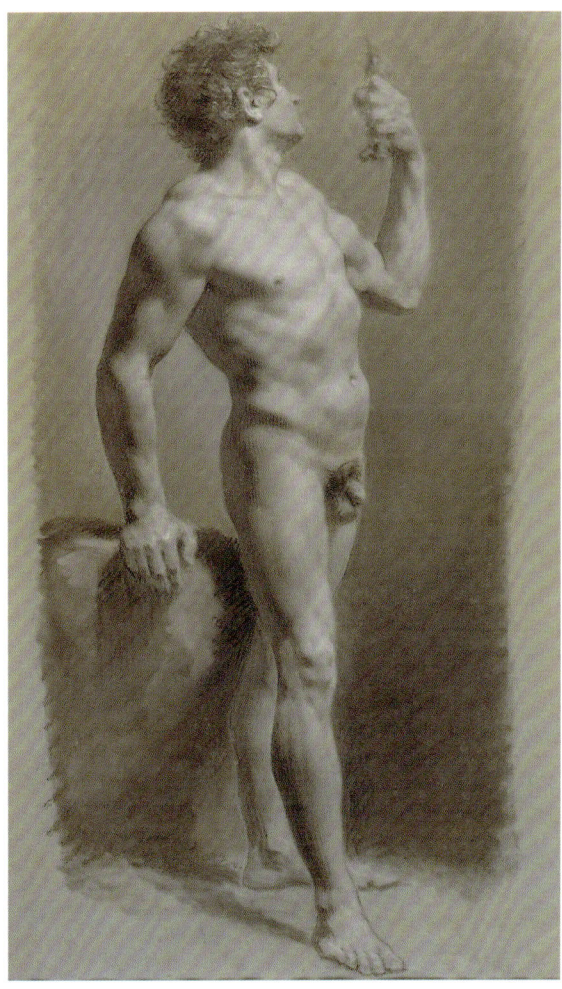

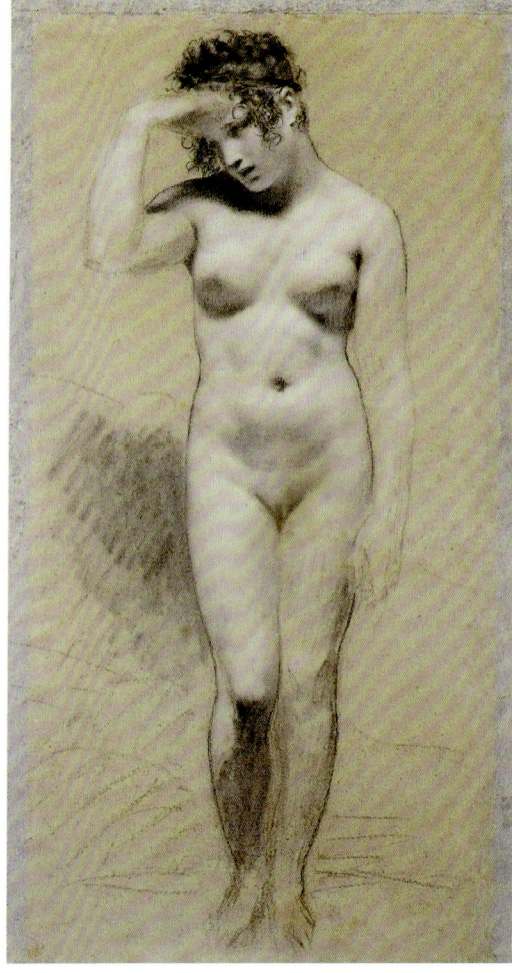

A CONTEMPORARY MASTER OF TONAL DRAWING

These two works by Richard Morris are beautiful examples of tonal drawing. *Sarah* is a charcoal drawing on toned paper in which the tonal rendering is achieved by gradual layering of charcoal, creating soft tonal passages. *Figure Study (Sarah)* is also on toned paper, but here Morris left the paper untouched where its value corresponded to the value of the skin of the model. Those areas are identifiable by the warm glow between the lighter and darker areas. Morris then applied charcoal to areas of darker value and white chalk to areas of lighter

BELOW: Richard Morris, *Sarah*, n.d., charcoal, 10 x 12 inches (25.40 × 30.48 cm). Courtesy of the artist.

RIGHT: Richard Morris, *Figure Study (Sarah)*, 2014, red, black, and white chalk on paper, 16 × 8 inches (40.64 × 20.32 cm). Courtesy of the artist.

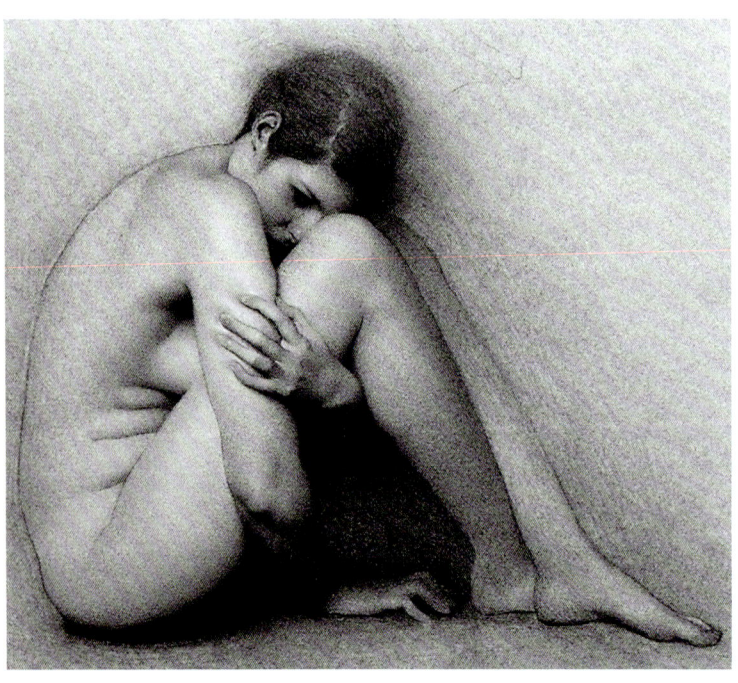

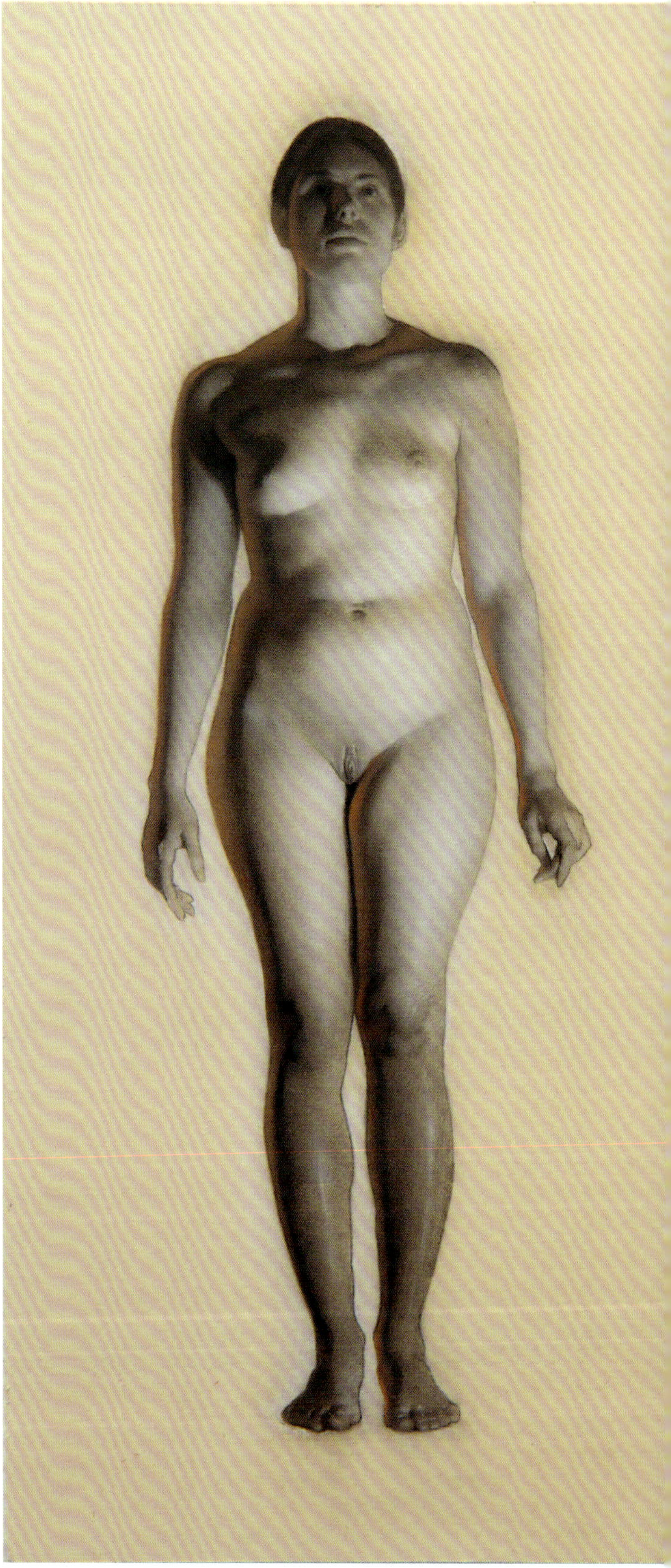

REDUCTION TECHNIQUE

The reduction technique, also called the subtractive technique, relies on the gradual removal of dry pigment from a paper surface that has been toned—typically using charcoal or conté crayon, either in sticks or powder form. The technique focuses on the light on the form and the contrast created between the areas of light and shadow.

Once the main areas of value are developed by removing pigment, either with an eraser or chamois cloth, the tonal rendering can be further developed by adding charcoal to the darker areas and white chalk to the lightest areas. (Usually, pure white cannot be obtained merely by removing the original ground applied to the paper.) With this last step, you're essentially following the same approach you would use on toned paper.

BELOW: I made this drawing of the head of Gianlorenzo Bernini's *David* for an online class demonstration using the reduction technique with charcoal and white chalk highlights.

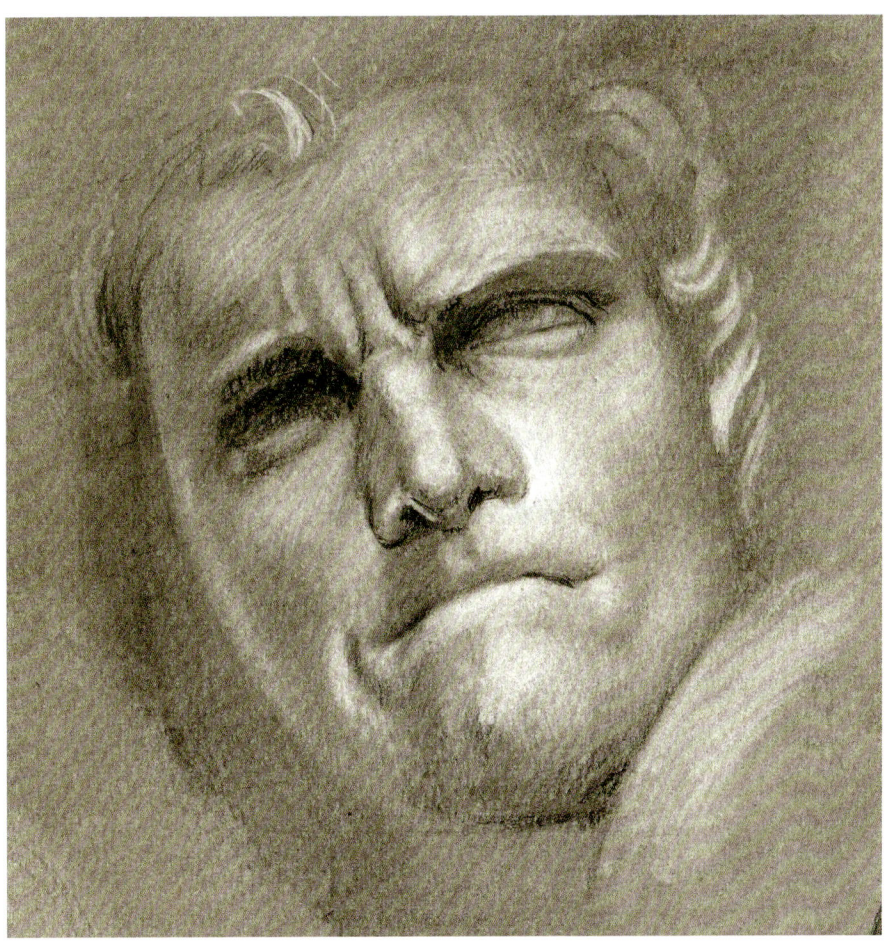

REDUCTION TECHNIQUE, CHARCOAL AND CHALK ON WHITE PAPER

To copy this demonstration, you'll need charcoal sticks or charcoal dust and a variety of erasing tools: chamois skin, a kneaded eraser, and one of those mechanical-pencil-type erasers. You'll also need white chalk in pencils or sticks as well as sandpaper to keep your drawing tools sharp.

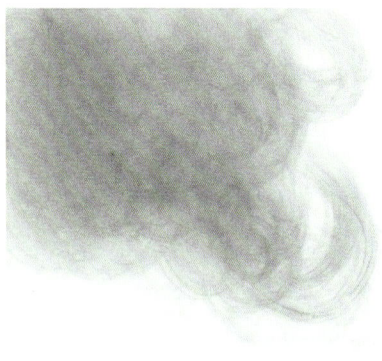

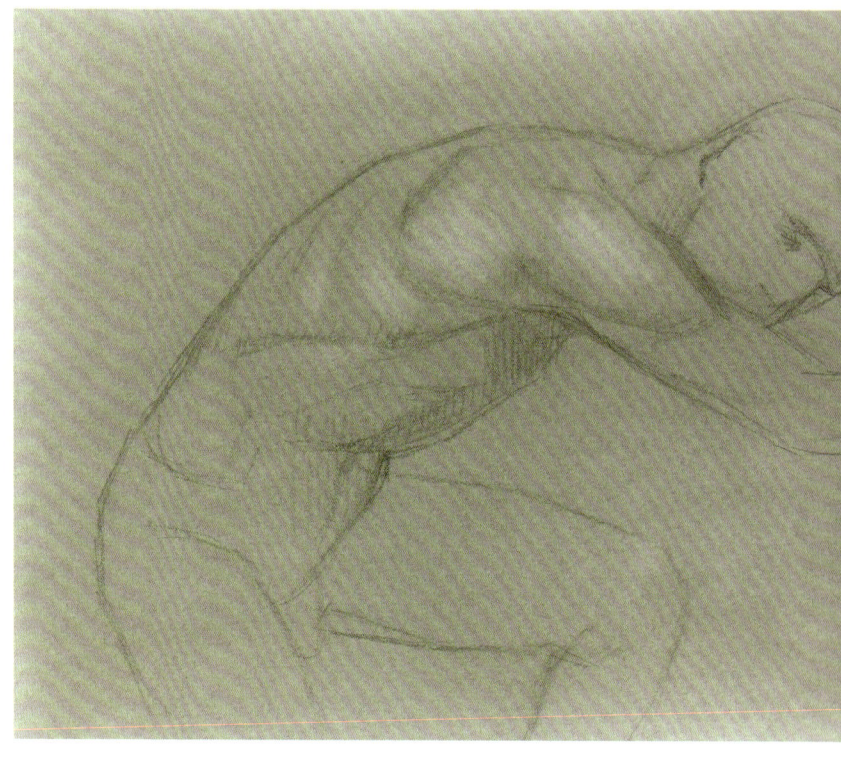

1

Start with a piece of paper, white or lightly toned, and smear it with charcoal, using powder or a stick. Rub the charcoal gently but thoroughly across the paper until it is saturated with pigment. Blow on the paper to get rid of any loose particles.

2

Sketch in the main outlines and volumes of your subject. Don't draw too much detail at this point—just the dominant volumes. Then, using a kneaded eraser or chamois, lift off the dominant areas of light.

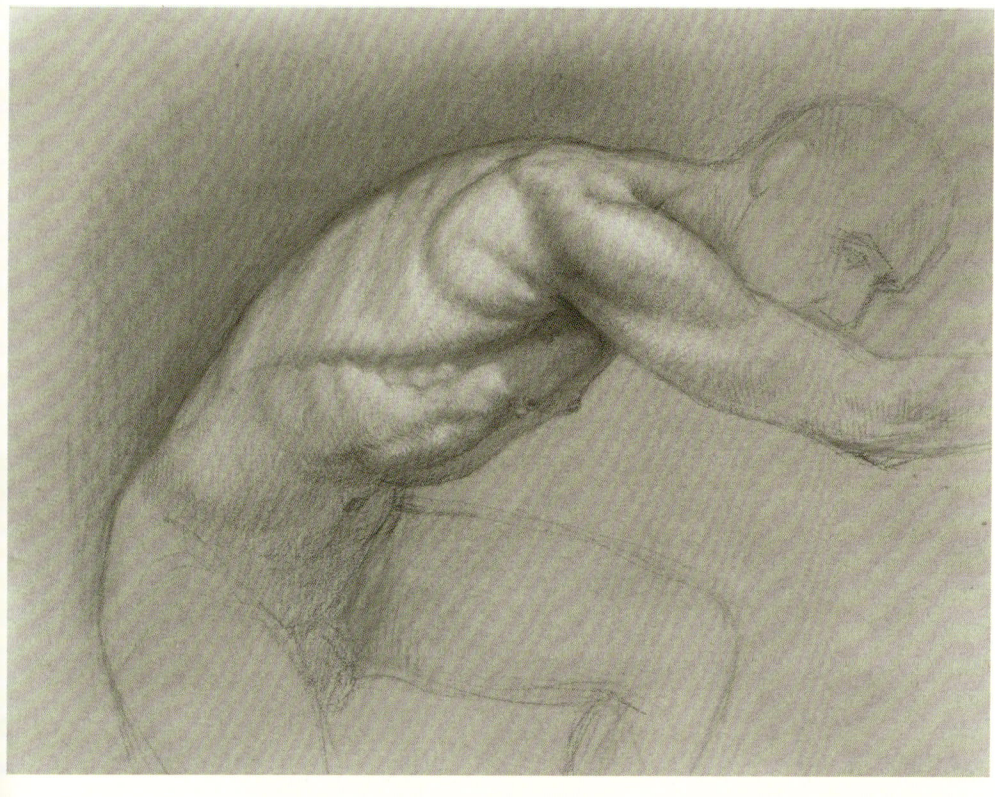

3

Keep erasing the charcoal with finer and finer erasing tools to extend the tonal scale in the light mass. At the same time, you can extend the values in the shadow mass by applying additional charcoal as needed.

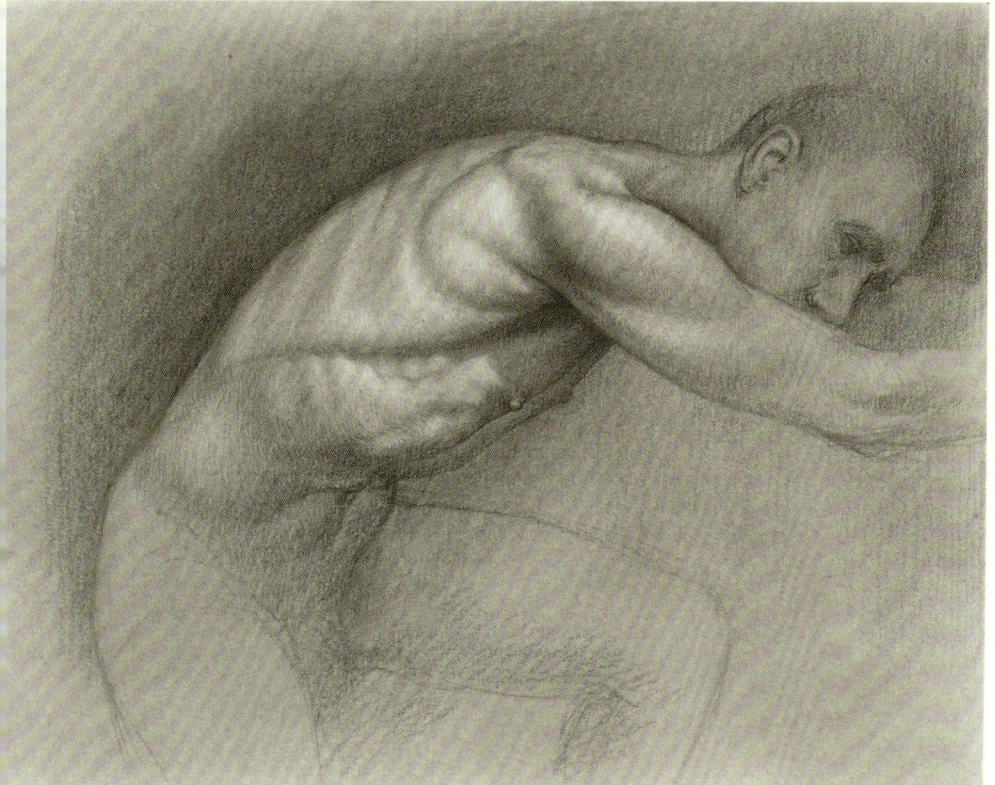

4

Gradually refine and define your drawing with charcoal and white chalk, if needed.

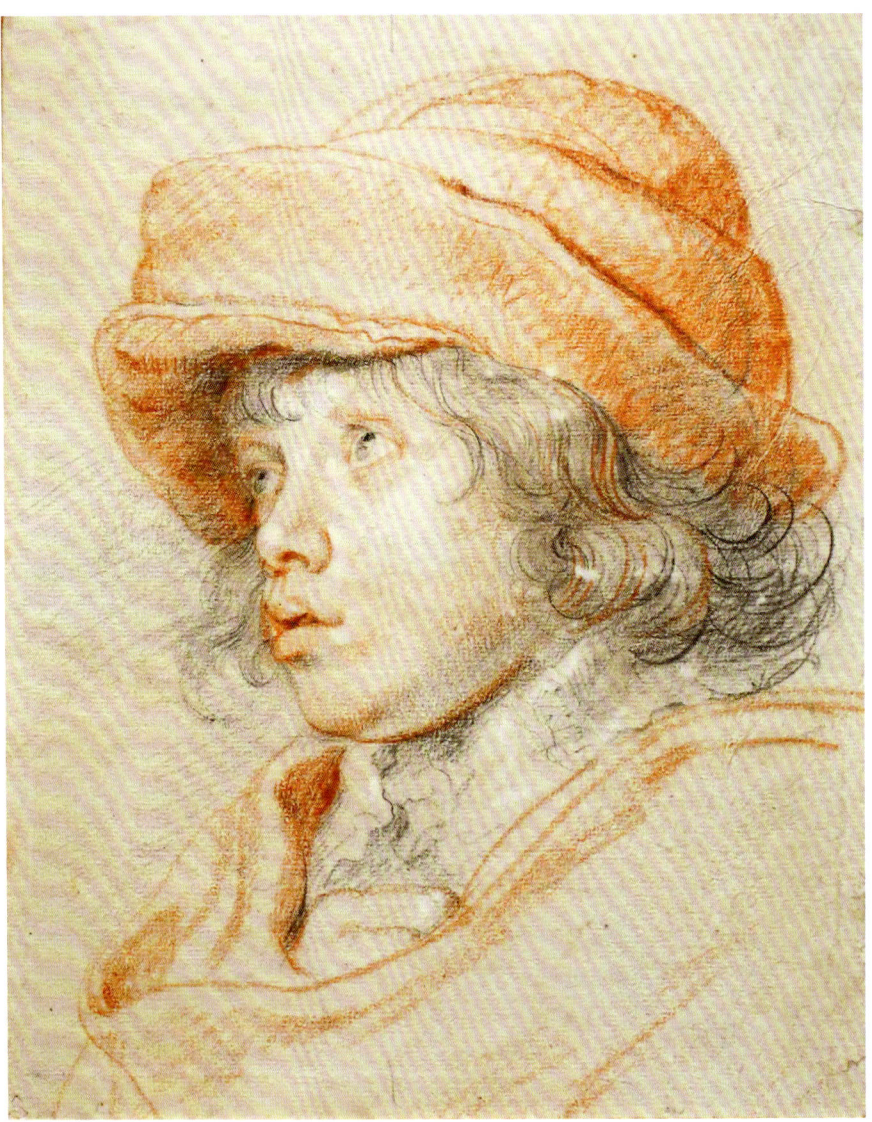

TROIS CRAYONS

Another essential technique is the cool-and-warm technique known as *trois crayons* because it requires three different-colored chalks or conté crayons: red, black, and white. *Trois crayons* is very useful for practicing the concepts of color temperature, high versus low chroma, tint and tone, and opacity versus transparency.

The *temperature* of a color can be defined as cool or warm depending on where it lies on the spectrum: for example, a vermilion red, which leans toward the orange/yellow side of the spectrum, is warmer than an alizarin crimson red, which instead leans toward the cooler blue/violet side of the spectrum.

Chroma refers to the intensity of a color. A color can be high chroma or low chroma: for example, vermilion is a high-chroma red while Venetian red is low chroma. Adding white to a color produces a *tint*, making the color lighter and cooler and lowering its chroma. Adding black produces a *tone*, lowering the chroma and also affecting the temperature, which that tends to cool down. Colors can also be laid down in *opaque*, *translucent*, or *transparent* layers. With this technique, thinly layered red and black tend to create a sense of depth, whereas a sense of volume is created by gradually increasing the brightness of highlights with opaque white chalk.

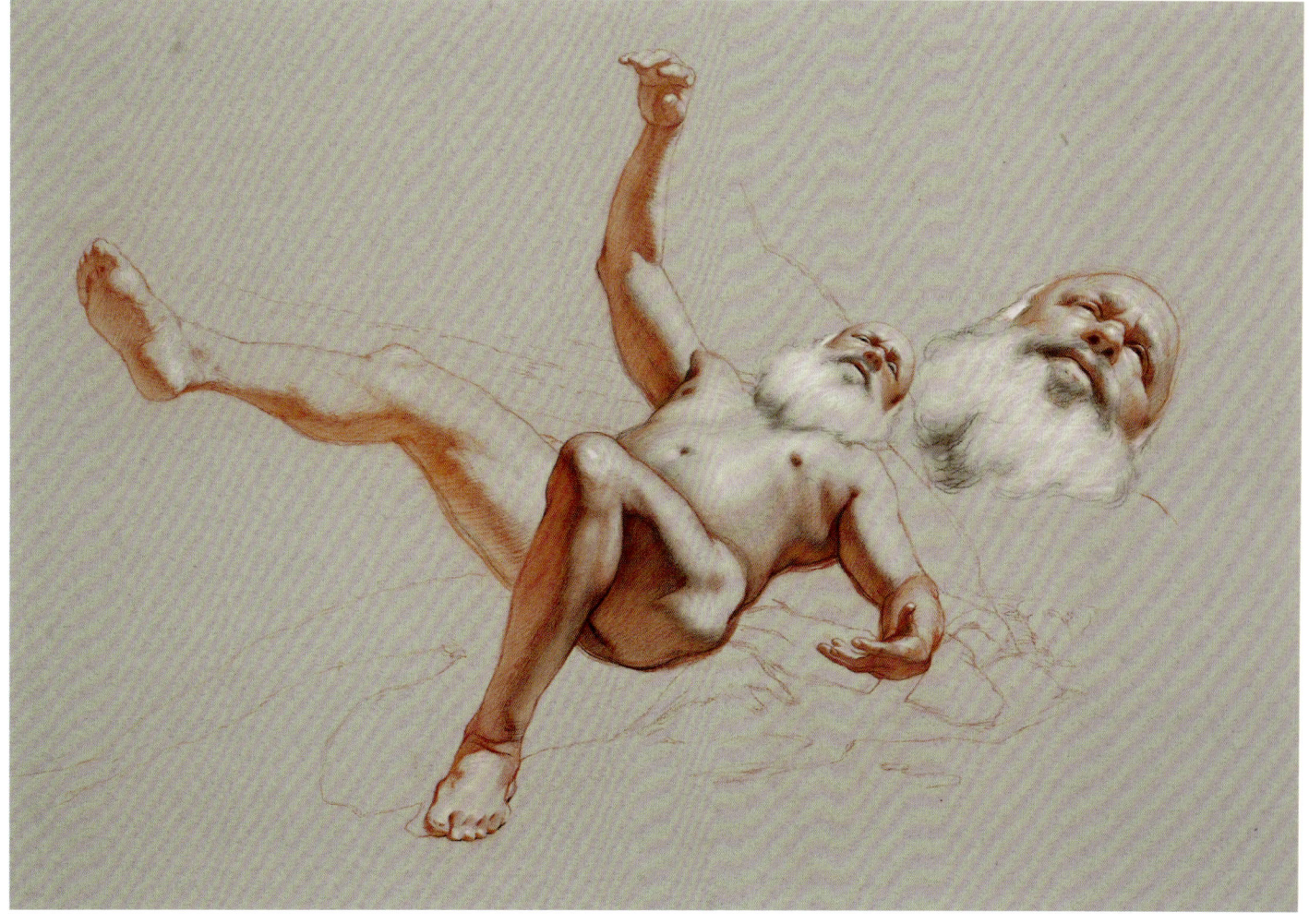

ABOVE: Noah Buchanan, *Study for Fallen Silenus,* 2020, red, black, and white chalk on toned paper, 15 × 18 inches (38.10 × 45.72 cm). Courtesy of the artist.

The *trois crayons* technique can also be used in a more detailed and deliberate way. This contemporary drawing by my colleague and friend Noah Buchanan was executed on a piece of cool gray toned paper using a purely additive approach, but the concepts of temperature, chroma, and transparency versus opacity apply here, as well.

TROIS CRAYONS AND REDUCTION TECHNIQUE ON WHITE PAPER TONED WITH RED PIGMENT

To summarize the *trois crayons* technique: Start drawing with red chalk or conté crayon on lightly toned paper, developing the figure tonally using only red in the light mass but both red chalk and black charcoal in the shadow mass. Use only red for higher-chroma areas—places hit directly by the light—to better distinguish them from the shadow-mass areas, where mixing black pigment with red will lower the chroma and create a darker tonal range, achieving a sense of depth, coolness, and transparency in the shadows. Add white only in the light-mass areas where you want to spotlight the lightest values. Do not mix white with red. Use white olny after you've removed all the red ground but find you still need to obtain a lighter value. Unlike red and black pigments, which can achieve a sense of transparency, white chalk is opaque, so you can obtain a progression from semitransparent to translucent to semi-opaque and, finally, opaque effects with progressive layering. The transparent shadow area will convey depth; the opaque light areas will create volume, enhancing the overall three-dimensional effect of your artwork.

The three steps here guide you through the essential aspects of the *trois crayons* technique. (The reduction technique in which pigment is lifted from the paper is also used.)

You will need white or lightly toned paper, red powdered pigment such as Cretacolor Sanguine Powder, a red earth conté crayon, white chalk, and charcoal. Colored pencils are also an option. You will also need erasing tools like those for the reduction technique.

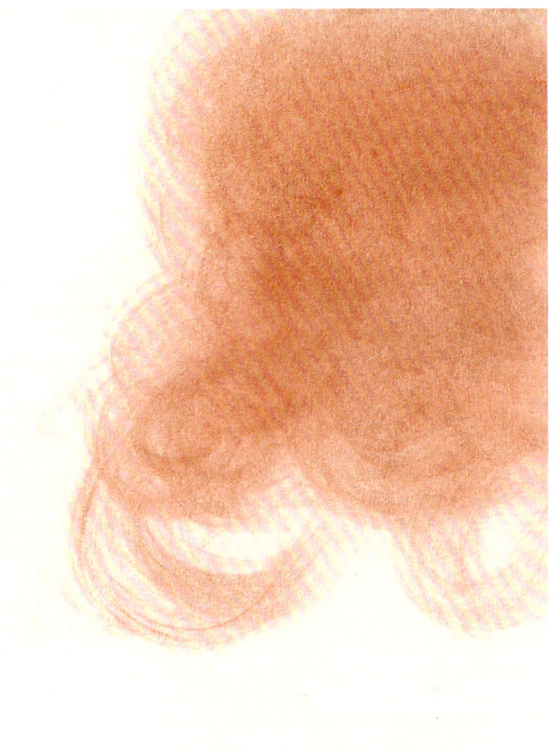

1
Smear red pigment powder (Pompeian red, sanguine red, or a similar red earth color) on a sheet of white paper.

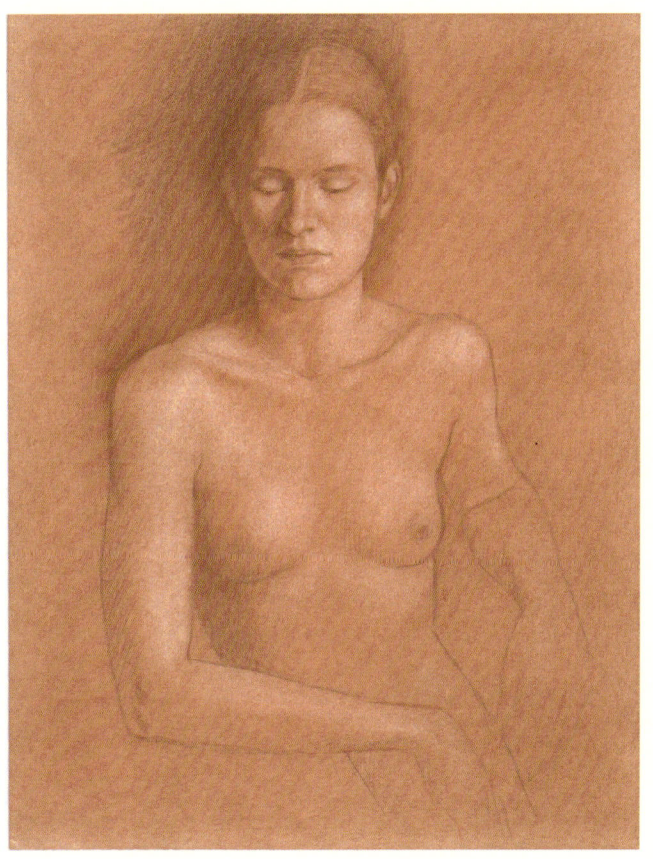

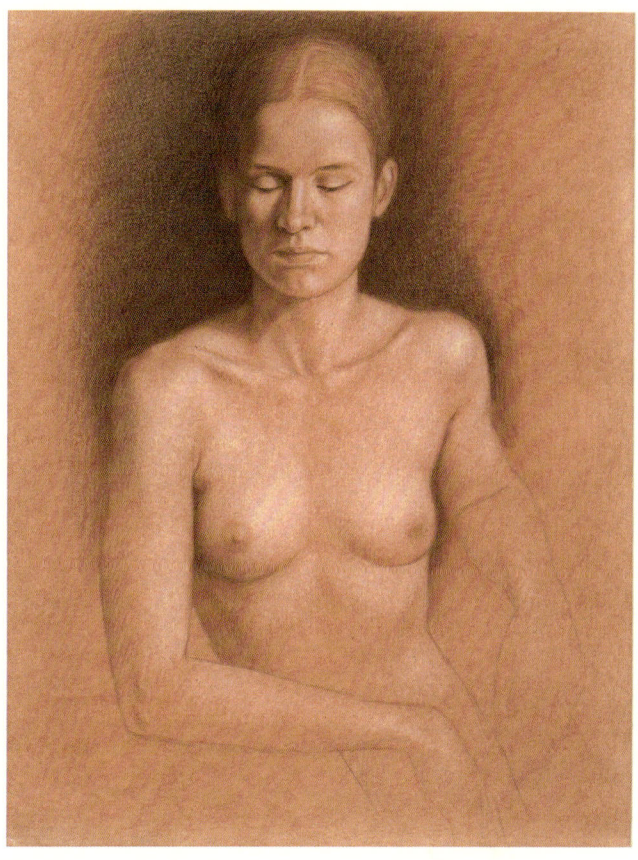

2
Next, block in the essential outlines of your drawing, then start refining the forms by lifting the highlights and developing the darker values with red pigment.

3
Finally, use the black to extend the tonal scale and lower the chroma in the shadows. Develop the light-mass area with the red and the highlights with white.

MEASURING AND ALIGNING USING THE CENTER LINE AND THE LINE OF THE CENTER OF GRAVITY

The center line (drawing *A* in the image below) and the line of center of gravity (drawing *B*) are useful for measuring a pose. These imaginary lines can be visualized, when straight, by aligning a plumb line or a knitting needle over the posing model. In drawing *A*, the center line divides the figure in two, making it easy to compare the symmetry of the two halves. In the central drawing *(B),* the line of center of gravity (red dotted line) goes through the center of the body starting from the top of the head, dividing it into two asymmetric halves that can easily be compared for an accurate measuring of the figure. Also notice how the center line (blue line) follows the external forms of the body, revealing their volumetric characteristics. The jugular fossa and seventh cervical vertebra are marked as the anterior and posterior starting points of the line of the center of gravity on the top of the ribcage. In figure *C*, the center line, following the middle of a figure in torsion, describes the relief of the forms of the body and divides it in two asymmetric halves that can be easily compared with each other for more accurate measurements, as shown by the blue arrows. The line of the center of gravity is projected on the outside of the ribcage at the jugular fossa.

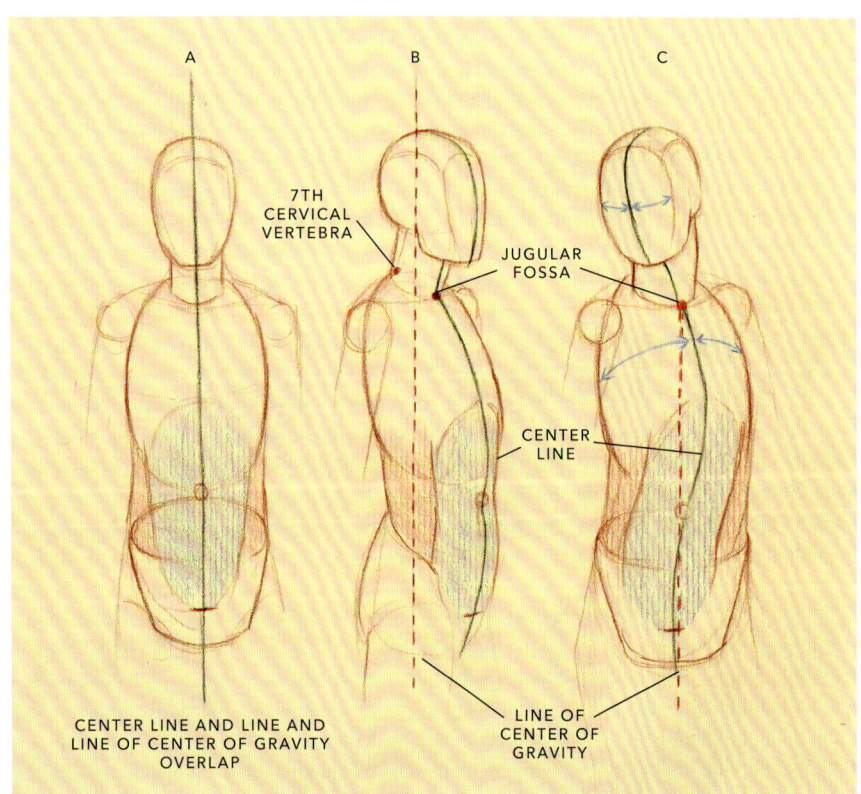

CENTER LINE AND LINE AND LINE OF CENTER OF GRAVITY OVERLAP

7TH CERVICAL VERTEBRA

JUGULAR FOSSA

CENTER LINE

LINE OF CENTER OF GRAVITY

EXERCISE

Demonstrate how much you've learned—and keep improving your skills—by doing a master copy of one or more of the master drawings in this chapter. Here are just a few possibilities—by Carracci and two contemporary artists (following pages).

BELOW: Annibale Caraccci, *Male Portrait* (full information on page 331).

OVERLEAF LEFT: Daniel Maidman, *MariYa,* 2017, black and white Prismacolor on Canford gunmetal gray paper, 15 x 17 inches (38.10 x 43.18 cm). Courtesy of the artist.

OVERLEAF RIGHT: Patricia Watwood, *Drawing of Rachel Seated,* 2018, sanguine and white prismacolor on apricot paper, 18 x 12½ inches (45.7 x 31.7 cm). Courtesy of the artist.

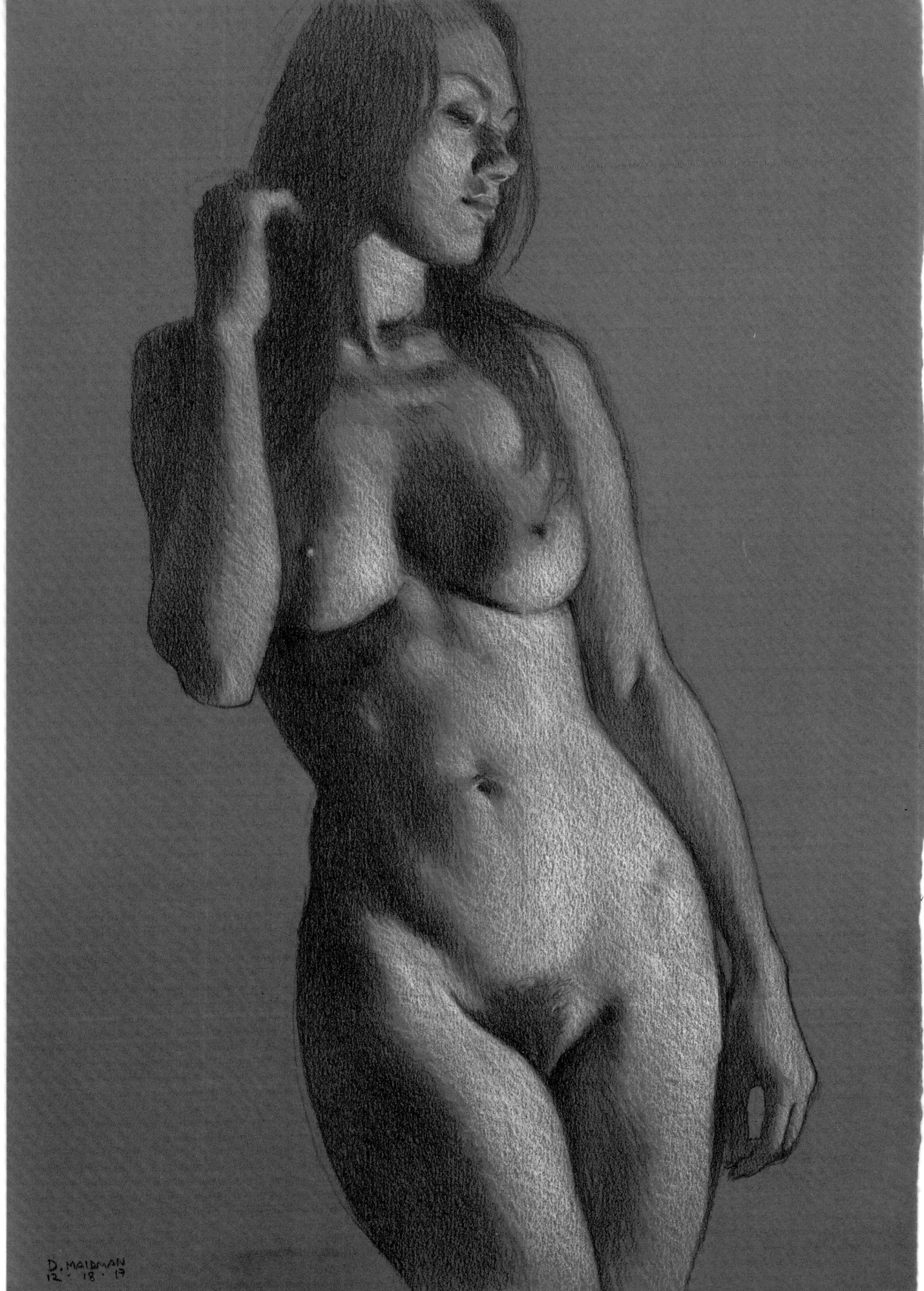

D. MAIDMAN
12 · 18 · 17

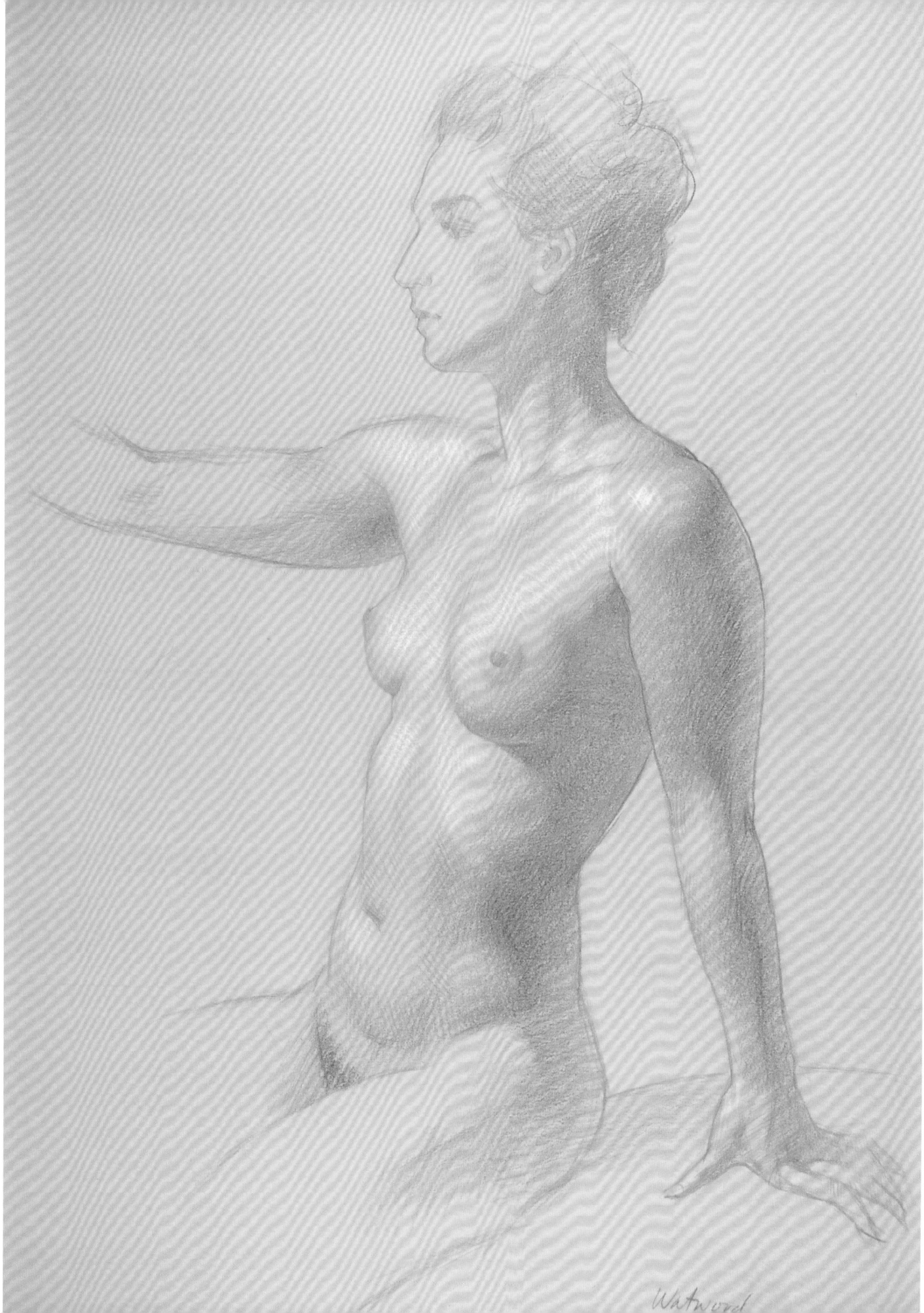

Watword

SELECTED BIBLIOGRAPHY

ANATOMY AND ART

Bammes, Gottfried. *Die Gestalt des Menschen*. Stuttgart: Urania, 2002.

———. *Complete Guide to Life Drawing*. Kent, U.K.: Search Press, 2011.

Goldfinger, Eliot. *Human Anatomy for Artists: The Elements of Form*. New York: Oxford University Press, 1991.

Lolli, Alberto, Mauro Zocchetta, and Renzo Peretti. *Struttura uomo: manuale di anatomia artistica*. Vicenza, Italy: Neri Pozza, 2000.

Osti, Roberto. *Basic Human Anatomy*. New York: Monacelli Studio, 2016.

Richer, Paul. *Artistic Anatomy*. New York: Watson-Guptill, 1986.

ANATOMY AND SCIENCE

Clemente, Carmine D. *Anatomy: A Regional Atlas of the Human Body*. Philadelphia: Lippincott, Williams & Wilkins, 2011.

Netter, Frank H. *Atlas of Human Anatomy*. Philadelphia: Saunders/Elsevier, 2014.

Sobotta, Johannes, et al. *Atlante di anatomia dell'uomo*. Florence: USES, 1996.

Spalteholz, Werner, et al. *Atlante di anatomia umana*, 6th ed. Milan: Vallardi, 1977.

Testut, L., and A. Latarjet. *Anatomia umana*. Turin: Unione Tipografico Editrice Torinese, 1971.

ANATOMY AND THE HISTORY OF ART

Caroli, Flavio. *Leonardo: studi di fisiognomica*. Milan: Electa, 2015.

Cazort, Mimi, Monique Kornell, and K. B. Roberts. *The Ingenious Machine of Nature: Four Centuries of Art and Anatomy*. Ottawa: National Gallery of Canada, 1996.

Hall, James. *Michelangelo and the Reinvention of the Human Body*. New York: Farrar, Straus and Giroux, 2005.

Hirst, Michael. *Michelangelo and His Drawings*. New Haven: Yale University Press, 1988.

Kwakkelstein, Michael. *Leonardo da Vinci as a Physiognomist*. Leiden, Netherlands: Primavera Pers, 1994.

Ministero per i beni culturali e ambientali, *Il compianto sul Cristo morto*. Bologna: Fondazione del Monte di Bologna e Ravenna, Rolo Banca 1473, 1996.

Premuda, Loris. *Storia dell'iconografia anatomica*. Milan: Ciba Edizioni, 1993.

Gisela Richter, *Kouroi: Archaic Greek Youths: A Study of the Development of the Kouros Type in Greek Sculpture*. 3rd ed. London: Phaidon, 1970.

Rifkin, Benjamin. *Human Anatomy from the Renaissance to the Digital Age*. New York: Harry N. Abrams, 2006.

Saunders, Gill. *The Nude, A New Perspective*. New York: Harper and Row, 1989.

Scribner, Charles III. *Gianlorenzo Bernini*. New York: Harry N. Abrams, 1991.

ABOUT THE AUTHOR

Roberto Osti studied at the State Institute of Art and the School of Anatomical and Surgical Drawing, University of Bologna, Italy, and earned an MFA from the New York Academy of Art in 2007. As a scientific illustrator, he has collaborated with many publications and publishers, including *Scientific American, The New York Times,* Rizzoli, Mondadori, and Scholastic. His illustrations have been exhibited at the Museum of Modern Art and the Aldrovandi Museum in Bologna, the Museum of Natural History in Milan, and the Oceanographic Museum in Monte Carlo, Monaco. His fine art paintings and drawings have been exhibited in galleries in New York, New Jersey, and Philadelphia and at other locations in the United States and abroad and have been included in publications such as *Creative Quarterly, American Artist,* and the Drawing Center's Drawing Papers. Osti has taught anatomy to artists since 2005, and currently teaches courses on anatomy and figure drawing at the University of the Arts in Philadelphia, the Pennsylvania Academy of the Fine Arts, and the New York Academy of Art. He also teaches online courses for universities and ateliers, as well as in-studio workshops. You can find him on the web at robertoosti.com, on Instagram at instagram.com/ostiroberto/, and on YouTube at youtube.com/c/RobertoOstiDrawing. He lives in New Jersey with his two children, Emilia and Massimo.

ACKNOWLEDGMENTS

I want to express my gratitude to the many people who were instrumental in the realization of this book, offering their help, advice, professional expertise, and support. First, I want to thank Victoria Craven, associate publisher of The Monacelli Press, for believing in this second book and closely following me throughout its laborious creation period. Many thanks to James Waller, who heroically and masterfully edited the book, giving it an elegant visual and reading flow.

Thanks to my friends Irvana Malabarba, for her invaluable help with iconographic research, and Massimo Demma, who expertly helped with the images that needed digital intervention, including the cover.

Many thanks also to these friends, colleagues, and former students who contributed their beautiful artworks, greatly enriching the book: Dan Thompson, Michael Grimaldi, Brian Booth Craig, Noah Buchanan, Scott Noel, Patricia Watwood, Daniel Maidman, Richard Morris, Gabriela Handal, Haley Manchon, He Lihuai, and Zachary Smith. Thanks too to my dear friend, colleague, and gifted artist Patrick Connors for his expert opinions about various topics in the book and the many hours he spent discussing them with me.

I developed this book's content and pedagogy (and those of my first book, as well) over the past twenty years, while teaching at the New York Academy of Art, the Pennsylvania Academy of the Fine Arts, and the University of the Arts, in Philadelphia. These schools' curriculums include courses on anatomy, figure anatomy, figure structure, and figure drawing, and they stubbornly and proudly continue a tradition that arcs back to Classical times and the Renaissance, providing their students with a formidable and thorough artistic education.

I must also acknowledge the fantastic models I've worked with, all dedicated professionals and sources of inspiration: the late Christophe Nayel, dear friend and passionate model, with whom I worked for almost two decades, as well as all the great models I work with now who are included in this book: Roger, Daro, Megan, Heather, Joseph, Frank, and David. Finally, I thank and remember my beloved late wife, Angela Conrad, Ph.D., for always supporting and encouraging me and for all the beautiful moments we lived together.

INDEX

Renaissance, 11–12, 33, 48–49, 139, 332

structural, 316–319, 328–331, 332

tonal, 313, 319, 333–334

trois crayons, 319, 338–341

drunken movement, 188

Dürer, Albrecht, 48, 50

dynamic flows, 186–192, 219–225

E

ears, 294

ecstasy, in arched-back pose, 191–192

elbow joint, 104–105

envelope method
of drawing, 254–256
of measuring subject, 322–326

Erasistratus, 28

Expressionism, 316

eyelids, 288, 298, 299

eyes
anatomical/structural characteristics of, 287–289
drawing, 313
expression of, 298–299

F

face
curvatures of, 295
ears, 294
eyes, 287–289
mouth, 292–293
muscles of, 296–297
nose, 291
parts of, 282–283
proportions of, 278–279, 281

facial expression
Archaic smile, 180, 181, 183, 274
basic emotions, 305–306, 313
complex, 307–311
drawing, 313

of eyes, 298–299

of mouth, 301–304

and muscles of face, 296, 307

in Renaissance art, 274, 275–277

facial volume, 280

Fairbanks, Avard T. and Eugene, 51

Fauvism, 316

fear, expression of, 303, 306, 313

female figure
back, 91
breasts, 82, 83
hips, 106, 108
pelvis, 82, 106, 108
proportions, 127
torso, 85–90
Venus of Willendorf, 154
Venus Pudica, 24

figure drawing
body movements, 194–198
extrapolating skeleton, 134, 140, 144
foreshortened pose, 132, 133, 258, 263, 324–327
geometric patterns in, 145
movement of figure, 204–210
muscular flows in, 176
from plaster casts, 172, 173
reconstructing muscular-skeletal connections, 134–151
reference charts for, 126–127
schematic, 130
sketching, 247, 262
technical and conceptual interaction in, 315–316
visualizing skeleton, 128, 137, 144
See also drawing techniques; measuring techniques; stereometric rendering; *specific parts of body*

fingers. *See* hand

flow, lines of. *See* muscular flows

foot and ankle, 118–119

foreshortened pose, 132, 133, 258, 263, 324–327

framing lines, 316

Francesca, Piero della, 275

G

geometric patterns, 70–75, 145

Giotto di Bondone, 274

Glyptothek museum, Munich, 25

Goethe, Johann Wolfgang von, *Theory of Colors*, 316

Goltzius, Hendrick, *The Great Hercules*, 37

Gothic style art, 274

Greek sculpture
anatomical accuracy of, 17–28
contrapposto pose in, 180–183
dynamic flows in, 186–187
facial expression in, 180, 181, 183, 273–274
proportional relationships in, 52–62

Greuze, Jean-Baptiste
Head of an Old Woman Looking Up, 316, 317, 319
Head of a Smiling Girl, 319

H

hand
analyzing/studying, 243
clasped, 267
cross-contour lines, 245
envelope method of drawing, 254–256, 265
freer approach to, 244, 246–249
holding objects, 263–264, 266
interlocked fingers, 268
light effects on, 248–251, 253
movement of, 252, 259–264
skeletal structure of, 238
sketching, 262
stereometric rendering of, 239–242

arm, 162–169, 230–234
asymmetries in, 216
dynamic, 186–192, 221
in figure drawing, 176
flexors and antagonists, 156
leg, 170–172
vs lines of action, 164
pathways of, 157
torso, 158–161
whole body, 174–175, 219–221
muscular-skeletal structure, 77
ankle and foot, 118–119
arm, 92–97, 102, 103
elbow joint, 104–105
female figure, 82–91, 106
as foundation, 77–78
hips, 106–107
identifying, 120–123
knee, 114–117
leg, 109–113
male torso, 78–81, 91
and movement, 211–221
reconstructing in figure drawing,
134–151
shoulder and scapula, 98–103
muscular volumes, 18, 96–97, 164
Muybrdige, Eadweard, movement studies
of, 193

N

Nabis, 316
names, anatomical, 15
narrative, projecting, 190
nipples, 82, 83
Noel, Scott, 63, 139, 178, 179
nose, size and shape of, 290–291

O

overlapping forms, 328
overlapping pose, 257

P

Paleolithic sculpture, 154
pankration athlete, 21
Passarotti, Bartolomeo, 78
pelvis
female, 82, 106, 108
reconstructing, 138, 143
tilt, 184
plaster casts, drawing from, 172, 173
Pliny the Elder, 26
plumb line, 203, 205
Pointillism, 316
Pollaiuolo, Antonio del, 23, 31
Polykleitos, 18, 50, 52, 54
The Canon, 48, 62
Pontormo, 316
pose
anatomical position, 129
arched-back, 191–192
contrapposto, 56–57, 181, 182–185,
188
dynamic, 205–206, 219–225, 252
foreshortened, 132, 133, 258, 263,
324–327
geometric patterns in, 73, 74–75
unbalanced, 188, 206
progressive method in figure drawing,
11–12
proportional relationships, 46–75
defined, 47
facial features, 278–279, 281
and geometric patterns, 70–75
head-to-body ratio, 52–53, 61–63
ideal and real, 48, 63
modular system, 54–60
and movement, 67–69
in Renaissance art, 48–49
uses of, 64–68
See also measuring techniques
Prud'hon, Pierre-Paul, tonal drawing of,
318, 319, 333

Q

quantum mechanics, 316

R

Raging Maenad, 191
Raphael, 316
Fighting Men, 221, 222
The Three Graces, 185
reduction drawing technique, 320, 335–
337, 340
Reformation, 316
religious content of art, 316
Renaissance art
and anatomical knowledge, 30–39,
316
drawing techniques, 11–12, 33, 48–49,
139, 332
facial expression in, 274, 275–277
movement in, 184–185, 188–192, 207
proportional relationships in, 48–49
technical and conceptual development
in, 316
Riace warriors, 22–23
Richer, Paul Marie Louis, 50
Richter, Gisela, 16
Rosso Fiorentino, 316
Rubens, Peter Paul, *trois crayons*
technique of, 338

S

sadness, expression of, 303, 306, 313
Salomon, Nanette, 24
Sarto, Andrea del, 207, 316
scapula. *See* shoulder and scapula
schematic drawing, 130, 131
S-curved lines, 183, 184, 185
searching lines, 246
shoulder and scapula
muscular flows, 168–169

muscular-skeletal structure, 98–103

sighting method of measuring, 321, 322, 327–328

skeletal landmarks, 18, 78

    See also muscular-skeletal structure

sketchbook studies, 247, 262

Skopas, 191

skull, planes of, 286

smile

    Archaic, 180, 181, 183, 274

    and muscles of mouth, 302, 303, 304

soft landmarks, 78

spine muscles, 89

spiraling action, 189

squinty eyes, 299

stereometric rendering

    of body, 199–201, 205

    of hand, 239–242

    of head, 200–201

    of moving figures, 205

    and visualization, 130–132

Stith, Zachary, 311

structural drawing technique, 316–319, 328–331, 332

subtractive (reduction) drawing technique, 320, 335–337

surprise, expression of, 306, 313

T

tendons, soft landmarks of, 78

Thermae Boxer, 181

Thompson, Dan, 307, 317

Tidemand, Adolph, *A Woman's Arm*, 236, 237

Titian, 23

    Saint Sebastian, 40, 41

tonal cross-contour hatching technique, 329

tonal drawing technique, 313, 319, 333–334

torso

    lines of flow, 158–162

    movement of, 198, 218

    muscular-skeletal structure (female), 85–90

    muscular-skeletal structure (male), 78–81, 91

    stereometric rendering of, 200–201, 226

Trecourt, Giacomo, 308

triceps, 101

trois crayons drawing technique, 319, 338–341

Turner, J.M.W., 316

V

Venus of Willendorf, 154

Venus Pudica, 24

Vesalius, *De humani corporis fabrica*, 31, 40

Vinci, Leonardo da. *See* Leonardo da Vinci

Vitruvius Pollio, Marcus, 48–49

W

Watwood, Patricia, 343, 345

Wounded Niobid, 186

wrinkles, 307

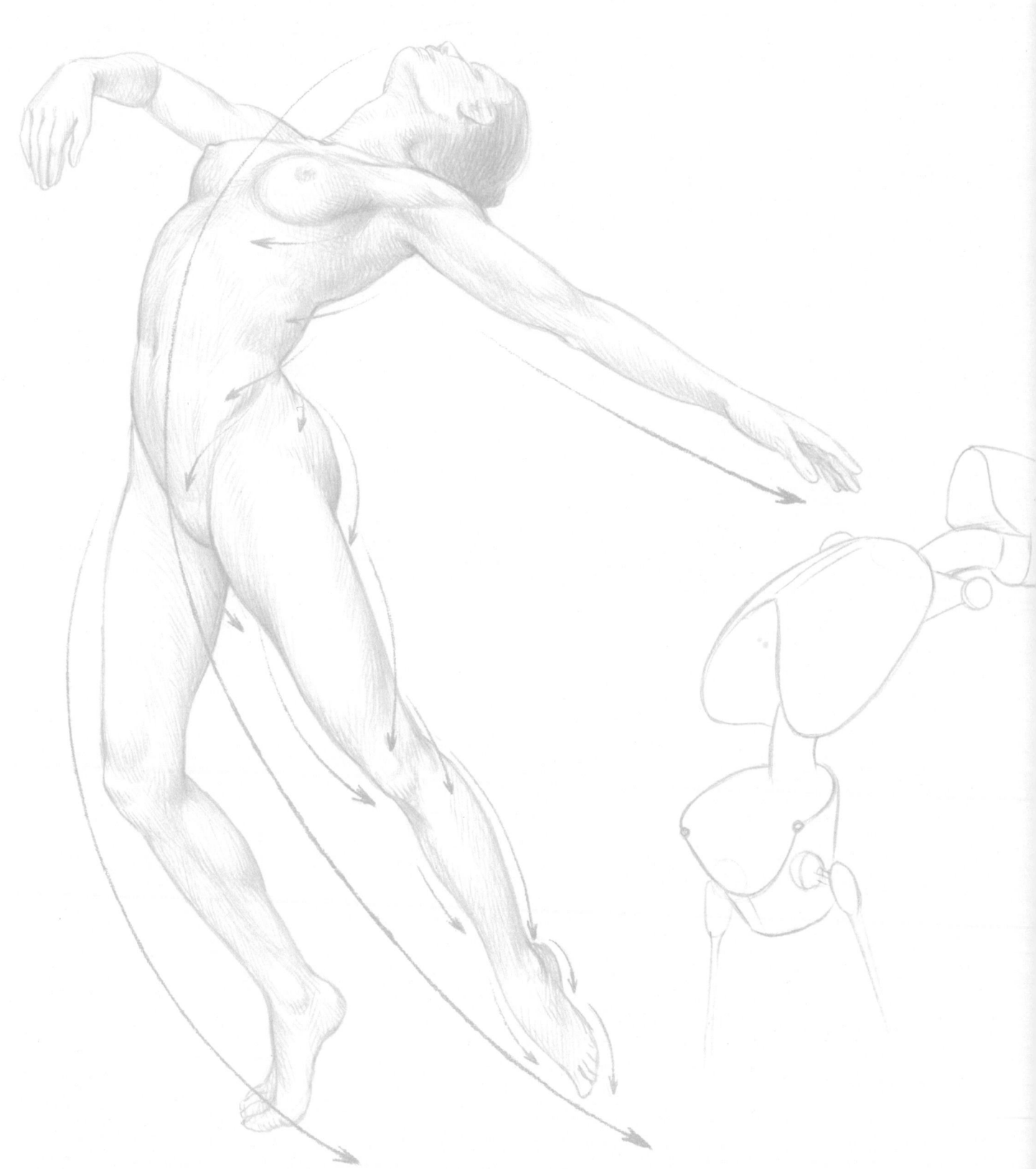